THE ADMINISTRATIVE PROFESSIONAL: TECHNOLOGY & PROCEDURES

13TH EDITION

PATSY FULTON-CALKINS, Ph.D.

Director of the Bill J. Priest Center for Community College Education
Don A. Buchholz Endowed Chair
University of North Texas
Denton, Texas

THOMSON
SOUTH-WESTERN

Australia • Brazil • Canada • Mexico • Singapore • Spain • United Kingdom • United States

THOMSON

™

SOUTH-WESTERN

The Administrative Professional: Technology & Procedures, Thirteenth Edition
Patsy Fulton-Calkins, Ph.D.

VP/Editorial Director:
Jack W. Calhoun

VP/Editor-in-Chief:
Karen Schmohe

Acquisitions Editor:
Jane Phelan

Project Manager:
Dr. Inell Bolls

Content Project Manager:
Darrell E. Frye

Marketing Manager:
Valerie A. Lauer

Marketing Coordinator:
Kelley Gilreath

Manufacturing Coordinator:
Charlene Taylor

Art Director:
Linda Helcher

Photo Researcher:
Darren Wright

Production House:
Graphic World Inc.

Printer:
QuebecorWorld
Dubuque, IA

Internal and Cover Designer:
Diane Gliebe

Cover Images:
Getty Images

For more information about our products, contact us at:

Thomson Higher Education
5191 Natorp Boulevard
Mason, OH 45040
USA

PREFACE

The Administrative Professional: Technology & Procedures, 13th Edition, is a complete learning package designed to push you to higher levels of accomplishment and add to your administrative professional skills. This is a capstone course—one that pulls together the skills you learned previously and adds to your knowledge and understanding of the technical and human-relation skills necessary to succeed in your chosen profession.

As you enter the business world and start your career as an administrative professional, you will be faced with many challenging experiences and opportunities. The work world that you will be entering is more diverse than ever before in the United States, and that diversity is expected to continue to increase. Additionally, we are living in an international work world—one where organizations frequently do business with international customers and clients. The international world is accessed immediately by going online or by using call centers that employ people in many countries outside the United States. This world demands that administrative professionals have not only technology skills but also a broad range of human-relation and critical-thinking skills.

The world of work requires your constant learning. When you leave your educational program in the near future, do not expect to leave learning behind. It is imperative for all of us who live in this fast-paced, ever-changing world to continue to learn throughout our lives. Your learning may not continue in a formal way, although you may choose to take some courses. However, your education will include learning on the job, ongoing research in your field, and becoming a member of professional organizations such as the International Association of Administrative Professionals (IAAP).

This text is organized into six parts, each focusing on an important aspect of the administrative field. Each part is divided into chapters to put emphasis on the main points of each subject. *The Administrative Professional: Technology & Procedures, 13th Edition,* includes:

- ▶ **Learning Objectives** that provide expected outcomes from studying each chapter.
- ▶ **Self Checks** to test your understanding of the concepts presented.
- ▶ A **Glossary** that highlights the key terms defined within each chapter.
- ▶ A **Summary** of main points at the end of each chapter.
- ▶ **Checkpoints** that provide an opportunity to check your understanding of the glossary terms.
- ▶ A **Data CD** that contains projects, forms, and other supplementary materials as well as communication drills to reinforce language skills.
- ▶ **Discussion Items** to test your understanding of the chapter.
- ▶ **Critical Thinking Cases** to reinforce critical-thinking skills provided at the end of each chapter.
- ▶ **Workplace Projects** to reinforce learning objectives, with objectives for each project, provided at the end of each chapter.
- ▶ **Workplace Icons** to direct students to the Internet 👆, teamwork 🌐, and communication power 🌀 .

▶ **Assessments of Chapter Objectives** that provide an opportunity to determine if chapter objectives have been met through a review of each objective.

These new features have been added to the text to enhance your learning experience:

▶ Part IV: Customer and Employee Satisfaction now includes a chapter focusing on customer service.
▶ Part VI: Your Career now includes an expanded chapter that covers the importance of and increasing demand for teleworkers/virtual assistants.
▶ An Integrated Project has been added to each part to combine chapter concepts and give practice on the skills learned.
▶ Spotlights in each chapter to focus on soft skill development such as ethics and communication.
▶ The importance of developing soft skills is reinforced through the Professional Growth Plan that begins in Chapter 1 and continues in each chapter of the text.
▶ This edition also provides updated administrative professional profiles, multinational company orientation, research integrated throughout each chapter, and projects in each chapter.

As the author, I have considered your learning needs throughout the book and made every effort to present the material in an understandable and relevant manner. In every chapter, you have a chance to develop and expand skills that will contribute to your success as an administrative professional.

The administrative professional role today is a challenging one due to constant advances in technology, our global economy, and an increasingly diverse workplace. It is my hope that from studying this book and completing the projects, you will not only learn and grow in your abilities and skills but also commit to continual learning as a lifelong goal. Best wishes to you for a challenging and successful course!

Dr. Patsy J. Fulton-Calkins

> START OFF ON THE RIGHT FOOT!

Spotlight on Success gives each part a jump start! All six parts begin with testimonials from professionals in the administrative field. The *Spotlight on Success* feature gives you insight into the real world and how hard work and determination can lead you to career success.

Learning Objectives move you in the right direction! When starting a new chapter, it is important to understand what you are expected to achieve. The *Learning Objectives* at the beginning of each chapter help you focus your study and use your time efficiently.

> BECOME AN ALL-AROUND SUCCESS!

Self Checks focus on learning needs. One way to find out where you need to apply yourself more in your learning is through testing your knowledge of the chapter topics. *Self Checks* provide the opportunity to quiz yourself on your understanding of the concepts presented throughout the chapter so you can focus on areas that require your attention.

Spotlights highlight the important soft skills you need. Soft skills are increasingly valued in today's workplace and are critical for career success. Throughout each chapter, *Spotlight* features—such as ethics, communication, and critical thinking—provide insight on critical areas of learning and development as well as professional-growth pointers.

> APPLY YOUR KNOWLEDGE!

Critical Thinking Cases challenge you to make the right decisions. At the end of each chapter, you are presented with a situation that may arise in the workplace. These cases require you to use critical-thinking skills to find a probable action and solution to solve your problem.

Workplace Projects use real-world scenarios to reinforce learning objectives. At the end of each chapter, there are multiple projects that challenge you to use the skills learned throughout the chapter. These tasks involve solving problems, making appropriate ethical decisions, and improving various soft skills.

Integrated Projects encourage using teamwork to accomplish your goal. At the end of each part, you combine chapter concepts with opportunities to practice the skills learned so that you can gain the most from the text.

> INSTRUCTOR RESOURCES

▶ The Instructor's Manual, now available in hard copy, includes learning objectives, chapter outlines, teaching suggestions, key to discussion items, suggested response to the critical-thinking activity, and solutions to projects.
▶ Testing software offers the instructor the opportunity to create printed tests and choose questions in rank order.
▶ PowerPoint® slides and other instructional aids are available for each chapter on the Web site.
▶ WebTutor on WebCT and WebTutor on Blackboard are also available for use as an online course for distance learning.

> ABOUT THE AUTHOR

Dr. Patsy J. Fulton-Calkins has extensive experience in the administrative field, including six years of corporate experience and completion of the CPS certification. Presently, she is the Director of the Bill J. Priest Center for Community College Education and the holder of the Don A. Buchholz Endowed Chair at the University of North Texas, Denton, Texas. Additionally, she teaches doctoral level courses in higher education.

PREFACE

Dr. Fulton-Calkins has taught senior level courses at the university, in addition to community college and high school levels. These courses include management capstone courses, diversity courses, business and society, office procedures, keyboarding, business communication, bookkeeping, business law, and general business. She also taught CPS review courses and community education courses.

In addition to her teaching experience, she has extensive leadership experience in the following positions.

▶ Chancellor of Oakland Community College (CEO), Oakland County, Michigan
▶ President of Brookhaven College, Dallas, Texas
▶ Vice President of Instruction, El Centro College, Dallas, Texas
▶ Division Chairperson of Business and Social Science, Cedar Valley College, Dallas, Texas

Her educational credentials include a B.B.A., and M.B.Ed., and a Ph.D. Honors include Outstanding Alumus, University of North Texas; Transformational Leader in Community Colleges; Who's Who in America; Outstanding Woman in Management; listed in *Michigan Women: Firsts and Founders;* Paul Harris Fellow of Rotary International; Beta Gamma Sigma, National Honorary Business Fraternity; and Piper Professor.

> ACKNOWLEDGMENTS

Thanks to the reviewers who spent many hours reviewing the chapters and making suggestions and comments. The reviewers are:

Margaret Stafford
Curriculum Coordinator
Valley College
Martinsburg, West Virginia

Paula S. McCord
Instructor
Trumbull Business College
Warren, Ohio

Christa R. Simmons, M.Ed.
Instructor, Business Systems
Tennessee Technology Center, Pulaski
Pulaski, Tennessee

Thanks also go to Ollie Rivers, San Antonio, Texas. Ms. Rivers is a co-author of business textbooks and a corporate trainer with more than 20 years of business experience. She holds an M.B.A. and a B.S. in accounting and management. Her contributions to Chapters 4 and 5 added depth to the material and are appreciated.

In addition, thanks go to Andrea Henne, Ed.D., Dean of Online Instruction, San Diego Community College, San Diego, California. Dr. Henne's contributions to Chapter 7 enhanced the information in this chapter, highlighting the necessity for maintaining effective records management.

CONTENTS

The Administrative Professional: Technology & Procedures

CONTENTS

CONTENTS

THE ADMINISTRATIVE PROFESSIONAL: TECHNOLOGY & PROCEDURES

AlVerta Harty, CPS/CAP
Executive Assistant/Department Coordinator
Berlex Biosciences, Richmond, California

SPOTLIGHT *on Success*

After graduation, I worked as a long distance operator with Bell Telephone. I received excellent interpersonal and communication training through their extensive 3-month course. Although I only worked for Bell Telephone for two years, the training I received and the skills I learned have served me well throughout my working career. When I returned to work after having my first daughter, I went to work for Capital Blue Cross as a subscriber service representative. I assisted callers by finding resolutions to problems with billing/payments, hospital and doctor claims, as well as referrals for out-of-plan issues.

In 1969, I moved to New York. I worked in Manhattan, first as a secretary in a food products company and then as secretary to a community psychiatric team at Roosevelt Hospital.

I returned to Pennsylvania in 1971 and went back to work at Blue Cross as secretary to the Medical Director and Claims Division, where nurses reviewed rejected claims. My restlessness continued to grow, but I bided my time. Harrisburg was only five miles away from Steelton, so I worked for the State of Pennsylvania for the Governor's Civil Tension Task Force.

A friend of mine who had moved to California kept inviting me to come for a visit. When I finally made arrangements to visit her, she called with the news that she was moving back to Philadelphia (the bad news) and got a promotion (the good news). Another friend invited me to come and stay with her since I had already paid for the trip, so off I went to San Francisco. After a week in the lovely San Francisco Bay area in August 1980, I knew this was where I wanted to live. After returning to Pennsylvania, I sold everything I could not carry in my car, put my two daughters in the car, and drove to California. My

TO WHAT DO I ATTRIBUTE MY SUCCESS?

My success comes from my work ethic. My grandmother owned a grocery store in the small town of Steelton, Pennsylvania, where I grew up. My first job at six years old was handing out penny candy to customers, giving the money to my grandmother, and if there was change, I gave it to the customers.

My responsibilities grew from handing out penny candy to stocking the shelves, ordering products, and even making change.

WHAT IS MY BACKGROUND?

My career background is extremely varied. When I was 16, I knew I wanted to be a secretary, so I signed up for business courses in high school. Unfortunately, my mom wanted me to go to college, so she made me change to college prep (in those days you listened to your parents—no questions asked). Not to be defeated, I taught myself Gregg Shorthand and took an elective keyboarding class.

Chapter 1:	The Ever-Changing Workplace
Chapter 2:	Ethics—Essential in the Workplace
Chapter 3:	Stress, Anger, and Time Management

intention was to become a music producer. Finally, my restlessness went away.

My first job in California was as a secretary in the Performance Monitoring Unit for San Francisco's Municipal Railway system. My soon-to-be manager expressed doubts about hiring me because of my ambition to become a music producer. In my interview, I informed her that if she hired me, she would have the best secretary she could ever have. She hired me and after six months, I received a call from a local jazz station DJ to be secretary for the first San Francisco International Jazz Festival. The problem was that they needed me in two days. I went to my manager, apologized up front and told her that although I wanted to take the job, if she said no I would stay. She thought about it and an hour later came back and said, "I do understand AlVerta. Your getting this call would be the same as my getting a call to play at Wimbledon." After the festival ended, I worked in both music and in the film and video industry between 1981 and 1996 as an independent production manager/line producer.

During slow times between jobs in the film/video industry, I temped as a secretary/administrative assistant/executive assistant through Kelly Services. Finally realizing that the work was getting more and more scarce as the industry moved south to L.A., I began to look for permanent work. I took a two-week temporary position at Berlex Biosciences as an executive assistant.

After two weeks, the administrative assistant came to me and asked me if I wanted the position. HR decided to try me for three months to see if it would work out. It worked out so well that even though an HR representative tried not to hire me permanently (she thought I "wouldn't be a good fit"), the vice president held his ground. Finally, the president informed HR that I would be the executive assistant to the Vice President of Cancer Research. I have been at Berlex for eight years.

WHAT IS THE MOST FUN PART OF MY JOB?

There is so much that is fun about my job. I enjoy the interaction with scientists from all over the world. Berlex is a subsidiary of an international pharmaceutical company, Schering AG, based in Berlin, Germany. I became the administrative assistant (Admin) for the Cancer Research Department, comprising 26 research scientists and technicians, and the RBA Dermatology Research Department, consisting of 11 research scientists and technicians and Post Docs. Responding to requests from each one is a class in prioritizing, interpersonal and writing skills, not to mention correcting miscommunications that can sometimes occur when English is a second language. After joining the International Association of Administrative Professionals (IAAP®) and receiving my Certified Professional Secretary (CPS®) certification, I was promoted to department coordinator, which included management responsibilities. All of my bosses have supported my membership in IAAP and pay for my attendance at conferences.

Another fun part of my job is meeting planning. My current boss has volunteered me to coordinate several meetings that involved speakers from the worldwide scientific research community. Because of my meeting planning successes, I have received CITE Awards that included half cash and half company stock awards.

I love challenges, and what better way to flex my skills than to be an executive assistant to an executive who throws challenges my way? Besides, if I make him look good, he appreciates me and shows me through raises, promotions (I am at the top of the ladder with the exception of working directly for the president), and his support of and encouragement for my IAAP membership.

WHAT IS THE MOST STRESSFUL PART OF MY JOB?

The most stressful part of my job is handling all the challenges that a job can deliver to an executive assistant.

WHAT ARE MY INTERESTS/HOBBIES?

I enjoy listening to contemporary jazz and gospel music and salsa dancing. I also like surfing the Internet and meeting people.

TO WHAT PROFESSIONAL ORGANIZATIONS DO I BELONG?

I joined the IAAP in 1997. In 1999, I was elected Secretary to the Board of Directors. After six months, the president moved to Colorado and I assumed the presidency. I was elected President for the next three years. In 2001, I passed the CPS® examination. When the first Certified Administrative Professional® (CAP) examination was offered, I started a study group with five members. All five of us passed the examination in 2001. This year I am running for vice president of the California Division.

After attending a seminar offered by another IAAP chapter, I passed the California Notary Examination in 2004 and now belong to the National Notary Association.

ALVERTA HARTY, CPS/CAP—CASE STUDY

In 2003, my company started a new department. The president called me into his office and told me that they did not have funds to hire an executive assistant for the department because it was too small. The company policy only allows departments with 15 or more people to have assistants. He asked me if I would be the executive assistant and department coordinator because he trusted that I would do a good job. I now had the responsibility of assisting two directors and 36 staff in two different buildings.

The director was a nice man, but it was obvious that he came from a previous company that allowed him unlimited spending and a lot of autonomy, which was the complete opposite of my company. I knew the limits my company would allow and I tried to explain them to him. No matter what I tried to do to keep him on an even keel, he would do just about everything contrary to policy and my advice.

I also spoke to him about some of his comments that were inappropriate in the office, but to no avail. He would compliment people so much until it seemed insincere. My frustration level increased and I felt something had to be done, both for my credibility and for my future with the company.

Decide how you would handle the situation. Then turn to page 431 for the case solution.

CHAPTER 1

THE EVER-CHANGING WORKPLACE

Learning Objectives

1. Describe the future workforce.
2. Determine changes in the work environment.
3. Define the types of business organizations and workplace structures.
4. Describe the role and responsibilities of administrative professionals.
5. Identify skills and qualities necessary for administrative professionals.
6. Begin the development of a professional growth plan.
7. Develop critical-thinking skills.

© Getty Images/Photodisc

> THE WORKPLACE—2050

What will work life be in 2050? According to projections by futurists, the workplace will be drastically different from our present day workplace. Here are a few projections from individuals writing in the field.

▶ Nearly all purchases will be made virtually. A tiny electronic device called an **information envelope** with a monitor in the office or home will tell a digital shopper (**DS**) what you want.
▶ Numerous jobs will be transferred from people to virtual programmers—a phenomenon known as **intelligence sourcing** or **I-sourcing.**
▶ Where we now have a keyboard or mouse, nearly all technology will be driven by voice recognition. We will talk to our office systems, our home, and our car.
▶ The **Telepresence (TP) Industry** will have been launched. These units will create the illusion of another location halfway around the world or just around the corner. They will make virtual travel possible because of their ability to convey the experience of another location convincingly. Nearly every room, at home and at work, will be equipped with telepresence devices.
▶ Nearly all new cars will have electric motors.
▶ Big leaps in computing power will have produced an infrastructure that allows cars to interact with each other and their surroundings, producing fewer accidents.
▶ The maximum [human] lifespan will be approximately 150 years.
▶ Quantum computers will enable the solving of incredibly complex problems like climate forecasting, missile defense, and traffic management.[1]

Reread the learning objectives given above. It is very important for you to begin each chapter understanding exactly what you are expected to achieve. The

---

[1]Peter Schwartz, "Future Shock," *Fortune,* April 5, 2004, pp. 260–266.

learning objectives will help you focus your study and use your time efficiently.

> THE LABOR FORCE

According to the U.S. Department of Labor, Bureau of Labor Statistics, the U.S. population as a whole is expected to grow by 24 million from 2002 to 2012, with the youth population growing by 7 percent and the **baby boomers** (people born between 1946–1964) growing by 43.6 percent.[2]

▷ Increasingly Diverse

This workforce will be increasingly diverse, with minorities and immigrants constituting a larger share of the workforce than today. White non-Hispanics are projected to be 65.5 percent of the workforce in 2012, falling from over 71.3 percent in early 2002.[3] From 2030–2050, the non-Hispanic White population will decline in size. African Americans, Asians, and Hispanics will outnumber Whites, with the Hispanic population growing much faster than the other groups.[4]

As you work in this diverse environment, you need to be aware of and sensitive to the various cultural differences and backgrounds. You must understand that individuals, because of their different backgrounds, may view situations differently than you do. Your openness to different ideas and perspectives is essential. It may not always be easy to remain

The workforce will be even more diverse in the future than it is today.

© Blend Images

open to differences, but the results will be well worth your effort. Only through awareness, understanding, and acceptance of different cultures can we expect to work in a harmonious, productive business world.

▷ Greater Numbers of Women

More women are in the workforce today, and that number is projected to grow. In fact, the number of women in the workforce is projected to grow at a faster rate than the number of men. By 2012, the number of women in the workforce is projected to increase by 14.3 percent (from 2002), whereas the men's share of the labor force is expected to decrease from 53.5 percent in 2002 to 52.5 percent in 2012.[5] Women, both single and married, continue to enter the workforce in greater numbers than in the past. Women, in 2005, represent 46.2 percent of the workforce, compared to 29 percent in 1950.[6] Women who have children are returning to the workforce today while their children are still preschool age. This is particularly true for families maintained by single women, a group that is growing significantly.

▷ Women in Positions of Greater Authority

More than ever before, women are assuming positions of greater authority and responsibility, and the positions traditionally filled exclusively by men are becoming more open to women. As women assume higher-level positions, even that of Chief Executive Officer (CEO), we must examine our assumptions about the way both men and women react in the workforce. One fairly common assumption about women has been that they are more emotional than men. Can we say that such an assumption is categorically true? No, we cannot. People with different backgrounds and different cultures react differently to situations, but it is not because they are male or female.

The socialization process in various cultures often encourages men and women to develop different traits. For example, if you were born in the United States and are female, you may have been encouraged to express your feelings openly. Males may have been taught to keep their feelings to themselves. Notice that "may have" is used.

---

[2]U.S. Department of Labor, Bureau of Labor Statistics, "Tomorrow's Jobs," <http://stats.bls.gov/oco/oco2003.htm> (accessed January 7, 2005).

[3]Ibid.

[4]"Diversity in the Work Force," <http:1164.233.179.104/search?q=CACHE:de3hwNcrw5Cj:WWW.NCCTE.ORG/PUBLICATIONS/INFOSYNTHESIS> (accessed January 7, 2005).

[5]Ibid., U.S. Department of Labor, Bureau of Labor Statistics, "Tomorrow's Jobs."

[6]"Diversity in the Work Force," <http:1164.233.179.104/search?q=cache:DE3HWnCRW5cJ:www.nccte.org/publications/infosynthesis> (accessed January 7, 2005).

We cannot say that all females born in the United States have been socialized in this manner. Neither can we say that all males have been. The point of this entire section is to remind you that we cannot **stereotype** individuals. We cannot assume that individuals have certain characteristics because of their gender. You need to be aware that stereotyping can occur and not let your attitudes or decisions be influenced by stereotypes. *Your focus must be on understanding and accepting differences.*

▷ More Senior Citizens

The number of workers 55 and older is expected to be 19.1 percent of the labor force by 2012 because of the aging of the baby-boom generation.[7] As medical technology continues to make advances that allow people to live longer, we can expect people to stay in the workforce beyond the traditional retirement age of 65, with 70 or older expected to be the new retirement age.

You will probably work with people aged 18 to 70 or older. Certainly, each generation of our population grows up with differing national and local influences in their lives. Demographers and writers in the field assign a name to groups of people according to their date of birth and then study their characteristics. Categories include the following:

Baby Boomers	1946–1964
Generation X	1965–1975
Generation Y	1976–1981
Millennial Generation	1982–2003

Each generation views the world through a different lens according to the events that were taking place during their formative years. For example, people in their early 20s have grown up in an age of computer applications. E-mail is common, with instant messaging an often-used feature; and cellphones are a standard piece of equipment for all. People walk around with their **BlackBerries** (wireless handheld communication devices offering various services such as e-mail and Internet access, the use of which has grown significantly since 9/11). Instant communication with the workplace and the home is extremely important. Video games are in common use by children and young adults alike. However, people in their forties and fifties had to acquire technology skills as adults; these skills were not something they mastered as young children or teenagers. Age differences in the workplace mean that people may view the world from different perspectives. In order to work together successfully, we have to listen closely to each other, attempt to understand the other person's perspective, and accept each other's differences.

Spotlight *on*

COMMUNICATION

America is composed of a mosaic of different cultures, races, and ethnicities. Such a world demands that we listen carefully to each other and that we are open to differences that exist.

▷ Higher Education Level

Because of our ever-increasing technological world, the level of education for jobs is higher than in the past. Numerous employers require an associate degree, while others require a bachelor's degree or higher. Education is essential in getting a job, and ongoing education is a must in keeping a job. Lifelong learning is necessary for all individuals who expect to remain productive workers. This ongoing education does not have to take a formal route (attendance at a technical/community college or a university). Often, informal education through reading, attending seminars and conferences, and being active in professional organizations is essential for maintaining and improving the knowledge and skills needed as work responsibilities change.

© Photodisc/Scott T. Baxter

Informal education through continued reading of current books and periodicals is essential.

---

[7]U.S. Department of Labor, Bureau of Labor Statistics, "Tomorrow's Jobs," <http://stats.bls.gov/oco/oco2003.htm> (accessed January 7, 2005).

> WORK ENVIRONMENT

The work environment today is constantly changing, with numerous events causing this change. These events include: globalization of the economy, telework, quality focus, downsizing, outsourcing, and flexible workweeks.

> Globalization of the Economy

You merely have to pick up a newspaper, read a business magazine, or listen to the news on television to see and hear the many references to our global economy. If you follow the stock market, you hear references to downturns and upturns in the market in Europe and Asia and the interrelatedness of these markets to the U.S. market. Go into an American electronics store, and you notice the number of products that are manufactured in Asia. Look at the labels on your clothes and shoes, and you become aware of the number of articles that are made outside the United States. Observe the automobiles that we drive, and you will notice the cars that are made by international firms. We also have a huge number of foreign investors in the United States. In fact, when the stock market takes a downturn in the United States, you hear financial experts expressing concern that foreign investors may take their money out of the United States, thus impacting the stock market even more. Virtually everyone is affected by the rapid globalization of the world economy.

> Telework

Today many workers have traded in the traditional work environment for **telework,** work that can be performed at any place and at any time using technology. The telecommuting-to-work lifestyle is here to stay. There were 44.4 million teleworkers in the United States in 2004, with 24.1 million employed by companies and 20.3 million self-employed.[8] Today telework is the word most frequently used. Telework is a broad term that means using telecommunications to work from a home office, a client's office, or a multitude of other locations. The term **teleworkers** refers to those individuals who are full- or part-time employees of an organization and work from home for part or all of the workweek. Also, **remote employment** (any working arrangement in which the worker performs a significant portion of work at some fixed location other than the traditional

workplace) and the **virtual office** (the operational domain of any organization that includes remote workers) are terms used in describing the concept of work that is done through technology in which an individual is physically present in one location and virtually present in another. You will learn more about telework in Chapter 15, Teleworker/Virtual Assistant.

The number of teleworkers in the United States continues to increase.

> Quality Focus

Whether the organization is national or international, its effectiveness and long life depend on the production of a quality product or service. Workforce teams have become an important part of producing quality work based on the concepts of Dr. W. Edwards Deming, an American statistician who developed the quality concept. He first introduced his concepts to businesses in the United States but failed to receive their support. In the 1950s, he took his concepts to Japan, where industrialists received him and his ideas enthusiastically. Significant productivity results began to emerge in Japanese industries. In fact, Japan began to surpass the United States in certain areas of production; e.g., technology and cars. As a result, American businesses began to pay attention to the processes being used in Japan and began to apply Deming's principles in their firms. Deming's concepts stressed the principle of continued improvement through **total quality management (TQM).** This approach is also referred to as **continuous quality improvement (CQI).** Deming's 14 principles are listed in Figure 1-1.

---

[8]FAQs about Telecommuting, <http://www.langhoff.com/faqs.html> (accessed January 7, 2005).

Figure 1-1   PRINCIPLES FOR AMERICAN MANAGEMENT

W. Edwards Deming

1. Create constancy of purpose for improvement of product and service, with the aim to become competitive, to stay in business, and to provide jobs.

2. Adopt a new philosophy. We are in a new economic age. Western management must awaken to the challenge, must learn their responsibilities and take on leadership for change.

3. Cease dependence on inspection to achieve quality. Eliminate a need for inspection on a mass basis by building quality into the product in the first place.

4. End the practice of awarding business on the basis of price tag alone. Instead minimize the total cost.

5. Improve constantly and forever the system of production and service.

6. Institute training on the job.

7. Institute leadership. The aim of leadership should be to help people do a better job.

8. Drive out fear so that everyone may work effectively for the company.

9. Break down barriers between departments. People in research, design, sales, and production must work as a team.

10. Eliminate slogans, exhortations, and targets for the workforce. Managers need to learn real ways of motivating people.

11. Eliminate work standards on the factory floor; substitute leadership. Eliminate management by numbers and numerical goals; substitute leadership.

12. Remove barriers that rob the hourly worker of his [or her] pride of workmanship. The responsibility of the supervisor must be changed from sheer numbers to quality. Remove barriers that rob people in management and engineering of their right to pride of workmanship.

13. Institute a vigorous program of education and self-improvement.

14. Put everyone in the company to work to accomplish the transformation. The transformation is everyone's job.

Excerpted from W. Edwards Deming, *Out of the Crisis,* Massachusetts: Massachusetts Institute of Technology, 1993.

How does TQM affect the administrative professional? How does it change your work? Here are some possibilities. You may find that you are:

▶ More involved in decisions that affect the direction of the organization.
▶ Part of a workforce team (perhaps even leading a team) that is responsible for improving a service or product.
▶ Expected to be a productive member of a team, making unique contributions that assist the company in improving the quality of its goods and services.
▶ More involved in helping to solve the problems of the organization.

▷ Downsizing

Downsizing, reducing the number of full-time employees in an organization, has become a large corporate movement. You merely have to be aware of

newspaper headlines to notice this trend. Newspapers and periodicals carry downsizing stories of corporations that reflect the national movement. Many major companies (such as Bank of America, Bristol-Myers, Hewlett Packard, and Verizon) downsized their companies in the last few years. There are two major reasons for downsizing—to streamline an organization so that it is more manageable and to cut **overhead costs** (salary and benefit costs) Additionally, such events as 9-11 have forced companies such as airlines to downsize. An employee can no longer assume that an organization is committed to lifetime employment.

▷ Outsourcing

Outsourcing, utilizing an outside company or a consultant to take over the performance of a particular part of an organization's business or to complete a project, is a cost-cutting measure being used extensively today. For example, an outside computer firm may be hired to perform the computer operations of a company. This approach can save the organization money in salary dollars and benefits often granted to employees, such as health insurance and retirement options.

A number of organizations use the assistance of **temporary agencies.** These temporary agencies supply the business with various types of workers, including accounting assistants, administrative professionals, and human resources assistants. Statistics show that twice as many temporary workers are employed by organizations today as in the past.

▷ Workweek

As you have already learned, the workplace may be the traditional office, the home office, or any number of other locations. Just as the workplace has changed, so has the workday. The workday may be nine-to-five or it may involve flexible hours. In addition to the flexible workday, the workweek may be compressed, may involve flextime, or may involve job sharing with another individual.

Job sharing can provide for more family time.

With a **compressed workweek,** employees work the usual number of hours (35 to 40); however, the hours are compressed into 4 days. For example, a 35-hour week may consist of 3 days of 9 hours each and a fourth day of 8 hours. Another departure from the workday is the **flextime** approach (the staggering of working hours to enable an employee to work the full quota of time but at periods defined by the company and the individual). Flextime helps to reduce traffic congestion at the traditional peak hours and allows employees needed flexibility in their schedules. Still another departure from the traditional workday is **job sharing.** Under this arrangement, two part-time employees perform a job that otherwise would be held by one full-time employee. Such a plan may be suitable for a mother or father with small children or workers who want to ease into retirement.

▷ The Office

The office today may be the traditional office in a building where people report to work each Monday morning and work through Friday afternoon in the traditional hours of 9 a.m. to 5 p.m. However, more and more people are working in places different from this traditional office, with growing types of offices being the *virtual office,* the *mobile office,* and the *home office.* The virtual office has no physical form and allows you to perform work from a variety of locations. You will learn more about this growing work opportunity in Chapter 15.

Mobile offices are temporary offices set up at almost any location that has workspace available. Places such as coffee houses, airport terminals, and hotels now have workspaces that allow individuals to set up a mobile office. Additionally, with the technology available, numerous people have **home offices** where they work from home on a full-time basis or a part-time basis. The capabilities of technology suggest that more and more workers will be working from virtual offices, mobile offices, or home offices in the future.

> ORGANIZATIONAL TYPES

The principal types of organizations are:

- ▸ Businesses.
- ▸ Not-for-Profit Entities.
- ▸ Governmental Units.

⊳ Businesses

The principal forms of business organizations are sole proprietorships, general partnerships, limited partnerships, corporations, limited liability companies, and cooperatives. No one form of business is applicable to all business needs. When setting up a business, the goal is to select the legal form that meets the needs of the business and its owners. Factors that need to be considered when forming a business include financing and liquidity of investments, management flexibility, liability, taxation, legal considerations, life of the business, and potential growth of the organization. For your overall understanding of the types of businesses, brief definitions of each type are given.

Sole Proprietorship

A **sole proprietorship** is a business owned and controlled by a single person. All responsibilities, profits and losses belong to the owner.

General Partnership

A **partnership** consists of an association of two or more people, as co-owners, of a business.

Limited Partnership

A **limited partnership** consists of an association of two or more owners, with at least one general partner and at least one limited partner. The partners share the profits or losses in proportion to their ownership agreement.

Corporations

A **corporation** is a legal entity in itself. Corporations are formed by following a formal process of incorporation set forth by state statutes, with the corporation publicly or privately owned. Owners (**stockholders**) hold shares of stock in the company.

Limited Liability Companies

A **limited liability company** (**LLC**) is a business form that combines the tax advantages of a partnership with the limited liability of a corporation. It must include two or more members. The rights of an LLC include conducting or promoting any lawful business or purpose that a partnership or individual may conduct or promote; it can own property, borrow money, loan money, enter into contracts, and elect or appoint managers or agents. An advantage of an LLC is that members receive limited personal liability from business activities. Professionals such as medical doctors, accountants, and lawyers may operate as an LLC.

Cooperatives

A **cooperative** is a type of corporation that is user owned and user controlled. The users are its customers or patrons; they are eligible to own stock, receive a share of the net income or profits, and control the cooperative as a voting member.

⊳ Not-for-Profit Entities

Not-for-profit entities (also known as **nonprofit corporations**) have several characteristics similar to profit-seeking business entities, including management processes and accounting systems. However, not-for-profits are exempt from income taxation on activities related to their exempt purpose. Additionally, these organizations typically have **fiduciary** (holding in trust for another) responsibility to their members and contributors. Numerous organizations, such as service organizations, performing arts groups, hospitals, faith-based organizations, charities, and private colleges and universities are set up as not-for-profit entities. However, some entities listed in this category, such as certain hospitals and schools, do operate as a business and seek to be profitable.

⊳ Governmental Units

Governmental units are not-for-profit units that operate at the local, state, and national levels. Examples of governmental units include city services, county services, state services, and national services. There are numerous departments, commissions, bureaus, and boards in all governmental units.

> WORKPLACE STRUCTURES

If you are to be an effective and productive administrative professional, you will find it crucial to learn as much as you can about how the entire organization functions. If the organization is a publicly held company, there are stockholders to consider in addition to the Board of Directors, the administrators, and employees of the organization. Although organizations operate differently, the major levels of an organization, along with an overview of the responsibilities of the individuals at this level, are given here.

Stockholders

Stockholders are investors in or owners of businesses. A stockholder owns a portion or a share of the business. Stockholders may be affected by the actions, decisions, policies, or practices of the business. For example, if the business has management issues, ethical issues, and/or financial problems, the value of the stock of the company may decrease. Thus, the stockholder loses money on his/her investment.

Board of Directors

Large corporations have **boards of directors** who have the major responsibility of establishing policies that guide the management of the organization. Boards are composed of community, civic, and business leaders, who meet monthly or every two or three months. In addition to making policy decisions, boards employ, evaluate, and dismiss (if necessary) the CEO of the corporation. Boards generally operate as a total board and also as committees of the board as a whole. For example, a major board committee is one that deals with the ethics and corporate responsibility of the entity. Board ethics committees are often involved in these activities: reviewing the ethical responsibilities of the company's employees and consultants; reviewing and assessing the company's policies and procedures; and addressing the resolution of conflicts of interest involving the company, its employees, officers, and directors.

Management

Individuals who carry out the direction of the board are classified as top or upper management. These people include the CEO, who reports directly to the Board, the **chief operating officer,** (COO) and the **chief financial officer** (CFO). Corporations also employ other officers of the company such as a president (who generally reports to the CEO), vice president, secretary, and treasurer, who are considered upper administration. Additionally, there are other administrators at lower levels responsible for the day-to-day operations of the organization. Figure 1-2 depicts a typical organizational chart. Many corporations use team management in which groups of

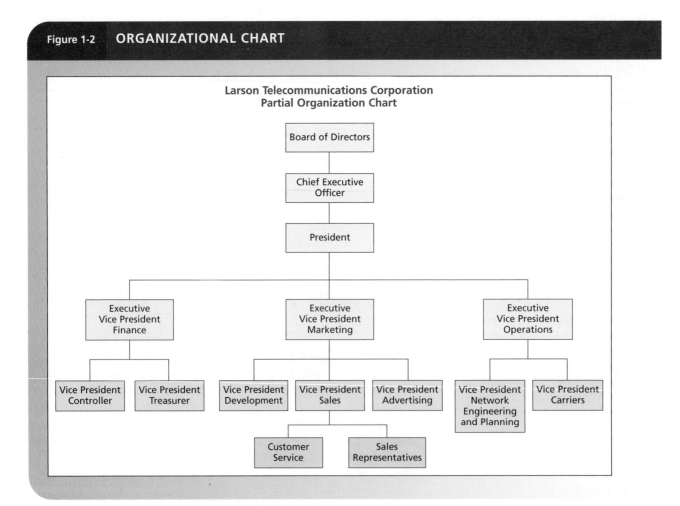

Figure 1-2   ORGANIZATIONAL CHART

Larson Telecommunications Corporation
Partial Organization Chart

Board of Directors

Chief Executive Officer

President

Executive Vice President Finance

Executive Vice President Marketing

Executive Vice President Operations

Vice President Controller

Vice President Treasurer

Vice President Development

Vice President Sales

Vice President Advertising

Vice President Network Engineering and Planning

Vice President Carriers

Customer Service

Sales Representatives

people within the organization serve on teams to address issues and operating procedures within the organization. These teams are often charged with making the final decisions, an approach that is referred to as **empowerment.**

⊳ Administrative Professional

An **administrative professional** is defined by the International Association of Administrative Professionals (IAAP) as an individual who possesses a mastery of office skills, demonstrates the ability to assume responsibility without direct supervision, exercises initiative and judgment, and makes decisions within the scope of assigned authority.

With the availability of technology and the emphasis on greater efficiency and productivity through **flattened organizational structures** (fewer management levels than the traditional structures of the past) and teams, administrative professionals of today and tomorrow will find that their role is continually shifting, with many administrative professionals assuming more responsibility than in the past.

Evolving Role

For years the administrative professional's title was confined to secretary, receptionist, and such specialized titles as legal and medical secretaries. Although the titles mentioned here are still used to a limited extent, the emerging titles today reflect the shifting role of the administrative professional. A few of these titles are administrative assistant, executive assistant, marketing assistant, payroll assistant, human resources assistant, office manager, and project manager.

Job Responsibilities

The evolving role is also reflected in the duties of the administrative professional, which include:

1. Researching and preparing reports (using the Web, as well as traditional research methods) complete with graphics and spreadsheets.

2. Assisting with the planning and direction of the company by leading TQM teams and working on organizational teams.

3. Administering computer networks.

4. Helping to upgrade and recommend office software.

5. Providing computer and software training.

6. Managing websites.

7. Working with outsourcing companies such as accounting and staffing firms.

Although job roles and responsibilities differ among the various positions, certain skills and knowledge sets are essential in all administrative professional roles. These skills and knowledge sets will be discussed in the next section and emphasized throughout this course. The term administrative professional will be used consistently throughout the text to denote the workplace support person.

Workplace Requirements

If the administrative professional is to succeed in a world of technology and rapid change, he or she needs certain skills and qualities. You should begin now to develop or improve these skills and qualities.

Success Skills. Numerous studies have been conducted with employers to determine the skills needed by administrative professionals. These skills most often listed are:

Interpersonal skills.
Teamwork skills.
Verbal and written communication skills.
Analytical/critical thinking skills.
Technology/computer skills.
Leadership skills.
Time, stress, and organizational management skills.
Verbal presentation skills.

The next section covers these skills in detail.

Administrative professionals often work in teams to accomplish an organizational task.

Interpersonal Skills. For a number of years, surveys have shown that when prospective employers are asked to rank the importance of candidate qualities and skills, the top five include communication skills, honesty and integrity, the ability to work on a team,

Self

Respond to the following comments with a yes or no answer.

	Yes	No
1. I understand that differences exist in culture, race, and ethnicity.	☐	☐
2. I respect others' differences in culture, race, and ethnicity.	☐	☐
3. I expect all individuals to react to situations just as I do.	☐	☐
4. I listen carefully when others are talking.	☐	☐
5. I ignore body language when others are talking.	☐	☐
6. I am conscious of the words I use in my written communications.	☐	☐
7. I avoid dealing with conflict.	☐	☐
8. I evaluate individuals when they are talking to me.	☐	☐
9. I trust people who are older than I am.	☐	☐
10. I think men are better supervisors than women.	☐	☐

interpersonal effectiveness, motivation and initiative, and a strong work ethic. These skills are often referred to as the **soft skills** (business-related nontechnical skills). Studies have also shown that more employees lose their jobs because of poor interpersonal skills than poor technology skills. As an administrative professional, you come in contact with a number of people. Within the company, you work with coworkers, your supervisor, and other executives. Contacts outside the company include customers and other visitors to your office, all with different backgrounds and experiences. If you are to be effective, you need to understand and accept the people with whom you work, both inside and outside the company. Interpersonal skills are like most of our other skills. We must constantly develop and improve these skills if we are to grow in our abilities.

Take the interpersonal skills Self-Check and compare your answers to the suggested responses at the end of the chapter. Where do you need to improve? Commit now to improving these areas during this course. You will have an opportunity to learn more about the importance of interpersonal skills and to continue to develop your skills throughout this course.

Teamwork Skills. You have learned in this chapter that organizations are using teams more and more in producing work. Obviously, if these teams are to be successful, individual team members must possess the ability to work well together. The word **team** can

be traced back to the Indo-European word *deuk,* meaning "to pull together." Successful teams in the work environment include groups of people who need each other to accomplish a given task. Teamwork skills are very similar to interpersonal skills in that they demand that you understand, accept, and respect the differences among your team members. Teamwork also demands that you engage in the following behaviors:

▶ Behave courteously to all team members.
▶ Build strong relationships with your team members so the team's goals can be accomplished.
▶ Learn collectively with your team. You must start with self-knowledge and self-mastery, but then you must look outward to develop knowledge and alignment with your team members.
▶ Take responsibility for producing high-quality work as an individual team member and encouraging a high-quality team project.

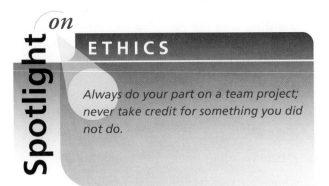

Spotlight *on* **ETHICS**

Always do your part on a team project; never take credit for something you did not do.

Verbal and Written Communication Skills. If you are to be an effective verbal communicator, you must be able to express yourself accurately, concisely, and tactfully. Additionally, you must be a good listener. Although we spend a large amount of our time listening, we do not always listen well. Even when we listen well, we may not grasp the full implication of what has been said. As you have already discovered, the office continues to become more diverse in ethnicity, gender, and age. This diversity demands your constant improvement in verbal communication so you can effectively work with the huge diversity of the workforce. You will learn more about verbal communication in Chapter 8.

In addition to verbal communication, written communication is extremely important in the office. Written communication takes the form of e-mails, letters, memorandums, faxes, and reports. You must express yourself accurately and concisely in written correspondence. You will learn more about written communication in Chapter 6.

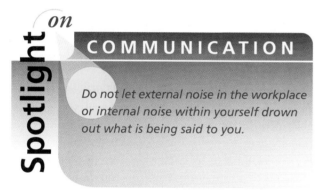

Spotlight *on* COMMUNICATION

Do not let external noise in the workplace or internal noise within yourself drown out what is being said to you.

Analytical/Critical Thinking Skills. **Analytical** is defined in the dictionary as "reasoning from a perception of the parts and interrelations of a subject."[9] In the fast-paced world of today, it is imperative that we understand the interrelatedness of problems and issues. For example, here are some questions that can be asked to help you think analytically.

▶ How many sides/issues are there to the problem?
▶ What steps should I take in order to view all sides of the problem/issue?
▶ What conclusions/recommendations follow from an analysis of the issue?

In our complex world, the administrative professional must think analytically about problems.

▶ How should I go about implementing these recommendations?

Critical thinking is closely related to analytical thinking. In fact, critical thinking is a form of analytical thinking. **Critical thinking** can be defined as a unique kind of purposeful thinking in which the thinker systematically and habitually imposes criteria and intellectual standards upon the thinking. Critical thinking involves:

▶ Taking charge of the construction of thinking,
▶ Guiding the construction of the thinking according to standards, and
▶ Assessing the effectiveness of the thinking according to the purpose, the criteria, and the standards.[10]

When we think critically about a subject, we try to see it from all sides before coming to a conclusion. Critical thinking requires us to see things from perspectives other than our own.

Both analytical and critical thinking are considered soft skills. Other soft skills are those relating to teamwork, leadership, and stress management. You will continue to learn about soft skills throughout this course. Although these skills are known as soft skills because they are nontechnical, do not make the mistake of assuming they are nonessential skills. In fact, job studies show that people are fired more because of their lack of understanding of soft skills and their inability to produce on soft skills than their lack of ability to produce in the technical area.

---

[9] *The American Heritage College Dictionary,* 3rd ed. (Boston: Houghton Mifflin Company, 1993), p. 48.
[10] Richard Paul, *Critical Thinking: How to Prepare Students for a Rapidly Changing World* (California: Foundation for Critical Thinking, 1993), p. 21.

Commit yourself now to improving your soft skills in this course and continuing to work in these areas throughout your career. Just as you must constantly learn new technical skills throughout your career because of changes in technology, so must you continue to improve your soft skills.

In each chapter throughout the course, the soft skill objective is italicized. This approach is used to remind you of the importance of soft skills and the need for you to concentrate on developing them.

If you are to succeed in the complex world of the 21st century, you must be able to think critically about the day-to-day decisions you make in the workplace. The Critical Thinking Cases and Workplace Projects in the course require that you demonstrate your continual growth in critical thinking. At the end of each chapter, a workplace situation is given in the Critical Thinking Case. You will be asked to critically analyze the activity and determine how it should be handled, using a critical-thinking approach. To help you understand more about how critical thinking is approached, read the list of questions in Figure 1-3. You should ask yourself these questions when you are attempting to critically analyze an issue.

Technology/Computer Skills. Success today demands that you be technologically competent. You must be

▶ Proficient on a computer.
▶ Knowledgeable about the most current software packages, including word processing, spreadsheets, databases, graphics, and presentation software.
▶ Competent in using telecommunications equipment.
▶ Competent in using printers/copiers.

▶ Willing to continually learn new workforce technology.

Leadership Skills. Leadership skills are developed over time. They are not something that we automatically have at birth. You begin to develop your leadership skills by seeking out and/or accepting leadership opportunities. For example, accepting the chairperson position of a committee helps you develop leadership skills. Accepting an office in one of your college organizations or in a professional organization to which you belong helps you develop leadership skills. The essential strategy for you to remember is to look for leadership opportunities and take advantage of each one. As you pursue and are granted certain leadership opportunities, learn from each one. Evaluate yourself or ask a close friend to evaluate your performance. What mistakes did you make? How can you correct your mistakes?

As you are promoted to higher-level positions, you may also have the responsibility of supervising one or more employees. Being an effective supervisor, one who is able to inspire people to produce at their maximum, demands that you understand and apply effective leadership and management principles. Chapter 16 will help you learn and apply these skills.

Time, Stress, and Organizational Management Skills. As an efficient administrative professional, you must be able to organize your time and your workload. Additionally, you must be able to effectively handle stress. You must be able to establish priorities, determining what needs to be done first. You must organize your workstation and files, whether they are paper or electronic. You must organize your time so your work flows

---

Figure 1-3   **CRITICAL THINKING STRATEGIES**

▶ What is the purpose of my thinking?

▶ What problem or question am I trying to answer?

▶ What facts do I need to address this problem or question?

▶ How do I interpret the facts or information I receive?

▶ What conclusions can I make from the information I received?

▶ Are my conclusions defensible?

▶ Have I dealt with the complexity of the situation?

▶ Have I avoided thinking in simple stereotypes?

▶ What will be the consequences if I put my conclusions into practice?

Richard Paul, *Critical Thinking: How to Prepare Students for a Rapidly Changing World.* (California: Foundation for Critical Thinking 1993), pp. 17–36.

smoothly and tasks are finished as needed. Chapter 3 will help you understand more about these important skills and give you a chance to practice them.

Verbal Presentation Skills. Administrative professionals today serve on project teams and may even chair a team. These project teams often make presentations of their findings and recommendations to peer groups or to executives within the workplace. You may also have occasion to speak at professional organizations to which you belong. If your presentations are to be successful, you must develop verbal presentation skills. Chapter 8 will help you develop these skills.

Other success skills such as ethical responsibility, problem solving, and continual learning will be discussed later.

Success Qualities
In addition to the skills that have been identified, there are certain qualities that are essential for the success of the administrative professional. These qualities include openness to change, creativity, dependability, confidentiality, integrity, initiative/motivation, and flexibility/adaptability.

Openness to Change. Because change will continue to play such an important role in the workplace, you must learn to cope with change as well as embrace it. Embracing change means accepting and preparing for change and being creative and flexible. Try to predict the changes you will face, and prepare yourself for them. For example, because you know technology will continue to play an important role in the workplace, keep current on the latest technological changes that might impact your workplace.

Creativity. **Creativity** is the ability to approach existing ideas or things in new ways. When a change occurs, you can usually connect that change to some

The administrative professional makes presentations to peer groups and others within the organization.

© Photodisc

already existing idea or way of doing something. Review the steps listed in Figure 1-4 to help you understand how to deal with change.

Dependability. **Dependability** means being trustworthy. It means being at work on time if you are working at an established location. If you are engaged in telework, it means being productive in performing your job. Dependability is the willingness to put in additional time on important assignments. It also means doing what you say you will do and when you say you will do it.

Confidentiality. As an administrative professional, you have access to information that is extremely confidential. For example, if you are working in the personnel department of an organization, you have

Figure 1-4   DEALING WITH CHANGE

Follow these steps in dealing effectively with change.

1. Understand why change is necessary. Determine what circumstances have occurred that have necessitated change.

2. Determine what objectives will be achieved by the changes that are proposed.

3. Establish guidelines for achieving those objectives.

4. Determine the benefits or rewards that will occur as a result of the change.

5. Once the change has occurred, evaluate the effectiveness of the change and your effectiveness in working through the change.

access to information about employees—their work history, performance evaluations, salaries, ages, and so on. If you work for a criminal attorney, you may have access to information about a client's case. If you work for a physician or other health care professional, you may have access to patients' files containing highly personal and confidential information about health issues. Your employer may occasionally talk with you about information that is highly confidential—perhaps a merger with another company that is pending. You may also overhear confidential conversations between executives. You must always maintain the **confidentiality** (secrecy) of the information received or the confidences shared. To let any confidential information leak outside your office may cause irreparable damage to your employer, to others within your organization, to customers, and to your organization.

Integrity. The dictionary definition of **integrity** is "adherence to a strict ethical code."[11] In the workplace environment, adherence means in part that you are honest. It means you do not take equipment or supplies that belong to the company for your own personal use. It means you spend your time on the job performing the duties of the job—not making and receiving personal telephone calls or writing personal e-mail messages. It means you uphold high standards of ethical behavior. You do not engage in activities in which your morals or values may be questioned.

Initiative/Motivation. The dictionary defines **initiative** as "the ability to begin and follow through on a plan or task."[12] Initiative is taking the tasks you are given and completing them in an appropriate manner. It means having the ability to set appropriate work goals for yourself. The most highly valued administrative professional has the ability to analyze a task, establish priorities, and see the work through to completion. The administrative professional takes the initiative to make suggestions to the employer about needed changes or revisions and is truly worth his or her weight in gold.

Motivation is closely related to initiative. Motivation means that someone is provided with an incentive to act—a move to action. In taking the initiative to begin a task, you may be motivated **extrinsically** (from outside) or **intrinsically** (from within). For example, you may be motivated to perform a task because it provides a monetary reward for you or external recognition from your supervisor, which is outside or extrinsic motivation. Additionally, you may be motivated to perform a task because you are committed to learning and growing—an example of intrinsic motivation. You understand that each task you perform provides you the opportunity to learn something new.

Flexibility/Adaptability. **Flexibility** is being responsive to change. **Adaptability** is being capable of adjusting. As you can readily determine, the two terms are closely related. In our fast-paced global and technology-driven world, we must respond and adjust to the changes that are constantly occurring not only in our work world but also in our personal life. You learned earlier in this chapter about the importance of being able to work with a diverse workforce. You also learned that mergers, downsizing, outsourcing, and telework can and often do make our work environment very different from the work environment of the past. All of these changes demand your flexibility and adaptability.

Professional Image

The administrative professional with a professional image constantly presents to the public the essential skills and success qualities discussed in the previous sections. In addition, the administrative professional must present a positive personal appearance. He or she dresses in appropriate business attire and is well groomed. The administrative professional pays attention to hairstyle, personal hygiene, appropriate jewelry and accessories, physical condition, good posture, and proper eating habits. Depending on the office, appropriate business attire may include a suit and tie for males and a suit or dress for females. Some workplaces may be more relaxed, allowing shirts without a tie for males and skirts or slacks and blouses or sweaters for females. A number of workplaces have a day once a month or even once a week when casual dress is appropriate, even if the remaining days are considered standard business attire. Some organizations allow employees to dress in business casual on a daily basis. Many organizations are becoming more casual in their dress considerations, while some are going back to standard business attire. If you are uncertain about the appropriate dress style in your organization, notice how respected people in the organization dress. You can generally follow their lead.

---

[11]*American Heritage College Dictionary*, 3rd ed. (Boston: Houghton Mifflin Company, 1993), p. 706.
[12]Ibid., p. 700.

Part I The Work Environment

A professional image is more than dressing appropriately, however. A positive personal appearance without the necessary skills and qualities is meaningless. If the administrative professional expects to succeed, he or she must combine the necessary skills and qualities with an appropriate personal appearance. A professional image is a combination of all of these areas.

Professional Growth

In our constantly changing world, you must be willing to continue your professional growth. This professional growth can be through:

- ▶ Attending classes at a college or university.
- ▶ Attending seminars and workshops provided by your company or outside firms.
- ▶ Reading business periodicals.
- ▶ Participating in professional organizations.

Periodicals. Numerous periodicals are available with articles to assist you in enhancing your knowledge and skills. Several of these periodicals are listed in Figure 1-5. Begin now to become familiar with them by reading selected articles. Visit your school or local library to see what periodicals on this list are available.

Organizations. Listed here are several organizations that provide growth opportunities for the administrative professional.

1. International Association of Administrative Professionals® (IAAP)—This organization is the world's largest association for administrative support staff, with nearly 700 chapters and 40,000 members and affiliates worldwide. IAAP administers two

| Figure 1-5 | **PROFESSIONAL PERIODICALS** |

OfficePro (published by International Association of Administrative Professionals)
  The Information Management Journal (published by the Association of Records Managers and Administrators)
  Business Week
  Fortune
  U.S. News & World Report
  Time
  The Wall Street Journal (a newspaper)
  PC Magazine
  PC World
  Pocket PC

professional certification programs—CPS (Certified Professional Secretary) and CAP (Certified Administrative Professional). The letters CPS or CAP after an administrative professional's name are indicative of the achievement of the highest professional standard within the field. Figure 1-6 gives more details about this certification. IAAP publishes a magazine called *OfficePro.* The Web address for IAAP is www.iaap-hq.org.

2. NALS—The Association for Legal Professionals—offers members and nonmembers the opportunity to obtain these certifications:
   ALS (the basic certification for legal professionals)
   PLS (the advanced certification for legal professionals)
   PP (a certification for those professionals performing paralegal duties)
   The Web address for NALS is www.nals.org.

| Figure 1-6 | **THE CERTIFIED PROFESSIONAL SECRETARY AND THE CERTIFIED ADMINISTRATIVE PROFESSIONAL** |

WHY CERTIFICATION?

Job Advancement—Certification gives you a competitive edge for hiring and promotion.

Professional Skills—You will learn more about office operations and build skills by studying for and taking the CPS or CAP examination.

Salary—A recent IAAP membership profile study shows that CPS holders earn an average of $2,228 more per year than those who do not have certification.

Esteem—Attaining certification demonstrates to your employer and yourself that you are committed as a professional.

College Credit—Many colleges and universities offer course credit for studying for and passing the CPS and CAP examinations.

Certification Seminar—Receive the benefit of annual state-of-the-art education and network with other professionals in the administrative field.

Excerpted from www.iaap-hq.org/cps/.

3. Legal Secretaries International confers the designation Board Certified Legal Secretary Specialist in areas such as civil litigation, real estate, probate, intellectual property, and business law to individuals who have five years of law-related experience and who pass the examination. The Web address for Legal Secretaries International is www.legalsecretaries.org.

4. American Association for Medical Transcription (AAMT)—This organization is for office staff, assistants, and technicians employed by physicians or hospitals. It sponsors a certification program, Certified Medical Transcriptionist (CMT), and publishes a magazine called the *Journal of the American Association for Medical Transcription.* The Web address for the American Association for Medical Transcription is www.aamt.org.

5. National Association of Educational Office Professionals (NAEOP)—NAEOP (at www.naeop.org) sponsors a program that issues certificates based on education, experience, and professional activity. It also publishes the *National Educational Secretary.*

6. ARMA International, the Association for Information Management Professionals—This association sponsors the Certified Records Manager (CRM) designation. It publishes *The Information Management Journal.* The Web address for ARMA is www.arma.org.

SUMMARY

Reinforce your learning in this chapter by studying this summary.

▶ The workplace of 2050 will be drastically different from our present day workplace, with continued innovations in technology changing our work life.

▶ The workplace of 2050 will reflect even more change, with numerous jobs being transferred from people to virtual programmers—a phenomenon known as intelligence sourcing.

▶ The workforce will become increasingly diverse, with minorities and immigrants constituting a larger share of the workforce.

▶ Greater numbers of women will be in the workforce, and women will hold positions of greater authority and responsibility.

▶ The number of workers 55 and older is expected to grow.

▶ Because of our ever-increasing technological world, the level of education for jobs will be higher than in the past. Lifelong learning will be essential for all workers.

▶ The number of teleworkers will continue to grow.

▶ The emphasis on quality and productivity will continue, with downsizing and outsourcing as viable business strategies.

▶ The traditional workweek will continue to change, with the compressed workweek, flextime, and job sharing remaining as alternatives to the nine-to-five concept.

▶ The principal types of organizations can be divided into three types: businesses, not-for-profit entities, and governmental units.

▶ The major levels of organization power and responsibility are stockholders, board of directors, and management.

▶ With the emphasis in organizations on getting more work done with fewer people, flattened organizational structures with fewer management levels and teams are two approaches to greater efficiency and productivity.

▶ The administrative professional role is continually shifting, with many administrative professionals assuming more responsibility than in the past.

▶ The job responsibilities of the administrative professional include research, report preparation, teamwork (with administrative professionals being team leaders), and management of websites, to name a few.

▶ Success skills needed by the administrative professional are interpersonal; teamwork; verbal and written communication; analytical/critical thinking; technology/computer; leadership, time, stress, and organizational management; and verbal presentation.

▶ Success qualities for the administrative professional include openness to change, creativity, dependability, confidentiality, integrity, initiative/motivation, and flexibility/adaptability.

▶ Administrative professionals must be willing to continue their professional growth throughout their careers. This growth can be through attending classes at a college or university, attending seminars and workshops, reading business periodicals, and/or participating in professional organizations.

GLOSSARY

Adaptability—Being capable of adjusting.

Administrative professionals—IAAP defines administrative professionals as individuals who possess a mastery of office skills, demonstrate the ability to assume responsibility without direct supervision, exercise initiative and judgment, and make decisions within the scope of assigned authority.

Analytical—Reasoning from a perception of the parts and interrelations of a subject.

Baby boomers—People born in the period 1946 through 1964.

BlackBerries—Wireless handheld devices offering various services such as e-mail and Internet access that have grown significantly since September 11, 2001.

Boards of directors—Persons with the main responsibility of establishing policies that guide management of the organization.

CEO—Chief Executive Officer.

CFO—Chief Financial Officer.

Compressed workweek—Regular workweek hours compressed into four days.

Confidentiality—Ability to maintain secrecy of information received or confidences shared.

COO—Chief Operating Officer.

Cooperative—A type of corporation that is user-owned and user-controlled.

Corporation—A legal entity in itself.

Creativity—The ability to approach existing ideas or things in new ways.

Critical thinking—A unique kind of purposeful thinking in which the thinker systematically imposes criteria and intellectual standards upon the thinking.

Dependability—Trustworthy.

Downsizing—Reducing the number of full-time employees in an organization.

DS—A digital shopper who will know your spending habits, financial ability, and taste in products.

Empowerment—Approach where teams are charged with making final decisions.

Extrinsically—Motivation from outside.

Fiduciary—Holding in trust for another.

Flattened organizational structures—Fewer management levels than the traditional organizational structures of the past.

Flexibility—Being responsive to change.

Flextime—Staggering of working hours to enable an employee to work the full quota of time but at periods defined by the company and the individual.

Generation X—People born in the period 1965 through 1975.

Generation Y—People born in the period 1976 through 1981.

Governmental units—Not-for-profit units that operate at the local, state, and national levels.

Home office—Offices in people's homes from which they work full- or part-time.

Information envelope—A tiny electronic device that will be used to tell a digital shopper what is needed.

Initiative—The ability to begin and follow through on a plan or task.

Integrity—Adherence to a strict ethical code.

Intelligence sourcing or I-Sourcing—Transferring jobs from people to virtual programmers.

Intrinsically—Motivation from within.

Job sharing—Two part-time employees performing a job that otherwise would be held by one full-time employee.

Limited liability company—A business form that combines the tax advantages of a partnership with the limited liability of a corporation.

Limited partnership—Association of two or more owners with at least one general partner and at least one limited partner.

Millennial Generation—People born in the period 1982 through 2003.

Mobile offices—Temporary offices set up at almost any location that has workspace available.

Motivation—Provided with an incentive to act, a move to action.

Not-for-profit entities (nonprofit corporations)—Organizations similar to profit-making ones, but exempt from income taxes related to exempt purpose. Service organizations, performing arts groups, hospitals, faith-based organizations, charities, and private colleges and universities are examples.

Outsourcing—Using an outside company or a consultant to take over the performance of a particular part of an organization's business or to complete a project.

Overhead costs—Salary and benefit costs.

Partnership—Consists of an association of two or more people as co-owners of a business.

Remote employment—Any working arrangement in which the worker performs a significant portion of work at some fixed location other than the traditional workplace.

Soft skills—Interpersonal skills such as communication skills, honesty, and integrity, and the ability to work with others as a team.

Sole proprietorship—A business owned and controlled by a single person.

Stereotype—A perception or an assumption held of people or things that may be favorable or unfavorable.

Stockholders—Individuals who hold shares of stock in a company.

Team—A word that means "to pull together" in order to accomplish a given task.

Telework—Using telecommunications to work from a home office, a client's office, or a multitude of other locations.

Teleworkers—Individuals who are full-time or part-time employees but work from home at least part of the workweek.

Temporary agencies—Companies that supply the business with various types of temporary workers.

Total quality management (TQM) or continuous quality improvement (CQI)—Emphasizes continued improvement of both goods and services through team approaches within a business, emphasizing leadership and pride in the work.

TP Industry—Telepresence industry in which virtual travel is possible due to a unit that can create the illusion of another location halfway around the world or just around the corner.

Virtual office—The operational domain of any organization that includes remote workers; it has no physical form and allows you to perform work from a variety of locations.

CHECKPOINT

Check your understanding of these terms by completing DCD1-a on the Data CD.

DISCUSSION ITEMS

These discussion items provide an opportunity to test your understanding of the chapter through written responses and/or discussion with your classmates and your instructor.

1. Explain how the work environment of 2012 and 2050 will be drastically different from our present workplace.

2. What is the projected diversity of the workforce of 2012?

3. How is the present work environment changing?

4. Explain the types of businesses, and define stockholders, board of directors, and management.

5. How is the administrative professional's role changing?

6. What skills are needed in the twenty-first century? In your response, explain the meaning of each skill.

CRITICAL THINKING CASE

JWay Nu-Systems Tech has introduced TQM in an effort to improve services provided to customers. You were asked to be part of a team that looks at the improvement of internal communication, and you took the assignment seriously. Before the first meeting, you identified several communication problems that seem to be ongoing in the organization. You brought these communication problems up at the meeting; i.e., failure to respond to e-mail promptly, failure to respond to voice mail, and communication issues within certain departments (ethnic and age diversity issues). Two of the individuals who work in your department became upset with you. They assumed that your statements referred to situations you had encountered with them. They exploded in the meeting, making these comments:

▶ I can't answer the e-mails you send me within the hour. Get off my back.

▶ The next time you have a complaint about me, talk with me personally.

▶ How am I to understand people who are 30 years older than I am? We grew up in a different era.

You let the individuals in your department know that you were not talking about individual cases. You were attempting to identify problems that needed to be addressed so the customer might be better served and communication might improve within departments. Since the meeting did not get off to a good start, you feel responsible. You want to be a contributor to the process. What should you do? Think through the following items and prepare responses.

▶ What is the problem?

▶ Do the upset employees have cause to be concerned about your behavior?

CRITICAL THINKING CASE *(continued)*

▶ Should you talk to these employees before the next meeting? If so, what should you say?

▶ How should you identify problems/issues that are negatively affecting office communication?

▶ How can you present problems/issues at the next meeting without causing the volatility of the last meeting?

Remember, your task is to critically analyze the situation given here. Before you attempt to answer the questions, review Figure 1-3.

CRITICAL THINKING

Critical thinking is a unique kind of purposeful thinking in which the thinker systematically and habitually

▶ Imposes criteria and intellectual standards upon the thinking;

▶ Takes charge of the construction of thinking;

▶ Guides the constructions of the thinking according to the standards;

▶ Assesses the effectiveness of the thinking according to the purpose, the criteria, and the standards.[13]

Questions to ask

▶ Is this belief defensible or indefensible? What is the basis for this belief?

▶ Is my position on this issue reasonable and rational?

▶ Am I willing to deal with complexity, or do I retreat into simple stereotypes to avoid it?

▶ Is it appropriate and wise to assume that my ideas and beliefs are accurate, clear, and reasonable if I have not tested them?

▶ Do I ever enter sympathetically into points of view that are very different from my own, or do I just assume that I am right?

▶ Do I know how to question my own ideas and to test them?

RESPONSES TO SELF-CHECK

The most appropriate answers are as follows:

1. Yes	3. No	5. No	7. No	9. Yes
2. Yes	4. Yes	6. Yes	8. No	10. No

WORKPLACE PROJECTS

PROJECT 1-1 CONDUCT WEB SEARCH

Describe the future workforce (Objective 1)

Determine changes in the work environment (Objective 2)

Search the Web for the following information:

▶ Articles on the changing office

▶ Diversity and age and gender statistics in your state presently

Prepare a short summary of the articles, giving the Web addresses; submit your summaries to your instructor.

PROJECT 1-2 PREPARE AN ORGANIZATION CHART

Define the types of business organizations and workplace structures (Objective 3)

With a team of two or three, engage in the following activities:

▶ Search the Web for information on establishing an LLC. Since JWay Nu-Systems Tech (your virtual company) was set up as an LLC, you want to learn more about how an LLC is established and how it operates. Prepare a short report of your findings on the memorandum form given on the file on your CD labeled DCD1-02.

---

[13]Richard Paul, *Critical Thinking: How to Prepare Students for a Rapidly Changing World* (California Foundation for Critical Thinking, 1993), p. 21.

▶ Prepare an organization chart for JWay. Refer to the organizational chart in Figure 1-2, as an example. Titles and reporting structures are as follows: The chief executive officer is the top position; the vice president of purchasing, the vice president of business development, and the vice president of finance report to the chief executive officer. The vice president of purchasing has a purchasing officer reporting; three buyers report to the purchasing officer. The vice president of business development has three senior account executives reporting; the senior account executive has six account executives reporting. The vice president of finance has a controller reporting; the controller has two credit assistants reporting.

PROJECT 1-3 CONDUCT INTERVIEWS

Determine changes in the work environment (Objectve 2)

Describe the role and responsibilities of administrative professionals (Objective 4)

Identify skills and qualities necessary for administrative professionals (Objective 5)

In teams of two or three, interview two administrative professionals. You do not have to interview these people in person; you may choose to do it by e-mail. Ask them the following questions:

▶ What are your roles and responsibilities?

▶ What skills and qualities do you need in order to be successful?

▶ What types of technology changes have occurred in your organization in the last five years? two years?

▶ Describe the diversity of personnel within your organization. Have there been any issues in dealing with this diversity? If so, what were those issues and how were they handled?

Report your findings verbally to the class.

PROJECT 1-4 PREPARE REPORT FROM RESEARCH

Identify skills and qualities necessary for administrative professionals (Objective 5)

In your job as an administrative professional, you constantly work with people. Explain how you will support JWay's value of "upholding excellence in all dealings with our customers." You choose to look at excellence from your position of dealing with customers. Using the Web and periodicals, research appropriate customer relations. Prepare a written report of your research. Submit your written report to your instructor by e-mail if your instructor approves.

PROJECT 1-5 WRITE PRODUCT DESCRIPTION

Describe the role and responsibilities of administrative professionals (Objective 4)

Identify skills and qualities necessary for administrative professionals (Objective 5)

Work in teams of three or four on this project. As new employees of JWay, you want to learn as much as you can about the company so that you may be effective. Using the Internet or computer periodicals, conduct research on the following products that JWay distributes: servers, networking equipment, processors, and tape libraries. If you have access to the technology center in your school, interview the manager and talk with her or him about the types of servers, networking equipment, and so forth that are used in your school. Write a description (as a group) of all of these products, citing your Web sources, periodicals, and/or personal interviews. Submit your report to your instructor; you may do so by e-mail if your instructor approves.

PROJECT 1-6 PREPARE PROFESSIONAL GROWTH PLAN

Begin development of a professional growth plan (Objective 6)

Begin the development of a Professional Growth Plan (PGP), which you will add to throughout the course. This plan should identify the periodicals you will read and/or the professional activities you will attend. For example, you might decide to attend two meetings of your local chapter of IAAP or some other professional organization. Prepare this plan and save it on a disk under "PGP1-6." You will be adding to this disk throughout the course. This portion of your PGP is to be titled "Improving My Knowledge of Today's Business World." You will be asked at the end of the course whether you accomplished the items listed on your professional growth plan.

PROJECT 1-7 REVIEW AND RESPOND TO CASE STUDY

Develop critical-thinking skills (Objective 7)

Read the Critical Thinking Case and respond to the items at the end of the activity. Submit your responses to your instructor by e-mail or by using the memorandum form on DCD1-07.

PROJECT 1-8 ANALYZE NEWS PROGRAMS

Develop critical-thinking skills (Objective 7)

View two current news programs on television (e.g., CNN and Fox); critically analyze whether or not the reporters are being objective in their reporting. Give reasons for your conclusions. Report your findings in a class discussion as directed by your instructor.

COMMUNICATION POWER

Use DCD1-b to assist you in improving your grammar skills.

ASSESSMENT OF CHAPTER OBJECTIVES

Now that you have completed the chapter and the projects, take a few minutes to review the chapter learning objectives. For your convenience, the objectives are repeated here. Did you accomplish these objectives? If you were unable to accomplish the objectives, give your reasons for not doing so; be specific and concise. Your instructor may prefer that your answers be submitted to her or him. If so, DCD1-c contains the Assessment of Chapter Objectives. Complete the Assessment of Chapter Objectives; submit your results to your instructor.

1. Describe the future workforce.   Yes ☐   No ☐

_____

_____

_____

2. Determine changes in the work environment.   Yes ☐   No ☐

_____

_____

_____

3. Define the types of business organizations and workplace structures.   Yes ☐   No ☐

_____

_____

_____

4. Describe the role and responsibilities of administrative professionals.   Yes ☐   No ☐

_____

_____

_____

5. Identify skills and qualities necessary for administrative professionals.   Yes ☐   No ☐

_____

_____

_____

6. Begin the development of a professional growth plan.   Yes ☐   No ☐

_____

_____

_____

7. Develop critical-thinking skills.   Yes ☐   No ☐

_____

_____

_____

YOUR VIRTUAL COMPANY

Throughout this course, you will be working for JWay Nu-Systems Tech, 1510 Eastern Drive, Dallas, TX 75275-0356. Your job title is administrative professional. You report to Jane Portosky, CEO. Read the following information to learn more about JWay Nu-Systems Tech.

WELCOME TO JWAY NU-SYSTEMS TECH

JWay Nu-Systems Tech is a young company, founded in 2004 and set up as an LLC. It is a computer products distributor; its products include servers, networking equipment, processors, storage (tape libraries), laptops, laptop accessories, and software. The company's sales during its first year were $10.4 million. The second year it went from $10.4 million to over $25 million in sales.

Jana Portosky, 34, and Wayne Wixom, 38, cofounded the company. There are presently 28 employees. Their staff is composed of knowledgeable, computer savvy, and extremely energetic personnel. Of the present 28 employees, 40% are white, 25% are African American, 20% are Hispanic, and 15% are Asian. Employee ages range from 19 to 70. Their work philosophy is evident in their state-of-the-art office, where music is constantly playing and there is an on-staff masseuse. They have established an annual company retreat, where all employees spend one week in such locations as Cancun and Cozumel. The purpose of these once yearly retreats is to evaluate the last year and determine strategic directions for the upcoming year.

Jana Portosky is the Chief Executive Officer of the company and Wayne Wixom is the Chief Operating Officer. Other titles within the company include vice president, business; vice president, corporate development; account executive; sales coordinator; buyer; and administrative professional.

During their first year of operation, the personnel developed the following mission and value statements:

Mission

JWay Nu-Systems Tech is dedicated to serving the technology needs of people throughout the United States. In serving these needs, we will continually live by our core company values.

Values

The personnel of JWay Nu-Systems Tech are committed to living the following values:
- Acting as responsible global citizens
- Building a diverse and knowledgeable company workforce
- Upholding excellence in all dealings with our customers
- Developing customer trust through the quality of our services

Branching into the Pacific Rim countries (countries bordering the Pacific Ocean from North and South America to Asia and Oceania) was discussed at last year's planning conference, with the projection that markets will be opened in Australia by the end of the fiscal year and in Taiwan within two years.

Although your title is administrative professional, you have been told by the CEO that, if business continues to grow and your work continues to be of the present high quality, you will be promoted within nine months to the title of office manager. You will have the responsibility of supervising two administrative assistants.

© Photodisc

CHAPTER 2

ETHICS—ESSENTIAL IN THE WORKPLACE

Learning Objectives

1. Recognize the importance of ethical behavior.
2. Explain the characteristics of an ethical organization.
3. Identify traits of an ethical employee.
4. Define steps necessary for ethical change.
5. Demonstrate a commitment to community involvement.

© Getty Images/Photodisc

> IMPORTANCE OF ETHICAL BEHAVIOR

Ethical malfeasance became more than a concept in the early 2000s when respected corporations, such as WorldCom, Enron, Arthur Andersen, Adelphia, and Rite Aid, were found guilty of mismanagement and even, in some cases, criminal activity. In addition to this mismanagement and criminal activity causing the corporations to lose millions of dollars, it also sent several upper-level executives to jail, caused innocent employees to lose their jobs, and contributed to a wave of stock market losses of more than $7 trillion.[1] Innocent investors lost large portions of their life savings, and a crisis of confidence in corporate America by much of the nation occurred.

Our government considered the situation serious enough to take action and signed into law the Sarbanes-Oxley Act, which is the most sweeping attempt to regulate public corporations since the Securities and Exchange Act of 1934. According to the White House Press Secretary release in 2002, "This law says to every American: there will not be a different ethical standard for corporate America than the standard that applies to everyone else. The honesty you expect in your small businesses, or in your workplaces, in your community or in your home, will be expected and enforced in every corporate suite in this country."[2]

The upholding of ethical standards by corporate America is extremely important, as it also is for employees within corporations and the general public. In this chapter, ethics is considered a **pragmatic** topic—one not only to be understood conceptually but also to be practiced in the day-to-day operation of businesses and in the lives of employees within the business.

[1]Randall Turk, "A Question of Ethics," *Sooner Magazine*, Winter 2003, <www.oufoundation.org/smwinter2003/thams.asp?ID=36> (accessed April 23, 2005).

[2]Breena E. Coates, "Rogue Corporations, Corporate Rogues & Ethics Compliance: The Sarbanes-Oxley Act, 2002," <www.pamij.com/8–3/pam8-3-6-coates.htm> (accessed January 30, 2005).

> BUSINESS ETHICS

Ethics is the systematic study of moral conduct, duty, and judgment. First, ethics involves learning what is right and what is wrong in particular situations. Second, ethics involves doing the right thing in that particular situation. Certainly, following ethical principles is not always easy. Even ethicists do not agree on how the "right thing" should be determined. Some ethicists assert that the right thing is based on moral principles, while others feel that the right thing may be based on the situation. Consider some of the ethical life-and-death situations we face today because of the advances in medical science.

Does an individual have the right to determine when he or she dies and to seek assistance with death? How long should a seriously ill patient be kept alive through artificial means? With the genetic work being done to determine links between genetics and diseases, is it ever "right" for parents to decide to abort a fetus? Is it ethical to use stem cells derived from embryos and fetuses in medical research?

Because the use of stem cells has become such a debated topic in our nation, the government has become involved. The Clinton Administration published guidelines governing the use of human embryonic stem cells in the Federal Register in August, 2000. In August of 2001, President Bush authorized funding of stem cell research using existing stem cell lines that were derived from human embryos before August 9, 2001. In 2002, the National Institutes of Health funded the first grants to conduct human embryonic stem cell research.[3] Congress is continuing to deal with the issues and the public continues to debate the pros and cons of stem cell research.

The ethical medical questions mentioned here have implications not only for individuals but also for the various health professions and pharmaceutical businesses. Obviously, these ethical questions are only a few of the issues our nation faces. As technology opens new vistas for all, ethical questions will continue to be raised. Wisdom is required on the part of business leaders and individuals employed by businesses to face and solve the ethical issues confronting us. An important aspect of this wisdom is **morality** (a set of ideas of right and wrong). All of us must strengthen our own ethical understandings and **moral integrity** (consistently adhering to a set of ideas of right and wrong), both within and outside the workplace.

Stem cell research is a fiercely debated topic today.

© Photodisc

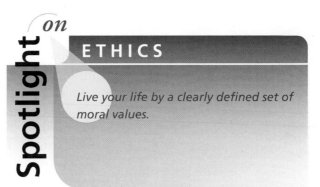

Spotlight *on* **ETHICS**

Live your life by a clearly defined set of moral values.

> OUR ETHICAL ROOTS

The major roots of today's ethical principles stem from religion and philosophy. Many of the major religions of the world are in basic agreement on the fundamental principles of ethical doctrine. Buddhism, Christianity, Confucianism, Hinduism, Islam, and Judaism teach the importance of acting responsibly toward all people and contributing to the general welfare of the world. The work ethic came from the **Protestant ethic,** a religious teaching carried by the early settlers to the United States from Europe. The Protestant ethic encouraged hard work, thrift, and dedication to a task.[4]

---

[3]Stem Cell Information: Pending Stem Cell Research and Legislation, <www.stemcells.nih.gov> (accessed February 19, 2005).

[4]D. Yankelovich, *New Rules: Searching for Self-Fulfillment in a World Turned Upside Down* (New York: Random House, 1981), p. 247.

The great philosophers added to the body of ethical knowledge with their teachings. Socrates taught that virtue and ethical behavior are associated with wisdom. Jeremy Bentham and John Mills taught that it is important to maximize the greatest benefit for the greatest number of people. Immanuel Kant taught that one must behave in such a way that one's actions can become universal law. Saint Thomas Aquinas taught that ethical behavior in business is necessary to achieve salvation.

> ETHICS—THE WHY

Why be ethical? What is ethical practice? How does one determine what is ethical and what is not ethical? Answers to these questions are never easy. They require constant evaluation of situations and constant analysis of what is right and wrong for individuals and organizations. A few of the benefits of placing a high priority on ethics in the workplace include adherence of a moral course in turbulent times, alignment of organizational behaviors with values, and integration of ethical guidelines with decision making.

You have already learned that businesses can succeed or fail based on their adherence or lack of adherence to appropriate ethical behaviors. Each year *Fortune* magazine prints a list of the "100 Best Companies to Work For." In 2005, W. L. Gore, Starbucks, and Griffin Hospital were in the top 11 companies to work for in the United States. Here are a few of the ethical guidelines and principles that these companies uphold in their work environments.

W. L. Gore is guided by four basic principles articulated by Bill Gore. These principles are:

1. Fairness to each other and everyone with whom we come in contact.

2. Freedom to encourage, help, and allow other associates to grow in knowledge, skill, and scope of responsibility.

3. The ability to make one's own commitments and keep them.

4. Consultation with other associates before undertaking actions that could impact the reputation of the company.[5]

Starbucks' six guiding principles are:

1. Provide a great work environment and treat each other with respect and dignity.

2. Embrace diversity as an essential component in the way we do business.

3. Apply the highest standards of excellence to the purchasing, roasting, and fresh delivery of our coffee.

4. Develop enthusiastically satisfied customers all of the time.

5. Contribute positively to our communities and our environment.

6. Recognize that profitability is essential to our future success.[6]

Griffin Hospital's values include embracing patients and families as partners in the care process, treating all people with compassion, attending to the mind and the spirit as well as the body, and preserving privacy and confidentiality.[7]

The statements by these three companies show a commitment to the communities they serve and to the employees who help make their companies successful.

> CHARACTERISTICS OF ETHICAL ORGANIZATIONS

Many organizations today are writing vision/mission statements. Such statements help the employees know the directions of the organization, what it values, and how it intends to live those values. Through such statements, the ethics and values of an organization become clear. Although the scope of this book will not allow for an exhaustive treatment of all the characteristics of an ethical organization, a number of ethical characteristics are covered in the next section.

▷ Environmentally Responsible

Ethical businesses understand that there are a number of environmental problems that the United States and the world face today, and unless businesses and individuals are environmentally responsible, we could

---

[5] *Corporate Culture,* <www.gore.com> (accessed January 30, 2005).

[6] "Starbucks Mission Statement," <www.starbucks.com> (accessed January 30, 2005).

[7] Patrick Charmel, "Changing the Face of Healthcare," <www.griffinhealth.org/AboutGriffin/Mission.aspx> (accessed January 30, 2005).

contribute to real and even life-threatening problems for future generations. One critical problem that is recognized universally is global warming. According to the Intergovernmental Panel on Climate Change, global temperatures could rise between 2.2 and 10.0 degrees Fahrenheit by 2100. Although this change may not seem significant, the temperature rose only 9 degrees from the last ice age to our current climate. In fact, the three warmest years in recorded history have occurred since 1998.[8] What is the result of continual global warming? Although experts in the field cannot predict with exact certainty what will happen, here are some projections.

▸ Oceans will rise and heat, resulting in some agricultural land too salty to be productive and coral ecosystems too warm to survive.
▸ The frequency of extreme weather events will increase, resulting in deteriorating human and non-human habitats.
▸ Some areas of the world, Great Britain and the northeastern United States, may experience cooling as the Gulf Stream changes course.
▸ Millions of animal and plant species may die off; other species will thrive from lack of competition.[9]

© Photodisc/Robert Glusie

Ethical businesses are environmentally responsible.

Although the United States currently represents only 4 percent of the world population, we account for one-fourth of the world's carbon dioxide emissions. We can make changes in our nation that will help us be a greener society. U.S. scientists, engineers, and manufacturers are working on the issues and have managed to improve America's energy efficiency by 46 percent in the past three decades. Energy companies have launched a multimillion-dollar initiative that will reforest six projects in Louisiana, Mississippi, and Arkansas to eventually capture more than 2 million tons of carbon dioxide from the atmosphere.[10] What can businesses do to help make the world of future generations a better place to live? What can individuals do?

▸ The automobile industry can produce more fuel-efficient vehicles. Attention is being paid to this issue, with a number of hybrids coming to market in 2005. The U.S. Department of Energy and the Environmental Protection Agency sponsor a website (fueleconomy.gov.) giving facts about fuel economy and greenhouse gas and toxic emissions of vehicles.
▸ Other businesses, such as office equipment, home electronics, and appliance companies, can produce and promote energy-efficient products.
▸ Individuals can be responsible energy users, saving energy at home and driving more fuel-efficient vehicles.

The examples given here are only a few of the many social and environmental problems that must be constantly addressed by businesses operating in the United States today. Valero Energy Corporation, one of *Fortune*'s "100 Best Companies to Work For" addresses some of the ways they are dealing with environmental issues.

▸ Valero was a national leader in the production of clean-burning fuels.
▸ Valero reduced their emissions by 50 percent between 1995 and 2004.[11]

In businesses across the United States, responsible executives take the necessary precautions to see that the environment is not polluted. They pay attention to government regulations regarding careful disposal of waste products. When building new buildings, they give top priority to cutting down as few trees as possible and protecting wetland areas and other areas that are environmentally important.

[8]"The Green Life, Simple, Healthy, Sustainable," *Global Warming*, <www.thegreenlife.org/globalwarming.html> (accessed January 15, 2005).
[9]Ibid.
[10]"Readers Report, How Business is Taking Global Warming Seriously," <www.businessweek.com/magazine> (accessed January 15, 2005).
[11]Valero Energy Corporation, "Environmental Stewardship," <www.valero.com> (accessed January 30, 2005).

▷ Internationally Aware

Ethical businesses, when working in other countries, understand the importance of learning the culture of the country. For example, a basic precept of Chinese culture is to put the best face on even the worst situation. Consequently, a smile, a nod, even a spoken affirmative in business negotiations may merely mean a reluctance to disappoint. There is a set ritual around conducting a meeting. For example, business is never conducted until tea is poured, business cards are exchanged, and introductions are made. The Chinese like to develop a strong relationship with those with whom they do business before a deal is closed. In contrast, the French get right down to business matters quickly; the French are formal and reserved in nature, and a casual attitude will alienate them during business dealings. In Mexico, eye contact must be unflinching; conversation is at a much closer distance than in the United States. Hugs after the second or third meeting are likely, and two-handed handshakes are common among mere acquaintances. Personal relationships are vital in Mexico for business, and it is important to spend time developing these relationships.[12]

When working with people who are ethnically diverse, seek to understand their culture.

© Photodisc/Andrew Wakeford

▷ Committed to Diversity

The ethical organization is committed to diversity in its hiring, promotion, and treatment of employees. The ethical organization

- ▶ Is intolerant of discrimination—racial/ethnic, gender, or age.
- ▶ Maintains a policy against sexual harassment.
- ▶ Provides for the physically challenged.

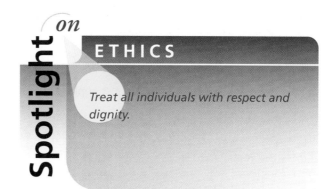

Spotlight *on*

ETHICS

Treat all individuals with respect and dignity.

▷ Intolerant of Race/ Ethnic Discrimination

Unfortunately, discrimination is ever present in our society. Businesses are made up of people who bring their own particular prejudices to the workplace. What does *prejudice* mean? **Prejudice** is defined in the dictionary as "an adverse judgment formed without knowledge or examination of the facts." When judgments are formed without knowledge or facts, they are often based on *learned* categories of distinctions and *learned* evaluation of these categories. When people act on such learned judgments (without consideration of the facts), prejudicial behavior is often the result. Prejudice can lead to acts of **discrimination**, which is defined in the dictionary as "the act, practice, or an instance of discriminating categorically rather than individual treatment or consideration based on class or category rather than individual merit."[13]

Discrimination may occur in many forms; race or ethnicity, gender, and age are some of the most likely forms. Discrimination may also involve sexual harassment.

Discrimination has been so prevalent in our society that laws have been enacted in an attempt to eliminate it. For example, Title VII of the Civil Rights Act of 1964 made it illegal to discriminate on the basis of race, color, religion, sex, or national origin. Since that time, other acts have been passed that address age, disability, equal pay, and pregnancy discrimination. Figure 2-1 lists some of these acts.

Racial/ethnic tensions have occurred in the United States from the time the first white settlers drove Native American Indians from their land and set up a system of labor based on black slavery.

---

[12]Terri Morrison, Wayne A. Conaway, and George A. Borden, *Kiss, Bow, or Shake Hands* (Avon, MA: Adams Media Corporation, 1994), pp. 55, 121, 230.

[13]*Webster's Ninth New Collegiate Dictionary* (Springfield, MA: Merriam-Webster, Inc., 1991), p. 362.

Figure 2-1   LAWS GOVERNING DISCRIMINATION

It is unlawful to discriminate against applicants and employees on the basis of

- ▶ Race.
- ▶ Religion.
- ▶ Color.
- ▶ National origin.
- ▶ Gender.
- ▶ Age.
- ▶ Height, weight.
- ▶ Marital status.
- ▶ Disability or handicap.

The following laws cover many of the rights of applicants and employees:

Social Security Act
Fair Labor Standards Act
Federal Unemployment Tax Act
Immigration Reform and Control Act
Occupational Safety and Health Act
Older Worker Benefit Protection Act
Consolidated Omnibus Budget Reconciliation Act (COBRA)
Worker Adjustment and Retraining Notification Act (WARN)
Employee Retirement Income Security Act (ERISA)
Civil Rights Act of 1964, Title VI and VII
Title IX of the Education Amendments of 1972
The Age Discrimination in Employment Act of 1967
The Americans with Disabilities Act of 1990
Civil Rights Act of 1991
The Equal Pay Act of 1963
The Pregnancy Discrimination Act of 1978
The Family Medical Leave Act of 1993
Health Insurance Portability and Accountability Act (HIPAA)

However, the existence of discrimination is no reason to accept it. Ethical businesses and individuals seek to eliminate discrimination. The ethical organization sets an example for its employees of nondiscriminatory behaviors and demands that its employees behave in nondiscriminatory ways. The ethical organization has a procedure for handling discrimination and provides the information to its employees.

Spotlight on ETHICS

Always behave in a nondiscriminatory manner.

▷ Intolerant of Gender Discrimination

Title VII covers gender discrimination as well as racial/ethnic discrimination. Employers may not advertise a job specifically for a man or woman unless the employer can prove that it is necessary that a person of a specific gender is needed. In other words, the question of gender may be asked only if it pertains to a bona fide occupational qualification; for example, a model for men's clothing. We recognize in our society that there are few gender-specific occupations. A person may apply for any job, and the hiring decision must be based on whether the individual has the knowledge and skills needed for the job, not on whether the person is male or female. Neither can employee pay be based on whether a person is male or female. The Equal Pay Act, a 1964 amendment to the Fair Labor Standards Act, prohibits pay discrimination because of sex. Men and women performing work in the same establishment under similar conditions must receive the same pay if their jobs require equal skill, effort, and responsibility.

Although sexual orientation is not covered under Title VII, most businesses today recognize that there can be no discrimination based on sexual orientation. Gay and lesbian organizations have become active in helping to ensure that the rights of individuals are not violated based only on their sexual preference.

▷ Intolerant of Age Discrimination

The Age Discrimination in Employment Act of 1967 (ADEA) "protects individuals who are 40 years of age or older from employment discrimination based on age. The ADEA's protections apply to both employees and job applicants. Under the ADEA, it is unlawful to discriminate against a person because of his or her age with respect to any term, condition, or privilege of employment—including, but not limited to, hiring, firing, promotion, layoff, compensation, benefits, job assignments, and training."[14]

No distinction can be made in age, either in the advertising or hiring process or once an employee is on the job. For example, an organization cannot print a job vacancy notice that specifies a particular age or age range for applicants.

▷ Maintains a Policy Against Sexual Harassment

Sexual harassment has been defined by the Equal Employment Opportunity Commission (EEOC) as:

> Unwelcome sexual advances, requests for sexual favors, and other verbal or physical conduct of a sexual nature constitutes sexual harassment when submission to or rejection of this conduct explicitly or implicitly affects an individual's employment, unreasonably interferes with an individual's work performance or creates an intimidating, hostile or offensive work environment.[15]

The Civil Rights Act makes the organization responsible for preventing and eliminating sexual harassment. The organization is liable for the behavior of its employees whether or not management is aware that sexual harassment has taken place. The organization is also responsible for the actions of non-employees on the company's premises. Because of these liabilities, many organizations have published policy statements that make it clear to all employees that sexual harassment is a violation of the law and of company policy. These statements generally include a clearly defined grievance procedure so an employee has a course of action to take if sexual harassment does occur. Figures 2-2 and 2-3 present steps for handling discrimination and sex harassment.

▷ Provides for the Physically Challenged

Physically challenged individuals (persons with physical handicaps) often face biases based on their physical challenges. They may be treated differently due to their disabilities. The ethical organization provides access for the physically challenged to all facilities, proper equipment and workspace, and ensures that initial employment practices do not discriminate against the physically challenged.

In summary, the organization that values diversity:

▶ Is intolerant of any type of discrimination—racial/ethnic, gender, age, physically challenged, and sexual harassment.

▶ Upholds its clearly stated policies and procedures that are committed to equal employment.

▶ Has a personnel department with expertise in assisting minorities and women with special issues.

Figure 2-2	STEPS FOR HANDLING DISCRIMINATION

▶ Know your rights and know the laws. Become familiar with how your organization handles racial discrimination and sexual harassment. The Human Resources Department should have a policy statement on both.

▶ Keep a record of all sexual harassment and racial discrimination infractions that you experience, noting the dates, incidents, and witnesses (if any).

▶ File a formal grievance with your company. If no formal grievance procedures exist, file a formal complaint with your employer in the form of a memorandum describing the incidents, identifying the individuals involved in the sexual harassment or racial discrimination, and requesting that disciplinary action be taken.

▶ If your employer is not responsive to your complaint, file charges of discrimination with the federal and state agencies that enforce civil rights laws, such as the EEOC (Equality Employment Opportunity Commission).

▶ Talk to friends, coworkers and relatives. Avoid isolation and self-blame. You are not alone; sexual harassment and racial discrimination do occur in the work sector.

▶ Consult an attorney to investigate legal alternatives to discriminatory or sexual harassment behavior.

---

[14]"Facts About Age Discrimination," The U.S. Equal Employment Opportunity Commission, 1997, <www.eeoc.gov/facts/age.html> (accessed March 19, 2005).
[15]"Legal Definitions of Sexual Harassment," <www.de.psu.edu/harassment/legal/> (accessed March 19, 2005).

Figure 2-3   PREVENTING SEXUAL HARASSMENT IN THE WORKPLACE

As you move up in an organization, you may be in a management position. If so, you need to understand how management should deal with sexual harassment. Here are several suggestions.

TAKE THE FOLLOWING STEPS

► Communicate with employees as to what constitutes sexual harassment.

► Designate a person or office where employees can bring concerns and complaints.

► Promptly and thoroughly investigate all complaints.

► Be observant of language and behavior of managers and employees. Confront them on any perceived sexual harassment.

► Maintain an environment free of retaliation or punitive actions against a complainant.

DO NOT

► Permit sexual jokes, teasing, or innuendo to become a routine part of the work environment.

► Allow social behavior to become confused with workplace behavior.

► Publishes grievance policies that are clearly stated and distributed to all employees.
► Provides diversity sensitivity training for its employees.
► Holds managers accountable for consistently supporting and ensuring diversity within the environment.

▷ Committed to the Community

The ethical organization understands its social responsibility to the community. Microsoft Corporation is an example of one organization that accepts that responsibility; these statements are made on the company's website.

> Our business is built on relationships—with our customers, partners, investors, employees, and with the communities where we live and work. Microsoft's 20-year history of community engagement has fostered a variety of key community partnerships built on the mutual commitment to find sustainable technology solutions that make real and lasting differences.

> In 2004 alone, Microsoft contributed a total of $264 million in cash and software to nearly 5,000 nonprofit organizations.[16]

The ethical organization is cognizant of the needs of its community and assists with meeting these needs when possible. For example, numerous organizations engage in the following types of activities:

Providing tutors for elementary and high school students

Engaging in mentoring programs for troubled youth

Working with colleges and universities in providing intern experiences for students

Providing technology to schools

Serving on community boards and commissions

Participating in local Chambers of Commerce

Contributing to community charities

Providing leadership to solicit funds for worthy causes, such as disabled children, healthcare for the indigent, and shelters for the homeless

Assisting with arts programs by providing leadership and/or monies.

▷ Respects the Needs and Rights of Employees

Promoting employee productivity is important to the ethical organization. An ethical organization understands that employees have needs. For example, they need to know the values and directions of the company, what is expected of them, how the organization will help the employees achieve organizational goals, and how they will be evaluated. Figure 2-4 illustrates several ways an organization can meet the needs of employees.

An ethical organization also understands that employees have rights. Two such rights are a right to due process and a right to privacy.

Right to Due Process

Generally, employees make a conscientious effort to contribute to an organization. In return, they expect to be treated fairly by an organization. People would not choose to work for an organization if they did not think they were going to be treated fairly. **Employment at will** (the doctrine that allows employees

---

[16]About Microsoft, "Everyone has potential," <www.microsoft.com> (accessed January 15, 2005).

Figure 2-4 | MEETING THE NEEDS OF EMPLOYEES

Provide employees with a copy of the values and goals of the organization; ask that managers go over these documents with the employees.

Encourage managers to consistently distribute important information about the organization.

Help employees set achievable goals that are consistent with the goals of the organization.

Administer employee performance evaluations fairly.

Support employees in learning new skills.

Reward employee creativity.

Challenge employees to generate new ideas.

Encourage collaboration and cooperation among employees.

Establish teams that work on significant organizational issues.

to be fired for good cause or for no cause) has been and still is an employment doctrine upheld by some states. In an unethical organization, adherence to such a doctrine can cause irreparable harm to employees. For example, companies have been known to call long-time employees into a supervisor's office, tell them they no longer have a job, and send them home immediately with no severance package and loss of all benefits. The doctrine of employment at will has come under considerable attack and is being replaced in most organizations by the right to due process. **Due process** means that managers impose sanctions on employees only after offering them a chance to correct the organizational grievance. An ideal system of due process is one in which employees are given the following:

A clearly written job description

Organizational policies and procedures

Assurance that all policies and procedures will be administered consistently and fairly without discrimination

A commitment by top management that managers will be responsible for adhering to the values and morals of the organization

A fair and impartial hearing if the rules are broken

Right to Privacy

Another right that the ethical organization grants to individual employees is the right to privacy. Certainly an organization has the right to information about an employee that affects the individual's performance. For example, if an individual has developed some type of physical illness that no longer allows the person to perform his or her job, the employer has a right to know about it. However, the employer does not have the right to know about illnesses that do not affect job performance. An employer does not have the right to know about a person's political or religious beliefs. In fact, in a job interview, the employer cannot ask questions about marital status, age, organizations to which the person belongs, where the person was born, or what the spouse does, for example. These questions are illegal. If an organization acquires information about an employee's personal life while doing a legitimate investigation, the organization has an obligation to destroy the information, especially if the data would embarrass or in some way injure the employee. Also, an organization must give employees the right to give or withhold consent before any private aspects of their lives are investigated.

▷ Establishes and Lives Organizational Values

Excerpts of mission/vision/value statements from two companies, Herman Miller and Genentech, follow:

> At Herman Miller, our conduct matters. Living with integrity and following a clear ethical code has produced a good business, a great place to work and a trustworthy investment.[17]

> We [Genentech] commit ourselves to high standards of integrity in contributing to the best interests of patients, the medical profession, our employees, and our communities.[18]

Once you know the company mission/value statement, it is your responsibility to behave in ways that support the mission. If you find yourself in a company where you cannot support the mission/values, it is time for you to find another position.

▷ Maintains a Safe and Healthy Environment

The public expects organizations to behave in ways that protect and maintain a safe and healthy environment for its customers. Additionally, the ethical

---

[17]Herman Miller, *Code of Conduct,* <www.hermanmiller.com> (accessed January 13, 2005).

[18]Arthur D. Levinson, Genentech, *About Us,* <www.gene.com> (accessed January 13, 2005).

organization is also committed to providing and maintaining a safe and healthy environment for its employees. For example, an ethical organization upholds the Occupational Safety and Health Administration's (OSHA) requirement that employers furnish a place of employment free from recognized hazards that can cause death, injury, or illness to its employees. Figure 2-5 gives a few of the guidelines that should be followed to keep the workplace safe.

Smoking

Smoking can be extremely dangerous to an individual's long-term health. Although the public is well aware of the dangers of smoking, some individuals within our environment continue to smoke. Nonsmokers complain of eye, nose, and throat irritations resulting from secondhand smoke. Almost all businesses have adopted smoking policies to protect the nonsmokers. These policies prohibit employees from smoking inside the building; smoking may be allowed at a designated place in the building or at an outside location.

Substance Abuse

Substance abuse is a huge problem in our society. **Substance abuse** refers to the use of alcohol or

drugs to an extent that is debilitating for the individual using the substance. Drug and alcohol users are absent an average of two to three times more than other employees. Employees with chemical dependence problems claim three times as many sickness benefits and file five times as many workers' compensation claims. Shoddy work and material waste are also evident with individuals who abuse substances. Mental and physical agility and concentration deteriorate with substance abuse. In many workplaces, 20 to 25 percent of accidents involve intoxicated people injuring themselves and innocent victims.[19]

> Provides an Ergonomically Sound Environment

The management of an organization is responsible for providing an environment where factors such as lighting, acoustics, equipment, and furniture are ergonomically sound. Although this chapter cannot provide an in-depth approach to ergonomics (entire books are written on the subject), several areas are addressed here.

It is the responsibility of management to provide an ergonomically sound environment.

© Digital Vision

| Figure 2-5 | SAFETY GUIDELINES |

Ask these safety questions about your workspace.

Is the space sufficient to perform tasks?
Is the space sufficient for equipment?
Can all items that are used frequently be easily reached?
Does flexibility exist to rearrange the workstation if needed?
Is the lighting sufficient?
Is the height of the work surface appropriate?
Is the height of the chair appropriate?
Can the chair be adjusted easily?
Does the chair feel sturdy?
Can the computer screen be tilted?
Is the work surface depth adequate to allow the computer screen to be placed at an appropriate distance?
Is the computer keyboard two inches lower than the desk surface?
Are document holders provided?
Is the equipment suitable for the work to be done?
Is adequate storage space provided?

Lighting

For employees to process information, an adequate lighting system must be maintained. Improper lighting can cause headaches, eye fatigue, neck and shoulder strain, and irritability. If improper lighting conditions continue, productivity and morale are lowered, which in turn can cost a business considerable dollars.

---

[19]SafeWork, *"Drug and alcohol abuse—an important workplace issue,"* <www.ilo.org/public/english/protection/safework/drug/impiss.htm> (accessed January 30, 2005).

Acoustics

Soft background music does not disrupt work; however, loud music, loud machines, and street sounds can cause employees to lose productivity. Noise can be controlled through the use of acoustical panels between workstations and by carpet, draperies, and acoustical ceilings.

Equipment and Furniture

Carpel tunnel syndrome, computer vision syndrome, back pain, and headaches can be caused by using computers and furniture incorrectly. Keyboards that help reduce problems include split keyboards and supportive keyboards with built-in wrist or palm rests. Additionally, desks that are a height where you can easily key with straight wrists and read or write without slumping forward or hunching your shoulders are helpful.

Document stands help reduce distortion of print that occurs when a document is slanted away from the eyes. Footrests allow different positions for the legs and feet. Task lights help reduce eyestrain by illuminating paperwork and reducing the need for bright light. Adjustable chairs help avoid back pain by supporting multiple postures.

▷ Honest

An ethical organization is honest. It makes its policies and procedures clear to both its customers and its employees. For example, its pricing policies are made clear to buyers; its product warranty is upheld. Employees understand salary and promotion policies. Executives within the organization are honest. The executive's word can be taken seriously; employees know and understand the direction of the company.

▷ Visionary

The **visionary organization** (an organization that has an understanding of what the future should be and leaders who inspire others to accept that vision) has the ability to look beyond the day-to-day activities of the organization. Executives within the ethical organization can help managers and employees understand where the company will be in 5, 10, or 15 years and assist others in formulating policies and objectives that will help the company achieve its goals. The organization, through its leadership, consistently articulates the vision of the company and constantly evaluates the daily operations of the company in relation to meeting the vision.

> THE ETHICAL ADMINISTRATIVE PROFESSIONAL

Ethical administrative professionals clearly know what they believe and how their beliefs were formed. Generally, the following people and beliefs influence our personal ethics:

- ▶ Our parents
- ▶ Significant individuals in our lives
- ▶ Our peer group
- ▶ The culture in which we grew up
- ▶ Our religious beliefs

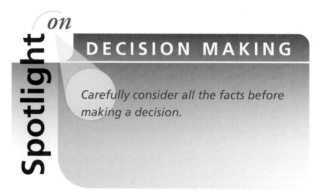

Spotlight *on* **DECISION MAKING**

Carefully consider all the facts before making a decision.

Although you may be clear about your beliefs, sometimes factors converge in organizations that make it difficult to determine what truly is right and wrong in a particular situation. Asking these questions can help you decide what is ethical.

What are the facts in the situation?

Who are the stakeholders, or who will be affected by my decision?

What are the ethical issues involved?

Are there different ways of looking at this problem? If so, what are they?

What are the practical constraints?

What actions should I take?

Are these actions practical?

If you are still unclear about what you should do, ask yourself these questions.

If my actions appeared in the newspaper or on television, would I feel right about everyone reading or watching what occurred?

Is what I anticipate doing legal?

Could I proudly tell my spouse, my parents, or my children about my actions?

Will I be proud of my actions one day, one week, and one year from now?

Do my actions fit with who I think I am?

▷ Accepts Constructive Criticism

Your supervisor is just that—your supervisor. She or he has not only the right but also the responsibility to help you do your job well. You should be willing to accept constructive criticism; i.e., criticism that can help you learn and grow. If your supervisor recommends that you do something differently, do not view his or her remarks personally. For example, assume you recently set up a meeting for your employer at a hotel where lunch was served. You had not previously planned a meeting, and you thought you did a good job. However, after the meeting, your employer told you the room arrangement was not satisfactory and the food was not good. How do you respond to such criticism? First of all, you deal with the issues at hand. You might say, "Can we talk about it further? How should the room have been arranged? What type of meal would you suggest?" Keep an open mind; realize that you have much to learn and that everyone makes mistakes. You might also suggest reviewing the arrangements with your supervisor before the next meeting.

Always avoid an emotional response to criticism. Try to separate the issue from the critic; realize the critic is merely concerned with improving the situation. If you respond emotionally to the critic, you may succeed only in upsetting yourself (and possibly the person who is doing the criticizing). Learn what you can from the situation, determine never to make the same mistake again, and then move on.

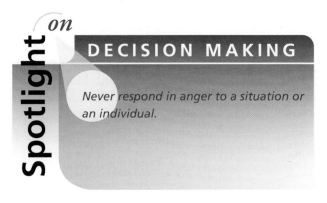

Spotlight *on*

DECISION MAKING

Never respond in anger to a situation or an individual.

▷ Respects Diversity

As the ethical organization is committed to diversity, so is the ethical employee. The ethical employee understands that the world is very diverse and that it

---

Self CHECK A

Respond to the following statements by circling your response: "always," "sometimes," or "never."

1. I accept constructive criticism.	Always	Sometimes	Never
2. I respect the privacy of others.	Always	Sometimes	Never
3. I become involved in office politics.	Always	Sometimes	Never
4. I am dependable.	Always	Sometimes	Never
5. I make excuses when I cannot finish a job.	Always	Sometimes	Never
6. I help others with a task if my job permits.	Always	Sometimes	Never
7. I am honest with customers.	Always	Sometimes	Never
8. I use the telephone for personal conversations.	Always	Sometimes	Never
9. I believe it is all right to accept gifts from clients.	Always	Sometimes	Never
10. I talk with my employer first about any job-related issues.	Always	Sometimes	Never

will continue to become even more diverse in the future. The ethical employee accepts and respects the diversity of all people—whether that diversity is in ethnicity, race, gender, or age. The ethical employee understands that there is no place in the office for telling jokes that have racial, ethnic, or gender overtones.

▷ Aware of Workplace Politics

Workplace politics are fed by networks of individuals where *who* you know can be more important than *what* you know. Favors may be handed out based on the existing networks. In a truly ethical world, office politics would not exist. Unfortunately, we do not live in such a world and probably never will.

So what do you do about workplace politics? When you begin a new job, notice what is happening around you. Be aware of the power bases. Be aware of who knows whom and what the relationships are. Then hold on to your own value system. Do your job to the best of your ability. Do not gossip about office politics. Use your awareness of the power bases to get your job done. In other words, do not fight a power base when you know you cannot win. Spend your energies in doing what is right.

Do not gossip about office politics.

© Photodisc/Ryan McVay

Generally, if you hold on to your values and perform your job extremely well, you will be recognized and respected for who you are.

▷ Respect Others' Privacy

Respect the privacy of others within the office. If someone confides a personal matter to you, do not spread the "juicy gossip." If you have access to personnel files that contain confidential information about others, keep the information confidential. You may at times be given information that is not specifically labeled "confidential," yet it should not be passed on to others. Be sensitive to the handling of this information. Do not hide behind the rationale, "But I was not told it was confidential." Use common sense. Ethical conduct dictates that you are always discreet. Remember the golden rule: Treat others as you would want to be treated.

▷ Honest

Being honest means the employee does not take anything that belongs to the company, is conscientious about using time wisely, and gives the company eight hours of productive work (or whatever the office hours may be) each day. Honesty dictates that the employee *not:*

Send email to family or friends on the office computer.

Take home office supplies such as paper, pens, and notepads.

Use the Internet for personal research or "chats."

Use the telephone for personal calls.

Use the computer for preparing personal correspondence.

Take longer than the time allocated by the organization for lunch or breaks.

Spend an inordinate amount of time repairing makeup or eating breakfast upon arriving at work.

Use the copier for personal use.

▷ Dependable

Do what you say you will do when you say you will do it. Do not make excuses for poor performance. Your employer or peers are never impressed; excuses merely make you look ridiculous for attempting to find a reason for irresponsible actions.

▷ Cooperative

You may believe that when your particular job is finished you need not worry about helping anyone else.

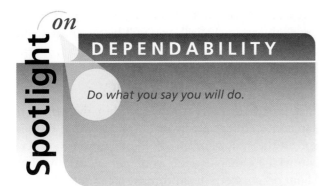

However, you are an employee of the company. Just because you have completed your tasks does not mean you can sit and do nothing; there is generally work that must be done. Remember, the time may come when you have more work than you can do and need the help of a coworker. When you help someone else, do not make that person feel obligated to you. Offer your help in the spirit of cooperation and with a desire to further the interests of the organization for which you work.

TO ENSURE YOUR FAILURE AS A PROFESSIONAL AND TO ALWAYS BE SEEN AS UNCOOPERATIVE, follow these simple guidelines.

Always have an excuse ready for why you cannot help someone else.

Point out how incompetent or lazy the individual needing help is.

Forget about the importance of office productivity and customer satisfaction.

Always look out for yourself. (You cannot possibly help because you have to go home early to take your sick pet to the veterinarian.)

▷ Respects Clients and Customers

As an administrative professional, you must be respectful of your clients and customers. The old adage that "the customer is always right" is true. Stop and think about that statement for a moment. Literally a customer may be wrong; he or she is human and makes mistakes. However, what the statement means is that in the context of service to the customer, he or she is always right. As an administrative professional, you may need to listen to numerous unhappy clients and customers. Let the clients and customers get their anger out; then proceed to address the issue. At times, you will not be able to say "yes" to the customer. When you cannot say "yes," explain the rationale of the company. Always act as your client's advocate within the company, getting the information or providing the service (if at all possible) your client needs. Value the client's time. Do not waste the client's time by keeping him or her on the phone for an inordinate amount of time or by being late for an appointment. Deal with irate clients calmly and professionally. Do not be defensive. Treat every client and customer as a VIP (very important person). Without clients and customers, the company would not be in business and you would not have a job.

Keep the Customer Informed

If there are production problems, material shortages, or other problems that prevent the customer from getting an order on time, tell the customer. Keep a computer file on the clients and customers with whom you work. Record important information in your file, and review it when a client calls. Remember that all clients are important, whether you deal with them once a year or once a month. You may have occasion to help entertain customers and clients. For example, you may be asked to take an out-of-town customer to dinner. If so, keep the situation on a purely professional basis. You also may occasionally receive gifts from clients and customers. Certainly a small gift may be appropriate, and you can accept it graciously. However, as a matter of ethics, you should not accept an extremely expensive gift, and some organizations have a policy prohibiting you from accepting *any* gifts. Be sure you know your organization's policy regarding the acceptance of gifts.

> ETHICAL CHANGE

We do not live in a world in which all individuals and organizations are ethical. This statement is not meant to be negative. It merely suggests the inevitable—we do not live in a perfect world. We do live in a world in which employees make ethical mistakes; however, in the majority of instances, they consistently strive to improve themselves and the organizations in which they work. Ethical organizations require people within the organization to behave ethically, including top management as well as all individuals throughout the organization. The process of achieving ethical change requires understanding, a systematic approach, commitment, cooperation, and hard work. Consider the following factors that impede ethical change as well as certain pragmatic steps that produce ethical change.

▷ Factors Impeding Ethical Change

Our backgrounds and beliefs often stand in the way of ethical change. Examine each of the following statements individually.

Organizations Are Amoral

Amoral is defined as "being neither moral nor immoral."[20] Generally, we readily accept that individuals should have ethics, but we are not so clear about what that means within the organizational framework. You may hear a statement such as: "The organization has no right to tell me how to behave." Yet, if an organization is to be ethical, its employees must be ethical. The two are inexorably linked—the organization is the people who comprise the organization, and the people within the organization are the organization. Managers have a right and an obligation to hold employees responsible for upholding the ethics of the organization and to hold them accountable for maintaining the skills required to produce the product or service of the organization.

Organizational Leadership Is Unethical

Certainly, there are organizations in which the leadership does not behave ethically. However, to assume automatically that all management is bad is negatively stereotyping management. If we do not want to behave ethically, it is easy to shift the blame for our lack of ethical behavior to management. Your first obligation is to uphold the organizational ethics yourself. Then, if you find through repeated incidences that management does not uphold the organizational ethics, you may decide to leave the organization. When organizational ethics are not embraced by management, the organization may not be a good place to work.

Values Cannot Be Changed

Clearly, we have difficulty changing our values because they are beliefs we have generally held from childhood. However, change is possible. Consider this example. Edgar learned at an early age that gender roles are fixed in our society—a female holds the more menial positions; a male, the management positions. Edgar has a female supervisor and has discovered that women can indeed hold high-level positions and be extremely competent in these positions. He has altered his view of women as a result of having a competent female supervisor. Organizations, by upholding a set of values and giving support to changes a person makes, can help an individual change or redefine his or her values.

Certain values are formed at an early age; however, you can change, redefine, or modify your values.

Labels Accurately Describe Individuals

When we attach a label to someone, we are usually not describing that individual accurately. For example, to describe a person as a "computer nerd" or a

---

[20] *Webster's Ninth New Collegiate Dictionary* (Springfield, MA: Merriam-Webster, 1991), p. 80.

"party animal" is restrictive of the whole person's qualities and traits. Remember that labeling hinders rather than helps the change process. Labeling individuals often restricts our view of them. We begin to see them only as the label we have attached. We ignore their other qualities. If we are committed to ethical change within an organization, we must avoid the use of restrictive labels.

▷ Factors Supporting Ethical Change

The organization and individuals committed to ethical change can take certain practical steps to produce the change. These steps include the following:

- ▶ Determine the ethical change needed.
- ▶ Determine steps required to achieve the objective.
- ▶ Practice the new behaviors.
- ▶ Seek feedback on the change.
- ▶ Reward the individual or group involved.
- ▶ Evaluate the effects of ethical change.

Consider this example of a situation in which ethical change is needed and is addressed within the organization.

A new Asian administrative professional has been hired by JWay Nu-Systems Tech; her name is Baysan Sheng; she has been with the company for three weeks. During that time you have invited her to have lunch with you twice. However, you notice no one else has asked her to lunch; you have also noticed that no one is helping her to "learn the ropes" at JWay, although you have given her several pointers. You have decided that there is racial bias being demonstrated among the administrative assistants and that it is important to try to help people work more closely together.

After thinking through the situation, you decide to approach three of the administrative professionals individually and discuss the situation with them. Two of the individuals (Ryan and Helena) admit that they have not tried to help Baysan; they believe that she needs help but have not known how to approach her since her culture is so different from their own. You suggest that the three of you work together in helping Baysan to understand the organization and her responsibilities. The third administrative professional tells you that she does not understand Chinese people and she has no intention of trying to help Baysan. You determine that an understanding of other ethnicities is the ethical change needed. You also talk with your supervisor and suggest that an outside consultant be invited to work with the administrative assistants on cultural differences. Baysan will be included in the group sessions since one of the purposes is to help the group have a greater understanding of all cultures. All administrative professionals will be invited to share their own culture.

You have engaged in the first two steps of the ethical change model: (1) Determine the ethical change needed and (2) determine the steps required to achieve the objective. Your next steps are as follows:

Practice the New Behaviors

After the consultant has worked with the group to help them understand cultural differences, the group needs to help each other in practicing open acceptance of all cultures.

Seek Feedback

Schedule a time for all administrative professionals to talk with each other about living their cultural values. Are they living their cultural values?

Provide Rewards

The group decides to have lunch together once each month to congratulate themselves on coming together as a multicultural group. The luncheon

CHECK B

Self

Respond to the following statements with a "true" or "false." Explain your answers.

		True	False
1. Organizations are amoral.		_____ True	_____ False
2. Organizational leadership is unethical.		_____ True	_____ False
3. Values cannot be changed.		_____ True	_____ False
4. Labels accurately describe individuals.		_____ True	_____ False

provides a chance to talk as a group and as individuals about their new cultural understandings and to further the newly developed team spirit.

Evaluate the Effects of Ethical Change

Observe whether the team's new understanding results in continued greater acceptance of diversity within the organization.

▷ Ethical Behavior—Your Call

Although you cannot impact the ethics of an entire organization unless you are in upper management, you can carefully check out an organization's ethics before you accept a position. Here are a few suggestions for how to check the ethics of an organization.

1. Read the organization's Web page information. Are the ethics of the organization mentioned? Is a commitment to diversity mentioned? Is a commitment to the external community mentioned? What type of programs do they have for employees?

2. Check the history of the organization. Have they ever made newspaper headlines for behaving unethically?

3. Talk with acquaintances who work for the organization. Ask them to describe the ethical environment of the company.

As an individual employee, you can commit to behaving in an ethical manner. You can do the following:

- ▸ Respect the organizational structure.
- ▸ Make ethical decisions.
- ▸ Accept constructive criticism.
- ▸ Respect diversity.
- ▸ Consider office politics.
- ▸ Respect others' privacy.
- ▸ Be honest.
- ▸ Be dependable.
- ▸ Be cooperative.
- ▸ Respect clients and customers.

You can also promise yourself that if for some reason (beyond your control) your organization engages in grossly unethical behaviors, you will seek employment in another organization. Consider this often told story. If you put a frog in a cup of tepid water, it will not jump out; the temperature is comfortable. If you continue to turn up the heat gradually until the water is boiling hot, the frog will continue to stay in the water and die.[21] The frog adjusts to the temperature as it is turned up and does not notice the difference in the environment or the threat to its safety. The moral of the story is this: Unless you are committed to observing the ethical behavior of an organization and behaving in an ethical manner yourself, you may stay in an organization that has become unethical and find yourself supporting those unethical behaviors to the detriment of your own value system and career growth. Commit now to "jumping out" of unethical waters before you "die" in them.

---

[21]Phillip A. Laplante, "Staying Clear of Boiling Frog Syndrome," *IEEE IT Professional*, Vol. 6, No. 2, March/April 2004, pp. 56–58, <http://www.computer.org/itpro/it2004/F2056.pdf> (accessed April 23, 2005).

Reinforce your learning in this chapter by studying this summary.

▶ The study of ethics and the ethical organization have been important to our society for a number of years. The lack of ethical behavior by businesses can impact our society and the individuals within it.

▶ The major roots of today's ethical principles stem from religion and philosophy. Many of the major religions of the world are in basic agreement on fundamental principles of ethical doctrine.

▶ The ethical organization is environmentally responsible, is internationally aware, is committed to diversity, maintains a policy against sexual harassment, provides for the physically challenged, respects the needs and rights of employees, establishes and lives organizational values, maintains a safe and healthy environment, provides an ergonomically sound environment, is honest, and is visionary.

▶ The ethical administrative professional accepts constructive criticism, respects diversity, is aware of workplace politics, respects others' privacy, is honest, is dependable and cooperative, and respects clients and customers.

GLOSSARY

Amoral—Neither moral nor immoral.

Discrimination—An act, practice, or an instance of discriminating categorically rather than individually.

Due process—The ability of managers to impose sanctions on employees only after offering them a chance to correct the organizational grievance.

Employment at will—The doctrine that allows employees to be fired for good cause or for no cause.

Ethics—A systematic study of moral conduct, duty, and judgment.

Moral integrity—Consistently adhering to a set of ideas of right and wrong.

Morality—A set of ideas of right and wrong.

Physically challenged—Persons with physical handicaps.

Pragmatic—A topic to be understood conceptually and practiced in the day-to-day operation of the organization.

Prejudice—A system of negative beliefs, feelings, and actions.

Protestant ethic—A religious teaching carried by the early settlers to the United States from Europe. The Protestant ethic encouraged hard work, thrift, and dedication to a task.

Sexual harassment—Persistent torment arising from sexual conduct that is unwelcome by the recipient and that may be either physical or verbal in nature.

Substance abuse—The use of alcohol or drugs to an extent that is debilitating for the individual using the substance.

Visionary organization—An organization that has an understanding of what the future should be and leaders who inspire others to accept that vision.

CHECKPOINT

Check your understanding of these terms by completing DCD2-a on the Data CD.

DISCUSSION ITEMS

These discussion items provide an opportunity to test your understanding of the chapter through written responses and/or discussion with your classmates and your instructor.

1. Explain why ethics is an important topic for organizations today.

2. Give examples of how business organizations address ethics.

3. List and explain six characteristics of an ethical business.

4. List and explain six characteristics of an ethical employee.

5. Can ethical change occur? If so, how?

CRITICAL THINKING CASE

Jana Portosky, your supervisor, has asked you to work on Saturdays for the last four weeks. You have worked for six hours each Saturday and have received no overtime pay for the work. She did tell you when she asked you to work that she expected you to work at your regular rate of pay on Saturday; you were surprised with her statement but decided that you would not make an issue of it. Now, she has asked you to work for the next month under the same arrangement. You feel that you are not being fairly treated as to salary. An additional consideration is your family. You have two small children at home who need you on Saturday. You also understand that JWay Nu-Systems Tech is extremely busy now and your supervisor needs your help. How should you handle the situation? What are the ethical dilemmas?

RESPONSES TO SELF-CHECK

A
The most appropriate answers are as follows:

1. Always
2. Always
3. Never
4. Always
5. Never
6. Always
7. Always
8. Never
9. Sometimes
10. Always

B
The most appropriate answers are as follows:

1. True*   2. False   3. False   4. False
*Remember, however, that organizations are made up of people who are responsible for ethical behavior.

WORKPLACE PROJECTS

PROJECT 2-1 CONTINUE PROFESSIONAL GROWTH PLAN

Recognize the importance of ethical behavior (Objective 1)

In this project, you are to examine your own ethics. Instructions are provided on DCD2–03. This project is a continuation of your Professional Growth Plan. Save your project on your Professional Growth Plan disk under "PGP2–1."

 ### PROJECT 2-2 CONDUCT INTERVIEWS

Recognize the importance of ethical behavior (Objective 1)

Explain the characteristics of an ethical organization (Objective 2)

Identify traits of an ethical employee (Objective 3)

Along with three of your classmates, interview three executives concerning the following:

▶ Importance of ethical behavior

▶ Characteristics of an ethical organization

▶ Traits of ethical employees

▶ As you are interviewing the executives, determine if their organizations have a vision or mission statement. If so, ask if you may have a copy of the statement.

Present your findings in a group report to the class.

Submit your written report to your instructor.

The interview may be done in person, by phone, or via e-mail.

PROJECT 2-3 READ AND RESPOND TO THE CASE

Define steps necessary for ethical change (Objective 4)

Read the following case, and respond to the questions given. Submit your responses to your instructor via e-mail or in a short memorandum using the memorandum form provided on DCD2–03.

Case
Helena Edwards has worked for JWay Nu-Systems Tech for six months. She is learning her job, but she has made a number of mistakes on projects. Each time that she makes a mistake, her supervisor has talked with her about it and explained that she needs to be more thorough in checking her work. You worked for her supervisor (Gordon Grant) for two years before being promoted six months ago. Helena replaced you in the job. You have always had an excellent relation with Gordon Grant. He respects your work, and you respect him as a supervisor. He called you last week and asked to talk with you confidentially about Helena. He explained that he wants Helena to succeed but that she is making too many errors. He asked for your help, suggesting that you might want to talk with Helena about how she can improve. You know Helena, but not well.

1. Reread the section on Ethical Change in this chapter.

2. Should you comply with Mr. Grant's request to help Helena with her work?

3. If your answer is "yes," what steps would you take to help Helena?

4. If your answer is "no," how will you respond to Mr. Grant?

PROJECT 2-4 MAKE A PLAN FOR WORKING IN THE COMMUNITY

Demonstrate a commitment to community involvement (Objective 5)

Add to your Professional Growth Plan that you began in Chapter 1 by describing how you can demonstrate a commitment to community involvement. For example, if you have an interest in assisting with the education of young children, you might volunteer to help in an elementary school. Or, if you enjoy working with the sick, you might volunteer to work in a hospital. The purpose of this project is to encourage you to think about the strengths and interests you have so you can assist your community. Remember, the ethical organization and individual seek to give back to the community in whatever way possible. Think futuristically and commit to working in your community in the future. You will not be engaging in this activity this semester unless you decide you want to do so. Save your plan on your Professional Growth Plan disk under "PGP2–4."

COMMUNICATION POWER

Use DCD2-b to assist you in improving your grammar skills.

ASSESSMENT OF CHAPTER OBJECTIVES

Now that you have completed the chapter and the projects, take a few minutes to review the chapter learning objectives. For your convenience, the objectives are repeated here. Did you accomplish these objectives? If you were unable to accomplish the objectives, give your reasons for not doing so; be specific and concise. Your instructor may prefer that your answers be submitted to her or him. If so, DCD2-c contains the Assessment of Chapter Objectives. Complete the Assessment of Chapter Objectives; submit your results to your instructor.

1. Recognize the importance of ethical behavior.   Yes ☐   No ☐

_____

_____

_____

2. Explain the characteristics of an ethical organization.   Yes ☐   No ☐

_____

_____

_____

3. Identify traits of an ethical employee.   Yes ☐   No ☐

_____

_____

_____

4. Define steps necessary for ethical change.   Yes ☐   No ☐

_____

_____

_____

5. Demonstrate a commitment to community involvement.   Yes ☐   No ☐

_____

_____

_____

STRESS, ANGER, AND TIME MANAGEMENT

Learning Objectives

1. Define the causes of stress.
2. Identify stress reducers.
3. Identify time wasters.
4. Manage time.
5. Control stress.
6. Manage anger.

© Getty Images/Photodisc

> STRESS IN OUR LIVES

Stress is an all too common word in our vocabulary today. The dictionary definition of stress is "a mentally or emotionally disruptive or upsetting condition occurring in response to adverse external influences and usually characterized by increased heart rate, a rise in blood pressure, muscular tension, irritability, and depression."[1] Stress can be and often is present in both our personal and work lives. This chapter focuses on **job stress** (harmful physical and emotional responses that occur when the requirements of the job do not match the capabilities, resources, or needs of the worker).[2] The reasons for stress are many, with change being a major one. Change occurs at whirlwind speed around us in our work and often in our personal lives as well. This constant change takes an increasing toll on our lives. Consider this all too common conversation between friends.

Gloria: "Your timing in leaving the company was great. Things have gone from bad to worse in the last two months. The company recently purchased new software. We are attending training sessions four hours each day, which puts us behind on work that must get done. So, we are being required to work twelve-hour days to finish our regular work. I'm exhausted. Morale is horrible; people are constantly complaining. I found myself yelling at one of my coworkers recently over nothing of any significance. When I finally get home at night I barely speak to my husband. My kids cry and I yell. I wish I had left the company with you."

Ruthie: "Well, unfortunately, I think I made a mistake in leaving. Your workload doesn't sound great, but I wish I were still there. This environment is terrible. At lunch, people tell stories about problems with their bosses, customers, and coworkers. I am trying to learn a new job, and everyone is too busy talking about their dislike for their own job to help me with mine. I

---

[1] *The American Heritage College Dictionary*, Third Edition (Boston: Houghton Mifflin Company, 1993), p. 1343.

[2] "SafeWork, What is Workplace Stress?" 2005, <http:www.ilo.org/public/english/protection/safework/stress/whatis.htm> (accessed March 10, 2005).

have asked my boss for help in learning my job, but he merely tells me to read the job description and the software manual. Both are poorly written and are no help. Even though you say it is bad there, at least you are having training sessions to help you learn the new software. I have unfamiliar software with no help."

Stress is a major problem for American businesses, and its cost to business is enormous, with the cost now estimated to be $300 billion annually.[3]

▶ One-fourth of employees view their jobs as the number one stressor in their lives.
▶ Three-fourths of employees believe the worker has more on-the-job stress than a generation ago.
▶ Problems at work are more strongly associated with health complaints than are any other life stressor—more so than even financial problems or family problems.[4]

Every week millions of people take medication for stress-related symptoms. According to research, these physical problems may be the result of stress: cardiovascular disease, musculoskeletal disorders such as back and neck problems, psychological disorders (depression and burnout), and workplace injuries. Additionally, studies suggest there may be a relationship between suicide, cancer, ulcers, and impaired immune functions; additional research needs to be done before firm conclusions can be drawn.[5]

Another major cause of stress is poor management of time. Some of the errors we make are:

1. Attempting to do too much in too little time.
2. Wasting time and becoming frustrated due to lack of productivity.
3. Not establishing appropriate priorities.

Stress and time management go hand in hand, with each contributing to the other. If we are stressed out, we cannot manage our time well. If we do not manage our time well, we become stressed out.

Closely related to stress management is anger management. Anger, with resulting violent conflicts in the workplace, has become one of corporate America's biggest problems. National polls taken of workers have shown that two of every ten employees have confessed to being angry enough to "hurt" a coworker. According to studies, as much as 42 percent of employee time is spent in engaging in conflict or in trying to resolve conflict.[6] Just as mismanagement of time produces stress, so does mismanagement of anger. The results of mismanagement of anger have become so serious in our world that each of us must give careful consideration to managing our anger and thus controlling our stress. This chapter can help you be a healthier and more productive individual by reducing your stress, controlling your anger, and managing your time.

> STRESS—ITS EFFECTS IN THE WORKPLACE

As knowledge continues to expand rapidly and ever-changing technology becomes the rule rather than the exception, we must constantly learn new ways of performing our jobs. As businesses **downsize** (reduce the number of employees) and **rightsize** (determine the most efficient and effective number of employees and organizational structure), we may lose our jobs and even change our careers. As telework becomes a reality for more and more employees, we must adjust to working in very different conditions than in the past—often by ourselves. Such situations force us to deal with change as well as embrace it if we are going to be successful workers in the twenty-first century. All of these occurrences can and often do contribute to stress.

▷ Healthy Stress

Although stress is usually considered negative, not all stress is harmful. In fact, **healthy stress** can cause us to enrich our lives—to be creative and productive. Our wants, needs, and desires are often satisfied through healthy stress. For example, if you did not feel a need to achieve, you would not be enrolled in this course. If you never felt a need to be productive, you would not accept a challenging job. Healthy stress can and does have a positive impact on our lives.

▷ Negative Stress

Now consider negative stress, often referred to as **distress.** For example, if someone you love is sick, you feel distress. If you are unable to keep up with

[3]Paul J. Rosch, The American Institute of Stress, <http:www.digipharm.com/12%20AIS/1201%20AIS.htm> (accessed April 8, 2005).
[4]NIOSH Stress, <http://www.cdc.gov/niosh/stdresswk.html> (accessed April 8, 2005).
[5]Ibid., <http://www.cdc.gov/niosh/stdresswk.html> (accessed April 8, 2005).
[6]Tony Fiore, *Anger and Your Health,* 2004, <http://1stholistic.com/Reading/health/A2004/health-anger-and-your-health.htm> (accessed April 8, 2005).

new technology in your work, you feel distress. If you receive a negative performance review on your job, you feel distress. When a distressful situation is prolonged, chronic stress occurs. Prolonged chronic stress can cause physical and emotional problems, as noted later in the chapter.

Causes of Negative Stress

In addition to the changes in our society that can cause stress, there are numerous other causes of negative stress. Some of the more common causes are discussed here.

Illness of a family member often causes negative stress.

Work Overload. Productivity is a key word in all organizations today. To compete in an international market, organizations are experiencing the need to be more productive; at the same time they are expected to reduce costs. Employees are often asked to produce more in less time with a greater degree of accuracy than ever before. Employees find themselves working long hours. In fact, Americans work an average of a full month longer each year

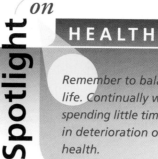
Spotlight *on*

HEALTH

Remember to balance work and family life. Continually working long hours and spending little time with family can result in deterioration of physical and mental health.

as compared to 20 years ago. Americans today work more hours than people in other major countries.

Dual-Career Families. In the majority of families today, both parents work. Parents must balance the pressures of the job with spending time with children and juggling the demands of grocery shopping, housework, and other responsibilities.

Single-Parent Families. The divorce rate in the United States continues to be high, and single-parent homes are prevalent. The responsibility for rearing children may fall on one parent. The responsibilities at home, along with the pressure of having to make enough money to meet the needs of the family, can cause stress.

Elderly Family Members. Americans are living longer than ever before. Many times this long life means that families include elderly family members who may require special care. Adult children may have to devote time and energy to assisting elderly parents in adapting to new living arrangements. Dealing with the challenges of the elderly family members can be difficult for everyone involved.

Economic Pressures. Even dual-career families may find it difficult to make ends meet. Individuals may work longer hours or take second jobs to bring in additional money for household needs. Single parents, too, may find themselves struggling to meet the financial needs of the family.

Distressing Work Conditions. Personality conflicts sometimes occur within the office. Coworkers can be unhappy in their personal lives, and this unhappiness may manifest itself on the job. You may be the innocent party who must face an unhappy individual at the office each day. You may also have to

© Rubberball Productions

deal with a difficult supervisor—one who is neither consistent nor considerate.

Time. People never seem to have enough time to satisfy the following needs and demands:

- ▶ Job requirements
- ▶ Professional expectations
- ▶ Spouse's needs
- ▶ Family's needs

Money. There is a very real relationship between time and money. The more money you spend, the more you need to work. The average person is in debt several thousand dollars, as reflected by national credit card statistics. Many people live from one paycheck to the next. Thus, individuals work more to have more money to pay their debts. They have less time to spend with family or on activities outside work. Their stress mounts higher, just as their debts do. It is a vicious cycle that millions in America have trouble breaking.

▷ Chronic Stress—Harmful to Your Health

Prolonged or **chronic stress** (occurrence of stress over an extended period of time) can cause a number of health problems, including the following:

1. Heart attacks
2. Hypertension[7]
3. Heightened muscle tension
4. Elevated blood pressure
5. Impaired immune functioning
6. Headaches
7. Chronic infections[8]

Chronic stress also can cause a number of emotional disorders, including the following:

1. Heightened anxiety
2. Depression
3. Anger
4. Phobias

5. Personality changes
6. Mental illness[9]

▷ Stress Reducers

Although we cannot avoid all negative stress, we can guard against stress becoming a prevalent part of our lives. Healthy individuals find ways to get rid of negative stress so their bodies will not be damaged. A number of stress reducers are listed in the next section.

Balance Work and Play

Many people comment that they work a 50- or 60-hour week, and the statement may be made with a sense of pride. Are these people producing a large amount of work? Perhaps not. Do they have demanding and challenging jobs? Perhaps. Are they appreciated and respected for their work contributions? Not necessarily. We know there is a relationship between hours worked and productivity. Of course, individuals differ in the number of productive hours they can work. However, for many people productivity decreases after extended periods. Most of us realize immediately when we are not being productive. When we become fatigued, the amount of work we produce goes down and our error rate goes up, signaling that it is time for us to slow down and take a break.

We actually can gain new energy by taking time to play. As adults we may have forgotten how to relax and, with complete abandon, enjoy the world around us. When we feel overtired or nonproductive on the job, it helps to stop for two to five minutes to play. For example, we might have toys at our desk—putty, a slinky, a kaleidoscope. Just a few minutes of working the putty, moving the slinky back and forth, or looking at the various shapes in

Spotlight *on* HEALTH

Play is good for you. Spend some time each day in play.

---

[7]Paul J. Rosch, The American Institute of Stress, <http://www.digipharm.com/12%20AIS/1201%20AIS.htm> (accessed April 9, 2005).

[8]Edward A. Charlesworth and Ronald G. Nathan, *Stress Management: A Comprehensive Guide to Wellness* (New York: Ballantine Books, 2004), p. 30.

[9]Ibid., p. 30.

the kaleidoscope can release stress through relaxation, pleasant thoughts, and smiles.

Laughter is also good for us. Laughter triggers the release of natural painkillers called endorphins. Laugher can enhance the immune system by raising the level of infection fighting T-cells and B-cells. Additionally, because laughter increases breathing, oxygen use, and heart rate, it can stimulate the circulatory system and lower blood pressure temporarily.[10] The positive emotions that result from laughter allow your body's natural healing systems to become fully engaged. The positive results from laughter can reduce the level of stress hormones, blood pressure, and pain. Positive emotions offset the negative emotions of anger, anxiety, and depression. When you are able to laugh at the stressors in your life, you have a greater sense of control over your daily moods. Laughter helps you maintain a more positive emotional state and gives you the resilience to cope with the next problem that undoubtedly will come your way. Your sense of humor grows stronger as it is used in managing the routine stress of your life.[11] Practice some of the following suggestions for helping you to see humor in your daily life:

1. Look for humor in past stressful events.

2. Take a few minutes each day to read your favorite cartoon in the newspaper.

3. Notice funny antics of your coworkers.

4. Keep a cartoon or joke calendar on your desk.

Another way to reduce tension quickly is to take a short exercise break. You might keep athletic shoes at your desk and during a break, spend five or ten minutes climbing stairs or walking briskly. Such physical activity allows you to release built-up tension, to open blocked thinking, and to trigger creative ideas.

Distinguish Between Achievement and Perfection

The dictionary definition of **perfectionism** is "a propensity for being displeased with anything that is not perfect or does not meet extremely high standards."[12] Whereas **achievement** is defined as "the act

of accomplishing or finishing."[13] Notice the difference; the word "perfect" does not appear in the definition of achievement. However, many of us seem to believe that we must do everything perfectly. Certainly, we must achieve and do things well; however, no human being can be perfect. If you blame yourself continually for not doing everything perfectly, you are engaging in energy-draining behavior. In fact, mistakes can be beneficial. Most of us have found ourselves in the position of making a mistake and thinking, *I learned a big lesson; I will never do that again.* One mark of mature individuals is their willingness to learn from errors and to continually grow and achieve.

Recognize Your Limits

You must recognize when you are working too hard. Everyone has a different energy level. You may be able to work ten hours a day quite successfully; someone else may be able to work productively only eight hours a day. How do you know when you are working too hard? One way to know that you are working too hard is to develop some of the stress symptoms mentioned earlier in this chapter, such as hypertension, elevated blood pressure, headaches, depression, and anger.

If you develop these symptoms, seek help. Many insurance programs provide for therapy sessions with psychologists or psychiatrists. These trained individuals can help you discover the causes of your stress and how you can alleviate it. You might want to check with your family physician; he or she can provide sources of assistance.

Exercise

Regular exercise has both physiological and psychological benefits, some of which are:

▶ Weight control.
▶ Increased physical fitness.
▶ Greater stamina, endurance, and muscular strength.
▶ Improved blood pressure and cholesterol level.
▶ Increased sense of well-being and self-esteem.[14]

What type of exercise should you do? Many exercises are good for your body—swimming, walking, and

---

[10] "Humor Therapy," <http://www.wholehealthmd.com/refshelf/substances_view/1,1525,10152,00.html> (accessed April 10, 2005).

[11] Edward A. Charlesworth and Ronald G. Nathan, *Stress Management: A Comprehensive Guide to Wellness* (New York: Ballantine Books, 2004), pp. 282–283.

[12] *The American Heritage College Dictionary,* Third Edition (Boston: Houghton Mifflin Company, 1993), p. 1015.

[13] Ibid., p. 11.

[14] Edward A. Charlesworth and Ronald G. Nathan, *Stress Management: A Comprehensive Guide to Wellness* (New York: Ballantine Books, 2004), pp. 302–303.

Exercise reduces tension.

bicycling, to name a few. Participate in an exercise that you enjoy. What time of day should you exercise? It depends on you. You may prefer to exercise in the morning, while someone else may find the evening a better time to exercise. You may choose to exercise while following along with a video or a television program. You may join a health club or the local Y (YMCA—Young Men's Christian Association, or YWCA—Young Women's Christian Association). Some clubs are open 24 hours a day. Most experts suggest exercising three to five times a week for 30 minutes to an hour. When you begin exercising, go slowly. Train your body; do not strain it. If you have any medical problems or you are just beginning an exercise program, consult your doctor about the type of exercise that is best for you.

Watch Your Diet

What you eat and drink affects your overall health. For example, excessive intake of caffeine is harmful to your health. Caffeine is found in drinks and food such as coffee, tea, chocolate, and certain soft drinks. Just as stress can cause physical health problems, too much caffeine can also cause health problems.

Although sugar provides a short-term energy boost, too much sugar in your diet can result in irritability, poor concentration, and depression. Too much

Self CHECK

Perfectionist Traits

Are you a perfectionist? Do you believe that everything you do must be done extremely well? Read and answer "yes" or "no" to the statements listed below.

	Yes	No
1. If I do not do something well, I feel as though I am a failure.	☐	☐
2. When I make a mistake, I spend many hours rethinking how I might have avoided the mistake.	☐	☐
3. I have a reputation of being someone who is hard to please.	☐	☐
4. When I am playing a sport (tennis, golf, baseball), I get angry with myself if I do not play my best game.	☐	☐
5. I will not start a project unless I know everything I can about what I am to do.	☐	☐
6. I do not like to try new things.	☐	☐
7. I lose patience with others when they do not do things well.	☐	☐
8. I expect every piece of work I produce to be perfect.	☐	☐

salt can also be harmful to your health; you should avoid eating foods that are high in salt content.[15]

Some fat in your diet is necessary; however, too much fat can cause health problems. According to guidelines recommended by the American Heart Association and the Surgeon General's office, fat should be no more than 30 percent of the total calories you consume each day. For people with heart disease, the fat percentage should be lower— no more than 10 to 20 percent of the total calories consumed.[16]

Your diet should include meals high in carbohydrates and fiber. Sources of carbohydrates include rice, pasta, potatoes, and bread. Nutritionists suggest that the carbohydrates present in a baked potato or a cup of rice will relieve the anxiety caused by a stressful day. Fruits, vegetables, and grains are good sources of fiber.[17]

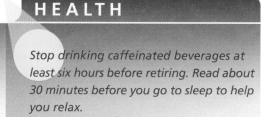

Spotlight *on*

HEALTH

Stop drinking caffeinated beverages at least six hours before retiring. Read about 30 minutes before you go to sleep to help you relax.

Get Enough Sleep

Not every person needs the same amount of sleep, with the amount of sleep needed by adults ranging from five hours to ten hours each night. However, the average adult functions best with seven to eight hours of sleep. Signs that you are not getting enough sleep include the following:

▸ Difficulty in waking up
▸ Inability to concentrate
▸ Falling asleep at work or in class
▸ Moodiness, irritability, depression, or anxiety

If you have trouble going to sleep, tips that will help you sleep include these: keeping a regular schedule, relaxing before going to bed (deep breathing exercises, warm baths), eating dinner two to three hours before bedtime, and drinking a cup of herbal tea.[18]

> ANGER—A GROWING PROBLEM

We are living in a time in which terms such as road rage, phone rage, and desk rage, to name a few, have become common terms. News stories such as the following appear often in newspapers and on television.

Road Rage (extreme anger on the roads and highways that can cause accidents and criminal behavior): Oklahoma City Woman Arrested Following a Series of Road Rage Incidents. A woman is in the Oklahoma County Jail charged with causing 14 accidents during a road rage attack in Oklahoma City.[19]

Phone Rage (extreme anger that can cause unprofessional and erratic behavior when talking on a cellphone or telephone): Phone rage causes $2000 in damage. An angry customer, fed up with bad cell phone service, decided to take action by throwing mobile phones across the cellphone store. After the incident, the man told authorities he only planned on yelling at the employees, but that claim was cast into doubt after it came out that he put on safety glasses before the throwing started.[20]

Desk Rage (extreme anger over a situation in the workplace that can cause irrational, destructive, or harmful behavior). An office worker slams her keyboard and shouts profanity when her computer freezes up.[21]

In addition to desk rage, even cubicle rage has been identified. Cubicle workers complain about noise (trying to concentrate over the sound of coworkers talking on the phone), crowded conditions (with cubicles extremely close together), and two or three workers having to share cubicles designed for one person.[22] One national study of more than 1,300 American workers revealed that 42 percent of the individuals surveyed said yelling and

[15]Holistic online, *Stress The Silent Killer,* <http://www.holistic-online.com/stress/stress_diet.htm> (accessed April 10, 2005).

[16]DietSite: Online dietitians serving your nutritional needs <http://www.dietsite.com/dt/diets/HeartHealthy/fatdictionary.asp> (accessed April 10, 2005).

[17]Holistic online.com. *Stress, The Silent Killer,* <http://www.holistic-online.com/stress/stress_diet.htm> (accessed April 10, 2005).

[18]"Getting the Sleep You Need: Sleep Stages, Sleep Tips and Aids," <http://www.helpguide.org/aging/sleeping.htm> (accessed April 10, 2005).

[19]Google Search: Road Rage, <http://news.google.com/news?q=road+rage&hl=en&lr=&sa=N&tab=nn&oi=newsr> (accessed September 30, 2005).

[20]Mobile Tracker: Cell phone news and reviews, "Phone rage causes $2000 in damage," <http://www.mobiletracker.net/archives/2004/05/14/phone_rage_caus.php> (accessed April 10, 2005).

[21]Jennifer Daw, (2001). *Road rage, air rage and now 'desk rage.'* <www.apa.org/monitor/julaug01/deskrage.html> (accessed April 8, 2005).

[22]Beth Nissen, (2000). *Overworked, overwrought: 'Desk rage' at work.* <http://www.archives.cnn.com/2000/CAREER/trends/11/15/rage> (accessed April 5, 2005).

verbal abuse took place where they worked. Half of the respondents said they are victims of daily verbal abuse, and 29 percent admitted that they have yelled at coworkers. Ten percent of the respondents said they work in organizations where physical violence has occurred. Fourteen percent of the workers said they work where an angry worker has damaged equipment.[23] Figure 3-1 suggests several steps for helping you to manage desk rage.

Because statistics show that we are becoming an angrier society and lashing out in anger many times, your task as an administrative professional is to understand that the problem exists and to learn positive steps that you may take to help you overcome anger. Listed here are some techniques that will help you not only deal with your anger but also help diffuse the anger of coworkers, customers, and clients with whom you come in contact.

▷ Its Positive Purpose

Although we do not generally think of the positive nature of anger, there is one. Anger as a positive is a messenger that tells us when something is wrong. Anger as a shield becomes negative because it allows us to hide our true feelings. Consider this example of how anger operates both as a messenger and a shield.

Rebecca wants to enroll in college, but she has a spouse who does not want her to do so. Rebecca and her husband have talked about the possibility for a time. After months of her spouse refusing to listen to her desires, Rebecca finds herself becoming angry. Her anger is serving as a messenger to tell her that something is wrong. In the past, her anger has also been serving as a shield. It has allowed her to mask her feelings and believe that her husband will eventually say it is okay. Individuals in such situations often get angry because it is easier than trying to understand the real problem and deal with it. However, whenever people use anger to mask a problem, they take a step closer to becoming angry individuals who see the world through a lens of anger that blinds them from being able to live a peaceful and happy life. If college truly is important to Rebecca, she must seek ways to convince her husband that she is serious.

▷ Anger Management

There are a number of proven techniques that can help you manage anger. These techniques, when used properly, can make you a more effective individual. Study carefully the following anger management techniques.

Relax

Deep-breathing exercises are one of the quickest ways to relax your body. Start by finding a comfortable position; sit in a comfortable chair. You may close your eyes if that makes you feel more at ease. Then slowly inhale air through your nose until you feel your lungs fill with air. Next, exhale the air

Spotlight *on*

HEALTH

Do not worry about things you cannot control.

Figure 3-1	TIPS FOR MANAGING DESK RAGE

1. Get away from your desk at lunch.

2. Take the vacation time you have earned.

3. Exercise.

4. Eat healthy.

5. Drink at least eight glasses of water daily.

6. Listen to your body. Headaches, upset stomachs, and back pain have a cause.

7. When confronted with a great deal of pressure, take three deep breaths and exhale with each breath.

8. Do not take on more projects than you can do.[24]

[23]Florence Stone, "Desk Rage: I've Been There, How About You?" 2004, American Management Association, <http://www.amanet.org/movingahead/editoria12002_2003/mar03_desk_rage.htm> (accessed April 5, 2005).

[24]Florence Stone, "Desk Rage: I've Been There, How About You?" 2004, American Management Association. <http:www.amanet.org/movingahead/editoria12003_2003/mar03_desk_rage.htm> (accessed March 10, 2005).

slowly, breathing out either through your nose or mouth.

Use Positive Self-Talk

If you are angry, negative self-talk can escalate your anger; positive self-talk can de-escalate your anger. For example, assume you are playing a game of tennis with a friend who is extremely good. You miss a ball and say to yourself, "I really am terrible!" You are engaging in negative self-talk, and negative self-talk on the tennis court causes you to miss more shots. In other words, your negative self-talk is a self-fulfilling prophecy. You decide you are terrible and you prove yourself right. Now consider a positive self-talk response. When you miss a ball, you say to yourself, "No big deal; I'll get the next one." And you do! You hit a terrific ball. When you find yourself engaging in negative self-talk, turn it around by engaging in these behaviors.

1. Recognize the negative self-talk

2. Stop it immediately

3. Begin positive self-talk

Walk Away

Walk away physically if you can; if you cannot, walk away emotionally. When you were a child, did your mother ever say, "Before you say or do anything when you are angry, count to ten"? Counting to ten allows you to interrupt your anger and cool off. It also allows you time to consider what other choices you might have. In your head, you are walking away from what is making you angry. Reflect on the following example, a common situation that often makes people angry.

You are waiting in line at the grocery store. Although there are self-check registers, the lines are longer at those registers than at the traditional ones. You choose the shortest line at the traditional register. The checker is slow, talking to customers as he scans their groceries. In addition, no grocery sackers are available, so the checker must sack the items. The person in front of you has forgotten two items and asks the checker if she can go get them; the checker agrees. You have an important appointment, and you must be on time. You find you are getting angrier and angrier. You are ready to scream at the person in front of you and at the checker.

What are your choices? You can walk away mentally—count to ten, sing a song to yourself, or envision yourself at one of your favorite places having a wonderful time. Or if you are going to be late for your appointment, you can physically walk away. Leave before you become angry and emotionally upset. You can always come back to the grocery store at another time.

As you perform your tasks as an administrative professional, there are times you will need to walk away mentally, take a deep breath, and tell yourself that tomorrow will be a better day.

Talk to a Friend

If a situation at work makes you angry, talk to a trusted friend about it. That person may be able to help you understand what is causing your anger and help you decide what you can do about the situation. For example, assume you have this situation at work.

You are chairing a team whose task is to recommend a records management system. The team has met three times, and you believe progress is being made on the task. You believe the team has worked well together. Yesterday your supervisor called you into her office, closed the door, and said that she needed to talk with you about a serious matter. She told you that two people on the records management team had complained that you were not listening to what the team was suggesting—that you apparently had already made up your mind about what the records management system should be and the team had almost no input. As she talked, you found yourself getting very angry. You believe that the accusations are totally false, and you do not understand why anyone would make such statements.

To address the issue and avoid excessive anger, you might take one of these two steps.

▸ Tell your supervisor that you have not made up your mind about the records management

To keep from becoming stressed, walk away (mentally or physically) when you are in a situation you cannot control.

system and that you feel the team is working well together. However, because two team members have complained, you will talk with the team, asking to hear their suggestions again. Tell your supervisor that you will be receptive to all suggestions, and you will set up an appointment to discuss the team's suggestions with her, along with your recommendations.

▶ Spend time talking with a trusted friend in the organization about the problem. Be open to the friend's comments concerning how you may be more inclusive. Then, develop a plan to address the team's concerns. Have another meeting with the team; hear their suggestions. Then talk with your supervisor, explaining what has been done.

Solve the Problem

Sometimes the same problem occurs frequently. For example, consider this situation.

You are the only woman in a department of men. Your job description is the same as that of the men. Each time an important assignment comes up, the work is given to one of the men. You do a good job, and your supervisor (who is male) has given you excellent evaluations. However, you are beginning to think he does not value your work. You believe that as long as you are passed over in the assignment of more challenging work, you will not have a chance to learn and grow on your job. You also believe that without having the opportunity to do the challenging assignments, you will not have a chance for promotion. You wonder if your supervisor is guilty of gender bias. You are beginning to feel anger not only toward your supervisor but also toward the other men in the department.

What do you do? The problem is important enough that you should attempt to solve it. You can use a problem-solving approach. Figure 3-2 illustrates the problem-solving steps. You can do the following:

1. Identify the problem. The problem in this case is that you are not being given any challenging assignments.

2. Collect and analyze information. Analyze the types of assignments that are available in your office; determine what work you are interested in and what your skills will allow you to handle.

3. List your alternatives. You can quit your job; you can talk to your supervisor; you can talk with the

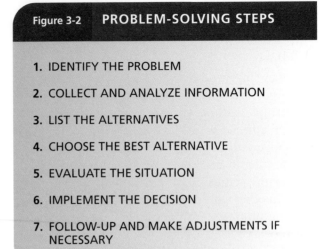

Figure 3-2 **PROBLEM-SOLVING STEPS**

1. IDENTIFY THE PROBLEM
2. COLLECT AND ANALYZE INFORMATION
3. LIST THE ALTERNATIVES
4. CHOOSE THE BEST ALTERNATIVE
5. EVALUATE THE SITUATION
6. IMPLEMENT THE DECISION
7. FOLLOW-UP AND MAKE ADJUSTMENTS IF NECESSARY

other males in the department; you can get angry and yell at everyone.

4. Choose the best alternative. The best alternative in this situation is to talk with your supervisor. He is the one controlling the job assignments. From the data that you have collected, give him examples of the types of projects you believe you have the skills and abilities to handle. Explain your interest in receiving more challenging work. Listen carefully to what he has to say.

5. Evaluate the situation. Was the talk successful? Did the supervisor explain his rationale successfully? Is he willing to give you more challenging assignments? Do you believe you now have a chance to move up in the organization if you continue to do a good job? Hopefully, the answers to these questions are positive. If they are not, you may be in a situation that you cannot change.

6. Implement the decision. If you are given the challenging assignment you have requested, prove to your employer that you can do the job well. Check with him in a few weeks to discuss your success in completing the assignments. If he does not consent to giving you more challenging assignments, you may ask for a transfer to another department (assuming there is an opening) or look for a position in another organization.

Take Breaks from Your Desk

Make it a practice to get away from your desk at noon; do not eat lunch at your desk. Take short

Part I The Work Environment

Do not make a practice of eating lunch at your desk; you deserve a break from the office.

© Digital Vision

We have 24 hours each day to manage effectively.

© Photodisc/Steve Cole

breaks from your desk in the morning and the afternoon.

Personalize Your Cubicle

If you work in a cubicle, personalize it to make it your office even if there is no door or walls that extend to the ceiling. Check to determine if your company has any regulations as to what you may add to your cubicle.

Put Family Photographs on Your Desk

Family photos help you remember what is really important in life and why you work so hard. However, before you put up photographs, be certain that your company has no regulations against doing so.

Get Help from a Professional

A number of companies offer counseling and stress-relief programs on site. Additionally, many companies provide insurance that includes outside counseling services. An important point to remember is that if you continually find yourself angry and stressed on the job, seek help. Do not assume that you can handle it by yourself.[25]

> TIME MANAGEMENT

Time management is really a misnomer since none of us can control the number of hours in a day. Time is finite; we cannot increase or decrease time by managing it. But we can learn to manage the way we use our time. Thus, time management

really refers to the way we manage ourselves and our tasks in relation to the time we have in a day, a week, or a year.

▷ Time Defined

Time is a resource, but it is a unique resource. It cannot be bought, sold, borrowed, rented, saved, or manufactured. It can be spent, and it is the only resource that must be spent the minute it is received. Every one of us receives the same amount of time to spend each day; we all have 24 hours each day to manage in relation to our professional and personal goals. We cannot speed the clock up or slow it down. Time passes at the same rate each minute, each hour, and each day. The difficulty with time management occurs as we try to manage ourselves in relation to the finite time we have; many of us do not understand how we spend our time. We do not understand our time wasters, and we certainly are not taking steps to manage ourselves more effectively in relation to our time. Many of us do not realize that once we have wasted time, it is gone and it cannot be replaced.

▷ Time Wasters

Before you begin to analyze how you might do a more effective job in managing yourself in relation to your time, look at some of the common time wasters. You may find that you have been guilty of many of these behaviors.

Ineffective Communication

As an administrative professional, you will communicate both verbally and in writing with people in

---

[25]Ibid.

Chapter 3 Stress, Anger, and Time Management

61

the workplace (your employer and coworkers) and outside the workplace (customers and clients). The lines of communication between you and others must be open and easily understood. Think of the time you will waste if you must rewrite a letter because you misunderstood the instructions from your employer; think of the profits the company may lose if you make a customer unhappy and lose an account as a result of misunderstood communication.

Inadequate Planning

Many individuals do not plan what they need to do on a particular day. Lack of planning can cause both you and your supervisor problems. Think about this situation. Your supervisor gives you a report on Friday afternoon that must be completed by 4 p.m. on Monday. You understand that the job is a high priority. The report is not lengthy, but you do not analyze how long you will need to produce it. On Monday morning, you have numerous interruptions; you do not begin the report until 1 p.m. As you get into the report, you see that it is very involved and that you will not be able to finish it by 4 p.m. You are embarrassed and frustrated when you have to admit to your employer that the report is not completed.

Your lack of planning resulted in an important report not being produced in a timely manner. Your employer is unhappy, and you know that if you continue to operate in this manner you could lose your job.

Improper Use of E-mail

E-mail is a valuable communication tool, both for its ease and for its speed. However, it must be used effectively. Improper uses of e-mail can cost you time and decrease your efficiency. Here are several tips for managing your e-mail properly.

▶ Determine times each day that you will check your e-mail. For example, it is a good idea to check it when you arrive at work to determine if there are any critical activities that you need to handle. Then, depending on the volume of e-mail correspondence that you receive, you may determine that you can check it again mid-morning and mid-afternoon.

▶ If you do not receive a large number of e-mails, determine that you will check only once each day.

▶ Do not spend valuable time checking your e-mail every 30 minutes. If there is something crucial that you need to handle, use IM (instant messaging), which is a type of communication service that allows you to create a private chat

room with another person. The system alerts you whenever someone is on your private line.

▶ Compose brief e-mails that are direct and specific. E-mail correspondence should never be repetitious or redundant.

▶ Answer your e-mails quickly; be clear and concise.

▶ Do not let e-mails take the place of all personal contact within your office. Clearly there are times that you need to meet face-to-face with someone.

▶ Remember that an e-mail is a communication tool to be wisely used. Say what you need to say courteously and directly.

▶ Do not send personal e-mails from your office computer; do not give your office e-mail address to friends. You may give it to immediate family members to be used for emergency situations only.

▶ Never generate or forward pornographic material by e-mail. Most organizations have strict policies that penalize employees who engage in such activity.

▶ Never generate or forward jokes by e-mail. Your company e-mail should only be used for company business.

Poor Telephone Usage

The telephone becomes a time waster when it is not used properly. Here are some of the mistakes that cause the telephone to be a time waster.

1. Engaging in personal conversations during work hours

2. Failing to give the proper information to a coworker, client, or customer

3. Failing to get the proper information from a caller; i.e., name, phone number, and reason for the call

4. Using the telephone when it would be more efficient to use e-mail or a fax

Improper Handling of Visitors

As an administrative professional, your responsibility is to make visitors feel comfortable and welcome. However, that does not mean you must entertain the visitors while they are waiting to see your employer. Also, you should not spend long periods of time chatting with coworkers who stop by your workspace to visit. Certainly if a coworker comes by on a work-related errand, you may engage in pleasantries such as "Good morning. How is your day going?" But you should not spend a lot of time in idle chitchat.

Disorganization

Does your desk have a pile of file folders on it, with their contents spilling out? Do you have half-finished projects, half-finished memorandums, and a stack of filing sitting around? Disorganized individuals are a serious liability to their organization. They cannot be depended on to provide information in a timely manner because they forget where the information is. They cannot meet deadlines because they forget to write them down. They waste an enormous amount of their time and other people's time searching for files, phone numbers, reports, and other necessary information.

Disorganization is a time waster; keep your desk organized so you can find information quickly.

▷ Techniques for Managing Time

Through the information presented earlier in this chapter, you know the importance of time management. You also understand that time is a resource that must be used well and that time wasters must be minimized. Now you must understand how to do a better job of managing yourself in relation to time. This area requires constant work. We never become such effective time managers that we can forget about the constraints of time. However, when we pay attention to effective management techniques, we find that not only do we seem to have more time to get our tasks done, but also we reduce the stress in our lives.

Set Goals

A **goal** is an objective, a purpose, or an end that is to be achieved. The idea of establishing goals makes many people feel uncomfortable—having to write them down and then being expected to achieve them. How many of us have set New Year's resolutions in good faith and then failed to reach any of them? Thinking of these resolutions at a later date results in a vague sense of guilt about not having accomplished what we set out to do. Goal setting can produce these same feelings of hesitancy and guilt. However, if we are to accomplish anything on our job and in our personal lives, we must set goals.

Organizational Goals. Most organizations are involved in strategic and organizational planning. When these plans are written, they include definite goals to be accomplished and deadlines to meet these goals. Employees are usually brought into the planning process. In fact, companies often ask employees to write action plans that reflect what they will accomplish to meet the goals of the organization. Then during their performance evaluations, these employees are evaluated on how well they met their goals.

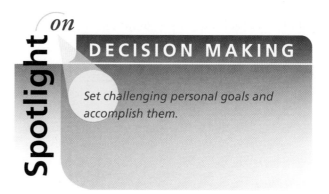

Spotlight *on*

DECISION MAKING

Set challenging personal goals and accomplish them.

Personal Goals. Personal goal setting is also important. For example, this goal setting can take the form of deciding what your career goals are and what you want to be doing in the next five or ten years. You may also set goals that involve your personal life such as when you purchase a house, start a family, and choose where you want to live.

Goal Attributes. A goal should challenge you and require you to do more than you have been doing. It should encourage you to reach a higher level of accomplishment. However, goals should not be unrealistically high. They should be achievable with hard work, appropriate skills, and dedication to the task. Goals should also be specific and measurable. If your goal is too vague, you will not know when you have achieved it. For example, "to become a more effective communicator" is a goal that is too vague. How can you become a more effective communicator? You should determine behaviors you will engage in to accomplish your goal. Your goal might be stated as: I am going to become a more effective communicator by using direct and simple language and listening to others.

Your next step is to establish methods for measuring the accomplishment of your objective. In the communication situation, you might determine that you are going to measure the accomplishment in the following manner: To determine if I have accomplished my objective, I will ask three people within my work group to evaluate my communication skills.

A Goal Must Have a Deadline. Deadlines allow us to see if the goal has been accomplished. In the communication example given previously, you might set yourself a deadline such as: Evaluation of my communication goal will occur by December 19 (within three months after it was set).

A Goal Should Be Flexible. Sometimes external conditions impact your goals to the point that you cannot accomplish them. When this occurs, do not cling stubbornly to something that is no longer possible but do not be too quick to eliminate the goal. By working smarter, you may be able to offset the external factors. Also, you may be able to revise your goal or establish a different time frame for completion.

Analyze How You Spend Your Time

Although you might think you know exactly how you spend your time, actually most people do not. Check periodically how you are spending your time. You might be surprised at what is taking up your time, and you might discover some time wasters.

One way to determine how you spend your time is to chart on a time log the amount of time you spend in various daily activities. Certainly you should not become a slave to the log, and you do not need to be accurate to the second or minute. However, you should be faithful to the process for a period of one or two weeks so you have a realistic picture of how you are spending your time. Figure 3-3 shows a time log.

The next step is to analyze your time log to discover ways in which you can improve the management of your time. Ask yourself these questions:

1. What was the most productive period of the day? Why?

2. What was the least productive period of the day? Why?

Figure 3-3   DAILY TIME LOG

Name _____ Day _____ Date _____

Time	Activity	Priority Nature of Interruptions

3. Who or what accounted for the interruptions?

4. Can the interruptions be minimized or eliminated?

5. What activities needed more time?

6. On what activities could I spend less time and still get the desired results?

Prepare an Action Plan

After you analyze your log, the next step is to prepare an action plan. The purpose of the plan is to set goals for yourself as to how you will increase your time management efficiency. The techniques given here will help you manage yourself in relation to your time.

Set Priorities

Many times you will not be able to do everything you have been asked to do in one day. Thus, you must be able to set priorities—to distinguish between the most important and least important jobs and determine the order in which they should be completed. If you are new to a job, you may need help from your supervisor to determine which tasks are the most important. When you learn more about your position and your supervisor, you should be able to establish priorities on your own.

Prepare Daily To-Do Lists

Before you leave work for the day, prepare a to-do list for the next day. List all the tasks, activities, and projects that you need to accomplish. Then review your list. Mark the most important items A, the less important items B, and those remaining C. Use your list, with priorities in place, to perform the following activities.

1. Arrange papers on your desk in priority order, with the A's in one pile, the B's in another pile, and the C's in still another pile.

2. Prioritize telephone messages, marking them A, B, or C.

3. The next day as you complete the items on your to-do list, mark them off. This step gives you a sense of accomplishment and calls your attention to what you still need to accomplish.

4. As you prepare your to-do list for the following day, use the present to-do list. If it still lists items you have not been able to accomplish, transfer these items to the to-do list for the next day. A sample to-do list is shown in Figure 3-4.

Figure 3-4   SAMPLE TO-DO LIST

TO-DO LIST
November 24, 20XX

1. E-mail the managers concerning the meeting on December 10.

2. Talk with Mike in Personnel concerning when the job vacancy notice should be submitted.

3. Complete the draft letter to Chien Pai for Ms. Portosky.

4. File the correspondence and reports from last week.

5. Begin the research on the industries in Australia for Ms. Portosky.

Simplify Repetitive Tasks

If you find yourself keyboarding a form numerous times, simplify the process. Prepare a template on your computer. Do you look up the same address or telephone number several times? Make yourself a list of frequently used addresses and telephone numbers. Store these on your computer or on a Rolodex file. Simplifying a repetitive task takes time to organize initially, but in the long run, the savings in time can be significant.

Conquer Procrastination

Procrastination is the postponement or needless delay of a project or task that must be done. Many of us are guilty of procrastination. We postpone a project because we are afraid we will fail at it, not interested in the work, and/or angry with the person who delegated it to us.

Of course, we do not want to admit any of these reasons, so we make excuses. We make statements similar to the following:

I have too many other projects.

I don't have what I need to do the job.

Before I can get started, I have to consult with my supervisor.

There really is no rush to begin; it's not due for three weeks.

Procrastinators are late for meetings, put off handling projects, and do not return telephone calls. Procrastinators may be such relaxed, easygoing people that their procrastination does not bother them as much as it bothers others. However, they can create stress for themselves with their last-minute efforts, and the stress they put on other members of their work group can be significant. If you know that you are a procrastinator, commit now to changing your behavior by following the tips given below.

TIPS FOR CONQUERING PROCRASTINATION

- ▷ Focus on one task at a time.
- ▷ Establish deadlines and then meet those deadlines.
- ▷ Tackle the most difficult tasks first.
- ▷ Do not let perfectionism paralyze you.
- ▷ Recognize that you have a habit of putting things off; take steps to correct the habit.
- ▷ Make a sign for your desk reminding you not to procrastinate.

Handle Paper Once

Do you ever find yourself rereading a piece of paper or shuffling it from the top of a stack to the bottom of the stack several times? Most of us do. In fact, many time management experts claim that handling paper over and over is the biggest paperwork time waster. The basic rule is to handle paper once. Read it, route it, file it, or answer it. Get it off your desk as quickly as possible.

Organize Your Work Area

As you start a new project, clear your desk of materials that relate to finished projects. Put these materials in a file folder, label the folder with the name of the project, and place the folder in your drawer. Keep in- and out-trays on your desk, and label the trays for incoming and outgoing material. If space permits, you may wish to have a tray on your desk for material to be filed. Keep frequently used supplies (such as pencils, pens, and paper clips) in your center desk drawer. Organize your paper into letterhead, plain bond, memorandum, and so on.

Use Time Effectively

Handling e-mail, telephone calls, and visitors effectively can be difficult at times. Figure 3-5 gives several suggestions for using your time well.

Use Good Communication Techniques

If your supervisor asks you to do something, be sure you understand exactly what you are to do. Paraphrase what you believe he or she said if you are not clear. Do not be afraid to ask questions. Transmit ideas in simple, clear terms. Define terms if necessary.

Listen carefully when someone is talking. When communicating with an individual face-to-face, look at her or him. Be sensitive to the person's body language as well as to the words the person is saying. Keep your mind open to new ideas; refrain from passing judgment on what the speaker is saying. Chapters 6 and 8 in this textbook focus on written and oral communication.

Practice Speed Reading

Numerous items that you must read will pass your desk. Before reading correspondence and other materials, organize the material in order of importance. Prepare folders, noting the dates when the materials must be read.

Read for the main thought or idea. If you are reading periodicals or company literature, scan the table of contents first. Then selectively read the articles. Read carefully only the sections that will enhance your knowledge of your job and your organization.

Use Electronic Time Management Systems

A number of time management systems allow you to organize your work quickly and efficiently by using electronic systems such as **PIMs** (personal information managers) and **PDAs** (personal digital assistants).

PIM software, which can be installed on your computer, allows you to organize to-do lists and keep track of meetings, phone calls, and business appointments. You can organize information by days, weeks, or months, or alphabetically or by priority. You can enter recurring activities and then view and

PDAs allow you to maintain contact with your office while traveling.

Figure 3-5   **USE TIME EFFECTIVELY**

E-mail

▶ Determine times each day that you will check your e-mail.

▶ Do not check your e-mail constantly.

▶ Compose brief e-mails that are direct and specific.

▶ Answer your e-mails clearly and concisely.

▶ Do not let e-mails take the place of personal contact.

▶ Remember that e-mail is a communication tool to be used wisely. Say what you need to say courteously and directly.

Telephone

▶ Give and record correct information during telephone calls.

▶ Do not engage in personal conversations during work hours unless there is an emergency situation.

▶ Get proper information from a caller; i.e., name, phone number, and reason for the call.

▶ Do not use the telephone when it would be more efficient to use an e-mail or a fax.

▶ Give and record correct information during telephone calls.

▶ When placing calls, identify yourself, your supervisor (if you are placing a call for her or him), and what you need.

▶ If the person called is not in, find out when the person will return.

▶ When taking incoming calls, find out who is calling and the nature of the call.

▶ If you are taking a call for your supervisor who is not in, let the person know when your supervisor is expected.

▶ If you take a message, repeat the name, phone number, and message to the caller to confirm the accuracy.

▶ When you have several calls to make, group them and make the calls when people are likely to be in the office. Early morning is usually a good time to reach people.

▶ Keep your personal calls to a minimum. Let your friends know they should not call you at the office.

▶ Use e-mail and faxes as an alternative to leaving and receiving phone messages.

Visitors

▶ Set up appointments for visitors. Discourage people from dropping by unexpectedly to see you or your supervisor.

▶ Make visitors welcome, but do not make small talk for extended periods. Continue with your work.

▶ Discourage coworkers from dropping by to socialize. You can socialize on breaks and at lunch. Make it clear that your responsibility during working hours is to work.

---

print daily, weekly, or monthly calendars. PIM software also allows you to store contact information, schedule meetings, and share schedules.

With PDAs, you can check your e-mail, retrieve telephone calls, access and download information from the Internet, check the financial markets, and key short letters and reports. PDAs and cell phone combination units, such as Sidekicks and BlackBerries, allow you to:

1. Send instant messages

2. E-mail

3. Take photos

4. Browse the Internet

5. Send and receive messages to and from cell phones

6. Organize your calendar and phone numbers

7. Make "To Do" notes

8. If your company has the appropriate server, you can have e-mails from the office automatically sent to your unit.

Set Up an Exercise Program

Cardiovascular specialists have found that regular aerobic exercise has numerous health benefits. Several of these benefits of physical activity are listed in

Figure 3-6. Aerobic exercise increases the heart and breathing rate while training the heart, lungs, and muscles to use oxygen more efficiently. A minimum of thirty minutes (and preferably one hour) of low to moderate-intensity aerobic activity (jogging, walking, cycling, stair climbing, swimming, rowing, or aerobics) five days per week is recommended.[26]

Figure 3-6	BENEFITS OF PHYSICAL EXERCISE

1. Improves the strength of the heart

2. Helps weight reduction

3. Improves flexibility and builds muscle

4. Decreases total and low-density lipoprotein cholesterol (bad cholesterol)

5. Increases high-density lipoprotein cholesterol (good cholesterol)

6. Increases energy

7. Increases tolerance to anxiety, stress, and depression

8. Decreases risk of orthopedic injury by improving flexibility

9. Helps build healthy bones, muscles and joints[27]

Get the Proper Amount of Sleep

The proper amount of sleep is essential to mental and physical health. Although the amount of sleep needed varies by individual, studies have shown that people who sleep seven to eight hours a night tend to live longer than people whose sleep is longer or shorter. If you have difficulty going to sleep, practice some of the techniques given in Figure 3-7.

Figure 3-7	SLEEP TECHNIQUES

▸ Take a warm bath

▸ Get a massage

▸ Listen to music

▸ Drink herb tea

▸ Sleep in a well-ventilated room

▸ Sleep on a firm bed

▸ Sleep on your back

▸ Get physical exercise during the day

▸ Keep regular bedtime hours

▸ Avoid naps

▸ Avoid illuminated bedroom clocks[28]

> YOUR POWER AND YOUR POTENTIAL

If you are to thrive in the business world today, you must master the multitude of changes that come your way in the form of technology, be productive and happy in your work, and be able to realize your full power and potential. When you are stressed to the point of being burned out on your job, angry a large part of the time, and finding too few hours in the day to accomplish what you must accomplish, you are not able to realize your full power and potential. By putting to use the techniques presented in this chapter, you have a chance to not only succeed in your job but also to thrive in the world of change.

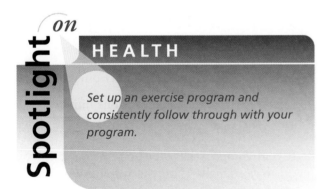

Spotlight *on* HEALTH

Set up an exercise program and consistently follow through with your program.

[26]Edward A. Charlesworth and Ronald G. Nathan, *Stress Management: A Comprehensive Guide to Wellness* (New York: Ballantine Books, 2004), p. 311.

[27]R. Iqbal, "Exercise and Cardiovascular Fitness," <http:www.dgfasli.nic.in/muscular.htm> (accessed March 13, 2005).

[28]Mick Winter. "30 Simple Steps to Help You Sleep," <www.well.com/user/mick/insomnia> (accessed March 10, 2005).

SUMMARY

Reinforce your learning in this chapter by studying this summary.

▸ Stress can be either positive or negative. Positive stress allows us to accomplish our wants, needs, and desires. Negative stress places our body under distress and can cause physical and emotional problems.

▸ Factors that contribute to negative stress are work overload, dual-career families, single-parent families, elderly family members, economic pressures, distressing work conditions, and lack of time and money.

▸ Stress reducers include balancing work and play, distinguishing between achievement and perfection, recognizing our limits, exercising, eating right, and getting enough sleep.

▸ Anger is a growing corporate problem. Over the past few years, incidences of violence in the workplace have increased.

▸ Techniques to help you reduce anger include relaxing, using positive self-talk, walking away, talking to a friend, solving the problem, taking breaks from your desk, personalizing your office space, and getting help from a professional.

▸ Time is a resource that cannot be bought, sold, borrowed, rented, saved, or manufactured.

▸ Time wasters include ineffective communication, inadequate planning, improper use of e-mail, poor telephone usage, improper handling of visitors, disorganization, and procrastination.

▸ Techniques for managing time include setting goals, analyzing the way time is spent, preparing an action plan, setting priorities, preparing daily to-do lists, simplifying repetitive tasks, conquering procrastination, handling paper once, organizing the work area, using time effectively, using good communication techniques, practicing speed reading, using electronic time management systems, setting up an exercise program, and getting the proper amount of sleep.

Achievement—The act of accomplishing or finishing.

Chronic stress—Occurs when a distressful situation is prolonged, allowing no rest or recuperation for the body; it can cause physical and emotional problems.

Desk rage—Extreme anger over a situation in the workplace that can cause irrational, destructive, and harmful behavior.

Distress—Negative stress caused from a troubling situation or event.

Downsize—Reduce the number of employees.

Goal—An objective, a purpose, or an end that is to be achieved.

Healthy stress—Our wants, needs, and desires are often satisfied through healthy stress.

Job stress—Harmful physical and emotional responses that occur when the requirements of the job do not match the capabilities, resources, or needs of the worker.

Perfectionism—A propensity for being displeased with anything that is not perfect or that does not meet extremely high standards.

PDA—Personal digital assistant; a small computer that allows the checking of e-mail, retrieving of telephone

calls, accessing and downloading of information from the Internet, checking of financial markets, keying of short reports, and so forth.

PIM—Personal information manager; software that allows organization of information.

Phone rage—Extreme anger that can cause unprofessional and erratic behavior when talking on a cell phone or telephone.

Procrastination—The postponement or needless delay of a project or task that must be done.

Rightsize—Determine the most efficient and effective number of employees and organizational structure.

Road rage—Extreme anger on the roads and highways that can cause accidents and criminal behavior.

Stress—A mentally or emotionally disruptive or upsetting condition occurring in response to adverse external influences and usually characterized by increased heart rate, an increase in blood pressure, muscular tension, irritability, and depression.

Time—A resource that cannot be bought, sold, borrowed, rented, saved, or manufactured; it is the only resource that must be spent the minute it is received.

Time management—The way we manage ourselves and our tasks in relation to the time we have.

CHECKPOINT

Check your understanding of these terms by completing DCD3-a on the Data CD.

DISCUSSION ITEMS

These discussion items provide an opportunity to test your understanding of the chapter through written responses and/or discussion with your classmates and your instructor.

1. Is all stress unhealthy? Explain your answer.

2. List and explain five causes of stress.

3. Explain five ways you can manage your anger.

4. Define five time wasters.

5. List and explain five techniques for managing time.

CRITICAL THINKING CASE

Claudia Shaeffer has worked in human resources at JWay Nu-Systems Tech for five years. Claudia is in charge of employee benefits. She is an excellent employee—very competent, knowledgeable about human resources (holds an MBA, with a specialty in management), loyal, dependable, and respected by her colleagues. Two years ago, a new director of human resources was hired. Claudia has tried to work with him, but she has not been successful in her attempts. The situation does not get better; it merely gets worse. He gives her inadequate information. He asks her at the last minute to prepare reports. He lies to her about company policies and directions. Then he yells at her about violating the directions of the company. On several occasions, Claudia has yelled back at him. She has talked with him repeatedly about the issues from her perspective. He seems to listen but never responds. He has never complained about her performance; she believes he is satisfied with her work. Claudia has considered leaving JWay; however, she likes all other aspects of her job. Recently, Claudia began to have health problems. She went to her physician, who said her illness was the result of stress. He also recommended that she take at least three months off. Claudia did so. The three months have passed, and Claudia is ready to come back to work.

What suggestions would you make to Claudia to decrease the stress on her job?

RESPONSES TO SELF-CHECK

The most appropriate answers are as follows:

1. No
2. No
3. No
4. No
5. Yes
6. No
7. No
8. No

WORKPLACE PROJECTS

PROJECT 3-1 ANALYZE AND RESPOND TO CASE

Define the causes of stress (Objective 1)

Identify stress reducers (Objective 2)

Control stress (Objective 5)

Analyze the case presented here. Then respond to the items following the case in a memorandum addressed to your instructor. Use the memorandum form on DCD3-01.

Johanna's Situation

One of your friends, Johanna, has worked for SP Engineering Corporation for three years. Recently, she was promoted to assistant to the president of the company. The job is a demanding one. Her responsibilities include setting up meetings, making travel arrangements for the president and the board of trustees, arranging meals before the monthly board meetings, and responding to calls from the board members about various items. In addition, she supervises two office assistants and takes minutes at the board meetings and at the biweekly staff meetings called by the president. She is responsible for numerous other projects as well.

Johanna is attempting to employ a new assistant. This task is taking a long time. She is using a temporary employee who needs close supervision until she can employ someone full time. Johanna has four children. She and her husband are in the process of getting a divorce, which has been a difficult, emotional process. The situation at home is very stressful. Johanna likes her job, but she is not being as effective as she usually is.

1. What are the stressors in Johanna's work environment?

2. What are the stressors in Johanna's home environment?

3. What might Johanna do to reduce some of the stress?

PROJECT 3-2 MAKE AN ACTION PLAN

Identify time wasters (Objective 3)

Manage time (Objective 4)

DCD3-02a contains a time log form. Print five copies of the form. For the next five days, use the form to log the time you spend on various activities. If you are employed, log the time you spend in workday activities. If you are not employed, log the time you spend in personal activities.

After you finish that part of the project, analyze the way you spent your time during the five days. DCD3-02b contains questions to help you analyze your time. DCD3-02c contains a Time Effectiveness Questionnaire, which provides general questions concerning the use of time. Respond to these items. After you have analyzed the way you use your time and considered your answers to the Time Effectiveness Questionnaire, prepare an action plan using the form on DCD3-02d. Indicate what you will be doing to make more effective use of your time. Print one copy of your action plan, and submit it to your instructor.

PROJECT 3-3 READ AND RESPOND TO CASE

Control stress (Objective 5)

Manage anger (Objective 6)

Frederick, a friend of yours who works for another company in your building, is extremely unhappy in his job. He has confided in you about the office situation and has asked for your analysis of what is happening. Respond to the questions at the end of this case by writing a memorandum to your instructor, giving your suggestions. Use the memorandum form on DCD3-03.

Frederick's Situation

Recently, several personnel cutbacks have taken place in Frederick's department. Now there are only two administrative professionals in the department; previously there were four. The other remaining administrative professional has been with the company for only six months. Since Frederick knows the operations well, having been with the company for two years, he has been asked to assume most of the responsibilities of the two assistants who left.

Frederick has always felt good about his abilities. He is able to produce large amounts of work quickly. However, for the last two months, he has not been able to see the top of his desk. His supervisor has become irritated with him on several occasions when work was not completed on time. There never seems to be an end to the amount of work stacked on his desk; he cannot get caught up. Frederick has not been feeling well or sleeping well lately. He wakes up two or three times a night, thinking about the office. He has resorted to taking sleeping pills to get some rest at night.

Additionally, Frederick has been having trouble with the other administrative professional, Maria Gustavo. Frederick has gotten very angry with her on several occasions. Frederick's anger has demonstrated itself in the following ways:

1. Frederick yelled at Maria for not helping him with his workload. Maria has been doing her job, but she has not offered to help Frederick. She does not believe she has the time; she can barely keep up with her own work.

2. Frederick called Maria incompetent when she asked for his help on an assignment. Frederick has always been willing to help Maria in the past; she does not understand why he is not willing to help her now. She believes she deserves the help since she has only been with the company for six months. The second time he called her incompetent, she became so upset that she screamed at him.

Identify the factors that have contributed to Frederick's anger and stress.
What steps can Frederick take to manage his anger?
What steps can Frederick take to control his stress?

 ## PROJECT 3-4 READ AND REPORT ON ARTICLES

Control stress (Objective 5)

Manage anger (Objective 6)

Work with three of your classmates on this project. Search the Internet for three recent articles on stress and anger control. Tip: You may want to use www.google.com as your search engine. Present your findings to the class. Turn in a written report of your findings to your instructor; cite all your references.

PROJECT 3-5 IDENTIFY AND RESOLVE STRESSORS IN LIFE

Control stress (Objective 5)

Manage anger (Objective 6)

Add to the Professional Growth Plan that you began in Chapter 1 by describing how you can control your stress and manage your anger in the future. In preparing this plan, identify the stressors you have in your life at the present time. These stressors may be at home, at school, or at the office. Identify ways in which you can relieve these stressors and effective ways of managing your anger. Save your plan on your Professional Growth Plan disk; file it as PGP3-5.

COMMUNICATION POWER

Use DCD3-b to assist you in improving your grammar skills.

ASSESSMENT OF CHAPTER OBJECTIVES

Now that you have completed the chapter and the projects, take a few minutes to review the chapter learning objectives. For your convenience, the objectives are repeated here. Did you accomplish these objectives? If you were unable to accomplish the objectives, give your reasons for not doing so; be specific and concise. Your instructor may prefer that your answers be submitted to her or him. If so, DCD3-c contains the Assessment of Chapter Objectives. Complete the Assessment of Chapter Objectives; submit the results to your instructor.

1. Define the causes of stress.   Yes ☐   No ☐

   _____

   _____

   _____

   _____

   _____

2. Identify stress reducers.   Yes ☐   No ☐

   _____

   _____

   _____

   _____

   _____

3. Identify time wasters.   Yes ☐   No ☐

   _____

   _____

   _____

   _____

   _____

4. Manage time.   Yes ☐   No ☐

   _____

   _____

   _____

   _____

   _____

5. Control stress.   Yes ☐   No ☐

_____

_____

_____

_____

_____

6. Manage anger.   Yes ☐   No ☐

_____

_____

_____

_____

_____

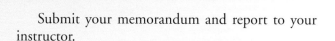

PART I: THE WORK ENVIRONMENT

Integrated Project

Note: You are to work in teams of three on this project.

Part 1: Engage in Research.

Prepare a Report.

Keep Time Log.

Write a Memo.

Your company, JWay Nu-Systems Tech, plans to begin operations in Australia by the end of this fiscal year. (Note: JWay's fiscal year is the same as the calendar year.) JWay also intends to begin operations in Taiwan within the next two years. Jana Portosky, the president of the company and your virtual employer throughout this course, has asked you to prepare information for the executives who will be going to these areas within the next two years. This information is to include the following: the history and culture of each country along with the high-tech industries presently in each country. Use your library and/or the Internet in researching this information.

Keep a record of the time you spend on this project. Prepare a time log; you may want to review the time log presented in Figure 3-3 of your textbook. However, use these headings (rather than the ones provided in Figure 3-3) for your log: Time, Activity, and Time Wasters. At the completion of this project, you will complete a Team Evaluation form (DCDIP1-5), which gives you the opportunity to evaluate how the team has worked together on this project. As a team, review the evaluation form before you start this project.

Write a cover memorandum to your instructor using the form on DCDIP1-1. Include the names of the team members in the memorandum.

Submit your memorandum and report to your instructor.

Part 2: Engage in Research.

Write a Memo.

JWay Nu-Systems Tech needs another administrative assistant. You have been asked to draft the qualifications section for the Personnel Office. Your task is to determine the skills, education, and experience needed for the position. You might want to check the qualifications given in your local paper for administrative assistants.

The administrative assistant will report to the Vice President of Corporate Development. Your recommendations are to be submitted to Antonio Orestes in the Personnel Department. Use the memorandum form on DCDIP1-2 to submit your recommendations. Record the time you spent as a team on the project on your time log. Provide a copy of your memorandum to your instructor.

Part 3: Research and Write Report.

Submit Time Log.

JWay is developing a company website. Your team has been asked to draft an ethics statement for JWay. Using the Internet, research the statement of ethics of three companies. You might want to use three of the companies listed as the "100 Best Companies to Work for in America." This list of companies is usually published in the January issue of *Fortune;* use the most recent list. Summarize the information that you find on the ethics of each of these companies. Write a concise report, giving the name of each company, along with the statement of ethics. Write a cover memorandum to Jane Portosky (the president of JWay); use the memorandum form on DCDIP1-3. Submit your memorandum and report to your instructor; using the memorandum form on DCDIP1-4, write a cover memorandum to your instructor. Report the time you spent on this project on your time log; submit your time log to your instructor.

Part 4: Team Evaluation.

Evaluate the Team's Ability to Work Together

Evaluate the team's ability in working together on these projects by completing DCDIP1-5.

Nilda Campbell
Personal Assistant to National President
New Zealand Educational Institute (NZEI)
Te Riu Roa

SPOTLIGHT *on Success*

WHAT IS MY BACKGROUND?

I was graduated from the University of the East, Philippines. I have a bachelor's degree in Business Administration with a major in management. While working on my degree, I was active in campus activities. Although I was an honor student, I started working during my last semester and could not keep up my grades sufficiently to graduate cum laude.

My parents wanted me to become a doctor, but my decision to pursue business management was influenced by an uncle who was then working at the university. When I started working, I discovered the interesting nature and diverse role of an administrative professional. Since then I have stuck to it and made it a career.

While in the Philippines, I was involved with the Philippine Association of Secretaries and served in different capacities. The company I worked for at that time conducted in-house seminars and encouraged professional development by allowing staff to attend seminars and workshops. The company also supported my attendance at international conferences abroad.

When I migrated to New Zealand, I was told I would have difficulty getting a job at the same level I had in the Philippines—a confidential secretary to the chairman of the board and president of the biggest real estate company in the country. Local experience was required and academic qualifications were essential. To get started, I accepted a job as a telex operator. My skills and competence in the job surfaced immediately, and my employers believed I should be given more responsibilities. I received training on computers and began doing more in the accounts department, overseeing accounts payable and receivable. After I had been with the company for five years, its New Zealand operations closed.

At this point, equipped with local experience, I found a job as an administrative secretary at the New Zealand Educational Institute (NZEI). After three years in this position, the personal assistant to the national president resigned. I applied for and was given this position.

PART **II** WORKPLACE TECHNOLOGIES

| Chapter 4: | *Information Processing* |
| Chapter 5: | *Telecommunications* |

WHAT ARE MY RESPONSIBILITIES?

My responsibilities include providing secretarial and personal assistance to the national president in all aspects of the organization and administration of the office. My duties involve communicating with other national executive members, communicating with staff and outside organizations, assisting in the preparation of executive meetings, organizing travel bookings, keeping track of meetings and appointments, hiring catering services, processing correspondence and other documents, and maintaining the mail flow to and from the office of the president.

WHAT IS THE MOST STRESSFUL PART OF MY JOB?

The most stressful part of my job is having several things to do that are all required "yesterday." I am fortunate to have an executive who understands my responsibilities and empathizes with me. Having a good relationship, communicating effectively, and understanding each other's role are important.

The national president is elected on an annual basis. Therefore, I have a new executive every year unless he or she is re-elected for a second term. As personal assistant to the national president, I must adapt to my executive's personality.

A newcomer in the administrative field should have a good attitude, good communication and human relations skills, and a willingness to keep abreast of technology. Spirituality also helps me a lot. I believe you should have faith in your ability to perform well at your job.

TO WHAT PROFESSIONAL ORGANIZATIONS DO I BELONG?

In this modern day, continuing education is important. One can achieve this through membership in professional organizations such as the International Association of Administrative Professionals® (IAAP) or a local professional group. As a member, you meet many people who can help you grow both personally and professionally.

WHAT ARE MY INTERESTS/HOBBIES?

I enjoy reading, creating tapestry, doing community work, and traveling with my husband when we have free time. I am a member of IAAP and the Association of Administrative Professionals, New Zealand (AAPNZ). I am also involved with the local Ethnic Council.

NILDA CAMPBELL—CASE STUDY

I work in an office of about 100 staff members inclusive of field staff. The office has no formal human resources department. Recruitment and induction of new staff members is done through individual departments or teams headed by a senior manager.

A new personal assistant (PA) was hired as a replacement for someone who resigned to move to another city. The new PA started a week and a half before the final departure of the current assistant to ensure that she had some training or induction into the job because she is a new migrant to the country.

I was to be part of the interview panel but something had come up, and I was not able to join the panel on the day of the interview, although I was given a copy of the new PA's curriculum vitae. The induction of the new PA was left to the departing assistant.

During the last week for the assistant on the job, she encountered some problems relating to the sale of their house and of course the transfer to another city. The departing assistant did not have much time for the new PA to give her the necessary induction. I was then involved in organizing the farewell function for the one leaving.

The new hire had experience working overseas, was efficient, and had the right attitude but was relatively new to the country. The expectation of the managers and staff was rather high and this new hire struggled somehow. Because it was nearing the holiday break and her manager went on holiday early, there was some time for the new PA to ask questions relating to the office and systems and procedures being followed in the organization.

In my case, what would you have done? Bear in mind that I am a migrant and speak a different language. Decide how you would have handled the situation. Then see page 431 for the case solution.

CHAPTER 4

INFORMATION PROCESSING

Learning Objectives

1. Identify information processing tasks.
2. Explain the functions of computer hardware.
3. Describe system and application software.
4. Describe electronic file management techniques.
5. Explain ergonomics and the role it plays in the health of employees.
6. Identify networking benefits and security issues.
7. Compare and contrast the Internet and the Web and explain how both are used in the workplace.
8. Explain the necessity for computer and Web ethics.
9. Demonstrate a commitment to continual learning about changing technologies.

©Getty Images/Photodisc

> INFORMATION PROCESSING AND THE ADMINISTRATIVE PROFESSIONAL

The value of accurate and timely information—about sales, expenses, products, suppliers, customers, employees, investors, and so forth—continues to grow for businesses that want to be competitive in today's complex global economy.

As an administrative professional, many of your daily tasks involve gathering data, processing that data into usable information, and then reporting the information to your supervisor, coworkers, suppliers, and customers. Typical information processing tasks you might complete are:

▶ *Preparing* correspondence
▶ *Compiling* and reporting sales and financial data
▶ *Updating* employee, supplier, and customer information
▶ *Researching* current business trends and statistics
▶ *Organizing* data from various sources into a single document

Figure 4-1 illustrates information processing. You will use workplace technologies, such as a desktop or laptop computer, a local area network, the Internet, and the World Wide Web to help you complete your information processing tasks. You will learn more about these and other information processing technologies in this chapter.

> DESKTOP AND MOBILE COMPUTING

Computers in use today can process data more quickly and accurately than the computers used just a few years ago; they are found everywhere in our modern society and are an essential tool for the workplace or home office.

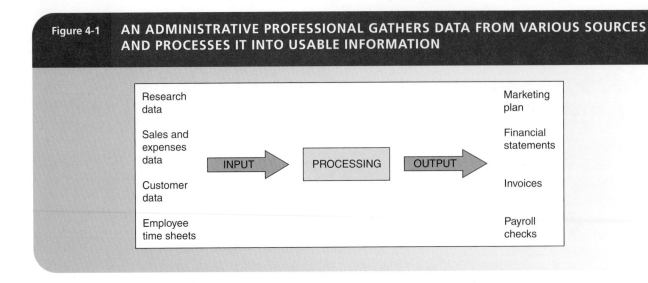

Computers come in all sizes, from tiny biomolecular computers used to detect disease to giant supercomputers used by the scientists at the National Aeronautics and Space Administration (NASA) for research.[1] The computer you are probably using in the workplace or home office is a small, powerful, and inexpensive machine called a **personal computer (PC)**. A personal computer can be either fixed in one location, such as on a desk, or it can be mobile to be taken from place to place as needed.

▷ Desktop

A PC that remains in a fixed location is also called a desktop computer. Desktop computers are used extensively in today's workplace, every employee—from the chief executive officer (CEO) to an administrative assistant—is apt to have one on his or her desk.

Desktop computers are also used widely for business or personal use in home offices. Personal use includes balancing checkbooks, paying bills, investing, completing homework assignments, and communicating with family and friends all over the world.

▷ Mobile

The demand for worker mobility in the workplace is increasing. Many workers today are highly mobile—visiting customers and vendors, traveling to branch offices, and attending training classes, seminars, and trade shows as part of their daily work. As you learned in Chapter 1, more and more workers are teleworkers, many splitting their work hours between the workplace and a home office. It is expected that more than 60 percent of U.S. workers will be mobile workers in the near future.[2] Portable

A computer is an important tool for an administrative professional.

© Photodisc/Ryan McVay

---

[1]Reuters, "Tiny Computer Could Fight Cancer," *Wired News,* April 28, 2004, <http://www.wired.com/news/technology/0,1282,63265,00.html> (accessed April 8, 2005).
[2]IDC, "The 'Wireless' Workforce Will Play an Increasingly Important Business Role," reported at *Athena Online.com,* <http://www.athenaonline.com/us/wireless.asp> (accessed March 29, 2005).

devices such as laptop computers, tablet PCs, personal digital assistants, and smartphones help mobile workers take their computing power wherever they go.

Laptop Computers and Tablet PCs

A laptop computer, sometimes called a notebook computer, is smaller in size and weight than a desktop computer, but it can be just as powerful. In some offices, laptop computers have replaced desktop computers completely. A worker uses his or her laptop in the office to process any number or kinds of documents. He or she then folds it up and puts it in a carrying case and off it goes to work in various types of situations and places.

A **tablet PC** is smaller and thinner than a laptop computer and uses handwriting and drawing to input data. Some tablet PCs are approximately the size of a letter-sized binder or notebook with less computing power than a laptop computer. Other convertible tablet PCs combine the power of a laptop computer with the handwriting and drawing capability of a tablet PC.

A laptop computer, tablet PC, or convertible tablet PC can be used in meetings, on a plane, in a hotel room, or in the car. For example, as an administrative professional, you may use a laptop computer or tablet PC to take notes during a conference and later process those notes into a report to be distributed to the conference attendees. Although generally more expensive than a desktop computer, the addition of portability makes a laptop computer or tablet PC a popular choice for the mobile worker.

Personal Digital Assistants and Smartphones

Another tool for the mobile worker is the **personal digital assistant (PDA)**. A PDA is a handheld computing device used to maintain an appointment calendar, an address book, a to-do list, or to communicate with others. Data from a PDA can be downloaded or transmitted to a desktop or laptop computer. A **smartphone** is a cell phone that combines traditional phone features with the computing capability of a PDA. You will learn more about these wireless devices and wireless communications for the mobile worker in Chapter 5.

A computer has many different parts; each part plays an important role in information processing.

Laptop computers and tablet PCs are popular tools for mobile workers.

© PR NewsWire Mindjet LLC

© Photodisc

© PR NewsWire Microsoft Corporation

© PR NewsWire Ttools, LLC

Courtesy of Blackberry

PDAs and smartphones help the mobile worker manage appointments and communicate with others.

> COMPUTER HARDWARE

The parts of a computer that you can see or touch are called **hardware.** Hardware components are used to input, process, and store data and then output usable information.

> Input Devices

The most commonly used **input devices**—equipment used to enter data—in the workplace include the keyboard, mouse, trackball, touchpad, stylus, touch screen, scanner, microphone, and digital camera.

A keyboard is a frequently used input device. A keyboard may connect to an outlet, called a **port,** on a computer via a thin cable or cord or it may be cordless, using instead a wireless connection.

Other input devices include the mouse, trackball, or a touchpad. A **mouse** fits under the palm of your hand and controls the movement and actions of a pointer, also called a **mouse pointer.** A mouse pointer is used to input computer commands. Like a keyboard, a mouse can be connected to a personal computer via cable or wireless technology.

The trackball and touchpad are alternatives to a standard mouse. A **trackball** combines a large ball that is rolled by hand to control the mouse pointer

with buttons to input commands. A **touchpad** is a small pad that uses motion and pressure by a finger to control the mouse pointer. It is accompanied by buttons used to input commands. Although originally developed for laptop computers, the trackball and touchpad are commonly used with desktop computers today.

Computer screens or monitors (**displays**) can be used either for input or for output. An example of using a display for input is the display on a convertible tablet PC. When left in an upright position, the display is used to view text and pictures. But swivel the display, fold it down, and lock it in place and it becomes an input device on which you can write or draw using a special type of pen called a **stylus** and digital ink. **Digital ink** is the electronic equivalent of liquid ink.

A stylus and digital ink are used to write and draw on a tablet PC.

You can also input data or commands by touching an item on a touch screen with your finger. Touch screens are used in a variety of settings, including:

▶ Hospitals, where medical professionals sign virtual prescriptions.
▶ Fast-food restaurants, where employees input food items ordered and then compute the amount of the checks.
▶ Gasoline stations, where customers start pumps by entering the appropriate type of gasoline.
▶ Office buildings, where visitors find the location of particular offices.

A **scanner** is an input device that converts a printed document, such as a black-and-white or color picture, drawing, graphic, or text, into an electronic

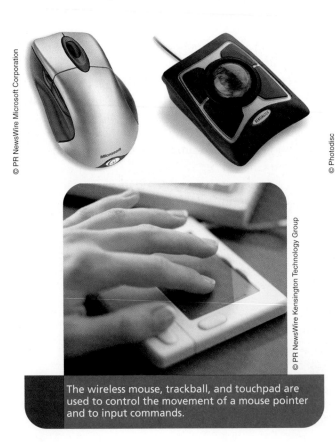
The wireless mouse, trackball, and touchpad are used to control the movement of a mouse pointer and to input commands.

document. You can store the electronic document on your computer and then edit, copy, and print it.

You can also interact with a personal computer by speaking into a headset microphone. A **microphone** is an input device that recognizes spoken words and commands. **Voice** or **speech recognition** technology has been used for many years; however, the technology was not a good choice until the last few years because of difficulty of use and poor recording accuracy. Older voice recognition technology, called discrete speech recognition, required the user to pause between individual words. A technological advance, called continuous speech recognition, now allows the user to speak naturally in complete phrases and sentences without pausing between individual words.

With practice and proper speaking patterns, speech recognition input can be highly accurate—a 95 percent or greater accuracy. Speech recognition technology is fast, allowing you to input text and commands at speeds of 140–160 error-free words per minute.[3] In addition to speed and accuracy, other advantages of speech recognition technology include:

▶ Reducing repetitive stress injuries, such as carpal tunnel syndrome, caused by using a keyboard or mouse over a long period of time.
▶ Providing access to the computer for people who have difficulty using a keyboard or mouse.
▶ Improving productivity for mobile workers who use handheld digital speech recorders to input memos, notes, and other data when "on the road."

Advances in speech recognition continue to make the technologies easier to use and more accurate. But it may be many, many years before speaking into a computer as the *only* means of data input is commonplace. Figure 4-2 lists popular speech recognition technologies.

Spotlight *on* ASSISTIVE TECHNOLOGIES

It is good business practice to hire physically challenged workers. Assistive technologies, such as speech recognition and large print keyboards, enable physically challenged workers to use computers productively in the workplace.

Advances in digital photography make it easier than in the past to dress up business documents, such as correspondence, marketing brochures, and employee records with inexpensive but professional-looking photographs. Digital cameras have quickly evolved from gadgets to serious photography tools designed for business users as well as professional photographers. Instead of film, a **digital camera** takes electronic images and becomes an input device

Digital cameras make it easy to add inexpensive and high-quality pictures to a variety of business documents.

© PR NewsWire Kyocera Optics, Inc.

Figure 4-2	**POPULAR SPEECH RECOGNITION TECHNOLOGIES**
Dragon NaturallySpeaking™	Offers specialized versions for the business, legal, and medical professions.
ViaVoice®	Provides customized templates for commonly used business documents.
SpeechMagic™	Available in more than 20 languages, including English, French, German, Spanish, and Dutch.

[3]"The Verdict Is in: Speech Recognition Software Can Increase Productivity in the Legal Environment," *ScanSoft*, 2004, <ftp://ftp.scansoft.com/pub/whitepapers/legal/cs_DNS_Legal.pdf> (accessed April 1, 2005).

when you download or transmit the electronic images to your computer.

Data you input must then be processed—formatted, calculated, or otherwise manipulated—into usable information.

▷ Processing

A PC is also called a microcomputer because its computing power comes from tiny silicon chips, called **microchips** or simply chips, on which electronic circuitry is placed. The chip that controls the processing function in a personal computer is called a **microprocessor.** Examples of microprocessors include the Pentium® processor, Athlon® processor, and PowerPC™ processor. Advances in microchip technologies—more electronic circuitry on ever-smaller chips—continue to increase the computing power of PCs.

Computers use two types of data storage—primary storage and secondary storage.

▷ Data Storage

Primary storage is also called main memory. The three types of main memory are **random access memory (RAM)**, **read-only memory (ROM)**, and **flash memory.** Active data and instructions are temporarily stored in RAM, which can be quickly accessed during processing. RAM is volatile, which means it requires an electrical current to store data and instructions. When a computer is turned off, the contents of RAM are lost.

On some computers, ROM is used to store the basic operating instructions needed when a computer is turned on. Because ROM is powered by a long-life coin battery inside the computer, its contents are not lost when a computer is turned off. Some computers use flash memory to store a computer's basic start up instructions. Flash memory is a nonvolatile memory chip that retains its data even when a computer is turned off. Flash memory is also used in cell phones, smartphones, and PDAs.

A **byte** is a single unit of computer storage. RAM is measured in million-byte units called megabytes (MB), billion-byte units called gigabytes (GB), and trillion-byte units called terabytes (TB). Personal computers generally have 128 MB, 256 MB, or 512 MB of RAM.

Because RAM is temporary storage and because its capacity is limited, data and computer instructions that must be reused require some type of more permanent mass storage.

You use a computer's **secondary** or **mass storage** the way you use a file cabinet—to organize, store, and retrieve data. Internal and external secondary storage devices include hard disks, diskettes, flash drives, and optical discs. Like primary storage, the capacity of secondary storage devices is measured in bytes:

- ▸ **Kilobytes** (1 KB = 1,024 bytes)
- ▸ **Megabytes** (1 MB = 1,024 kilobytes)
- ▸ **Gigabytes** (1 GB = 1,024 megabytes)
- ▸ **Terabytes** (1 TB = 1,024 gigabytes)
- ▸ **Petabytes** (1 PB = 1, 024 terabytes)

A **hard disk,** also called a hard drive, is a storage device named for its hard, inflexible platters on which data and computer instructions are electronically recorded. Typically, a PC has a single internal hard disk with a storage capacity of from 40 to 80 GB. If additional hard disk capacity is required, one or more external hard disks that plug into a computer port can be easily added. External hard disk storage capacities range from 10 GB to more than 1 TB.

Unlike a hard disk with its rigid platters, the electronic media in a **diskette** or floppy disk is flexible. This flexibility is the reason the term *floppy* was coined for the early 5.25-inch soft-cover disks rarely used today. The 3.5-inch diskette housed in a rigid plastic case commonly used today is still sometimes called a floppy disk.

Spotlight on SECONDARY STORAGE

A typical typewritten page can be stored in about 2 KB.[4] That means a 3.5 inch, 1.44 MB high-density diskette can store approximately 700 pages; a 250 MB Zip® disk about 128,000 pages. A 4 GB flash drive more than 2 million pages, and a 4.7 GB optical disc more than 2,460,000 pages.

---

[4]Roy Williams, "Data Powers of Ten," *California Institute of Technology,* as reported by the *University of California at Berkeley,* 2000, <http://www.sims.berkeley.edu/research/projects/how-much-info/datapowers.html> (accessed March 30, 2005).

© PR NewsWire Memorex

A high-capacity flash drive is useful for moving data from one computer to another.

At one time, diskettes were an indispensable secondary storage medium for a PC. Today, other types of higher-capacity external storage—Zip® disks, flash drives, and optical discs—are gaining on the diskette in popularity in the workplace and home office.

Zip® disks are very high capacity diskettes and are available in 100 MB, 250 MB, and 750 MB capacities. Zip® disks are typically used to store large documents containing graphic images. They are also used to archive old documents that are no longer used but still must be maintained. A PC must have an internal or external Zip® drive to read a Zip® disk.

A **flash drive,** also known as a jump, keychain, pen, or thumb drive is a small, portable, secondary storage device about the size of a package of gum. Flash drives have a storage capacity from 32 MB to 4 GB and can be used on any computer that has a special type of port, called a USB port. Because of its small physical size and portability, a flash drive is a popular choice for moving data from one computer to another.

Another type of high-capacity storage is the optical disc. An **optical disc** is a thin, round, lightweight plastic disc that can be read from or written to using laser technology. Optical discs come in a variety of formats, including CD-ROM, CD-R, CD-RW, DVD-ROM, and DVD+RW. Typical storage capacity is 700 to 800 MB for a CD-R optical disc and 4.7 GB for a DVD+RW optical disc. A DVD-ROM can store up to 17 GB. Keep in mind that RW means that the disc can be read from and written to multiple times and can be erased. The R means it can be read from and written to once but cannot be erased. Without either of these letters, the disc can be read from but not written to or erased (meaning it is read only).

DVD-ROM storage is expected to eventually replace the CD-ROM storage because of its greater capacity, faster access speeds, and ability to take advantage of high-quality video and audio capabilities that are added to many DVD-ROM-equipped computers.

Figure 4-3 lists ways to care for your diskettes, Zip® disks, and optical discs.

Figure 4-3	TIPS FOR CARE AND HANDLING OF YOUR DISKETTES, ZIP® DISKS, AND OPTICAL DISCS
Diskettes and Zip® Disks	▶ Never open the hard plastic case nor touch the media inside the case. ▶ Label a diskette or Zip® disk using an adhesive label; write on the adhesive label before applying it and remove old labels before applying a new one. ▶ Remove diskettes or Zip® disks from their drives when not in use; store them in specially designed containers. ▶ Protect diskettes and Zip® disks from liquids, dust, smoke, direct sunshine, heat, and x-rays such as those used at airports.
Optical Discs	▶ Handle an optical disc by the outside edges or center hole; do not touch the surface. ▶ Use a felt-tipped pen and water-soluble ink to label optical discs; do not use adhesive labels. ▶ Protect optical discs from extremes in heat and humidity. ▶ Clean optical discs with a lint-free cloth and a special CD/DVD cleaning detergent or alcohol; wipe from the center of a disc to the outside edge, never wipe in a circular motion.

Source: Fred R. Byers, "Care and Handling of CDs and DVDs," *National Institute of Standards and Technology,* October, 2003, <http://www.itl.nist.gov/div895/carefordisc/CDandDVDCareandHandlingGuide.pdf> (accessed April 1, 2005).

The information output from processing raw data can be both viewed on a computer's monitor and printed on paper.

▷ Output Devices

Earlier in this chapter you learned that a PC monitor may be used to input or output data. The other most commonly used output device is a printer.

Soft copy output is information shown on the monitor only; **hard copy** output is information printed on paper. For example, as an administrative professional you will use a PC to prepare letters and reports. A draft of a letter or report that you view on your personal computer monitor as you key and edit its contents is soft copy; the printed letter or report that you mail or distribute is hard copy.

The two primary computer monitor technologies are the traditional **cathode ray tube** (**CRT**) and the newer **liquid crystal display** (**LCD**). A CRT uses vacuum tube technology like a television screen. CRT technology has stayed basically the same for years with the changes being mainly in size and color quality. An LCD uses liquid crystals and an electrical current to light each pixel (picture element; a spot on a grid of millions of spots that make an image) on the screen. First introduced with laptop computers, LCDs are now a popular monitor choice for desktop computers.

The two major advantages of an LCD over a traditional CRT are size and reduced energy costs. A CRT is a foot or more deep and takes up a lot of space on a desktop. In contrast, an LCD is only a few inches deep, making it practical for normal desktops and for cramped quarters, such as workplace cubicles. The energy-consumption for an LCD can be one half to two-thirds that of a CRT. Plus, an LCD is cooler to operate, which can translate into less energy consumed to cool the workplace or home office. The amount of money that can be saved depends on the number of LCDs in place and a company's location. For example, a company with 20 LCDs located in the Midwestern United States might save about $400 a year; a company with 50 LCDs located in the Eastern United States might save around $1,600 a year in energy costs.[5]

The most commonly used output device is the printer. The printers most often found in the workplace or home office are inkjet and laser printers. An **inkjet printer** works by spraying ink onto the paper. Another type of printer that is gaining in popularity is a photo printer. A **photo printer** prints high-resolution photographs on glossy photo paper directly from a digital camera, personal computer, or mobile device. Most photo printers use inkjet technologies to create an image. A **laser printer** uses a beam of light to form images on paper. Both inkjet and laser printers can print in black and white and color; they both produce high-quality graphics and text. The primary differences between the two are printing speed and operating costs.

Inkjet printers can be inexpensive to purchase, with prices ranging from $50 to $350. However, the cost of ink cartridges can be quite high because of the relatively small number of pages that can be printed with a single ink cartridge. Additionally, inkjet printers usually have a slower printing speed than laser printers. Printing speed for black-and-white text ranges from two to nine pages per minute; printing speeds for color printing can be half that of black and white printing.[6] An inkjet printer may be a good choice for a home office if high-volume text printing is not required.

Businesses use laser printers for their high-volume printing needs.

---

[5]U.S. Department of Energy and U.S Environmental Protection Agency, "LCD Basics," *ENERGY STAR*, <http://www.energystar.gov/index.cfm?c=monitors.lcd> (accessed April 7, 2005).

[6]"Ratings: Printers (Inkjet models)," *ConsumerReports.org*, September, 2004, <http://www.consumerreports.org> (accessed March 31, 2005).

Because of their fast printing speed and lower operating costs, laser printers are most often used in the workplace where the need for high-volume text printing is common. For example, a low-end laser printer that prints in black and white has a purchase price around $200; can print from 10 to 17 pages per minute; and has operating costs of less than four cents per page.[7] High-end laser printers that also print in color can cost several hundred dollars; however, laser printers in this range can comfortably print from 35,000 to 100,000 pages per month.[8]

It is important to keep your computer hardware clean and dust free. Figure 4-4 lists tips for caring for your computer.

Software provides the instructions a computer needs to process data.

Figure 4-4   COMPUTER CARE TIPS

Avoid spilling food or drink on your keyboard or mouse. Make certain your computer is plugged into a surge protector or an uninterruptible power supply (UPS) battery backup to avoid damage from power surges.

To clean your computer, first turn it off, then:

▶ Use a dry lint-free cloth to wipe down the computer case and monitor. Dampen the cloth with warm water to wipe off stains; then use a dry cloth to dry the area. Do not use paper products that can scratch or ammonia-based cleaners that can damage a display.

▶ Vacuum the computer's air ducts and keyboard.

▶ Use cleaning wipes to wipe down the outside of the mouse and cables.

▶ Clean the ball on a mechanical mouse with rubbing alcohol. Follow the manufacturers' cleaning instructions for other pointing devices.

▶ Use special cleaning disks to clean diskette drives or optical disc drives.

To maximize your hard disk space and improve the disk's performance, periodically reorganize the files and delete unnecessary files. If you are using the Windows® operating system, the Disk Defragmenter utility gathers and reassembles fragments of files scattered across the hard disk. The Disk Cleanup utility removes temporary and unused application software files.

Source: Bill Howard, "Clean Your PC," *PC Magazine*, January 12, 2005, <http://www.pcmag.com/article2/0, 1759,1747017,00.asp> (accessed April 19, 2006).

CHECK A

Self

Respond to the following comments by checking True or False.

	True	False
1. In the workplace, data and information mean the same thing.	☐	☐
2. Hardware provides the instructions a computer needs to operate.	☐	☐
3. A keyboard is a commonly used input device.	☐	☐
4. Computer monitors are used for both input and output.	☐	☐
5. A personal computer is called a microcomputer because it can fit on your lap.	☐	☐
6. An optical disc is an example of a secondary storage device.	☐	☐
7. An LCD display uses vacuum tube technology.	☐	☐
8. An inkjet printer uses a beam of light to form images on paper.	☐	☐

---

[7]"Ratings: Printers (Laser models)," *ConsumerReports.org*, September 2004, <http://www.consumerreports.org> (accessed March 31, 2005).

[8]"Color Laser Printers Review," *ConsumerSearch*, December 2004, <http://www.consumersearch.com/www/computers/color_laser_printers/> (accessed March 30, 2005).

> COMPUTER SOFTWARE

A personal computer receives instructions from **software.** The two general categories of software are system software and application software.

▷ System Software

System software includes any instructions or programs that are used to manage and control computer functions. The operating system (OS) of your PC is part of its system software. The **operating system** is the program that provides an easy-to-use interface between you and your computer's hardware and software, accepts your keyboard and mouse commands, and manages the interactions between input, processing, storage, and output devices. The operating system launches and takes control of your computer as soon as you turn the computer on. An operating system is also responsible for managing the application software you use to perform specific tasks.

▷ Application Software

Software that performs a specific function is called **application software.** As an administrative professional, you will use a variety of application software programs separately or in combination to complete your daily tasks. For example, suppose you are preparing for a quarterly sales meeting.

Here is how you might use your computer and application software to get ready for the meeting. You can use:

1. *Spreadsheet* software to analyze the quarterly sales data and chart it.

2. *Presentation* software to create a slide show for the meeting that includes the sales data and chart.

3. *Database management* software to access the names and addresses of individuals who will be attending the meeting.

4. *Word processing* software to write an interoffice memorandum or letter inviting attendees to the meeting.

5. *Personal information management* software to schedule the meeting in your and your supervisor's calendars and book a conference room for the meeting.

6. *Groupware* to participate in a virtual conference with other employees preparing for the meeting.

Spotlight *on* **APPLICATION SOFTWARE**

Remember to use the Help command or button in your application software window if you need more information about how to use the software's tools to complete a task.

Several software manufacturers combine popular application software programs in one package called a business or productivity software suite. Popular software suites are Microsoft® Office, Corel WordPerfect® Office, Lotus® SmartSuite®, and Sun Microsystems StarOffice™. Other software sometimes included in a business or productivity software suite is publishing software used to create newsletters, brochures, and multimedia documents. Figure 4-5 lists examples of popular application software for the workplace or home office.

Figure 4-5	POPULAR APPLICATION SOFTWARE
Word processing	Create text documents
Spreadsheet	Analyze numbers
Presentation	Create slide shows and printed handouts
Database management	Organize and manipulate large amounts of data
Graphics	Create drawings and edit photos
Accounting	Maintain financial data
Publishing	Create brochures, catalogs, business cards, and multi-media documents
Personal information	Schedule appointments, maintain an address book, manage a "to-do" list
Groupware	Coordinate workplace team communications

One of your tasks as an administrative professional is to solve as many of the computer hardware or software problems that occur as possible. When computer hardware or software problems occur, they must be solved quickly. To do this, you must become adept at troubleshooting (tracing and correcting computer or software problems). Figure 4-6 lists the important information you should have handy as you troubleshoot a hardware or software problem. Both operating system and application software are updated by their manufacturers as needed to improve performance or fix problems. Making certain that these software updates are installed on your computer is an important administrative task. Failure to update your software when notified by the manufacturer may lead to loss of data or processing errors.

Managing the electronic files you create using application software is another important administrative task.

> ELECTRONIC FILE MANAGEMENT

An electronic file contains data and information stored or saved to some type of secondary storage, such as a hard disk, a diskette, or flash drive. Electronic files can include all types of business data, including employee data, vendor invoices, correspondence, customer invoices, mailing lists, accounting data, and so forth.

You will create many files as you complete your varied administrative tasks. Some files will be archived as a permanent record of business transactions while others, such as electronic forms, will be used over and over again. Carefully naming a file as you save it ensures that you can easily find it when you need it.

Figure 4-6 **INFORMATION TO HAVE HANDY FOR TROUBLE-SHOOTING HARDWARE AND SOFTWARE PROBLEMS**

1. A written description of the problem and steps you have taken to try and resolve it

2. The name and version of your personal computer's operating system

3. A description of the hardware devices connected to your computer and the name, address, and contact information for each device vendor

4. The name and version of each application software program installed plus the vendor's name and customer support contact information

5. The name and contact number of an in-house computer technician or other administrative professional who can help

6. Hardware and software manuals provided by each vendor

7. Third-party hardware and software manuals, if available

▷ File Names

Most application software programs assign a temporary name to each file you create. As you save the file, you must give it a unique, meaningful name. For example, suppose you create a letter to John Jones on March 31 and save it in a file on your hard disk. Naming the file "John Jones letter 3.31" makes it easier to find it again.

A file name generally can contain letters, numbers, and spaces. It cannot contain certain special characters: the forward slash (/), the backward slash (\), the colon (:), the semicolon (;), the pipe symbol (|), the question mark (?), the less than symbol (<), the greater than symbol (>), the asterisk (*), and the quotation mark (").

Another way to ensure that you can quickly find your saved files is to organize them in electronic folders.

> Folders

An electronic folder is similar to a paper folder you might place inside a file cabinet drawer. Logically organizing your files in folders saves time and effort when you are looking for a specific file. You can organize your files in folders in several ways, for example:

▶ By type of file—Create separate folders for word processing, spreadsheet, presentation, and database files.

▶ By business activity—Create separate folders for sales, marketing, accounting, and other business activity files.

▶ By customer or vendor—Create separate folders for each customer's and vendor's files.

▶ By project—Create separate folders for each project's files.

The best folder organization is the one that works for you and your supervisor. Use your computer's operating system file management tool to create and name your folders. If you are using the Windows® operating system, use the Windows Explorer file management tool.

An administrative professional must also plan for the unexpected when managing his or her files. Processing errors can occur, data can be lost, and files can be accidentally deleted. To avoid disaster, make certain to have duplicate copies of all your important files.

> File Backup

Nothing is more important in managing your files than creating duplicate copies of your important files. This process is called backing up your files. It is a very good idea to keep handy a backup copy of those files you use on a regular basis—sample documents, electronic forms, mailing lists, and so forth—that would be difficult or impossible to recreate quickly. Business-critical files, such as financial data, should be backed up on a regular basis and the storage media taken offsite to a safe, protected location.

In the workplace, it is generally the responsibility of a computer technician to back up files stored on shared storage devices. But be aware that each individual is usually responsible for backing up files stored on his or her own computer's hard disk, on individual diskettes, or on flash drives.

An individual who works at a computer for more than two hours each day should take special care to protect his or her body from injury.

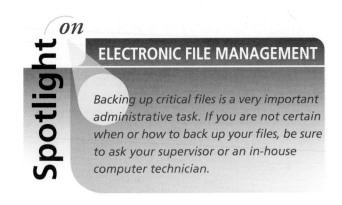

Spotlight on

ELECTRONIC FILE MANAGEMENT

Backing up critical files is a very important administrative task. If you are not certain when or how to back up your files, be sure to ask your supervisor or an in-house computer technician.

> COMPUTER ERGONOMICS

As an administrative professional, you will spend many hours each day using your computer to complete your tasks. Continuous keyboard and mouse actions can cause **repetitive strain injuries (RSIs)** to tendons, muscles, and nerves from prolonged repetitive motions, such as keying. A type of RSI is **carpal tunnel syndrome.** Carpal tunnel syndrome occurs when the large nerve, the median nerve, is compressed as it passes through a tunnel composed of bone and ligaments in the wrist. Symptoms include

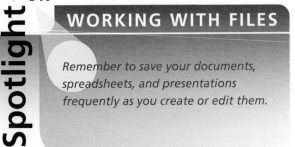

Spotlight on

WORKING WITH FILES

Remember to save your documents, spreadsheets, and presentations frequently as you create or edit them.

a gradual onset of numbness and a tingling or burning in the thumb and fingers.

Other types of overuse injuries, which occur as a result of sitting at the computer for long periods of time, include **computer vision syndrome** (vision problem associated with screen glare) and back problems (from chairs that are not the right height or configuration for the user). Vision problems associated with computer use include eye fatigue, blurred vision, dry eyes, and headaches. These conditions may also be accompanied by neck, shoulder, and back pain because those with vision problems often hunch over their work.

Some basic work habits that may reduce eyestrain include

- Keep the hard copy close to the screen.
- Take breaks—use the 20/20/20 rule—every 20 minutes, take 20 seconds, and look 20 feet away.
- Blink regularly.
- Move the monitor so that it is at least 20 inches away.
- Have your eyes checked annually.[9]

Ergonomics is the term used to describe the fit among people, the tools they use, and the physical setting in which they work. You should use ergonomically sound computer equipment and furniture in the workplace or your home office. It is also important to position your keyboard and other devices so they are easy to reach; position your monitor so that it is easy to see without moving your head up or down. Use glare screens on your computer to protect your eyes.

Pay attention to your posture while sitting at your computer. Poor posture can also lead to injury. Figure 4-7 itemizes ways that ergonomics can contribute to a better work environment and less risk to your body when working at your computer.

The National Telecommunications Safety Panel has published guidelines for those who work in telecommunications that align with OSHA recommendations. Some of these guidelines follow: Chairs should be adjustable for seat back (height, angle, tension); armrests should also be adjustable. The base of chairs should have five wheels. The seat cushion height needs to be adjustable as well as being able to swivel. Taking care of chair

---

Figure 4-7   ERGONOMICS TIPS

Your Posture

- Relax your head and neck and keep them in-line with your body
- Keep your upper arms and elbows close to your body
- Keep your forearms, wrists, and hands straight
- Make sure your body is perpendicular to the floor and your feet are flat on the floor

Work Area

- Position your keyboard and mouse next to each other
- Position the top of the monitor at or just below eye level
- Locate the monitor directly in front of you
- Reduce or eliminate screen glare

- Keep adequate clearance below your work surface for legs, feet, and thighs
- Support your back by sitting straight against the back of your chair
- Make certain your chair's seat width, depth, and length are adequate

Relaxation

- Take several short breaks throughout the day to stand, stretch, and move about
- Look away from the display screen for a few minutes every hour
- Remember to alternate computer tasks with non-computer tasks

Source: "eTools: Computer Workstations," *U.S. Department of Labor, Occupational Safety & Health Administration*, August, 2003, <http://www.osha.gov/SLTC/etools/computerworkstations/index.html> (accessed April 1, 2005).

---

[9]Karen Fritscher-Porter, "Ergonomic Advice: How Ergonomically Friendly Is Your Workplace?" *Office Solutions*, January–February 2003, p. 23, as cited in Odgers, *Administrative Office Management*, 13e, 2005, p. 381.

adjustments will often alleviate back pain from postural problems.

Reaching activities have been found to contribute to worker problems. Such activities as reaching above shoulder height for reference materials, reaching for the telephone, the keyboard, or the mouse may impact worker injuries if these are improperly placed. Even reaching for a trash can or a tower located under the work surface can contribute to awkward movements.

Suggestions to avoid these situations include using a telephone handset and a wider keyboard, which will eliminate reaching. Workstations can be equipped with bookcases or cabinets to store reference materials for easier reach.

A footrest to support the legs and bring them into alignment to alleviate pressure on the back of the leg is an adjustment that may make computer work more comfortable.[10]

In addition, you may wish to check out ergonomic keyboards, trackballs, and mice. Some of the features of ergonomic keyboards are as follows:

► Split keyboards
► Built-in wrist rest
► Detachable wrist rest
► Chair-mounted keyboards
► Foot-switch support
► Mouse functions through keys

Trackballs are the device of choice for many people whose hands cramp when they use a conventional mouse device. Also available is a mouse that vibrates, helping the user find an exact location on cluttered Web pages and software displayed on the screen with less hand motion.

Spotlight *on*

ERGONOMICS

Take care every day to check your posture. Take short breaks to stretch and rest your eyes. Make certain your keyboard, pointing device, and screen are positioned correctly.

Ergonomic exercises recommended by the National Telecommunications Safety Panel include shoulder rolls, elbow stretches, arm stretches, and upper and lower back stretches to help eliminate muscle pain.[11]

Many businesses link their employees' computers, printers, and other devices together to create a network.

> NETWORKS, THE INTERNET, AND THE WORLD WIDE WEB

In the workplace and in the home office, computers and other devices are commonly linked together to form a computer network. A **computer network** is two or more computers and their attached devices, such as printers and storage devices, linked together by communication media. The computers and devices on a network may be connected by some type of cable or by wireless RF (radio frequency) technologies. Computer networks can be classified by the geographical area they cover as local area networks, metropolitan area networks, and wide area networks.

⊵ Local Area Networks

A **local area network (LAN)** covers a small geographical area and links computers, printers, and other devices within a single office, a building, or several nearby buildings. Today, LANs are common in the workplace and in many home offices. Your workplace or school computer is likely connected to a LAN. Some of the benefits of being on a LAN are that one or two printers can accommodate everyone on the network. The network administrator can manage the installation of software for all employees and the back up of files stored on the file servers (network storage). Fast electronic messages can be sent between users on the network. Figure 4-8 illustrates a small office LAN.

LAN Security

To use a computer on a LAN you are required to identify yourself by keying a unique username and password in a process called logging in to the network. You may even be required to log in to a computer that is not on a network. Your supervisor or network

---

[10]Bill Wright, "National Telecommunications Safety Panel Aligns with OSHA," February 26, 2004, U.S. Department of Labor, Occupational Safety & Health Administration, Office of Communication, <http://www.telsafe.org/htsp/Publications/FINALversionALL%209_09-04%20.pdf> (accessed May 17, 2005).
[11]Ibid.

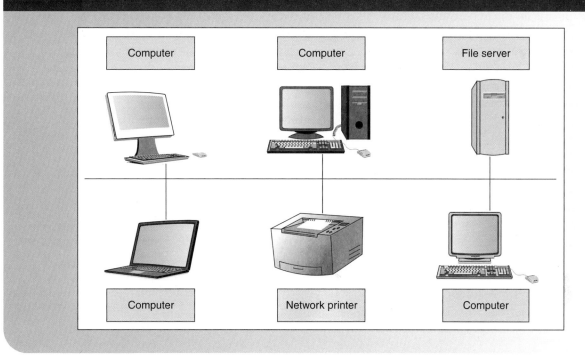

administrator may assign you an identifying **username** but you may be responsible for creating your own, unique password. Be careful! Passwords containing readily available information—your birthday, a pet's name, or a common word from the dictionary—may be known or easily guessed by others.

A well-crafted **password** contains eight or more mixed uppercase and lowercase letters, numbers, and symbols. It should be easily remembered, but not easily guessed. A good password example is *Z3!62f87*. A poor password example is *Fluffy23*, where "Fluffy" is a pet's name. Passwords should remain secret. Do not share your password with others. Do not write down your password and then leave it in an easily accessible place in your work area.

Other threats to a computer or network include viruses, Trojan horses, worms, and hackers. A computer **virus** is a destructive program that infects data files or other software programs with which it comes in contact. Viruses can cause unexpected messages to pop up on your display, delete data, damage your operating system, and shut down your computer. Viruses can be introduced into your system by retrieving an infected file from secondary storage or by sharing infected files across a network.

A Trojan horse and a computer worm are similar to a virus. A **Trojan horse** is destructive software designed to look like something useful. A Trojan horse does not attach itself to other programs. Instead it is deliberately included as part of otherwise useful software or passed between users who mistake it for useful software. A **worm** is a malicious self-replicating program that does not need to attach itself to other software. Worms can delete files, transmit data, overload primary storage, or create a **back door** or secret electronic entrance into a network. Here are some ways to protect against viruses, Trojan horses, and worms:

▶ Install antivirus software. Installing antivirus software manufactured by vendors such as McAfee® or Norton™ is the most important action you can take to protect against these threats.

▶ Keep your antivirus software updated. Antivirus software vendors publish regular updates, which can be automatically downloaded over the network and installed. To maintain maximum protection using your antivirus software, keep it updated.

▶ Stay informed by paying attention to news reports about new computer viruses, Trojan horses, and worms.

▶ Accept files on diskette, flash drives, or optical discs from trusted sources only.

- Transfer files over a network to and from trusted sources only.
- Remember to have backup copies of your critical files just in case an infection occurs.

Shared Document Security

An administrative professional must collaborate with others both inside and outside his or her company to accomplish tasks. Sharing electronic files or documents such as letters, spreadsheets, and presentations stored on a LAN file server or attached to electronic messages makes collaborating with others easier and more efficient. But doing so can expose a company to certain document security risks.

Productivity software, such as the Microsoft® Office Suite, adds hidden information to documents. This hidden information, called **metadata,** includes:

- Document properties—author, date created, title, subject
- Tracked changes—insertions, deletions, and repositioned text
- List of reviewers—document users who made, accepted, or rejected tracked changes
- Comments—notes added by author or reviewers
- Document statistics—dates the document was opened, printed, and saved.

Hidden metadata travels with a document and can place a company at risk by exposing confidential or potentially embarrassing information. Productivity software utilities, such as TRACE by Workshare and iScrub by iOffice System can be used to check for and remove metadata from shared documents.

Computers may also fall victim to a **hacker,** which is a common term for an individual who uses his or her computer skills to gain unauthorized access to a network. Criminal hackers break into networks to steal data—credit card numbers, Social Security numbers, intellectual property—or to commit vandalism or terrorism. For example, in 2005 one credit card company reported that more than 40 million credit card numbers belonging to U.S. consumers were accessed by a computer hacker.[12]

Sometimes hackers break into a networked computer and install keylogging software, software that records keystrokes. Hackers use the keylogging software to retrieve passwords and other sensitive data entered from a keyboard. Network security software or hardware called a **firewall** protects the network against hackers by filtering or controlling the traffic that can come into or leave a network. Inexpensive firewall software can be installed on a home office computer; businesses use more complex combinations of hardware and software firewalls.

Stay alert against strangers in the workplace or unusual inquiries about network login procedures. A workplace intruder or criminal hacker may try to use a common technique, called **social engineering,** to gain your trust and trick you into opening a locked door, revealing the location of your network facilities, or revealing your username and password. Why do criminals attempt social engineering? Because it works! Security professionals commonly use social engineering techniques, with great success, to try and breach network and office security during audits.[13]

Networks that cover a larger geographical area than a LAN are the Metropolitan and Wide Area Networks.

▷ Metropolitan and Wide Area Networks

A high-speed network that links computers and other devices across a city or region is called a **metropolitan and wide area network (MAN).** A college or university network that links several city or regional campuses is an example of a MAN. A network that connects computers and other devices over the largest geographical area—perhaps hundreds of thousands of miles—is a **wide area network (WAN).** International businesses can link their offices around the world with a private WAN. The largest public WAN is the Internet.

▷ The Internet

The Internet is a worldwide public network that connects private networks. The Internet has revolutionized the way people communicate and the way business is conducted. People around the world use the Internet to access information, communicate with family and friends, and purchase products and services. Businesses around the world use the Internet to communicate with vendors and customers, to sell their products and services, and to provide customer support after the sale.

---

[12]Jonathan Krim and Michael Barbaro, "40 Million Credit Card Numbers Hacked," <http://www.washingtonpost.com/wpdyn/content/article/2005/0617/AR2005061701031.html> (accessed October 10, 2005).

[13]Darren W. Miller, "Social Engineering: You Have Been a Victim," *CASTLECOPS,* March 15, 2005, <http://castlecops.com/article-5807-nested-0-0.html> (accessed April 7, 2005).

Self

Respond to the following comments by checking True or False.

	True	False
1. Application software performs a specific function, such as word processing.	☐	☐
2. Operating system software provides an easy-to-use interface to a computer.	☐	☐
3. A workplace computer technician typically creates backup copies of all electronic files no matter where they are stored.	☐	☐
4. An individual who works at a computer several hours each day must take special care to protect his or her body from injury.	☐	☐
5. Viruses, Trojan Horses, worms, and hackers are all threats to computers on a LAN.	☐	☐
6. A well-crafted password contains easy-to-remember dates, such as a birthday, or names, such as the name of your favorite pet.	☐	☐
7. You should be helpful and cooperative with strangers who ask for your username and password or directions to your network facilities.	☐	☐

History

The Internet began in the 1960s as an experimental networking project of the U.S. Department of Defense. When the network was turned over to commercial providers in the 1990s, the Internet was born. Since then Internet use has grown exponentially, with more than 850 million Internet users worldwide.[14]

The power of the Internet lies in its ability to facilitate communication between individuals, businesses, and other organizations. Figure 4-9 explains the many ways people communicate using the Internet. You will learn more about these Internet communication tools and how you, as an administrative professional, will use them in the workplace or home office in Chapter 5.

Individuals, businesses, and other organizations connect to the Internet in a variety of ways.

Connections

An **Internet Service Provider (ISP)** is a private company that connects directly to the Internet and then sells Internet access to other organizations and to individuals. America Online (AOL), EarthLink, NetZero, Netscape, AT&T, and Time Warner are all examples of ISPs. A business or home office LAN

Figure 4-9	INTERNET COMMUNICATION TYPES

Internet Communications	Description
Electronic mail (e-mail)	Written messages sent between two or more people and delivered to electronic mailboxes
Instant messaging	Short messages between people connected to the Internet at the same time
Web-based discussion groups and newsgroups	Electronic "bulletin boards" or discussion groups
Mailing lists	Topic-specific e-mail sent to a list of subscribers
Weblogs or blogs	Electronic diaries to which users can post their thoughts
Telephony	Telephone calls transmitted using Internet technologies

---

[14]"Internet Usage Statistics—The Big Picture," *Internet World Stats*, March 24, 2005, <http://www.internetworldstats.com/stats.htm> (accessed April 3, 2005).

is commonly connected to an ISP, allowing network users to share an Internet connection. An individual connects his or her computer directly to the ISP. The most common ways to connect to an ISP are regular analog dial-up, high-speed analog dial-up, DSL, cable, fixed wireless, or satellite.

Connecting to the Internet via an **analog dial-up** telephone line requires that a computer connect to a telephone line through a modem. A **modem** is a device that converts a computer's digital signal into an analog signal for transmission over telephone lines. At the transmission's destination, another modem converts the analog signal back into a digital signal. A regular analog dial-up connection is the slowest and least expensive type of Internet connection.

Some ISPs now offer high-speed analog dial-up as an alternative. **High-speed analog dial-up** is achieved by shortening the time it takes for an ISP to authenticate a computer's dial-up connection and by routing the data request through an acceleration server. High-speed analog dial-up can be up to five times faster than regular analog dial-up for most data transmissions. Figure 4-10 illustrates an analog dial-up Internet connection.

Businesses—and increasingly home office users—use digital telephone or cable technologies for high-speed or **broadband Internet** connections. **Digital Subscriber Line (DSL)** technologies allow digital data transmissions over regular telephone lines. A DSL can be used for both high-speed data transmissions and voice transmissions. The high-speed data capabilities of a DSL are "always on," meaning the connection to the ISP and the Internet is continuous.

Cable broadband is a competing high-speed, always on connection to an ISP and the Internet across cable TV lines. Cable broadband uses a cable modem to manage the data transmissions between a computer and the cable TV network. Cable broadband Internet connections are very fast. But just like cable TV, multiple cable users in the same neighborhood share the same data transmission capacity, called **bandwidth.** The more users sharing the bandwidth, the slower the transmissions can become for each user. Cable providers compensate by adding additional cable capacity to a neighborhood when necessary.

In areas where DSL and cable broadband are not available, access to an ISP and the Internet may be available either through fixed wireless or satellite. **Fixed wireless** technologies use microwave signals relayed through a network of repeaters mounted on utility poles, streetlights, and so on to a **Wireless Internet Service Provider (WISP).** Each fixed wireless user has a small radio receiver and directional antenna oriented toward the nearest repeater. Figure 4-11 illustrates a fixed wireless Internet connection.

The only broadband Internet service available for those in rural areas may be a communication satellite. A communication **satellite** is a radio signal receiver/transmitter that orbits the earth and uses microwave signals to transmit data. Satellite Internet access is generally more expensive than DSL or cable broadband.

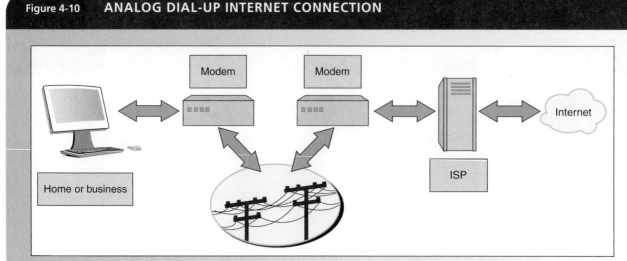

Figure 4-10   ANALOG DIAL-UP INTERNET CONNECTION

Modem   Modem

Internet

Home or business   ISP

Figure 4-11   HOW FIXED WIRELESS WORKS

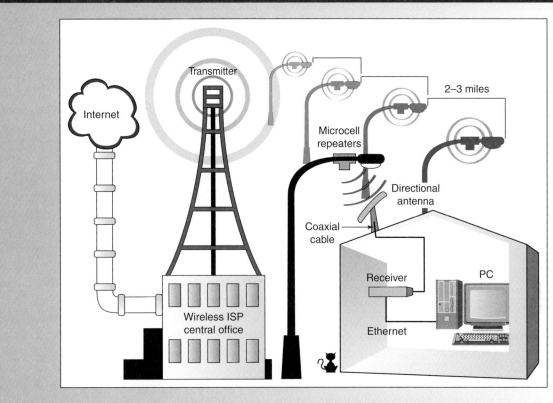

Source: Cassimir Medford, "Pipe Dreams," *PC Magazine,* February 6, 2001, 156.

Signal interference during bad weather is another problem with satellite Internet access.

One of the most popular aspects of connecting to the Internet is having access to the World Wide Web.

▷ The World Wide Web

The **World Wide Web (Web)** consists of computers called Web servers that can be accessed with an Internet connection. **Web servers** store multimedia documents that can contain text, graphics, video, and audio. These documents, called **Web pages,** are linked to other multimedia documents. A group of related Web pages is called a **website.** Web page links are called **hyperlinks** or just links. Links can be created using text or pictures.

The application software used to access and view Web pages is called a **Web browser.** Popular Web browsers include Firefox, Opera, Internet Explorer, and the Netscape browser. When viewing a Web page in a browser, you click a link to "jump" to a different position in the same page, to view a different page at the same website or a page at a different website. Figure 4-12 lists additional Web terminology.

History

In the late 1980s Tim Berners-Lee, a computer consultant at the Swiss research laboratory CERN, was looking for ways to help physicists at the laboratory share research data. He adapted an older and mostly theoretical technology called hypertext—text linked to other text—to solve the problem. Berners-Lee used hypertext concepts to develop the first Web page, Web server, and Web access technologies and then called his vision of globally connected documents the "WorldWideWeb."

Many people today consider the Internet and the Web indispensable and use both extensively for communications, research, entertainment, and shopping. Commercial activity over the Internet and the Web, called electronic commerce, or **e-commerce,** is an ever-growing part of the global economy. For example, in the United States, e-commerce retail sales

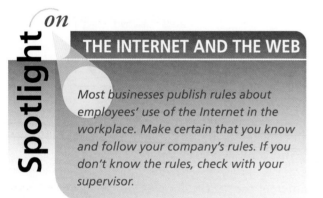

Spotlight *on*

THE INTERNET AND THE WEB

Most businesses publish rules about employees' use of the Internet in the workplace. Make certain that you know and follow your company's rules. If you don't know the rules, check with your supervisor.

alone climbed to more than $65 billion annually by 2005.[15]

Many millions of pages are now available on the Web. Web page authors use application software, such as Microsoft®, FrontPage®, Macromedia®, and Dreamweaver®, to create business or personal Web pages that contain text, pictures, links, audio, and video files. The pages are uploaded to a Web server where they can be accessed by others. To find just the right data on these pages requires special Web search tools.

Search Tools

One of the biggest challenges to using the Web for research is finding the right Web page or pages with data

that meets your needs. Two search tools—directories and search engines—can help you with this process by allowing you to search their Web page indexes. A **directory** builds its index of Web pages by accepting information on new pages from individual submissions. The directory then catalogs the Web page information by category, much like old library card catalogs. Users click a category link to "drill down" through a specific category until they find the page they want. The Yahoo! search tool was one of the first and most powerful Web directories.

A **search engine** uses software called a spider or bot that travels the Web looking for new Web pages to add to its index. Bot is a term used for a software program that is a software agent. The term comes from the word "robot," reflecting the autonomy of the concept. Bots interact with other network services intended for people as if they are real people. Bots are used to gather information.[16] Users access a search engine's index using keywords. AltaVista was one of the first popular Web search engines. The line between directories and search engines quickly became blurred as directories added search engine access and search engines added Web page category links. Today, popular search tools, such as Google, Yahoo!, AlltheWeb, WiseNut, and Teoma, are hybrids combining different methods to build their indexes. Figure 4-13 lists tips on using search tools.

Browsing the Web to find useful information will expose your computer to spyware and cookies.

Web Privacy

Spyware is a general term for software that gathers information that is installed on your computer without your knowledge or approval. A **cookie** is a small text file installed on your computer when you visit a website. Most cookies are harmless and are used to store information about how you use the website: customized features, contents of a shopping cart, website login passwords, and so forth. These types of cookies are beneficial and make the Web browsing experience more useful.

But some malignant cookies are installed by third-party advertisers to track your website viewing habits. For example, a common spyware application is **adware,** software installed on your computer as part of other software or when you visit a website. Adware works with third-party cookies to control

---

[15]"Quarterly Retail E-Commerce Sales," *U.S. Department of Commerce, U.S. Census Bureau,* February 24, 2005, <http://www.census.gov/mrts/www/ecomm.html> (accessed April 5, 2005).

[16]Dictionary. LaborLawTalk.com, <http://encyclopedia.laborlawtalk.com/bot> (accessed October 10, 2005).

Figure 4-13 TIPS FOR SEARCHING THE WEB

Search tools have different methods of indexing Web pages and presenting search results. Check out a search tool's Help section before you use it for the first time to better understand how the search tool works. Pay attention to the basic search features and the advanced search features. The following general rules apply to most search tools.

▶ The more keywords you use in a search, the more targeted the search results will be. For example, when searching for information about photo printers, using both keywords *photo printers* instead of just *printers* will return more targeted search results.

▶ Using quote marks around keywords indicates a phrase. For example, using the keywords *"employment statistics"* surrounded by quote marks means each Web page returned in the search results must contain the two words together as a phrase.

▶ Learn to use Boolean operators in your search to better target the search results.

Boolean operators include *and* and the plus sign (+), *or,* and *not* and the minus sign (−).

▶ Using *and* or the + sign means the keyword that follows must appear in every page in the search results. For example, to search for government Web pages that must contain the keywords *computer* and *ergonomics,* use +*computer* +*ergonomics* +*.gov* (government page URLs end in .gov).

▶ Using *or* between two keywords means that only one of the keywords is required, not both.

▶ Using *not* or the − sign means to exclude the keyword that follows.

▶ Some search tools automatically assume the *and* relationship between keywords unless you indicate otherwise by using *or* or *not.*

Check out your Web browser's search tool feature for easy access to the most popular search tools.

Spotlight *on*

SEARCH TOOLS

Remember that Web search tools have different indexes and use different methods for evaluating the Web pages. You should become comfortable using multiple search tools.

the type of advertising you see at websites and to collect information about your Web page viewing habits. To protect your privacy as you browse the Web, you may choose to use special anti-spyware software to regularly scan your computer's hard disk to find and delete spyware and malignant cookies. Some ISPs, such as AOL, provide Spyware Zappers to help protect your computer from spyware.

Businesses also use Web and Internet technologies to communicate with their employees and business partners via intranets and extranets.

Intranets and Extranets

An **intranet** is a private "Web" that uses Web pages and other Web technologies and is accessible only by an organization's employees through their LAN. Intranets are used to share information that needs to be quickly and easily disseminated, such as company policies and in-house newsletters.

An **extranet** also uses Web technologies but is available to certain individuals, companies, and others outside an organization. Access to an extranet is controlled by usernames and passwords. These same usernames and passwords also control what users can see and do when logged in to the extranet. An extranet may be used by financial institutions to provide clients with account information and performance reports; by health institutions to access medical records; or by businesses to allow stockholders to view financial information.

Computers, the Internet, and the Web have spawned behaviors by some individuals that are illegal or unethical.

> COMPUTER AND WEB ETHICS

Just as you need to be ever vigilant about behaving ethically in the workplace, you need to be certain you are living your business and personal values as you complete tasks using the computer and the Web.

One pervasive problem is software piracy, the illegal copying of software. Unfortunately, people

CHECK C

Briefly answer the following questions.

1. Define the Internet and the Web.
2. Discuss the difference between an analog dial-up Internet connection and a broadband Internet connection.
3. Compare and contrast an intranet and an extranet.
4. Describe a search engine, a directory, and a hybrid search tool.

Self

sometimes rationalize that "software vendors are getting rich anyway so it is okay to copy software for their personal use." Other people engage in software piracy to make money by reselling illegally made copies. For whatever reason it is done, software piracy is illegal in the United States.

U.S. copyright law provides for both civil and criminal penalties for making and distributing illegal copies of copyrighted material, including software. Penalties under Title 17 of the United States Code include imprisonment for up to five years and fines of up to $250,000 for the unauthorized reproduction or distribution of 10 or more copies of software with a total retail value exceeding $2,500. An exception to copying software is made for one backup copy. Not only is copying of software unethical and illegal, software copies might introduce viruses into your computer and then infect an entire network.

Additionally, the cost to the global economy from lost revenues, taxes, and jobs as a result of software piracy is a serious matter. Researchers estimate that the retail market value of copied software will exceed $40 billion in the near future.[17] Finally, individuals who copy software deprive themselves of the benefits of technical support and training provided by many software vendors and the ability to buy software upgrades at reduced rates.

Another major problem is personal use of business computers and network resources, including Internet access. Employees who use workplace computers and Internet connections for personal reasons during the workday contribute to a 40 percent loss in employee productivity for U.S. businesses.[18] Downloading personal files can use up expensive

bandwidth needed for business transactions and expose the network to security breaches. Sending offensive and inappropriate messages or downloading pornography can expose a business to charges of workplace harassment.

Employees sometimes believe it is acceptable to use a workplace computer after the workday has ended for personal use or even to take a few minutes during the day to send an e-mail to a friend or shop on the Web. It is not okay to do so without permission. Most businesses today publish strict computer and Internet use policies. However, never assume that the absence of a policy regarding acceptable computer and Internet usage implicitly gives you the right to do as you please. It is unethical to use your workplace computer to:

▶ Access your company's data for non–work-related purposes.
▶ Steal a coworker's username and password to log into the network.
▶ Allow a coworker to use your password and username to access data for which he or she is not authorized.
▶ Access a coworker's electronic files to read, edit, or delete them.
▶ Send and receive personal e-mail.
▶ Use the Web for personal shopping or entertainment.
▶ Download non–work-related files.
▶ Send racist, sexist, or offensive messages and attachments to anyone.

In addition to the problems or issues discussed above, some rules to keep in mind are:

---

[17]"First Annual BSA and ID Global Software Piracy Study," *Business Software Alliance*, July 2004, <http://www.caast.org/resources/IDC_Global_Software_Piracy_Study_2004.pdf> (accessed April 5, 2005).

[18]"Did You Know?" *Gartner Group* as reported by *Spector CNE*, 2005, <http://www.spectorcne.com/Solutions/Productivity.html> (accessed April 25, 2005).

- Remember there is a person on the other end of the e-mail who has feelings and values.
- Respect the time of those with whom you communicate by keeping messages short and concise.
- Never forward or write offensive e-mails.
- Leave sensitive or confidential issues to face-to-face communications if at all possible. If not, a telephone call may be advisable since e-mails are rarely secure.
- Be conscientious about those to whom you send messages and copy others on the address. Remember the right to know and the need to know should guide whether someone gets a copy.
- Avoid forwarding any e-mail that contains sensitive or confidential information.
- If you receive an angry e-mail, stop and evaluate your response before you send it. You may want to walk away from the computer to calm down before you compose a reply. Put yourself in the shoes of the receiver: would you be happy to receive this reply? Would you want to see or hear it mentioned on the national news on television? If not, revise your response for a more humane approach.

Some businesses and individuals try to exploit the unregulated nature of the Internet and the Web together with easy access to perpetrate other types of abuses including:

- Using information gathered at a website for purposes other than those represented at the site.
- Selling e-mail addresses and other personal information without the owner's permission.

- Releasing patient medical information to the wrong people.
- Intercepting private electronic messages.

Concern about easy access to information though the Web has prompted the Federal government to establish laws protecting the privacy of personally identifiable information. For example, the Health Insurance Portability and Accountability Act (HIPAA) now contains provisions requiring health care providers, health insurance companies, and health information clearinghouses to take specific steps to secure the privacy of the patient information they maintain. The Electronic Communications Privacy Act (ECPA) prohibits the interception of electronic messages except in specific circumstances.

Another problem is plagiarism of Web content. Millions of Web pages along with the data and images they contain are at your fingertips. You must be vigilant in your ethical use of the data and images you find on the Web. Remember that Web page content is protected by U.S. copyright law. Do not copy Web page data and use it as your own work; cite the source of Web page data that you use in documents and reports. Do not download Web page images without permission from the site owner. As an administrative professional, it is your responsibility to make certain to use your workplace computer, the Internet, and the Web ethically.

Computer, Internet, and Web technologies will continue to evolve and play an important role in tomorrow's workplace. The challenge for the

Self CHECK D

Respond to the following comments by checking True or False.

	True	False
1. It is ethical to shop online for a personal gift during work hours.	☐	☐
2. It is acceptable to copy application software without paying for it because everyone does it.	☐	☐
3. Downloading large files for personal use using your company's broadband Internet connection is all right because no one will notice.	☐	☐
4. Sending offensive and inappropriate messages through a company's e-mail system can expose the company to charges of workplace harassment.	☐	☐
5. All the information you find on the Web is free to use as you wish.	☐	☐

administrative professional is to keep his or her information processing skills current in the face of rapid technological change.

> THE FUTURE

In the workplace of the future, speech recognition may be the primary method used to input data; quantum computers that store data in atoms may provide very fast processing capabilities; and employees may participate in conferences as three-dimensional holographic images.

In the workplace of the not-so-distant future, you may find marvels such as photonic computers that use infrared (IR) technologies to perform calculations instead of electrical current. You may store your data as three-dimensional holographic images.[19] Logging into your computer may be as simple as clicking a picture. Or, instead of keying your username and password or clicking a picture, you may wear an identity badge that automatically logs you into the computer and network as you enter your work area.

No matter how the information processing technologies of the future evolve, one thing is certain—you *must* continue to learn if you are to be a productive citizen in our modern society. Here are some suggestions for you as you commit yourself to continual learning.

▸ Learn where to find information, starting with the Web, computer periodicals, and books.
▸ Develop an inquiring mind. Ask questions when you do not understand something. Do not be afraid to admit that you do not have all the answers.
▸ Commit to continuing your formal education. Take classes offered by your organization or classes offered at a college or university. Take a course through distance learning.

Devote time to learning. Learning does take time, but the results are well worth the time spent.

Continual learning is a must for an administrative professional.

© PR NewsWire Lexmark International, Inc.

---

[19]John Goff, "In the Year 2025," *CFO.com,* March 1, 2005, <http://www.cfo.com/article.cfm/3709826> (accessed April 6, 2005).

SUMMARY

Reinforce your learning in this chapter by studying this summary.

▶ Information processing involves changing raw data into usable information. The workplace technologies an administrative professional uses to do this include computers, the Internet, and the World Wide Web.

▶ Personal computers are used extensively in the workplace and can be fixed in one location, such as desktop computers. They may be mobile and taken from place to place, such as a laptop computer or tablet PC. Other mobile computing devices include PDAs and smartphones.

▶ Computer hardware consists of parts you can see and touch. Hardware can be used for data input, processing, storage, and output.

▶ Input devices include keyboards, mouses, touch screens, trackballs, touchpads, monitors (displays), scanners, microphones, and digital cameras.

▶ The processing power of a PC comes from tiny microchips, called microprocessors, on which electronic circuits are placed.

▶ Primary storage consists of RAM in which active data and instructions are temporarily stored and ROM or flash memory, which are used to store basic startup instructions.

▶ Secondary storage is permanent or mass storage. Secondary storage devices include hard disks, diskettes, Zip® disks, flash drives, and optical discs.

▶ The two primary output devices are monitors and printers. Inkjet and laser printers are the most common types of printers in the workplace. Photo printers that print high-resolution photographs on photographic paper are becoming more common.

▶ Computer software contains the instructions a computer uses to perform various tasks. The two general categories of software are system software and application software. System software is used to manage and control computer functions. Application software is used to perform specific tasks.

▶ The three important electronic file management techniques are (1) assigning meaningful, unique file names; (2) creating a logical system of electronic folders in which to store the files; and (3) making backup copies of all critical files.

▶ Computer ergonomics involves using ergonomically sound furniture and computer equipment, good posture, and correct positioning of your equipment to protect your body from injury.

▶ Computer networks are classified by geographical area as local, metropolitan, or wide area networks. Local area networks (LANs) are common in the workplace and home offices.

▶ Connecting computers, printers, and other devices on a LAN saves time and money because users can share resources and communicate faster via electronic messages.

▶ Security threats to a computer or network include viruses, Trojan horses, worms, hackers, and physical intruders. Usernames and passwords, firewalls, and antivirus software are all tools used to protect a LAN from internal and external threats.

▶ The largest public WAN is the Internet, a public network of private networks.

▶ Individuals and businesses connect to the Internet through an ISP. The physical connection to the ISP and Internet can be made in a number of ways. The slowest and less expensive method is analog and high-speed analog dial-up over standard telephone lines. High-speed broadband connections are made using DSL, cable, fixed wireless, or satellite connections.

▶ The World Wide Web (Web) is part of the Internet. The Web consists of Web servers on which are stored Web pages linked together by hyperlinks. The Web is used by individuals for research, entertainment, and shopping. Businesses use the Web to conduct all types of business transactions.

▶ It is the responsibility of an administrative professional to use workplace computers, software, workplace Internet access, and Web content legally and ethically.

▶ Information technologies continue to evolve. To meet the challenge of staying current with information processing skills, an administrative professional must make a commitment to continual learning.

GLOSSARY

Adware—Spyware that works with cookies to control the website advertisements you see when you browse the Web.

Analog dial-up—A slow and inexpensive Internet connection made by dialing up to an ISP over regular telephone lines.

Application software—Software that performs a specific task, such as word processing software.

Back door—A secret electronic entrance into a network that a hacker can use to gain unauthorized access to the network.

Bandwidth—A measure of data transmission capacity.

Broadband Internet—High-speed Internet access via DSL, cable, fixed wireless, or satellite.

Byte—A single unit of computer storage.

Cable broadband—Broadband Internet connections over cable TV lines.

Carpal tunnel syndrome—A repetitive strain injury of the wrist.

Cathode ray tube (CRT)—A display that uses vacuum tube technology similar to a television tube.

Computer network—Two or more computers and their devices, such as printers, linked by communication media.

Computer vision syndrome—Injuries to the eyes from prolonged computer screen glare.

Cookie—A small text file installed on your computer when you visit a website.

Digital camera—A camera that takes electronic images.

Digital ink—The electronic equivalent of liquid ink used by a stylus.

Digital Subscriber Line (DSL)—An "always on" high-speed Internet connection over regular telephone lines that can carry both data and voice.

Directory—A Web-based search tool that organizes its index of Web pages by category.

Diskette—A small 3 ½-inch secondary storage device with a rigid plastic case.

Display—A viewing device on a computer.

E-commerce—Business transactions conducted over the Web.

Ergonomics—The term used to describe the fit among people, the tools they use, and the physical setting in which they work.

Extranet—A restricted-access private "Web" available to a company's business partners.

Firewall—Network security software or hardware that filters incoming and outgoing traffic to control access to the network.

Fixed wireless—A high-speed Internet connection that uses microwave signals relayed from the user to a Wireless Internet Service Provider (WISP) over a network of signal repeaters.

Flash drive—A small high-capacity secondary storage device about the size of a package of gum.

Flash memory—A nonvolatile chip used to store a computer's basic start up instructions.

Gigabytes (GB)—One billion bytes; 1,024 megabytes.

Hacker—A term for an individual who uses his or her computer skills to gain unauthorized access to a network.

Hard copy—Information output to the printer.

Hard disk—A secondary storage device named for its hard, inflexible platters on which data and instructions are electronically recorded.

Hardware—The parts of a computer that you can see and touch.

High-speed analog dial-up—An analog dial-up Internet connection in which the ISP shortens the time it takes to authenticate the computer's connection and then passes the user's request through an acceleration server.

Hyperlink—Text or picture in a Web page that connects the page to another place in the same page, to another page at the same website, or to a page at a different websites.

Inkjet printer—A printer that creates images by spraying ink on the paper.

Input devices—Equipment used to enter data.

Internet Service Provider (ISP)—A private company that connects directly to the Internet and then sells Internet access to organizations and individuals.

Intranet—A private "Web" restricted to employees, that uses Web pages and other Web technologies to disseminate intra-company information.

Kilobytes (KB)—1,024 bytes.

Laser printer—A printer that uses a beam of light to create images on the paper.

Liquid crystal display (LCD)—A display that uses liquid crystals and electric current to light individual pixels on a screen.

Local area network (LAN)—A computer network that covers a small geographical area, such as a single office, a building, or several nearby buildings.

Megabytes (MB)—1,024 kilobytes.

Metadata—Hidden document information including document properties, tracked changes, reviewers, comments, and document statistics.

Metropolitan area network (MAN)—A high-speed network that spans a city or region.

Microchip—A tiny silicon chip on which electronic circuits are placed.

Microphone—An input device that recognizes spoken words and commands.

Microprocessor—The microchip that controls the processing functions in a personal computer.

Modem—A device that converts a computer's digital signal into an analog signal or converts an analog signal back into a digital signal.

Mouse—An input device that fits under the palm of your hand; controls the actions of the mouse pointer.

Mouse pointer—A pointer on a computer's display screen used to input computer commands.

Operating system—The program that provides an easy-to-use interface, accepts commands from a keyboard or mouse, and manages the interactions between a computer's various hardware devices.

Optical disc—A thin, round lightweight plastic disc that can be read from or written to using laser technology.

Password—A secret combination of letters, numbers, and symbols that identifies a user on a network.

Personal computer (PC)—A small, powerful, and inexpensive computer used in the workplace or home office.

Personal digital assistant (PDA)—A handheld computing device used to maintain an appointment calendar, an address book, a to-do list, or to communicate with others.

Petabytes (PB)—1,024 terabytes.

Photo printer—An inkjet printer that prints high-resolution photographs.

Port—An outlet on a computer used to plug in other hardware.

Primary storage—A computer's internal storage area or main memory.

Random access memory (RAM)—Temporary primary storage for active data and commands; the contents of RAM are lost when the computer is turned off.

Read-only memory (ROM)—Battery-operated primary storage for basic instructions the computer needs at startup.

Repetitive strain injury (RSI)—Injury to tendons, muscles, and nerves from prolonged repetitive motion.

Satellite—A radio signal receiver/transmitter that orbits the earth and uses microwave signals to transmit data.

Scanner—An input device that converts a hard copy document or picture into an electronic file.

Search engine—A Web-based search tool that builds its index of Web pages automatically using software called a bot or spider.

Secondary or mass storage—Permanent internal and external storage including hard disks, diskettes, flash drives, and optical discs.

Smartphone—A cell phone that combines traditional phone features with the computing capability of a PDA.

Social engineering—A technique used by criminal hackers and intruders to gain a person's confidence and trust.

Soft copy—Information output to a display.

Software—Computer instructions used to perform various tasks.

Speech recognition—An input technology that converts spoken words into electronic data and commands.

Spyware—Software installed on your computer without your knowledge or permission to gather information.

Stylus—A pen used to draw or write on a tablet PC.

System software—Instructions used to manage and control computer functions.

Tablet PC—A small, thin computer that uses hand-writing and drawing to input data.

Terabytes (TB)—1,024 gigabytes.

Touchpad—A pointing device that uses a small pad, finger motion, and pressure to control the mouse pointer.

Trackball—A pointing device that combines a large ball to control the mouse pointer with buttons to enter commands.

Trojan horse—Malicious software designed to look like useful software.

Username—A name that identifies a user on a network.

Virus—A destructive program that infects data files or other software programs.

Voice recognition—See speech recognition.

Web browser—The application software used to access and view Web pages.

Web page—A hyperlinked document containing text, pictures, audio, and video stored on a Web server.

Web servers—Computers on which Web pages are stored.

Website—A group of related Web pages.

Wide area network (WAN)—A high-speed network that covers the largest geographical area.

Wireless Internet Service Provider (WISP)—An ISP that offers wireless Internet access.

World Wide Web (Web)—A system of computers called Web servers that store multimedia documents called Web pages.

Worm—A malicious self-replicating program.

Zip® disk—High capacity diskette.

CHECKPOINT

Check your understanding of these terms by completing DCD4-a on the Data CD.

DISCUSSION ITEMS

These discussion items provide an opportunity to test your understanding of the chapter through written responses and/or discussion with your classmates and your instructor.

1. Explain the difference between computers in use today and those in use only a few years ago.

2. List and describe the computing devices used by mobile workers. How do mobile workers benefit from these devices?

3. Explain how speech recognition technologies can be used to improve productivity in the workplace.

4. Explain how ergonomics can protect users from injury when working at a computer.

5. Discuss software piracy and its affect on the global economy.

CRITICAL THINKING CASE

Your supervisor, Jana Portosky, just received a phone call from an important client who has questions about a sales agreement he and one of your coworkers, Dave Smith, are negotiating. Dave, who travels frequently on business, is out and won't be back in the office until later this afternoon. He left no number where he could be reached. Ms. Portosky asks you to quickly retrieve and print a copy of the most current agreement draft from the hard disk on Dave's computer.

Logging in to the network at Dave's computer is easy; he taped a note with his username and password, Dave1, to his computer's display. You find that Dave has hundreds of unorganized files on his hard disk named

Sales Agreement1 final, Sales Agreement2 draft, and so forth. You are unable to locate the correct file on the hard disk. Next, you check Dave's desk and file cabinet for a backup copy of the latest negotiated agreement on diskette or CD. You can find no backup copies of Dave's files. Finally, you look for a hard copy of the agreement—but find none. Dave has taken the client's file with him. Out of options for a quick solution to the problem, you break the bad news to Ms. Portosky.

Ms. Portosky apologizes to the client and arranges to call back the next morning. Then she asks you to analyze the situation to make suggestions that will help avoid similar situations in the future.

CRITICAL THINKING CASE *(continued)*

Questions to ask:

▶ What administrative management issues did this situation expose? Think carefully—this situation exposed several different issues that must be addressed.

▶ Are the issues widespread or do they just involve Dave? How can you find out?

▶ What policies and procedures could be put in place to prevent similar situations in the future?

▶ What are some ways to address the issues with Dave and, if necessary, with other employees?

RESPONSES TO SELF-CHECK

A
The most appropriate answers are as follows:

1. False	3. True	5. False	7. False
2. False	4. True	6. True	8. False

B
The most appropriate answers are as follows:

1. True	3. False	5. True	7. False
2. True	4. True	6. False	

C
The most appropriate answers are as follows:

1. The Internet is a worldwide computer network made up of smaller, interconnected networks that span the globe. The Web is a huge collection of computer files scattered across the Internet.

2. An analog dial-up Internet connection uses a standard telephone line and a modem to convert a computer's digital signals to analog and vice versa at the signals' destination. An analog dial-up connection is a temporary connection. A broadband Internet connection is an "always on" high-speed connection using cable, DSL, fixed wireless, or satellite connections.

3. An intranet is a company's internal "Web" accessible to employees though their local area network. An extranet is a "Web" to which a company allows certain individuals outside the company access depending on the individual's needs.

4. A search engine is a Web-based search tool that uses software in the form of a spider or bot to search the Web and add pages to the search engine's index. A directory is a Web-based search tool that creates its index of Web pages by accepting individual submissions; it then organizes its index of Web pages by category. Most search tools have evolved into hybrids that use multiple ways to add new Web pages to indexes and provide both keyword searching and category links for users.

D
The most appropriate answers are as follows:

1. False	3. False	5. False
2. False	4. True	

PROJECT 4-1 UPDATE A DIAGRAM

Identify information processing tasks (Objective 1)

Use the instructions provided on DCD4-01 to update an information processing diagram.

PROJECT 4-2 STUDY HARDWARE/SOFTWARE AND WRITE A REPORT

Explain the functions of computer hardware (Objective 2)

Describe system and application software (Objective 3)

Explore the computer hardware and software used in your workplace, classroom, computer lab, or home office, and then write a short report that:

1. Lists the input, processing, storage, and output hardware devices and explains their functions.

2. Identifies the operating system.

3. Names at least four application software packages and explains how they are used.

Submit your report to your instructor.

PROJECT 4-3 ANALYZE ELECTRONIC FILE MANAGEMENT METHODS

Describe electronic file management techniques (Objective 4)

Use the instructions provided on DCD4-03 to explain three critical aspects of electronic file management.

PROJECT 4-4 EVALUATE ERGONOMIC ISSUES

Explain ergonomics and the role it plays in the health of employees (Objective 5)

Working with a classmate, create your own checklist of ergonomic issues related to furniture, computer device placement, and posture. Then use the checklist to evaluate the computer work areas in a workplace, classroom, computer lab, or home office. Are the chairs ergonomically sound? Are the positions of the keyboard, pointing device, and monitor ergonomically correct? Are you and your classmate using correct posture at the computer? Report back to the class on what you and your classmate found during your evaluation and what changes, if any, should be made.

PROJECT 4-5 RESEARCH AND LABEL NETWORKS

Identify networking benefits and security issues (Objective 6)

Use the instructions provided on DCD4-05 to label three types of networks and to explain networking benefits and security issues.

PROJECT 4-6 PREPARE A SEMINAR PRESENTATION

Compare and contrast the Internet and the Web and explain how both are used in the workplace (Objective 7)

Explain the necessity for computer and Web ethics (Objective 8)

Your supervisor, Ms. Portosky, asks you to prepare a short seminar to introduce new mailroom employees to the Internet and the Web and to explain how employees at JWay use both.

Create a handout for your seminar. Your handout should include a description of the Internet and the World Wide Web with examples of how each is used. It should also include a list of at least five Web page reference tools (dictionaries, encyclopedias, and other reference desk material). Include the URL and a description of each page. Finally, include information about ethical use of computers and the Web by employees at JWay.

Use the Google (www.google.com), Yahoo! (www.yahoo.com), and AltaVista (www.altavista.com) search tools to locate the Web page reference tools. You may use DCD4-06 file as the starting point for your handout.

Distribute your handout to a team of classmates, chosen by your instructor, who play the role of the new mailroom employees. Then conduct your seminar.

PROJECT 4-7 CREATE A PLAN FOR CONTINUAL LEARNING

Demonstrate a commitment to continual learning about changing technologies (Objective 9)

Use the AlltheWeb (www.AlltheWeb.com), Teoma (www.teoma.com), and LookSmart (www.looksmart.com) search tools to find five websites that can contribute to your continual learning about information processing technologies.

Then using your computer and word processing software, add to your Professional Growth Plan by creating a document and saving it as PGP4-7. Title your document "My Plan for Continual Learning about Technologies." Use the document to list and describe each website. Then create a schedule for reviewing each of the websites every two weeks for six weeks. Record in your document what new things you learn during each review. If you use personal information management software, schedule each website review date in your electronic calendar.

COMMUNICATION POWER

Use DCD4-b to assist you in improving your grammar skills.

ASSESSMENT OF CHAPTER OBJECTIVES

Now that you have completed the chapter and the projects, take a few minutes to review the chapter learning objectives. For your convenience, the objectives are repeated here. Did you accomplish these objectives? If you were unable to accomplish the objectives, give your reasons for not doing so; be specific and concise. Your instructor may prefer that your answers be submitted to her or him. If so, DCD4-c contains the Assessment of Chapter Objectives. Complete the Assessment of Chapter Objectives; submit your results to your instructor.

1. Identify information processing tasks.   Yes ☐   No ☐

   _____

   _____

   _____

2. Explain the functions of computer hardware.   Yes ☐   No ☐

   _____

   _____

   _____

3. Describe system and application software.   Yes ☐   No ☐

   _____

   _____

   _____

4. Describe electronic file management techniques.   Yes ☐   No ☐

   _____

   _____

   _____

5. Explain ergonomics and the role it plays in the health of employees. Yes ☐   No ☐

   _____

   _____

   _____

6. Identify networking benefits and security issues.   Yes ☐   No ☐

   _____

   _____

   _____

7. Compare and contrast the Internet and the Web and explain how both   Yes ☐   No ☐
   are used in the workplace.

   _____

   _____

   _____

8. Explain the necessity for computer and Web ethics.   Yes ☐   No ☐

_____

_____

_____

9. Demonstrate a commitment to continual learning about changing   Yes ☐   No ☐
   technologies.

_____

_____

_____

CHAPTER 5

TELECOMMUNICATIONS

Learning Objectives

1. Explore the present and future of telecommunication technologies.
2. Define workplace collaboration tools and explain how they are used.
3. Describe how to protect against spam, phishing, pharming, and spim.
4. Explain the importance of e-mail use policies.
5. Describe telephone communications over PSTN, VoIP, and handheld devices.
6. Explain the importance of professional call management skills.

©Getty Images/Photodisc

> THE TELECOMMUNICATION REVOLUTION

A revolution is taking place in the field of **telecommunication**—the electronic transmission of text, data, voice, video, and images (graphics and pictures) from one location to another—that is rapidly changing the way an administrative professional communicates and collaborates with others in the workplace.

This telecommunication revolution is apparent in the movement from traditional circuit-switched telephone networks developed to transmit voice messages to packet-switched networks for transmitting data and today to converged networks capable of both voice and data transmissions. Another facet of the telecommunication revolution is the proliferation of wireless communication devices and wireless broadband technologies that promise a "workplace without walls." Figure 5-1 summarizes some key telecommunication terms used to describe different aspects of the telecommunication revolution.

In this chapter, you learn more about the development of converged networks and the workplace collaboration tools they make possible. You also learn ways to manage professional telecommunications, including e-mail, fax, and telephone communication. Finally, you learn how the ongoing telecommunication revolution may affect the workplace of the future.

▷ Circuit-Switched Networks

For many years the telephone was the primary method of sending and receiving electronic messages in the workplace. Regular telephone voice messages are transmitted electronically over a telephone company's circuit-switched network. A **circuit-switched network** provides a single dedicated connection or path from sender to receiver. No one

Figure 5-1

Figure 5-1   TELECOMMUNICATION TERMS

Backbone—The part of the network used as the main path for carrying traffic between network endpoints.

Bluetooth—A short-range wireless communication standard used to connect cell phones, PDAs, smartphones, and laptops with each other and with other devices, such as printers.

Broadband—Short for broad bandwidth; a high-speed network able to carry video as well as voice. Bandwidth describes the throughput of a network per unit of time, measured in kilobits, megabits, or gigabits per second.

Cognitive Radio—Automatic radio spectrum sharing.

Ethernet—The IEEE 802.3 protocol for transmitting data packets over a LAN.

GPRS—General Packet Radio Service; a technology for high-speed wireless communications including Internet access and data transmissions.

Fiber-optic cable—Glass fibers over which data and voice are transmitted using pulses of light.

Hotspot—A location or area that offers free or fee-based Wi-Fi access for laptops and handheld devices.

Ultra broadband—Very high-speed data transmissions at 10 Mbps or higher.

VoIP—Voice over Internet Protocol; IP telephony.

Wi-Fi—The general name for the 802.11 family of wireless fidelity protocols for wireless LAN communications.

WiMax—Long-range wireless broadband.

WLAN—A wireless LAN.

---

else can use the connection or path for the duration of the call. Circuit-switched networks have been the primary telecommunication technology for the workplace for more than 125 years.

The development of packet-switched networks changed how electronic messages are transmitted.

▷ Packet-Switched Networks

The first big step in the modern telecommunication revolution occurred with the early development of networks and the Internet that you learned about in Chapter 4. Two technological breakthroughs during that time made communications over a network

Telephone calls over a circuit-switched network use a dedicated circuit for the duration of the call.

possible: packet-switching and the Transmission Control Protocol/Internet Protocol (TCP/IP) set of communication rules.

On a **packet-switched network,** such as a workplace local area network (LAN) or the Internet, data is broken into small pieces, called **packets,** before transmission. Each packet contains the data's destination address. The individual packets are routed over the network and are assembled again at their destination. **Transmission Control Protocol/Internet Protocol (TCP/IP)** ensures that the packets are delivered error free to the correct destination. TCP/IP is the mandated telecommunications protocol for the Internet. Most private networks also use the TCP/IP communications protocol. Networks using TCP/IP are referred to as **IP networks.** Figure 5-2 illustrates data packets sent over a packet-switched or IP network.

Packet switching allows multiple users to share the same path or connection. For many years, the only electronic messages sent across packet-switched or IP networks were data in the form of text, numbers, and pictures. The next step in the telecommunication revolution was the convergence of voice and data across IP networks.

⊳ Converged Networks

Telephone companies are joining other telecommunication service providers in the process of transforming the traditional services that connect *people to people* to services that connect *people to people* and *people to machines* over a converged network. A **converged network** is an IP network that supports the transmission of all types of electronic messages, including voice, data, and video. The development of converged networks is changing the telecommunication marketplace.

Telecommunication companies such as AT&T are redefining themselves from domestic long-distance telephone service providers to global all-distance providers of broadband communication services. Gone are the days when one or two giant companies controlled the whole telecommunication infrastructure. New telecommunication carriers are entering the marketplace to provide voice and other types of electronic messaging over the Internet.

Traditional telecommunication companies are merging with companies that offer completely different products and services, such as entertainment, publishing, or broadcasting. Combining telecommunication with these types of businesses opens up new channels for delivering products and services to customers via computers, cell phones, personal digital assistants, televisions, and a combination of these devices over a converged network.

This chapter is designed to help you understand the telecommunication revolution and the communication technologies—e-mail and other workplace

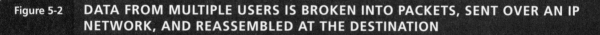

Figure 5-2 DATA FROM MULTIPLE USERS IS BROKEN INTO PACKETS, SENT OVER AN IP NETWORK, AND REASSEMBLED AT THE DESTINATION

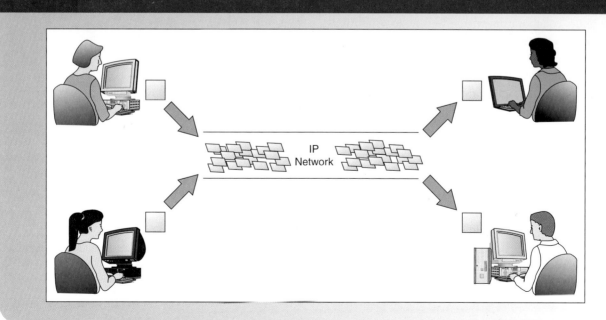

IP Network

collaboration tools, fax, telephone, and wireless devices—you will use in today's modern workplace.

> WORKPLACE COLLABORATION TOOLS

As an administrative professional, you will spend many hours collaborating with others to accomplish a variety of tasks, such as creating and revising documents. Studies show that about 70 percent of all office work is **collaborative work** in which teams of workers share resources to complete a specific task.[1] In Chapter 4, you learned about business or productivity software suites, such as Microsoft® Office. For some time, productivity suites have contained basic collaboration tools that allow you to schedule, host, and participate in electronic meetings and send and receive e-mail. Productivity suites also contain features that allow you to route documents across an IP network to coworkers who then review, revise, and return them.

IP networks make possible several other useful electronic collaboration tools—instant messaging, shared workspaces, weblogs, wikis, and Web conferencing—that are becoming essential for collaboration in the modern workplace. Network and Web-based software that assists in workplace collaboration is commonly called **groupware.** Groupware examples include IBM Lotus Team Workplace (QuickPlace) and Lotus Notes, Microsoft SharePoint™ Services, Novell GroupWise, TikiWiki, Groove Networks Virtual Office, and EMC Documentum eRoom.

▷ Electronic Mail

The most popular workplace collaboration tool is **e-mail**—electronic text messages sent from one computer to another over an IP network, such as a LAN or the Internet. Surveys suggest that worldwide person-to-person e-mail messages will exceed 10 trillion annually by 2008.[2] Today, e-mail is an indispensable tool for workplace communication because e-mail messages:

▸ Can be composed, sent, and delivered in minutes no matter the destination.

---

[1]"Workspace, The Final Frontier," *Samsung Future Working,* 2005, <http://www.samsungexplore.com/working/future/future_article01.html> (accessed April 15, 2005).
[2]"The Spam You Never See Can Hurt You," *IDC* as reported by *eMarketer,* April 18, 2005, <http://www.emarketer.com/Article.aspx?1003355> (accessed April 19, 2005).

- Are sent when convenient to the sender and read when convenient to the recipient.
- Can be used to transfer files across the network as e-mail attachments.
- Can be accessed from a number of locations and devices.
- Are a low-cost method of communicating.
- Can be saved as a permanent record of a business activity.

To receive e-mail, you must have an e-mail address and an electronic mailbox on a network computer called a **mail server** (hosts electronic mailboxes and temporarily stores incoming e-mails). An **e-mail address** has three parts: a name or nickname that identifies the recipient, the @ sign, and a host name. The host name is the identifying name of the mail server where the electronic mailbox is located. Jana.Portosky@hostname.net is an example of an e-mail address. The destination mail server where the electronic mailbox is located may be connected to a business LAN or it may be part of an e-mail service provider's network.

To access the e-mail messages in an electronic mailbox, you can use e-mail client software or Web mail.

E-mail Client Software

An **e-mail client** is software used to create, send, receive, retrieve, reply to, and save e-mail messages. You can also access an electronic address book with an e-mail client. Network groupware, such Novell GroupWise, contains e-mail clients. Other popular e-mail clients include Microsoft® Outlook, Windows® Outlook Express, Mozilla Thunderbird, and QUALCOMM Eudora®. Figure 5-3 illustrates an e-mail client.

An e-mail client downloads e-mail messages from a destination mail server to a folder on your computer's hard disk generally called an Inbox. An e-mail client also provides additional folders for temporarily storing outgoing messages, copies of the messages you send, drafts of messages you are in the process of creating, and messages you delete. You can also create custom folders to organize your saved messages.

Web Mail

Another way to access e-mail is with a Web browser. Popular Web-based e-mail services include Yahoo! Mail, EarthLink Web Mail, and MSN Hotmail. An advantage of Web-based e-mail is its portability. You can access a Web-based e-mail account from any computer that has a Web browser and Internet

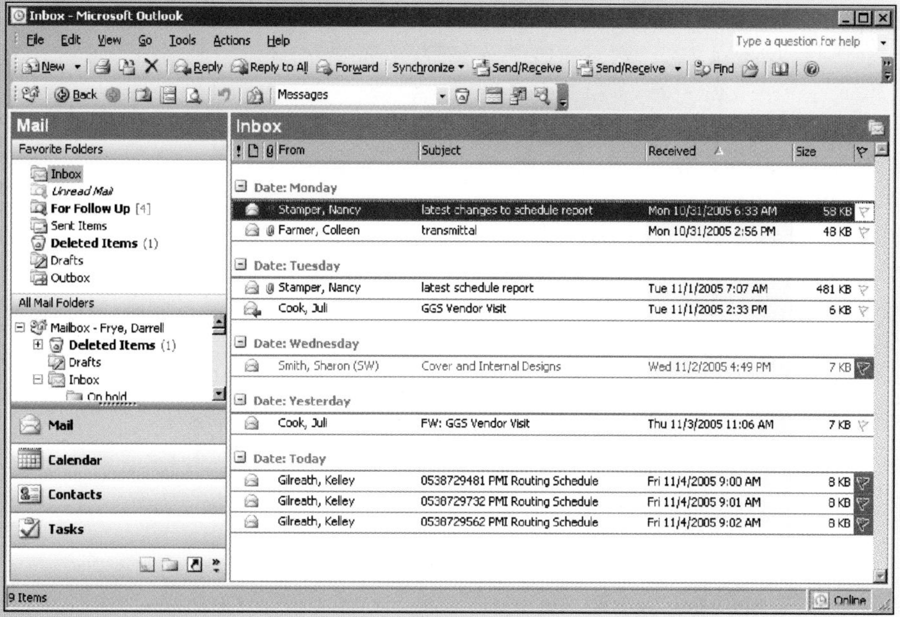

Figure 5-3   AN E-MAIL CLIENT IS SOFTWARE USED TO ACCESS AN ELECTRONIC MAILBOX ON A MAIL SERVER

connection. Figure 5-4 illustrates access to an electronic mailbox using Web mail.

Spam, Phishing, and Pharming

Spam is the term used to describe unwanted and unsolicited electronic messages. Recent studies show that over 50 percent of all e-mail messages are spam. Spam received in the workplace and home office costs businesses worldwide more than $40 billion each year.[3] Spam messages are more than just unsolicited advertising. Spam brings with it the risk of viruses, worms, financial fraud, identity theft, and more.

Online criminals send spam that looks as though it is from a legitimate financial institution or business, such as an ISP, requesting credit card numbers or Social Security numbers or other personal information. The e-mail will be dressed up with company logos and contact information to make it look legitimate. It may contain a link that appears to be to the institution's or ISP's website. Do not fall for it. This is an online scam called **phishing.**

A legitimate business should never ask you to provide personal and sensitive information via e-mail. Be suspicious of every message from an unknown source. *Don't click any links in a suspected message!* Clicking a link in a spam message lets the sender know that the message found an active address, increasing the chances you will get even more spam. Clicking a link can also expose your computer or network to other threats, such as viruses or

| Figure 5-4 | WEB-BASED E-MAIL CAN BE ACCESSED FROM ANY COMPUTER WITH A WEB BROWSER AND AN INTERNET CONNECTION |

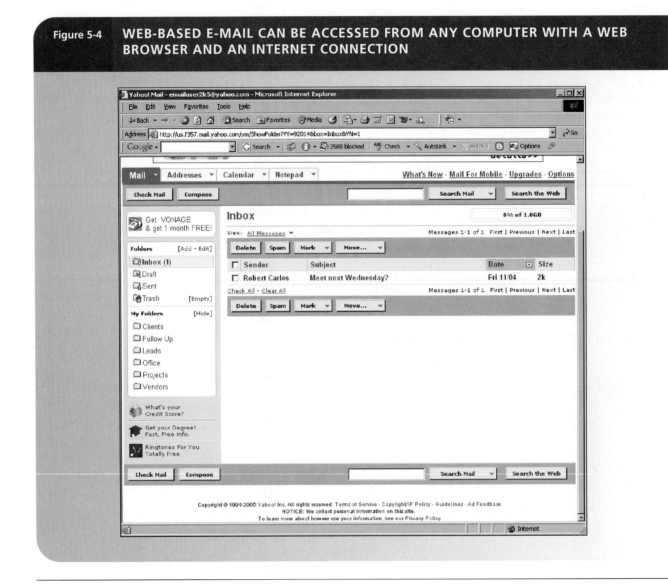

---

[3]Jon Surmacz, "Safety in Numbers: Spam Costs Business Billions," *Radicati Group* as reported by *CSO Online,* February 24, 2004, <http://www.csoonline.com/metrics/viewmetric. cfm?id=665> (accessed April 16, 2005), as cited in Radicati Group Source.

Part II Workplace Technologies

worms. A link in a phishing message will jump to a fraudulent copy of an actual business website created specifically to collect personal information from unsuspecting users.

Another online scam that currently concerns Internet security professionals is called **pharming**—the manipulation of a legitimate website address to direct unsuspecting users to a fraudulent copy of the site designed to gather personal information for criminal purposes. The best way to combat pharming is to keep your Web browser updates installed and be very careful about submitting personal information at any website.[4]

Spam-blocking or filtering software can be installed on mail servers and on user computers in an attempt to block spam. E-mail client software generally contains some features for managing unwanted messages. Although the CAN-SPAM Act of 2003 makes sending bulk spam illegal, spammers continue to flood the Internet with spam messages. Spam remains a serious problem for businesses both in the workplace and the home office. You must remain constantly vigilant to protect yourself and your company from spam risks. Figure 5-5 provides tips to avoid being a spam victim.

Figure 5-5	**SPAM PROTECTION TIPS**

- Be suspicious of all e-mail messages from strangers.

- Don't open an e-mail attachment unless you are certain it is from a trusted source.

- Install anti-virus software and keep it updated. Make certain the software feature that checks e-mail message content and e-mail attachments is turned on.

- Read all messages carefully before you reply.

- Remember that a legitimate financial institution, ISP, or other business should never request personal information via e-mail. Never send personal or financial information via an e-mail message.

- Don't click links in e-mail messages. Use your Web browser to access the Web site.

Source: Dan Tynan and Scott Spanbauer, "Safety Cheat Sheet: Avoid Being Played for a Sucker," *PCWorld*, March 8, 2005, <http://www.pcworld.com/news/article/0,aid,119943,00.asp> (accessed April 16, 2005).

Spotlight on

E-MAIL SPAM

Do not contribute to spam by sending or forwarding junk e-mail, jokes, or offensive material to your coworkers.

E-mail is a powerful business tool for increased collaboration between coworkers and for communicating with clients, vendors, investors, and others. But e-mail abuse also poses potential problems for a business.

E-mail Use Policies

Sending personal e-mails from workplace computers reduces employee productivity. Forwarding jokes, junk mail, and chain letters to others stresses the e-mail system and reduces productivity. Offensive e-mail content can place a company at risk for charges of workplace harassment. Many businesses protect themselves from these risks by using network software to monitor their employees e-mail.

Another way to protect against e-mail abuse is a clearly stated and strongly enforced company-wide e-mail policy. Every business should have a formal e-mail policy that each employee agrees to follow. As an administrative professional, you may be called on to help establish your company's e-mail policy. Figure 5-6 lists items that should be addressed in an e-mail policy.

E-mail plays a primary role in workplace collaboration. But other workplace collaboration tools such as instant messaging, shared workspaces, discussion groups, wikis, weblogs, and Web conferencing are growing in importance. Fax transmissions are still used in the workplace or home office to send copies of documents to coworkers, vendors, and customers.

▷ Instant Messaging

Instant messaging (IM) has moved with lightning speed from a toy for teenagers to an important

---

[4]Bill Husted, "Computing Hazards Likely to Get Worse in Next Year," *The Columbus Dispatch*, April 18, 2005, p. E4.

Figure 5-6   **E-MAIL POLICIES**

- ▶ Make clear whether or not personal e-mail sent at the workplace is permitted.

- ▶ Let employees know that all e-mail accounts, messages, and attachments sent via the workplace e-mail system are the property of the company—not the employee.

- ▶ Let employees know if their e-mail is being monitored. Describe how and why messages are being monitored.

- ▶ Include a description of the type of e-mail message content that is not permitted, such as offensive, illegal, or discriminatory content or confidential information.

- ▶ Explain what types of e-mail attachments are permitted and the maximum file size of an attachment.

- ▶ State the company's position on sending or forwarding spam and other junk mail.

- ▶ Outline the company's guidelines for creating professional business e-mail messages.

- ▶ Explain how employees should handle standard e-mail replies and urgent e-mail replies.

- ▶ Explain that e-mail messages are permanent business records. Tell employees when and how to archive their e-mail messages.

- ▶ Make clear what employees should do if they have questions about company e-mail policies.

- ▶ Have employees formally acknowledge the company's e-mail policies by signing an e-mail policy agreement. If the e-mail policies change, have new agreements signed by all employees.

- ▶ Periodically remind employees about the company's e-mail policies through seminars and memos.

- ▶ Explain the disciplinary actions that can be taken for violation of e-mail policies.

- ▶ Enforce the stated policies.

business communication tool. A 2004 survey of employees at 840 U.S. businesses by the American Management Association showed that 90 percent of survey respondents used instant messaging in the workplace up to 90 minutes each workday.[5]

An **instant message** is an electronic message sent and received by two or more people who are connected to a network at the same time. The instant message opens in a small window on the recipient's computer screen. Instant messaging services support text, video, and audio messaging. Participating in instant messaging that includes video and audio requires a microphone, speakers, video camera, and application software, such as Windows Media Player or Real-Player. Figure 5-7 illustrates an instant message.

Like e-mail, you can also transfer electronic files across the network by attaching them to an instant message. Popular instant messaging services include AOL Instant Messenger, ICQ Instant Messenger, Microsoft Windows Messenger, Yahoo! Messenger, MSN Messenger, and IBM Lotus Messenger.

As a workplace collaboration tool, instant messaging has some real advantages. It is easy to use, gets faster response than e-mail, and can save more time than making a phone call. However, concerns do exist in the workplace about the use of instant messaging. For example, security risks include the possible unauthorized interception of messages or sending viruses with instant message attachments.

Some workers find instant messages popping up on their screens a distraction. To quote one analyst: "To me, it's kind of like opening someone's door and barging in and asking them a question."[6] Also, productivity can be lost by workers sending personal instant messages during work hours. Businesses that permit instant messaging are increasingly establishing company-wide procedures for using instant messaging in the workplace. Additionally, businesses are installing network software to monitor and secure their employees' instant messages.

Instant messaging is quick and easy to use, but just like e-mail messages you must always be careful

---

[5]"2004 Workplace E-mail and Instant Messaging Survey Summary," *American Management Association* as reported by the *ePolicy Institute*, 2004, <http://www.epolicyinstitute.com/survey/survey04.pdf> (accessed April 16, 2005).

[6]Kris Maher, "Instant Messaging at Work Can Create Problems Instantly," *CareerJournal.com, The Wall Street Journal Online*, October 6, 2004, <http://www.careerjournal.com/jobhunting/jungle/20041006-jungle.html> (accessed April 16, 2005).

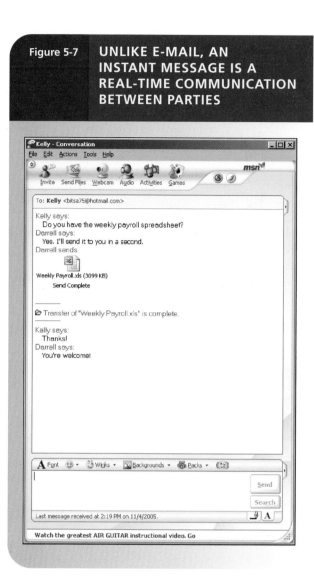

Figure 5-7 UNLIKE E-MAIL, AN INSTANT MESSAGE IS A REAL-TIME COMMUNICATION BETWEEN PARTIES

about what you say and how you say it. Keep your instant messages short and to the point. Send instant messages only when you must get a prompt reply to a question or send urgent information. Remember that you must not disclose private or confidential information or spread office gossip via instant messaging. To do so is both embarrassing and unethical. Being too casual with coworkers and supervisors in your instant messages may be viewed as unprofessional.

As is true with e-mail, instant message users are at risk for unwanted and unsolicited messages, which are referred to as **spam via IM** or **spim**. A recent survey indicated that at least 30 percent of instant message users are victims of spim.[7]

Shared Workspaces

An IP network allows collaborative team members to come together in a **shared workspace,** a virtual work area hosted by a Web server and accessed via a Web browser. Team members can work together in the shared workspace to create and revise documents, view the status of projects, and share project calendars. Features of a shared workspace include:

- ▶ Names and contact information for each team member.
- ▶ Links to other Web-based information needed by the team members.
- ▶ Document libraries containing stored documents related to the specific project.
- ▶ Tasks assigned to each team member and the tasks' status.

The application software in some productivity suites can be used as an interface to a shared workspace when combined with Web server technologies.

▶ Discussion Groups

A **discussion group** is an online forum in which participants discuss or receive information on a specific topic. Discussion groups include **newsgroups** (virtual bulletin boards), **mailing lists** (e-mail newsletters), and **Web-based forums** (messages posted via a Web browser). Businesses use mailing lists and Web-based forums to keep customers updated with new products and to provide customer service. Professionals can use discussion groups to connect with peers and stay updated with the latest information in their field. Figure 5-8 lists useful netiquette tips for participating in instant messaging and discussion groups.

▶ Wikis

A **wiki** is a website or group of Web pages on which anyone can add, edit, or delete content. An example of a wiki is the *Wikipedia,* a popular Web-based free encyclopedia to which anyone can contribute. **Hypertext Markup Language (HTML)** is the markup language used to create and edit Web pages. Wiki contributors do not have to know HTML to contribute to or edit a wiki—wikis can be added to, changed, or deleted by anyone using a Web browser.[8] In the workplace, businesses host wikis on their

---

[7]Jon Surmacz, "Safety in Numbers: Spam Comes to IM," *Pew Internet and American Life Project* as reported by *CSO Online,* March 2, 2005, <http://www.csoonline.com/metrics/viewmetric.cfm?id=778> (accessed April 16, 2005), as cited from Pew Internet and American Life Project.

[8]Paul Barnard, "Wiki 101," *Really Strategies Newsletter 10,* January, 2004, <http://www.reallysi.com/newsletter10_3.htm> (accessed April 16, 2005).

secure intranets to enable work groups to build knowledge bases on specific work-related topics.

▷ Weblogs

Weblogs or **blogs** are Web-based journals in which participants express their opinions, thoughts, and feelings. Posting to a weblog is called **blogging**. Although a wiki and a weblog are both Web-based, they are used differently. Unlike a wiki, postings to a weblog are added chronologically and generally follow conversational threads or ideas. Postings to a weblog may be monitored by a moderator and edited to remove inappropriate content. Examples of public weblogs include the weblogs hosted by reporters and columnists at online news sites such as MSNBC or CNN.com.

Businesses are increasingly using public weblogs to create forums for exchanging product information between users. An example of this type of weblog is one hosted by an application software manufacturer for its users. Users can share ways to use and troubleshoot the software and make suggestions for software updates and new features. Users testing a manufacturer's latest software version can share their testing results with other testers. A business may encourage its executives to host public weblogs that present a "human face" to the business's customers. Small business owners use weblogs to connect with other entrepreneurs. Private business weblogs hosted on an intranet can be used to help work groups manage their projects.

Spotlight on BLOGGING

Never post private or confidential information to a weblog. Doing so is unethical and may also jeopardize your job. If you are unsure about the confidentiality of information, check with your supervisor.

▷ Video, Internet, and Web Conferencing

A **video conference** is a live, interactive conference between two or more people located in separate geographical areas. Video conferencing uses telephony and video technologies to connect participants. The equipment and facilities needed to host or participate in a video conference can be expensive.

A lower-cost alternative to a video conference is an Internet or Web conference. An **Internet conference** is hosted over an IP network and may include video, audio, and shared resources between two or more persons. You can use application software, such as Microsoft® NetMeeting, to participate in an Internet conference. A **Web conference** also uses an IP network, such as the Internet, to bring people together who are physically located in different geographic areas; however, attendees access the conference using a website interface. Internet and Web conferencing allows businesses to save time and money by eliminating the unproductive time workers spend traveling, reducing travel costs, and eliminating the need for expensive equipment and facilities.

Interacting during an Internet or Web conference with sound and video requires a microphone, speakers, and a video camera, called a **Webcam**, connected to the computer. Participants in a Web conference may need special software downloaded from the conference service provider or they may only need a browser and a connection to the network. Web conferencing can be hosted on a business's own LAN or intranet. Alternatively a Web conference can be hosted by a Web conferencing service provider. Popular Web conferencing solutions include Microsoft® Live Meeting, Citrix GoToMeeting, and WebEx.

Workplace collaboration tools have forever changed the way tasks get done in the workplace and how team members communicate with each other. But another more traditional workplace communication tool—a fax machine—still plays an important role.

▷ Fax Communications

The facsimile or fax machine is a standard piece of telecommunication equipment in the workplace and the home office. You can communicate with other people within the same building, in the same city, across the nation, or across the world by sending them a fax message.

Fax Machines

A **fax machine** copies or scans a document containing text or pictures treating both as an image. The fax machine then sends the image over telephone lines to a destination telephone number assigned to another device: another fax machine, printer, or computer. Two fax modems are involved: one to convert the outgoing signals so that they can be sent over the phone lines and one to convert the incoming signals back into a format the receiving device can read. The ability to attach documents to outgoing e-mail messages has eliminated much of the faxing previously done.

Multifunction Machines

Fax machines are often **multifunction machines,** combining printing, faxing, copying, and scanning into one machine. The multifunction machines are inexpensive and particularly useful in a home office in which cost and space are considerations. When considering purchasing a multifunction machine, be aware of:

▶ Space available—One multifunction device takes up far less space than the machines it replaces and can be installed more easily because only one connection to a computer is needed.

CHECK B

Self

Check your understanding of collaborative tools by answering the following questions:

1. Why is e-mail an indispensable workplace collaboration tool?

2. How are wikis and weblogs similar? How are they different?

3. What is a shared workspace?

- Capability and cost—Multifunction machines are available with various speeds, print resolutions, and capabilities. The cost of the machine increases with more capabilities.
- Downtime—When a multifunction device malfunctions, you may lose all features—the copier, printer, scanner, and fax. This is an important factor to consider, especially in a small business or home office in which there are no backup machines.

Fax Spam and Message Security

Two issues that can make communication using a fax machine problematic are fax spam and fax security. **Fax spam** is the term used for unwanted, unsolicited advertising messages sent to fax machines. Dealing with fax spam in the workplace is time consuming and increases costs for paper and fax machine toner. Never use a fax machine to broadcast unsolicited advertising or other messages. Sending fax spam is illegal in the United States.

Securing fax messages is another problem, especially in the workplace. Fax messages are generally

automatically printed at their destination; they can remain unsecured and available to anyone who walks by the fax machine. Always take the appropriate measures to secure any fax transmissions—both outgoing and incoming messages. Figure 5-9 lists fax security guidelines for the workplace.

Another telecommunication technology that you use regularly is the telephone.

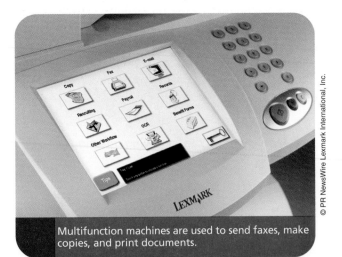

Multifunction machines are used to send faxes, make copies, and print documents.

© PR NewsWire Lexmark International, Inc.

| Figure 5-9 | **FAX SECURITY GUIDELINES** |

- When possible, designate a single individual to pick up, check page count, and distribute faxes in the workplace.

- To prevent unauthorized employees from reading incoming faxes, locate the fax machine in an area that is not easily accessible.

- Use a standard cover sheet containing name, address, and fax telephone numbers for both sender and receiver. Include the number of pages you are faxing, especially if it is a long document.

- Request a confirmation that the fax has been successfully transmitted.

- When faxing sensitive or confidential information, phone ahead so the recipient can be waiting at the destination machine.

- To avoid sending a fax to the wrong number, keep the list of fax numbers current.

- Verify the entered fax number before transmitting the fax.

- Notify the sender if a fax is received in error and determine how to handle the situation: by returning the fax via mail, by destroying it, or by forwarding it on to the appropriate party.

Source: Ann Cavoukian, Ph.D., "Guidelines on Facsimile Transmission Security," *Information and Privacy Commissioner of Ontario*, January, 2003. <http://www.ipc.on.ca/docs/fax-gd-e.pdf> (accessed April 12, 2005).

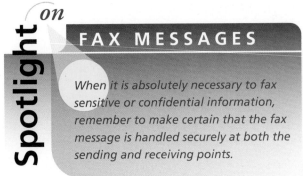

Spotlight *on*

FAX MESSAGES

When it is absolutely necessary to fax sensitive or confidential information, remember to make certain that the fax message is handled securely at both the sending and receiving points.

> TELEPHONE COMMUNICATION

In Chapter 4, you learned that standard telephone lines carry analog signals using technology that has been around for years. This type of telephone service is provided by a **Public-Switched Telephone Network (PSTN)**, sometimes referred to as **Plain Old**

Telephone Service (POTS). The telecommunication revolution is moving voice telecommunication from analog PSTN to IP telephony over private LANs and public networks, such as the Internet.

⊳ IP Telephony

One technology changing voice communication drastically in both the workplace and the home office is **Voice over Internet Protocol (VoIP)**, also called **IP telephony.** IP telephony involves breaking telephone calls into voice packets and routing them over a corporate private IP network or a public IP network such as the Internet. The primary advantage of IP telephony is reduced cost. For example, sending and receiving voice messages over the Internet or a private MAN or WAN eliminates the cost of long distance phone charges. Businesses can also reduce service and maintenance costs by supporting just one network—the IP network—instead of operating two networks, one for data and one for voice. Other IP telephony advantages include:

▸ Area code flexibility—Because IP telephony is not connected to a PSTN telephone exchange, users are not tied to one area code and may even be given a choice of area codes by their service provider. There is no need to transfer phone service when moving to new office space or a new city.
▸ Voice mail can be routed to a computer's electronic mailbox.
▸ Phone numbers kept in a user's personal information management (PIM) software can be dialed from a computer.

IP telephony is also available for the home office in two ways. A standard telephone can be plugged into an analog telephone adapter that, in turn, is plugged into a home network router or DSL or cable modem. This makes voice communication over the Internet using a standard telephone possible. Another method is the **softphone,** which is application software that allows IP telephony from a computer or PDA. One popular freeware softphone example is Skype™. Users can download Skype and then call other Skype users around the world free of charge using their computers equipped with a microphone and speakers or a headset. A small fee is charged for calling regular PSTN phone numbers and mobile phones.

There are some disadvantages to IP telephony. While IP telephony message quality is continuing to improve, in some circumstances voice message quality may not be equal to PSTN voice quality. A broadband Internet connection is required and connection reliability depends on an ISP's service reliability. If the broadband Internet connection is not available, there is no phone service. Softphone software may be vulnerable to worms, viruses, and Trojan horses and **Spam over Internet Telephony (SPIT),** unwanted and unsolicited voice messages.[9]

IP telephony users are expected to grow to more than 27 million by 2008.[10] Because of its rising popularity, IP telephony is now commonly offered by traditional telecommunication providers, ISPs, cable companies, and telecommunication providers new to the marketplace.

The telephone equipment and features found in the modern workplace make it easier for an administrative professional to manage his or her calls.

⊳ Telephone Equipment

You will find a variety of telephone equipment in the workplace including standard PSTN phone sets, IP telephony sets, cordless sets, conference call speakers, and headsets to use with computers and software. Common features on business phone sets include multiple buttons for answering multiple phone lines, built-in speaker phones, LCD displays to view caller identification information, and programmable buttons for setting up call management features.

IP telephony sets have special ports used to connect the sets to an IP network. Some sets have ports that are enabled for wireless infrared (IF) communication, allowing users to dial out through the set from their IF-equipped PDA or smartphone.

Modern telephone systems support several useful call management features.

Call Management Features
Popular call management features include call forwarding, waiting, holding, parking, conferencing, redialing, transferring, and speed dialing.

---

[9]Wayne Rash, "Severe Vulnerabilities are Possible in VoIP, Official Warns," *eWeek,* April 5, 2005, <http://www.eweek.com/article2/0,1759,1782914,00.asp> (accessed April 15, 2005).

[10]The Associated Press, "The New Telephony," as reported by *CNN.com,* April 13, 2005, <http://www.cnn.com/2005/TECH/internet/04/13/new.telephony.ap/index.html> (accessed April 14, 2005).

- Call forwarding—sending incoming calls to a different phone number or office extension when you are away from your desk or out of your office. Some systems can provide automatic call forwarding if your line is busy or if you do not answer your line within a few rings.
- Call waiting—a beep or signal telling you that another call is coming in when you are already on the line. The caller hears a busy signal.
- Call holding—placing a call in a waiting queue to be answered in a few seconds.
- Call parking—placing a call on hold and then picking it up from any phone set in the office, not just your own.
- Conferencing—adding multiple callers to the same conversation.
- Redialing—calling back the most recently received incoming call.
- Transferring—sending an incoming call to another person.
- Speed dialing—setting up frequently called numbers to be dialed by the push of one or two buttons.

Intercom features are also useful. A phone system may provide a two-way intercom feature through which two parties—perhaps you and your supervisor—can hold a conversation. A group intercom feature allows multiple team members working on a project to collaborate via a telephone conference.

Another popular, but sometimes problematic, phone feature is voice mail.

Voice Mail

Voice mail or voice messaging is an efficient method of managing incoming calls when the call recipients are unavailable. The voice mail feature plays a recorded announcement, records, and stores voice messages. Most workplace telephone systems today use voice mail for both inside calls between employees

Telephone equipment for the modern office includes multifunction telephone sets, conference speakers, and headsets.

and incoming calls from outside the company. Voice mail is also used in the home office, often as a built-in feature of softphone software or as a subscription service from the PSTN or IP telephony provider.

Voice messages are delivered to a call recipient's voice mail box, from which they can be retrieved, forwarded, and erased. A voice mail box is generally set up with a private access code known only to its owner. The private access code must be entered to access the mail box's contents. This prevents anyone other than the user from listening to and forwarding or erasing messages.

A voice mail box owner usually accesses his or her voice mail box from a phone inside the workplace. Many voice mail systems also permit mail box access from a phone outside the workplace. Some voice mail systems also provide automatic notification that messages are waiting for the mail box owner via his or her PDA, cell phone, or pager. Many voice mail systems also support message broadcasting, or the sending of the same message to multiple voice mail boxes. Some callers do not like to leave voice mail messages; therefore, most voice mail systems provide a return to operator feature that allows callers to access a live person.

Spotlight *on*

VOICE MAIL

Always check your voice mail immediately upon returning to your desk. Answer all messages promptly.

The proper use of voice mail in the workplace or home office increases productivity and saves time and money. For example:

- ▶ Workers can leave a voice message instead of placing repeated calls to someone who is not available.
- ▶ Voice messages are to the point, eliminating extraneous conversation.
- ▶ Business travelers can communicate with the workplace at any time.
- ▶ Message delivery speed can be increased even between differences in time zones because a voice message can be left any time of the day or night.

As an administrative professional, you may be assigned the task of setting up your telephone system's voice mail announcement—the first message a caller may hear when he or she calls your company. If your voice mail system must have multiple levels of call routing, give callers no more than four options. Callers strongly dislike trying to follow a maze of instructions to record their messages.

Remember to keep caller instructions short—under 15 seconds if possible. Provide the most important information or answer the most frequently asked questions first. When recording step-by-step instructions, tell the caller exactly what you want him or her to do first—then explain what action to take. For example, "To transfer your call to our receptionist, press zero."

Be certain your instructions tell the caller how to reach a live person. Callers dislike getting lost in a voice message system that never allows them to speak to a live person.

Voice mail can be a very effective tool in the modern workplace; however, care must be given to announcement or individual message content and length to maintain effectiveness and efficiency. Figure 5-10 provides tips for effective voice mail.

Whether answering incoming calls or making outgoing calls, professional call management skills are essential in the workplace.

Figure 5-10   VOICE MAIL TIPS

- ▶ The voice mail outgoing message a caller hears is very important as it can create either a favorable or an unfavorable impression. A well-crafted announcement succinctly provides key information, such as the mail box owner's name, the current date, in-office or out-of-office information, and whom to contact if the call is urgent.

- ▶ Remember that the sound and tone of your voice message greeting must create a favorable impression. When recording your outgoing message, vary your vocal tone; do not talk in a monotone.

- ▶ Be careful to avoid background noise when recording your message.

- ▶ Don't misuse voice mail. Answer your calls whenever possible.

- ▶ When leaving a voice message for someone else, make it short and to the point.

VOICE MAIL

Be certain to keep your telephone system's voice mail programming instructions handy in case you need to change your voice mailbox access code or outgoing announcement.

▷ Call Management Skills

An administrative professional must constantly improve his or her communication and human relations skills to succeed. This is especially true when making or receiving phone calls because you will communicate daily with numerous individuals without ever seeing or meeting them. Regardless of the calling technology you use—PSTN, IP telephony, or wireless—remember that good human relations skills are crucial to leave a positive impression of yourself and your company with the person on the other end of the call.

Always give a positive impression of yourself and your company when on the phone.

© Photodisc

Call management is an extremely important part of business communication. Attention must be paid to handling both incoming and outgoing calls professionally. Never forget that a human being is on the receiving end of your call.

Professional Approach

Chances are you do make errors when using the phone; we all do. You probably have been the victim of ineffective calling techniques used by others.

Keep a Smile in Your Voice. Visitors to your office appreciate a cheerful smile, a cup of coffee, and perhaps a magazine when they have to wait. You rely on your voice and your manner to make the person-to-person contact as pleasant as possible. Using your voice to make a caller feel as if a smile is coming through the receiver is just as important.

How do you develop such a smile in your voice? One way is to smile as you pick up the telephone receiver. When you are smiling, it is much easier to project a smile in your voice. Treat the voice on the other end of the line as you would treat a person who is standing in front of you.

▸ Let the individual know you are interested in him or her.
▸ Maintain a caring attitude.
▸ Never answer the phone in a curt or rude manner.
▸ Do not speak in a monotone; vary your voice modulation.
▸ Be alert to what you are saying.

Listen Carefully. Listen carefully to what the other person says and never interrupt. If the caller is unhappy about some situation, allow him or her to explain why. More good listening skills include:

▸ Listening for facts and feelings.
▸ Trying to understand what the caller is saying, both from the words and from the tone of voice.
▸ Searching for hidden or subtle meanings in the caller's voice or demeanor.
▸ Being patient.
▸ Helping the caller by responding to what the caller wants or asks. Do not just try—do it!

Be Discreet. Be discreet when you must tell a caller that your supervisor is unavailable. Carefully explain why your supervisor cannot answer his or her phone—but don't say too much. You may say, "Ms. Portosky is away from the office now. I expect her back in approximately an hour. May I have her call you when she returns?" Never say, "Ms. Portosky is not here yet" (at 10 a.m.), "She's gone for the day" (at 2 p.m.), or "She's out sick" (at any time of day). A good rule to remember is to be helpful about when

Self Check

Respond to the following comments with a yes or no answer.

	Yes	No
1. I always have a smile in my voice when I answer a call.	☐	☐
2. I never listen carefully to the caller.	☐	☐
3. I use correct English when answering a call or making one.	☐	☐
4. I forget to take messages completely and accurately.	☐	☐
5. I indicate my respect for the caller by using his or her name.	☐	☐
6. I never discriminate in words or actions when using the phone.	☐	☐
7. I explain the reason and ask permission before I transfer a call.	☐	☐
8. I never request permission before I put a call on hold.	☐	☐
9. I never bother with a list of frequently called numbers.	☐	☐
10. I follow through on promises I make to callers.	☐	☐

your supervisor is returning but not specific about where he or she is or whom he or she may be with at the time.

Use Correct English. Be careful to use correct English and watch your word pronunciation. Using slang in the workplace is unprofessional. Figure 5-11 gives you some suggestions to avoid using slang.

Take Messages Completely and Accurately. One way to keep track of messages is to record them using special software. Another way is to record messages manually using paper message pads. Paper message pads may have single or duplicate sheets. Duplicate sheets allow a permanent record of the call. When manually recording a message, be careful. Incomplete messages are frustrating to the recipient and may result in an incomplete or inaccurate response.

Figure 5-11	SLANG AND REPLACEMENT WORDS

Avoid saying	*Instead, say*
Yeah	Certainly
OK	Yes
Uh-huh	Of course
Bye-bye	Goodbye
Huh?	I did not understand.
	or
	Would you please repeat that?

Remember to ask the caller for complete information, if necessary. Always get the following information:

▶ the caller's name spelled correctly (Ask the caller to spell his or her name if you are not certain how it is spelled.)
▶ company name
▶ telephone number (with area code)
▶ time of call
▶ exact message text

Repeat the message to the caller so you can be certain it is accurate.

Use the Caller's Name. Callers appreciate being recognized and called by name. Responding with "Yes, Mr. Bradshaw. I will be happy to get the information." and "It was nice to talk with you, Mr. Bradshaw" indicates to the caller that you know who he is and that you care about him.

Ask Tactful Questions. Be careful when asking a caller questions. Ask only necessary questions, such as "May I tell Ms. Portosky who is calling?" or "When Ms. Portosky returns, may I tell her who called?" Never ask "Who is calling?" The caller may be offended by such a blunt question. If your supervisor is not in or cannot take the call for some reason, ask about the nature of the call so you can handle the call or refer it to someone else. For example, you may say, "If you tell me the nature of your call, perhaps I can help you or refer you to someone who can."

Speak Distinctly and Clearly. Make sure the caller can understand what you say. You cannot speak distinctly with gum, candy, or a pencil in your mouth. Also speak in a voice that can be heard. You do not want to shout or whisper.

▸ Place the receiver firmly against your ear.
▸ Place the center of the mouthpiece about an inch from the center of your lips.
▸ Speak in a normal voice. Watch the speed of your voice. Do not talk too fast or too slow. Speak at a moderate rate.

Handle Problem Calls Carefully. Most callers are pleasant, especially if you are courteous to them. Occasionally you may have a caller who has had a difficult day or for some other reason is unhappy. An angry caller can often be defused by taking the time to listen to his or her story. Remember that the caller is not angry with you, but rather with a situation or an event. Do not become emotionally involved in the situation.

Once you have listened to the caller's story, try to assist him or her in getting the problem solved. This approach may mean that you suggest a solution or that you tell the person you will have someone who can solve the problem call him or her back. Do not put the person on hold or mishandle the call by transferring it to an individual who cannot help. Such approaches merely make the caller angrier.

From time to time, you may answer a call for your supervisor and the caller will refuse to give you his or her name. You should discuss this possibility with your supervisor and understand exactly what you are expected to do in such a situation. However, if you are unsure what to do, put the caller on hold and explain the situation to your supervisor. He or she can then decide whether or not to speak to the caller.

Use Words to Identify Letters. Some callers may be difficult to understand over the telephone; certain letters are also difficult to understand when spoken quickly or softly. If you need to clarify what you hear, repeat what the caller has said using words to identify letters in the spelling. Say something like "That is Joan D. (as in David) Singleton, correct?" Figure 5-12 gives you some additional examples.

Do Not Discriminate. Have you ever found yourself being nicer over the telephone to the president of your company than to a caller you do not know? If the answer is "yes," make a point of being friendly

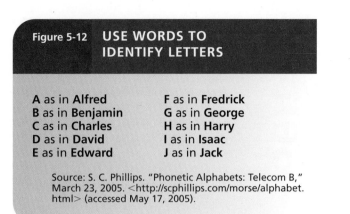

Figure 5-12 USE WORDS TO IDENTIFY LETTERS

A as in **Alfred**   F as in **Fredrick**
B as in **Benjamin**   G as in **George**
C as in **Charles**   H as in **Harry**
D as in **David**   I as in **Isaac**
E as in **Edward**   J as in **Jack**

Source: S. C. Phillips. "Phonetic Alphabets: Telecom B," March 23, 2005. <http://scphillips.com/morse/alphabet.html> (accessed May 17, 2005).

before you know who is on the other end of the line. Try saying to yourself "A friend is calling" before answering the phone. Remember that all assistants are not female and all executives are not male. If you answer the telephone and the voice on the other end is female, do not assume she is an assistant and ask to speak to her supervisor. When addressing anyone, use terms that connote respect. Do not refer to a woman as a girl, a young lady, a beautiful young thing, a gal, or any other term that can be construed as gender biased. Do not refer to a man as a boy, a hunk, or a guy.

Be Aware of Time Zone Differences. Because of the multinational nature of business today, you will likely place business calls to places all around the world. Obviously, time zone differences must be taken into consideration when making calls. In the United States, the time zones are Eastern, Central, Mountain, and Pacific as shown in Figure 5-13. The international time zones are shown in Figure 5-14.

Maintain a List of Frequently Called Numbers. Maintaining a list of frequently called numbers is an excellent time saver. If you use personal information management (PIM) software, frequently called numbers can be stored with other contact information. Telephone software, such as softphone or cell phone software, also provides features you can use to store frequently called numbers.

Incoming Calls

The techniques you learned in the previous section apply to all calls. Here are some special techniques for handling incoming calls.

Answer Calls Promptly. When your telephone rings, answer promptly—on the first ring if possible and

Figure 5-13   **A TIME ZONE MAP**

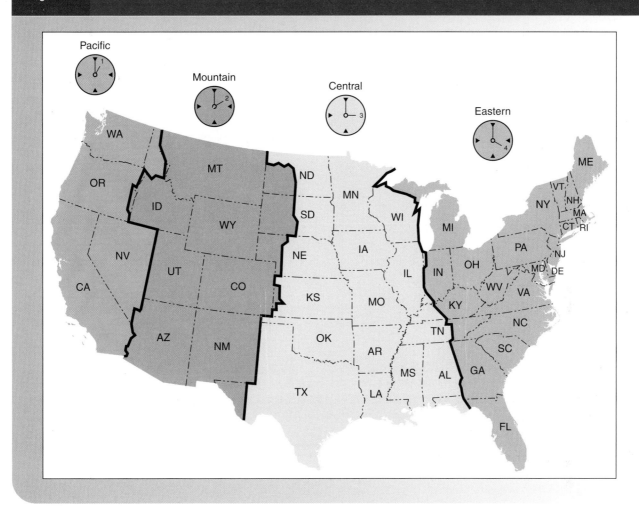

certainly by the third ring. You may lose a potential customer if you are slow in answering the telephone.

Identify Yourself and Your Company. Most businesses and supervisors have specific procedures for answering the telephone. In large businesses, calls are often routed first to a person whose job it is to greet telephone or in-person visitors. This person identifies the company and then routes the incoming call to the appropriate party, which may be his or her administrative professional. For example, if the target of the call is Ms. Portosky, you might answer her line as "Ms. Portosky's office, Adele Wilson." If you are the target of the call, you might answer "Good morning. JWay Nu-Systems Tech, Adele Wilson. How may I help you?"

Transfer Calls Carefully. Make certain you know how to transfer calls on your telephone system.

Callers dislike being told they are going to be transferred and then getting disconnected due to incorrect transferring procedures. Before you transfer a call, explain to the caller why it must be transferred. Make sure the caller is willing to be transferred. For example, you may say "Ms. Portosky is out, but James Gonzales can give you the information. May I transfer you to Mr. Gonzales?" You may also want to give the caller the complete number or the extension of the person to whom the caller is being transferred in case the transfer is not completed. The caller can then place the call to the new party without having to call you again.

Request Permission to Place Calls on Hold. A caller may sometimes request information that you do not have at your fingertips. You may need to check with someone else or go to your files to get the information. Or you may be answering your supervisor's line

Figure 5-14 **AN INTERNATIONAL TIME ZONE MAP**

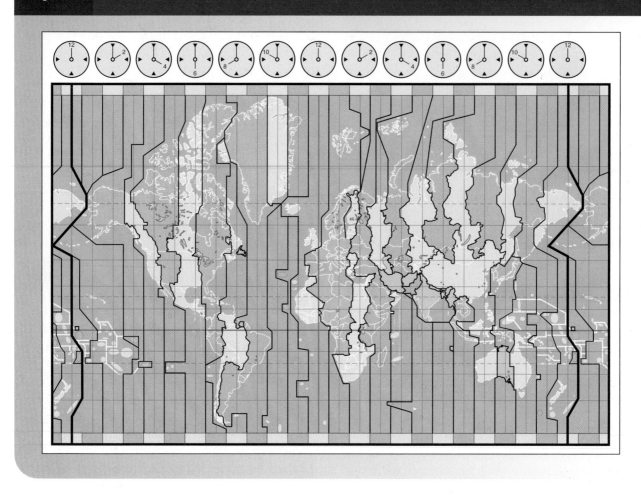

because he or she is not immediately available to take a call. If you must place the caller on hold until your supervisor is available or until you retrieve the necessary information, do so only with the caller's permission. Do not assume that a caller is willing to be placed on hold. You may say "I need to pull the information from my files. Would you like to hold for a moment while I get it, or shall I call you back?" Or "Ms. Portosky is on another call. Would you like to hold?" If the caller agrees to hold, try to get back to him or her as soon as possible. Nothing irritates a caller more than to be left on hold for a long time. When you return to the line, let the caller know you are back by saying "Thank you for waiting." If there is a delay in responding to the call, return to the line and ask the caller if he or she wants to continue to hold or leave a message; apologize for the length of time it is taking to complete the call. If the caller leaves a message, make certain that the message is delivered promptly.

Handle Multiple Calls. You may be responsible for answering more than one line. If so, at times you will be answering a call on one line when another line rings. When this happens, you must remember that the caller on the second line does not know you are already on the phone. The caller is expecting to get an answer immediately. Excuse yourself politely by saying to the first caller, "May I place you on hold for a moment? I must answer another line." If the second call is going to take awhile, ask the caller for a number so you can call back as soon as you finish the first call. Then go back to the first caller with "Thank you for waiting." Your responsibility is to handle all calls as quickly and efficiently as possible.

Defer Business Cell Phone Calls. Interrupting your interaction with others—clients, vendors, coworkers—to answer your business cell phone is discourteous. Taking these calls conveys the impression that you have something more important to do than what you are currently doing. Be courteous by turning your business cell phone to silent mode when working with others. If you are expecting an urgent call on your business cell phone, be sure the client, vendor, or coworker with whom you are working understands this before you answer the call. You may say, "We may be interrupted by a call I must take, but I promise to be as quick as possible." If the call comes through, excuse yourself and keep the conversation as brief as possible. Personal cell phone calls should not be made or accepted during business hours unless you have permission from your supervisor.

Screen Calls as Instructed. Many supervisors have one telephone number that is published for callers and another private number that is not published. The unpublished number is often used to make outgoing calls or may be given out to close friends or family members. An administrative professional usually is expected to screen incoming calls from the published number. For example, when the supervisor receives a call, an administrative professional is expected to determine who is calling and why and then route to others those calls that the supervisor will not take, such as unsolicited sales calls. If someone else in your company can handle the call, transfer it to that person after requesting permission from the caller to transfer the call. If no one is available to take the call, let the person know courteously that your employer is not interested. One response might be "I appreciate the information; however, Ms. Portosky is not interested in pursuing the matter at the present time."

Leave a Message in Your Absence. If you are going to be away from your desk for some time, you may choose to record a brief message on your phone system and have the system automatically transfer all incoming calls to voice mail, your cell phone, or pager. If you have to leave your desk for a short time, you may choose to arrange for a coworker to answer your calls. Tell the coworker where you can be reached and what time you will be back. If your supervisor is also out, tell the coworker in general terms where your employer is and when he or she will be back. You might say, "Ms. Portosky is in a meeting and will be available around 3 p.m."

Follow Through on Promises. If you make a promise to call back with information, do so. A broken promise can cause a canceled order or a lost customer. A kept promise can enhance a reputation for

reliability and trustworthiness. Help your supervisor remember promises made. If you know of information that your supervisor has promised a customer but has not followed through on, provide a tactful reminder of the need to follow through. Your supervisor will appreciate your assistance.

Outgoing Calls

As an administrative professional, you may be responsible for placing calls for your supervisor; certainly you will make your own business calls. Professional handling of outgoing calls is just as important as for incoming calls.

Plan Your Call. When calling for your supervisor or yourself, take a few minutes to plan your call before you make it. Know the purpose of your call and what you intend to say. Your call may be answered first by a receptionist or the administrative professional to the person you are calling. Always identify yourself and your company and be prepared to state the purpose of your call clearly and concisely. For example, you may say, "This is Adele Wilson of JWay Nu-Systems Tech. I'm calling to verify Mr. Bradshaw's attendance at the breakfast meeting tomorrow at 7 a.m. at the Executive Club." If transferred to the person you are calling, be prepared to restate the purpose of the call clearly and concisely. Although you may exchange pleasantries, don't forget that the main purpose is to get your message across without wasting his or her time.

Place Calls Properly. Supervisors usually place their own calls to save time; however, you may be asked to place your supervisor's calls. If so, be sure to identify your supervisor when you make the call. For example, you may say, "Ms. Portosky of JWay Nu-Systems Tech is calling." Then transfer the call to Ms. Portosky's line. Make certain your supervisor is ready to accept the call before you make it. You might say, "Ms. Portosky, are you going to be available for a few minutes? I want to place the call you requested to Mr. Bradshaw."

The ongoing telecommunication revolution presents both challenges and rewards for the administrative professional.

> THE ONGOING REVOLUTION

The telecommunication revolution continues with advances in wired networks, voice technologies, wireless connections, and other technologies that may create a workplace without walls.

▷ Fiber-optic Networks

Futurists expect that in the not-so-distant future most wired workplace telecommunications will occur over pure fiber-optic networks. A **fiber-optic network** permits very high-quality and high-speed communications using light and glass fibers to transmit digital signals. Fiber-optic networks deliver bandwidth that is far greater than what cable, DSL, or satellite can offer. It is also expected that, in time, fiber-optic network connections will also be widely available in home offices, providing ultra-fast Internet connections.

▷ Voice Technologies

Today we are seeing an increase in the use of voice technologies to input data and commands into laptops, cell phones, PDAs, and smartphones. The future promises an even greater increase in the use of voice technologies and voice browsers to mine the Internet for just about any kind of information—all without touching a keypad. Scientists and researchers continue to develop the underlying technologies that will permit more extensive use of voice technologies in the workplace.

▷ Wireless Technologies

Wireless technologies, such as the Wi-Fi, Bluetooth, and GPRS make it possible for today's mobile worker to stay connected to his or her LAN, the Internet, and coworkers no matter where he or she is at the moment.

More and more often the workplace or home office LAN is a **Wireless LAN (WLAN)** and its users connect with Wi-Fi enabled devices. **Wi-Fi,** or wireless fidelity, is the general name for a family of wireless networking protocols that follow the IEEE 802.11 wireless communication standards. For example, a laptop with a Wi-Fi networking card can connect to a WLAN or to a wired LAN using RF technologies and a transceiver called an **access point.** A public location that provides a wireless access point is called a **hotspot.** Mobile workers can find hotspots in a variety of places, such as airports, hotels, coffee bars, and restaurants. Some cities, such as Philadelphia, Pennsylvania, are making plans to become one large wireless hotspot to enable wireless connections from anywhere in the city.

Bluetooth is a short-range RF technology that links PDAs and smartphones to laptops, printers, and other handheld devices. Bluetooth enabled devices can be used to easily exchange small electronic files, such as contact information, between coworkers. **GPRS** (General Packet Radio Service) is a packet-switching wireless communication technology that enables high-speed wireless Internet connections and data transmissions from smartphones and PDAs.

Another way mobile workers can stay in touch with the workplace is with a wireless messaging service and a **pager,** a small portable messaging device. Originally designed for one-way number or text messaging over a paging service network, some pagers now support two-way wireless messaging and Internet access over a wireless messaging service or a cellular phone network. However, the ability to send and receive text messages using PDAs and smartphones has made pagers a less popular choice for many mobile workers.

Using wireless technologies and devices to stay connected is growing more and more popular and important in the workplace. For example, a recent survey by the Pew Internet & American Life project indicates that more than 40 percent of all U.S. Internet users—56 million people—have access to a laptop, smartphone, or PDA that provides a wireless connection to the Internet.[11] The number of people making wireless connections to the Internet and other IP networks is expected to explode as new wireless technologies being developed become reality. These technologies include **WiMax** (long-range wireless broadband) and **Cognitive Radio** (automatic radio spectrum sharing).

Electronic perception technologies combine sensor chip technology with image processing software to enable electronic devices to "see" and respond to nearby objects. An intriguing application of electronic perception technologies is the projection keyboard for PDAs and smartphones. Because of their small size, complex data entry on wireless handheld devices—such as a PalmOne Trēo smartphone or a BlackBerry PDA—can be difficult and time consuming. This problem may be solved by using a **projection keyboard,** which is a virtual QWERTY keyboard projected on a flat surface. Finger movements on the virtual keyboard are recorded as

---

[11]John B. Horrigan, "Pew Internet Project Data Memo, May 2004" *Pew Internet & American Life,* <http://www.pewinternet.org/pdfs/PIP_Wireless_Ready_Data_0504.pdf> (accessed April 18, 2005).

keystrokes. A projection keyboard allows mobile workers to create complex documents and spreadsheets on their handheld devices more easily.

▷ A Workplace Without Walls

Telecommunication providers are today working on other advances in wireless technologies that will push IP networking and VoIP out to laptops, tablet PCs, smartphones, and PDAs. The combination of IP networking, VoIP, and wireless broadband is expected to ultimately lead to a workplace without walls. In a workplace without walls, physical location is unimportant and every worker is a teleworker. Work is conducted wherever the teleworker is at any given moment—a central workplace, a home office, a restaurant, or an airport.

Futurists expect that the central workplace will also become a workplace without walls. Work areas will be open and unassigned, used on a first-come basis. All computing and communicating will be conducted over an IP network using portable devices.[12] **Intelligent agent software**—software that acts on behalf of its user—will convert incoming e-mail, instant messages, or voice messages as necessary and automatically route them to whatever device a teleworker has at hand at any given moment.[13]

Having faster IP networks and improved wireless technologies will enable greater teleworker team collaboration. For example, one teleworker's work area may become a virtual three-dimensional video conference room for an entire teleworker team with just the touch of a button. Desk, table, and wall surfaces may convert to shared writing areas called **white boards** accessible by all team attendees. Instead of whiteboards, attendees may use groupware to work together on documents displayed on giant wrap-around plasma screens.[14]

The convergence of voice and data over very high-speed IP networks is also expected to change the way businesses interact with their customers and vendors, as well as their employees. As Donald Peterson, a telecommunications executive, noted in an interview for the Association for Computing Machinery:

> We've gone through a stage where the network has enabled any-to-any connection—anybody, anywhere, anytime, anyplace. That's been done. Today, we are at a stage of the right person at the right time in the right place. Whereas we used to call a location, we now can call a device. In the future, we're going to call a person and it's going to be the right person because the application is going to know who the right person is, and the network is going to know the person's availability. Think about whole companies becoming call centers—any employee is available to any customer at any time with the information needed to really be of use to that customer.[15]

---

[12]Michael Kanellos, "The Office of the Future?" *ZDNet Australia,* November 3, 2005, <http://www.zdnet.com.au/insight/communications/0,39023754,39165271,00.htm> (accessed April 16, 2005).

[13]Ibid.

[14]Olga Kharif, "Sneak Peeks at Tomorrow's Office," *Business Week Online,* April 13, 2004 <http://www.businessweek.com/technology/content/apr2004/tc20040413_0505_tc146.htm> (accessed April 15, 2005).

[15]"A Conversation with Don Peterson," *Queue,* as reported by *AVAYA,* September, 2004 <http://www.avaya.com/gcm/master-usa/en-us/resource/assets/articles/dpinqueue.pdf> (accessed April 12, 2005).

SUMMARY

Reinforce your learning in this chapter by studying this summary.

▶ An administrative professional uses telecommunication technologies daily to send and receive electronic messages containing voice, text, numbers, audio, video, and pictures.

▶ A revolution in the field of telecommunication technologies is the move from traditional circuit-switched networks to packet-switched networks to converged networks.

▶ On a circuit-switched network, a voice call between parties is made on a dedicated circuit for the duration of the call. No one else can use the circuit.

▶ On a packet-switched network, data and voice messages are broken into small packets, sent across the network, and reassembled at the destination.

▶ A packet-switched network uses TCP/IP to control the accuracy and destination of the packets. A packet-switched network is also called an IP network. The Internet is an example of an IP network.

▶ IP networks make possible various workplace collaboration tools, including e-mail, instant messages, shared workspaces, wikis, weblogs, and Web conferencing.

▶ E-mail is still the most popular workplace collaboration tool. To receive e-mail, a recipient must have an e-mail address and an electronic mailbox hosted on a mail server either on his or her corporate LAN or on the e-mail service provider's network. E-mail messages can be accessed using an e-mail client or with a Web browser.

▶ Spam (unwanted and unsolicited electronic messages) and phishing (online scams) are serious e-mail threats. Dealing with spam costs businesses billions of dollars each year. Unwary e-mail users may respond to a phishing message and send criminals sensitive information such as credit card numbers or Social Security numbers.

▶ Instant messaging is growing in popularity as a workplace collaboration tool because it is easy to use, gets a fast response, and saves time. Disadvantages of instant messaging include distraction, lost productivity from sending personal messages, viruses and worms sent along with attached files, and spam via IM, or spim.

▶ Businesses use online discussion groups to support customers and maintain a high industry profile. Professionals use discussion groups to stay up-to-date with industry trends and to connect with peers.

▶ Wikis and weblogs are two Web-based collaboration tools. Wikis are used in business to build worker knowledge bases. Weblogs are used much like discussion groups.

▶ Businesses save time and money by hosting Internet or Web conferences on their LANs or through a conference provider. To participate in an Internet conference, you may need special software installed on your computer. To participate in a Web-based conference, you may need software downloaded from a conference service provider or simply a Web browser and Internet connection. To interact with others during an Internet or Web conference, you may need a microphone, speakers, and a Webcam connected to your computer.

▶ A fax machine is a copier used to send an image consisting of text and pictures over telephone lines to another device, such as another fax machine, computer, or printer.

▶ Voice messages have traditionally been sent over a PSTN's circuit-switched network. IP telephony or VoIP is replacing circuit-switched networks as the preferred means of sending and receiving voice messages.

▶ Modern telephone equipment for the workplace includes standard and IP telephony sets, cordless sets, standalone conference call speakers, and headsets. Telephone systems support a wide array of call management features which include call forwarding, waiting, holding, parking, and voice mail.

▶ Voice mail is used extensively in the workplace or home office to store and retrieve messages. The proper use of voice mail increases productivity and saves time and money.

▶ Call management skills are critical for an administrative professional. Attention must be paid to both incoming and outgoing calls. Remember! There is a human being on the other end of every call.

▶ Telecommunication technologies of the future include widespread use of fiber optic networks for wired communication and very high speed and long distance wireless communication.

GLOSSARY

Access point—An RF transceiver that provides access to a WLAN or wired LAN from a Wi-Fi-enabled wireless device.

Blogging—Posting messages to a weblog.

Bluetooth—A short-range RF wireless technology for connecting handheld devices and laptops to other devices.

Circuit-switched network—A single dedicated circuit or path for each call from sender to receiver.

Cognitive Radio—A future technology that provides for automatic radio spectrum sharing between multiple wireless service providers.

Collaborative work—Office work completed by teams of coworkers.

Converged network—An IP network that transmits data, voice, and video.

Discussion group—An online forum in which participants discuss or receive information on a specific topic.

Electronic perception technologies—Technologies that use sensor chips and image processing software to allow electronic devices to "see" and respond to nearby objects.

E-mail—Electronic mail; messages sent from one computer to another over an IP network.

E-mail address—The destination address of an e-mail message consisting of three parts: the recipient's identifying name or nickname, the @ sign, and the name of the mail server where the recipient's electronic mailbox is located.

E-mail client—Software used to receive, retrieve, send, create, reply to, and save e-mail messages.

Fax machine—Also called a facsimile machine; a copier that scans a document containing text or pictures and treats both as an image, then sends the image over telephone lines to another fax machine, a computer, or a printer.

Fax spam—Unwanted and unsolicited fax messages.

Fiber-optic network—Light and glass fibers used to transmit high-speed electronic messages and data.

GPRS—General Packet Radio Service; a packet-switching wireless communications technology that enables high-speed Internet connections and data transmissions.

Groupware—Software that assists workplace collaboration.

Hotspot—A public location that provides a wireless access point.

Hypertext Markup Language—Also called HTML; the markup language used to create and edit Web pages.

Instant message—An electronic message sent to two or more people connected to the network at the same time.

Intelligent agent software—Software that acts on behalf of its user.

Internet conference—A conference hosted over an IP network that may use video, audio, and shared resources and is attended by two or more persons

IP network—See packet-switched network and TCP/IP.

IP telephony—See Voice over Internet Protocol (VoIP).

Mail server—The computer on an IP network that hosts electronic mailboxes and temporarily stores incoming e-mail.

Mailing lists—E-mail newsletters sent to subscribers.

Multifunction machine—Machines that combine fax, copier, scanning, and printer functions.

Newsgroup—A virtual bulletin board.

Packet—A small piece of a data or voice message sent across an IP network.

Packet-switched network—A network that transmits data and voice in small packets. Multiple users can send their messages across the network at one time.

Pager—Small portable messaging device used for one-way messaging over a paging service network or two-way messaging over a wireless messaging service or cellular phone network.

Pharming—The manipulation of a legitimate website address to direct unsuspecting users to a fraudulent copy of the site designed to gather personal information for criminal purposes.

Phishing—Online scams designed to gather sensitive information, such as credit card numbers or Social Security numbers.

Plain Old Telephone Service (POTS)—See Public Switched Telephone Network.

Projection keyboard—Virtual QWERTY keyboard projected on a flat service and used for complex data input on handheld wireless devices.

Public Switched Telephone Network (PSTN)—A traditional circuit-switched telephone network.

Shared workspace—A virtual work area hosted on a Web server used by workers collaborating on a task or project.

Softphone—Application software that allows IP telephony from a computer or PDA.

Spam—Unwanted and unsolicited electronic messages.

Spam over Internet Telephony (SPIT)—Unwanted and unsolicited voice messages sent over an IP network.

Spam via IM—Also called spim; spam sent via instant messaging.

TCP/IP—the Transmission Control Protocol/Internet Protocol rules for transmitting data over a packet-switched network, also called an IP network.

Telecommunication—The electronic transmission of text, data, voice, video, and images from one location to another.

Video conference—A live, interactive conference that uses telephony and video technology to bring geographically diverse participants together.

Voice mail—Voice messages left in an electronic mailbox.

Voice over Internet Protocol (VoIP)—Also called IP telephony; voice messages sent over an IP network.

Web conference—A conference hosted over an IP network; participants may need software downloaded from the conference service provider or may only need a Web browser and an Internet connection to participate.

Web-based forums—Messages posted via a Web browser.

Webcam—A video camera that connects to a computer.

Weblog—Also called a blog; a Web-based journal to which participants post their opinions, thoughts, and feelings.

White board—Virtual shared writing area.

Wi-Fi—Wireless fidelity; general name for the IEEE 802.11 family of wireless networking protocols.

Wiki—A website or a group of Web pages whose content can be added to, edited, or deleted by anyone with a Web browser.

WiMax—A future wireless technology that provides long-range wireless broadband.

Wireless LAN (WLAN)—A LAN that users connect to with Wi-Fi enabled devices.

CHECKPOINT

Check your understanding of these terms by completing DCD5-a on the Data CD.

DISCUSSION ITEMS

These discussion items provide an opportunity to test your understanding of the chapter through written responses and/or discussion with your classmates and your instructor.

1. Compare how voice is transmitted over a PSTN with how voice and data are transmitted over an IP network.

2. Discuss how converged networks are changing the telecommunication marketplace.

3. Explain why workplace collaboration tools accessed over an IP network are so important in today's workplace.

4. Why is it important for an administrative professional to use good call management skills?

5. Discuss how wireless technologies are changing the workplace.

CRITICAL THINKING CASE

What a busy Friday! Ms. Portosky is traveling on business so you are taking her calls as well as yours. An angry client just called Ms. Portosky and was upset because her call to accounting to solve a billing problem was put on hold for 10 minutes without anyone getting back to her. She finally hung up and called back to complain to Ms. Portosky.

The quarterly sales meeting is around the corner and you must have the agenda, the sales report, and Ms. Portosky's presentation ready for her review when she returns on Monday. An important fax message containing confidential sales data from Marlene, one of the account executives, has not been received. When you call Marlene, she tells you that she faxed the sales data over an hour ago. You go to the fax machine, but no fax. Judy, the receptionist, finally finds the fax message. Someone walking by the fax machine picked up the fax message and dropped it on Judy's desk.

Betty in accounting keeps sending you instant messages about a dinner party she is planning. Attached to her last instant message is a file containing recipes

that she downloaded from a website. You check your and Ms. Portosky's e-mail and find that Tom in marketing has again forwarded an e-mail chain letter to everyone in the office. Julie in the mail room has sent you a message containing an offensive joke. Several spam advertisements fill your inbox. You are getting frustrated because you just can't get anything done!

Questions to ask:

► What administrative management problems did this situation expose? Think carefully: this situation exposed several different problems that must be addressed.

► How should you personally handle the frustrations caused by these problems?

► Should you discuss the problems with Ms. Portosky on her return or should you just ignore them?

► How can these problems be minimized or prevented in the future?

RESPONSES TO SELF-CHECK

A

The most appropriate answers are as follows:

1. Voice messages over a circuit-switched network use a single dedicated circuit for the duration of the call. No one but the parties to the call share the circuit for the duration of the call.

2. Converged networks—voice, data, and video on the same network—are providing new marketing possibilities for traditional telecommunication companies. New telecommunication providers are entering the marketplace. Traditional telecommunication companies are merging with companies from other industries providing additional distribution channels for products and services.

B

The most appropriate answers are as follows:

1. E-mail is inexpensive, fast, convenient, and can be used to transfer files across the network.

2. Wikis and weblogs both involve Web pages and a Web browser. Wiki content can be added to, edited, or deleted by anyone using a Web browser. A weblog is a chronological list of individual postings. A weblog may be monitored and postings edited to remove inappropriate content.

3. A shared workspace is a virtual room or work area in which team members can share information and other resources needed to complete a specific project.

C

The most appropriate answers are as follows:

1. Yes	3. Yes	5. Yes	7. Yes	9. No
2. No	4. No	6. Yes	8. No	10. Yes

WORKPLACE PROJECTS

PROJECT 5-1 PREPARE AND PRESENT A REPORT

Explore the present and future of telecommunication technologies (Objective 1)

Using your word processing or presentation software, create a report or presentation that describes the following stages of the telecommunication revolution:

1. Circuit-switched networks

2. Packet-switched networks

3. VoIP

4. Fiber-optic networks

5. Wireless broadband

Submit your report to your instructor. With permission, present your report or presentation to your classmates.

PROJECT 5-2 WRITE ABOUT WORKPLACE TOOLS

Define workplace collaboration tools and explain how they are used (Objective 2)

Use the instructions provided on DCD5-02 to define workplace collaboration tools.

PROJECT 5-3 WRITE POLICIES

Define workplace collaboration tools and explain how they are used (Objective 2)

Explain the importance of e-mail use policies (Objective 4)

Working with a team of two or three classmates, draft an e-mail and instant message use policy for JWay Nu-Systems Tech. Use your word processing software to formalize the policy document. Submit the document to your instructor. You may use DCD5-03 to create your formal policy document.

PROJECT 5-4 WRITE A MEMORANDUM

Describe how to protect against spam, phishing, pharming, and spim (Objective 3)

Write an interoffice memorandum from Ms. Portosky to all employees discussing the threat of spam, phishing, pharming, and spim and how employees should protect themselves and the company. You may use DCD5-04 to create the memorandum.

PROJECT 5-5 PREPARE AND PRESENT A REPORT FROM RESEARCH

Describe telephone communications over PSTN, VoIP, and handheld devices (Objective 5)

Working with a classmate, use your word processor or presentation software to create a report or presentation containing:

1. Illustrations of voice communications over PSTN and VoIP. Use the software's drawing tools and pictures to create your illustrations. If necessary, check the software's Help feature to answer questions you may have about using the drawing features or inserting pictures.

2. Information on how voice technologies are used with PDAs, smartphones, and cell phones. Use Google (www.google.com) to research voice technologies and wireless handheld devices.

Submit your report to your instructor. With permission, present your report or presentation to your classmates.

PROJECT 5-6 WRITE A MEMORANDUM FROM RESEARCH

Define workplace collaboration tools and explain how they are used (Objective 2)

Use Google (www.google.com), Yahoo! (www.yahoo.com), and WiseNut (www.wisenut.com) to research the latest fax and multifunction machines. Then write a memorandum to Ms. Portosky recommending one of the machines for the office. Include in your recommendations new fax security procedures. You may use DCD5-06 to create the memorandum.

PROJECT 5-7 PREPARE PROFESSIONAL DEVELOPMENT PLAN

Explain the importance of professional call management skills (Objective 6)

You will work with a team of classmates on this activity. But first, using your word processing software, create a document and save it as PGP5-7. Title your document "My Plan for Improving My Professional Call Management Skills." Use the document to create a checklist of call management skills discussed in this chapter. Print and distribute a copy of the checklist to each team member.

Then, working with a classmate who assumes the role of a caller, and you the role of administrative professional, use a phone and simulate separate scenarios. Practice each of the listed skills. Allow other team members to indicate on their copy of the handout which skills need more practice. Switch roles and take turns until everyone in the team has been evaluated.

Review the checklist comments and practice those skills that need improvement. Repeat the activity in two or three weeks. How have your call management skills improved? What skills still need improvement? Record your answers in your document.

COMMUNICATION POWER

Use DCD5-b to assist you in improving your grammar skills.

ASSESSMENT OF CHAPTER OBJECTIVES

Now that you have completed the chapter and the projects, take a few minutes to review the chapter learning objectives. For your convenience, the objectives are repeated here. Did you accomplish these objectives? If you were unable to accomplish the objectives, give your reasons for not doing so; be specific and concise. Your instructor may prefer that your answers be submitted to him or her. If so, DCD5-c contains the Assessment of Chapter Objectives. Complete the Assessment of Chapter Objectives; submit your results to your instructor.

1. Explore the present and future of telecommunication technologies.   Yes ☐   No ☐

_____

_____

_____

_____

2. Define workplace collaboration tools and explain how they are used.   Yes ☐   No ☐

_____

_____

_____

_____

3. Describe how to protect against spam, phishing, pharming, and spim.   Yes ☐   No ☐

_____

_____

_____

_____

4. Explain the importance of e-mail use policies.   Yes ☐   No ☐

_____

_____

_____

_____

5. Describe telephone communications over PSTN, VoIP, and handheld devices.   Yes ☐   No ☐

_____

_____

_____

_____

6. Explain the importance of professional call management skills.   Yes ☐   No ☐

_____

_____

_____

_____

PART II: WORKPLACE TECHNOLOGIES

Integrated Project

Note: You are to work in teams of three on this project.

Ms. Portosky thinks that it is time to upgrade the employees' computers. More and more of JWay's employees will be traveling on business both domestically and internationally to help with the expansion of the business into the Pacific Rim. Because of the increased need for communication mobility and computing portability, Ms. Portosky wants to replace all the employees' desktop computers with either laptops or convertible tablet PCs.

Additionally, she wants all of the account executives, the senior management staff, and the administrative assistants to have a new handheld communication device, either a PDA or smartphone—she does not know which is best. Ms. Portosky wants to present the new equipment recommendations to the JWay management committee at its next meeting. She has assigned you to lead a workplace team to research the new equipment and make recommendations. You have invited an account executive and a computer technician from the IT department to work with you on the project.

Ms. Portosky has provided the team with the following guidelines. Each handheld device should cost no more than $500 and have features that support:

- Making incoming and outgoing phone calls both domestically and internationally.
- Maintaining an address book.
- Maintaining a schedule of appointments.
- Sending text messages.
- Accessing the Internet and company website and sending e-mail.
- Connecting with other devices such as PDAs, laptops, and printers.

Each laptop or convertible tablet PC should cost no more than $2,000. Required features include:

- A minimum 40-GB hard disk.
- A CDR/W/DVD-ROM drive.
- Windows® operating system.
- Both wireless and nonwireless networking capability.

Any other available features for laptops, convertible tablet PCs, and handheld devices are acceptable as long as the cost does not exceed Ms. Portosky's suggested maximums.

Effective workplace collaboration is an important part of completing this project. Team members should use all available workplace collaboration tools including (but not limited to) telephone, e-mail, and instant messaging to coordinate efforts. Team members should use a variety of Web search tools to research features and pricing for laptops, convertible tablet PCs, and handheld devices. As part of their research, team members may choose to visit offline stores that sell these items.

Use appropriate application software to organize the research, create the reports and memorandums, and schedule team meetings and activities. Remember to cite all report references in proper footnote format. If you have questions about proper citation formats, check a reference source or follow the citation format provided by your instructor.

Before beginning the project, team members should determine standard file naming rules for all team documents. Then each team member must create an appropriately named electronic folder in which to store his or her documents. Every team member should follow the file naming and folder naming rules established by the team. Then one backup copy of all documents must be created and the backup media submitted to your instructor with all printed documents.

Part 1: Create Spreadsheet, Report, and Compose Memo

Research handheld communication devices (PDAs and smartphones) and organize the research in a spreadsheet. Then create a report comparing features and price for the team's top three choices. Write an interoffice memorandum advising Ms. Portosky of the team's first choice. Remember to give the reasons for the choice. Attach the spreadsheet and report to the memorandum and turn it in to your instructor. Use DCDIP2-1 for your memorandum.

Part 2: Create Spreadsheet, Report, and Compose Memo

Research laptop and convertible tablet PCs and record the research in a spreadsheet. Then prepare a report comparing features and price for the team's top three laptop and top three convertible tablet PC choices. Compose an interoffice memorandum advising Ms. Portosky of the team's first choice for each. Remember to give the reasons for the choices. Attach the spreadsheet and report to the memorandum and submit it to your instructor. Use DCDIP2-2 for your memorandum.

Part 3: Create a Slide Presentation

Using presentation software, create a slide show for Ms. Portosky to use at the next management meeting. The presentation should illustrate the new equipment recommendations, including features and pricing. Print the slides and attach them to an interoffice memorandum to Ms. Portosky. Use DCDIP2-3 for your memorandum.

Part 4: Create a Time Log

Each team member must keep a record of his or her time spent on Parts 1–3 of this project in a time log. Follow the guidelines in Chapter 3 for a time log. The time log should also contain a notation of the types of workplace collaboration tools the team used. All time logs should be submitted to your instructor attached to a single memorandum that lists the names of each team member, the total amount of time he or she spent on the project, and a paragraph discussing the effectiveness of the workplace collaboration tools used. Use DCDIP2-4 for your memorandum.

Janet K. Radosevich, CPS/CAP
Sr. Administrative Assistant
Fisher Controls International—Valve Division
Emerson Process Management
Marshalltown, Iowa

SPOTLIGHT *on Success*

TO WHAT DO I ATTRIBUTE MY SUCCESS?

My success as an administrative professional has come from many sources. My parents were advocates of receiving a good education and maintaining good grades while promoting involvement in extracurricular activities throughout my high school years. My high school business teacher set extremely high standards of excellence, which influenced my administrative professional career. I attended college for one year in the General Secretarial Program at Mankato State College to develop the technical skills needed to obtain a position in the administrative professional field. During the past 30 years in the workforce, I have worked for many supervisors who have shown their confidence and trust in my abilities to achieve the success I have attained. Below are attributes I have that helped me to succeed.

1. Adaptable: manage multiple projects and change with a minimum amount of stress.

2. High degree of integrity: making daily ethical choices for myself, my executive, and company.

3. Commitment to education and training: computer skills, leadership, and other continuing education through seminars; continue to learn new skills on the job. Without the drive to keep learning and growing, a skill set becomes obsolete. The difference between success and mediocrity is to never stop learning.

4. Expect to be treated as an equal.

5. Flexibility: work well with others. Have concern and interest for others.

6. People skills: at ease with myself and others; not defensive.

7. Commitment and loyalty to the people and the organization for whom I work.

8. Competent and accountable for actions.

9. Proactive: anticipate the needs of my executives and what is to be accomplished.

10. Drive and ambition to be the best.

WHAT IS MY BACKGROUND?

My background includes business classes in high school, involvement in speech contests, and participation in 4-H. At Mankato State College, I was awarded the One-Year General Secretary of the Year award upon completion of my certificate program.

TO WHAT PROFESSIONAL ORGANIZATIONS DO I BELONG?

To keep myself involved in my profession, I joined the International Association of Administrative Professionals®

Chapter 6:	*Written Communication*
Chapter 7:	*Records Management*
Chapter 8:	*Presentations*

(IAAP) and achieved the Certified Professional Secretary® (CPS) rating in 1995 and the Certified Administrative Professional® (CAP) rating in 2001, and continue to maintain my certification. I am actively involved in IAAP and have served on various committees and as president of the Iowa-Nebraska Division in 2003. Culminating my presidency, I received the following international awards: Outstanding Division President in Membership, Outstanding Division President in New Chapter Development, and Distinguished Division President. I give credit to my chapter presidents and members who helped me achieve success during my year as division president.

I have always believed in improving my skills and have taken advantage of numerous professional development seminars including time management, diversity training, ethics training, conflict management, teamwork, listening skills, and leadership through my involvement in IAPP.

WHAT IS THE MOST FUN PART OF MY JOB?

I like the variety of managing multiple projects at once. It is interesting, exciting, and challenging. I produce presentations given by top management to executives as well as employees. Some days I feel I "live" in PowerPoint®, but I thoroughly enjoy developing meaningful presentations with my executive. I enjoy coordinating travel and communicating with administrative assistants and executives throughout the world as my supervisors travel to our many locations worldwide. I enjoy being an innovative thinker and sharing my positive "whatever it takes" attitude with my supervisors and coworkers.

I plan and coordinate the logistics for several large meetings throughout the year with 10 to 12 people preparing individual presentations. We have various reviews before the final meeting. I coordinate room setup, computer/projector/screen setup, preparation of meeting books, and load presentations to various computer files for screen viewing. These meetings are time-consuming, but very rewarding when the finished product is presented.

WHAT ARE SOME OF THE DEMANDING PARTS OF MY JOB?

Some of the demanding portions of my job include trying to coordinate various events and meetings, scheduling/canceling/rescheduling meetings, and keeping up with the day-to-day activities in my position. Constant change and not having time to accomplish everything I would like to in a given day can be stressful. I work for great executives—they expect exceptional work, and I want to deliver exceptional work. Having high expectations to achieve this can be stressful.

WHAT ARE MY HOBBIES/INTERESTS?

My hobbies and interests include many fitness activities. In warm weather, I enjoy being outdoors and playing golf and taking four-mile walks. Cold-weather activities include snow skiing, aerobics, yoga, weight training, and cycling classes. I enjoy traveling, reading, cooking/baking, and counted-cross stitch.

WHAT ADVICE WOULD I GIVE SOMEONE JUST BEGINNING IN THIS FIELD?

The advice I would give to someone beginning this field is to:

1. Attend college, either two or four-year course work to broaden your knowledge.

2. Join a professional organization. If you want to be considered a professional, join a professional group or organization and be an active and involved participant.

3. Study successful people: what choices have they made to reach a level of success?

4. Embrace lifelong learning: read publications on your profession, and refresh professional certifications and credentials. Read newspapers/magazines every day.

5. Control attitude: be optimistic toward yourself and others, and success will be achieved.

6. Write and speak in a simple, straight-forward manner.

7. Admit mistakes.

8. Network with peers to help accelerate learning and elevate expertise.

JANET RADOSEVICH—CASE STUDY

My case study is a situation that took place 13 years ago when my company was going through major restructuring and downsizing at our local facility.

I was notified that my employment with the company would be ending as we were downsizing. Although I had been employed as an administrative assistant at the company for 14 years, I did not have sufficient seniority to maintain my employment. It was communicated to me that I had the option of severance or lay off with recall rights. An office person, who was not a trained administrative assistant, was chosen to replace me. It was thought that she would be able to handle the duties of this position.

Within two weeks, I was asked to stay on and train my replacement for the next several months. I was working for a vice president who had responsibilities for our worldwide locations. After several months of training, this individual was not able to handle the entire workload, and I was given a desk nearby to work with her. At that time, I was asked to take on additional responsibilities that I had not handled previously, while continuing to work with my replacement.

I continued to demonstrate a positive attitude when assisting my coworker with questions or any problems she encountered. I have always been very detail oriented, and believe my supervisor realized that this was an important asset needed to support him in his position.

With my additional responsibilities, I was asked to learn new presentation software and was able to share that knowledge with other coworkers who later needed to use the software. I continued to show confidence in what I was asked to do and took a proactive approach in assisting my peers when questions were asked. I focused on my strengths of knowledge, hard work, and positive attitude. I continued to build working relationships throughout my company, and refrained from any negativity.

How would you have handled this very sensitive situation? See page 432 for the case solution.

CHAPTER 6

WRITTEN COMMUNICATION

Learning Objectives

1. Choose the appropriate written communication method.
2. Identify the steps in planning and organizing written materials.
3. Produce effective instant messages, e-mail, memorandums, and letters.
4. Research and write a report.
5. Observe appropriate ethical and legal practices in writing.

Comstock Images

> WRITTEN COMMUNICATION—
IMPORTANT IN THE WORKPLACE

Is written communication as important in the workplace today as it was ten years ago?

The answer is a resounding *yes*. In fact, because e-mail is a major written communication vehicle in today's office, administrative assistants probably write more than in the past. Many administrative professionals spend a greater amount of time writing e-mails to their coworkers than they do telephoning their coworkers. Written communication in all of its forms remains extremely important. Ineffective written communication costs the organization greatly, often resulting in misunderstandings among coworkers and thus increased time on tasks and greater personnel costs, loss of customers, and resultant loss of profits.

Organizations produce numerous types of written communication each day. In addition to e-mail, office workers use instant messaging via the Internet and write memorandums, letters, and reports. Effectively written correspondence brings not only business but also goodwill for the organization, while ineffectively written correspondence can cost the organization greatly in unhappy clients and customers. The costs include, but are not limited to, loss of business, profits, customer satisfaction, and goodwill. These costs over time can bankrupt a for-profit organization or render ineffective a not-for-profit organization. Consider these examples of poorly written communications:

▶ A software company produces an instruction manual that is not readable for 80 percent of its customers (as a result, the software company loses business).
▶ A recent graduate sends a letter of application to a company that has three grammatical errors in it. (The poorly written letter results in the individual not being considered for an interview and thus losing the chance for a job with the organization.)

E-mail is a major written communication vehicle in today's workplace.

▶ A graphic designer puts the wrong price ($500 lower than the real price) on a sales brochure that was sent to 10,000 prospective customers; 3,000 customers buy the product at the price given in the brochure. (The company loses $1,500,000 due to one pricing mistake.)

As you can readily see from each of these examples, there is a cost to the company or individual, such as loss of business, loss of a job prospect, and/or loss of money.

Ineffective and/or inaccurate writing increases the liability and risks of any organization. As an administrative professional, a major portion of your job is to produce correspondence that is both effective in tone and content and free of grammatical and/or factual errors. This chapter will help you attain the necessary skills; practice will help you perfect these skills.

> CHOOSING A COMMUNICATION METHOD

As an administrative professional, you may be faced with determining the type of communication medium that you use to deliver your message. The five types of written communication discussed in this chapter are not new to you; they are e-mail, instant messages, memorandums, letters, and reports. You have probably keyed a number of these types of messages, starting with your beginning keyboarding course and continuing throughout your program of study. However, in this course, your task becomes more than keying the document. You will be responsible for selecting the most appropriate communication medium for the task, as well as writing and producing the document.

When choosing the most appropriate communication medium, there are a number of factors that must be considered, including (but not limited to):

1. Your purpose/objective for writing.

2. Your target audience.

3. The length of your message.

4. How quickly the information needs to be disseminated.

5. The cost of distribution, along with the budget available.

> E-mail

The number of people around the world using e-mail regularly is projected to grow to 850 million by the end of 2008, with the number of messages sent daily projected to be 147.5 billion.[1] Figure 6-1 depicts this growth. With the number of e-mails continually escalating, it is extremely important that they be well written. Have you ever not opened an e-mail because the subject did not appear to be something you were interested in? Or, the person(s) writing the e-mail were unknown to you? Many of us would say that we are in information overload today because of the amount of written information that we receive in numerous ways. Consequently, if we expect our e-mails to be read, we must take care to write them effectively, paying attention to all details, including the subject line.

Guidelines

Although e-mail is less formal than an office memorandum or letter, there are a number of guidelines that need to be followed.

---

[1]"ITFacts," CNET Networks, Inc., 2004, <http://www.itfacts.biz/index.php?id+C20_8_1> (accessed April 29, 2004).

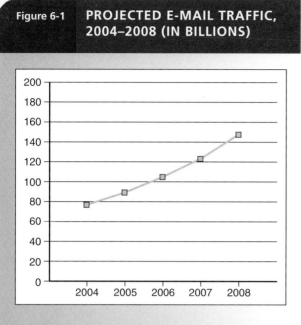

Figure 6-1 PROJECTED E-MAIL TRAFFIC, 2004–2008 (IN BILLIONS)

Source: "691 e-mail users globally," <http://www.itfacts.biz/index.php?id=C20_8_1> (accessed May 5, 2005).

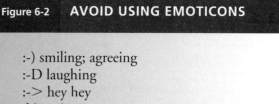

Figure 6-2 AVOID USING EMOTICONS

:-) smiling; agreeing
:-D laughing
:-> hey hey
:'-) crying
:* kisses
^5 high five
>:-< angry
(:1 egghead
:0 shocked

devoid of body language). Figure 6-2 shows several emoticons.

Ethics

Because of the large number of e-mails sent daily from businesses and organizations, management has found it necessary to develop codes of ethics. Figure 6-3 shows a portion of the code of ethics for JWay Tech. Listed here are a number of statements that, when followed, help ensure ethical behavior in writing and sending e-mails.

1. Do not send personal e-mail from your office computer. When people send personal e-mail to your office, let them know politely that you cannot receive it. You might say, "I would love to hear from you, but please send any personal e-mail to my home. I cannot receive it at the office."

2. Do not use e-mail to berate or reprimand an individual.

3. Do not use e-mail to fire someone.

4. Do not forward junk mail or chain letters; both are inappropriate in a work setting.

5. Do not engage in **bombing** (repeatedly sending an e-mail message to a particular address at a specific site), **spamming** (sending e-mail to hundreds or thousands of users or lists that expand to many users),[2] or **spoofing** (e-mail that appears to have originated from one source when it actually was sent from another source).[3] Most organizations have a policy against such usage. One study found

▶ Always use the subject line provided on the e-mail form. This line should be concise yet give enough information so that the receiver knows the purpose of the message at a glance.

▶ Think through the purpose of the e-mail before you begin writing.

▶ Keep the message short. E-mail should not be longer than one screen. Readers become frustrated when they must scroll from screen to screen and then scroll back to reread something.

▶ Edit and proofread carefully. Do not send an e-mail that contains inaccuracies or incorrect grammar. Most e-mail programs have spelling and grammar checks.

▶ Use complete sentences.

▶ Capitalize and punctuate properly. Do not key in all capitals.

▶ Assume that any message you send is permanent.

▶ Single-space your message.

▶ Be cautious when using humor or sarcasm. Since electronic communication is devoid of body language, the slightest hint of sarcasm could be misinterpreted.

▶ Avoid using **emoticons** (faces produced by the Internet counterculture in answer to e-mail being

---

[2] Cert Coordination Center, Carnegie Mellon University, 2002, "Email Bombing and Spamming," <http://www.cert.org/tech_tips/email_bombing_spamming.html> (accessed May 5, 2005).

[3] Cert Coordination Center, Carnegie Mellon University, 2002, "Spoofed/Forged Email," <http://www.cert.org/tech_tips/email_spoofing, html> (accessed May 5, 2005).

that spam accounted for 77 percent of all e-mail traffic in 2004.[4]

6. Do not use e-mail to send information that might involve legal action.

7. Remember that even if you delete e-mail, it may not actually be deleted. Some organizations make backup tapes of all electronic files. Think carefully before writing an e-mail.

8. Do not respond to unsolicited e-mail.

9. Do not include credit card numbers in e-mail messages. It is possible to intercept e-mail in transit. An unscrupulous individual can steal and use someone else's credit card number.

Etiquette

Just as it is important to observe ethical rules in sending and receiving e-mail, so is it important to use proper etiquette. Figure 6-4 lists a number of important e-mail etiquette tips. Read it carefully and observe proper etiquette as you write e-mails.

▷ Instant Messaging

Instant messaging (IM) is a form of e-mail that "allows the user to communicate in real time with other users who have the same instant messaging application. Instant messaging includes **presence technology,** which means that when users launch the application, they can see who on their contact list is online. Icons on the contact list also indicate who is online but not available for instant messaging, and whether or not the contact is using a mobile device."[5]

Figure 6-3	PORTION OF CODE OF ETHICS FOR JWAY NU-SYSTEMS TECH

▸ Do not engage in e-mail bombing, spamming, or spoofing.

▸ Do not forward an unsolicited e-mail that has been sent to you.

▸ Do not send personal e-mail messages to anyone within the company or outside the company.

▸ Do not engage in harassment via e-mail.

▸ Do not use someone else's e-mail to send messages.

▸ Do not forward chain letters via e-mail.

Figure 6-4	E-MAIL ETIQUETTE TIPS

▸ Be concise and to the point.

▸ Answer all questions; anticipate and pre-empt further questions by giving additional information that is needed.

▸ Use proper spelling, grammar, and punctuation.

▸ Answer swiftly.

▸ Do not attach unnecessary files.

▸ Do not write in CAPITALS.

▸ Read the e-mail before you send it.

▸ Do not copy a message or attachment without permission.

▸ Do not use e-mail to discuss confidential information.

▸ Use a meaningful subject.

▸ Use active instead of passive voice when writing.

▸ Avoid long sentences.

▸ Do not send or forward e-mails containing libelous, defamatory, offensive, racist, or obscene remarks.

▸ Keep language gender neutral.[6]

▸ Avoid sending messages when you are angry. Give yourself time to settle down and think about the situation before you send or reply to an e-mail in anger. Take a walk around your office; drink a cup of hot tea to soothe your nerves.

---

[4]Ibid. (accessed April 30, 2004).

[5]"Learn it: Instant Messaging in the Enterprise," April 6, 2005, <http://searchcio.techtarget.com/sDefinition/0..sid19_gci934583.00.html.> (accessed April 29, 2005).

[6]Email Etiquette, 2001–2004, <http://www.emailreplies.com> (accessed July 18, 2005).

According to projections, there will be 670 million instant messaging users around the world by 2008. Globally, in 2004, only 20 percent of corporate users thought IM was a valid communication tool for business. It is projected that by 2008 this number will quadruple to 80 percent. However, America is ahead of the world in its acceptance of IM as a viable business tool. In 2004, 85 percent of Americans considered instant messaging a viable business tool.[7] It is also estimated that 90 percent of American businesses today are already engaging in some level of instant messaging.[8]

The pros, cons, and writing tips of instant messaging include the following:

Pros

1. Instant real-time communication

2. Enhanced customer service

3. Improved employee productivity

4. Greater accountability of off-site employees through the ability to check to see if employees are online

5. Cost savings on long distance and travel

6. Elimination of phone tag

7. Compatibility with wireless handhelds and other portable devices

Cons

1. Content concerns, with employees possibly using IM as a tool for casual conversation

2. Governmental and industry regulations governing IM content, privacy, and retention

3. Monitoring and retention headaches, with business records that must be retained for legal purposes

4. Decrease in employee productivity as chat increases

5. Assumption of false identities and appropriation of corporate domain names by nonemployees or ex-employees[9]

Writing Tips

1. Use IM for more than chats.

2. Keep personal information to a minimum.[10]

3. Do not include jokes in correspondence.

4. Do not use sexual innuendos.

5. Do not use obscene language.[11]

Spotlight on INSTANT MESSAGING

Never use instant messaging in the office for personal conversations.

With both e-mail and instant messaging, it is important to take precautions against virus infections by using anti-virus software. Research has shown that IM and Web-based attacks increased by 300 percent in the first quarter of 2005, compared to the last quarter of 2004. It is also anticipated that by 2008, 450 million people will be using an IM product, with few businesses prepared to handle the increase in usage.[12] In addition to viruses, today we have spyware, which is defined as "any application that makes potentially unwanted changes to your computer while collecting information about your computer activities."[13] Spyware can come bundled with freeware or shareware, through e-mail or instant messaging, or by someone with access to your computer. Spyware is not only difficult to detect, but it is also difficult to remove.[14]

It is important to guard against both viruses and spyware by having anti-virus and spyware protection programs on your computer, as well as a firewall.

---

[7]"WWW, 670 mln instant messaging users by 2008," April 6, 2004, <http://www.itfacts.biz/index.php?id=P1159> (accessed April 29, 2005).

[8]Harry Wessel, "IM: Two Little Letters Equal a Big Help to Some Businesses," *Orlando Sentinel*, June 25, 2003, G1.

[9]Nancy Flynn, *Instant Messaging Rules: A Business Guide to Managing, Policies, Security, and Legal Issues for Safe IM Communication* (New York: American Management Association, 2004), pp. 41–44.

[10]"Using IM: Know the lingo (and 4 other tips)," <http://www.microsoft.com/smallbusiness/issues/technology/communications/using_im_kn> (accessed May 17, 2005).

[11]Nancy Flynn, loc.cit., pp. 81–87.

[12]Science and Technology, "Talking Tech: IM Riding Along the Information Superhighway—Avoid Being Road Kill," <http://www.richmond.com/business/output.aspx?ID=3605918&Vertical_ID=5&tier=2&position=5> (accessed May 7, 2005).

[13]"Spyware Defined," *Australian IT,* February 2004, <http://www.webroot.com/spywareinformation/spywaredefined> (accessed May 7, 2005).

[14]Ibid. (accessed May 7, 2005).

⊳ Memorandums

Although e-mail is the tool of choice for internal correspondence in most organizations, memorandums continue to have a place in the work environment. The hard-copy memorandum generally is written when the message is fairly long (more than one screen).

A memorandum usually is written in the same format throughout the organization, with a common format including these elements: *To* line, *From* line, *Date* line, and *Subject* line. In addition to the name of the individual in the *To* line, a job title may also be used, although it is not absolutely necessary. Many organizations do not use titles in memorandums. Figure 6-5 illustrates an appropriate format. When sending memorandums, specially designed envelopes are often used. These envelopes are reusable and are generally large enough that standard-size stationery can be inserted without folding.

Additional guidelines for writing memorandums include the following:

▸ If you are sending a memorandum to more than one individual, list the names in alphabetical order or by hierarchical order within the company.
▸ List c (copy), cc (courtesy copy), or pc (photocopy) recipients alphabetically or hierarchically.
▸ If you are addressing a memo to a large group of people (generally ten or more), use a generic classification, such as *Budget Committee.*

The Audience

You might think that writing an effective memorandum to your coworker is much easier than writing a letter to a customer. However, if you think so, you are not necessarily correct. Why? Here are a few reasons.

1. As a general rule, organizations today are less hierarchical. The line of authority is not as clearly drawn in many companies as in the past. Most employees may see themselves as peers rather than as subordinates.

2. Generation X (born between 1965 and 1975) and Y (born between 1976 and 1981) do not respect their elders as much as Baby Boomers (born between 1946 and 1964) did. The word of a senior employee is not necessarily taken as correct or binding; they often have to convince others that their ideas are worthwhile.

3. The pace of work is faster in general, with people being less cordial and civil to each other and with less time to spend on communication.[15]

Memo Writing Tips

Before writing a memo, get the facts. Why are you writing? What is the need? Who is your audience? What do you want your audience to do after reading the memo? Memorandums must be complete, clear, accurate, prompt, concise, courteous, and positive. In style, they are slightly more formal than an e-mail, but less formal than a letter.

When writing a memo, get to the point of the correspondence quickly. Explain the purpose of your writing. Give the facts that are needed by the recipients, but do not burden them with unnecessary details. State your needs/requests clearly, logically, and as briefly as possible. Although a memo is generally longer than an e-mail, it should not be considerably longer. Most effective memorandums can be written in one-half to one page. The tone of the memorandum is informal. The people you are writing are your coworkers. However, being informal does not mean that you are careless or negative.

Once you have completed the memorandum, proofread carefully; use your grammar and spell check. Do not assume that errors do not matter because it is an in-house document. Ask yourself if you were complete, clear, accurate, prompt, concise, courteous, and positive.

⊳ Letters

Although organizations communicate extensively with their customers, clients, and employees via telephone,

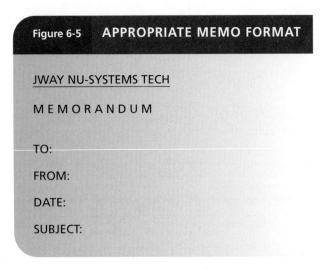

| Figure 6-5 | **APPROPRIATE MEMO FORMAT** |

JWAY NU-SYSTEMS TECH

MEMORANDUM

TO:

FROM:

DATE:

SUBJECT:

[15]Robert W. Bly, *Webster's New World Letter Writing Handbook* (Indianapolis: Wiley Publishing, Inc., 2004), p. 189.

memorandum, and e-mail, letters remain an important part of organizational communication. Letters are more formal and are the preferred method of communication when writing to current and prospective clients and customers. Additional information on writing letters is provided later in this chapter.

▷ Reports

In addition to e-mail, instant messaging, memorandums, and letters, numerous reports are prepared in the workplace. These reports may be informal ones of two or three pages, or they may be formal reports containing the table of contents, body of the report (with footnotes or endnotes), bibliography, and appendices. Because reports are often presented orally, in addition to distribution of the written copy, PowerPoint® slides can be an effective visual. Information on preparing PowerPoint slides, as well as information on report writing, is presented later in this chapter.

> PLANNING AND ORGANIZING WRITTEN MATERIALS

Inherent in writing success is the ability to organize. Effective writing is based on determining the purpose or goal to be accomplished, considering the costs, analyzing the reader/audience, gathering the appropriate information, organizing the content, determining graphics, drafting the correspondence, editing, and preparing the final correspondence. An appropriate step as you plan and organize is to make an outline listing the steps you should take.

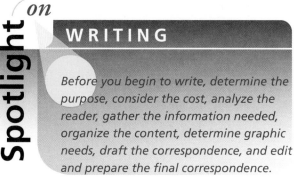

Spotlight on WRITING

Before you begin to write, determine the purpose, consider the cost, analyze the reader, gather the information needed, organize the content, determine graphic needs, draft the correspondence, and edit and prepare the final correspondence.

▷ Determine the Purpose or Goal

Why am I writing this letter or report? What is the objective? What do I hope to accomplish? Business messages generally have one of three primary objectives: to inform the reader, to request action or information, and/or to persuade the reader to take action or accept an idea. Some business messages have more than one objective. For example, the objectives may be to inform and persuade.

▷ Consider the Cost

Have you ever read a poorly written e-mail, letter, or report? The answer is probably a resounding *yes!* You have probably read an e-mail or a memorandum that failed to give necessary information concerning a meeting, such as the time and place. You may have read a letter that had a number of typographical and/or grammatical errors in it which gave you a very poor impression of the organization and the person writing the letter. You have probably read a report in which the technical terms used were well above the level of the audience's understanding. Money and time are often wasted in the writing process.

The costs of written correspondence can be considerable. For example, assume that you are an administrative assistant making $32,000 a year, which equates to slightly over $15 per hour. You spend approximately 20 hours each week in writing, for a total writing cost of approximately $300 per week, or approximately $15,600 a year. If you are not an effective and efficient writer, you can cost your organization thousands of dollars each year.

In addition to actual writing and rewriting time, there are other costs associated with ineffective writing, including unclear instructions, lack of understanding of the reader, and inadequate information to produce the document.

▷ Analyze the Reader

If your employer is not clear with you concerning who is receiving the correspondence, do not be afraid to ask. It is imperative that you get all the necessary information before you begin to write.

How much does the person receiving the document know about the subject? Is the reader familiar with technical jargon that might be used? What is the educational level of the reader? What effect will the message have on the reader? Will the reader react favorably or unfavorably to the message? How much time does the reader have? Is the reader knowledgeable about the subject and thus would prefer a short, concise memo, letter, or report? Or, does the reader need a great deal of supporting information and detail? Will the reader resist the message? Does the reader come from a different background? If so, what is that background? When the reader is from another country, you need to take additional steps to make certain that you are clear and not offending the reader in any way. Figure 6-6 lists several general principles to observe when writing for international audiences.

▷ Gather the Appropriate Information

You may check the organization's files on the subject, talk with your employer concerning any background information, and/or research the topic. Ask yourself the "W" questions: Who? What? When? Where? Why? For example, if the item you are writing is a report, here are several "W" questions you might ask.

- Who is the audience? Who will read the report?
- What level of expertise about the subject do the readers have?
- Where can I obtain the information needed for the report? Do I need to research the subject? Is information available through secondary research or must I do original research?

- What level of formality is needed? Should there be a title page? A table of contents? An executive summary?
- Who should review the draft document of the report?

▷ Organize the Content

Make an outline of the key points that should be covered; arrange your points logically. **Brainstorm** (a sudden idea; a group problem-solving technique) with others if the project is a collaborative one. Write down everything that comes to mind. Then group your ideas, getting all similar ideas together. Next determine which idea logically goes first, which second, and so on. The basic organizational structure uses a three-pronged approach. The first part of the document conveys the purpose of the correspondence. The second part supports, informs, and/or convinces the reader. The last part states the desired results, the action, or a summary of the findings.

▷ Determine Graphic Needs

If there are graphic needs, determine what they are and who is responsible for preparing the graphics.

Figure 6-6	GENERAL WRITING PRINCIPLES FOR INTERNATIONAL AUDIENCES

- Use relatively formal language. Always address the individual by his or her title. Never use first names.

- Do not use expressions unique to the United States; do not refer to events that are common only to the United States.

- Use the dictionary meanings of words; do not use slang.

- Be extremely courteous; use *thank you* and *please* often.

- Be complimentary when appropriate (but always sincere).

- Ask questions tactfully.

- Do not use humor; it may be misunderstood.

- Respect all customs of the country (social, religious, and so on).

- Learn all you can about the particular countries where you write frequent letters.

- Talk with individuals who are from the countries; read books about their customs and cultures.

- Translate correspondence into the native language of the country.

- Send business cards that are printed in the native language of the country.

- Ask nonnative English speakers who are familiar with the country to review your work.

- Avoid jargon.[16]

- Use visual clues (indentation, bullets, symbols) to increase comprehension.

- Use key terms or phrases consistently.

- Use active voice whenever possible.[17]

[16]Michael Knowles, "How to Write for the International Audience," <http://www.writethinking.net/Articles/How-to/international/international.html> (accessed May 19, 2005).
[17]"Editing for an International Audience," <http://www.editexpress.com/article_intl-audience.html> (accessed May 19, 2005).

You may be responsible if the graphics are minimal. With the graphic capabilities of computers, many graphics can be produced with relative ease. However, if the graphic needs are extensive, most large companies or organizations will have graphic design departments. If you work for a small company, you may have an outside printer do the graphics and printing. If you are preparing a report, you may have the responsibility of preparing PowerPoint® slides.

▷ Draft the Correspondence

Your goal when drafting correspondence is to write down everything you want to say in rough-draft form. Do not spend time agonizing over each word and mark of punctuation. Get your ideas down.

▷ Edit

Your next step is to edit the correspondence. Now that you have completed the draft, you need to answer the following questions as to its grammatical correctness and its readability level.

- Are the paragraphs effective?
- Is the sentence structure appropriate?
- Have you used the active voice?
- Is the readability level appropriate?

> ASSURING EFFECTIVE CORRESPONDENCE

Certain characteristics of effective correspondence are common to letters, e-mails, memorandums, and reports. As you write, you must pay careful attention to each of the following points.

▷ Concise

Conciseness in writing demands that you express the necessary information in as few words as possible. Say what you need to say without cluttering your correspondence with irrelevant information, needless words, or flowery phrases. The following principles will assist you in writing concisely.

Keep Your Sentences Short

Sentences should vary in structure and in length but on average should be no more than 15 to 20 words. Consider the following example of a sentence that is too long and then reflect on the shortened, more effective sentence.

Long sentence: *In answer to your letter of May 4, I wish to tell you how pleased and happy I am with your asking me to speak at the meeting on May 25 and to tell you that it will give me great pleasure to speak to your group.*

Short sentence: *Thank you for the invitation to speak at your meeting on May 25. I will be delighted to do so.*

Use a Simple Approach

If a shorter word will suffice, use it. You should not try to impress the reader with the breadth of your vocabulary. Your aim is to get your purpose across in a simple, concise manner. Write to express rather than impress. An effective writer is able to express complex ideas in clear, simple terms. For example, rather than writing *elucidate your meaning,* use *clarify your meaning.*

Write as You Speak

Ask yourself how you would say something if the reader were sitting next to you. A conversational tone is usually appropriate. However, such a tone may not be suitable for international correspondence. An exception to this rule might be appropriate if you have developed a relationship with the international person over a period of time. Then, the person knows and understands you. However, be very cautious about using a conversational tone even in such a case. Read Figure 6-6 on page 156 again to refresh your thoughts concerning general writing principles for international audiences.

Edit Unnecessary Words

Using too many words weakens writing. Edit unnecessary words. Study the following example containing unnecessary words and its concise rewrite:

Excessive: *At this point in time, I must tell you that our plant will be closed due to the remodeling of our facilities. We have wanted to remodel our facilities for the last five years but have been unable to do so due to the large demands of our customers for products. We have every confidence in our ability to complete the remodeling and get your order out by July 16.*

Concise: *Because our plant is being remodeled, we will ship your order on July16 by air. We appreciate your business and look forward to continuing to serve you.*

Use the Active Voice

A verb is in the active voice when the subject performs the action. A verb is in the passive voice when the subject receives the action. Review the following examples of active and passive voice.

- *The group chose the delegates.* (Active voice: "The group" performed the action.)
- *The delegates were chosen by the group.* (Passive voice: "The delegates" receive the action; the action is indirect.) The passive voice often results in wordy phrasing.

Avoid Clichés

Notice the following clichés and the improved wording.

Cliché: *At the present time*
Improved: *Now*
Cliché: *By return mail*
Improved: *Mail today*
Cliché: *Your kind letter*
Improved: Omit *kind.* People, not letters, are kind.

Here are some additional clichés that are often used. Avoid them; they should not be used in business correspondence.

- among those present
- perfect in every detail
- cool as a cucumber
- powers that be
- words are inadequate

▷ Complete

A business document is complete if it gives the reader all the information needed to achieve the intended results. To help achieve completeness, ask these W questions.

Why is the correspondence being written?
What is the goal of the correspondence?
What information is needed before writing the correspondence?
Who needs to receive the correspondence?
What information needs to be included in the correspondence?

▷ Considerate

Treat the reader with respect and friendliness; write as if you care about the reader. When dealing with people face to face, courtesy and consideration are necessary to develop and maintain goodwill. The same or even greater concern must be evident in written correspondence because only the written word conveys the message.

Never express your anger in business correspondence. You may be extremely unhappy about a situation; however, expressing it only compounds the problem. Both parties may end up yelling at each other through the written word, with little of value being accomplished. Always be considerate of the other person.

▷ Grammatically Correct

Spelling, grammar, punctuation, capitalization, and sentence structure must be correct. To assist you in catching errors, use the spelling and grammar check on your computer. However, remember that this feature does not catch all errors. For example, if you use *your* rather than *you're,* the error will not be detected. In addition to good grammar and spelling skills, you must be a good proofreader. Proofreading tips are given in Figure 6-7.

▷ Prompt

Prompt replies to messages convey to the reader that the writer and organization care. Conversely, late messages convey negative impressions. The basic promptness rules for effective, courteous replies are:

Reply to e-mail on the same day of receipt.
Reply to instant messages immediately.
Reply to memorandums within one day.
Reply to letters within three to five days.
Respond to reports within the timeline established by the cover letter or memorandum.
If there is no timeline established, reply within a week, depending on the nature and urgency of the report.

▷ Positive Tone

People hear the word *yes* more easily than they hear the word *no.* It is easier to accept a concern than it is to accept a complaint. Positivism gives the reader a favorable impression of the writer or organization. A positive tone is set by the words the writer chooses. Some words possess positive qualities while other words possess negative qualities. Figure 6-8 gives some positive and negative expressions. However, even a negative statement can be written in a positive tone. For example, "Do not litter" can be changed to "Please deposit all trash in the nearest receptacle." Figure 6-9 lists several tips for setting a positive tone in your writing.

▷ Effective Paragraphs

Effective paragraphs possess unity, coherence, and parallel construction.

- Unity. A paragraph has unity when all its sentences clarify or help support the main idea. The

Figure 6-7 PROOFREADING TIPS

▸ Use your grammar and spell check feature.

▸ Proofread your document on the screen before you print. Scroll to the beginning of the document, and use the top of the screen as a guide for your eye in reading each line.

▸ Proofread a document in three steps.

  a. General appearance and format

  b. Spelling and keyboarding errors

  c. Punctuation, word usage, and content

▸ Read from right to left for spelling and keyboarding errors.

▸ If possible, do not proofread a document right after keying it; let it sit while you perform some other task.

▸ Pay attention to dates. Do not assume that they are correct. Check to determine that Friday, May 8, is actually a Friday, for example. Check the correctness of the year.

▸ Do not overlook proofreading the date, the subject, the enclosure notation, and the names and addresses of the recipients.

▸ Use a thesaurus if you are not certain a word is appropriate.

▸ Watch closely for omissions of -ed, -ing, or -s at the end of words.

▸ Check your punctuation.

▸ Check numbers.

▸ Be consistent in format.

▸ Keep a reference manual at your desk to look up any grammar or punctuation rules you question.

Figure 6-8 POSITIVE AND NEGATIVE EXPRESSIONS

Positive	Negative
Glad	Sorry
Pleasure	Displeasure
Satisfactory	Unsatisfactory
Please let us know	You failed to let us know.
Please send your check	You neglected to send your check.
Your order will be shipped	I hate to inform you that your order has not been shipped.

sentence that contains the main idea of a paragraph is called the **topic sentence.** In this paragraph, the topic sentence is at the beginning. However, it may also be at the end of the paragraph. The point to remember is that the topic sentence helps the writer stay focused on the main idea of the paragraph.

▸ Coherence. A paragraph has coherence when its sentences relate to each other in content, grammatical construction, and choice of words. One method of achieving coherence is to repeat key words in a paragraph or to use certain words for emphasis. Consider the following use of repetitive words in an article in *Fortune* magazine.

Shakespeare got it wrong when his Othello said, "Who steals my purse steals trash . . . but he that filches from me my good name robs me of that which not enriches him, and makes me poor indeed." Were Othello alive today to witness the modern crime of identity theft, he might have said, "Who steals my trash steals my purse, and enriches him by filching my good name." And then the noble Moor would have set out hotly to fetch himself a shredder.[18]

Notice how effectively the writer uses the quote from Shakespeare and then repeats the quote with slight changes. Notice also how the writer uses "and" at the beginning of a sentence. The rule of never using a conjunction at the beginning of a sentence no longer holds true. As in the above paragraph, it is sometimes extremely effective to use "and" at the beginning of a sentence.

Notice in the following passage how the writer effectively uses contractions (which were once always considered inappropriate in formal writing).

---

[18]Peter Lewis, "Taking A Bite Out of Identity Theft," *Fortune,* May 2, 2005, p. 36.

Figure 6-9 TIPS FOR SETTING A POSITIVE TONE

- Ask and answer these questions

  Why am I writing this document?

  Who am I writing to and what do I want them to understand?

  What kind of tone should I use?

- Be confident

- Be courteous and sincere

- Use nondiscriminatory language; e.g., chairperson rather than chairman

- Stress the benefits for the reader

- Write at an appropriate level of difficulty for the individual or audience[19]

Then again, what's a little mustard on your shirt when a Dumpster dive might yield those missing Bank of America backup tapes containing detailed financial records. . . .[20]

> Parallel structure. Keeping items parallel helps you achieve coherence in a paragraph. **Parallelism** is created when grammatically equivalent forms are used within a sentence. Note the non-parallel construction used in the following sentence.

Superstitions are sometimes smiled at, sometimes frowned on, and also superstitions may be considered as backwoods.

Now, study the same sentence in a parallel format. Do you see how much more effective the sentence becomes?

Superstitions are sometimes smiled at, sometimes frowned at, and sometimes seen as backwoods.

▷ Error Free

In addition to being well written, correspondence must be error free—free from factual errors, keying errors, and spelling errors. In order to ensure freedom from factual errors, check your facts several times. Be certain that you have included accurate information. You might also have a knowledgeable colleague review it for errors of fact. If you know that you are a poor speller, be certain that you use spell check on your

CHECK A

Self

Determine whether the following words are spelled correctly. If they are spelled incorrectly, correct the spelling. Check your work with the responses at the end of this chapter.

1. accesible _____
2. accomodate _____
3. accurate _____
4. appearence _____
5. calendar _____
6. changeable _____
7. commitment _____
8. dilema _____
9. embarrass _____
10. exorbitant _____
11. fourty _____
12. harass _____
13. inadvertant _____

14. maintenence _____
15. milage _____
16. ninty _____
17. occasionally _____
18. parallel _____
19. perseverence _____
20. receive _____
21. separate _____
22. succeed _____
23. superintendant _____
24. transferable _____
25. withold _____

---

[19]"Tone in Business Writing," <http://owl.english.purdue.edu/handouts/pw/p_tone.html> (accessed May 10, 2005).
[20]Lewis, Loc. Cit.

computer. An incorrectly spelled word can render ineffective an otherwise well-written document. Many people associate a spelling error with sloppy work.

▷ Appropriate Reading Level

Readability is the degree of difficulty of the message. Items that contribute to a greater reading difficulty include long sentences and words with several syllables and/or very technical terms. Readability formulas such as the Gunning Fog Index and the Flesch-Kincaid Index provide readability indices. The higher the readability index, the less readable the message. As a rule, the writer should achieve a readability index of between seventh- and eleventh-grade levels for the average business reader. However, there are exceptions. If you are writing a technical report for an expert audience, you may write at the fourteenth or higher grade level. Writers must understand the background and educational level of their audience.

You can check the readability level of your document by activating the "tools" bar and then clicking on the "spelling and grammar" bar. Additionally, you can obtain word count, sentences per paragraph, words per sentence, and passive sentences from this bar. Figure 6-10 shows readability statistics available in Microsoft Word. If you are using a Macintosh computer, you may have different features on your tool bar and/or different formulas for computing readability.

Spotlight *on* **READABILITY**

Know your audience and write for their level of understanding.

> WRITING LETTERS

Letters are more formal than e-mail or memorandums. A letter represents the company to the outside public—customers, clients, and prospective customers and clients. A well-written letter can win friends and customers. Conversely, a poorly written letter can lose customers and make enemies of prospective customers. One of your tasks as an administrative professional is assisting your employer with writing effective letters or writing letters yourself for her or his signature. Here are additional suggestions for writing effective letters.

▷ Determine the Basic Purpose

Before you begin to write a letter, you must determine the basic purpose for writing. Generally, letters fall into six types:

1. Requesting information or seeking routine action
2. Providing information
3. Acknowledging information
4. Conveying negative information
5. Seeking action
6. Persuading

▷ Basic Approaches

The first three types of letters (requesting information, providing information, and acknowledging information) are letters in which the reader's reaction to the message will be favorable or neutral. The next two types of letters (conveying negative information and seeking action) are letters in which the reader's reaction may be unfavorable. These first five types of letters can be placed into one of two writing approaches—direct or indirect.

Figure 6-10 READABILITY STATISTICS

Readability Statistics ⊠

Counts
Words	16151
Characters	86718
Paragraphs	681
Sentences	1045

Averages
Sentences per Paragraph	2.5
Words per Sentence	14.6
Characters per Word	5.1

Readability
Passive Sentences	11%
Flesch Reading Ease	40.7
Flesch-Kincaid Grade Level	11.1

OK

The sixth type, persuading, uses an indirect approach with special characteristics.

Direct Approach

The **direct approach** in correspondence begins with the reason for the correspondence. The direct approach is used for positive or neutral correspondence. If you are making a request or an inquiry, state it. Continue with whatever explanation is necessary so the reader will understand the message. Close the letter with a courteous thank you for action taken or with a request for action by a specific time.

Indirect Approach

When using the **indirect approach** in correspondence, use this format: (1) Begin with an opening statement that is pleasant but neutral; (2) review the circumstances and give the negative information;

(3) close the correspondence on a pleasant and positive note. Request what action you want taken or what you plan to do. Figure 6-11 illustrates a letter using the indirect approach.

Persuasive Approach

The **persuasive approach** is used when you want to convince someone to do something or to change an indifferent or negative reader reaction. By using this approach, you can hopefully change the reader's initial negative or indifferent attitude to a positive one. Persuasive correspondence should follow these guidelines.

▶ Begin with the **you approach.** This approach requires the writer to place the reader at the center of the message. Rather than using *I* or *we,* the writer puts herself or himself in the

---

Figure 6-11 INDIRECT APPROACH LETTER

JWAY NU-SYSTEMS TECH
1510 Eastern Drive
Dallas, TX 75275-0356

October 24, 200X

Dr. Alan Mossavi
Southwestern State College
1800 Boswick Boulevard
Dallas, TX 75001-4839

Dear Alan:

Your invitation to speak at the conference on December 15 is an honor. Unfortunately, the demands on my time now are very heavy. We are opening two locations in the Pacific Rim, and I have been engaged in a significant amount of traveling to both areas. Since I would not want to accept your invitation without having adequate time to prepare, I must say no this time. However, if you need a speaker in the future, please remember me.

Have you met Rachael Stanhope, one of our extremely bright administrators, with expertise on such topics as international relations and global expansion? She is an excellent presenter. Although I have not spoken to her about your needs, I think she may be available. Her number is 214-555-4888.

Please accept my best wishes for the success of your program.

Sincerely,

Alexander R. Ramon

Alexander R. Ramon
Vice President, Corporate Development

smt

shoes of the reader and uses *you* frequently. The *you* approach involves the use of **empathy** (mentally entering into the feeling or spirit of a person). If the writer is trying to sell a product or service, she or he must look at the benefits the product or service will offer to the reader, *not the amount of the sales commission.* If the message involves something as routine as setting up a meeting, the writer must stress the benefits of the meeting to the reader. Such writing emphasizes *you* and *your* and de-emphasizes the *I, we, mine,* and *ours.*

▶ Be sincere when carrying out the *you* approach. Do not overuse it to the point of being dishonest. Your goal is not to flatter the reader; rather, your goal is to see the situation from the reader's point of view and to respond accordingly. Sincerity dictates that you be genuine. Be honest and empathic with the reader.

▶ Continue by creating interest and desire. For example, you might write: *The Effective Letter Writer is packed with powerful techniques and writing tips to help you become an effective writer.*

▶ Close by asking for the action that you seek. For example, you might write: *To order The Effective Letter Writer, complete the enclosed card. Put it in the mail today. By following our proven letter-writing techniques given in this book, you will find your writing job is not only easier but also much more productive.*

Notice how the following examples of writing from the *I-we* viewpoint have been changed to the *you* viewpoint. The changes may seem small, but the meaning and tone are quite different.

I-We Viewpoint: *We received your order for 50 laptop computers on June 8.*

You Viewpoint: *Your order for 50 laptop computers was received on June 8.*

I-We Viewpoint: *I will be glad to attend the conference.*

You Viewpoint: *Thank you for asking me to attend the conference. I am delighted to accept your invitation.*

Take a few minutes now to check your understanding of what you have learned. Rewrite the sentences in Self-Check B so they are effective. When you have finished, check your responses with those given at the end of the chapter.

▷ Edit, Proofread, and Format

Once you have written a letter, you are responsible for editing and proofreading the document. The grammar and spelling software on your computer can aid you in this job. However, the software will

Once you have a written piece of correspondence, you must carefully edit and proofread the document. You do not want any correspondence going out with an error in it.

© Digital Vision

CHECK B

Self

1. I wish to thank you for your recent order.

2. The information was presented by the Chairman of the Board, Ms. Michelle Edwards.

3. By return mail I am sending you the information you requested.

4. Since you did not respond when I requested the information for the report, I cannot furnish you a copy of the information. I was very clear in my initial communication that only participants in the study would receive a copy of it.

5. Your claim that we made an error in your bill is incorrect.

6. People's propensity to consume goods is insatiable.

not catch all errors, and certain errors noted by the software may not in fact be errors. Therefore, you must have a good command of grammar and proofread carefully. You also might ask someone else to proofread the document; it is sometimes difficult to see your own mistakes.

> PREPARING REPORTS

The administrative assistant's role in preparing reports varies. You may have the responsibility of keying the report, producing the final copies, and distributing the report to the appropriate individuals. Or, your role may involve assisting with the creation of Power-Point® visuals for the report (charts and graphs), researching, and even drafting some or all portions of the report. Figure 6-12 gives several tips for preparing PowerPoint slides.

Figure 6-12   TIPS FOR PREPARING POWERPOINT® VISUALS

- ▶ Create an outline before you begin.

- ▶ Create a title slide for the person who is giving the presentation; include the title of the presentation, the presenter's name, title, and affiliation.

- ▶ Use five or fewer words for each title.

- ▶ Use type size of 30 to 36 point for headings and at least 24 points for body copy.

- ▶ Use 20 or fewer words per slide.

- ▶ Double space between bullet points.

- ▶ Observe copyright laws.

- ▶ Use one main idea per visual.

- ▶ If using charts or graphs, label them clearly.

- ▶ Make sure visuals are in the proper sequence.[21]

Technology has opened up new opportunities for administrative professionals, with one possibility being a **virtual assistant** (work-at-home professionals who provide numerous business support services, including making appointments, laying out reports, organizing files, and so on). The virtual assistant may work for a particular organization or be self-employed. If you are a self-employed virtual assistant, you may write a **business plan** before you establish your company. Such a plan provides strategic direction for your company's ongoing activities and is also used, for example, to help you borrow money from a financial institution to begin your business. You will learn more about the world of the virtual assistant in Chapter 15. The point here is that administrative professionals may be involved in writing numerous types of reports. As a student, you need to understand the importance of developing your report writing skills. You may work for an organization or be self-employed; in either case, a comprehensive set of writing skills will be a valuable asset for you.

▷ Planning Steps

The planning steps involved in the writing of a report include the following:

- ▶ Determine the purpose of the report.
- ▶ Analyze the audience who will receive the report.
- ▶ Prepare a summary of what should be included in the report.
- ▶ Gather information for the report.
- ▶ Prepare an outline of the report.
- ▶ Draft the report.
- ▶ Prepare any necessary graphics, charts, and tables.
- ▶ Read, edit, and proofread the report.
- ▶ Prepare the executive summary and proof the entire document once again.
- ▶ Print and distribute the report.

▷ Reference Sources

Most reports involve some type of research. The research may be primary research—the collecting of original data through surveys, observations, or experiments. The research also may be secondary research—data or material that other people have discovered and reported via the Internet, books, periodicals, and various other publications.

Primary Research
If you are conducting primary research, you must decide how to gather the information. You may decide to take these steps: (1) observe situations and individuals; (2) survey or interview groups of individuals; (3) perform an experiment.

---

[21]"Tips for Preparing Your PowerPoint Presentation," <http://64.233.187.104/search?q+cache:buf0Zxnz-oJ:www.iosc.org/docs/2005_Preparing?your?plat> (accessed May 10, 2005).

Observational research involves collecting data through observations of an event or of actions. Survey research involves collecting data through some type of survey or interview. An interview is usually done in person; however, it may be done over the telephone. Sometimes **focus groups** are brought together to talk with an interviewer about their opinions of certain events or issues. In political campaigns, focus groups are often used extensively to learn the opinions of people on various issues. A survey is generally done by e-mail or mail; however, it may be administered in person also. For example, you may decide to assemble several people in your company and distribute a survey to be completed immediately. You generally get a better **response rate** (the number of people responding to a survey or questionnaire) on surveys administered in person than those done by mail.

Experimental research has generally been used in the sciences; however, it is popular with businesses also. It may involve a researcher selecting two or more sample groups and exposing them to certain treatments. For example, a business may decide to test a marketing strategy before implementing a marketing campaign. Experimental groups may be selected and the marketing strategy implemented with the group. Based on the outcome of the research, the business may proceed with the marketing strategy or modify it.

Focus groups bring together a group to discuss with an interviewer their opinions of events, products, or issues.

© Dex Image

Secondary Research

Secondary research involves using printed information available from sources such as books, periodicals, and the Internet. In the not-too-distant past, research was associated with libraries and librarians helping you find what you needed. You may still go to a brick-and-mortar library to do research (although some libraries are closing their doors due to the impact of the Internet on research). Libraries do have a number of advantages, a few of these advantages being:

1. Libraries carry a huge collection of materials that may offer considerable depth in the subject matter you are interested in researching.

2. Libraries have materials that may not be on the Internet, including historical, highly specialized, and often quite rare materials.

3. Libraries employ librarians to assist you in finding what you need. These people have degrees in library science or another equivalent field and can assist you in finding information in their own libraries as well as libraries in other U.S. or world cities.

4. Many libraries have some type of presence on the Internet; it may include only their location, hours, and general information. However, many libraries provide extensive collections online.

One of the most difficult parts of searching the Internet for information is clarifying your search so you can get the information you need. If you do not clarify your search sufficiently, you may find yourself looking at hundreds of articles that do not match your needs. Ask yourself these questions to assist you in clarifying your search:

▶ Is the Internet the best place to look? If you know very little about a topic and believe you are going to need help in narrowing the field, you may decide that the help you can receive from your local library staff is essential.
▶ What information do I want? For example, assume you are interested in finding information on ethics. Do you want a history of ethics in the United States? Do you want a history that goes back to early philosophers? Are you interested in business ethics? Are you interested in societal ethics? In other words, you need to narrow your search so you can obtain information that is helpful for your project.
▶ When keying in your search words, enter the most clarifying word first.

Information Evaluation. Because anyone can place information on the Internet, you must determine the credibility of the company or individual providing the information, along with the date the information was put on the Internet. Do you need historical information? Or, do you need current information? Check the date on the website. Additionally, ask yourself these questions: Who has written the information? What education does the person have? Is the person representing a respected organization? The website may provide some information about the author. If not, you can do a Web search on the author's name or visit the library for credentials on the individual.

Copyrighted Information. Just as you give credit for a library resource, you must give credit for a Web resource. If no author is listed, which is often the case, list the name of the article or the name of the website and the date you accessed the information. If an author is given, list the author's name first, followed by the title of the article. You have probably noticed that a number of websites have been accessed in doing research for this book. Notice the format that has been used in documenting the Web source. Formats can vary; however, the format used in this book is one acceptable style.

⊵ Parts of the Report

An informal report may have only one or two parts, with those parts being the body and an **executive summary** (a one- or two-page summary of the report). An informal report is written in conversational style. Personal pronouns such as *I, you, me, we,* and *us* may be used. Contractions are usually acceptable in an informal report. Before you begin writing a report, be certain that you determine whether the report is considered formal or informal.

Formal reports usually contain several parts, which are the executive summary, title page, table of contents, list of tables and illustrations, body, bibliography or reference section, and appendix.

Executive Summary

The executive summary is a one- or two-page summary of the document. It is written for the busy executive who wishes to preview the report but does not need a detailed understanding of all aspects of the report. The executive summary contains these parts: (1) background—establishing why the report was written and identifying the problem or issues; (2) major findings—explaining what was discovered; and (3) the recommendations—recommending future

steps that need to be taken to solve the problem and/or address the issues that were discovered.

Title Page

The title page contains the title of the report, the writer's name, title, and department or division, and the date the report is being submitted.

Table of Contents

The table of contents lists each major section of the report and the page number of the first page of that section. Although a table of contents is not required in an informal report, it helps the reader find particular parts of the report.

List of Tables and Illustrations

If numerous tables and illustrations are within the report, list the title of each one with the respective page number. This procedure helps the reader quickly locate and scan the data presented.

Body of the Report

The body is divided into the following major sections:

- ▸ Introduction
- ▸ Problem statement
- ▸ Research methods
- ▸ Findings and discussion
- ▸ Conclusions
- ▸ Recommendations

Bibliography or Reference Section

All references used in a report should be included in a bibliography or reference section. The complete name of the author(s), the title of the book or periodical, the date of publication, the publishing company, and the page numbers are standard information given.

Appendix

A formal report may contain an appendix that includes supporting information such as tables and statistics. Items in an appendix are listed as Appendix A, Appendix B, and so on. The appendix is the last part of the report.

Reference citations or footnotes are usually placed at the bottom of the page in the body. If endnotes are used, they are placed at the conclusion of the document. Internal citations appear within the context of the document.

> WRITING COLLABORATIVELY

Teams are used extensively in organizations today, with teams writing reports being relatively common. Following these collaborative guidelines will help you be a more valuable member of a team writing project.

- ▶ Determine the purpose of the writing assignment. What is the team to produce? What is the deadline? Must certain stipulations be met?
- ▶ Determine who the audience is. Who is to receive the final report? What is the receivers' background? How much do they know about the subject matter? In other words, determine what your style of writing should be and how much information to give the recipient(s).
- ▶ Select a team leader. The team leader is responsible for setting the procedures for the team writing meetings; facilitating the meetings; and helping the group meet deadlines, solve problems, and produce the document.
- ▶ Set a work schedule. Decide when and where you are going to meet. Set timelines and stick to them.
- ▶ Allocate the work. Define the tasks of each team member. Determine each team member's writing strengths, and use these strengths when assigning tasks.
- ▶ Monitor the progress. The group must stay focused and produce the written product by the deadline established.
- ▶ Reduce the chance of conflict by actively listening to each group member; paying attention to culture, age, and gender differences; and acknowledging the work of other group members and their points of view.

> WRITING INTERNATIONALLY

Throughout this book, you are reminded of the global nature of business and what that means for you as an administrative professional. Chances are great that, at some point in your career, you will be communicating in writing with individuals from various countries. This chapter has focused on written communication using the principles appropriate for firms in the United States, with reminders that internal communication is different. If you become employed in an organization that communicates frequently with an international country, remember that it is important for you to learn about appropriate communication with that country. You cannot assume that standard communication techniques observed in the United States will be appropriate for your international audience. The result of such knowledge and understanding will be clear, concise, and appropriate communications with international businesses.

Spotlight *on*

WRITING INTERNATIONALLY

With many U.S. companies engaged in activities abroad, consideration must be given to appropriate written communications for a world audience.

> OBSERVING ETHICAL AND LEGAL CONSIDERATIONS

You were introduced to the importance of ethical behavior in Chapter 2. Almost every day we hear a story about business ethics or lack thereof on television or read it in a newspaper. Ethical problems are often difficult to resolve precisely because generally there are no exact rules to determine when something is ethical or unethical. Each organization and individual must make that determination unless the issue is covered by federal or state laws.

In written correspondence, the organization must act ethically in regard to its public responsibilities. Organizations must tell the truth about their products and/or services. For example, airlines have an ethical obligation to the public to meet the scheduled flight times unless circumstances such as weather or mechanical problems arise. They also have an ethical obligation to be honest with the public as to why a flight is late. Automotive companies have an ethical obligation to the public to present correct written specifications of all vehicles. Not-for-profit organizations have an ethical obligation to present in writing to the public how their dollars are spent in meeting the needs of the underprivileged. Unethical behavior by businesses can result in loss of business, loss of the public's goodwill, and costly lawsuits.

SUMMARY

Reinforce your learning in this chapter by studying this summary.

▶ Written communication in the office today is extremely important; the increase in the use of written correspondence through the use of instant messaging and e-mail has increased the time that the administrative professional spends writing.

▶ Thought needs to be given to the most appropriate communication medium when writing for both internal and external audiences.

▶ Codes of ethics have become even more important due to the large number of both internal and external written communication.

▶ Along with being ethical when writing, proper etiquette must be used.

▶ Memorandums continue to be an important vehicle of internal written communication.

▶ Inherent in writing success is the ability to plan and organize the necessary materials.

▶ Considerations when writing include determining the purpose or goal of the correspondence, evaluating the cost, analyzing to learn who the reader is, gathering appropriate information, organizing the content, determining the graphic needs, drafting, and editing the correspondence.

▶ Effective correspondence is clear, concise, complete, considerate, prompt, grammatically correct, positive in tone, effective in paragraphing, error free, and written at the appropriate reading level.

▶ When writing letters, it is necessary to determine the basic purpose and approach of the letter, along with editing, proofreading, and formatting.

▶ Letters can be categorized into three basic writing approaches: direct, indirect, and persuasive.

▶ Report writing steps include determining the purpose of the report, analyzing the audience who will receive the report, preparing a summary of what should be included in the report, gathering information, preparing an outline, drafting the report, preparing necessary graphics, reading and editing, preparing an executive summary, proofreading the final copy, and printing and distributing the document.

▶ In writing reports, both primary and secondary research is often used.

▶ Parts of a formal report include the executive summary, title page, table of contents, list of tables and illustrations, body of the report, bibliography or reference section, and appendix.

▶ When writing collaboratively, follow these steps: determine the purpose, determine the audience, select a team leader, set a work schedule, allocate the work, monitor the progress, and reduce the chance of group conflict through appropriate human relations techniques.

▶ The golden rule of writing is to be both ethically and legally correct.

GLOSSARY

Bombing—Repeatedly sending an e-mail message to a particular address at a specific site.

Brainstorm—A sudden idea; a group problem-solving technique.

Business plan—Plan written to establish a business.

Direct approach—Begins with the reason for the correspondence.

Emoticons—Faces produced by the Internet counterculture in answer to e-mail being devoid of body language.

Empathy—Mentally entering into the feeling or spirit of a person.

Executive summary—One- or two-page summary of a report.

Focus groups—Group brought together to talk with an interviewer about their opinions of certain events or issues.

Indirect approach—Begins with an opening statement that is pleasant but neutral; reviews the circumstances and gives the negative information; closes on a pleasant and positive approach.

Parallelism—Created when grammatically equivalent forms are used within a sentence.

Persuasive approach—Used when you want to convince someone to do something or change an indifferent or negative reader reaction.

Presence technology—When users launch an instant message, they can see who on their contact list is online.

Readability—Degree of difficulty of a message.

Response rate—Number of people responding to a survey or questionnaire.

Spamming—Sending e-mail to hundreds or thousands of users or lists that expand to many users.

Spoofing—E-mail that appears to have originated from one source when it actually was sent from another source.

Topic sentence—Contains the main idea of a paragraph.

You approach—Places the reader in the center of the message.

Virtual assistant—Work-at-home professionals who provide numerous business support services, including making appointments, laying out reports, organizing files, and so on.

CHECKPOINT

Check your understanding of these terms by completing DCD6-a on the Data CD.

DISCUSSION ITEMS

These discussion items provide an opportunity to test your understanding of the chapter through written responses and/or discussion with your classmates and your instructor.

1. Explain what factors should be considered when choosing a communication method.

2. Identify six ethical guidelines to be considered when sending e-mail.

3. Identify the steps in planning and organizing written materials.

4. Identify the characteristics of effective correspondence that are common to letters, e-mails, memorandums, and reports.

CRITICAL THINKING CASE

Ms. Portosky asks that you draft a congratulatory letter for her to the newly elected mayor of Dallas, Horatio Gutierrez. Prior to becoming mayor, Mr. Guiterrez was on the Dallas City Council. He has been active for the past ten years in civic organizations. Ms. Portosky first met Mr. Guiterrez five years previously when he was on the City Council; they have worked together on several city projects, including downtown revitalization. His address is: City Hall, 8302 Avenue A, Dallas, TX 75112. Draft the letter for Ms. Portosky to review.

A

1. Incorrect—accessible
2. Incorrect—accommodate
3. Correct
4. Incorrect—appearance
5. Correct
6. Correct
7. Correct
8. Incorrect—dilemma
9. Correct
10. Correct
11. Incorrect—forty
12. Correct
13. Incorrect—inadvertent
14. Incorrect—maintenance
15. Incorrect—mileage
16. Incorrect—ninety
17. Correct
18. Correct
19. Correct
20. Correct
21. Correct
22. Correct
23. Incorrect—superintendent
24. Correct
25. Incorrect—withhold

B

1. Thank you for your May 15 order. (Use current date.)
2. Ms. Michelle Edwards, Chair of the Board, presented the information.
3. The information you requested is being sent today, Monday, May 15, by first-class mail.
4. Although I am unable to send you the complete report due to its confidential nature, I am sending you a summary today. I appreciate your interest in this information and believe you will find the summary helpful.
5. The total charge on your bill is $125; I am enclosing an itemized statement of the individual charges. If I can be of further assistance, please let me know.
6. Our society consumes a large amount of goods.

WORKPLACE PROJECTS

PROJECT 6-1 PREPARE MEMORANDUM

Choose the appropriate written communication method (Objective 1)

Observe appropriate ethical and legal practices in writing (Objective 5)

In a memorandum to your instructor, explain the communication medium you would use in each of the following situations, giving your rationale. Use the JWay memorandum form DCD6-01.

1. Ms. Portosky asks you to send a communication to upper administration announcing a planning retreat within the next two weeks. The retreat will be at the Lone Star Lodge for three days, starting with lunch on the first day and ending in the afternoon of the third day. The administrators are to be ready to discuss strategic directions for JWay, along with strategic directions for their particular unit.

2. There will be a written communication workshop for all administrative assistants in the company within the next three weeks. The communication workshop will begin at 9 a.m. and conclude at 4 p.m. for two days. Your responsibility is to send a communication to all administrative assistants in JWay Nu-Systems Tech.

3. You will be out of the office tomorrow; you need to let the person know who sits in for you when you are gone. It is now 3:30 p.m. in your office.

PROJECT 6-2 PREPARE MEMORANDUM

Identify the steps in planning and organizing written materials (Objective 2)

In a memorandum to your instructor, list and explain the guidelines that need to be followed when preparing the following types of correspondence: e-mail, instant messaging, memorandums, letters, and reports. Use the JWay memorandum form DCD6-02.

PROJECT 6-3 COMPOSE CORRESPONDENCE

Produce effective instant messages, e-mail, memorandums, and letters (Objective 3)

Observe appropriate ethical and legal practices in writing (Objective 5)

Prepare the appropriate communication for the situations given in Project 6-1. Use the JWay memorandum form on DCD6-03 if you are preparing a memo.

PROJECT 6-4 COMPOSE LETTERS

Produce effective instant messages, e-mail, memorandums, and letters (Objective 3)

One of your friends, Velma Powell, has recently received a promotion to office manager for Bartlemen Corporation, 2005 Cascade Drive, Southlake, TX 76036. Write a letter of congratulations to her. Use the JWay letterhead on DCD6-04.

PROJECT 6-5 COMPOSE LETTERS

Produce effective instant messages, e-mail, memorandums, and letters (Objective 3)

You have been asked to speak on "Ethics in the Office" at the next meeting of IAAP. Write a letter to the president of the local chapter of IAAP, Janet Wolfly, Griffin Corporation, 4832 Gold Mountain Road, Hurst, TX 76035, accepting the invitation. Give her the title of your presentation, any special equipment you will need, the number of minutes you will speak (no more than 30 minutes), and any special room setup. You are going to be using PowerPoint® slides in your presentation. Use the JWay letterhead on DCD6-05.

PROJECT 6-6 WRITE A REPORT

Research and write a report (Objective 4)

 Observe appropriate ethical and legal practices in writing (Objective 5)

Working in teams of three, research and write a report on the subject of effective office communication. The report is to be given to all administrative professionals at JWay. Use the Internet as one reference source and at least three books from your college library. You are to have at least nine references in total. Include a section on appropriate ethical and legal practices. Save your report; you will present it in Chapter 8.

PROJECT 6-7 ADD TO PROFESSIONAL GROWTH PLAN

Observe appropriate ethical and legal practices in writing (Objective 5)

Add to your Professional Growth Plan by determining how you will continue to observe ethical and legal obligations in your written correspondence. Save your plan on your Professional Growth Plan disk as PGP6-7.

COMMUNICATION POWER

Use DCD6-b to assist you in improving your grammar skills.

ASSESSMENT OF CHAPTER OBJECTIVES

Now that you have completed the chapter and the projects, take a few minutes to review the chapter learning objectives. For your convenience, the objectives are repeated here. Did you accomplish these objectives? If you were unable to accomplish the objectives, give your reasons for not doing so; be specific and concise. Your instructor may prefer that your answers be submitted to her or him. If so, DCD6-c contains the Assessment of Chapter Objectives. Complete the Assessment of Chapter Objectives; submit your results to your instructor.

1. Choose the appropriate written communication method.   Yes ☐   No ☐

   _____

   _____

   _____

2. Identify the steps in planning and organizing written materials.   Yes ☐   No ☐

   _____

   _____

   _____

3. Produce effective instant messages, e-mail, memorandums, and letters.   Yes ☐   No ☐

   _____

   _____

   _____

4. Research and write a report.   Yes ☐   No ☐
   _____
   _____
   _____

5. Observe appropriate ethical and legal practices in writing.   Yes ☐   No ☐
   _____
   _____
   _____

CHAPTER 7

RECORDS MANAGEMENT

Learning Objectives

1. Explain what records management is and how records management applies to administrative professionals.
2. Identify best practices for managing records.
3. Describe the types of storage systems for paper and electronic records.
4. Determine records retention requirements and prepare a retention schedule.
5. Apply the rules for indexing records.
6. Increase decision-making skills.

Comstock Images

> PAPERLESS OFFICE: MYTH . . . OR REALITY?

With e-mail, instant messaging, the Internet, networked file servers, and electronic document tools, paper files would seem to be unnecessary in an organization. Yet the reality is that as more information is made available in digital format, more people want to print it and read the paper-based version. The global consumption of paper has increased by nearly 25 percent over the last ten years and is expected to almost double by the year 2010![1]

How does a company manage the paper that flows throughout the organization? What are the guidelines and requirements for managing electronic records? These are among the important questions that you need to address as an administrative professional. Proficiency with managing both electronic and paper-based records management systems is a requirement that affects vital areas of the business.

As the information flows in and out of an organization at an ever-increasing rate, it is often difficult and sometimes impossible to find essential information when it is needed. This inability to find a record quickly is not only a frustrating process but also a costly one. It can

- ▶ Cost the organization hundreds or thousands of dollars.
- ▶ Force the management of a company to make decisions based on incomplete information.
- ▶ Result in the loss of a valuable client.
- ▶ Hinder a legal case because of lack of information.

The administrative professional is the individual most often held responsible for being unable to locate a record or for not doing so in a timely

---

[1] Nick Robins and Sarah Roberts, September 1996, "Rethinking Paper Consumption," International Institute for Environment and Development, <http://www.iied.org/smg/pubs/rethink1.html> (accessed April 29, 2005).

manner. An understanding of records management procedures and techniques can simplify the process for you and allow you to become known as the person who can locate needed materials instantly—a skill that can make you invaluable to your supervisor and the organization. This chapter will help you learn the basics of records management. Your ongoing task regarding records management is to keep current on new developments in the field.

The successful administrative professional is able to locate records quickly.

The administrative professional may be responsible for compliance of files with laws or acts passed that affect business records. For example, a 2002 U.S. law, the Sarbanes-Oxley Act, was passed to strengthen corporate governance and restore investor confidence. The Act was passed in response to a number of scandals as a result of corporate accounting practices. Public trust was lost because of problems in accounting and reporting practices. Sarbanes-Oxley establishes new standards for corporate and audit committees as well as a standard for and penalties for management.[2]

A company must have adequate internal controls on access to its data (records). All confidential information on a network must be protected. For these reasons, a company needs to ensure adequate protection of all of its records stored in any format or in any location, electronic or paper.

In addition, an administrative professional must be sure that the company records are in compliance with the Health Insurance Portability and Accountability Act (HIPAA) of 1996. The Act provides that any company sponsoring healthcare plans for its employees will be held accountable for the record-keeping procedures protected by HIPAA. No matter how your company records or communicates health information—electronic, written, or spoken—these records are protected by HIPAA. Among other things, a company must put into place safeguards to protect the privacy of health information. Vendors must conduct any transaction electronically in the format required by HIPAA's electronic data interchange provisions.[3] As an employee involved in records management, you will want to secure training in HIPAA rules to help you work in compliance with them.

> WHAT IS RECORDS MANAGEMENT?

A **record** is a unit of recorded information either received or created within an organization. While most records are documents, recorded information may also take the form of an e-mail message, instant message, letter, report, spreadsheet, contract, human resources record, content on a website, personal digital assistant (PDA), flash drive, server, or any other type of organizational file that provides evidence of an event, activity, or business transaction. **Records**

---

[2]Six Sigma Tutorial, 2004, <http://sixsigmatutorial.com/SOX/sarbanes-oxley.aspx?ref=aw> (accessed June 22, 2005).
[3]Tim King, "The New HIPAA Rules: What Small Biz CEOs Need to Know," *Columbus C.E.O.,* February 2004, p. 56.

management is the systematic control of records from the creation of the record to its final disposition—the complete life cycle of records.

For a records management system to function, there must be information, equipment, and trained people. Information is generated by many sources and can appear in many forms—as a paper record or as an electronic record stored on a computer's hard drive, on a networked file server, on a compact disc, on numerous other electronic media, or on microfilm. Equipment in a records management system includes all of the hardware used in processing documents. People include the necessary personnel who understand the life cycle of records and are able to get the right documents to the right individuals with the greatest efficiency. Because both electronic and paper (hard copy) systems are used in most organizations today, this chapter will emphasize both paper and electronic records management procedures.

> COMPONENTS OF A RECORDS MANAGEMENT SYSTEM

Every organization needs an effective records management system. Recent legislation and regulations concerning security and compliance are causing public and private businesses to formalize their records management systems. With a records management system in place, the records in an organization are managed throughout their life cycle.

The most effective systems are those that are flexible and customized to the needs of the company and its employees while following generally accepted practices. The main components of a records management system as shown in Figure 7-1:

▶ An organizational set of policies and procedures for managing the lifecycle of records

▶ Records storage system(s)
▶ Alphabetic and numeric indexing rules
▶ Appropriate filing supplies
▶ Necessary equipment and media
▶ Retention schedules
▶ Active to inactive file procedures

In addition to these components, manuals and on-going training of all persons using the filing system are necessary. Provisions must also be in place for updating the system before it becomes ineffective or inefficient.

These components are necessary for an electronic system, a manual system, or a system that combines the two (prevalent in most organizations). The components of the records management system are explained in detail in the next sections.

▷ Organizationwide Records Management System

The records management department or the person in charge of records management must clearly define the policies and procedures for managing the life cycle of the organization's records. The organization's file structure must be developed according to a logical scheme that is systematically applied throughout the organization. This structure should be comprehensive in approach; that is, the structure should include how records are to be filed, how long they are to be kept in active status, and how inactive records are to be stored. Without such clarity, personnel within each department may file records in very different ways, resulting in great confusion, mishandling of records, and loss of important records. The records management system (RMS) needs to be documented and made available to the organization in the form of a manual or website.

▷ Records Storage Systems

An important consideration in any records management system, whether that system is electronic or manual, is how the records are stored. **Records storage systems** include alphabetic (alphabetical order) and numeric (numerical order). Both of these systems have several variations that are explained in the following paragraphs. Records in a manual or electronic system may be stored by either of these methods.

Alphabetic Storage Methods
The **alphabetic storage** method uses letters of the alphabet to determine the order in which the record is

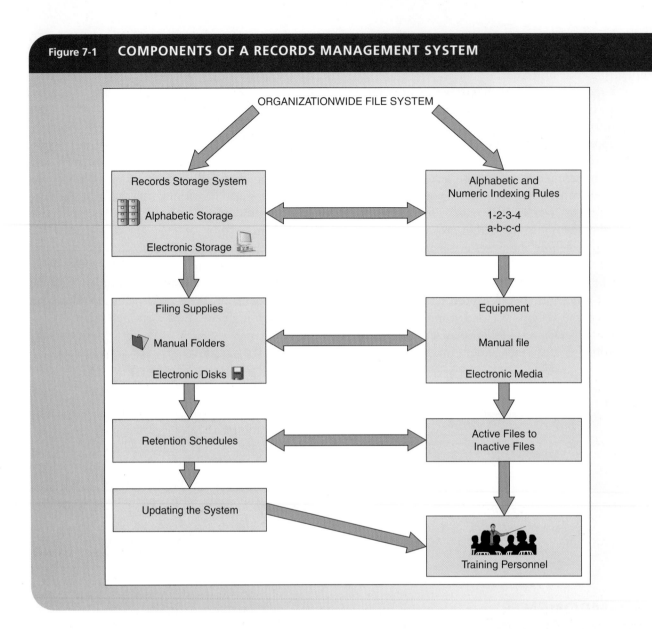

Figure 7-1   COMPONENTS OF A RECORDS MANAGEMENT SYSTEM

ORGANIZATIONWIDE FILE SYSTEM

Records Storage System
- Alphabetic Storage
- Electronic Storage

Alphabetic and Numeric Indexing Rules
1-2-3-4
a-b-c-d

Filing Supplies
- Manual Folders
- Electronic Disks

Equipment
Manual file
Electronic Media

Retention Schedules

Active Files to Inactive Files

Updating the System

Training Personnel

---

filed. This is the most common method used and is found in one form or another in every organization. Figure 7-2 illustrates a manual alphabetic file. Alphabetical ordering can be performed electronically by using the sort function in a word processing program, as illustrated by the electronic alphabetic screen in Figure 7-3. Documents are filed according to the basic alphabetic filing rules, which are given in a later section of this chapter.

Advantages of an alphabetic system are as follows:

▶ It is a **direct access** system. There is no need to refer to anything except the file to find the name.
▶ The dictionary arrangement is simple to understand.
▶ Misfiling is easily checked by alphabetic sequence.

Figure 7-2   MANUAL ALPHABETIC FILE

C
- COX CABLE
- COSTUMES BY J

B
- BOOTS 'N THINGS
- OUT
- BERNIE'S DELI

A
- AXEL COMPANY
- ARNOUX G E
- APPLE PRODUCTIONS

Figure 7-3   ELECTRONIC ALPHABETIC SCREEN

Figure 7-3   ELECTRONIC ALPHABETIC SCREEN

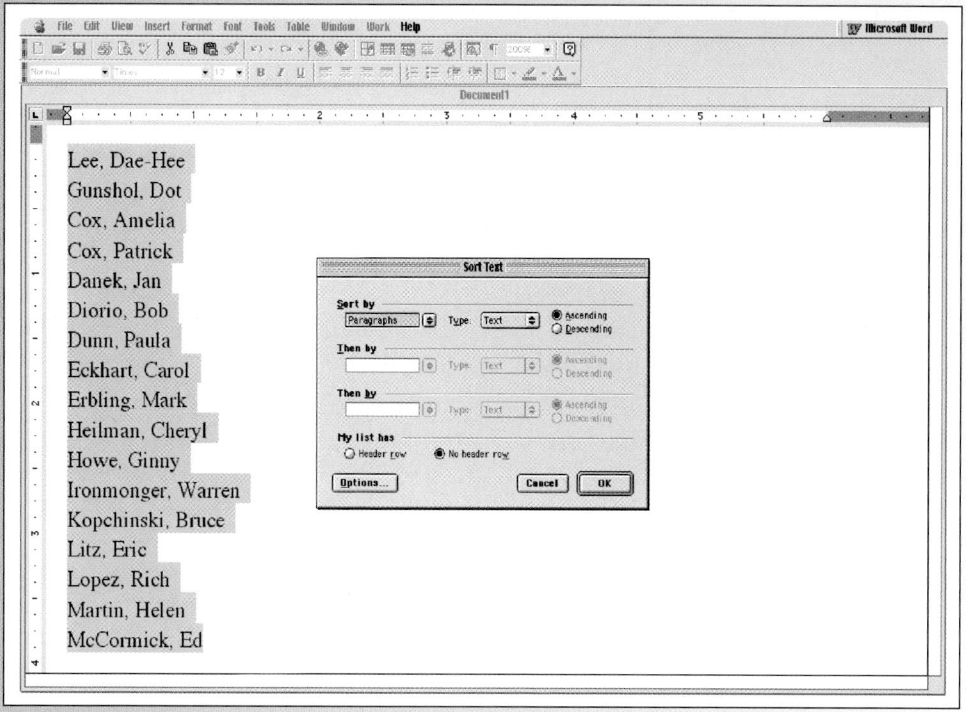

Variations of the alphabetic storage method include **subject filing** (arranging records by their subject) and **geographic filing** (arranging records by geographic location).

Subject Filing. Subject filing is widely used in organizations. An illustration of a manual subject file is shown in Figure 7-4.

Figure 7-4   MANUAL SUBJECT FILE

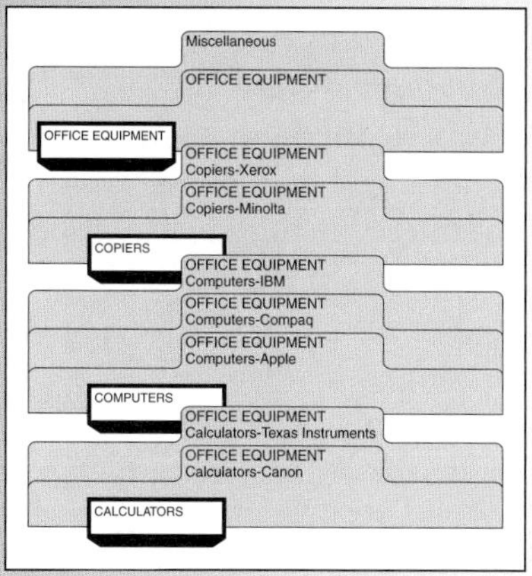

Filing by subject requires that each record be read completely to determine the subject—a time-consuming process. It is a difficult method to control because one person may read a record and determine the subject to be one thing and another person may read the record and decide the subject is something entirely different. For example, one person classifying records concerning personnel grievances may determine that the subject is grievances while another person may determine that the subject is personnel—grievances.

You learned earlier that an alphabetic system is a direct system (direct access)—a file can be found by going directly to the name of the file. A subject system can be considered direct or indirect. When the system is direct, the subject file is a simple one (with few subjects consisting of only a single sheet of titles) and access can be obtained directly through its alphabetic title. Keeping the subjects in alphabetical order is necessary. However, most subject systems are more complex and require some type of index. For electronic systems, **cross-reference** (a method of filing under a separate name when the record may be called for by more than one name) terms can be incorporated within the index. Without an index, it is almost impossible for the subject storage method to function satisfactorily. This index may include several levels or several cross-references. Figure 7-5 illustrates two- and three-level subject indexes. The index should be kept up-to-date as new subjects are added and old ones eliminated. When new subjects are added, the index provides guidance to avoid the duplication of subjects.

The index to the Yellow Pages of the telephone directory is a good example of a subject index. Take a few minutes now to look at your Yellow Pages. Notice the index that precedes the directory. The index gives you the subject areas. If this subject area is not where the information is located, the user is directed to the correct subject area. Here are some examples.

Forms-Business See
    Business Forms & Systems
    Office Supplies
    Printers
    Printers—Business Forms
Doctors
    Clinics
    Hospitals
       Physicians & Surgeons—M.D. & D.O.
       Physicians & Surgeons—Optometrists—
          Doctors of Optometry (O.D.)
       Physicians & Surgeons—Podiatrist—D.P.M.
          (Foot)

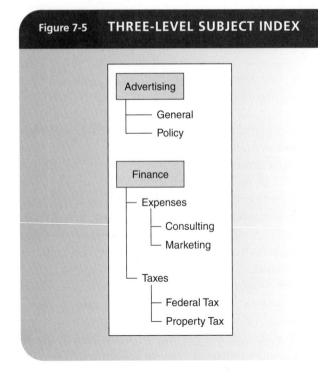

Figure 7-5   THREE-LEVEL SUBJECT INDEX

One of the major advantages of the subject method is that all records about one subject are grouped together. For example, notice that all doctors are grouped together; all hospitals are grouped together, and so on. If this information was filed using a straight alphabetic method, each individual doctor would be listed by name and each individual hospital would be listed by name. Obviously, such a system is not helpful in finding information if you do not know the name of a hospital or a doctor.

Geographic Filing. Another variation of an alphabetic system is the geographic method, with related records grouped by place or location. Geographic filing is considered a direct method if you know the location of the file needed. If you do not, it is an indirect system and requires a separate geographic file in a manual system or the appropriate **keywords** (unique identifiers) set up for an electronic system so you can query the system in a variety of ways. Geographic filing is particularly useful for the organizations listed here.

▶ Utility companies where street names and numbers are of primary importance in troubleshooting
▶ Real estate firms that have listings according to land areas
▶ Sales organizations that are concerned with the geographic location of their customers
▶ Government agencies that file records by state, county, or other geographic division

In a manual geographic file by state and city, file guides are used to indicate the state and city. File folders are arranged alphabetically behind the guides with tabs indicating the company or individual. Figure 7-6 shows a manual geographic arrangement.

Numeric Storage Methods

Under the **numeric method**, records are given numbers that are arranged in a numeric sequence when stored. The numeric method is particularly useful to the following organizations:

▶ Insurance companies that keep records according to policy numbers
▶ Law firms that assign a case number to each client
▶ Real estate agencies that list properties by code numbers

Figure 7-6 MANUAL GEOGRAPHIC FILE

DAYTON	OH Dayton
	OH Columbus
	OH Columbus McMullins Farm Supply
	OH Columbus Effers Beauty Salon
COLUMBUS	
	OH Cincinnati
	OH Cincinnati Pearson Gift Shop
	OH Cincinnati Pearlmark Office Supply
	OH Cincinnati Ismael Laboratory
CINCINNATI	
	OH Akron
	OH Akron Laura X Stationery
	OH Akron Haydens Rotisserie
	OH Akron Akron Dry Cleaning Co. 3900 Plymouth Street
AKRON	
OHIO	

The manual numeric file has four basic parts.

▶ Numeric file
▶ Alphabetic general file
▶ A file containing the names of the clients, customers, and/or companies with the number that has been assigned to the individual or company
▶ A file containing a list of the numbers that have been used

In practice, here is how the manual numeric method works.

1. When a document is ready to be filed, the file containing the names of the clients and customers is consulted to get the number of the particular client or customer.

2. The number established is placed on the document; the document is placed in the numeric file.

3. If the client or customer is new and no number is established, the document may be placed in the alphabetic file until the client or customer has enough documents to open an individual numeric file.

4. If it is necessary to establish a new numeric file, the file containing the list of numbers is consulted to determine the next number to be used.

Figure 7-7 illustrates the manual numeric method. Here are three variations of numeric filing.

▶ Chronological filing
▶ Terminal-digit filing
▶ Alphanumeric filing

Figure 7-7 MANUAL NUMERIC FILE

Chronological Filing. **Chronological filing** is the arrangement of records by date, usually by year, month, or day. Additionally, other calendar divisions (such as weeks, months, or quarters) may be used as key sort fields for document groupings. Chronological filing is also used for **tickler files** (files used to tickle your memory and remind you to take certain actions). An example of a tickler file is the calendar file that is used on wireless PDAs. The to-do items are arranged by the date the item is due. Once the items have been keyed into the PDA, you can readily call up what you are to accomplish each day.

Terminal-Digit Filing. In the basic numeric method, as the files increase, the numbers assigned become higher. Each new file needs to be placed behind all the lower-numbered files, which means that the file arrangement expands at the back. This can be inconvenient. One remedy to this difficulty is the use of **terminal-digit filing,** in which a number is divided into three groups. For example, 129845 becomes 12-98-45. By adding zeros to the left of a smaller number, three groups are created. The number 68559 becomes 06-85-59. The purpose is to indicate primary (first), secondary, and tertiary (final) groupings of numbers. These primary, secondary, and tertiary numbers tell the location of the record.

06	**85**	**59**
Tertiary	secondary	primary
(Folder	(Guide	File Section, Shelf,
number)	number)	or Drawer number)

To locate the record 06-85-59, you would first go to the 59 shelf, look behind the 85 guide to locate the 06 folder. Note that you are reading the numbers from right to left in terminal digit filing. The next number (folder) to be assigned would be 07-85-59. After 99-85-59, a new guide, 86 would be created. The first new number in Guide 86 would be 01-86-59.

Alphanumeric Filing. **Alphanumeric filing** combines alphabetic and numeric characters. For example, RM-01 Records Management may be the main directory, with the subdirectories being RM-01-01 Manual Filing Methods and RM-01-02 Electronic Filing Methods.

▷ Manual Filing Procedures

When filing manual records, certain procedures should be followed before placing the record in the file, including:

- ▶ **Inspecting**—Checking to see that the record is ready to be filed. A release mark (such as the supervisor's initials, a "File" stamp, or some other agreed-upon designation) lets you know the record is ready to be filed.
- ▶ **Indexing**—Determining the way the record is to be filed—the name, the subject, the number, or the geographic location.
- ▶ **Coding**—Marking the record by the name, subject, location, or number that was determined in the indexing process.

When filing records electronically, you must also follow certain procedures. For example, if you are using a subject file, you must have the appropriate keywords so the system can display information in a variety of ways. Software database and document

on

Spotlight

ELECTRONIC BUSINESS RECORDS

Employee e-mail and instant messages (IM) can be subpoenaed in a lawsuit or legal investigation as a primary source of evidence.

CHECK **A**

Self

Complete Self-Check A to determine if you understand the different types of records storage systems.

Fill in the name of the records storage system:

1. Arrangement of records by date _____

2. Uses a dictionary arrangement _____

3. Records are grouped by place or location _____

4. Requires an index for manual or electronic records _____

5. Combines alphabetic and numeric characters _____

management software are particularly helpful in filing electronic records.

▷Database Software

Database software programs most widely used are FileMaker Pro®, Microsoft Access®, Paradox, and QuickBase, among others. Free database programs are also available on the Web.

With **database software** programs, the user can organize, enter, process, index, sort, select, link related files, store, and retrieve information. Data can be shared within the organization, across the organization's intranet, and displayed on data-driven Web pages over the Internet. **Electronic indexing** sorts the records and stores the information based on one or more key fields or **metadata fields** (database of information about the documents). Each key field contains a unique identifier or keyword either generated automatically by the software or chosen by the person performing the indexing. For example, if you are working in a human resources department and entering employee information, the keyword might be the employee identification number. In this case,

you would be using a numeric filing system. This system is similar to the inspecting, indexing, and coding mentioned previously that is necessary when filing documents manually. You can **query** (ask) the database to display information in a variety of ways. For example, you might ask for employees who are making a certain salary level or employees who have been employed for a specified period of time. Information may be stored on a variety of media, including DVDs and CDs. **Integrated packages or software suites** combine database software with spreadsheet, presentation, and word-processing software so users can easily move stored information from one application to another. Figure 7-8 illustrates the cycle.

▷ Document Management Systems

Document management systems are also available to assist an organization in managing electronic, microimage, and paper systems. The features of most document management systems enable faster and more powerful access to an organization's documents

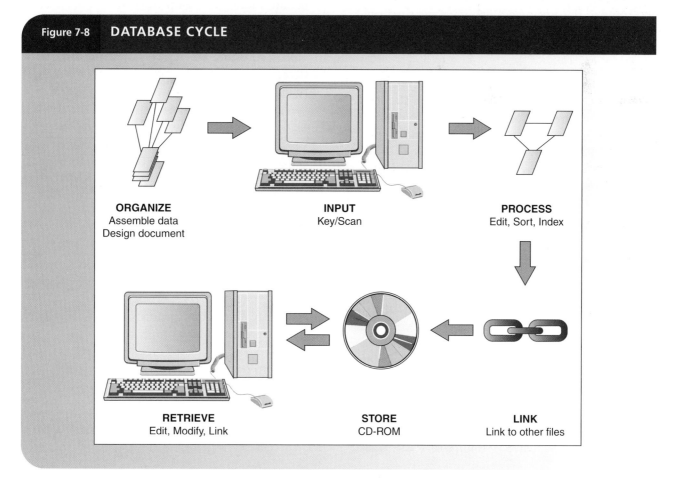

Figure 7-8   **DATABASE CYCLE**

ORGANIZE
Assemble data
Design document

INPUT
Key/Scan

PROCESS
Edit, Sort, Index

RETRIEVE
Edit, Modify, Link

STORE
CD-ROM

LINK
Link to other files

via a computer system or network. The database of a document management system captures complete information about each document, including the following information[4]:

Author: who wrote or contributed to the document

Main topics: what subjects are covered in the document

Related documents: what other documents are relevant to this document

Version tracking: how a document evolves over time

Document sharing: what business processes use and reuse the document

Document security: provides different permission levels for accessing the document

Documentum®, Xerox®, and IBM® are among today's leading providers of document management systems. Document management programs are helpful if an organization decides to move from a manual to an electronic system. For example, with document management software, paper documents can be digitized and stored on a variety of media, including CDs, optical media, hard drives, or even online.

Some of the advantages of a document management system are as follows:

▸ Retrieving documents faster
▸ Reducing labor costs involved in processing files
▸ Viewing, printing, faxing, e-mailing, or annotating any document from your PC
▸ Recovering manual filing and storage space for other business use
▸ Storing backup copies of all files in a safe location
▸ Generating activity reports by department and user
▸ Generating records retention and disposal guidelines

You have already learned that you must perform certain functions before filing a record manually, such as inspecting, indexing, and coding. You must also perform certain functions before filing an electronic record. You must determine how you want the information sorted. For example, do you want to sort by name, by location, or by number? If you want to sort by location, will you sort by state, by city, and then by name? In other words, you have to pay careful attention to setting up your electronic file system in a manner that lets you retrieve the data quickly and accurately. When filing numerically,

caution is advised to add zeros to achieve alignment of numbers one through nine with numbers containing additional digits.

▷ Indexing Rules

The rules for filing may vary slightly from organization to organization based on specific business and legal needs. The organization must be clear and consistent about its indexing rules and communicate these rules through published policy and procedures documents to all its administrative professionals. ARMA International, the Association for Information Management Professionals, has established the official set of indexing rules. You can find these rules later in this chapter. Familiarize yourself with these rules and refer to them as needed. ARMA provides additional services, some of which are listed here.

▸ *The Information Management Journal* is published bimonthly and is considered to be the authoritative source of information on records management with articles written by experts in the field.

▸ Standards and best practices guidelines to assist organizations to develop and implement effective records management policies and procedures.

▸ An online bookstore to order publications, videos, software, articles, audio recordings, and streaming media presentations on records management.

▸ Professional certification for those in the RIM field (Records and Information Management) of Certified Records Manager (CRM). The CRM is designed for experienced professionals with management-level responsibilities. ARMA International has contracted with the Institute of Certified Records Managers (ICRM) to be its certifying body.

▸ Through ARMA International's Career Placement Services, employers may post a position and applicants may search the job bank for a position.

You may obtain more information about ARMA from their website at www.arma.org.

▷ Storage Supplies, Equipment, and Media

The selection and arrangement of records storage supplies, equipment, and electronic media depend on whether the organization's records management

---

[4]Todd Freter, 2002, "XML: Document and Information Management," <http:/www.sun.com/980908/xml> (accessed April 22, 2005).

system is manual, electronic, or both. As you learned earlier in this chapter, most organizations have business records that include:

- ▶ Traditional paper documents such as forms, correspondence, contracts, reports, and hardcopy printouts of e-mail or Web pages.
- ▶ Electronic records stored on personal computers, network file servers, databases, and CDs/DVDs.
- ▶ Records that take the form of microfilm, videos, tape recordings, or photographs.
- ▶ Selection of systems and equipment to manage this wide array of business records is best achieved when personnel are knowledgeable about the available systems, equipment, and supplies.

Basic Manual Filing Supplies

Basic manual filing supplies include file folders, hanging or suspension folders, file guides, and labels.

File Folders. A file folder is generally a manila folder either 8½ by 11 inches or 8½ by 14 inches in size. A variety of colored folders is available. The filing designation for the paper document(s) that are placed in the folder is keyed on a label and then affixed to the tab of the folder. The tab may be at the top of the folder for traditional drawer files or on the side of the folder for open-shelf filing (a type of filing in which files are placed on shelves similar to books on a shelf). Folders are made with tabs of various widths, called **cuts.** The cuts are straight cut, one-half cut, one-third cut, and one-fifth cut. File folders may be purchased with these cuts in various positions. For example, if you are buying folders with one-third cuts, you may want to have all the tabs in first position. Or you may want to have the tabs in first, second, and third positions. By choosing tabs in three positions, you are able to see the file captions on three folders at once. Figure 7-9 illustrates the cuts in various positions.

Suspension Folders. In addition to standard file folders, suspension folders are available. These folders are sometimes called hanging file folders because small metal rods attached to the folders allow them to hang on the sides of the file drawer. Plastic tabs and insertable labels are used with the folders. These tabs and labels may be placed in any position using the precut slots on the folder.

Open shelf filing is often used in medical offices.
© PhotoDisc/Jack Hollingsworth

Figure 7-9   FOLDER CUTS

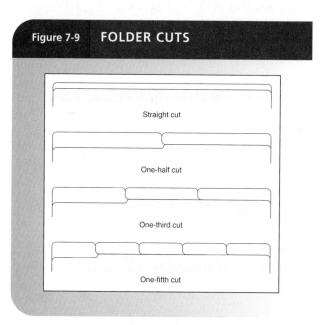
Straight cut
One-half cut
One-third cut
One-fifth cut

File Guides. A file guide is usually made of heavy pressboard and is used to separate the file drawer into various sections. Each guide has a tab on which is printed a name, a number, or a letter representing a section of the file drawer in accordance with the filing system. Guides with hollow tabs in which labels are inserted are also available. The filing designation is keyed on the label and inserted in the table. Figure 7-10 illustrates one type of file guide. Guides are always placed in front of the file folders.

File Folder Labels. File folder labels may be purchased in various configurations, including continuous folder strips, separate strips, rolls in boxes, or pressure-sensitive adhesive labels. Different colored labels can speed up the process of filing and finding records and

Figure 7-10 FILE GUIDE

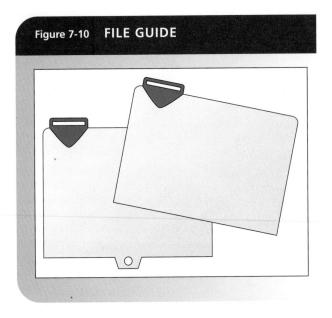

eliminate much misfiling. It is easy to spot a colored label that has been misfiled because that color stands out from the other colors that surround it.

Some of the ways in which colored labels may be used are to

▶ Designate a particular subject (e.g., green labels may designate budget items; blue labels, personnel items).
▶ Indicate geographic divisions of the country.
▶ Designate particular sections of the file.

When preparing labels for files, consistency should be observed in keying them. Suggestions for preparing labels are given here.

▶ Key label captions in all capitals or lower case letters with no punctuation.
▶ Begin the caption two spaces from the left edge of the label; key any additional information five spaces to the right.
▶ Always key the name on the label in correct indexing order.
▶ Use the same style of labels on all folders. For example, if you decide to use labels with color strips, be consistent. If you decide to use colored labels, be consistent.
▶ Key wraparound side-tab labels for lateral file cabinets both above and below the color bar separator so the information is readable from both sides.

Some computer software programs have features to format these standard label sizes. Using the software features makes creating and printing labels easy.

Manual Equipment

Vertical drawer cabinets are the traditional storage cabinet, with the most common vertical file having four drawers. Lateral files are similar to vertical files except the drawer rolls out sideways, exposing the entire contents of the file drawer at once. Less aisle space is needed for a lateral file than for a vertical file.

Movable-aisle systems consist of modular units of open-shelf files mounted on tracks in the floor. Files are placed directly against each other. Wheels or rails permit the individual units to be moved apart for access. The movable racks are electrically powered. Because these movable systems take up less space than standard files, they are being used more and more today. Movable systems may be manual,

Movable-aisle systems save space.

© The Smead Manufacturing Company

mechanical, or electrical. Manual systems are small, with two to four carriages. They require no power; the user merely pushes the files apart. Mechanical systems operate by turning a crank. Electrical systems move carriages with motors. Features that provide safety both for the administrative professional using the system and for the file contents are a top priority of companies. Protection devices are available for all systems. The most basic device is a key-operated carriage lock that prevents the system from rolling on the rails. Another safety device is a strip that runs the length of the file cabinet at floor level. Pressure of more than a few ounces stops cabinet movement. Still another safety device is an infrared photoelectric beam. If a person or an object breaks the beam, the system stops moving. When the person or object is no longer breaking the beam, the system resets itself. To ensure safety of materials, users may have a badge that is swiped through a badge reader to allow entrance to the system or they may enter a password code. Also, some systems can be fitted with locking doors.

Electronic Equipment

The personal computer has become a major electronic filing equipment component. With database and document management software, which you learned about earlier, the personal computer that is networked with other PCs can

- Provide electronic document storage and retrieval.
- Serve as an access device for scanned and electronically generated documents.
- Maintain records inventories.
- Retrieve documents stored electronically.
- Store records retention and destruction data.

Also included in the electronic equipment category are networked file servers, server log files, and backup tapes for disaster recovery.

Electronic Media

In addition to electronic records being stored on the hard drive of a computer, they may be stored on a variety of external storage media. (The major ones are listed here.) The storage capacities shown were correct at the time this book was published. However, storage capacities are constantly being increased with the introduction of new electronic media.

- Floppy disks—double-sided and high-density 3.5-inch disks store 1.44 MB
- Zip® disks—750 MB used with Zip drives provide portable storage for backup of computer
- Jaz disks—2 GB
- Flash Drive/Thumb Drive–up to 5 GB
- A variety of CD (compact disc) technology, including CD-R (CD-recordable) and CD-RW (CD-rewritable). CD-R is WORM (write once, read many) technology. This technology has become popular in digital archiving because information stored in this manner cannot be modified or erased but can be read any number of times. If the information stored on the CD needs to be revised, then CD-RW technology is used. CDs provide 700 MB of storage. It is expected that CD storage will be replaced by DVDs.
- A variety of DVD (digital versatile disc) technology is available, including DVD-ROM (read-only, manufactured by a press), DVD-R/RW (recordable once/rewritable), and DVD-RAM (random access memory-rewritable). A DVD can contain:
- DVD-Video (containing movies [video and sound])
- DVD-Audio (containing high-definition sound)
- DVD-Data (containing data)

The disc may have one or two sides, and one or two layers of data per side; the number of sides and layers determines the disc capacity, which can range from 4.7 GB for single-sides to 17 GB for double-sided (double-sided formats are becoming much less common.)

Microform Storage

In addition to the storage of records in paper and electronic form, microforms may be used to store records. *Microform* is a general term for microimage media such as microfilm and microfiche. Most applications of microform storage are for records that are inactive or infrequently accessed. For example, personnel departments have stored personnel records of former employees on microforms and libraries have stored research information on microforms. Magnification equipment is required to read the microimages. There are two types of microforms—**microfilm** (a roll of film containing a series of frames or images) or **microfiche** (a sheet of film containing a series of images arranged in a grid pattern).

▶ Advantages of microfilm include its cost effectiveness for maintaining the security and file integrity of records.
▶ Microfiche (or small card) is easier to handle than rolls of microfilm because each fiche has a title that can be read without magnification and each fiche holds approximately 90 pages of information. Additional microfiche can be added to the file as needed, making updates easier than with microfilm.

Organizations that need to manage large amounts of computer-mainframe-generated data often move to optical media systems, known as Electronic Report Management (ERM)/Computer Output to Laser Disc (**COLD**) to manage information that was historically stored on microforms. COLD systems automatically process, index, compress, store data, and generate reports that are viewed on a company's computer network, Intranet, or over the Internet, permitting simultaneous access to information across an organization.

▷Retention Schedules

In both electronic and manual systems, it is important to know how long records should be retained by the organization. The cost of maintaining documents that are no longer of any use can be significant, particularly in manual systems, because of the floor space necessary for the files. Additionally, even though electronic storage is not nearly so space-intensive, there is some cost to maintaining unneeded documents. Here are some additional benefits to an organization that follows a **records retention schedule:**

▶ Vital legal, financial, compliance, regulatory, or administrative records will not be disposed of prematurely.
▶ Valuable historical records will be preserved.
▶ Records that are no longer needed can be disposed of systematically.
▶ Clear procedures for when to transfer records from active to inactive storage and whether to convert to microform or digital format will be established.

The retention schedule should identify

▶ The time a record should be retained.
▶ How long records are needed in the active area of the organization.
▶ The time records should be retained in inactive storage.

As an administrative professional, you generally will not make retention schedule decisions. The general approach is to consult with the legal counsel of the organization (or if it is a small organization, an outside legal firm), then develop appropriate retention schedules. A sample retention schedule is shown in Figure 7-11. If the company does not have a records retention schedule, the administrative professional should check with the supervisor before making any decisions about how documents should be transferred or destroyed.

Figure 7-11   RETENTION SCHEDULE

	Retention Schedule		
Record Category	**Retention Period**	**Retained in Active File**	**Retained in Inactive File**
Employee Personnel Records (after termination)	7 years	2 years	5 years
Payroll Records	7 years	3 years	4 years
Audit Reports	Permanent	Permanent	

The United States government has an independent federal agency serving as the nation's record-keeper, called National Archives and Records Administration (NARA) that provides initiatives and publications concerning records management. Some of the recent initiatives are listed here.[5]

- Records Management Guidance for PKI (Public Key Infrastructure) Digital Signature Authenticated and Secured Transaction Records
- Vital Records and Disaster Recovery
- Electronic Records Management Initiative
- Electronic Records Archives (ERA) Program

Spotlight *on* SECURITY

When disposing of records, shred anything that has names, addresses, social security numbers, account numbers, and/or credit card numbers to avoid the threat of identity theft.

To understand more about retention schedules, review the following categories into which records can be classified:

Vital Records
Records that cannot be replaced and should never be destroyed are called **vital records.** These records are essential to the effective continued operation of the organization. Some examples of vital records are corporate charters, deeds, tax returns, constitutions and bylaws, insurance policies, procedures manuals, audited financial statements, patents, and copyrights.

Important Records
Records that are necessary to an orderly continuation of the business and are replaceable only with considerable expenditure of time and money are known as **important records.** Such records may be transferred to inactive storage but are not destroyed. Examples of important records are financial statements, operating and statistical records,

physical inventories, electronic business records, and board minutes.

Useful Records
Useful records are those that are needed for the smooth, effective operation of the organization. Such records are replaceable, but their loss involves delay or inconvenience to the organization. These records may be transferred to inactive files or destroyed after a certain period of time. Examples include letters, memorandums, reports, and bank records.

Nonessential Records
Records that have no future value to the organization are considered **nonessential.** Once the purpose for which they were created has been fulfilled, they may be destroyed. For example, a memorandum that is written to arrange a meeting generally has no value once the meeting has occurred.

Active to Inactive File Procedures
At some point in the life of a record, based on records retention information, you either decide to destroy it, retain it permanently, or transfer it to inactive storage. Two common methods of transfer are perpetual and periodic.

Perpetual Transfer. With **perpetual transfer**, records are continuously transferred from the active to the inactive files. The advantage of this method is that all files are kept current because any inactive material is immediately transferred to storage. The perpetual transfer method works well in offices where projects or tasks are completed. For example, when a lawyer finishes a case, the file is complete and probably will not need to be referred to at all or certainly not frequently. Therefore, it can be transferred to the inactive files. When distinguishing between active and inactive records, the following categories should be used:

- Active records—Used three or more times a month; should be kept in an accessible area.
- Inactive records—Used less than 15 times a year; may be stored in less accessible areas than active records.
- Archive records—Have historical value to the organization; are preserved permanently.

---

[5]NARA, "Records Management," <http://www.archives.gov/records_management/> (accessed April 24, 2005).

Periodic Transfer. With **periodic transfer**, active records are transferred to inactive status at the end of a stated time. For example, you may transfer records that are over six months old to the inactive file and maintain records that are less than six months old in the active file. Every six months you follow this procedure.

▷ Maintaining and Updating the File Management System

The records management needs of an organization change. New manual and electronic systems, equipment, and storage possibilities become available. Organizations must keep current on what is available and change systems as appropriate. Although changing systems can be expensive in the short term, new systems often save money in the long term by offering improved speed and accuracy and requiring less staff time to operate. For example, with electronic filing of records, new software is available that offers more features for improving a records management system. New features can save the organization considerable dollars and provide for more efficient management of records. If the organization is a large one, generally at least one person in a management position

is responsible for the ongoing maintenance and updating of the system.

▷ Ongoing Training of Personnel

With changes in records management systems and new equipment, ongoing training should be provided to those personnel involved in records management. The organizational person in charge of records management generally provides this training. Other sources of training include courses and publications from major organizations, such as NARA–U.S. National Archives and Records Administration.[6]

Here is a sample of the many records management courses offered by NARA:

- ▸ Records Management Fundamentals
- ▸ Records Scheduling
- ▸ Records Schedule Implementation
- ▸ Asset and Risk Management
- ▸ Records Management Program Development
- ▸ Managing Special Records
- ▸ Planning for Digital Imaging Success
- ▸ Disaster Preparedness and Response
- ▸ Vital Records
- ▸ Managing Electronic Records

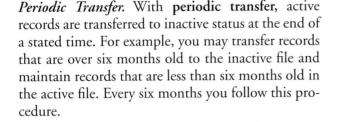

CHECK B

Self

Complete Self-Check B to see if you understand how records are classified for retention.
Categories of records:
    (a) Vital Records
    (b) Important Records
    (c) Useful Records
    (d) Nonessential Records
Select a, b, c, or d for each of the following documents.

1. Memo written to remind coworkers about Chris's birthday   _____

2. Minutes of the Board of Trustees   _____

3. Fax from corporate office to HR about new job posting   _____

4. E-Mail Policy Manual for Employees   _____

5. Computer Hardware Inventory Report from Department of Information Technology   _____

---

[6]NARA, Records Management, "Records Management Training Course Descriptions," <http://www.archives.gov/records_management/training/descriptions_fy05.html> (accessed April 24, 2005).

- ► Electronic Recordkeeping
- ► Electronic Records Issues
- ► Information Technology

ARMA–ARMA International, the Association of Information Management Professionals[7] offers on-line courses and Web seminars:

- ► E-mail, Voice Mail & Instant Messaging: A Legal Perspective
- ► Electronic Discovery in 2010
- ► HIPAA Privacy Essentials
- ► Issues and Approaches in Archiving Electronic Records
- ► The 1-2-3 Guide to Organizing Files & Records
- ► Vital Records: Preparing for the Unexpected

AIIM–Association of Image and Information Management[8] offers various professional development Webinars as well as a certificate program in Enterprise Content Management.

> INDEXING RULES

A systematic set of rules for storing and retrieving records results in an accurate, efficient records management system. ARMA, the professional organization of records managers, has published a standard set of indexing rules for filing documents. These rules include alphabetic indexing and cross-referencing and apply to electronic and manual systems of managing records.

If you are presently working in an organization or beginning your career, you may find that the indexing rules used are slightly different from the ones presented in this text. At times, organizations deviate from these rules for reasons that support their own internal needs. At other times, deviation from the rules may merely mean the individuals setting up the filing system were not aware of the most recent indexing rules. You might want to call attention to the differences if they are significant. However, wait until your supervisor has come to respect your competence.

> Alphabetic Indexing

The rules in this chapter are compatible with ARMA's *Alphabetic Filing Rules.*[9]

Rule 1: Filing Rules for Personal Names

A. Personal Names—Standard Form

- ► Use the last name (surname) as the first filing unit.
- ► The first name or initial is the second filing unit.
- ► Subsequent names or initials are filed as successive units.

Rule 1A Personal Names— Standard Form

Name as Written	Unit 1	Unit 2	Unit 3
Russ Evans	Evans	Russ	
Ruth T. Evans	Evans	Ruth	T
Sam Thomas Evans	Evans	Sam	Thomas

B. Personal Names with Prefixes

Surnames that include a prefix are filed as one unit, even if a space or punctuation mark follows the prefix. Spaces and non-alphabetic characters are removed and the surname is considered as one filing unit.

Rule 1B Personal Names with Prefixes

Name as Written	Unit 1	Unit 2	Unit 3
David DaVern	DaVern	David	
Marilyn Da'Vos	DaVos	Marilyn	
Edward Thomas Da Waters	DaWaters	Edward	Thomas

---

[7]ARMA International, Online Learning, 2005, <http://www.arma.org/learningcenter/index.cfm> (accessed April 24, 2005).

[8]AIIM, <http://www.aiim.org/elearning.asp> (accessed April 24, 2005).

[9]Mary L. Ginn, Editorial Consultant, *Establishing Alphabetic, Numeric, and Subject Filing Systems* (Kansas: ARMA International, ANSI/ARMA 12-2005, Standard for Records and Information Management), pp. 17–22.

C. Personal Names with Titles, Suffixes, and Numbers
Titles and suffixes are not used as filing units except when needed to distinguish between two or more identical names. When needed, the title or suffix is the last filing unit (with the exception of royal and religious titles) and is filed as written without punctuation. The title or suffix should be recorded for the record in case it is needed.

Exception for royal and religious titles: Royal and religious titles followed by either a given name or a surname only (Father John) are indexed and filed as written.

Numbers (Arabic and Roman) as part of name: Arabic (e.g., 1, 2, 3, etc.) and Roman (e.g., I, II, III, etc.) numbers are filed sequentially before alphabetic characters. Arabic numerals precede all Roman numerals. (This sequencing may not be possible in an automated system without using a separate field for the numeric data because the characters used for Roman numerals are alphabetic characters and will sort as such in an automated system.)[10]

Rule 1C: Personal Names with Titles and Suffixes

Name as Written	Unit 1	Unit 2	Unit 3	Unit 4
Father Harrod	Father	Harrod		
S. R. Harrod, 2nd	Harrod	S	R	2
S. R. Harrod, 3rd	Harrod	S	R	3
S. R. Harrod, II	Harrod	S	R	II
S. R. Harrod, III	Harrod	S	R	III
S. R. Harrod, CPA	Harrod	S	R	CPA
S. R. Harrod, MD	Harrod	S	R	MD
S. R. Harrod, Ph.D.	Harrod	S	R	PhD
Sister Margaret	Sister	Margaret		

Rule 1D: Non-English Names

Name as Written	Unit 1	Unit 2	Unit 3	Unit 4
Yen Sufi	Sufi	Yen		
Lim Yauwn Tjin	Tjin	Lim	Yauwn	
Tai Se Yang	Yang	Tai	Se	
Yen Sufi	Yen	Sufi		
	(See Sufi, Yen)			

D. Non-English Names
If the surname is identifiable, file the name as any other personal name. If the surname is uncertain, use the last name as the first filing unit and cross-reference the name as written.

[10]Ibid., p. 17.

Rule 1E Nicknames

Name as written	Unit 1	Unit 2	Unit 3
Missy (Michele) Edwards	Edwards	Missy	
	Edwards	Michele	
	(See Edwards, Missy)		
Ricky (Ricardo) Sanchez	Sanchez	Ricky	
	Sanchez	Ricardo	
	(See Sanchez, Ricky)		

E. Nicknames
When a person commonly uses a nickname as a first name, file using the nickname. Include a cross-reference to the given name only if necessary.

Rule 1F Pseudonyms

Name as written	Unit 1	Unit 2
Tiger Woods	Tiger	Woods
Grandma Moses	Grandma	Moses
Max Factor	Max	Factor
Stephen King	Stephen	King

F. Pseudonyms
Pseudonyms are filed as written.

Rule 1G Hyphenated Names

Name as written	Unit 1	Unit 2
Sue Loaring-Clark	LoaringClark	Sue
Mary-Kay Matthey	Matthey	MaryKay
Michael Win-Row	WinRow	Michael

G. Hyphenated Names
Remove the hyphen, combine the words, and file as one unit.

Rule 1H Identical Personal Names

Name as written	Unit 1	Unit 2	Unit 3	Unit 4
Helen Greer	Greer	Helen	Dallas	Texas
Helen Greer	Greer	Helen	Fort Worth	Texas

H. Identical Personal Names
When personal names are identical, filing order is determined by the addresses. Compare addresses in the following order: city names, state names, and street names.

Complete Self-Check C to determine if you understand the indexing rules for personal names by placing the names in proper indexing and alphabetical order. Check your answers with those at the end of this chapter.

	Units			
	1	2	3	4
L. Mark Greeson				
Dan E. LeWaters				
Jackson E. Matthews, Ph.D.				
Jackson E. Matthews, 2nd				
Jackson E Matthews, Jr.				
Jackson E. Matthews, III				
Sister Mary Kay				
Yao Tungsun				
Lim Yauwn Tjin				
Dizzy Dean				
Susan Clark-Edwards				

Rule 2: Specific Filing Rules for Business and Organization Names

2A: Business and organizational names are filed as written using the general filing rules applied to the name obtained from the most authoritative source; e.g., letterhead, company files, and/or registered business names. When business names are identical, filing order is determined by the address, in this order: city, state, and street.

Because the word "the" is often used as the first word in a filing segment, it is moved from the beginning of the filing segment to the end.

2B: Subsidiaries of businesses are filed under their own name with a cross-reference to the parent company if needed. Additional information is given on cross-referencing on pages 194–195.

Rule 2A Business Names—Standard Form

Name as Written	Unit 1	Unit 2	Unit 3
3M	3M		
Juarez Foods	Juarez	Foods	
Tom's Foods	Toms	Foods	
The Orchard Market	Orchard	Market	The

Rule 2B Subsidiaries of Businesses

Name as Written	Unit 1	Unit 2	Unit 3
Essex Group	Essex	Group	
	See Superior Essex Communications		
Superior Essex Communications	Superior	Essex	Communications
United Health Group	United	Health	Group
United HealthCare	United	HealthCare	
	See United Health Group		

Rule 2C Geographic Names in Business Names

Name as Written	Unit 1	Unit 2	Unit 3
Fort Worth Lighting	Fort	Worth	Lighting
Fort Worth Pediatrics	Fort	Worth	Pediatrics

2C: Follow general filing rules when filing geographic place names in business names.

Rule 2D Compass Terms in Business Names

Name as Written	Unit 1	Unit 2	Unit 3	Unit 4
North East Telecommunications	North	East	Telecommunications	
Northeast Jewelry	Northeast	Jewelry		
Northwest National Bank	Northwest	National	Bank	

2D: Each word/unit in a business organization filing segment containing compass terms is considered a separate filing unit. If the name includes more than one compass point, treat it as it is written. Prepare cross-references when needed.

Rule 3: Governmental and Political Designation Filing Rules

Rule 3A: When filing governmental or political material, the name of the major entity is filed first and followed by the distinctive name of the department, bureau, and so forth. This rule covers all governmental and political divisions, agencies, departments, and committees from the federal to the county/parish, city district, and ward levels. When filing federal government entities, the first unit is "United States Government." The second and third levels depend on the information. The words "Department," "Bureau," "Agency," and so forth should be retained. The words "of" and "of the" should not be considered as units and are placed in parentheses. Notice the examples given below.

Rule 3A Governmental and Political Designations

Name as Written	Unit 1	Unit 2	Unit 3	Unit 4
Health and Human Services Department, United States Government	United States Government	Health (and) Human Services Department		
Commerce Department United States Government	United States Government	Commerce Department		
Department of Labor United States Government	United States Government	Labor Department (of)		

Rule 3B Military

Name as Written	Unit 1	Unit 2
Camp Pendleton United States Government	United States Government	Camp Pendleton
Fort Benning United States Government	United States Government	Fort Benning
Fort Bliss United States Government	United States Government	Fort Bliss

Rule 3B: Military. Camps, forts, arsenals, bases, stations, and depots are indexed in the second level of indexing after the first level of "United States Government."

Rule 3C State and Local

Name as Written	Unit 1	Unit 2	Unit 3	Unit 4	Unit 5
Commerce Department State of Alabama	Commerce	Department	State	of	Alabama
City of Roanoke	Roanoke	City	of		
Nevada Department of Highways	Nevada	Highways	Department	of	

Rule 3C: State and Local. State, county, provincial, parish, city, town, township, and village governments or political divisions are filed by their distinctive names. To avoid confusion and to ensure efficient, accurate information retrieval, the words "County of," "City of," "Department of," etc., should be retained and used for indexing. However, if "of" is not part of the official name do not use it for indexing.

Rule 3D Non-U.S. Governments

Name as Written	Unit 1	Unit 2	Unit 3	Unit 4	Unit 5	Unit 6
Commonwealth of Australia	Australia	Commonwealth	of			
Ministry of the Interior, Paris, France	Paris	France	Ministry	of	the	Interior

Rule 3D: Non-U.S. Governments. The Distinctive English name is the first filing unit. If needed, the balance of the formal name of the government forms the next filing units. Divisions, departments, and branches follow in sequential order, reversing the written order where necessary to give the distinctive name precedence in the filing arrangement.

States, colonies, provinces, cities, and other divisions of foreign governments are filed by their distinctive or official names as spelled in English.

Cross-reference the written English name to the official native name where necessary.

If you are dealing with non-U.S. government names frequently, you may want to use a current copy of *The World Almanac and Book of Facts* as a reference source.

▷ Cross-Referencing

Cross-referencing should be done when a record may be filed under more than one name. Here are some rules for cross-referencing personal and business names.

Cross-Referencing Personal Names
Cross-references should be prepared for the following types of personal names:

1. Unusual Names. When it is difficult to determine the last name, index the last name first on the original record. Prepare a cross-reference with the first name indexed first.

Name as Written	Cross-Reference
Andrew Scott	Scott Andrew
	See Andrew Scott

2. Hyphenated Surnames.

Name as Written	Cross-Reference
Helen Edwards-Moore	Moore Helen Edwards
	See EdwardsMoore Helen

3. Similar Names. SEE ALSO cross-references are prepared for all possible spellings.

Baier	Bauer	Bayer
See also	See also	See also
Bauer, Bayer	Bayer, Baier	Baier, Bauer

Cross-Referencing Business Names
Cross-references should be prepared for the following types of business names:

1. Compound Names. When a business name includes two or more individual surnames, prepare a cross-reference for each surname other than the first.

Name	Cross-Reference
Peat Marwick and Main	Marwick Main and Peat
	See Peat Marwick and Main
	Main Peat and Marwick
	See Peat Marwick and Main

2. Abbreviations and Acronyms. When a business is commonly known by an abbreviation or an acronym, a cross-reference is prepared for the full name.

Name	Cross-Reference
YMCA	Young Mens Christian Association

3. Changed Names. When a business changes its name, a cross-reference is prepared for the former name and all records are filed under the new name.

Name	Cross-Reference
DaimlerChrysler	Chrysler
	See DaimlerChrysler

4. Foreign Business Names. The name of a foreign business is often spelled in the foreign language. The English translation should be written on the document and the document stored under the English spelling. A cross-reference should be placed under the foreign spelling.

Name as Written	Cross-Reference
French Academy	Academie Francaise

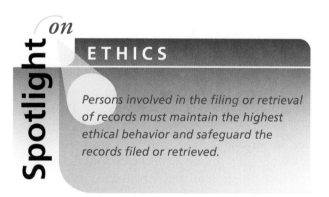

Spotlight on ETHICS

Persons involved in the filing or retrieval of records must maintain the highest ethical behavior and safeguard the records filed or retrieved.

> EFFECTIVE DECISION MAKING

Effective decision making is clearly important in all areas of your work as an administrative professional. Making the right decision about how to file any document, paper or electronic, means that you must think ahead about the decisions you will make. How will the document be asked for again, how often will it be required, and what will be the time frame for accessing it from the files?

Now using a records management scenario, assume you are the records management professional. You recently have been hired by a small company to assist in setting up a coordinated records management program. The company has been in existence only

CHECK D

Complete Self-Check D to determine if you understand the indexing rules for business and organization names by determining the units in each name in numerical order.

	Units					
	1	2	3	4	5	6
5H Health Foods						
Harold's Market						
Texas Health Group						
Texas Health Association						
Fort Myers Dry Cleaners						
Northwest Grocery						
North West Computers						
United States Government						
Department of the Treasury						
Fort Bragg						
United States Government						
Dallas County Health Department						

two years, but it is growing rapidly. A manual file system has been used in the past, with a few individuals filing information on their computers in certain situations. Each individual has decided how he or she would file the documents electronically. There is no overall records management strategy. In using the decision-making model, you make these decisions.

► The problem is to establish an effective, coordinated records management program.
► In establishing the criteria, you determine that you want to establish both a manual and electronic filing system that can be used by all employees in storing and finding materials quickly and easily. You want to avoid a high-cost system, but you also need to provide a system that can grow as the company grows.
► The alternatives you generate are as follows:
(a) Establish a manual system with the assistance of internal staff.
(b) Establish an electronic system with the assistance of internal staff.
(c) Employ a firm to assist with both the manual and the electronic system.
(d) Determine the type of database and document management software available and implement the system with limited internal support.

► After reviewing the alternatives, you decide to use database and document management software to implement the electronic system and provide detailed standards for manual filing. You have extensive experience in database and document management software; you have also identified two experienced individuals within the company who can assist you. Additionally, you have identified one individual who can assist with setting up the manual filing system.
► Once the records management system is designed, implemented, and used for six months, you evaluate its effectiveness. The system is working well, so you feel the correct decision was made. However, you discover that you did not provide enough training on the electronic system for some individuals within the organization. You immediately implement an ongoing training program, and you begin writing a comprehensive document management manual.

Review the way the administrative professional handled the above situation. Would you have followed the same decision-making steps? If not, what would you have done differently?

> THE FUTURE OF RECORDS MANAGEMENT

As you have seen, technology has affected the filing and storage of records tremendously. For that reason, you need to know the correct procedures for managing not only paper records but also records recorded on digital media. Stored information is useful only if it can be accessed when needed. What advances in technology will change the way you are involved in records creation, retrieval, and disposal? Likely the technology will provide emphasis on protection of records from unauthorized access through various software programs for electronic storage. Technology will also likely offer additional measures for protecting off-site and large file rooms housed in large companies. Increased security will always be critical for computer systems and networks. Since vital records must never be destroyed, appropriate measures will be advanced to protect records from destruction from not only fire, water, and other climatic concerns, but also from sabbotage or any type of intrusion or similar disaster.

As an administrative professional, you should always be alert to new systems and new procedures that may make your job of records management easier and more effective.

SUMMARY

Reinforce your learning in this chapter by studying this summary.

▶ A record is a unit of recorded information either received or created within an organization. While most records are documents, recorded information also takes the form of an e-mail message, letter, report, spreadsheet, contract, human resources record, content on a website, PDA, flash drive, server, or any other type of organizational file that provides evidence of an event, activity, or business transaction.

▶ Records management is the systematic control of records from the creation of the record to its final disposition—the complete lifecycle of records.

▶ An effective records management system has these components:
(a) An organizational set of policies and procedures for managing the lifecycle of records
(b) Records storage system(s)
(c) Alphabetic and numeric indexing rules
(d) Appropriate supplies, equipment, and media (electronic or manual)
(e) Retention schedules
(f) Active to inactive file procedures
(g) Records management manuals and ongoing training for personnel
(h) Procedures for updating the management system

▶ There are two basic records storage systems—alphabetic and numeric.

▶ The alphabetic storage method uses letters of the alphabet to determine the order in which the record is filed. Variations of the alphabetic storage method include subject filing (arranging records by their subject) and geographic filing (arranging records by geographic location).

▶ Numeric records are given numbers that are arranged in a numeric sequence when stored. Variations of a numeric file include chronological filing, terminal-digit filing, and alphanumeric filing.

▶ In the filing of manual records, the procedures to be followed include inspecting, indexing, and coding.

▶ In the filing of documents electronically, database and document management software are available to assist you.

▶ Consistent filing rules should be used. ARMA has developed indexing rules that are widely used.

▶ Basic manual filing supplies include file folders, suspension folders, file guides, and file folder labels.

▶ Manual equipment includes vertical drawer cabinets, lateral files, and movable-aisle systems (including open shelf files).

▶ Electronic filing equipment includes PCs, networked file servers, server log files, and backup tapes for disaster recovery.

▶ Electronic filing media include floppy disks, Zip® and Jaz disks, Flash drives, CDs, and DVDs.

▶ Microform filing media includes microfilm and microfiche.

▶ Electronic Report Management (ERM)/COLD systems automatically process, index, compress, and store data, and generate reports that are viewed on a company's computer network, intranet, or over the Internet, permitting simultaneous access to information across an organization.

▶ Retention schedules (providing the length of time a record should be maintained) are essential to effective records management systems.

▶ Vital records are those records that cannot be replaced and should never be destroyed.

▶ Important records are those records necessary to an orderly continuation of the business.

▶ Useful records are those that are useful for the smooth, effective operation of the organization.

- Nonessential records have no future value to the organization once the purpose for which they were created has been fulfilled.

- Records may be transferred to inactive files through perpetual or periodic transfer.

- The records management system should be able to be changed to meet the needs of the organization.

- With changes in records management and when new equipment is secured, training is necessary for all involved in records management.

- ARMA rules have been established to provide guidelines for accurate indexing of all materials, electronic or paper.

- Cross-referencing is necessary when a record may be filed under more than one name.

- Administrative professionals need to be alert to decisions for filing every document whether in paper or electronic format. Being alert to new systems, procedures, methods, and laws are also pertinent duties of the administrative professional.

GLOSSARY

Alphabetic storage—Uses letters of the alphabet to determine the order in which a record is filed.

Alphanumeric filing—Using a combination of alphabetic and numeric characters in filing.

Chronological filing—The arrangement of records by date, usually by year, month, or day.

Coding—Marking the record by the name, subject, location, or number that was determined in the indexing process.

COLD—Computer output to laser disc.

Cross-reference—A method of filing under a separate name when the record may be called for by more than one name.

Cuts—Tabs on folders made in various widths.

Database software—Allows the user to organize, enter, process, index, sort, select, link to related files, store, and retrieve information.

Direct access—A system that does not require referring to anything but the file to find the name.

Document management systems—Assists in managing electronic, microimage, and paper filing systems.

Electronic indexing—Sorts the records and stores the information based on one or more key fields or metadata fields.

Geographic filing—Arranging records by geographic location.

Important records—Records that are necessary to an orderly continuation of a business and are replaceable only with considerable expenditure of time and money.

Indexing—Determining the way the record is to be filed—the name, the subject, the number, or the geographic location.

Inspecting—Checking to see that the correspondence is ready to be filed.

Integrated packages or software suites—Combine database software with spreadsheet and word-processing software so users can easily move stored information from one application to another.

Keywords—Unique identifiers.

Metadata fields—Database of information about the documents.

Microfiche—A sheet of film containing a series of images arranged in grid patterns.

Microfilm—A roll of film containing a series of frames or images.

Nonessential records—records that have no future value to an organization.

Numeric method—Records given numbers that are arranged in numeric sequence.

Periodic transfer—Active records transferred to inactive status at the end of a stated period.

Perpetual transfer—Records continuously transferred from the active to the inactive files.

Query—Asking the electronic system to display information in a certain way.

Record—Any type of recorded information, a unit of recorded information either received or created within an organization.

Records management—The systematic control of records from the creation of the record to its final disposition.

Records retention schedule—A statement to identify how long a record should be retained and where in the organization.

Records storage systems—A method of filing records that includes alphabetic and numeric systems.

Subject filing—Arranging records by their subject.

Terminal-digit filing—A numeric filing order in which the final digits of a number are used as the first filing unit.

Tickler files—Files used to tickle your memory and remind you to take certain actions.

Useful records—Records that are useful for the smooth, effective operation of an organization.

Vital records—Records that cannot be replaced and should never be destroyed.

CHECKPOINT

Check your understanding of these terms by completing DCD7-a on the Data CD.

DISCUSSION ITEMS

These discussion items provide an opportunity to express your thoughts and demonstrate your understanding of the chapter through written responses and/or discussion with your classmates and your instructor.

1. What is the importance to an administrative professional of managing the flow of records throughout the company? What effect have HIPAA rules had on records management?

2. Explain what it means to have a systematic approach to records management.

3. Compare the capacities of the different electronic external storage media and discuss their advantages and disadvantages.

4. What is the future of paper records and what impact, if any, will this have on the responsibilities of an administrative professional?

5. List and explain the steps for effective decision making as it applies to the records management function.

CRITICAL THINKING CASE

JWay Nu-Systems Tech, although a fairly new company, already is facing the challenge of managing the steady stream of records being generated by its executive, finance, operations, sales, and human resources areas. Each department is maintaining both manual and electronic systems. The lateral file equipment throughout the company has insufficient capacity to store the manual records, and many departments have requested the purchase of additional sets of lateral file cabinets. The electronic records are being kept on individual users' hard drives. As a new company, JWay has yet to establish a company policy and procedures manual for the management of records, either manual or electronic, including the management of e-mail records. There is no official records retention policy, so all the records are currently in active storage. Wayne Wilson, COO, has asked you to lead a committee that will research best practices in records management, examine the records management needs of JWay, and develop company policies for records management. Using the decision-making model presented in this chapter, describe how you would proceed in accomplishing this task.

RESPONSES TO SELF-CHECK

A

1. Arrangement of records by date—chronological system

2. Uses a dictionary arrangement—alphabetical system

3. Records are grouped by place or location—geographic system

4. Requires an index for manual or electronic records—numeric system; some subject systems

5. Combines alphabetic and numeric characters—alphanumeric system

B

1. Memo written to remind coworkers about Chris's Birthday   _d_
2. Minutes of the Board of Trustees   _b_
3. Fax from corporate office to HR about new job posting   _c_
4. E-Mail Policy Manual for Employees   _a_
5. Computer Hardware Inventory Report from Department of   _b_
   Information Technology

C

Name as Written	Unit 1	Unit 2	Unit 3	Unit 4
Susan Clark-Edwards	ClarkEdwards	Susan		
Dizzy Dean	Dizzy	Dean		
L. Mark Greeson	Greeson	L	Mark	
Dan E. LeWaters	LeWaters	Dan	E	
Jackson E. Matthews, 2nd	Matthews	Jackson	E	2
Jackson E. Matthews, III	Matthews	Jackson	E	III
Jackson E. Matthews, Jr.	Matthews	Jackson	E	Jr
Jackson E. Matthews, Ph.D.	Matthews	Jackson	E	PhD
Sister Mary Kay	Sister	Mary	Kay	
Lim Yauwn Tjin	Tjin	Lim	Yauwn	
Yao Tungsun	Tungsun	Yao		

D

Name as Written	Unit 1	Unit 2	Unit 3	Unit 4
5H Health Foods	5H	Health	Foods	
Fort Myers Dry Cleaners	Fort	Myers	Dry	Cleaners
Harold's Market	Harolds	Market		
Dallas County Health Department	Dallas	County	Health	Department
North West Computers	North	West	Computers	
Northwest Grocery	Northwest	Grocery		
Texas Health Association	Texas	Health	Association	
Texas Health Group	Texas	Health	Group	
	See Texas Health Association			
United States Government Department of the Treasury	United States Government	Treasury Department (of the)		
Fort Bragg United States Government	United States Government	Fort Bragg		

WORKPLACE PROJECTS

PROJECT 7-1 CONDUCT INTERVIEW AND REPORT ON FINDINGS

Explain what records management is and how records management applies to administrative professionals (Objective 1)

Team with two or three of your classmates on this collaborative project. Interview two administrative professionals, one from a small-to-medium company that employs 50 or fewer people; and one from a large company that employs more than 100 employees. Your interviews may be conducted via telephone, in person, or via e-mail. Ask the questions listed below plus two other questions that your team develops. Report your findings orally to the class.

1. What types of records flow through your organization?

2. Are the records in your organization managed within each department, or is there a centralized records management department?

3. What records management system(s) is used in your organization (manual, electronic, or a combination of these systems)?

4. Describe the storage and retrieval methods (alphabetic or numeric) you use for managing paper records.
   a. If you use alphabetic, do you use subject and/or geographic? Please describe.
   b. If you use numeric, do you use chronological, terminal-digit, or alphanumeric? Please describe.

5. What is your level of familiarity with ARMA's indexing rules?

6. Do you use database or document management software to manage records? Please describe.

7. Does your company have a records retention schedule? If so, may I please have a copy?

8. As an administrative professional, what challenges do you currently face or do you foresee occurring in the future concerning records management; and what suggestions do you have to meet these challenges?

9. and 10. Team develops two of its own questions.

PROJECT 7-2 WRITE A REPORT FROM WEB SEARCH

Identify best practices for managing records (Objective 2)

Explore the information that is available to assist administrative professionals in records management on the ARMA website at http://www.arma.org, Click on the **Topic Areas: Standards/Best Practices** (http://www.arma.org/standards/) and **Records/Info Management** (http://www.arma.org/rim/index.cfm) or other areas of the website that interest you.

Write a brief description to give to your instructor of two areas of the ARMA website that you believe would be useful to an administrative professional in keeping up to date with the latest records management standards and best practices. Include the Web addresses of those pages in your descriptions so that your classmates can visit the areas you have recommended.

PROJECT 7-3 DESCRIBE ELECTRONIC MEDIA STORAGE SYSTEMS

Describe the types of storage systems for paper and electronic records (Objective 3)

Visit a computer supply store either in your community or online. Research what types of storage systems are available for electronic media, such as CD holders and

racks, DVD towers and carousels. If your office needed to organize the stacks of CDs, DVDs, floppy disks, or Zip disks that were currently disorganized, what storage systems would you recommend and why? Use the form on DCD7-03 to describe the features of at least three different storage systems, along with the pros and cons and pricing information to give to your instructor. Based on your exploration, what procedures should an administrative professional follow in choosing an electronic media storage system?

PROJECT 7-4 INDEX AND FILE NAMES

Apply the rules for indexing records (Objective 5)

Access DCD7-04 and review the names. For each group of names, indicate the indexing units and file each group alphabetically. The correct response is given for the first group as an example. Key your responses and submit your work to your instructor.

PROJECT 7-5 INDEX GEOGRAPHICALLY A LIST OF NAMES

Apply the rules for indexing records (Objective 5)

Print the list of clients on DCD7-05 as a working copy. Then key the list in proper geographic sequence arranged as shown below. Arrange the Client Name in indexing order. Print a copy of your work for your instructor.

State

City

Client Name

PROJECT 7-6 PREPARE RECORDS RETENTION SCHEDULE

Determine records retention requirements and prepare a retention schedule (Objective 4)

DCD7-06 contains a set of policy guidelines to determine how long to keep records in your company, JWay Nu-Systems Tech.

Based on the guidelines, prepare a records retention schedule that applies to the records listed.

Submit your schedule to your instructor.

PROJECT 7-7 SEARCH THE WEB AND REPORT ON DOCUMENT MANAGEMENT SOFTWARE

Describe the types of storage systems for paper and electronic records (Objective 3)

Increase decision-making skills (Objective 6)

Using one or more search engines on the Web, locate the websites for database and document management software. Read the features and descriptions of what is available for managing an organization's records. If you were setting up an electronic storage system, which systems would you recommend and why? Write an e-mail to your instructor using the form on DCD7-07. In your e-mail, explain to your instructor:

1. What search engines or Web sources you used and the search terms you keyed into the search engine to locate the websites.

2. The names and Web addresses of three database and document management software programs that you located on the Web.

3. What systems you would use and why.

PROJECT 7-8 PREPARE A RETENTION SCHEDULE AND IMPROVE SKILLS IN MAKING DECISIONS

Determine records retention requirements and prepare a retention schedule (Objective 4)

Increase decision-making skills (Objective 6)

Continuing with the Records Retention Schedule for JWay Nu-Systems Tech that you created in Project 7-6,

you are now asked to decide how long to retain the records in the Active and Inactive files. Using the form on DCD7-06, key the number of years you would retain the records as Active or Inactive. Below the table, write a brief explanation to your instructor of your reasons for deciding how many years to keep each record in the Active and Inactive files. Submit your revised schedule to your instructor.

PROJECT 7-9 INCREASE SKILLS IN MAKING DECISIONS, PROFESSIONAL GROWTH

Increase decision-making skills (Objective 6)

Add to your Professional Growth Plan that you began in Chapter 1 by determining what training courses or workshops are available for an administrative professional who wants to improve his or her decision-making skills. Save your training ideas on your Professional Growth Plan file as PGP7-9.

 COMMUNICATION POWER

Use DCD7-b to assist you in improving your grammar skills.

ASSESSMENT OF CHAPTER OBJECTIVES

Now that you have completed the chapter and the projects, take a few minutes to review the chapter learning objectives. For your convenience, the objectives are repeated here. Did you accomplish these objectives? If you were unable to accomplish the objectives, give your reasons for not doing so; be specific and concise. Your instructor may prefer that your answers be submitted to her or him. If so, DCD7-c contains the Assessment of Chapter Objectives. Complete the Assessment of Chapter Objectives; submit your results to your instructor.

1. Explain what records management is and how records management applies to administrative professionals.　　　　　　　　　　　　　　　　　　　　　　Yes ☐　　No ☐

_____

_____

_____

2. Identify best practices for managing records.　　　　　　Yes ☐　　No ☐

_____

_____

_____

3. Describe the types of storage systems for paper and electronic records.　　Yes ☐　　No ☐

_____

_____

_____

4. Determine records retention requirements and prepare a retention schedule.   Yes ☐   No ☐

_____

_____

_____

5. Apply the rules for indexing records.   Yes ☐   No ☐

_____

_____

_____

6. Increase decision-making skills.   Yes ☐   No ☐

_____

_____

_____

CHAPTER 8

PRESENTATIONS

Learning Objectives

1. Develop and deliver individual and group verbal presentations using visuals.
2. Release your creativity.
3. Conquer presentation fears.

Comstock Images

> ENHANCE WRITTEN AND VERBAL SKILLS

Both verbal and written communications are significant parts of the administrative professional's job. In Chapter 6 you had the opportunity to increase your written communication skills. In this chapter, you have the opportunity to enhance your written and verbal communication skills.

Many people experience stage fright and presentation anxiety. In fact, surveys show that fear of speaking in front of groups is one of the greatest fears people have. Some people believe giving a speech is more frightening than falling off a cliff, encountering financial difficulties, or even being in a pit with snakes.[1] Numerous individuals lack the confidence and skill to make effective presentations. You can probably cite several incidences in which you have observed ineffectiveness at the podium. You might have found that in addition to showing fear, the speaker was not confident, the subject matter was presented in a boring manner, the speaker did not seem to have a command of the subject matter, or the visuals were poorly presented. Additionally, you might have been in an audience in which the speaker was so boring that half the audience went to sleep, with you included in that half.

In addition to the bad experiences, you have probably had the opportunity to hear some outstanding speakers, ones in which you heard every word the speaker said and felt energized and motivated as you left the presentation. As an administrative professional, you may not speak before large audiences often; however, you will have numerous opportunities to speak before small groups. In fact, your job may demand that you lead small teams of people and present the teams' reports to groups of people within your organization. Also, as you become a member of professional organizations such as the International Association of

---

[1]Making Effective Oral Presentations," <http://web.cba.neu.edu/~ewertheim/skills/oral.htm> (accessed May 21, 2005).

Giving verbal presentations to an audience is one of the top fears of most individuals.

© Digital Vision

Administrative Professionals (IAAP), you will have the chance to assume leadership roles, with these roles giving you the opportunity to preside over a small group in your own chapter of IAAP or even a large group at a national convention of IAAP. For your own professional growth, it is important that you develop your presentation skills.

> PREPARE MENTALLY FOR THE VERBAL PRESENTATION

To help you prepare mentally for the presentation, you should ask and answer the following questions.

▶ What are my goals in giving this presentation? Do I want to inform my audience? Do I want to entertain my audience? Most of the time as an administrative professional, your goal in giving a presentation is to inform your audience. For example, if you have chaired a committee in your organization on strategic directions for your unit for the next year, your goal is to inform your audience of those strategic directions.

▶ What strategy will I use in presenting my ideas? How will I tailor the message to the audience?

▶ How will I structure my presentation so that the audience has these basic questions answered?

1. Why should I pay attention to you? What credibility do you have on the subject?

2. What relevance does what you are saying have for my life?

3. What should I do with the information you are giving me?

> Develop Audience Rapport

Without prior knowledge and planning for a particular audience, it is almost impossible to develop **rapport** (a mutually trusting relationship). In getting to know your audience, here are several considerations.

Who Is the Audience?

How old are they? Are they men, women, or both? What are their demographics? For example, if you have a number of people in the audience who are from countries outside the United States, you may need to define terms that are specific to the United States. What are their interests? What do they know? What knowledge do they have of the topic that you plan to present? What do they want to learn from your presentation? Based on who they are and what they know, should you be informing or persuading your audience?

Spotlight *on*

COMMUNICATION

Before your presentation, find out all you can about your audience.

Why Are They Attending?

Is it a job requirement that they be in attendance? If so, what relevance does the topic have for their job? Will they be able to use the information you are giving them immediately? Will it make their work life easier or more productive? Individuals who are required by their supervisors to attend are sometimes a more difficult audience. You have to convince them early in your presentation that the time they are spending listening to you will be worthwhile. You can expect people who are voluntarily attending your session to be initially more receptive to your message. After all, they chose to come, so they must have some interest in the topic. However, if you have not prepared your talk well, it is possible to have these initially interested people leave with the feeling that they have wasted their time.

Is Your Topic Controversial?

If you are presenting a topic that is controversial, your task is much more difficult. You must convince the audience that the subject being presented can enrich their lives in some way. For example, they will be more informed by what you have presented; they will change their viewpoint because of your presentation; or they will change some direction in their life as a result of your presentation.

▷ Release Your Creativity

What do creativity and learning how to release your creativity have to do with presenting? Have you ever been to a presentation that was boring? Dull? Ill prepared? Chances are that you answered these questions with a resounding yes. If so, you clearly understand the connection between creativity and presentations. Creativity is a necessary ingredient of successful presentations.

Creativity Defined

The dictionary definition of **creativity** is "having the ability or power to create" or "characterized by originality and expressiveness; imaginative."[2] Creativity is a process. It is a way of thinking and doing. It is a way of making new connections or new links. It is solving a problem in a new and different way. Consider this example:

> *You have a problem convincing one of your coworkers that PowerPoint slides are important in an upcoming presentation the two of you are preparing. You keep telling her how important visuals are and how they can help an audience remember more of what they hear. She constantly rejects your ideas. You decide to invite her to a presentation at your local IAAP chapter, where you know the presenter will be using visuals. You have heard the speaker on previous occasions, and you know he is an excellent presenter. Your coworker agrees to go. After the presentation, she remarked that the visuals he used were extremely beneficial in helping her remember his main points. Then she laughingly remarked, "I understand your point. I'm willing to use visuals in our presentation if you are willing to help prepare them."*

You used your creativity. You presented an important concept to an individual in more than one way. You helped bring about change in her thinking.

Information is retained longer when presented both orally and visually.

© Image Source

▷ Steps in Releasing Creativity

As you commit to getting in touch with your creative self, remember that it is a process. You cannot decide one day to become more creative and then suddenly be more creative the next day. Developing creativity is a process that occurs over time; engaging in the following techniques will help you.

- ▸ Have faith in your ability to become creative.
- ▸ Try problem-solving techniques.
- ▸ Observe children.
- ▸ Control your judgmental self.
- ▸ Let your creativity soar.

Have Faith in Your Creativity

Have you ever said to yourself or others, "I do not have a creative bone in my body"? You were not being **self-deprecating** (disapproving of self) or even modest; you merely were stating facts about your abilities as you saw them. Becoming creative is a process. First, it demands that you believe in yourself. Next, it demands that you nurture the development of your creativity. If you have an idea about something that is different from the ideas of other individuals, do not immediately assume you are wrong. Try it out. Your idea may be the creative spark to solving a complex problem.

Try Problem-Solving Techniques

Assume that you have this problem at work.

> *The records management system JWay is using is not working well. Several of the administrative professionals have complained that they can never find anything. You,*

---

[2] *The American Heritage Dictionary,* Third Edition (Boston: Houghton Mifflin Company, 1993), p. 311.

CHECK A

Self

Select a problem that you have at work or school. Use a technique called *incubating*. As you are falling asleep, review the problem and several solutions that you have considered for solving the problem. Then go to sleep and let your subconscious work. Engage in this same activity three nights in a row. Then ask yourself if your subconscious produced an answer for you.[3]

too, are concerned about the system. You talk with Ms. Portosky; she asks you what changes you would make to have an effective system. You do not have an answer; however, you tell her that you will do some research. You decide to ask some of your associates in the local IAAP chapter what suggestions they have for developing an effective records management system. They give you several names to contact. You proceed to do so. You spend time going to the companies and looking at the systems. You talk with the administrative professionals who manage the systems. As a result of your research, you decide on two companies that have what you believe are effective systems. You are pleased and excited about adopting a system that works. Ms. Portosky has promised to support financially any sound changes to the system. However, she asks that you present your research and ideas to the other administrative assistants at JWay. You believe they will be extremely pleased with the possibility of getting a new system.

You call a meeting of the administrative professionals. Before the meeting, you spend hours preparing your presentation. You have all the facts and figures. You have PowerPoint slides explaining the major points. You practice before presenting. However, you notice as you are presenting that your coworkers do not seem to be interested. You wonder why since you have heard so many of them complain in the past. When you complete your presentation, several administration professionals begin to tell you why the ideas you presented will not work. They are angry with you; you are upset and frustrated. You have worked hours on the project. Your motives were not self-motivated ones. You were motivated by the needs of JWay. You did your research, and you presented some very workable recommendations.

What went wrong? You saw a problem. You received the support of your employer. You did the research.

You presented a solution to a problem that administrative professionals had been complaining about for at least six months. You exercised creativity and commitment to JWay in your work.

Clearly, you were creative in your approach. You thought through a situation, received support from administration, and found possible solutions to the problem. However, you were not creative in your involvement of people. You took a task that involved all administrative professionals in the company and attempted to solve it alone. You did not consider the needs of others for involvement. How can you creatively correct the problem? You know you have several solid suggestions. How can you get the administrative professionals to consider them? You might employ one of the teachings of **Aikido,** a Japanese art of self-defense that uses the principles of nonresistance to debilitate the strength of the opponent.[4] Rather than getting angry at the group, respond to their concerns with a non-confrontational statement. Invite them to look at the systems that you have seen. Get their ideas on how the records management system could be more effective. Bringing the group into the planning and recommendation process will probably dissipate their anger. The group does know there is a problem, and they are interested in developing an effective records management system. They are not willing to let you solve the problem by yourself; they want to be involved.

Observe Children

Children allow their creativity to run unabated. Their imagination generally knows no boundaries. Think back to the child who was once within you; the one you pushed out of your consciousness because you grew up. Let that child back in. Play

---

[3]Kris Cole, *The Complete Idiot's Guide to Clear Communication,* (Indianapolis: Alpha Books, 2002), p. 302.

[4]Farlex, "The Free Dictionary.com," as cited in *The American Heritage Dictionary of the English Language,* Fourth Edition (Boston: Houghton Mifflin Company, 2003), <http://www.thefreedictionary.com/aikido> (accessed May 21, 2005).

Self

Engage in positive self-talk. Think of a mistake that you have made at work or school recently. Once you realized that you had made a mistake, what did you do? Did you engage in negative self-talk? If so, the next time you make a mistake, try the opposite, engage in positive self-talk. Say to yourself, "I've learned through this experience; I will not make the same mistake again." Continue to behave in this manner for approximately two weeks. Have you modified your behavior? Are you less likely to berate yourself for making a mistake? Do you find you are making fewer mistakes?

games. Have a water fight; get out the squirt guns and play! Ask a child how to solve a problem; you might be amazed at the creative ideas you hear. Push the boundaries aside; your ideas are limited only by the boundaries that you set on your adult imagination.[5]

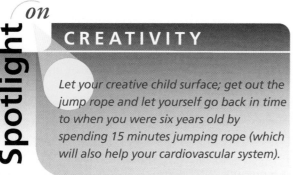

Spotlight on CREATIVITY

Let your creative child surface; get out the jump rope and let yourself go back in time to when you were six years old by spending 15 minutes jumping rope (which will also help your cardiovascular system).

Control Your Judgmental Self

As you are thinking through a problem or an issue, do not be judgmental. Let your thoughts flow freely. Do not discard any of them. Do not let your mind tell you that an idea is no good or ridiculous. To help you control your **judgmental** (exercise judgment or criticism) self (which is not easy to do), pay attention to each thought you have. If you begin to become critical of your thoughts, attack the judgmental you. Say to yourself, *judgmental self, retreat!*

Let Your Creativity Soar

According to Jean Piaget, a noted professor of psychology who contributed greatly to the educational world, the principle goal of education is to create

individuals who are capable of doing new things, not simply of repeating what other generations have done. The Chinese word "to learn" consists of two characters. One character is a picture of a moose, which refers to the "self" of each individual. The other character consists of a pair of wings, with the wings resting above the self. To the Chinese, the truly educated person is one who lets the self soar.[6] It takes both learning and freedom (the freedom to create, to learn new things, to experiment) to be the most creative person you can be. Review Figure 8-1, which lists several other steps for boosting your creativity.

> PREPARE YOUR PRESENTATION

Have you ever heard a speaker deliver an excellent presentation that had no relevance for the audience? If so, you probably saw an audience who demonstrated numerous signs of disinterest—fidgeting, yawning, talking to their neighbor, or even "dozing off." As you begin to prepare, give thought to who the audience will be and what their interests are. Have you been asked to speak on a particular topic or has the group given you free reign? If you have not been given a topic, review the suggestions given at the beginning of this chapter, which are: know your audience and determine their interests. The "kiss of death" for a presentation is often due to the presenter not considering who the audience will be and what their interests are.

As an administrative professional, you will generally give presentations to three basic types of audiences.

[5]Karen Keubler, "Developing Your Personal Creativity—a Powerful Force!" 2001, <http://blessingsforlife.com/money/personalcreativity.htm> (accessed May 21, 2005).
[6]"Developing Creativity," <http://www.chemistrycoach.com/on.htm> (accessed May 21, 2005).

Figure 8-1 STEPS FOR BOOSTING YOUR CREATIVITY

1. Sit down with a drawing pad and sketch drawings of things you did as a child that were creative.

2. Make a list of things that your company or school has done that were creative.

3. Interview 12 strangers in one day and ask them for their definition of creativity.

4. Write down the names of six famous people who have inspired you and examples of why you find them inspiring.

5. Ask yourself this question: Why are the best teachers creative?

6. Pick a problem from your past. Make a list of 12 different people who had nothing to do with your problem. Write down how they might have defined your problem from their perspectives.[7]

7. If you cannot think, go for a walk. A change of atmosphere is good for you and gentle exercise helps shake up the brain cells.

8. Read as much as you can about everything possible. Books exercise your brain, provide inspiration, and fill you with information that allows you to make creative connections easily.[8]

▸ Coworkers in your organization
▸ Workplace teams containing a cross section of people within your organization
▸ Colleagues within professional organizations to which you belong

The following steps will help you make your presentation confidently and expertly if practiced every time you make a presentation.

▷ Plan

Planning involves gathering and arranging your thoughts, developing your ideas, and finding unique ways to express them. Using your creativity in the process will help you put together a memorable presentation that holds the audience's attention and allows you to get your message across. As you are planning, think about talking to individuals, and the word *individuals* is important here. You want each individual to take something "home" from your presentation; something that will allow that person to grow in his or her professional life.

As soon as you know you are going to give a presentation, start a folder. Put whatever comes to your mind in the folder—for example, ideas, questions, and quotations. You may even wake up in the middle of the night with an idea. Keep a pad and pencil by your bed to use in jotting down your thoughts. You do not want to forget them.

▷ Determine Your Purpose and Role

What is your purpose? Do you want to inform your audience? Do you want to inform and persuade your audience? Is your role one of coach? Advocate? Teacher? Spend some time determining your purpose and your role. If you do not understand both, no one else will. Once you have determined it, write it down in one clear, concise statement. As you prepare your presentation, review the statement frequently to stay on track.

▷ Research the Topic

Research your topic on the Web or in a library. Generally, there is a wealth of material available on the Web. This type of research is referred to as secondary research (information gathered through published sources). You also may want to conduct primary research (information gathered through interaction with people) if you have a topic that lends itself to such an activity. For example, you may be asked to deliver a presentation to your local chapter of IAAP on professional ethics. If so, you may do primary research with a group of IAAP members on ethical and/or unethical practices in the profession.

▷ Determine the Location and Time

The location and time of your presentation and any other activities that will occur around the same time are important to know. Ask these questions about the setting.

▸ Where will I be presenting? Will it be in the workplace? A hotel? A conference center? A school?

---

[7]Robert Alan Black, "Creativity Exercises," 2002, <http://www.cre8ng.com/newsletter/news23.shtml> (accessed May 12, 2005).
[8]Jeffrey Baumgartner, "10 Steps for Boosting Creativity," 2003, <http://www.jpb.com/creative/creative.php> (accessed May 12, 2005).

- What time is the presentation? Morning? During or after breakfast? Immediately after lunch? In the afternoon? In the evening?
- Are there other activities occurring before or after your presentation? You need this information so that you will know when the room can be set up and when it is possible for you to remove any materials or equipment once your presentation is over.
- What is the size of the room? What is the configuration of the seating? If the audience is small, should the audience sit around a table? As the presenter, you have the latitude to determine the seating arrangements.

Be certain the size of the room is appropriate. You do not want to be giving a presentation to 12 people in a room designed for 100 people. It will look as though you gave a party and no one came. Nor do you want to give a presentation to 50 people in a room designed for 25. People are not comfortable when they are crowded. Check out the room (if possible) well before your presentation. Talk with the person(s) responsible for the room arrangements. Provide input if possible. Ask that someone check the room on the morning of the presentation to be certain that the temperature is pleasant, the room is clean, the lighting is appropriate, and the acoustics are good.

▷ Determine the Length

As a general rule, presentations should be no longer than 20 minutes, with 30 to 40 minutes the maximum. Why? There is a large variance between the audience's listening skills and the presenter's speaking skills. Studies have shown that generally individuals' speaking rate is approximately 125 to 150 words per minute. Our mental capacity for understanding speaking is approximately 400 words per minute. With this difference in speaking speed and thought speed, listeners are using only 25 percent of their capacity.[9] With 75 percent of their time, listeners can engage in something else—such as letting their minds wander or evaluating the speaker's dress, voice, and mannerisms. When a speaker goes beyond the 30-minute maximum, the audience generally becomes bored and restless.

An exception to this rule exists if you are delivering a presentation in which the audience is actively

The audience may become restless when a presentation is long.

© Stockbyte

involved. For example, you may be a workshop presenter, with numerous activities in which the audience participates as small groups. You may present for 20 minutes, give small groups a task to do, get feedback from the small groups, and then have another 15 or 20 minutes when you present, followed by additional small group activities.

▷ Organize the Material

What is the most effective organization? The answer is the one that works best for you, taking into consideration the material you are presenting. Here are often used methods of organization; pick the style that works best for you.

- Make an outline.
- Talk out the presentation with a close friend; then make an outline.
- Prepare a numerical list of the points you want to cover; do this on 3 × 5 cards if you wish. You can shuffle the order easily on the cards; you can also carry them around with you and jot down ideas as they occur to you.
- Group your related ideas.

▷ Write the Presentation

Once you have planned and researched adequately, you are ready to begin the writing process. Your

---

[9]Dick Lee and Delmar Hatesohl, "Listening: Our Most Used Communication Skill," 1993, <http://muextension.missouri.edu/explore/comm/cm0150.htm> (accessed May 24, 2005).

Spotlight *on*

ORGANIZATION

Organize your materials before you start writing; this approach forces you to think through the important parts of your presentation and the order in which they should be delivered.

writing tasks include developing an opening, developing a strong body, and preparing an appropriate conclusion. As you write, you should continue to think of ways that you can make your presentation interesting for your audience. Several suggestions are given in this section, along with preparing visuals.

Develop an Opening

The opening should immediately get the audience's attention. You might tell a story, use a quotation, ask a question, or refer to a current event. Begin with the unexpected and the unpredictable. Also, know what you do best. If you are a good joke teller, you might open with a joke. However, if you are not, stay away from a joke like you would stay away from poison. Nothing can be worse than starting a presentation with a joke that is in poor taste, offends someone in the audience, or one that the audience does not think is funny.

Another possibility is to open with a story if you tell stories well. If you decide to tell a story, ask and answer these questions for yourself.

▶ Is there a link between the story and the presentation?
▶ Is it a new story?
▶ Am I telling it as succinctly as possible? You do not want to spend one-third of your time on your opening story.

However you decide to begin your presentation, remember that its purpose is to set the stage for your message. Make the opening not only strong but also one that relates directly to the central message of your presentation.

Develop a Strong Message

Start with your strongest points. Get to your major points quickly; do not spend time on irrelevant facts. As you develop this message, keep your focus

on your projected audience. Keep asking these questions of yourself as you write:

1. What is my message?

2. Am I developing the right message for my audience?

3. Am I using current examples to illustrate concepts?

4. Do I have current facts and figures?

5. Do my quotations relate to a point in my presentation? Do not use too many quotes; such a practice can be deadly for the audience.

6. Am I using direct language? Do not try to impress your audience with multi-syllable words or little used terminology.

7. Am I using active voice rather than passive voice? For example, do not say, "It is believed . . . ," say, "I believe . . ."

8. Is the message of my presentation a sincere, knowledgeable, and credible one?

Remember that repetition is one key to your audience remembering your message. Take every opportunity as you write to reinforce the point that you are making by saying it over and over or by giving different explanations of the same point. A good rule to follow throughout your presentation is one that you have probably heard often: First tell the audience what you are going to say, then tell them, then tell them what you have said.

Anticipate Questions

Determine if you are going to allow the audience to ask questions. If your answer is *yes,* think through the ten most likely questions that you may be asked. Then, plan the answer to these questions. When you open up the session for questions, use these guidelines:

1. Understand the question; repeat the question or paraphrase it if needed.

2. Be honest; if you cannot answer the question, say so.

3. Control interchanges: if a questioner becomes a heckler, try to enlist the audience. If a questioner digresses, gently remind the questioner of the presentation goal.

4. Use the last question to summarize what has been said.

Develop a Strong Closing

As you have learned, the opening should be an appropriate attention-getter. In the body, you must develop the heart of your presentation. The conclusion is your destination. It is the part of your presentation that takes your audience where you want them to be—what you want them to learn or what you want them to do.

A good conclusion gets the audience's attention. It helps them see the relationship between each part of your presentation—between the opening and the body and the body and the conclusion. The closing puts the pieces of the presentation together in a creative and interesting way so the audience leaves thinking you have helped them learn and/or have motivated them to some action.

Let the audience know you are ready to conclude by stating simply, "In conclusion . . ." or "My final point is. . . ." Make the conclusion short (about 5 percent to 10 percent of your talk) and powerful. The conclusion can be a moving statement, a story, a call to action, or a challenge. For example, if you are delivering a presentation on human potential, you might end by saying:

I leave you with three challenges—to be the best person you can be, to constantly grow and learn, and to reach your unreachable star.

The conclusion gives you an opportunity to connect with your audience for one final minute or so. For example, you can urge them to action, make them think about new possibilities, or even make them laugh. The final impression you make on the audience is the one they will remember the most. You must plan your last few sentences with care; you want to leave your audience energized to reach the goal you established in the beginning of your presentation. Figure 8-2 provides several tips for delivering presentations effectively.

Prepare and Use Visuals Effectively

When used properly, visual aids can be very effective. According to research studies, on average, people retain the following percentages of what they see; hear; see and hear; and see, hear, and do.

Figure 8-2 TIPS FOR DELIVERING PRESENTATIONS

1. Don't think about delivering a speech; think about talking to people.

2. Make frequent eye contact.

3. Rehearse your explanations of charts and diagrams.

4. Prepare for disasters—computer not working, lights going out, and so forth.

5. Use visuals to help you explain, not as substitutes for an explanation.

6. Watch the time.

7. Take questions in the middle of the presentation.[10]

- 20 percent of what they see
- 30 percent of what they hear
- 50 percent of what they see and hear, and up to
- 80 percent of what they see, hear, and do simultaneously[11]

However, if visuals are not used well, they can distract from the presentation. You have probably sat through a few presentations where visuals were not effective. Perhaps you could not read them—the print was too small. Perhaps the visuals had very little relevance to the presentation; apparently, the presenter did not spend much time in thinking about what the visuals should be. Or, perhaps the visuals were so ineffectively presented that they actually distracted from the speaker's message. If you want your audience to remember what you said, show them effective visuals during your presentation. Review Figure 6-12 in Chapter 6 to refresh your memory on preparation of visuals.

▷ Write Your Introduction

One way to build credibility with the audience is to give them your credentials. How do you do this? First, find out who will be introducing you. Then write a succinct statement—one that will take no more than two minutes to deliver. Highlight your major accomplishments. Do not send a

---

[10]Dennis G. Jerz, "Oral Presentations: Delivering Information Face-to-Face," 2003, <http://jerz.setonhill.edu/writing/technical/oral.htm> (accessed May 12, 2005).

[11]Actstream Technologies, Services, 2005, <http://www.actstream.com/services> (accessed May 24, 2005).

packet with pages of information about you and leave it up to the introducer to determine the highlights; the person may miss a major piece of information that you want the audience to know. You should take a copy of the introduction with you in case the introducer has misplaced the copy you sent. If you are not being introduced, introduce yourself as you begin.

> REHEARSE

Make arrangements, if at all possible, to rehearse in the room where you are giving the presentation. Sometimes this is not possible if you are delivering a presentation out of town and are not able to fly or drive in a day or several hours before you will be giving the presentation. However, generally you will be giving the presentation to a local audience, and you can rehearse the presentation in the room in which you will be delivering it.

Rehearse the presentation just as you are going to give it. For example, if you will be standing at a lectern during the presentation, stand at a lectern during rehearsal. If you are going to be using a microphone, use a microphone during your rehearsal. Be certain that you know before the presentation what type of microphone you will use. You might want a stationary microphone; however, remember if you choose this type you cannot walk away from it. Its advantage is that you do not have to be concerned with holding it or being certain that it is positioned on your clothing correctly. The main disadvantage to a stationary microphone is a major one—it ties you to the podium. In most cases, it is not advantageous for a speaker to be tied to the podium.

As you rehearse, include the visuals that you are going to use. If you are using PowerPoint, check out the computer to be certain that you know how to show the PowerPoint slides. If you are too uncomfortable with attempting to use the PowerPoint when you are presenting, get someone to assist you. If you choose this approach, the person who is assisting you must rehearse several times with you to be certain that he or she knows exactly when each slide is to be used. Provide the person assisting you a copy of your presentation to follow if possible. Certainly, it is possible to render a presentation ineffective quickly through poor use of PowerPoint slides.

Ask a respected colleague to listen to your practice session and provide constructive criticism. Go over your presentation completely three or four times. With repeated rehearsals, the text becomes part of your memory; you will be more at ease because you are not likely to forget important points during your presentation. Figure 8-3 lists several common mistakes people make in presentations. You can avoid these mistakes by planning and rehearsing.

| Figure 8-3 | **COMMON MISTAKES PEOPLE MAKE IN PRESENTATIONS** |

1. The speaker lives in his or her own little world of research. He believes that all background information needed to appreciate the meaning of the work is common knowledge. This is seldom the case.

2. The structure of the presentation is unclear. Important matters such as problem identification or motivation are insufficiently clear.

3. Visual aids are inadequate, confusing, unreadable, too small, too crowded, etc.

4. The speaker uses long, complicated sentences and jargon.

5. The speaker reads the speech.

6. The speaker uses monotonous sentences, spoken either too quickly or too slowly, with lack of emphasis and unclear pronunciation.[12]

Before you leave the facility where you will be giving the presentation, get a name of a contact person who can help you with last minute details of room arrangement or equipment on the day of your presentation. You never know when something might occur at the last minute that demands some assistance from a person who knows the facility and can get you additional equipment if there is a malfunction of equipment.

> DRESS APPROPRIATELY

Determine what you will wear several days before the presentation. The usual attire for a woman is a suit or dress; for a man, it is a suit and tie. Wear

---

[12]"How to Give a Successful Oral Presentation," <http://www.efcats.org/pages/presentation/oralpresentation.html> (accessed May 12, 2005).

something you are comfortable in and that looks good on you. Bright colors are perfectly okay. Women should avoid necklaces and earrings that are too large and distracting. Rings and bracelets are appropriate; however, large, noisy bracelets are inappropriate because of the distraction they can cause for audience members. Men may wear colored shirts and bright ties. Both women and men should wear a color that looks particularly good on them. Hair for both men and women should be well groomed. For women, this is not a time to try out a new hairstyle.

> CONTROL FEAR

Realize that nervousness and even fear are normal reactions of many people when they think about presenting before an audience. A number of well-known performers have performance fears. Donny Osmond, Barbara Streisand, and Kim Basinger are a few performers who have dealt with this fear. Barbara Streisand's social phobia prevented her from singing in public for 27 years. Early in her career, she forgot the words to several songs while performing. From then on, Streisand worried that she might make the same mistake again if she performed in public. She gradually conquered her fear of performing by starting with a small show, then a national tour, and then performing in front of a large television audience. The gradual accumulation of positive experiences helped her overcome her fear.[13]

Fear can definitely work to your advantage. It generally makes you work harder to understand your audience and what type of presentation will be beneficial for them. A well-prepared and well-rehearsed presentation can eliminate many of your fears. Visualizing success can also help you control fear.

Remind yourself that you have prepared well. You have followed all of the steps mentioned previously, such as knowing your audience, having faith in your own creativity, preparing your presentation well, and rehearsing. Now is the time to burn off some of your nervousness by exercising. Go jogging, walking, or biking. Whatever your favorite exercise is, do it.

Give yourself a break from working too hard on your job. Try not to push yourself to the limit with work responsibilities a few days before your presentation. When you are overly tired, you increase your chances of not doing a good job.

> PRESENTATION DAY

Arrive early enough to check out the layout of the room, the equipment, and the microphone. Take the name and telephone number of the contact person at the location where you are giving your presentation with you in case you have last minute changes.

▷ Practice Relaxation Techniques

In the 10 or 15 minutes before your presentation is to begin, find a private place (maybe a small room away from the gathering audience) and try these relaxation techniques.

- ▶ Sit in a straight chair, carry your rib cage high, and breathe deeply. As you exhale, push the air over your lower teeth in a *ssss* sound. Focus your efforts entirely on your breathing.
- ▶ Walk around. Take a brisk walk for a minute or two. Do some jumping jacks.
- ▶ Work off nervous tension by taking deep breaths.
- ▶ Realize that some nervousness is normal and can help you. You can channel your nervousness into your talk, which can become a positive energy source that adds to your effectiveness.
- ▶ Right before you enter the room, swing your arms a few times.
- ▶ Remember that the audience is your friend; those in the audience want you to succeed.

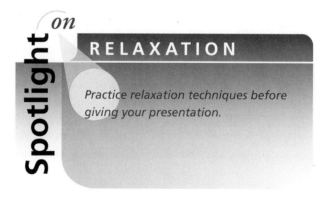

Spotlight *on*

RELAXATION

Practice relaxation techniques before giving your presentation.

▷ Attend to Your Introduction

Pay attention to your body language as you are being introduced. Look at the introducer and then look slowly at the audience. As you approach the lectern, walk with confidence. As you reach the lectern, look at the audience and smile. Place your notes as high

---

[13]"Famous People Who Have Suffered from Social Anxiety," <http://www.socialanxietyassist.com.au/famous_people.shtml> (accessed May 24, 2005).

as possible on the lectern so you can refer to them easily. Respond to the introduction, but make your response brief. You might say *thank you very much* and exchange a firm handshake with the introducer. If you are not being introduced, you will need to introduce yourself.

▷ Deliver Your Presentation

Pause for just a moment before beginning your presentation. Let your eyes sweep the room. Do not draw attention to your hands, which may be shaking as you begin. Leave your notes on the lectern; you do not want to call attention to shaking papers. Attempt to create rapport with the audience in the first minute; if you do so, you will generally keep them for the remainder of your presentation.

Observe Nonverbal Feedback

During the presentation, observe the nonverbal feedback from the audience. Puzzled looks or blank stares are cues that the audience does not understand what you are saying. You may need to modify the rate of your voice or give another example or two to clarify what you mean. Smiles and nodding heads are positive reactions.

Maintain Eye Contact with the Audience

If you are in a small group, look at each individual briefly. When you are in a large group, move your eyes from one side of the room to the other, concentrating for approximately five or six seconds on the individual or group before moving to another individual or group. Eyes can be used to convince the audience of your honesty, openness, and confidence in what you are saying.[14] Use natural gestures. You may use your arms and hands to emphasize points. However, avoid too many arm and hand gestures; they can be distracting to the audience. Be natural; do not perform. Speak in a normal tone of voice; do not speak too fast. Articulate carefully. For example, do not drop your *g's;* say *learning,* not *learnin.*

Speak with Credibility

Credibility is defined as "capable of being believed, worthy of confidence."[15] As you speak, demonstrate your competence. Let the audience know you are experienced in your field. Make a few relevant comments about your past experiences. Do not talk too fast; slow down and take your time. Vary your inflection. Speaking in a monotone can put an audience to sleep quickly. It sends a message to the audience that shouts, *boring, boring, boring.* Be animated in your speech as well as in your expression. Just as in a normal conversation, your facial expression reinforces what you are saying; the same is true when delivering a presentation. Make certain that your normal expressive self comes through as you speak.

Repeat Your Main Points

Repetition is often important when talking one on one to an individual. It is doubly important when speaking to a group. Although most presenters do not like to admit that the audience may get bored and "tune out" for a few minutes, it clearly happens. Even with the best of speakers, audiences may tune out at some point because of their own personal concerns or needs. Have you ever been listening to a speaker and something that was said triggered you to think of an office problem? If so, as you turned your attention to something else for a few seconds, you missed an important point the speaker made. Thus, for the speaker, it is important to repeat the main points a second time. You may not word the points exactly as you did the first time; however, you should repeat them, thus reinforcing the major points of your presentation for all audience members—those who may have tuned out for a second or two and those who did not. As you close your presentation, it is also important to repeat your important points. Such an approach gives the audience a final chance to remember what you have said.

Keep Your Audience's Attention

Stories are good attention-getters. It is generally smart to sprinkle a few stories within the context of your speech. Make certain that the stories are relevant to the subject of your presentation. Do not overuse the stories. Three or four short stories are generally enough in a 30-minute presentation.

Watch Your Time

If you have been asked to deliver a 20-minute presentation, do so. Do not allow yourself to go over the time limit. Because you rehearsed your presentation several times before giving it, you have a definite feel

---

[14]Shared Learning, "Oral Communication–Presentation Skills," 2003, <http://www.sharedlearning.org.uk/html_pages/oral_communication_presentations_three.htm> (accessed May 24, 2005).

[15]*The American Heritage College Dictionary,* Fourth Edition (Boston: Houghton Mifflin Company, 1993) p. 334.

for how long it will take. However, it is essential that you watch the time during your presentation; do not be obvious about it. Such behavior would be distracting for the audience. Some speakers find it helpful to take off their watch and place it on the podium. Determine a plan that works for you, with no audience distraction.

If you go over your limit by several minutes, the audience will usually let you know by some subtle message such as fidgeting in their chairs or a not so subtle message, such as leaving the room.

Spotlight on TIME

If you are asked to deliver a 20-minute presentation, do so. Do not let it become a 30-minute presentation.

Deliver a Strong Closing

Your conclusion should be announced clearly and tie in with your opening statements. Assume the title of your presentation is Your Creativity: Use It or Lose It! You began your presentation by saying that true creativity is available to everyone—not just musicians or visual artists—but to all who seek it. You continued by stating there are a number of steps one can take to boost creativity. You proceeded to identify and explain ten such steps. Throughout your presentation you made the point that anyone can be creative and you continued to give suggestions for discovering your creative self.

In your closing, you might say: *I am closing with a challenge for you! I ask you to let your creative self out! Try for one week just one of the techniques that I have given you to increase your creativity. Write down the creative ideas that you have had during the week. Write down the creative solutions that you found for problems that you were facing. Post your notes on the refrigerator door or some other familiar place. The next week, try another technique that I have given you. Follow the same procedures as you did the first week. Watch your creativity grow. CONGRATULATE YOURSELF FOR ALLOWING YOUR CREATIVE SELF TO EMERGE! REWARD YOURSELF. If you take my suggestions seriously, I know that you will* have more creative ideas the second week than you had the first.

Avoid Common Mistakes

People commonly make these ten mistakes when delivering a presentation. Your task is to avoid them.

1. Failing to prepare with the audience's interests and needs in mind.

2. Failing to rehearse sufficiently.

3. Failing to rehearse with visuals.

4. Failing to check the room configuration.

5. Not knowing when to stop; in other words, speaking too long.

6. Preparing too much material.

7. Beginning with an inappropriate story or joke that does not fit the situation or is in poor taste.

8. Ignoring the body language of the audience; failing to modify the message if the audience does not understand it.

9. Attempting to appear knowledgeable when you are not.

10. Failing to prepare a short and powerful conclusion that motivates the audience to action, challenges them, or motivates them to learn more about the subject.

Review Figure 8-3 again to remind yourself of additional kinds of mistakes people make so that you can avoid them.

> AFTER THE PRESENTATION

Within a day after the presentation, critique your performance. In evaluating yourself be kind, but honest. List the good along with the not-so-good. Pick one or two things to improve before you deliver your next presentation. Realize evaluation is an ongoing process. After your next presentation, pick one or two more things to improve. Pat yourself on the back for the improvements you have made from your prior presentations.

Additionally, get feedback from other people. Ask a respected colleague to evaluate you. You or the individuals who asked you to speak may provide evaluation forms for the people in the audience. Ask to see copies of the completed forms; review them carefully. Do not let yourself become upset over a few negative comments. Know that there will always be some negatives. However, take seriously the points that are made in the critique. Before you speak again, concentrate on how you might improve your presentation techniques. Tell yourself that you are growing as a speaker; with each presentation, you become better than you were the last time you presented!

> TEAM PRESENTATIONS

Teams are used extensively in organizations today. Although the techniques presented in the previous section still apply, team presentations require certain different skills and offer some benefits that a single presenter does not have. Consider these benefits:

- Because of the different people presenting, variety is built in. This variety can increase and hold the attention of an audience if used effectively.
- One team member can be responsible for the visual aids that are being used; for example, handling the PowerPoint® or changing overheads. Note that although PowerPoint is generally the visual of choice for most presenters, overhead transparencies remain effective if used correctly. Overheads provide the opportunity to record information that may be offered by the audience in informal types of presentations. Certainly, this approach can also be used with PowerPoint with one individual recording the information at the computer and then showing it on the screen. White boards may be used in giving presentations within the workplace. These boards allow an individual to sketch ideas or work processes as he or she talks. Also, attachments to white boards are available that allow speakers to capture whatever is on the white board and send it via e-mail to individuals who are out of the workplace. Speakers can also save the notes or illustrations for later use by connecting the attachment to a USB port. These notes can then be downloaded and printed.[16]

- Greater experience and expertise is available because of the number of team members as opposed to one presenter.
- If the audience works in small groups on a particular assignment, team members are available to mingle with the small groups and provide expertise and leadership.

▷ Select the Team

One of the ingredients of a successful team is finding the right people for the team. What should you consider when assembling the team? Here are a few suggestions.

1. What are the strengths and weaknesses of each individual being considered?

2. How does the strength of each individual add to the strength of the team?

3. Do the team members collectively have a breadth of knowledge of the topic to be presented?

4. What particular knowledge of the topic does each individual have? Do individual team members have the technical knowledge needed for the presentation?

5. What people skills does each presenter possess? For example, is the person a team player? An effective communicator? A good listener?

▷ Select the Team Leader

Once the group has been selected, the next task becomes selecting a strong team leader. The individual selected not only should have leadership ability but also should be able to make decisions. The leader is the one who will ultimately be responsible for the team delivering an excellent presentation or a series of presentations. The leader can emerge from a team discussion of various strengths and weaknesses of the group. Team members need to be willing to engage in this discussion non-defensively. Such a discussion should not be thought of as being critical of each other, but merely trying to find the person with the strongest skills in each area needed. A second possibility, if the team is going to be working within an

---

[16]Arik Hesseldahl, "White Boards Get Wired," 2002, <http://www.forbes.com/2002/02/14/0214tentech.html> (accessed June 15, 2005).

organization for a period of time, includes upper administration appointing the leader. A third possibility, if it is a presentation to be delivered to an external group, is the person who was initially contacted by the external group. That person can take the lead responsibility and assemble a team that she or he chooses.

▷ Determine the Purpose

Each team member and the team collectively should know exactly what the purpose of the presentation(s) will be. The team leader should be the facilitator in this session. Questions that need to be asked and answered are:

▶ What do we want our audience to know when we finish?
▶ How will the audience understand this message best?

▷ Identify Team Members' Subject Matter and Presentation Strengths

Factors that need to be considered when deciding who will be responsible for individual subject areas in the presentation and the portion of the presentation he or she will deliver include:

▶ Individual area of expertise in the subject matter to be presented.
▶ Presentation style and skill—who will be the lead presenter, who will conclude, and who will deliver each section.
▶ Understanding of the audience concerning the subject matter. For example, is a technical expert important?
▶ Purpose of the presentation. If it is to persuade, who is the most effective salesperson in the group?

▷ Continually Build the Presenter Team

Team members may stay together for a number of presentations. If so, the team leader and team members

Continually build the team's skills.

© PhotoDisc/Ryan McVay

are responsible for continually building the team, from the time of its inception to the day of the presentation. These techniques will help the team become a more cohesive group.[17]

1. Maintain an unwavering commitment to improve team communication and teamwork skills.

2. Never have one person prepare a section unless there is coordination with the team members and other sections of the presentation before the research begins. Be certain that each section integrates effectively into the whole.

3. Ask that team members give candid feedback to each other, particularly on ways to improve.[18]

4. Rehearse several times. A good way to identify weaknesses is to do a videotape of the rehearsal. You also might have a colleague listen to the team's presentation and critique it.

---

[17]"The Group Presentation," <http://www.sheridanc.on.ca/> (accessed May 25, 2005).
[18]Ibid., pp. 6–7.

Reinforce your learning in this chapter by studying this summary.

▶ Both verbal and written communications are significant parts of the administrative professional's job.

▶ Delivering a verbal presentation is one of the top fears of most individuals.

▶ Preparing mentally for a verbal presentation will help you do it well. When preparing mentally, ask these questions: What are my goals in giving this presentation? What strategy will I use in presenting my ideas? How will I structure my presentation so that the audience has basic questions answered?

▶ Develop audience rapport by paying attention to who the audience is and why they are attending. If your topic is controversial, you must convince the audience that it can enrich their lives in some way.

▶ Creativity is a necessary ingredient of successful presentations.

▶ You can develop and increase your creativity by engaging in these techniques: Having faith in your ability to be creative; trying problem-solving techniques; observing children; controlling your judgmental self, and letting your creativity soar.

▶ The steps in preparing a presentation include planning, determining your purpose and role, researching the topic, determining the location and time, determining the length, organizing the material, and writing the presentation.

▶ In writing the presentation, it is important to develop a strong message, anticipate questions, develop a strong closing, and prepare and use visuals effectively.

▶ As a presenter, you should write your own introduction rather than letting someone else write it. When you write it, you maintain control over the information that is given to the audience.

▶ If at all possible, it is important to rehearse your presentation in the room where you will be presenting. Rehearse just as you will be giving it; for example, if you will be standing at a lectern during the presentation, stand at a lectern during rehearsal.

▶ Ask a respected colleague to listen to your rehearsal and provide constructive criticism.

▶ Dress appropriately for the presentation. Determine what you will wear several days before the presentation. The usual attire for a woman is a suit or dress; for a man, it is a suit and tie.

▶ Take steps to control your fear. Realize that nervousness and even fear are normal reactions. In fact, fear can work to your advantage. It generally makes you work harder to understand your audience and what type of presentation will be beneficial for them.

▶ On presentation day, arrive early enough to check out the room, the equipment, and the microphone. Practice relaxation techniques before your presentation.

▶ As you are delivering your presentation, observe the nonverbal feedback of the audience, maintain eye contact with the audience, speak with credibility, repeat your main points, keep your audience's attention, watch your time, and deliver a strong closing.

▶ Within a day after the presentation, critique your performance. In evaluating yourself, be honest. List the good along with the not-so-good. Also get feedback from other people. Ask a respected colleague to evaluate you; have evaluation forms completed by the audience.

▶ Team presentations are used often today. The advantages of team presentations include the variety built on when members of a team present, greater experience and expertise available, and the ability to have groups work in teams, with individual team members available to work with small groups.

▶ When putting together a team presentation, consideration should be given to selecting the team leader, determining the purpose of the presentation, and identifying individual team members' subject matter and presentation strengths.

▶ Additionally, it is important to continually build the team. For example, a team may stay together during a number of presentations; if so, team members must give consideration to constantly improving their skills.

GLOSSARY

Aikido—Japanese art of self-defense that uses the principles of nonresistance in order to debilitate the strength of the opponent.

Creativity—Having the ability or power to create or characterized by originality and expressiveness; imaginative.

Credibility—Capable of being believed; worthy of confidence.

Judgmental—To exercise judgment or criticism.

Rapport—Relationship, especially one of mutual trust.

Self-deprecating—Disapproval of self.

CHECKPOINT

Check your understanding of these terms by completing DCD8-a on the Data CD.

DISCUSSION ITEMS

These discussion items provide an opportunity to test your understanding of the chapter through written responses and/or discussion with your classmates and your instructor.

1. Explain the mental preparation steps that are necessary before you develop a presentation.

2. List and explain the steps in developing a presentation.

3. Explain how you can help control fear both before and on the presentation day.

4. List and explain eight tips for delivering a successful presentation.

5. What are the benefits of a team presentation?

6. Discuss how you can continue to build a presenter team.

CRITICAL THINKING CASE

You are a member of your local chapter of IAAP. You have been asked to speak at the national meeting of IAAP, which will be held in Boston this year. Your speech is not a keynote; you will be presenting at a session on the first afternoon of the conference—from 2 p.m. to 3 p.m.; there will be four sessions (including yours) going on at the same time. You have been given the prerogative of choosing your own topic and whether or not you will present as an individual or make it a team effort. The theme of the conference is: *Letting Your Best Self Soar.* You decide you will do a team presentation; there are two additional people within your chapter who have agreed to present with you. (Work with two of your classmates on this project.) As a group, explain the steps that you will take in brainstorming and preparing the presentation, including steps to limit the fear factor. Develop a title for the presentation and an outline. Additionally, develop an introduction for each person.

RESPONSES TO SELF-CHECK

A

When you tried incubating, did you come up with a solution to your problem? If so, write that solution in the space provided here.

_____

_____

_____

_____

_____

_____

B

Did you engage in positive self-talk when you made a mistake?

Yes ___ No ___

If your answer is *yes,* have you found that you are more confident in your work at school or in the office?

Yes ___ No ___

Do you find you are making fewer mistakes?

Yes ___ No ___

WORKPLACE PROJECTS

PROJECT 8-1 WRITE AND DELIVER A PRESENTATION

Develop and deliver individual and group verbal presentations using visuals (Objective 1)

Release your creativity (Objective 2)

Conquer presentation fears (Objective 3)

Prepare a written presentation to be delivered to your class on a subject of your choosing. Use your creativity to determine a topic that will not only be of interest to you but also will be of interest to your classmates. The presentation should be no longer than 20 minutes in length. You are to prepare PowerPoint visuals (assuming your classroom is equipped to do so). Turn in a written copy of your presentation to your instructor, along with copies of your PowerPoint slides.

PROJECT 8-2 DELIVER A PRESENTATION AS A TEAM; ADD TO YOUR PROFESSIONAL GROWTH PLAN

Develop and deliver individual and group verbal presentations using visuals (Objective 1)

Release your creativity (Objective 2)

Conquer presentation fears (Objective 3)

In Project 6-6, Chapter 6, you worked as a team to develop a report on the subject of effective office communication. You were asked to save this report for use in this chapter. Working as a team (the same team that wrote the report), prepare a presentation for the class. The presentation should be no longer than 20 minutes. Prepare PowerPoint visuals (assuming your classroom is equipped to do so). Additionally, prepare a Presentation Evaluation to be given to your classmates after they hear your report. A sample evaluation form is on DCD8-02A. You may modify this form or prepare an entirely new form. After your presentation, ask that your classmates complete the forms; then tally the results. Discuss as a group how you might improve your presentation skills. In a memorandum to your instructor, explain what your group plans to do to improve its presentation skills. Use the memorandum form on DCD8-02B. Add to your Professional Growth Plan by determining how you will improve your presentation skills. Save your plan on your disk as PGP8-2.

 COMMUNICATION POWER

Use DCD8-b to assist you in improving your grammar skills.

ASSESSMENT OF CHAPTER OBJECTIVES

Now that you have completed the chapter and the projects, take a few minutes to review the chapter learning objectives. For your convenience, the objectives are repeated here. Did you accomplish these objectives? If you were unable to accomplish the objectives, give your reasons for not doing so; be specific and concise. Your instructor may prefer that your answers be submitted to her or him. If so, DCD8-c contains the Assessment of Chapter Objectives. Complete the Assessment of Chapter Objectives; submit your results to your instructor.

1. Develop and deliver individual and group verbal presentations using visuals.   Yes ☐   No ☐

_____

_____

_____

_____

_____

_____

_____

_____

_____

_____

2. *Release your creativity.*   Yes ☐   No ☐

_____

_____

_____

_____

_____

_____

_____

_____

_____

_____

3. Conquer presentation fears.   Yes ☐   No ☐

_____

_____

_____

_____

_____

_____

_____

_____

PART III: WRITTEN COMMUNICATION, RECORDS, AND PRESENTATIONS

Integrated Project

Class members are to work in teams of three on this project. The situation is as follows.

Activity 1: Plan a Conference

Situation: The three of you who are on this team are members of the local chapter of IAAP. Your chapter is having a regional conference in six months; your team is in charge of planning the conference. Approximately 200 people are expected to attend. Your responsibilities include the following:

1. Determining the theme of the conference.
2. Providing a draft of the brochure to be sent out to the IAAP members in your region announcing the conference. You are not responsible for the final brochure; your team is only responsible for doing an outline of what the brochure should contain. Your plan is for a professional firm to take your ideas and tentative mock up to prepare the final document.
3. Deciding where the conference should be held. It will be in your city; however, you need to determine what hotel or other facility such as a conference center will be used.
4. Scheduling the number of meeting rooms necessary. The conference is for two days, with the opening session beginning at 12 noon on the first day; there will be a luncheon prior to the speaker. An afternoon session will occur on the first day

and morning and afternoon sessions will occur on the second day.
5. Your team is also going to do a presentation at the conference; your team is to determine the topic of your presentation (consistent with the theme of the conference) and prepare a presentation outline.

Activity 2: Set Up a Records Management System

As you work on this project, set up a records management system that will contain hotel names, printers, your presentation preparation (topic and outline) and any other related information that you need. File your information on a thumb drive if you have availability to one or on a floppy disk if not.

Activity 3: Develop a Proposed Outline for the Conference

Your task is to let your creativity flow and come up with a theme and a proposed outline of an exciting and informative conference for all IAAP attendees. You are to present your ideas to your class members in outline form, along with your group's presentation topic and outline.

LaVetta Hunley
Administrative Assistant II
Competitive Business Plan Coordinator
Water Services Department
Kansas City, Missouri

Spotlight on Success

I also attribute my success to being a risk taker. Many of the jobs I have held are attributed to the fact that no one else wanted to take the risk of accepting them because of the responsibilities involved. Most were vacant for a long time or newly created so I was the first one in the position. When starting a new job, I go in with a positive attitude with the intent of making it better than it was when I started and upon departing making it more appealing for someone else.

WHAT IS MY BACKGROUND?

Since October 1993, I have been employed by the City of Kansas City, Missouri. I began as an information processor in the City Planning Department and was subsequently promoted to secretary to the Assistant Director of Economic Development in the Aviation Department at Mid-Continent Airport (MCI). When the Assistant Director was promoted to the Director of Aviation at MCI, he asked me to serve as his executive assistant. That director later accepted a position at an airport in another city; however, I remained the executive assistant to two aviation directors until I decided that I wanted a more project-oriented position. I changed my career path by accepting my current position as Administrative Assistant II, Competitive Business Plan Coordinator with the Water Services Department.

WHAT IS THE MOST FUN PART OF MY JOB?

The fun part of my job is meeting people who hold very different jobs from those I have had and have vastly different backgrounds from mine. Every moment is fun because I enjoy everything I do. The opportunities are endless. I continue to move up the career ladder based solely on the many skills I have learned along the way.

TO WHOM AND TO WHAT DO I ATTRIBUTE MY SUCCESS?

I acknowledge my mother for my success, who as a single mother, always worked in the administrative field, primarily with the federal government. I thank her for encouraging me to take a keyboarding course throughout junior and senior high school because becoming familiar with a keyboard would be the key to my career and future. She remains my role model as a mother, wife, and administrative professional. My children, Jay and Alishia, are a source of pride for me, and I thank God that we are a strong family unit.

I followed in my mother's footsteps by participating in the office education program as a junior and senior in high school. I worked half days as an insurance clerk for Armed Forces Insurance during my senior year; then, I received a promotion to Insurance Counselor at Armed Forces, I remained there for a total of five years. Since then, I held a variety of administrative positions until I entered the city government workforce. I have completed 15 credit hours toward a degree in business administration and aspire to complete my education.

Chapter 9:	*The Workplace Team*
Chapter 10:	*Customer Service*

I am the only employee in the city government with the title of Competitive Business Plan Coordinator. I know that what I do affects all of the nearly 900 employees in the department. Remaining positive and enthusiastic about the Plan can be stressful at times, but I realize the outcomes are tremendous. The success of the Plan may open many doors of opportunity for me.

WHAT ADVICE WOULD I GIVE SOMEONE JUST BEGINNING IN THIS FIELD?

The advice I would give to someone entering the field is to first and foremost always act in a professional manner. Consider the administrative field as your profession, no matter what your working title may be—file clerk, secretary, administrative assistant, or senior executive assistant. Remember, regardless of what corporation or industry, big or small, administrative professionals are always needed to make an organization a success. Never under estimate your abilities and always strive to be the best you can be. Being an administrative professional will enable you to climb the ladder of success. Your opportunities are unlimited. Never do anything that would be an embarrassment to you, your manager, or your employer.

WHAT ARE MY HOBBIES/INTERESTS?

My hobbies include reading romance novels, watching soap operas, and singing in the young adult choir, the Voices of Palestine, at Palestine Missionary Baptist Church. My interest is learning more about becoming a virtual assistant.

TO WHAT PROFESSIONAL ORGANIZATIONS DO I BELONG?

My professional affiliations include the International Association of Administrative Professionals (IAAP), Heart of America Chapter. I serve as the Administrative Professionals Week Event Chairperson. In 2006 to 2007, I will serve as the IAAP Missouri Division, APW Committee Chairperson.

LAVETTA HUNLEY—CASE STUDY

A little background: As the Competitive Business Plan (CBP) Coordinator, it is my responsibility to monitor and track the 47 performance measures and numerous action items as stated in the Competitive Business Plan implemented in 2002. The Plan is a ten-year plan and is based on an agreement between the Water Services Department (WSD) and the City of Kansas City, Missouri (KCMO). It was implemented as a basis to prevent privatization of the Water Department. The Water Services Department is the first and only department in the city to have such a plan.

One of the performance measures of the CBP is that every WSD associate must complete 40 hours of training (job specific and mandatory) within each fiscal year. I realized that this would be a difficult task for the administrative staff. As an active member of IAAP, I recommended the OPTIONS training program (one of IAAP's educational programs) as an ideal way for the department's administrative staff to achieve this goal.

The OPTIONS training program is designed as a self-study program; however, I implemented a plan for the WSD administrative staff to participate in either the self-study or in monthly classroom study. In doing so, I agreed to facilitate the monthly classes for three of the four skill levels (skill level four participants are solely self-study), track the progress of the 35 to 40 participants, and coordinate with IAAP Headquarters regarding the receipt and distribution for the certificates of completion. For each book completed, each participant receives four hours of training toward the 40 hours per year goal, as well as 0.2 Continuing Education Units.

In my situation, what would you have done to make this training program run smoothly and efficiently? Decide how you would have handled the situation. Then turn to the end of the text (page 432) to see how I solved the situation.

CHAPTER 9

THE WORKPLACE TEAM

Learning Objectives

1. Cite the changing demographics of the future workforce.
2. Identify the types of workforce teams.
3. Determine characteristics of successful teams.
4. Develop effective verbal and nonverbal communication processes.

©Getty Images/Photodisc

> BUILDING TEAMS

Because teams are a vital part of almost any organization today, your effectiveness in working in a team is crucial. Although being a vital and contributing member of a team is not easy, the rewards from successful teamwork are substantial. First of all, teamwork within the organization in which you work allows you to not only get to know the people well, but also to understand individual strengths and weaknesses. In the diverse world in which we live today, you have an opportunity to work with a group of people who are not only diverse in age and gender, but also are more and more diverse in ethnicity and background. Learning more about various cultures, ethnicities, and age groups may help you be more successful and productive in today's workforce.

> DEMOGRAPHICS OF THE PRESENT AND FUTURE WORKFORCE

In Chapter 1 you were introduced to a few of the demographics of the workforce of 2012, indicating a projected increase of Hispanics, blacks, and Asians. Also mentioned were women and senior citizens (age 65 and up), with an anticipated increase in the numbers of both groups in the workforce by 2012. Because the composition of the workforce is extremely important as you consider the workplace team for the future, additional workforce diversity numbers by age and by ethnicity are presented in this chapter.

▷ Population Diversity

Every ten years, a census is taken by the U.S. Census Bureau; the last one taken in the United States was in 2000. At that time, the racial

| Figure 9-1 | ACTUAL POPULATION OF THE UNITED STATES BY AGE, 2000, AND PROJECTED POPULATION BY 2050 |

Year	All Ages	0–4	5–19	20–44	45–64	65–84	85+
2000	100%	6.8%	21.8%	37.0%	22.0%	10.9%	1.5%
2030	100%	6.7%	19.5%	31.6%	22.6%	17.0%	2.6%
2050	100%	6.7%	19.3%	31.2%	22.2%	15.7%	5.0%

Source: "U.S. Census Bureau, Demographic Trends in the 20th Century, Census 2000 Special Reports, CENSR-4, Table 5, November 2002, http://www.michigan.gov/documents/hal_lm_USProj04age_87545_7.pdf (accessed May 25, 2005).

distribution of the United States was: white, 71.6 percent black, 12.8 percent; American Indian, 0.9 percent; Asian and Pacific Islander, 4.4 percent; and Hispanic, 11.3 percent. The age distribution of the population in 2000 and the projected population in 2030 and 2050 are shown in Figure 9-1. The distribution of the population by ethnicity in 2000 and the projected population by ethnicity in 2025 and 2050 are shown in Figure 9-2.

Notice that we have an increasing Hispanic population (projected to be the second largest growth group), with the white population the slowest-growing among the groups during 2000 to 2050. The black population is projected to be the second slowest-growing in all regions except the South, where it will rank third. The Hispanic and Asian populations are the fastest-growing groups.[1]

▷ Aging Population

The actual figures for 2000 are from the census of that year, and projected figures for 2030 and 2050 show the extent to which our population is expected to change. Notice that we have an aging population that is living longer (because of medical research and personal care) than ever before. According to projections released by the Bureau of the Census, the elderly population (age 65 and up) will account for more than 20 percent of the total population; i.e., one in every five Americans, by 2050[2]—almost double the number in 2000.

▷ Women in the Workforce

Additionally, another statistic to take into consideration is the percentage of women in the workforce

| Figure 9-2 | PERCENT OF THE POPULATION BY RACE AND HISPANIC ORIGIN, 2000, AND PROJECTED PERCENT OF POPULATION BY RACE AND HISPANIC ORIGIN, 2025 AND 2050 |

Year	White	Black	American Indian, Eskimo, and Aleut	Asian and Pacific Islander	Hispanic Origin
2000	71.6%	12.8%	0.9%	4.4%	11.3%
2025	62.0%	14.2%	1.0%	7.5%	16.8%
2050	52.5%	15.7%	1.1%	10.3%	22.5%

Source: "U.S. Census Bureau, Population Division and Housing and Household Economic Statistics Division," http://www.census.gov/population/www/pop-profile/natproj.html (accessed May 25, 2005). Note: Figures for 2025 and 2050 total to slightly more than 100% due to rounding.

---

[1]"Population Projections for States by Age, Sex, Race, and Hispanic Origin: 1995 to 2025," http://www.census.gov/population/www/projections/pp147.html. (accessed May 31, 2005).

[2]"Actual and Projected Population of the United States by Age, 1900-2050," <http://72.14.207/search?q+cache:HgAUAsKuS10J:www.michigan.gov/douments/hal> (accessed May 31, 2005).

today. In 2000, women accounted for 47 percent of the labor force, up from 40 percent in 1975. In married-couple families where both wife and husband work, about one-fifth of the wives earn more than their husbands. Nearly three-fourths of all mothers are in the labor force. More than 60 percent of mothers with young children are in the labor force.[3]

> GLOBAL NATURE OF ORGANIZATIONS

The global nature of our society is an extremely important area for consideration; we can say without hesitation that the world is becoming the market for America. Many large corporations are establishing a presence in numerous countries. An example of this is evident on the website of Citigroup, where this statement is made:

> With a presence in more than 100 countries, where 98 percent of our employees are hired locally, Citigroup is perhaps the most diverse company in the world. . . . At Citigroup, we have worked hard to create a workplace with an emphasis on inclusion, innovation, and merit, each rooted in our shared values and respect for our colleagues and the millions of people we serve. We are proud of our work to promote diversity in our world and the community, including and engaging minority—and women—owned enterprises in the United States, which are worth $590 million of business.[4]

As organizations continue to become more and more global, your understanding of people in other cultures and countries is crucial. You may be working with virtual teams composed of people from a variety of cultures and backgrounds.

> GENERATIONAL CHARACTERISTICS

You learned in Chapter 1 that, according to sociologists studying and writing in the field, various generations have different characteristics and values depending on the year in which they were born. For example, according to Tapscott in "Growing Up

Digital: The Net Generation," the Millennial Generation or **N-Geners**—born between 1982 and 2003—want the following:

▶ Freedom. N-Geners feel they can reach the world via technology.
▶ Customization. They like the freedom of picking and choosing. For example, they enjoy customizing their cars.
▶ Accessibility. N-Geners want to get their hands on every piece of technology (hardware, software, and the like) over the Internet.
▶ Honesty. They do not want to be tricked into something. They want advertising to be up front. They do not want to be told what to do.
▶ Diversity. The Internet imposes no boundaries on N-Geners. Online identities are formed without regard to age, income, ethnicity, sexual orientation, or gender.[5]

Team opportunities in our diverse work world allow employees to learn and grow professionally.

© Digital Vision

> TEAMWORK—A MUST

What does what you have just read mean for teamwork in today's organizations? It means that you are going to have to work at understanding the diversity of people who make up the workplace of today and continue to work at understanding as your workplace becomes even more diverse. A challenging task? Yes, but a task that must be taken seriously if you expect to be a contributing member of a workplace team. Without

[3]"Workforce Development Facts," <http://www.ecwdb.org/facts.cfm> (accessed May 30, 2005).

[4]Citigroup: Corporate Citizenship, "Diversity—Working Paper," <http://www.citigroup.com/citigroup/citizen/diversity/workingpaper.htm> (accessed May 30, 2005).

[5]"Future Leaders," <http://www.growingupdigital.com/Lfuture.html> (accessed May 30, 2005).

such understanding, you may not be an effective member of a team. And, organizations today use teams extensively. In fact, in the last fifteen or twenty years, organizations have undergone a shift from individual work to an increasing emphasis on work teams and groups. This shift is largely due to globalization, downsizing, and the need for technological efficiency. As the tasks become more complex in organizations, individual specialists are needed as part of a team in solving problems. Technology-driven tasks have become far too complex for one person to handle alone; organizations create work teams to accomplish collective goals. Additionally, downsizing has resulted in fewer people to complete the more complex tasks that exist in the workplace. Teams allow management to capitalize on a positive synergy that hopefully results in significant increases in productivity.[6]

As you have looked at job vacancy notices, have you discovered that the ability to work in teams is often a requirement? A number of organizations list teamwork in their job vacancy notices or emphasize the importance of teamwork in their mission statements. As you prepare your résumé, consultants will often advise you to include teamwork skills as one of your important abilities.

▷ Team Definition

A team is defined in the dictionary as "A group organized to work together."[7] In the workplace, a team is a group of individuals who work together to achieve defined goals; in other words, the team members are linked by a common purpose.

▷ Types of Teams

As an administrative professional, you will usually be involved in two types of ongoing teams: (1) the

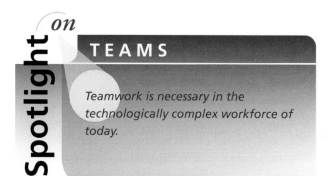

Spotlight on TEAMS

Teamwork is necessary in the technologically complex workforce of today.

Self CHECK A

Respond to the following comments with a *yes* or *no* answer.	Yes	No
1. The workforce of today resembles the workforce of the previous generation.	☐	☐
2. Our population is less diverse than 10 years ago.	☐	☐
3. The white population is one of the fastest growing groups in the United States.	☐	☐
4. Statistics show that approximately one-fifth of wives earn more than their husbands.	☐	☐
5. Statistics show that the Asian population in the United States is expected to be the slowest-growing group.	☐	☐
6. Women account for roughly 47 percent of the labor force today.	☐	☐
7. The elderly population will account for over 30 percent of the population by 2030.	☐	☐
8. A number of corporations in the United States have a global workforce.	☐	☐
9. N-Geners reach the world via technology.	☐	☐
10. An understanding of various cultures, ethnicities, and age groups is crucial in our world.	☐	☐

---

[6]Asim Khan, "Understanding Work Teams," <http://www.themanager.org/HR/Understanding_Work_Teams.htm> (accessed June 1, 2005).
[7]*The American Heritage Dictionary,* Third Edition (Boston: Houghton Mifflin Company, 1993), p. 1414.

232   **Part IV** Customer and Employee Satisfaction

administrative professional/supervisor team, and (2) the administrative professional/coworker team.

Administrative Professional and Supervisor Team

Your relationship with your supervisor is of primary importance. The two of you must be a good **permanent team.** Your major role in the team is that of support. Without your support, your supervisor is handicapped; she or he may not be able to complete the necessary projects as efficiently. Conversely, without your supervisor's trust in your abilities, you do not have the latitude to perform at your highest level. For example, if you must have your supervisor's approval on every task that you undertake, the amount of work that you and your supervisor are able to produce is reduced.

Administrative Professional and Coworker Team

Another important team consists of you and your coworkers—the other administrative professionals and support staff within the workplace. Have you ever worked in a situation in which there was constant bickering among a workforce team? If you have, you understand the importance of having a cohesive workforce team of administrative professionals. What are the characteristics of that team? There are several, including cooperation, acceptance of each other's strengths and weaknesses, fairness in your work with others, and willingness to assist each other.

Additionally, as an administrative professional there are teams that you will be involved in that are **temporary teams,** with these teams being the following:

▸ **Task forces**—a temporary team assembled to investigate a specific issue or problem. For example, a task force may be set up to improve communication flow within the office.
▸ **Problem-solving teams**—a temporary team set up to solve a specific problem. For example, this team may be set up to establish a more effective records management system.
▸ **A committee**—a temporary or permanent group of people in charge of a specific activity or acting upon some matter. A committee, for example, may be appointed once each year to plan special functions within the workplace such as employee orientations.
▸ **Quality circles**—a group of employees who meet regularly to solve work-related problems and to

seek work improvement opportunities. For example, a quality circle may be set up to improve the strategic planning process that occurs each fiscal year.
▸ **Virtual teams**—the virtual team is a relatively new team to the workplace. It is made up of people who communicate electronically with each other. Its members may never meet except in cyberspace and may be from countries all over the world. Software designed for virtual teams—such as **groupware**—is becoming increasingly sophisticated. Figures 9-3 and 9-4 give effective characteristics of virtual teams and tips for effective leadership of virtual teams.

Because virtual teams are in their infancy, there is much to learn about the successful operation of such teams. One study done from the Graduate School of Business at the University of Texas at Austin found these behaviors surfaced when an analysis was done of 12 virtual teams.

▸ The teams that began and finished with low trust had these characteristics in common: unequally distributed communication, shallow ideas, lack of task focus, and little feedback.
▸ Teams that began and finished the project with high trust had these characteristics in common: were able to dynamically address issues of who would do what, when, and with whom; provided detailed explanations of content contributions; quickly responded to others' initiatives; and were immersed in the task.
▸ Conclusions from the study included these: Social exchanges appear to facilitate trust early in

Figure 9-3	**CHARACTERISTICS OF EFFECTIVE VIRTUAL TEAMS**

▸ Accomplish their goals.

▸ Can be trusted to do their jobs when you cannot see them.

▸ Utilize occasional face-to-face meetings.

▸ Efficient workgroup as the team matures and processes are put in place.

Source: Virtual Organization, "Leading Virtual Teams," <http://www.seanet.com~daveg/ltv.htm> (accessed June 1, 2005).

Figure 9-4 — EFFECTIVE LEADERSHIP OF VIRTUAL TEAMS

► Deal with communication problems.

► Give team members a sense of how the overall project is going.

► Establish a code of conduct, such as acknowledging a request for information within a certain period of time.

► Do not let team members vanish into cyberspace.

► Develop trust.

► Keep everyone focused on the task.

► Determine leadership by expertise on issue/problem—not by corporate hierarchy.

Source: Virtual Organization, "Leading Virtual Teams," <http://www.seanet.com~daveg/ltv.htm> (accessed June 1, 2005).

the team's existence; enthusiastic and optimistic communication resulted in a virtual family. Conversely, inequitable, irregular, and unpredictable communication hindered trust. Teams with ineffective and/or negative leadership described the work and experience as extremely frustrating.[8]

▷ Successful Teams

Successful teams are made up of individuals who not only understand themselves, knowing what they value and living their values, but also value others. Successful teams use effective verbal communication techniques.

> VERBAL COMMUNICATION PROCESS

If you are to be an effective member of a team, you must not only understand the communication process but also you must be an excellent verbal communicator. This section will help you improve your verbal communication skills.

▷ Originator

The **originator** is the sender of the original message. The originator transmits information, ideas, and feelings through speaking, writing, or gesturing. Although the originator is often a person, the originator also may be a committee or a company.

▷ Message

The **message** is the idea being presented by the originator. Words are usually used in communicating the idea, but hand signals, gestures, or a combination of words and gestures may also be used. The transmission of these words or gestures usually takes the form of face-to-face exchanges, telephone conversations, voice mail, or written correspondence such as e-mail, instant messages, faxes, letters, and memorandums.

▷ Receiver

The **receiver** is the person who translates the message into meaning. For example, if your employer asks you to prepare a letter and gives you a deadline of early afternoon to have the letter ready for signature, you attach meaning to "early afternoon." You may decide that the letter should be ready by 2 p.m. At 1 p.m., you receive a call from your employer asking if the letter is ready. You apologize and say you will get it done. You quickly understand that the meaning you attached to the communication was not the same as the message the communicator intended.

▷ Response

The **response** (feedback) of the receiver lets the originator know whether the communication is understood. In the example given in the previous paragraph, the assumption was made by the administrative professional that early afternoon meant 2 p.m. to the originator of the message. However, it did not; it meant 1 p.m. Because there was no attempt to check the meaning of the message sent by the originator, an error occurred.

It is important for the originator to be clear and exact in his or her message; it is also important for the receiver to verify his or her understanding of the communication. For example, in the situation given previously, the originator could have said, "I need the letter by 1 p.m. this afternoon." The receiver can

---

[8]Sirkka L. Jarvenpaa and Dorothy E. Leidner, "Communication and Trust in Global Virtual Teams," <http://www.ascusc.org/jcmc/vol3/issue4/jarvenpaa.html> (accessed May 31, 2005).

then respond, "I will have it on your desk by 1 p.m." With exactness and clarity, the originator has stated the time the letter is to be completed, and the receiver has responded with the time expected. Such a response from the receiver verifies her or his understanding of the communication.

Each element of the communication process is important. If the originator does not clearly state his or her message, problems can occur. If the receiver interprets the message incorrectly and responds inappropriately, there may be problems. Each person in the communication process has an obligation to communicate as clearly as possible, to frame his or her message well, and to ask questions if the message or response is unclear.

Spotlight *on*

VERBAL COMMUNICATION

Make a point to be exact in your verbal communication; give all the information necessary for the receiver to understand and act upon (if necessary) the message.

> INDIVIDUAL AND TEAM VALUES

Values are an extremely important variable in the communication process. Through our communication, if someone is listening closely or maybe even not so closely, he or she can pick up many of our values. The word **value** comes from the French verb *valoir,* meaning "to be worth." Values are our beliefs. They determine how we live on a day-to-day basis. We may or may not spend much time thinking about what we value, but the decisions we make each day are influenced by the values we have.

Our early values are learned from significant people in our environment, such as our parents and other family members. Additionally, values are learned from our educational, social, and religious structures, such as our schools and places of worship. However, our values are not static; that is, as we

grow and change, our values may change. Your value system shapes what you believe, how you live and work, and how you relate to others.

Because values are learned from significant people in our environment, what is happening in our world during our formative years does matter in shaping our values. Tom Brokaw, who wrote a book entitled *The Greatest Generation,*[9] discusses the common values held by the men and women who came of age during the Great Depression and the Second World War. These people, known as the Silent Generation, were born between 1930 and 1945. Brokaw lists several values that are common for this generation—duty, honor, courage, service, and responsibility for oneself. In contrast to the Silent Generation, Generation X's (born between 1965 and 1981) values and characteristics have been identified as tolerance (accepting of most everything except narrowmindedness), spiritual, and relational (value good friends).

The generation that is now beginning to enter corporate America has been defined by Tapscott[10] as N-Geners (born between 1982 and 2003 and also referred to as the Millennial Generation). They demonstrate these values: caring deeply about social issues; strong belief in individual rights, alienation from formal politics, and non-trusting of traditional institutions' ability to provide the good life for them. N-Geners see themselves as authorities on the technological revolution that is changing every institution in society. They have grown up with technology and do not fear it. For them it is a way of life, and there is a widening gap between these Internet-savvy young people and the earlier generations. In a study by the Pew Internet & American Life Project in Washington, DC, one of the young people summed up representatives of this generation by saying that he and his classmates think it is a pity that schools do not understand in the way that this generation does how the Internet should be used. This new technological culture in which N-Geners are so immersed is just beginning to be imposed on the workplace as these young people show the older generations new ideas about how business can be changed through technology.[11]

As you can determine from this cursory analysis of the values of different generations, individuals who grow up in different times may have different

[9]Tom Brokaw, *The Greatest Generation* (New York: Random House, Inc., 1998).

[10]Don Tapscott, *Growing Up Digital: The Rise of the Net Generation* (New York: McGraw-Hill, 1998.)

[11]Unisys, "The Generation Gap at Work," <http://www.cioinsight.com/print_article2/0,2533,a+103326,00.asp> (accessed May 31, 2005).

values. However, recognizing these different values does not give one the right to make judgments about individuals based on their ages. The importance of this information as applied to the work world is that differences in values may exist because of age that impact the way people understand and live in the work world. Your task as you work in teams becomes to recognize these differences and help teams understand how to use the values of diverse groups of people in promoting the goals of the organization.

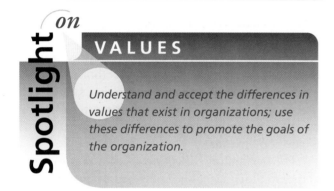

Spotlight *on*

VALUES

Understand and accept the differences in values that exist in organizations; use these differences to promote the goals of the organization.

> VERBAL COMMUNICATION BARRIERS

Encountering barriers to our verbal communication are common. Such barriers are not generally thrown up on purpose; they merely arise because of the complexity of our lives and the differences in the way we view situations. You learned earlier in this chapter about the increasing diversity of people in the work environment. Certainly, this diversity can and does cause barriers; these barriers exist not intentionally, for the most part, but merely because individuals with extremely diverse backgrounds have had very different experiences. In other words, the diverse individuals in the workforce do not understand the world in the same way. Thus, verbal communication becomes more difficult. What are these verbal communication barriers and how do you overcome them? The next section of this chapter deals with several common barriers and gives suggestions for alleviating them.

▷ Listening

Listening is the complete process by which verbal language, communicated by a source, is received,

recognized, attended to, comprehended, and retained. The listener attends to the verbal language of the source with the intent of acquiring meaning. The main components of listening, however, are not located in the ears, just as the main components of seeing are not located in the eyes. Our ears hear the sound vibrations to which we attend and comprehend; but our listening is based on our needs, desires, interests, previous experiences, and learning.

Listening is a complex phenomenon involving the total individual. As we listen, our process of thought, which is composed of many separate and independent concepts, flows into ideas and emotions and affects what we hear.

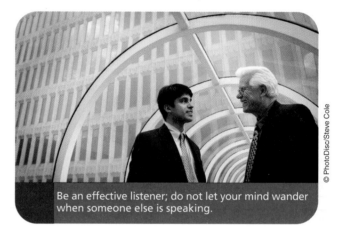

© PhotoDisc/Steve Cole

Be an effective listener; do not let your mind wander when someone else is speaking.

Communication studies show that individuals spend 70 percent to 80 percent of their waking hours in some form of communication. Of that time, 9 percent is spent in writing, 16 percent in reading, 30 percent speaking, and 45 percent listening. Studies also confirm that most of us are inefficient listeners.[12]

Spotlight *on*

LISTENING

Use the differences between speaking rates and listening rates to process information that you receive: do not let your mind wander to unrelated areas.

---

[12]Dick Lee and Delmar Hatesohl, "Listening: Our Most Used Communication Skill," <http://muextension.missouri.edu/explore/comm/cm0150.htm> (accessed June 1, 2005).

CHECK B

Do you consider yourself a good listener? Complete this self-check to determine your listening effectiveness.

Respond to the following comments with *always, sometimes,* or *never.*

1. When people talk to me, I find it difficult to keep my mind on the subject. _____

2. I listen only for facts. _____

3. Certain words and ideas can prejudice me against a speaker to the point that I cannot listen objectively to what is being said. _____

4. I can tell by a person's appearance if the person will have something worthwhile to say. _____

5. When someone is speaking to me, I am easily distracted by outside sights and sounds. _____

6. I interrupt the speaker to get my point across. _____

7. When someone else is talking, I plan what I will say next. _____

8. I frequently criticize the speaker's delivery or mannerisms. _____

9. I use the difference between the talking time of the speaker and my own comprehension time to analyze and relate to the speaker's points. _____

10. I am aware of the nonverbal communication of others. _____

11. I try to understand what the speaker is feeling as the speaker talks. _____

We know from studies that we think faster than someone else can speak. Most people speak at the rate of approximately 125 to 150 words per minute; we have the mental capacity to understand and process someone speaking at 400 words per minute. The difference between speaking speed and thought speed means that we use only 25 percent of our mental capacity when listening. Thus, we still have 75 percent of our mental capacity to use in different ways. Thus, many of us let our minds wander.[13] Additionally, studies also show that immediately after listening to a 10-minute oral presentation, the average listener hears, understands, and retains only 50 percent of what was said. Within 48 hours, that retention rate drops another 50 percent to a final retention level of only 25 percent listening efficiency. In other words, we retain only one fourth of what we hear.[14]

Studies also indicate that listening skills suffer as we get older. Experiments with students from first grade through high school indicate the following:

- First and second graders showed a 90 percent listening rate.
- Junior high students showed only a 44 percent listening rate.
- High school students showed an average of 28 percent listening rate.[15]

Take Self-Check B now. How did you do on the Self-Check? Did you recognize yourself as an ineffective listener? If you are like most of us, you probably need to spend more time concentrating on being an effective listener. Why are you an ineffective listener? There are numerous characteristics that produce poor listening; consider the following ineffective habits.

Talking

Unfortunately, many of us are so intent on discussing what has happened to us that we have difficulty waiting for the other person to finish so we can begin talking. In fact, many times the eager talker will interrupt the speaker to get his or her point across. Such individuals absorb little of what the other person says.

---

[13]Dick Lee and Delmar Hatesohl, "Listening: Our Most Used Communication Skill," <http://muextension.missouri.edu/explore/comm/cm0150.htm> (accessed June 1, 2005).

[14]R. G. Nichols, "Listening is a 10-Part Skill," *National Business* 75 (Sept. 1987), p. 40.

[15]Ibid. Lee and Hatesohl.

Distractions

As you have already learned, most people speak at approximately 125 or 150 words per minute, with the mental capacity to process speaking at 400 words per minute. These speed differences allow the listener to turn his or her attention to something else easily. Distractions can be in the form of **external noise** (physical sounds that hinder the listening process) or **internal noise** (distractions that occur within the listener), such as a personal or work problem that concerns the listener. Both external noise and internal noise create distortion in the message being sent and prevent us from understanding the message as it was intended. Although the distracted individual has the ability to hear what the speaker said and also spend some time thinking about his or her own problems, many times the distracted person becomes so involved in the personal/professional issue that he or she fails to tune back in to the speaker. If the speaker stops talking and asks a question, the person has to admit that the speaker's message was not heard.

Outguessing

Have you ever known someone who would not let you finish a sentence, always finishing it for you? Most of us have. Many times the outguesser makes an inaccurate assumption concerning what you intended to say. Thus, you have to stop and explain to the outguesser that she or he made a wrong assumption.

▷ Language Usage

The language we use often prevents clear communication. Words in isolation have no meaning. They have meaning only because people have agreed to a particular meaning. What about the dictionary; doesn't it contain the correct meanings of words? Yes and no are both correct answers. It contains the correct meaning as agreed to by **etymologists** (specialists in the study of words[16]). However, cultural differences impact the meaning of certain words. Although people in England speak the same language as people in the United States, the words they use often have different meanings. For example, in England an *elevator* is called a *lift; standing in line* is referred to by the British as *queuing up*.

Words do not always have the same meaning in different countries; in England, an elevator is referred to as a "lift."

Words also change with time. For example, in our technological world, how many words can you name that have a different meaning from the meanings in the past? A bulletin board no longer means only a board that is hung on the wall for notes to be attached. It can now mean a public-access message system via the computer. A chat room is not a physical room with four walls, but a computer location where people any place in the world can talk with each other through a Web connection.

▷ Evaluation

A major barrier to communication is the tendency to judge the individual making a statement and then to accept or reject the statement based on the **evaluation** (to judge carefully[17]) of the individual. The evaluation is made from the listener's frame of reference and experience. If what is said agrees with the listener's experiences, the listener tends to make a

---

[16]*The American Heritage College Dictionary,* Fourth Edition (Boston: Houghton Mifflin Company, 2002), p. 481.
[17]Ibid., p. 483.

Part IV Customer and Employee Satisfaction

positive evaluation. If what is said does not agree with the listener's experience, he or she may make a negative evaluation.

▷ Inference

Inference (process of deriving logical conclusions from premises known or assumed to be true[18]) causes a problem when individuals act upon what they believe to be true when it is not true. Consider Figures 9-5 and 9-6. What do you see? Compare your answers with a classmate. Did you see the same thing in both pictures?

Generally, people think or assume that they see things or situations exactly as they are; in other words, we believe we are objective in our assessment of what we see. When other people disagree with us, we immediately think something is wrong with them. In actuality, we see the world through our own filter—a filter that has been established through our values, our culture, our background, our teachings, and even our generation (as you learned earlier in this chapter). What does that mean for us in our work environment? It means that we must be careful when we are making decisions. We must look at the picture (the situation) from many sides; we must be slow to jump

Figure 9-6 WHAT DO YOU SEE? AN OLD WOMAN OR A YOUNG GIRL?

Figure 9-5 WHAT DO YOU SEE? A RABBIT OR A DUCK?

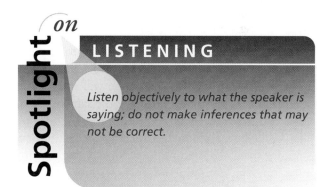

Spotlight *on* **LISTENING**

Listen objectively to what the speaker is saying; do not make inferences that may not be correct.

to conclusions. We must be fair in our analysis. The problem is that none of these suggestions is easy; it is difficult to separate ourselves from the world we believe we know and look objectively at situations without making inferences that may be completely wrong.

▷ Cultural and Language Differences

Culture makes a great difference in communication; we learn to speak and give nonverbal

---

[18] *The American Heritage College Dictionary,* Fourth Edition (Boston: Houghton Mifflin Company, 2002), p. 710.

messages (which you will learn more about in the next section of this chapter) based on our culture. You have already learned in this chapter that age differences do impact what we believe is true and important in our lives. People growing up in one generation experience different situations in their formative years than do people growing up in a different generation. Individuals growing up in different cultures, with different languages, often attach meaning to verbal communication in vastly different ways.

Non-Equivalent Words

Ethnoscience (branch of anthropology concerned with the cultural aspects of cognitive structure[19]) gives us insight into the way different cultures use words. The findings of ethnoscience and comparative semantics suggest that it is a rare thing to find a word in one language that is exactly equivalent to a word in an unrelated language. For example, the Eskimo has six names for snow, whereas North Americans have one word—snow.

Silence

Consider another example of how culture influences language. The North American society is a talk society. Silence is uncomfortable; it is difficult for a North American to spend more than a few moments in silence. Silence is not usually considered appropriate in the American workplace. When an American has been reprimanded he or she is allowed to respond verbally to show that the offense has been understood and to explain how he or she will correct the situation in the future or not make the same mistake again. However, a Filipino, for example, remains silent while being rebuked. Any spoken word shows a lack of respect. The Filipino tends to apologize with an action; e.g., extending a favor to the one who has been offended, but saying nothing.[20]

Time and Space

Time and space are other cultural differences that impact communication. In the United States many of us seem to have a reverence for efficient time usage. In fact, you have probably heard a number of times in your life the saying "time is money." Such an approach to time is called **monochromic** (having or appearing to have only one color[21]); this approach favors linear structure and focuses on one event or interaction at a time. Compare this understanding of time to the East, in which there is an unlimited continuity—an unraveling rather than a boundary.

This approach to time where many things are happening at one time is referred to as **polychromous** (having many or various colors).[22] India is a good place to observe time moving endlessly through various cycles. Time stretches far beyond the human ego or lifetime. There is a certain timeless quality to time. The Western concept of time as a straight line emanating from no one in particular suggests that there are no purposeful forces at work in time. In Eastern thought, time is alive with purpose.

Space and how we use it tells us something about ourselves and our objectives. How we arrange chairs and whether we like an open office space sends a message about the formality or informality with which we view our communication environment.[23]

> EFFECTIVE VERBAL COMMUNICATION

To counter the many negatives that can occur during verbal communication, we must employ processes and techniques that offset the negatives and give us a chance to truly understand what the person communicating with us verbally is saying. Here are several suggestions.

▸ Be non-judgmental. Do not judge an individual's values, culture, intelligence, appearance, or other characteristics. Listen to what the person says. In other words, give the person a chance to get the message across, without forming judgments.
▸ Question. If you do not understand what someone is saying to you, **question** (technique used to understand verbal communication through questions) the person speaking.
▸ Give feedback. Use clarifying statements and questions such as these:
  Let me see if I can review the main points we have discussed.
  I understand your major concerns are . . .

---

[19]David Hesselgrave, "Verbal and Nonverbal Communication," <http://home.snu.edu/~hculbert/verbal.htm> (accessed June 2, 2005).
[20]David Hesselgrave, "Verbal and Nonverbal," <http://home.snu.edu/~hculbert/verbal.htm> (accessed June 3, 2005).
[21]*The American Heritage College Dictionary*, Fourth Edition (Boston: Houghton Mifflin Company, 2002), p. 899.
[22]*The American Heritage College Dictionary*, Fourth Edition (Boston: Houghton Mifflin Company, 2002), p. 1079.
[23]Mary Ellen Guffey, *Business Communication: Process and Product* (Cincinnati: Thomson South-Western, 2003), p. 82.

Did I hear you correctly?

As I understand you, your major objections are. . . .

Have I stated them correctly? Do you have any other objectives?

Spotlight *on*

NONVERBAL COMMUNICATION

Do not assume that you can interpret all verbal communication in the same way.

> NONVERBAL COMMUNICATION

Nonverbal communication is an extremely important element of communication. Edward T. Hall, a social anthropologist, claimed that 60 percent of our communication is nonverbal.[24] Gestures and body language can communicate as effectively as words when in face-to-face contact with individuals. In fact, nonverbal communication can be another barrier to effective communication. However, before you consider this, keep the following point in mind. Just as the same words spoken in different languages can be interpreted in vastly different ways based on the culture of the individual, so can nonverbal communication be interpreted differently in different cultures.

▷ Cultural Differences

People of different cultures give different meanings to gestures. Listed are several meanings given to gestures by people of China, Japan, the Philippines, and Taiwan.

▷ China

- Hugging and kissing when greeting are uncommon.
- When walking in public places, direct eye contact is uncommon.

- Personal space is limited in China; Chinese will stand closer than Westerners.
- Silence is perfectly acceptable and customary.

▷ Japan

- The graceful act of bowing is the traditional greeting; however, they have adopted the western custom of shaking hands.
- Hugging and kissing are avoided when greeting.
- Prolonged direct eye contact is considered impolite.
- It is considered rude to stand with your hands in your pockets.
- Smiling covers a gamut of emotions: happiness, anger, confusion, apologies, and sadness.

▷ Philippines

- Handshaking is the common custom for both men and women.
- Prolonged direct eye contact is considered impolite and even intimidating.
- Speaking in a loud voice is considered ill-mannered and rude.

▷ Taiwan

- The Taiwanese are not a touch-oriented society.
- Public displays of affection are rare.
- The open hand is used to point.
- Loud, boisterous, or rude behavior is a strong taboo.[25]

When talking with people of other cultures, you must constantly keep in mind that how you interpret gestures may not be the same as how others interpret gestures. Conclusions cannot be drawn from only one element of nonverbal communication. You must take all the elements of nonverbal communication as a whole. Additionally, you must be cautious about your interpretations.

One might ask the following questions for the future in regard to communication in the world: (1) What does the continual emergence of a truly global society mean for verbal communication? (2) Will we understand each other better as we become that global society? (3) What role does the Internet play in verbal communication? As we communicate more and more through e-mail (which is devoid of gestures), will we become a more united society, understanding and

---

[24]Gary Imai, "Gestures: Body Language and Nonverbal Communication," <http://www.intranet.csupomona.edu/~tassi/gestures.htm> (accessed June 3, 2005).
[25]Ibid.

accepting each other's differences rather than evaluating those differences?

⊳ Nonverbal Categories

Nonverbal categories include these: personal behavior, personal space, eye contact, facial expression, voice quality, and space and time. Consider this situation.

Personal Behavior

You are talking very intently with someone; that person is leaning back in the chair with his arms crossed, frowning. Throughout your conversation, he has exhibited this same type of behavior. Do you think the individual is interested in what you are saying? Bored with the whole exchange? Or not believing a word you are saying?

Nonverbal behaviors include posture and facial expressions.

© Digital Vision

You probably answered "no" to the first question and "yes" to the next two questions. We would assume that all of the nonverbal signs indicate that the message is not being received. The listener may have no confidence in you or even be angry with you. Or, the listener may not be unhappy with you at all, but may merely not agree with what you are saying.

Although body language is important, one gesture may not have significant meaning. When evaluating body language, consider all the gestures a person makes, along with what the person says. Review these additional categories of nonverbal communication.

Personal Space

This category refers to the distance people use when approaching others. People in countries such as Latin America or the Middle East feel more comfortable standing close to each other, while persons in the United States and people of Northern European descent generally prefer a greater distance.

Eye Contact

Americans value eye contact; in fact, looking away from someone who is talking to you is considered not only rude but also can be considered as avoidance of contact or even deviousness.

Facial Expression

Facial expression can portray many emotions, some of which are:

▶ Amusement.
▶ Sadness.
▶ Confusion.
▶ Anxiousness.
▶ Thoughtfulness.

Voice Quality

A loud tone of voice is usually associated with anger; a soft tone of voice with calmness and poise. A person's voice is usually pitched higher when she or he is tense, anxious, or nervous. Additionally, a person usually talks faster when angry or tense. A low pitch and a slow pace usually indicate a relaxed tone. Additional forms of voice communication include the nervous giggle; a quivering, emotional voice; a breaking, stressful voice; and a whiny, upset voice.

Space and Time

Space is treated differently in different cultures. In the United States, we tend to lay claim to a certain territory and defend it if someone else tries to take our space, which is defined as **territoriality.** In the workplace, we use space in special ways. For example, the president's office is usually larger than the vice-president's office. As one continues to go down the hierarchical structure, generally the offices continue to get smaller. However, as you learned in Chapter 1, some organizations are now going to large common areas in which people share space or have their own defined space.

In the United States, time is extremely important. If a deadline is set, the expectation by organizations is that the deadline will be met. To behave differently by not meeting the deadline often results in no promotions or even firing. As a student, you have probably already learned that time is important in education. Timelines that are not met, such as a paper not being submitted to the instructor on time, generally result in some type of grade penalty. To be late for a job interview can send such a negative signal that the interviewee may not even be considered for the job, although the person may have excellent qualifications.

> AN EFFECTIVE WORKPLACE TEAM

An effective workplace team is one that understands the demographics of the present and projected workplace. Additionally, the effective workplace team accepts the differences of others and commits to working successfully with all team members, using both effective verbal and nonverbal communication patterns.

SUMMARY

Reinforce your learning in this chapter by studying this summary.

▶ Teams are a vital part of most organizations today; the administrative professional's effectiveness in a team is crucial.

▶ America has a population that is living longer. By 2050, the Bureau of the Census projects that over 20 percent of the total population will be elderly—65 and older.

▶ America's population is projected to continually become more diverse, with Hispanics and Asians as the largest-growth groups.

▶ Women are expected to continue to enter the workforce in large numbers. Women in 2000 accounted for 47 percent of the workforce, up from 40 percent in 1975.

▶ Our society is more global today than ever before. Many organizations now have a presence in companies scattered all over the world. For example, Citigroup has a presence in more than 100 countries.

▶ With the age span of people in the workforce, generational characteristics become an important consideration.

▶ The diversity of ethnicity and ages in the workforce today demands that individuals entering the workforce understand how to work with major differences in thought and background.

▶ Because of the increased number of teams being utilized by organizations today, teamwork is essential.

▶ A team by definition is a group organized to work together. In the workplace, a team is a group of individuals who work together to achieve defined goals.

▶ The types of teams presented in this chapter include (1) the administrative professional and supervisor team, (2) the administrative professional and coworker team, (3) task

forces, (4) problem-solving teams, (5) committees, (6) quality circles, and (7) virtual teams.

▶ The virtual team is a relatively new team to the workplace. It is made up of people who communicate electronically with each other. Its members may never meet except in cyberspace.

▶ Conclusions from virtual team studies indicate that social exchanges appear to facilitate trust early in the team's existence and enthusiastic and optimistic communication results in a virtual family. Conversely, inequitable, irregular, and unpredictable communication hinders trust.

▶ Successful teams of all types use effective verbal communication techniques.

▶ The verbal communication process consists of the originator, message, receiver, and response.

▶ Individual and team values are an extremely important variable in the communication process.

▶ Our early values are learned from significant people in our environment, such as our parents and other family members.

▶ Research has shown that each generation develops a relatively common set of overall values. For example, people born in the Silent Generation (1930–1945) value duty, honor, courage, service, and responsibility to oneself.

▶ People entering corporate America today are defined as N-Geners (born between 1982 and 2003). They demonstrate these values: young navigators, who are non-trusting of traditional institutions' ability to provide the good life; concern for social issues; belief in strong individual rights; and alienation from formal politics.

▶ Barriers to verbal communication exist, with one barrier being the diversity that is present today in the workforce. These barriers exist not intentionally, for the most part, but merely because individuals with extremely diverse backgrounds have had very different experiences.

▶ Barriers to effective verbal communication include listening, language usage, evaluation, inference, and cultural and language differences.

▶ Effective verbal communication includes being non-judgmental, questioning, and giving feedback.

▶ Nonverbal communication is also an important element of communicating. Nonverbal communication is made more difficult because of the huge diversity of the people in the workplace.

▶ Nonverbal categories of communication include personal behavior, personal space, eye contact, facial expression, voice quality, and space and time.

▶ An effective workplace team is one who understands the demographics of the present and projected workforce. Additionally, the effective workforce team accepts the differences of others and commits to working successfully with all team members, using both effective verbal and nonverbal communication patterns.

GLOSSARY

Committee—A temporary or permanent group of people in charge of a specific activity or acting upon some matter.

Ethnoscience—Branch of anthropology concerned with the cultural aspects of cognitive structure.

Etymologists—Specialists in the study of words.

Evaluation—The process of judging carefully.

External noise—Physical sounds that hinder the listening process.

Groupware—Software designed for virtual teams.

Inference—Process of deriving logical conclusions from premises known or assumed to be true.

Internal noise—Distractions that occur within the listener.

Listening—Complete process by which verbal language, communicated by a source, is received, recognized, attended to, comprehended, and retained.

Message—Idea being presented by the originator.

Monochromic—Having only one color.

N-Geners—People born between 1982 and 2003.

Originator—Sender of an original message.

Permanent team—A team composed of the supervisor and administrative professional is considered a permanent team within the organization.

Polychromous—Having many or various colors.

Problem-solving team—A temporary team set up to solve a specific problem.

Quality circle—A group of employees who meet regularly to solve work-related problems and to seek work improvement opportunities.

Question—Technique used to understand verbal communication through questions.

Receiver—Person who translates the message into meaning.

Response—Feedback from the receiver that lets the originator know whether or not the communication is understood.

Task force—A temporary team assembled to investigate a specific issue or problem. For example, a task force may be set up to improve communication flow within the office.

Temporary teams—Consist of task forces, problem-solving teams, committees, quality circles, and virtual teams.

Territoriality—Laying claim to a certain territory and defending it if someone else attempts to take the space.

Value—Comes from the French *valoir* meaning "to be worth." Values are our beliefs.

Virtual team—A team made up of people who communicate electronically with each other.

CHECKPOINT

Check your understanding of these terms by completing DCD9-a on the Data CD.

These discussion items provide an opportunity to test your understanding of the chapter through written responses and/or discussion with your classmates and your instructor.

1. Explain how the demographics of the future workforce are changing. How might these changes influence you as part of that workforce?

2. What types of teams might the administrative professional be a part of in the workplace? What roles may the administrative professional take in the teams? On what types of teams may the administrative professional serve?

3. Describe three characteristics of successful teams.

4. List and describe the elements of the verbal communication process.

CRITICAL THINKING CASE

You have been working with a team of four administrative professionals at JWay Nu-Systems Tech for the last two weeks; the team has met a total of four times. The team is a temporary one, charged with making recommendations concerning the necessary hiring qualifications for administrative assistants. The recommendations are due to the human resources department at the end of next week. You, as the chairperson of the team, have scheduled two meetings for next week. However, you are extremely concerned that the team is not going to finish the recommendations in the timeframe established. Two members of the team are very disruptive.

Each meeting has been scheduled for two hours, and these two team members spend most of their time arguing with each other and any other team member who tries to make a contribution. They came in with ideas as to what the qualifications for administrative assistants should be, and each has been unwavering in her opinion. You are totally frustrated and feel strongly that you have not been an effective team chairperson. What strategy might you use at the next team meeting to allow others to participate (without totally alienating these two team members) and be assured that the team will deliver a quality product in the established timeframe?

RESPONSES TO SELF-CHECK

A
The most appropriate answers are as follows:

1. No	3. No.	5. No	7. No	9. Yes
2. No	4. Yes	6. Yes	8. Yes	10. Yes

B
The most appropriate answers are as follows:

1. Never	4. Never	6. Never	8. Never	10. Always
2. Never	5. Never	7. Never	9. Always	11. Always
3. Never				

WORKPLACE PROJECTS

PROJECT 9-1 CONDUCT WEB RESEARCH AND EVALUATION

Cite the changing demographics of the future workforce (Objective 1)

Working as a team of five, determine the following demographics for your state and city:

▶ White, black, American Indian, Asian and Pacific Islander, and Hispanic for the last census year.

▶ The number of women in the workforce for the last census year or for the current year.

Use the Web as one source of information for finding your statistics. If you are not able to find data for your city on the Web, contact the Chamber of Commerce or the City Council. Both of these groups generally have statistical population data. Prepare charts showing your results. Save your results; your data will be used in Project 9-2.

All team members are to evaluate the work of the team using an evaluation form developed by the team. You are to address verbal communication processes, along with any other areas that your group thinks should be considered. Distribute the form to each team member; compile the results. Distribute the results to the team. If the team could have been more effective in certain areas, discuss what needs to be done to increase effectiveness. You will submit your work to your instructor after completing Project 9-2.

PROJECT 9-2 CONDUCT ORIGINAL RESEARCH; ADD TO PROFESSIONAL DEVELOPMENT PLAN

Identify the types of workforce teams (Objective 2)

Determine characteristics of successful teams (Objective 3)

Develop effective verbal and nonverbal communication processes (Objective 4)

Working as a team of 5 (same team as in Project 9-1), conduct primary research by interviewing two adminis-

trative professionals in your city. You may do the interview by e-mail or telephone. Ask these questions:

Administrative Professionals
1. Have you been a part of what you considered a successful team?
2. What were the strengths of the team?
3. What weaknesses did the team have?
4. Did communication problems occur? If so, what were they?
5. If you had the latitude to work in teams or individually on a project, which would you choose? Why?

Prepare a written report of the information you received. Have the team complete a second team evaluation form; you may use the same form you prepared in Project 9-1. Have one or two team members compile the results; go over the results as a team. Submit your written report of both research projects (9-1 and 9-2) to your instructor. Also submit the areas of teamwork improvement that were identified by your team. Develop a list of tips to help you become a more effective team member and researcher. Add this list to your disk as PGP9-2.

COMMUNICATION POWER

Use DCD9-b to assist you in improving your grammar skills.

ASSESSMENT OF CHAPTER OBJECTIVES

Now that you have completed the chapter and the projects, take a few minutes to review the chapter learning objectives. For your convenience, the objectives are repeated here. Did you accomplish these objectives? If you were unable to accomplish the objectives, give your reasons for not doing so; be specific and concise. Your instructor may prefer that your answers be submitted to her or him. If so, DCD9-c contains the Assessment of Chapter Objectives. Complete the Assessment of Chapter Objectives; submit your results to your instructor.

1. Cite the changing demographics of the future workforce. Yes ☐ No ☐

_____

_____

_____

2. Identify the types of workforce teams. Yes ☐ No ☐

_____

_____

_____

3. Determine characteristics of successful teams.   Yes ☐   No ☐

_____

_____

_____

4. Develop effective verbal and nonverbal communication processes.   Yes ☐   No ☐

_____

_____

_____

CHAPTER **10**

CUSTOMER SERVICE

Learning Objectives

1. Discover the characteristics of a customer service organization.
2. Determine who the future customers will be.
3. Develop and evaluate your customer service skills.

©Getty Images/Photodisc

> THE CUSTOMER SERVICE ORGANIZATION

Customer service is a concept that is generally accepted as extremely important in our society. What is the definition of **customer service?** Customer service can be defined as the ability of an organization to constantly and consistently give customers what they want and need. As customers, what do we expect? How do we evaluate customer service? As a partial answer to this question, consider **call centers** (centralized offices that answer incoming calls from customers—via a phone, e-mail, website, or fax—and make outgoing contacts with customers).[1] Most of us with cell phones and computers have used call centers several times. We probably have an immediate reaction as to whether or not we think the centers offer quality service. The Service & Support Professionals Association (SSPA), a call center association that was founded in 1989, determines its winners for the Star Awards Hall of Fame by using the following criteria:

▶ Innovative support
▶ Mission-critical support
▶ Sustained performance

In 2004, EMC Corporation (a call center), a world leader in information storage and management, received its fourth consecutive SSPA Star Award for world-class mission-critical support—one of the categories determined essential for winning an award. In accepting this award, Leo Colborne, EMC senior vice president, made these remarks:

---

[1]"Web Definitions for Call Centers," <http://www.google.com/search?biw=818&hl=en&q=Definition+of+call+centers&btnG=G.> (accessed June 21, 2005).

Call centers are increasing in number both nationally and internationally.

© Photodisc

Winning our fourth consecutive SSPA award for mission-critical support is a testament to the people driving our 'customer first mentality' in our support centers around the world.[2]

One aspect of outstanding customer service, according to EMC Corporation is a *customer first mentality*. Certainly because call centers are growing (notice the statistics given in the Call Center Growth below) and more and more customer service is being offered through call centers, we can readily accept the importance of the customer first mentality as one aspect of quality customer service. How does an organization maintain a customer first mentality? Throughout this chapter, that question will be discussed.

▷ Growth of Call Centers Around the World

According to 2004 statistics, there were 50,600 call centers in the U.S. and 4,500 call centers in Canada, with 5,300 call centers predicted by 2008. Call centers in Europe, the Middle East, and Africa were approximately 45,000 in 2005, with over 2.1 million agents.[3]

▷ Values of a Customer Service Organization

Customer service organizations value four broad areas, which affect all aspects of an organization. These areas are: the right mission, the right vision, the right leadership, and the right employees.

The Right Mission

Organizations dedicated to customer service take time to ask and answer the question: What is our **mission?** A mission statement addresses what an organization does. It is a statement of purpose that can be used to initiate, evaluate, and refine an organization's directions. For example, Disney World has defined its mission as "to make people happy."[4] Mission statements are not static but dynamic. Each year the mission statement should be reviewed and modified or changed according to the new directions of the organization that may have emerged.

The Right Vision

A **vision** statement addresses what the organization wants to become; it is a picture of the future. Walt Disney, when he started his theme parks, had a clear vision. His picture of the future was that when guests left the parks, they would have the same smile on their faces as when they entered the park. "Keep our guests smiling" was the rallying call.[5] The successful service organization not only has a mission statement that is reviewed yearly, but a vision of where the organization will be in the future.

The Right Leadership

Leadership in this context does not mean only the officers and administrators of an organization. It means all employees who take any kind of leadership roles in the organization. Robert Greenleaf, in his book *Servant Leadership: A Journey into the Nature of Legitimate Power and Greatness* (a book that has spawned the Greenleaf Center for Servant Leadership located in Indianapolis, Indiana) identified these characteristics as those of a servant leader.

Leadership is a calling. Servant leaders have a natural desire to serve others. This calling is rooted in a strong value-based decision process. These **leaders** have a strong desire to make a difference in the world—to make the world a better place to live. A servant leader does not serve from a position of his or her needs, but from a position of what is right and good for others.

▸ Leaders are listeners. Servant leaders are receptive and genuinely interested in the views of others.

[2]"EMC Wins Fourth Consecutive SSPA Star Award for World-Class Mission Critical Support," <http://www.emc.com/news/> (accessed June 20, 2005).

[3]Call Center Industry Statistics Related to Market Size/Demographics," <http://www.incoming.com/statistics/demographics.aspx?SelectedNode+Statistics> (accessed June 20, 2005).

[4]Paul B. Thornton, "The Foundation: Mission, Vision and Values," <http://www.refresher.com/!thefoundation.html> (accessed June 20, 2005).

[5]Ken Blanchard, et al., *Customer Mania!* (New York: Free Press, 2004), pp. 34–35.

- Leaders have empathy. Servant leaders understand the problems of others; they empathize with others' concerns and issues.
- Leaders are persuasive. Servant leaders offer compelling reasons for why they make requests. They attempt to develop people rather than to demand that they operate in a specific way.
- Leaders have a strong sense of stewardship. Servant leaders prepare the organization to contribute to the greater good of the world.
- Leaders help people grow. Servant leaders believe that all people have something to offer to the world; they help people understand and develop their strengths.
- Leaders build community. Servant leaders believe that individuals in the organization are part of not only a local community but also a larger community that is capable of changing the world.[6]

The Right Employees

The remainder of this chapter focuses on the skills crucial for successful customer service employees. The following sections are designed to help you develop and/or improve your customer service skills.

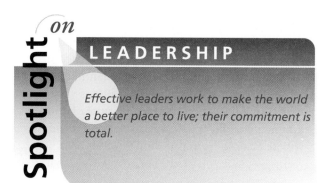

Spotlight on

LEADERSHIP

Effective leaders work to make the world a better place to live; their commitment is total.

> FUTURE CUSTOMERS

As you learned in Chapter 9, the demographics of the population are changing radically. The population is already more diverse than it has ever been in age, race, and ethnicity. Thus, the future customers of any organization will be extremely diverse. If you are dealing directly with customers in your organization, the chances are that you will deal with people who are very different from you. These people will come from various cultures that may not resemble your culture at all. They may not be of the same race; they may be recent immigrants to the United States.

These customers may not live in the United States at all; they may be communicating with you from China, Brazil, New Zealand, or from a multitude of other locations. Additionally, you may never talk with them. Americans working in corporations receive an average of 200 messages per day, with the largest number of messages being electronic ones. When you cannot see or sometimes even hear your customers, it is more difficult to communicate effectively. Written messages can be misinterpreted. In fact, it is much easier to be difficult or even nasty to someone through an electronic message. Our internal responses to what we perceive to be a difficult person over the phone or e-mail are often to become more difficult than the person with whom we are communicating. After all, we may reason, who cares? The person cannot physically hit you. You may rationalize your behavior by saying to yourself, he or she "started it," so I will be even nastier than the other person in my response.

Customers for United States products increasingly buy them on the Web.

© Photodisc

What does the information mean that you have just read in this chapter? What does the aforementioned information have to do with effective customer service? What difference does it make to

[6]John E. Barbuto, Jr., and Daniel W. Wheeler, "Becoming a Servant Leader: Do You Have What It Takes?" <http://ianrpubs.unl.edu/misc/g1481.htm> (accessed June 20, 2005).

you? What you have read impacts not only your work life but also your ability to function well within an organization. Here is what it means to you as an employee and as an effective member of a service organization, one who cares about providing excellent service to customers and about helping employees become excellent providers of customer service.

- The **values** [principles that guide a person's life such as honesty and fairness], mission, and vision that an organization, through its top and middle management, lives do affect organizational culture. Management must be held accountable for living the values, mission, and vision. Management must help employees understand the values, mission, and vision through written statements and constant adherence to them in actions. Figure 10-1 is a value statement of JWay Nu-Systems Tech, your virtual company.
- Employees need to be held accountable for knowing and living the values, mission, and vision of an organization.
- Customer service includes customers you see and have a chance to talk with face-to-face. Customer service also includes customers with whom you communicate with only through cyberspace—via e-mail, voice mail, fax—or by telephone. Additionally, customer service is sometimes interpreted as including your relationships with your coworkers, with the customer being defined as your coworker. For example, if you have a report to write with a coworker, and you fail to do your part of the writing in a timely manner, your coworker is impacted negatively. You may want

Figure 10-1 JWAY VALUES

COMMITMENT TO CUSTOMERS
We serve the needs of our national and international customers.
We listen carefully to what our customers tell us about our products.
We respond to our customers' needs through constantly improving our present line of products.
We constantly seek new products to serve the technological needs of our national and international market.

COMMITMENT TO EMPLOYEES
We listen to better customer service ideas from our employees.
We respond to their ideas by modifying and improving our service to customers.
We trust our employees to consistently produce quality work.
We provide training for our employees on all new products.
We believe that successful ideas emerge from groups who are given support and encouragement.

to review Chapter 9 to reinforce the importance of working effectively with your coworkers.
- These customers may have vastly different backgrounds from your own. They may not speak the English language very well. They may be difficult to understand not only because of their accents but also because of their lack of understanding of the nuances of the English language, just as you have difficulty understanding them because of your lack of understanding of their language and its nuances.
- These customers may be much older or much younger than you are because of people living

CHECK A

Take a few moments to list the customers of organizations today. Next list your projections for customers of the future. Think creatively and futuristically.

1. Today's Customers: Who Are They?

_____
_____
_____

2. Tomorrow's Customers: Who Are They?

_____
_____
_____

Part IV Customer and Employee Satisfaction

longer in our society than ever before. Age differences do matter. As you learned in Chapter 9, each generation grows up with a different set of values because of world and personal events during their formative years.

You may be saying to yourself right now, "Well, what do I do with all of this information? I have no control over it as an employee in an organization. I am just at the mercy of the administrators or the world environment." The answer is, "No, you are not." Certainly, administrators and the world environment can impact you; however, you do have significant control. The next sections of this chapter give you some practical suggestions for being a superior customer service agent in our complex environment. Remember, however, that your effectiveness depends on your ability to think, listen, learn, and grow.

> CUSTOMER SERVICE— A DEFINITION

If you were asked to define what customer service is, what would your definition be? At the beginning of this chapter customer service was defined as "the ability of an organization to constantly and consistently give customers what they want and need." That definition is correct; however, it needs to be expanded; it is too narrow. Customer service includes listening with empathy to customers when they have a problem and providing options and alternatives when you cannot give the customer exactly what she or he wants.[7]

Your role as an administrative professional may include the first contact a customer has with your organization. If so, you play an extremely important part in customer service. What you do or say can determine if the customer will do business with your organization. You may not always be able to satisfy a customer's need but you can listen with empathy to the need and provide appropriate options and/or alternatives for the customer.

> DEVELOP YOUR CUSTOMER SERVICE SKILLS

Customer service is important in any organization. You may be saying to yourself:

I do not believe that statement; schools do not have customers, they have students.

Yes, that is true. But, are not students customers in the broadest sense? College students are buying a service; the chance for an education that benefits them throughout their life. An education does not merely allow you to be employed in an organization and in a position that you enjoy, but it also expands your mind on many subjects that can help you be a better citizen of our world.

You might be saying, "Wait a minute; all students do not pay. What about elementary students?" Yes, the student does not pay but the parents or some adult in the student's life does pay through taxes. Consider this definition of a customer. A **customer** is the person who receives the services or products that are offered by an organization. When you define customers in this manner, you understand that all of us are customers at some time.

▷ The Customer Is Always Right

Most of us have heard this statement numerous times. Is it true? No, it isn't. *Customers are people, and people are not always all right.* Customers do not make reasonable requests at times; sometime their requests cannot be fulfilled by an organization. Let's take a simple but realistic situation and examine it. Assume you have just taken a test. You get your test

Customers deserve to be treated well, even if you cannot meet all of their demands.

© Photodisc

[7]Karen Leland and Keith Bailey, *Customer Service for Dummies* (New York: Wiley Publishing, Inc., 1999), p. 10.

back, and you feel you answered a question correctly for which you were given no credit. You talk with your instructor; she or he explains that your answer is not correct and refers you to a source for the correct answer. If the instructor had agreed that you were right when you were not, you would have gone away with incorrect information, which would not help you to learn and grow. However, when the customer is not right, the customer still deserves to be treated well. In the example just given, the instructor referred you to a source where you could get the correct answer, which helps you learn. And, the instructor did so without denigrating you. In other words, the customer should expect to be treated with respect, to be given an explanation if there is a question about the product or service, and to be not only listened to but also heard by a representative of the organization.

▷ Prepare Yourself

Because all of us are customers and most of us are either working or going to school or both, we need to understand not only how to deliver quality service but also what to expect from an organization from which we are receiving services. What basics do you need to know before you can begin to deliver excellent customer service? Here are several of the basics.

- Be extremely familiar with your organization's objectives and values.
- Where is your organization headed?
- Who is it attempting to serve?
- What is its mission?
- What is its vision?
- What is the philosophy of leadership?

The previous sections have emphasized several of the crucial organizational elements necessary in effective organizations—ones that consider their customers' needs and help their employees grow and learn. This section is devoted to giving you a number of practical suggestions for effectively dealing with customers.

Visualize Success

Know who you are and what your strengths are. Be honest about your weaknesses. However, do not let your weaknesses define you. We learn and grow by recognizing what we do know and deciding to do something about what we do not know. In visualizing success, you might say, "I have much to learn about being effective in a customer service environment.

However, I am willing to learn and I know I can." In other words, you visualize your success in the environment.

STOP! Sit quietly in a chair for a minute or two to clear your mind of the day's activities. Next, close your eyes and visualize yourself in a successful customer service environment. Now, write down what you saw. What were you doing? What were you saying? How were customers reacting to you?

_____

_____

_____

Take Responsibility

When working in a customer service environment, you are going to make mistakes. In fact, when working in any environment, you will make mistakes. We all do, unfortunately; it is part of being human. However, the mature individual willingly takes responsibility for his or her mistakes and actually learns from them. In a customer service environment, it is important to take time at the end of the day to think through what went right and what went wrong, both with internal customers and external customers. Ask yourself, "What can I learn from each experience?" Then, do so—learn from the positives and negatives. Reinforce the positives and move on. Peak performers know what they need to do, and they keep their eyes focused on their goals.

Admit Mistakes

When you make a mistake in your personal life, do you admit it or try to hide the fact that you have made a mistake? If you answered honestly, you probably had to say that there have been times in your life when you did not admit a personal mistake. If so, have you ever been found out? If your answer to this question is yes, did it hurt your relationship with the person? Does that person now think of you as a "liar" or a "dishonest" person? Chances are good that the answer, if not a resounding "yes," is a "perhaps." When such a situation occurs, you have to work almost twice as hard to get back the person's trust.

If you as a business employee fail to admit a mistake to a customer, you not only run the risk of being seen as a liar but also you run the risk of the individual seeing your entire company lying and thus possibly losing thousands of dollars of business for the company. When you make a mistake or your company makes a mistake, the key is to apologize quickly for the error and then solve the problem.

Go the Extra Mile

Have you ever complained about a product you received and the customer service representative listened intently to your concerns and then said, "Our company is so sorry that we caused you this inconvenience; we will reduce the cost of your next order 5 percent"? If something similar has happened to you, how did you feel? Did you decide that everyone makes an error occasionally and that the company is not as incompetent as you had originally thought? Did you decide that you would give the company a second chance? Most of us would probably answer in the affirmative to the last two questions. By going the extra mile, the company has maintained a valued customer for a small cost.

However, never do anything that violates company ethics or standards just to keep a customer happy. A good question to ask yourself is: Would I be comfortable explaining what I did to my supervisor the next day?

> FACE-TO-FACE CUSTOMER SERVICE SKILLS

Many times in a customer service organization, you encounter the customer on a face-to-face basis. The skills that you use in face-to-face contacts are somewhat different from the skills that you need to use when talking with a customer over the telephone or in cyberspace. Listed here are several skills you will need when working with the customer in person.

▷ Make Eye Contact

Body language is an extremely important element in verbal communication. Body language can be divided into five forms—eye contact, facial expressions, posture, gestures, and space. Eye contact is an extremely powerful form of body language. It lets customers know that you are interested and attentive to what they are saying. You should make immediate eye contact with a customer. However, you should also look away from time to time. A gaze that lasts longer than ten seconds can be interpreted as a stare, which makes people uncomfortable.[8] Figure 10-2 gives several other forms of body language and the interpretation that can be given to the language.

▷ Smile

Generally a warm smile is extremely valuable. It signals that you care about the customer and are eager to help her or him. However, if the customer is extremely upset, a smile can signal that you are laughing at the individual, suggesting to the customer that you are not taking his or her issue seriously or possibly laughing at her or him.

▷ Maintain Appropriate Interpersonal Distance

Interpersonal space boundaries are cultural and individual. Some cultures, such as the Hispanic culture,

---

CHECK B

Self

List the body language behaviors that cause you to feel uncomfortable when you are talking with someone in person. Arrange them in hierarchical order by listing the body language element that causes you the most discomfort, followed by the second most uncomfortable, and finishing with the least uncomfortable element.
Body Language Behaviors that Make Me Uncomfortable

_____

_____

_____

_____

_____

---

[8]"Body Language," <http://faculty.ecpi.edu/Bmccabe/190Body.htm> (accessed June 21, 2005).

Figure 10-2	BODY LANGUAGE INTERPRETATIONS

Body Language	Interpretation
Tightly crossed arms	Defensive and uninterested
Rolling on your heels	Insecure and childish
Shoulder shrug	Signals disbelief of what is being said
Playing with your hair	Implies an inner build-up of anxiety
Pulling your ear	Gives the impression that you are struggling to reach a decision
Touching your face	Nervousness or possibly even dishonesty
Wringing your hands	Concern
Fidgeting	Worry
Foot tapping	Impatience
Pen drumming	Boredom[9]

tend to have small interpersonal space zones; people get close together to talk. However, most Americans will back away if you get too close to them; again, it is a cultural issue.

When you are working with customers, respect their personal space requirements. If you get too close, you will notice that people will back away. Honor their need for you to not violate their personal space. Sometimes, people will use space as an intimidation factor; they will get "in your face" and possibly even yell if they are angry enough or shake their finger at you. Such an approach is never an acceptable way to deal with customers; it only makes people angrier and nothing gets accomplished.

▷ Call the Customer by Name

When a company representative whom you have just met immediately calls you by name, how do you feel? Do you feel as if the representative is interested in you and your concerns? Most of us would answer with a "yes." When someone takes the time to actually hear your name and then uses it, you tend to feel that the representative and the company care about you.

▷ Let the Customer Talk

Have you ever had the experience, when you called a company to report lack of receipt of all items that you ordered, of being interrupted by the company employee before you could finish your statement? If you have, you understand the importance of letting a customer tell you the story. Do not interrupt midway into the story. Even though it is time consuming to hear a customer's entire story when you think you understood all that was necessary to solve the problem at the first of the conversation, it is important to let the customer finish her or his statement. You may be wrong; you may not have understood the real problem. Let the customer talk freely without your interruption. Review the statement in Figure 10-3.

Figure 10-3	THE COMMUNICATOR'S PLEDGE

Whether or not I agree or disagree with what you say, I will respect your right to say it and I will try to understand it from your point of view. This, in turn, helps me to communicate my point of view to you more effectively.[10]

▷ Listen to the Customer

You learned in Chapter 9 that studies show that individuals spend 70 percent to 80 percent of their waking hours in some form of communication, with 45 percent of that time spent in listening. Several listening techniques are given in this chapter. You might wish to review those now. Additionally, read carefully the information in Figure 10-4; observing these tips will help you listen well to customers.

Listening cannot be overemphasized when you are dealing with customers. Listening says to the customer that you believe she or he is important, that you are paying attention to the customer's concerns, and that you care about the individual. One effective listening technique is to repeat back to the customer what you believe the customer said. Even though we think we are listening effectively, we certainly can misunderstand, particularly when the customer is upset. For example, you might say to the customer, "I understand that our shipment to you included eight laptops and you had ordered ten. Did I understand you correctly?"

Occasionally, you might have a customer who swears or yells at you. You need to continue to listen in such a situation; if you get mad, the situation only

[9]Barbara Oaff, "Body Language: Posture v Performance," <http://www.ivillage.co.uk/workcareer/survive/prodskills/articles/0,,156472_176844,00.html> (accessed June 21, 2005).

[10]Kris Cole, *The Complete Idiot's Guide to Clear Communication* (Australia: Pearson Education, Inc., 2002), p. 89.

Figure 10-4 **LISTENING TIPS**

1. Develop patience. Stay focused on listening.

2. Listen to what is not said; observe the body language of the speaker.

3. Listen with your eyes, mind, and heart as well as your ears.

4. Pay attention to the speaker's tempo; match your own tempo with the speaker.

5. Remember that you do not need to agree. You are listening in an effort to understand.

6. Wait out thoughtful silences.

7. Summarize your understanding of what has been said.[11]

over the telephone? The answer is probably a resounding "yes." Most of us have; we generally think that the person is yelling at us, demeaning us, and often misunderstanding us. Over the telephone, tone of voice influences 86 percent of the encounter, with words only 14 percent. Tone of voice often reveals not only what you think, but also how you feel. Notice the following examples:

► A monotone and flat voice can be interpreted as not being interested in the customer and/or boredom.
► A low-pitched and slow speed voice can indicate that the person wants to be left alone or is depressed.
► A loud voice many times indicates anger.[12]

Here are several suggestions for using your voice effectively when talking with customers.

gets worse. Try to find a neutral place where the two of you can meet; also try empathy statements. Consider the following conversation.

> Customer: Your organization is totally incompetent. I bought this (bleep) printer in here two days ago, and I have had nothing but (bleep) problems. I expect your (bleep) organization to do something about it immediately.
>
> Employee: It's frustrating, isn't it, when something does not work properly, particularly when you are under a deadline to get something out. I can understand; I've been in situations such as this myself. Let's see what we can do.

Generally such an approach will help diffuse the person's anger. The next step is to see what is wrong (if anything) with the printer. It could merely be that the person does not know how to set it up.

1. Keep the pitch of your voice fairly low; deeper voices sound more confident and competent than high voices.

2. Breathe deeply and relax your neck muscles and vocal cords to give your voice more volume and richness.[13]

3. Speak at a moderate rate of speed—not too fast or too slow. Vary your rate of speed for emphasis. A faster rate of speed usually indicates excitement, enthusiasm, and energy. Slow down to sound more thoughtful and serious.

4. Enunciate words clearly.[14]

▷ Use Empathy Statements

Empathy is defined as "identification with and understanding of another's situation, feelings, and motives."[15] Empathy is a skill that must be practiced; you must listen to what the person is saying without evaluation. Review again the communicator's pledge given in Figure 10-3. Empathy does not involve agreeing or disagreeing; it does involve respecting the other person's right to express a point of view. It does involve attempting to understand the other person's point of view.

▷ Use Voice Tone Effectively

Voice tone is always important, but it is extremely important when talking with someone over the telephone. Have you ever become extremely angry when someone actually raised his or her voice to you

---

[11]Kris Cole, *The Complete Idiot's Guide to Clear Communication* (Australia: Pearson Education, Inc., 2002), pp. 158–159.

[12]Leland and Bailey, p. 82.

[13]Kris Cole, *The Complete Idiot's Guide to Clear Communication* (Australia: Pearson Education Inc., 2002), p. 100.

[14]Ibid.

[15]*The American Heritage College Dictionary* (Boston: Houghton Mifflin Company, 2002), p. 459.

Respect International Differences

It is never easy to attempt to communicate when you and the other individual have very little if any knowledge of each other's language. Both caring and patience are needed to attempt to understand the other person. It is helpful if you have someone in the organization who speaks the same language as the individual. However, if you do not, you must attempt to do your best. Here are several suggestions.

► Break down the conversation into short sentences and questions.
► Attempt to use questions that can be answered with a yes or no.
► Be patient; remember that the situation is frustrating for both individuals.
► Avoid all signs of frustration.
► Do not yell. Have you ever asked yourself why we tend to yell when talking to someone who does not understand? Do we think yelling will help them understand? Obviously, it will not. Hearing is not the problem.
► Speak slowly and clearly.[16]

In addition to being sensitive to language difficulties when dealing with the international customer, pay attention to body language. Listed here are touching behaviors of four different countries.

1. China is not generally a touch-oriented society. A nod is an acceptable way to greet customers from China.

2. In France, a light handshake (rather than the firm handshake of North America) is appropriate.

3. In the Middle East, touching in public between opposite genders is not appropriate; handshaking is appropriate for those of the same sex.

4. Latin America is an extremely touch-oriented culture. Almost every hello and goodbye is accompanied by a warm handshake or a hug.[17]

Explain the Situation

Have you ever been in a situation in which you spoke clearly; you articulated well; you used empathy; and still the individual to whom you were talking did not understand you? Most of us would answer in the affirmative to such a question. Why? The basic reason is that the person is not using the same frame of reference that you use. Consider this story. Two individuals were talking and one said, "The car is a lemon." The other person responds, "I did not know that you bought a yellow car." You almost laugh out loud, because you are so surprised. However, you restrain yourself and try to clear up the matter. You explain you have had one mechanical problem after another with the car. What you thought was a simple statement turned into a communication problem. However, at least the person let you know what she was thinking. Often, you do not know; thus, it is important for you to explain clearly what you mean. Then, you might give the person a chance to let you know if she or he understands by asking, "Does this make sense to you?" With such a statement, you are giving the individual a chance to tell you whether or not you have been clear in your communication.

Assist Difficult People

Some people are going to be difficult no matter how helpful and professional you are. Do not take it personally. Take a deep breath and tell yourself you have done the best you can. Use positive self-talk. Here are some statements you can make to yourself:

► I will not get angry.
► I have been successful in situations such as this one in the past, and I will be successful again.
► I care about people, and I know that most people are not difficult.

Even when a customer is difficult, you should remain positive and helpful.

© Photodisc

---

[16]Robert Bacal, *Perfect Phrases for Customer Service* (New York: McGraw-Hill, 2005), pp. 77–78.
[17]Leland and Bailey, pp. 75–76.

> TELEPHONE CUSTOMER SERVICE SKILLS

Although we use e-mail and instant messaging extensively, the telephone remains an important tool of the workplace environment. As an administrative professional, you must be effective in your telephone communications. In Chapter 5 you were given these effective telephone techniques, which are also appropriate when working with customers.

1. Keep a smile in your voice.

2. Listen carefully.

3. Be discreet.

4. Use correct English.

5. Ask questions tactfully.

6. Transfer calls carefully.

Given here are some additional skills that you need to acquire when working with customers. Without appropriate telephone customer skills, you may not only make customers angry but also lose customers for your organization.

◁ Answer the Phone Professionally and Quickly

When your telephone rings, answer quickly, between the first and second ring if possible, and certainly before the third ring. You may lose a potential customer if you are slow in answering the telephone.

◁ Answer With Appropriate Information

Greet the caller, state the name or department of your organization, introduce yourself, and offer your help. For example, you might say: *Good morning, Rogers Electronics, Marjorie Edwards speaking. Thanks for calling. How may I help you?*

◁ Show Enthusiasm and Remember to Smile

Have you ever made a call and the person who answered the phone sounded as if she or he wished you had not called? Most of us have. A tired or unhappy voice is readily discernible over the telephone and instantly makes a bad impression on the customer or potential customer. Remember to smile as you pick up the telephone. It might even help to have a mirror on your desk and the word "smile" taped on your phone.[18]

◁ Transfer When You Cannot Help

If the caller has dialed your number by mistake or has inadvertently chosen the wrong department, tell the caller immediately. Do not say, "I cannot help you." You can help; you can get the caller to the appropriate person. For example, you might say, "Jacqueline Edwards in our customer service department can assist you. Her number is 555-388-0234; may I transfer you?"

◁ Listen Intently

As you are speaking with the caller, visualize the person. Speak with the person, not at the telephone. Listen politely to what the person is saying; do not interrupt. If the caller is unhappy about an experience with the organization, listen to the person's complaint. Use good listening skills, such as:

▶ Listen for facts.
▶ Search for subtle meanings.
▶ Be patient.
▶ Do not evaluate.
▶ Act on what the caller is saying.

Spotlight *on* **LISTENING**

Always speak with the customer—not at the customer.

If there is a problem, listen with understanding. Make statements such as, "I'm sorry you have been inconvenienced. Tell me what happened so that I can help you." Paraphrase and record what

---

[18]"Customer Service Skills on the Telephone," <http://www.tsuccess.dircon.co.uk> (accessed June 24, 2005).

the customer tells you. Whenever you hear an important point, say, "Let me make sure I understand." Then, repeat the complaint and follow with, "Is that correct?" Find out what the customer wants. Does he or she want a refund, credit, or replacement?[19]

Next, solve the problem if you can. If the scope is such that you do not have the authority to solve it, tell the customer that you must transfer her or him, asking permission to make the transfer. Give the customer the name of the person to whom you are transferring the call. Also, give the customer your name and number so that she or he can contact you later if needed. Thank the caller and say, "I have enjoyed talking with you; I hope your problem is solved soon."

Take notes during a long or involved conversation so you will remember all the information. Use words such as "thank you" often. Let the caller know you care. Additionally, reread the following sections under Face-to-Face Customer Service Skills; these sections also apply to telephone customers:

- ▶ Call the customer by name.
- ▶ Let the customer talk.
- ▶ Listen to the customer.
- ▶ Use voice tone effectively.
- ▶ Use empathy statements.
- ▶ Respect international differences.
- ▶ Explain the situation.
- ▶ Assist difficult people.

Figure 10-4 gives several other listening tips; review that figure again now.

▷ Deal With an Abusive Customer

Usually, you cannot help the customer until she or he calms down. Do not let yourself become angry; it merely escalates the situation. Look for points of agreement with the customer and voice those points. These techniques generally work well, and you can then begin to help solve the problem with the customer. If the customer continues to be abusive, you do have the right to hang up. However, many organizations have a policy concerning difficult situations. Find out what the policy is and observe it. If there is no policy, you might say, "I'm sorry that I cannot assist you now, but you are certainly welcome to call back later if you wish. My number is 555-102-8000."

▷ Close the Call Courteously

As you finish the call, thank the caller and let her or him know that you appreciate the business.

> E-MAIL CUSTOMER SERVICE SKILLS

The volume of corporation e-mail is constantly increasing and the projections are that it will continue to increase.[20] Effectively managing the amount of e-mail that is received by businesses has become a major issue. Why has the amount of e-mail increased so greatly? Here are several reasons for this occurrence.

▷ Advantages of E-mail

- ▶ Less expensive than regular mail.
- ▶ Does not require that the parties involved be available at the same time.
- ▶ Easy to send the same information to multiple people at the same time.[21]
- ▶ Not limited to an 8 to 5 timeframe; e-mail can be sent at any time of the day or night.

▷ E-mail Etiquette

Certainly, you should answer your e-mail as soon as possible. In other words, it should not sit in your e-mail box for days before you open your e-mail. However, neither can you be expected to answer your e-mail within five minutes of receiving it unless it is marked urgent. One way to handle your e-mail effectively and still be productive at the other work you must do is to schedule specific times of the day that you will write and respond to e-mail. You will need to determine the scheduling times based on the volume of your e-mail. For example, if most of your job requires handling e-mail customers, then you will need to check your e-mail every hour or every two hours (depending on the volume of e-mail). However, if only a portion of your job requires handling e-mail customers, you may want to check your e-mail only three or four times a day. What you need to keep in mind is that the customer must be served in a timely, caring, and efficient manner.

---

[19]"Customer Service Skills on the Telephone," <http://www.tsuccess.dircon.co.uk> (accessed June 24, 2005).

[20]Ed Frauenheim, "Report: E-Mail Volume Grows Rapidly," <http://news.com.com/2110-1032_3-5085956.html?tag+prntfr> (accessed June 23, 2005).

[21]Leland and Bailey, p. 329.

▷ Write Effective E-mails

Even though e-mails are seen as more informal than letters, you need to be certain the customer has all the information she or he needs to buy your product or service. Here are several suggestions for writing effective e-mails.

- Use the subject line so the reader will know at a glance why the e-mail is being written.
- Do not use acronyms when writing for customers, such as FYI (for your information) and IMO (in my opinion). You will have some customers who do not understand the acronyms, and it is also very informal. You may use acronyms internally within the organization, but not for customers.
- As you would when writing letters, be clear and concise. Good e-mail messages sell the product or service to the customer by giving the necessary information but not belaboring the point.
- Read your e-mail carefully before you send it; it is extremely important to give the customer clear, correct, and complete information. Your e-mail should also be free of grammatical or typographical errors, errors that can say to the customer that your organization is sloppy and thus your product or service may be inferior.
- Check the e-mail address of the individual. You do not want to send an e-mail message to the wrong individual.

> CALL CENTER CUSTOMER SERVICE SKILLS

At the beginning of this chapter, you were introduced briefly to call centers. Although centers vary as to the types of services offered, a call center can be defined as a centralized office that answers incoming calls from customers (via a phone, e-mail, website, or fax) and makes outgoing telephone calls to customers (telemarketing). **Telemarketing** is the act of selling, soliciting, or promoting a product or service on the telephone. Call centers may also respond to letters, faxes, e-mail, and similar written correspondence.[22] A number of these centers are open all hours of the day and night. They are not places that have direct (person-to-person) customer contact.

These centers can provide pre-sales, sales and sales support, or a variety of other types of service.

Call centers, regardless of their size, often become the public face of the company, thus the customer's call center experience can become a key driver of a company's success. Research by the Technical Assistance Research Project has shown that 96 percent of unhappy customers will not report their frustration to the company. Of those unhappy customers, over 90 percent will simply not come back. However, they will tell ten people about their bad experience.[23] In contrast, research has shown that if customers have a good experience, 89 percent are likely to repurchase a product.[24]

▷ Call Center Sectors

Although call centers exist in all types of businesses and organizations, here are a few of the sectors:

- Energy and utility industries
- Prescription dispensing centers
- Technology
- Software
- Utilities
- Banking/finance
- Insurance
- Tourism
- Mass distribution centers

▷ Worldwide Operation

Call centers continue to grow in number, with centers located all over the world, including the United States, France, the United Kingdom, Germany, and India. For the last few years, the growth rate of call centers has been over 10 percent a year, with a projected increase in jobs of 150,000 by 2006.[25]

▷ Call Center Employment

As an administrative professional, you may or may not be employed by a call center. However, the organization for which you work may employ a call center to handle some of its customer service functions. You need to be knowledgeable concerning these centers. The customer service skills that have been stressed in this chapter are applicable to call centers. According to research done with call center workers, one of the biggest challenges is remaining

---

[22]"Web Definitions for Call Centers," <http://www.google.com/search?biw=818&hl=en&q=Definition+of+call+centers&btnG=G.> (accessed June 24, 2005).

[23]"Industry/Call Center," <http://www.telrex.com/cr_callcenter.htm> (accessed June 23, 2005).

[24]Alice Dragoon, "Put Your Money Where Your Mouthpiece Is," <http://www.darwinmag.com/read/020102/mouthpiece.html> (accessed June 23, 2005).

[25]"Customer Service Centers," <http://www.investinfrance.org/France/KeySectors/Operations/?p=call_centers&1=en> (accessed June 21, 2005).

resilient in the face of the anger and hostility that can come from call center customers.[26]

> WEB CUSTOMER SERVICE

Millions of people in countries all over the world use the Web. For example, there were over 200 million Web users in the United States as of February 2005 (67.8 percent population penetration), with Canada having 20,450,000 users (63.8 percent population penetration).[27] Customers use the Web for booking travel reservations, banking, and shopping for sundry products. Businesses today see the Web as a market for sales and services. The Web offers the possibility of pricing products and services from a large group of vendors without ever leaving your business or your home.

Listed here are several questions that are appropriate to ask when offering services on the Web.

▶ Is it easy for customers to navigate through your site?
▶ Is your site visually appealing?
▶ Do you make it easy for customers to find your site?
▶ Do you offer a menu of communication options, such as e-mail, fax, and telephone?[28]

Spotlight on

THE WEB CUSTOMER

Is your website appealing to customers? Is it easy to find your products and services?

> INAPPROPRIATE CUSTOMER BEHAVIOR

You learned earlier in this chapter that the customer is not always right. However, the concept is an extremely good one. As you work in customer service organizations, you must treat each customer with respect and follow the suggestions that have been given in this chapter in regard to working with customers.

However, there are times when you encounter individuals who behave in threatening, racist, or sexist ways. Read the next sections to understand your options when such situations arise.

▷ Handling a Customer Who Threatens Bodily Harm

Although all verbal threats of bodily harm are just that—threats—you as a customer service representative do not know which threats are serious and which threats are not. Thus, you must behave in a way that protects not only you, but also other workers within the organization. Workplace violence is indeed a consideration. For example, the U.S. Department of Labor reported that workplace violence rose in 2003, but many employers are still not addressing the issue. The United States Occupational Safety and Health Administration mandates that employers provide a safe working environment for employees.[29] It is best to report all threats immediately, either to management or, if the threat puts you or others in serious danger, to the police. If you are ever in such a situation, you need to remain as calm as possible. You will also want to make some notes about the situation as soon as the imminent danger threat is no longer viable. Your organization probably has guidelines and procedures for these types of situations. Make it a priority to know the policy and follow it if ever such a situation arises.[30]

▷ Handling Racist and Sexist Comments

When a racist and/or sexist comment is made to you by a customer, it is good idea not to let yourself be drawn into the situation. Realize that you are probably not going to change a customer's mind about either area, so it is generally best to ignore the remark and focus the conversation on the business needs of the customer. The person is a stranger to you; and even if you chose to engage the customer in a dialog concerning appropriate racial and/or sexist

---

[26]"Call Centers: How to Reduce Burnout, Increase Efficiency," <http://www.whartonsp.com/articles/article.asp?p+393303&rl+1> (accessed June 20, 2005).

[27]"Internet World Stats: Usage and Population Statistics," <http://www.internetworldstats.com/america.htm> (accessed June 23, 2005).

[28]Leland and Bailey, p. 360.

[29]"Most Workplace Violence Avoidable," <http://www.huffmaster.com/emails/april_2005> (accessed June 26, 2005).

[30]Robert Bacal, *Perfect Phrases for Customer Service* (New York: McGraw-Hill, 2005), pp. 136–139.

behaviors, you are probably not going to change his or her mind.

However, if an employee in the organization makes these statements, you have the right to report the situation to the Human Relations Office. You should be aware of your organization's guidelines in relation to sexual and racial/ethnic discrimination, along with **Equal Employment Opportunity Commission (EEOC)** guidelines. See Figure 10-5, which gives these guidelines.

Figure 10-5   GUIDELINES FOR HANDLING SEXUAL AND RACIAL/ETHNIC DISCRIMINATION

1. Know your rights. Know your organization's position on racial discrimination and sexual harassment, what is legal under the EEOC (Equal Employment Opportunity Commission) guidelines, and what your employer's responsibility is. Know what redress is provided by federal laws.

2. Keep a record of all harassment infractions, noting the dates, incidents, and witnesses (if any).

3. File a formal grievance with your organization. Check your organization's policy and procedures manual or talk with the director of human resources as to the grievance procedure. If no formal grievance procedure exists, file a formal complaint with your employer in the form of a memorandum describing the incidents, identifying the individuals involved in the harassment or discrimination, and requesting disciplinary action.

4. If your employer is not responsive to your complaint, you may wish to file charges with the federal and state agencies that enforce civil rights laws, such as EEOC.

5. Talk to friends, coworkers, and relatives. Avoid isolation and self-blame. You are not alone; sexual harassment and racial discrimination do occur in the work sector.

6. Consult an attorney to investigate legal alternatives to discriminatory or sexual harassment behavior.

SUMMARY

Reinforce your learning in this chapter by studying this summary.

▶ Customer service can be defined as the ability of an organization to constantly and consistently give customers what they want and need.

▶ Customer service organizations value four broad areas that affect all aspects of an organization; these areas are the right mission, the right vision, the right leadership, and the right employees.

▶ In providing customer service, an organization needs to determine its mission, its vision, and constantly pay attention to its leadership through increasing leadership strengths and decreasing leadership weaknesses. The values, mission, and vision that an organization, through its top and middle management lives, do affect organizational culture.

▶ Customers of organizations today are global. Customer service includes customers you see and have a chance to talk with face-to-face and customers that you communicate with through cyberspace—via e-mail, voice mail, fax—or by telephone.

▶ Customers, because of our technological expertise, are worldwide today.

▶ Customer service is the ability of an organization to constantly and consistently give customers what they want and need. Customer service includes listening with empathy to customers when they have a problem and providing options and alternatives when you cannot give the customer exactly what she or he wants.

▶ The customer is not always right; however, the customer does deserve to be treated well.

▶ Here are several important keys to serving customers well: visualize success, take responsibility, admit mistakes, and go the extra mile.

▶ In serving face-to-face customers, make eye contact, smile, maintain appropriate interpersonal distance, call the customer by name, let the customer talk, listen to the customer, use voice tone effectively, use empathy statements, respect international differences, explain the situation, and assist difficult people.

▶ In serving telephone customers, answer the phone professionally and quickly, answer with appropriate information, show enthusiasm, remember to smile, transfer when you cannot help, listen intently, deal with an abusive customer, and close the call courteously.

▶ The volume of corporation e-mail is constantly increasing and projections are that it will continue to increase. E-mail etiquette demands that e-mail be answered in a timely fashion. However, that does not mean within five minutes of receiving it unless it is marked urgent. A good approach is to schedule specific times of the day that you will write and respond to e-mail.

▶ When writing effective e-mails; use the subject line; be clear and concise; read your e-mail before you send it; and check the e-mail address carefully.

▶ Call centers can be defined as a centralized office that answers incoming calls from customers (via a phone, e-mail, website, or fax) and makes outgoing telephone calls to customers (telemarketing).

▶ Call centers often become the public face of the company.

▶ Call center sectors exist in all types of businesses and organizations, with a few of the sectors being energy and utility industries, prescription dispensing centers, technology, software, utilities, banking/finance, insurance, tourism, and mass distribution centers.

▶ Millions of people worldwide use the Web; it has become a very effective marketing tool for businesses and organizations.

▶ Customers are not always right, although keep in mind in that you should treat each customer with respect. However, when customers threaten bodily harm or engage in inappropriate racist and/or sexist behaviors, you have the right and responsibility to deal appropriately with such incidences.

GLOSSARY

Call Centers—Centralized offices that answer incoming calls from customers via a phone, e-mail, website, or fax and make outgoing contacts with customers.

Customer—A person who receives the services or products that are offered by an organization.

Customer service—Ability of an organization to constantly and consistently give customers what they want and need.

EEOC—Equal Employment Opportunity Commission.

Leaders—Individuals who have a strong desire to make a difference in the world; people who influence others to achieve group and/or organizational goals.

Mission—A statement that addresses what an organization does.

Telemarketing—The act of selling, soliciting, or promoting a product or service over the telephone.

Values—Principles that guide a person's life, such as honesty, fairness.

Vision—Statement that addresses what the organization wants to become.

CHECKPOINT

Check your understanding of these terms by completing DCD10-a on the Data CD.

DISCUSSION ITEMS

These discussion items provide an opportunity to test your understanding of the chapter through written responses and/or discussion with your classmates and your instructor.

1. Explain what is meant by customer service.

2. Describe the characteristics of a customer service organization.

3. List and explain six important customer service skills.

CRITICAL THINKING CASE

You have been dealing with a customer over the telephone for several months. He continues to buy telecommunications equipment from your customer service organization. At this point, he has spent approximately $100,000 with the organization. You have never had any problems with him; he has been very professional in his conduct with you, as you have with him. When he calls, he always asks for you by name. He has been extremely polite and businesslike. However, he recently, on two occasions, has told you that you sound so nice over the telephone that he would like to meet you. You have made statements such as, "Thanks for the compliments; I do care about customers." You have evaded the suggestion that you meet him, thinking that he would not insist. The last time he called to place an order, he repeated his interest in meeting you, making a threatening statement (you believe) that he will stop ordering from the company unless you are willing to meet him. He did laugh after he made the statement, but you believe he is serious. You know your employer values his business; he has mentioned to you that he appreciates your help with this valuable customer. You are single, but you do not think that it would be wise to meet him. How should you handle this difficult situation? Should you talk with your employer?

A

Answers will vary; the important point is to think creatively and futuristically about customers.

1. Today's customers are people who buy services or products in person, over the telephone, by e-mail, through call centers, and through the Web. These customers are local, national, or international.

2. Tomorrow's customers are people who buy services or products in the same ways, but it is projected that there will be an increase in buying through call centers, e-mail, and Web services. Additionally, the projection is that we will continue to become a global society and that more of our customers will be international than they are today.

It is also projected that call centers will continue to increase in volume of business.

B

Answers will vary. Students may list a variety of behaviors that make them uncomfortable.

WORKPLACE PROJECTS

PROJECT 10-1 PREPARE A REPORT

Discover the characteristics of a customer service organization (Objective 1)

Determine who the future customers will be (Objective 2)

Team with three of your classmates on this activity. Interview three administrative professionals who work in organizations that sell a product directly to customers. If possible interview people whose organizations sell by telephone, e-mail, and via the Web. Ask them the following questions:

1. Who are your customers? Are they local? National? International?

2. Whom do you expect your customers to be in the next 5 years? 10 years? 15 years?

3. Have you encountered problems in serving customers? If so, how have you handled them? What suggestions would you make to an administrative professional starting out in the field as to handling external customers?

4. Does your organization have vision and mission statements that include the importance of customers? If so, may we have a copy?

If you were able to obtain vision and mission statements from a customer service organization, use what you have learned from it to write a new mission statement for JWay Nu-Systems Tech—one that will include its service to Australia and Taiwan. If you were not able to get a statement, compose one as a group.

If you are able to find demographics on your city as to the projected workforce for the future as to age, ethnicity and race, and gender, include this information in your report.

Prepare your findings on the questions you asked in your interview in report format. Additionally, include any demographics concerning the future workforce in your city. Deliver the information verbally to the class and submit a written report to your instructor. Also, present a copy of your mission and vision statements to the group.

PROJECT 10-2 ADD TO YOUR PROFESSIONAL GROWTH PLAN

Develop and evaluate your customer service skills (Objective 3)

Add to your professional growth plan by describing the customer service skills that you believe you presently have (face-to-face customer service, telephone service, and e-mail service). Next, describe how you intend to improve the weaknesses that you have. Save your statements as PGP10-2.

COMMUNICATION POWER

Use DCD10-b to assist you in improving your grammar skills.

ASSESSMENT OF CHAPTER OBJECTIVES

Now that you have completed the chapter and the projects, take a few minutes to review the chapter learning objectives. For your convenience, the objectives are repeated here. Did you accomplish these objectives? If you were unable to accomplish the objectives, give your reasons for not doing so; be specific and concise. Your instructor may prefer that your answers be submitted to her or him. If so, DCD10-c contains the Assessment of Chapter Objectives. Complete the Assessment of Chapter Objectives; submit your results to your instructor.

1. Discover the characteristics of a customer service organization.   Yes ☐   No ☐

_____

_____

_____

2. Determine who the future customers will be.   Yes ☐   No ☐

_____

_____

_____

3. Develop and evaluate your customer service skills.   Yes ☐   No ☐

_____

_____

_____

PART IV: CUSTOMER AND EMPLOYEE SATISFACTION

Integrated Project

Note: You are to work in a team of three on this project.

In the Integrated Project for Part 1, you were told that JWay Nu-Systems Tech plans to begin operations in Australia by the end of this fiscal year, which for JWay is the same as the calendar year.

Setting Up a Call Center for JWay

JWay intends to set up a call center in Australia. This center will take calls for JWay products from customers in the United States and Australia. Additionally, since JWay plans to expand to Taiwan within the next two years, Jana Portosky, Chief Executive Officer, and Wayne Wixon, Chief Operating Officer, have made several significant business contacts with prospective customers in Taiwan. Several $100,000 plus orders have already come in from Taiwan and more are expected. The call center will also take calls from Taiwan. The plans are to begin the call center with a group of seven people, with three of the people being responsible for taking calls from the United States, Australia, and Taiwan. Additionally, the group will consist of a center manager and three salespeople, who will be traveling between Australia and Taiwan seeking new business.

Task 1: Recommendations for Call Center Staffing

Jana Portosky has asked you to work with two other administrative assistants in making recommendations to her on the following areas:

- A job description for the three call center assistants
- A training program for the call center assistants; it is your responsibility to determine what the training program should include and the length of the training program. (In preparing this report, you must look at who the future customers are, individuals from Taiwan, Australia, and the United States, and what information the call center assistants must have about culture, language, and so forth. You also must decide if one of the assistants must speak Chinese or if you anticipate that your customers from Taiwan will speak both Chinese and English.)

Task 2: Submit Your Report in Report Format, with a Cover Memorandum to Jana Portosky

Nancy Upchurch, CPS/CAP
Senior Marketing Coordinator
Hensel Phelps Construction Company
Greeley, Colorado

SPOTLIGHT *on Success*

WHAT ARE SOME OF THE REASONS I LIKE MY PROFESSION?

One of the reasons I have always liked my profession is because it never gets boring, and each year, that becomes more of an understatement. Each day I have to wear a number of different hats—administrator, human resource manager, marketer, financial planner, trainer, educator—and sometimes I've had to be a little psychic—but I've also had to learn about being a professional.

Throughout our profession's long and proud history, successful administrative assistants have one universal quality in common—and that quality is "professionalism."

What do I mean when I say someone is a "professional"? It means you care enough about your profession to continually seek out ways to develop your skills and knowledge. It means you stay connected with peers and continually seek out advice from mentors.

TO WHAT PROFESSIONAL ORGANIZATIONS DO I BELONG?

Education is one way I continue to increase and enhance my knowledge of the administrative professional. My membership in the International Association of Administrative Professionals® (IAAP) is a positive reinforcement in presenting myself as a professional. I have always felt that what goes out of the office is a product of me and if it is not professional, it should not be seen.

Earning the Certified Professional Secretary® (CPS) rating in 1992 and the Certified Administrative Professional® (CAP) rating in 2001 not only helped build my self-esteem but also reflected the expanding responsibilities, specialization, and skills needed for today's administrative support staff. The CPS and CAP ratings offer me a

WHAT IS MY BACKGROUND?

I have been an admin—in one sense or another—since my senior year in high school. I attended a small school where the principal picked one of the business class students to be his "secretary" for the year—I was fortunate to be that student. What an experience—it started my career as an administrative professional.

Having seen the many role changes of the secretary and the discord of the "just a secretary" classification, I have been a proponent in changing this negative perception by sharing my knowledge and skills with other office professionals.

Our jobs, now more than ever, have been a balancing act. Sometimes I feel like the picture in the Dr. Seuss book, *The Cat in the Hat,* when he is trying to juggle numerous things with only two hands and two feet.

PART V

MAIL, TRAVEL, MEETINGS, AND CONFERENCES

significant, measurable, and attainable goal for the career-oriented administrative professional that I am. The ratings also provide me the assurance that comes from having met and accepted professional standards.

WHAT ARE SOME OF THE ASSETS I BRING TO THE PROFESSION?

Some of the assets I bring to my profession include:

- Dedication/dependability/reliability.
- Computer skills (training for eight district offices).
- Knowledge of all office equipment and its uses.
- Grammar, punctuation, and language skills in writing and editing; document layout skills.
- Leadership qualities.
- Positive attitude.
- Willingness to share my knowledge with others.
- Willingness to change, adapt, and learn.
- Hardworking—I do what it takes to get the job done.
- Team Player!

It seems like everywhere one turns these days, one hears about what will be required of tomorrow's worker and the challenge in preparing and retraining employees to accept a more advanced and functionally demanding job. I

am one of "tomorrow's workers" and I prepare for these challenges by taking advantage of all opportunities provided me. IAAP and my employer play positive roles in helping me attain these goals of professional development, thus making me a better admin—for them and for me.

In short, mastering technology effectively is using interpersonal and communication skills, giving me the ability to track and organize and be creative in solving problems, and most importantly, having the willingness to learn, grow, and accept challenges.

Until you test the limits of what you can achieve, you cannot truly know what your possibilities are. The odds change in your favor when you begin to challenge them. I believe that if you truly want to succeed at something, you have to be willing to work at it. You have to have a passion for what you are pursuing. If you want to improve yourself and your professional image, join others who share that dream.

WHAT ARE MY INTERESTS/HOBBIES?

My hobbies include active involvement in IAAP, camping, hiking, being with family and friends, and using my creative skills through the computer.

Although I have faced many different challenges in my years as an administrative professional, the one that stands out the most is one that helped create continuity with my current employer.

THE SITUATION

Hired some 20 years ago at my current company, I came from a very forward-thinking, technology-driven company, only to find a setback in this company's office equipment.

After six months of using the Memory Writer as a "computer" of sorts, I did a company-wide study, knowing that computers were used in the field. I developed a spreadsheet asking employees what type of computers they were using and any related software. I found that each jobsite was purchasing whatever type of computer was the least expensive and using the software that came with it. In this situation, what would you have done to bring about standardization in equipment as well as in purchasing of replacement or new computers? Decide how you would have handled the situation. Then, see page 433 for the case solution.

CHAPTER 11

WORKPLACE MAIL AND COPIERS

Learning Objectives

1. Identify USPS mail services and mail classifications; identify private mail services.
2. Explain how to process both incoming and outgoing mail.
3. Describe copier types and features.
4. Explain the benefits of recycling to organizations and our environment.
5. Explain the importance of ethics and etiquette when making copies.

Image 100

> MAIL AND OTHER SPECIAL SERVICES

Mail in the workplace of today is delivered in a variety of forms—through the **United States Postal Service®** (USPS), e-mail, instant messaging, fax, and by private companies such as FedEx®, United Parcel Service of America, Inc.® (UPS), and others. In Chapter 5, e-mail and fax processes were presented. This chapter will focus on USPS mail and private mail services. Additionally, copier types, features, and ethical considerations are presented.

> USPS SERVICES

On July 26, 1775, members of the Second Continental Congress meeting in Philadelphia agreed ". . . that a postmaster general be appointed for the United states."[1] With the appointing of Benjamin Franklin as the first Postmaster General, the USPS was born. At that point the United States was a confederation of colonies scattered along the eastern seaboard. The postal system created by Congress helped bind the new nation together, support the growth of commerce, and ensure a free flow of ideas and information.[2] The USPS is now the eighth largest organization in the country, with annual revenues approaching $68 billion and employing a workforce of nearly 800,000 people.[3]

Today, however, the USPS faces a number of challenges, including a soft economy, changing global markets, new technologies, and the need to deliver mail to an ever-increasing number of addresses, along with a decline in revenue partly because of a reduction in First-Class Mail® (the

---

[1]"History of the Post Office," <http://www.ceol.com/vvpo/history.html> (accessed June 7, 2005).
[2]Ibid.
[3]John E. Potter, "Executive Summary," <http://www.usps.com/strategicplanning/transformatio/tppr2004/pmgletter.htm> (accessed June 7, 2005).

The USPS is the eighth largest organization in the country.

© Photodisc

largest mail class in terms of both volume and revenue). From 1999 to 2004, First-Class Mail volume declined 5.4 percent.[4] Because of these challenges, the Congress and the General Accounting Office asked the Postal Service to prepare a Comprehensive Transformation Plan to address its challenges; this plan was completed in 2002. A progress report was prepared in 2004. According to a letter from the Postmaster General & CEO, John Potter, the goals of the Transformation Plan, which include debt reduction, increased productivity, and rate stabilization, are being achieved. However, ongoing improvement is seen as essential.[5]

Although the challenges of the USPS mentioned in the previous paragraphs require constant attention, the main provider of mail services in the United States remains the USPS. Regular and special mail services provided by the USPS, international mail, and private mail services are presented in the next section.

If you work in a large organization, you are not likely to be responsible for processing mail. It is more efficient when an organization receives and sends a large amount of mail each day to have a mail room to handle all processing. However, if you work in a small organization, you may be responsible for processing the outgoing mail. In order to be efficient at your task, you must keep current on postal services, classifications, and rates. The United States Postal Service maintains an extensive website at www.usps.com.

> U.S. POSTAL SERVICE CLASSIFICATIONS

The following standard classifications are used by the United States Postal Service.

▷ Express Mail®

The fastest delivery available from the USPS is **Express Mail.** This service offers next-day delivery by 3 p.m. to many destinations. Express Mail is delivered 365 days a year with no extra charge for Saturday, Sunday, or holiday delivery. It is automatically insured for $100 against loss or damage. Proof of delivery is provided upon request; tracking information is available.[6]

Self CHECK A

To help you become more familiar with the services provided by the USPS, check out their website at www.usps.com. List three services that you had not been aware of in the past in the space provided below.

Three services provided by the USPS are:

1. _____

2. _____

3. _____

[4] "Financial Review," <http://www.usps.com/history/anrpt04/freview_006.htm> (accessed June 7, 2005).
[5] Ibid.
[6] "Express Mail," <http://www.usps.com/shipping/expressmail.htm> (accessed June 8, 2005).

▷ First-Class Mail

First-Class Mail includes letters, greeting cards, large envelopes, and packages. The maximum weight for First-Class Mail is 13 ounces—over 13 ounces becomes Priority Mail®. First-Class Mail includes the following types:

First-Class Mail cards—the least expensive, most immediate way to reach someone.

First-Class Mail letters—the everyday letter mail.

First-Class Mail large envelopes—material in large envelopes.

First-Class Mail packages—letters, envelopes, and small packages weighing 13 ounces or less.

Presorted First-Class Mail—used for high volume business mail.[7]

▷ Priority Mail

All first-class mail exceeding 13 ounces is designated **Priority Mail.** No shipment weighing over 13 ounces should be sent by Priority Mail until it has been determined that Priority Mail is the most cost-effective method. Non–First-Class Mail items (large and/or irregular shipments) should be examined to see if an express-type common carrier would be more cost effective. Priority Mail must be prominently displayed on the package or envelope to ensure proper handling. Without the marking, mail sent via USPS will receive standard mail service at first-class cost.[8]

▷ Standard Mail™

Standard Mail offers a lower price on postage because of the work that is performed by the sender. The sender does some of the preparing, sorting, and entering of the mail. An annual mailing fee of $150 is required. The mail piece must weigh less than 16 ounces.

Standard Mail requires a minimum of 200 pieces or 50 pounds per mailing. It cannot be used for sending personal correspondence, handwritten or typewritten letters, or bills and statements of account. Rates are based on weight, shape, preparation, and entry. Standard Mail is often used to send printed matter, flyers, circulars, newsletters, bulletins, catalogs, and small packages.[9]

▷ Package Services

The **Package Services** class is intended for merchandise, catalogs, and other printed material. The four classes of package services include Parcel Post®, Bound Printed Matter, Media Mail®, and Library Mail.

1. Parcel Post. This service is used for mailing merchandise, books, circulars, catalogs, and other printed mater. Bulk rates are available, in addition to a barcoded discount.

2. Bound Printed Matter. This class is reserved for advertising, promotional, directory, or editorial material. The material must be securely bound by permanent fastenings such as staples and spiral binding. Loose-leaf binders are not considered permanent.

3. Media Mail. This mail is generally used for books of at least eight pages, film, printed music, printed test materials, sound recordings, play scripts, and so forth. There are presorted rates available for bulk quantities of mail (300 pieces or more) and barcoded discounts.

4. Library Mail. This mail is used by qualifying institutions such as libraries, universities, zoos, and research institutions to mail educational and research material. There is also a barcode discount for Library Mail.[10]

▷ Special Mail Services

In addition to being familiar with USPS mail classifications, you also need to know about special services available. Some of the major services are as follows.

Certificate of Mailing

A **Certificate of Mailing** provides evidence that an item has been mailed. There is a minimal charge for this service, and you must purchase the certificate at the time of mailing. This service is available for First-Class Mail, Priority Mail, Parcel Post, Bound Printed Matter, and Media Mail.

Registered Mail™

Registering mail provides maximum protection and security for valuable items. **Registered Mail** is available

---

[7]"First-Class Mail," <http://www.usps.com/send/waystosendmail/senditwithintheus/firstclassmail.htm> (accessed June 8, 2005).

[8]Internal Revenue Service IRS.Gov, Department of the Treasury, Classes of Mail and United States Postal Service (USPS) Special Services," <http://www.irs.gov/irm/part1/ch15s02.html> (accessed July 30, 2005).

[9]"Standard Mail," <http://www.usps.com/send/waystosendmail/senditwithintheus/standardmail.htm> (accessed June 8, 2005).

[10]"Business Mail 101," <http://www.usps.com/businessmai1101/classes/welcome.htm> (accessed June 8, 2005).

for First-Class or Priority Mail only. When you register an item with no declared value, no insurance is necessary. However, if you declare a value on the item, insurance is mandatory. You can combine Registered Mail with Collect on Delivery (COD), Restricted Delivery, or Return Receipt service.

Return Receipt

Return Receipt is a service that provides the mailer with evidence of delivery. You should request a return receipt before the item is mailed.

Signature Confirmation™

You can also purchase **Signature Confirmation** service for an additional fee. This service provides signature proof of delivery as well as the date and time of delivery or attempted delivery. Mailers can track the delivery information online.

Collect on Delivery

Collect on Delivery (COD) allows the mailer to collect the price of goods and/or postage on the item ordered by the addressee when delivered. The amount to be collected cannot exceed $1,000.

Certified Mail™

For materials that have no monetary value but for which you need a record of delivery, use **Certified Mail.** The mailer is provided with a mailing receipt, and a record is kept at the recipient's post office. An additional fee is charged for Certified Mail.

Insured Mail

You can obtain coverage against loss or damage through **insured mail** (a service to individuals who pay a special fee to obtain reimbursement for lost or damaged mail). You cannot insure items for more than their value.

▷ International Mail

With organizations continuing to expand into international markets, you may need to send paper mail internationally. The principal categories of international mail provided by the USPS are: Global Express Guaranteed®, Global Priority Mail®, and Global Express Mail®.

Global Express Guaranteed

Global Express Guaranteed (GXG) is a service that takes from one to two days for most major international markets and three days for other international destinations. Reliable, date-certain shipping to more than 190 countries and territories worldwide is available. Additional services available through GXG are date-certain delivery, refunds for delayed packages, and online tracking and confirmation service. Insurance covering up to $100 for loss, damage, rifling, or document reconstruction is included at no additional charge. Volume discounts are also available.

Global Priority Mail

Global Priority Mail (GPM) is an accelerated airmail service that provides a reliable and economical way of sending correspondence, printed matter, and merchandise that weighs four pounds and under to over 51 countries and territories worldwide.

Global Express Mail

Global Express Mail (EMS) is a high-speed service for mailing time-sensitive items to international

Self CHECK B

Take a few minutes now to check your understanding of what you have learned to this point about USPS mail classifications. Answer the following questions:

1. Describe the following types of U.S. mail: Express Mail, Priority Mail, and First-Class Mail.

_____

_____

_____

2. Describe the following types of international mail: Global Express Guaranteed and Global Priority Mail.

_____

_____

_____

locations. Customers who pay postage through an Express Mail Corporate Account receive a 5 percent discount off the single piece EMS rates.

International Mail—Addressing

The USPS recommends that international addresses be in all uppercase letters, with no more than five lines if possible. The last line of the address block must include only the complete country name. The following information and order are correct for international mail.

Line 1: Name of addressee
Line 2: Street address or post office box number
Line 3: City or town name, other principal subdivision
Line 4: Country name[11]

A properly formatted delivery address is as follows:

MR COLIN FRANKS
3135 CANTEBERRY ROAD
LONDON WIP 5HQ
ENGLAND

> PRIVATE MAIL SERVICES

Several private companies within the United States offer both national and international services worldwide, three of which are FedEx, United Parcel Service of America, Inc. (UPS), and DHL Worldwide Express. You can find information about each of these companies on their websites.

Here are a few of the services offered by these companies:

1. Document exchange that is an electronic delivery service, enabling customers to send time-sensitive documents, images, and software for immediate worldwide delivery via the Internet

2. Same-day delivery service to virtually anywhere in the continental United States as well as from many international business centers 24 hours a day, 365 days a year

3. Overnight delivery of letters, documents, and packages

4. Daily pickup services

5. Online tools that allow users to select services, calculate rates, look up addresses, validate and print labels, and track shipping history using criteria defined by the user

Additionally, private mail services include messenger and courier services, which are available in large cities. If you wish to have a document delivered

© Photodisc

Courier mail delivery services are available in large cities.

Self CHECK C

Check the websites of two of the private mail services listed in the section Private Mail Services. Record below three services for each company that are not listed in that section.

Name of private mail service: _____

Services provided: _____

_____

Name of private mail service: _____

Services provided: _____

_____

[11]"Categories of International Mail," <http://pe.usps.gov/text/pub51/pub51.html> (accessed June 8, 2005).

to a customer across town, you can call the service to pick up the document and deliver it to the receiver. Private companies such as Mail Boxes ETC.® (which has merged with UPS) and Pak Mail also provide mailing services for individuals and small businesses. These services include: packing and shipping, insuring, package tracking, stuffing envelopes, and holding and forwarding mail.

> OUTGOING AND INCOMING MAIL

An administrative professional's responsibilities for handling outgoing mail will vary depending on how the organization handles incoming and outgoing mail. Research in 2004 indicated that 41 percent of mailroom work was sent to third parties for processing, up significantly from 2003, with the projection that **outsourcing** (handled by an outside firm) will continue to increase in the future. The basic reason for outsourcing mail is a financial one. For example, American Express Company's financial advisory group reduced 50 employees—or more than half of its mailroom staff—to save $1.5 million in salaries.[12] Other cost savings come in the form of the release of valuable office space and reduced storage costs.[13]

Still another reason for outsourcing has to do with the threat of anthrax-contaminated mail, which has become very real for our nation after the 2001 anthrax terrorist attacks on mailrooms. There is also the fear that infection may be spread even if letters are not opened. Many companies that are not outsourcing are equipping their mailrooms with high-technology detection and disinfection gear. Additional measures being used include bomb-sniffing dogs to inspect incoming cars and deliveries. Mail may also be sent to a special location where mailroom employees wear gas masks and protective suits and gloves while sorting the mail.[14]

A third trend that is changing the work of administrative professionals and mailroom staff is converting the paper to digital. Companies, in an attempt to understand and control the vast amount of paper information that is confronting them, are moving to adopting software that converts letters, faxes, and other paper into electronic files, which automatically sort the information. However, moving from printed documents to digital documents does not mean that less paper will be used by organizations. As a result of the rapid growth in data, the number of printed pages is predicted to double from 2005 to 2010.[15]

> Administrative Professional's Mail Handling Responsibilities

Although a big percentage of large organizations outsource mail, small companies generally do not. Thus, it is important that you understand how mail should be handled; you certainly cannot assume presently that all mail will be outsourced or automated to the extent that the administrative professional will have no mail handling responsibilities.

Outgoing Mail

The administrative professional in a large company may be responsible for preparing the mail for processing by mailroom employees. Several important steps to ensure that you handle outgoing mail properly are described in the next section.

Interoffice Mail. Place all interoffice correspondence in appropriate envelopes with the name and department of the addressee listed on the envelope.

Enclosures. An **enclosure** or **attachment notation** at the bottom of a document serves as a flag to the recipient. Use *attachment* when an item is attached to the document. Use *enclosure* when the item is placed behind the document without being attached. If there is more than one enclosure or attachment, the number should be placed in parentheses after the word *enclosures* or *attachments*.

Envelopes. Key the address carefully; once it is keyed, check the inside address against the envelope address. An additional precaution that you can take to be certain that you have the correct address is to check the address against the letterhead of previous

[12]"American Express Financial Advisory Group Implements Digital Mailroom Technology and is On Tract to Save $1.5 Million," <http://www.captivasoftware.com/products/casestudies/casestudies_view.asp?wes_id=53> (accessed August 25, 2005).

[13]Natasha Gray, "Abbey National Banks on Innovation by Outsourcing Document Management," <http://www.outsourcing-financial-services.com/abbey.html> (accessed June 8, 2005).

[14]"Paul Glader and William Bulkeley, "Corporate Mailrooms Across U.S. Tighten Their Security Measures, Special Report: Aftermath of Terror," <http://www.mosaicvp.com/Home/newsclip/20010ctober/Silanis2.htm> (accessed June 8, 2005).

[15]Roger Gann, "How managing documents better can help your business," <http://www.techworld.com/applications/features/index.cfm?FeatureID=1493> (accessed August 28, 2005).

278   **Part V** Mail, Travel, Meetings, and Conferences

correspondence with the organization. You might also want to keep a list of frequently used addresses; be certain that this list is always up to date. Before placing a letter in an envelope, check to see that it is signed; you never want to send out an unsigned letter.

Automation Requirements. As you address envelopes to be read by optical character readers (**OCRs**), key the address in all capital letters. Omit punctuation except for the hyphen in the ZIP + 4 designation. Figure 11-1 shows a correctly addressed domestic envelope.

Seal and Stamp. If you work in a medium to large organization, the outgoing mail may be sent to a mailroom or outsourced. If you work in a small office, you may seal and stamp envelopes using a postage meter. Envelopes are fed into the meter and are stacked, sealed, weighed, meter-stamped, and counted in one continuous operation. The metered mail imprint serves as postage payment, a postmark, and a cancellation mark. A postage meter either prints directly on envelopes or on adhesive strips that are then affixed to packages.

Electronic Postage. In 1999, the USPS began allowing stamps to be provided through Internet-based postage. Stamps.com is a service that allows you to print official United States Postal Service postage directly from your computer and printer. No special hardware is needed.

Mailing Lists. Most companies have correspondence they send to certain groups of individuals on a regular basis. As an administrative professional, your responsibility is to maintain a current mailing list on your computer. From this computerized list, you can print envelopes and address labels with barcodes.

Periodic updating of addresses is essential, as is adding new names to the mailing list.

Incoming Mail

Just as outgoing mail responsibilities depend largely on the size of the company, so do incoming mail responsibilities. One of your responsibilities as an administrative professional in a small firm may be to receive and process mail. In large companies, a big percentage of mail functions are now outsourced to independent companies. If mail is not outsourced, however, large companies have centralized mail departments that receive and distribute mail. Mail is generally delivered by mailroom employees at set times twice each day (in the morning and the afternoon). Some organizations use electronic carts that are self-powered and unattended. These carts use a photoelectric guidance system to follow invisible chemical paths painted on carpeting, floor tile, or other surfaces. The cart is programmed to make stops at particular locations, where the administrative professional can retrieve the mail from the cart.

© Photodisc

Some organizations use photoelectric mail carts that are self-powered and unattended.

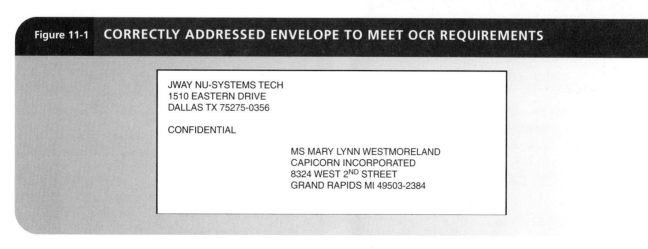

Figure 11-1 **CORRECTLY ADDRESSED ENVELOPE TO MEET OCR REQUIREMENTS**

JWAY NU-SYSTEMS TECH
1510 EASTERN DRIVE
DALLAS TX 75275-0356

CONFIDENTIAL

MS MARY LYNN WESTMORELAND
CAPICORN INCORPORATED
8324 WEST 2ND STREET
GRAND RAPIDS MI 49503-2384

In small organizations, a USPS carrier may deliver the mail directly to the organization. If the small organization maintains a post office box, you may have the responsibility for picking up the mail.

Sort. Once you receive the mail in your office or department, you must do a preliminary mail sort. If several individuals work in the department, sort the mail according to the addressee. An alphabetical sorter is handy if you are sorting mail for a number of individuals. Once the mail is sorted, place the mail for each individual into separate stacks.

When this preliminary sort is completed, sort each person's mail in this order:

▸ Personal and confidential. The administrative professional should not open mail marked *personal* or *confidential.* Place this mail to one side so you do not inadvertently open it.
▸ Special Delivery, Registered Mail, or Certified Mail. This mail is important and should be placed so the individual to whom it is addressed sees it first.
▸ Regular business mail (First-Class Mail). Mail from customers, clients, and suppliers is also considered important and should be sorted so it receives priority.
▸ Interoffice communications. E-mail has become pervasive in the workplace; however, there are still times when the interoffice memorandum is more appropriate, particularly when the correspondence is relatively long, more than one-third to one-half page. Interoffice memorandums are generally sent in a distinctive interoffice envelope.
▸ Advertisements and circulars. Advertisements and circulars are considered relatively unimportant and can be handled after the other correspondence is answered.
▸ Newspapers, magazines, and catalogs. These materials should be placed at the bottom of the correspondence stack since they may be read at the executive's convenience.

Open. Mail may be opened in the mailroom or in the individual's office. Mail opened in an individual's office is usually opened by hand, using an envelope opener. When opening mail, follow the procedures given here.

▸ Have necessary supplies readily available. These supplies include an envelope opener, a date and time stamp, routing and action slips, a stapler, paper clips, and a pen or pencil.
▸ Before opening an envelope, tap the lower edge of the envelope on the desk so the contents fall to the bottom and are not cut when the envelope is opened.
▸ After the correspondence is opened, check the envelope carefully to be certain all items have been removed.
▸ Fasten any enclosures to the correspondence. Attach small enclosures to the front of the correspondence. Attach enclosures larger than the correspondence to the back.
▸ Mend any torn paper with tape.
▸ If a personal or confidential letter is opened by mistake, do not remove it from the envelope. Write "Opened by Mistake" on the front of the envelope, add your initials, and reseal the envelope with tape.
▸ Stack the envelopes on the desk in the same order as the opened mail in case it becomes necessary to refer to the envelopes. A good practice is to save all envelopes for at least one day in case they are needed for reference. Then they may be thrown away.

Keep Selected Envelopes. Certain envelopes should be retained. Keep the envelope when one or more of the following situations exist:

1. An incorrectly addressed envelope—You or your supervisor may want to call attention to this fact when answering the correspondence.

2. A letter with no return address—The envelope usually will have the return address.

3. An envelope that has a significantly different postmark from the date on the document—The document date may be compared with the postmark date to determine the delay in receiving the document.

4. A letter specifying an enclosure that is not enclosed—Write *No Enclosure* on the letter and attach the envelope.

5. A letter containing a bid, an offer, or an acceptance of a contract—the postmark date may be needed as legal evidence.

6. An envelope that appears to contain any suspicious substance or other materials. Proper procedures for handling suspicious mail should be in place.

Date and Time Stamp. Although all organizations do not use date and time stamping procedures, it can be an important step. It furnishes a record of when the correspondence was received. For example, a letter may arrive too late to handle the matter mentioned in the letter. Therefore, the stamped date of receipt is a recorded confirmation of the day the letter was received and of the resultant inability to take care of the matter. Sometimes the correspondence is not dated; the date stamped on the letter shows the approximate date of writing. Date and time stamping may be done with a hand stamp or a small machine that prints the date and time.

Read and Annotate. Busy executives need help with the large amount of mail that crosses their desks each day. As an administrative professional, you can help by scanning the mail for the executive and noting important parts of the correspondence. You can underline the important words and phrases with a colored pen or pencil. You should also check mathematical calculations and verify dates that appear in correspondence.

One of the responsibilities of an administrative professional in handling the mail is reading and annotating.

© Photodisc

The next step is to **annotate** (to make notations about previous action taken or facts that will assist the reader). You can annotate by writing notes in the margin of the correspondence or by using Post-it® notes. The advantage of Post-it notes is that they can be peeled off and destroyed when you and the executive are finished with them.

If an enclosure is missing from the letter, make an annotation. If a bill is received, check the computations. Note any discrepancies by annotating. If the correspondence refers to a previous piece of correspondence written by the executive, pull that correspondence and attach it to the new correspondence. Note that the previous correspondence is being attached. Annotations may also be used to remind the executive of a previous commitment. For example, the executive might have agreed to have lunch with the person who signed the correspondence. When answering the letter, the executive may want to refer to their lunch plans.

Organize and Present. After you have completed the preliminary mail sorts and have opened, date and time stamped, read, and annotated, you are ready to do a final sort. Here is one arrangement that may be used.

1. Immediate action. This mail must be handled on the day of receipt or shortly thereafter.

2. Routine correspondence. Such mail includes memorandums and other types of non-urgent mail.

3. Informational mail. Periodicals, newspapers, advertisements, and other types of mail that do not require answering but are for the executive's reading should be included here.

4. Sort mail into color-coded folders, using an appropriate label. Review the suggestions in the Spotlight on Handling Mail.

Spotlight *on*

HANDLING MAIL

Incoming mail may be sorted into folders with these labels: Urgent Mail (includes mail to be signed)—red folder; Routine Mail—blue folder; Periodicals and Printed Matter—yellow folder.

The executive may ask that you present the mail two times a day. For example, if external mail is received in the morning and afternoon, the executive may ask that you organize and present it approximately 30 minutes after you receive the mail. If you have been with the company and the executive for a period of time, she or he may not want to see all mail; you may handle a large portion of it.

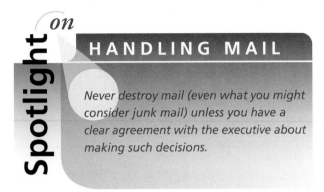

Spotlight on

HANDLING MAIL

Never destroy mail (even what you might consider junk mail) unless you have a clear agreement with the executive about making such decisions.

Route. At times, more than one person may need to read a piece of correspondence. In that case, make photocopies of the correspondence and send a copy to each individual on the list or route the correspondence to all individuals, using a routing slip. When determining whether to make photocopies, ask yourself if it is urgent that all individuals receive the information contained in the correspondence immediately. If so, it is best to photocopy the document. If not, it generally is best to use a routing slip, particularly if the correspondence is lengthy.

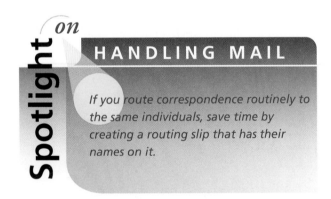

Spotlight on

HANDLING MAIL

If you route correspondence routinely to the same individuals, save time by creating a routing slip that has their names on it.

Handle E-Mail. E-mail usage continues to increase. Some executives, because of the large number of e-mails, expect the administrative professional to assist with their e-mails. If you are expected to assist with the executive's e-mail, be certain that you are clear on how she or he wants you to handle them. You might be expected to answer routine e-mail; if so, your employer needs to know that you have done so. Here are some suggestions for the handling of your employer's e-mail.

▶ Check the e-mail three or four times per day, depending on your employer's wishes. For example, you may check it at 9 a.m., 11 a.m., 2 p.m., and 4 p.m.

▶ Do not open e-mail marked confidential unless your employer instructs you to do so.

▶ Read the e-mail, reply to the e-mail (if appropriate), and forward, if necessary, the e-mail to appropriate individuals.

▶ If the individual does not know that you routinely handle the e-mail of your employer, be explicit in the e-mail when you answer it. Say, for example, "Mr. Livingston has asked that I respond to your e-mail."

▶ If you cannot handle the e-mail, send a note to your employer informing him or her of the e-mail you have not been able to handle. If your employer needs to handle it immediately, mark your e-mail as urgent.

▶ When your employer is out of town, handle the e-mail as usual assuming you have been authorized to do so. If not, forward the e-mail to the appropriate person who is in charge during your employer's absence.

Handle Mail During the Executive's Absence. Talk with the executive before she or he leaves concerning your responsibilities in handling the mail. Be specific with any questions so you have a clear understanding of what should be done. Mistakes in handling mail can be costly to the company. Follow these general guidelines when handling mail.

1. When urgent mail (any mail, including e-mail, containing a matter to be handled immediately) comes in, respond to the correspondence the same day. If you cannot answer the mail, send it to the appropriate person in your organization who can answer the correspondence. Usually your employer will have designated someone who is in charge in her or his absence. You must see that the person receives the urgent correspondence quickly.

2. Answer mail that falls within your area of responsibility in a timely manner.

3. Maintain mail that has been answered, along with a copy of the answer, in a separate folder. The executive may want to review it when she or he returns.

4. Maintain mail that can wait for the executive's return in a separate folder. Retrieve any previous

Part V Mail, Travel, Meetings, and Conferences

correspondence that the executive will need when reviewing the mail. Place this correspondence in the folder also.

File E-mail. A study conducted by Account Temps and published in the *Wall Street Journal* estimated that office workers spend an average of six weeks per year looking for things. It is imperative that you establish a logical filing system on your computer. Here are several suggested steps for doing so.

► Mirror your paper filing system (assuming it is an effective one) on your computer. A good system that is consistent for both paper and computer filing makes it easier to find documents. For example, if you generally reference your work by client/customer, then set up your e-mail folders by client/customer name.

► When new e-mails come in, do not let them stay in your mailbox. Read them on a schedule (probably at least twice each day), reply, forward the message if needed, and file the message in an appropriate folder. If it is a message that you clearly do not need, delete it.

► Delete old e-mail that you no longer need.

► Delete any spam that may be hanging around.[16]

> OFFICE COPIERS

The **information age,** which began in the last quarter of the twentieth century when information became easily accessible through computers and computer networks, spawned the term **paperless office.** The paperless office was seen as a probability by people writing in the field, because of the information being available on computers, through electronic transmission, and the ability to store the data electronically. However, as we now know, the information age did not spawn a paperless office. In fact, the exact opposite has been true. The traditional workplace and even the home workplace, although having numerous technological capabilities, still generate enormous amounts of paper, with no decrease in paper usage seen on the horizon.

Today, we use workplace and home copiers (which are available relatively inexpensively) to copy a tremendous amount of information. Additionally, businesses have sprung up that generate income

Spotlight *on* E-MAIL

Establish a filing system that mirrors the paper filing system.

Self CHECK D

Check yourself on processing incoming mail. List eight steps to follow when handling incoming mail.

1. _____
2. _____
3. _____
4. _____
5. _____
6. _____
7. _____
8. _____

[16]"Filing email and electronic documents," <http://www.records.uts.edu.au/procedures/documents/filing-email.html> (accessed June 10, 2005).

around copying materials for the public. No doubt you have used such businesses at least once and perhaps numerous times in assisting you to make copies of important documents. The Information Age has produced **information junkies,** who have a tremendous amount of information on a wide variety of topics. Have you ever copied a document from the Web because you thought it might be useful later and then never referred to it? Have you ever thought you needed five copies of a document but made eight instead just in case you needed them? Most of us would have to answer "yes" to those questions.

Although we often are guilty of making too many copies of information, most offices today would have trouble existing without a copier. This portion of the chapter is devoted to an overview of copier capacities and functions. As an administrative professional, you will use copiers extensively. It is important that you are knowledgeable concerning the capabilities of copiers, and also that you are judicious in your use of copiers. The last section of this chapter will deal with the importance of recycling paper.

▷ Copier Technology

Xerox first introduced the plain-paper copier in 1959. Today, the copier industry generates billions of dollars in revenue each year. The huge market for copiers drives manufacturers to constantly improve their offerings. The traditional copier was created using **analog** technology, in which the image is translated as a fluctuating electronic signal. However, today the analog copier (although still available) is becoming obsolete.[17] Most manufacturers have stopped introducing new analog models. The **digital** copier (transfers data as a series of bits rather than as a signal) has become the most commonly used copier. The digital copiers have fewer moving parts, which results in fewer mechanical breakdowns, make less noise than the analog copier, and are better at reproducing fine lines and photographs. Although the analog is simpler to operate than the digital, you can learn to operate a digital copier with only a minimal training period.

▷ Questions to Ask When Choosing a Copier

Before you choose a copier, you should ask and get the answers to the following questions:

▶ What do I need a copier to do? Do I need a copier that supports color? Do I need a multifunction product—one that can print, copy, scan, and fax?

▶ What volume do I need? If a copier is going to be used as a network printer, the volume will generally be increased by 30 percent to 50 percent.

▶ At what speed does the copier need to perform? Copier speed is measured in copies per minute (cpm), or outputs per minute (opm).[18]

Additional questions are given in Figure 11-2.

▷ Copier Classifications

Copiers are classified into four basic categories, depending on their speed, with these categories being: low volume, mid volume, high volume, and copier/duplicators.

Low-Volume Copiers

Low-volume copiers typically produce copies in the range of 18 to 30 **cpm** (copies per minute) and 5,000 to 10,000 **ppm** (pages per month).

Mid-Volume Copiers

Mid-volume copiers produce approximately 25 to 60 cpm and 80,000 ppm.

High-Volume Copiers

High-volume copiers produce approximately 50 to 140 cpm and 500,000 ppm.

Copy/Duplicators

Copy-duplicators are high-performance machines generally found in specialized copy/duplication centers or in print shops. They are fast and cost-effective alternatives to the large-volume copy machine when a large number of copies must be completed.

▷ Copier Features

Copier features differ; however, a few of the features are mentioned here.

Reduction and Enlargement

This feature allows you to reduce the size of the original document. For example, reduced copies can be made of large documents so all filed copies are uniform in size. An enlargement feature also allows an

---

[17]"Business Copiers Introduction," <http://www.buyerzone.com/office_equipment/copiers-digital/buyers_guide1.html> (accessed June 6, 2005).

[18]"Choosing an Office Copier: Digital Copiers Buyer's Guide," <http://www.buyerzone.com/office_equipment/copiers-digital/buyers_guide2.html?click=1> (accessed June 6, 2005).

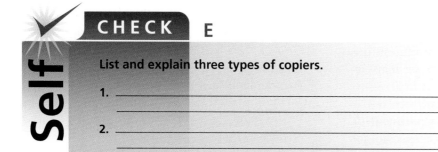

CHECK E

List and explain three types of copiers.

1. _____

2. _____

3. _____

Self

original document to be magnified. Fine details on an original can be made more legible by using this feature.

Automatic Document Feeding

The **automatic document feeder (ADF)** allows you to copy multipage documents without having to lift and lower the platen cover for every sheet.

Duplexing

Copying on both sides of a sheet of paper is known as **duplexing.** This feature saves paper. An operator makes copies on both sides of the paper by pushing the proper buttons, requiring no other intervention by the operator.

Editing

A number of copiers have built-in editing features. These features include border erasing, centering, color adjusting, marker editing, and masking. **Marker editing** lets you change the color of specific sections of a document to highlight these areas; **masking** allows you to block out areas of sensitive or confidential information.

▷ Systems Control

If you have worked in an organization, you are probably aware of the copying abuses that persist. For example, employees often make ten copies of a document when only six are needed. The additional copies are made "just in case." More often than not the extra

---

Figure 11-2   COPIER SELECTION QUESTIONS

Questions for the Organization

▸ How many people will be using the copier?

▸ How many copies will be made per month?

▸ Is there a projected increase or decrease in copy volume over the next three years?

▸ What features are needed?

▸ Will color copying be needed?

▸ What space limitations exist for the copier?

▸ Should a maintenance contract be purchased?

▸ What dollars are available for the copier purchase?

Questions to be Asked During the Demonstration

▸ What is the quality of the copy?

▸ If it is a color copier, are the colors clear?

▸ Is the machine easy to operate?

▸ Is it easy to remove jammed paper? Replace toner?

Questions to be Answered Concerning the Dealer/Vendor

▸ How long has the dealer been in business?

▸ Have any complaints been filed against the dealer with the Better Business Bureau?

▸ Does the vendor offer service agreements? If so, what is the cost?

▸ If service contracts are provided, what is the response time on a typical service request?

▸ Does the price of the copier compare favorably with a similar copier from another dealer?

---

copies are thrown away. Unfortunately, another wide-spread abuse is the copying of materials for personal use. Such behavior is clearly an ethical violation.

To curb copying abuses, many organizations use copy control devices. For example, the user may enter an account number on a keypad to gain access to the copier or a card may be used to gain access to the computer. With such systems, each department or division can check copy costs against specific accounts. If abuses seem to be occurring, appropriate fact gathering can be done by department. If there is an abuse, appropriate action can be taken.

▷ Ethical and Etiquette Considerations

Each employee in a company should be ethical in the use of copying machines. Each employee should also be aware of the legal restrictions on the copying of certain documents. Behaving ethically when copying means that you do not engage in the following activities:

1. You do not copy documents for your own personal use.

2. You do not copy cartoons and jokes for distribution to coworkers.

3. You do not make copies of documents that you need for an outside professional group, unless you have approval from your organization to do so.

4. You do not copy materials restricted by the Copyright Law, such as birth certificates, passports, driver's licenses, and so on. If you have questions about what is legal to copy, check with your organization's attorney or check the Copyright Law.

5. You are prudent in making the appropriate number of copies needed.

In addition to ethical considerations, it is also important to observe basic courtesies when copying materials. Figure 11-3 lists several etiquette items for your consideration.

> SHREDDERS

For those times when a machine malfunctions and copies must be destroyed, businesses often place a

| Figure 11-3 | ETIQUETTE CONSIDERATIONS WHEN COPYING MATERIALS |

When sharing a copier with several people, be considerate of their time. Observe the basic courtesies listed here.

▶ If you are involved in an extensive copying job, let your colleagues interrupt when they have only a few pages to copy.

▶ If the machine malfunctions while you are copying, try to fix the problem. If you cannot do so, call the key operator in your company or call a service repairperson. Do not walk away, leaving the problem for the next person to handle.

▶ When toner runs out, refill it.

▶ When paper runs out, add more.

▶ When paper jams, remove it.

▶ If you are using additional supplies such as paper clips, scissors, and so on, return them to their location before leaving the copier.

▶ If you have run copies that are not usable, destroy them. Put them in a shredder and/or a recycle bin. Do not leave a messy work area for the next person to clean up.

▶ Return the copier to its standard settings.

shredder in proximity to the copier. A shredder cuts paper into strips or confetti-like material. Today shredded paper is recycled by many businesses as packing material. Since mailrooms process a large amount of paper and often pack materials for shipping, they use shredders also.

Shredders are being used more extensively today because of identity theft. Statistics from the General Accounting Office Report to Congressional Requesters found that the prevalence and cost of identity theft is increasing. One study estimates that the cost of identity theft to financial institutions will be $3.6 billion by the end of 2006.[19]

> RECYCLING

Our technological age is spawning the use of more paper rather than less. This increase in the use of paper can have serious repercussions for our environment. We are losing valuable forests and land (in

---

[19]"Fact Sheet: Identity Theft," <http://www.privcom.gc.ca/fs-fi102_05-d_10_e.asp> (accessed June 10, 2005).

establishing landfills). Recycling can save millions of tons of paper each year. Other benefits of recycling include these:

▶ Saving money—Recycling services can be cheaper than trash disposal services.
▶ Divert material from disposal—Keeping paper out of the waste stream saves landfill space and reduces pollution through avoided incineration.
▶ Conserving natural resources—By using recycled paper, fewer trees have to be cut down.
▶ Saving energy—Less energy is used in recycling products than in processing virgin materials.
▶ Reducing greenhouse gas emissions—By reducing the amount of energy used by industry,

recycling reduces greenhouse gas emissions that may lead to global warming.[20]

Additionally, organizations can reduce the paper used by asking employees to use both sides of the page (duplex documents), convert scratch paper into memo pads and telephone answering slips, print only the number of copies needed, increase the use of e-mail, shred used paper and use it to package materials instead of using plastic pellets, and use recycled paper. One ton of paper using recycled fiber saves the following: 17 trees, 3.3 cubic yards of landfill space, 360 gallons of water, 100 gallons of gasoline, 60 pounds of air pollutants, and 10,401 kilowatts of electricity.[21]

SUMMARY

Reinforce your learning in this chapter by studying this summary.

▶ Mail today is delivered in a variety of forms, including USPS, e-mail, instant messaging, fax, and private companies such as FedEx and UPS.

▶ USPS mail is classified as Express Mail, Priority Mail, First-Class Mail, and Standard Mail.

▶ USPS mail services include Certificate of Mailing, Registered Mail, Return Receipt, Signature Confirmation, Collect on Delivery, Certified Mail, Insured Mail, and international mail.

▶ When handling outgoing mail, the following steps are important: Prepare interoffice mail, key envelopes carefully, include the appropriate enclosures, use the correct ZIP code, key envelopes carefully, apply electronic postage if appropriate, and keep mailing lists current.

▶ When handling incoming mail, sort the mail by categories, keep selected envelopes (ones with incorrect addresses, etc.), date and time stamp, read and annotate, organize and present, and route if necessary.

▶ Establish procedures to handle mail during the executive's absence.

▶ File e-mail.

▶ Office copiers are classified by the number of copies they produce. Low-volume copiers produce 18 to 30 cpm and 5,000 to 10,00 ppm; mid-volume copiers produce 25 to 60 cpm and 80,000 ppm; high-volume copiers produce 50 to 140 cpm and 500,000 ppm.

▶ Copy-duplicators are high-performance machines generally found in specialized copy/duplication centers or in print shops.

▶ Copier features, to name a few, include reduction and enlargement, automatic document feeding, duplexing, and editing.

▶ When copying, these ethical and etiquette considerations are important: do not copy documents for your own personal use; do not copy cartoons and jokes; do not make copies of documents you need for outside professional groups unless you have approval from your organization; do not copy materials restricted by copyright law.

---

[20]"Information on Recycling Paper," <http://www.wastecap.org/wastecap/commodities/paper/paper.htm> (accessed June 10, 2005).
[21]Ibid.

- Shredders can save paper by using the shredded paper as packaging materials; shredders also help curb identity theft, which is on the increase in our nation.

- Using recycled paper can help an organization and our environment by saving money for the organization, saving landfill space and reducing pollution, conserving natural resources, saving energy, and reducing greenhouse gas emissions.

GLOSSARY

Analog—Image is translated as a fluctuating electronic signal.

Annotate—To make notations about previous action taken or facts that will assist the reader.

Automatic document feeder (ADF)—Allows you to copy multipage documents without having to lift and lower the platen cover for every sheet.

Certificate of Mailing—Provides evidence that an item has been mailed.

Certified Mail—For materials that have no monetary value but for which you need a record of delivery.

Collect on Delivery (COD)—Allows the mailer to collect the price of goods and/or postage on the item ordered by the addressee when delivered.

Copy-duplicators—High-performance machines generally found in specialized copy/duplication centers or print shops.

Cpm—Copies per minute.

Digital—Transfers data as a series of bits rather than as a signal.

Duplexing—Copying on both sides of a sheet of paper.

Enclosure or attachment notation—Serves as a flag to the recipient that an item is enclosed or attached.

Express Mail—USPS service that offers next-day delivery by 3 p.m. to many destinations.

First-Class Mail—Includes letters, greeting cards, large envelopes, and pages that weigh 13 ounces or less.

Global Express Guaranteed (GXG)—Service that takes from one to two days for most major international markets and three days for other international destinations.

Global Express Mail (EMS)—A high-speed service for mailing time-sensitive items to international locations.

Global Priority Mail (GPM)—Accelerated airmail service that provides a reliable and economical way of sending correspondence, printer matter, and merchandise that weighs four pounds and under to over 51 countries and territories worldwide.

High-volume copier—produces approximately 50 to 140 cpm and 500,000 ppm.

Information age—Began in the last quarter of the twentieth century when information became easily accessible through computers and computer networks.

Information junkies—People who seem to revel in having a tremendous amount of information on a variety of topics.

Insured Mail—A service to individuals who pay a special fee to obtain reimbursement for lost or damaged mail.

Low-volume copier—Copier that produces 18 to 30 copies per minute and 5,000 to 10,000 pages per month.

Marker editing—Lets you change the color of specific sections of a document to highlight these areas.

Masking—Allows you to block out areas of sensitive or confidential information.

Mid-volume copier—produces approximately 25 to 60 cpm and 80,000 ppm.

OCR—Optical character reader.

Outsourcing—Mail handled by an outside firm.

Package Services—Merchandise, catalogs, other printed material.

Paperless office—Little paper, with most documents stored electronically.

Ppm—Pages per month.

Priority Mail—All First-Class Mail exceeding 13 ounces is designated Priority Mail. This mail must be marked Priority Mail prominently to ensure proper handling.

Registered Mail—Available for First-Class or Priority Mail; provides maximum protection and security for valuable items.

Return Receipt—Service that provides the mailer with evidence of delivery.

Shredder—Cuts paper into strips or confetti-like material.

Signature Confirmation—Provides signature proof of delivery as well as the date and time of delivery or attempted delivery.

Standard Mail—Mail in which sender does some of the preparing, sorting, and entering of the mail for a lower postal cost.

USPS—United States Postal Service.

CHECKPOINT

Check your understanding of these terms by completing DCD11-a on the Data CD.

DISCUSSION ITEMS

These discussion items provide an opportunity to test your understanding of the chapter through written responses and/or discussion with your classmates and your instructor.

1. Define the major categories of USPS mail.

2. Define the types of special mail services offered by USPS.

3. Explain how the administrative professional should handle outgoing and incoming mail.

4. Explain the differences in the capabilities of low-volume, mid-volume, high-volume and copier duplicators.

5. Explain why it is important to recycle.

CRITICAL THINKING CASE

Your employer, Jana Portosky, was out of town for two weeks recently. During the time she was out, you became sick and had to take three days off. You called in and talked with Roger Garrett, one of the other administrative assistants in the office; he agreed to handle the mail and other items that came up. You came back two days before Ms. Portosky returned. You did not have a chance to go over the mail that was received in your absence; however, Roger did leave you written information concerning the mail. Ms. Portosky did not understand several of his notes; she asked you to explain. You could not since you had not talked with him. She was upset with you and proceeded to tell you that you should have the information she needed; she asked that you talk with him and get it immediately. You did so, but you felt terrible about your mistake. You know that she feels you did not perform your job well. Explain what you can do now.

A

You were to list three services from the USPS that you were not aware of previously by going to the USPS website. What services did you list?

_____

_____

_____

B

You were to describe several types of USPS mail classifications and types of international mail. Look back over your descriptions on Self-Check B, p. 276; to check your answers, review the USPS and international mail descriptions in the chapter.

C

You were to check the websites of two private mail services. What mail services did you check?

_____

_____

D

You were to list eight steps to follow when handling incoming mail. Check your responses by the following steps:

Do a preliminary sort and then sort each person's mail.

Open the mail, following the procedures given in the text or by the procedures established in your office.

Keep selected envelopes that may be needed to verify addresses, or other problems with the incoming mail, such as enclosures not in the envelope or the postmark needed to establish the date of mailing.

Date and time stamp the mail.

Read and annotate for the executives if that procedure is approved by your supervisor.

Organize and present the mail to your executive as he or she directs.

E

List and explain three types of copiers.

Review the specifications for low-volume copiers, mid-volume copiers, and high-volume copiers. Check your understanding about the technical specifications using the information presented in the section under Copier Classifications in the text.

WORKPLACE PROJECTS

PROJECT 11-1 WRITE A MEMORANDUM

Identify USPS mail services and mail classifications; identify private mail services (Objective 1)

Using your textbook information and/or USPS website at www.usps.com, determine what class of mail or mail service you would use to send the following items. Write a memorandum to your instructor with your responses; use the memorandum form on DCD11-01a.

1. A letter that must be delivered to the addressee before noon tomorrow

2. Valuables that are worth $30,000

3. A letter that must be received in Thailand in two days

4. A package that weighs ten pounds and is worth $500

5. A letter for which you need evidence of delivery and that must reach its destination the next day

Using a private mail website (FedEx, UPS, or DHL), describe the services provided by the company. Prepare a memorandum to your instructor explaining these services. Use DCD11-01b for the second memorandum.

PROJECT 11-2 PREPARE LETTERS AND ENVELOPES

Explain how to process both incoming and outgoing mail (Objective 2)

DCD11-02a contains a mailing list of 20 names and a letter that is to be sent to the names on the list. Add the eight names that are given below to the mailing list; place the names in alphabetical order. Make these changes to the letter: (1) The luncheon is now scheduled for the second Tuesday of April at noon. (2) The session will be held in the Board Room of JWay Nu-Systems Tech. If you notice any other necessary changes in the letter, make those changes.

Prepare the letters for the 20 names on the mailing list, plus the additional eight names below. Use JWay Nu-Systems Tech letterhead on DCD11-02b. Address envelopes for each of the letters. Sign the letter for Jana Portosky, with your initials under her signature. Fold and place the letters in the envelopes. Submit the package to your instructor.

Names and Addresses

Mr. Maxwell Neill
Neill Corporation
3001 Angle Drive
Dallas, TX 75398-0034

Ms. Sandra Gonzales
Plover Corporation
4045 Meridian Drive
Dallas, TX 75390-0788

Mr. David F. Williams
Williams Financial Services
1501 Rippet Drive
Dallas, TX 75379-8902

Ms. LaTanya Neticent
Myers Incorporated
1144 Cockrell Avenue
Dallas, TX 75371-0344

Mr. Tailor Grace
One Main Place
301 W. Green Oaks Blvd.
Dallas, TX 75398-0021

Ms. Ricco Ramando
Reynolds Corporation
5445 Lake Powell Drive
Dallas, TX 75374-3892

Mr. Edward Caneel
Caneel, Inc.
5400 East Loop 620
Dallas, TX 75389-0011

Mr. T. D. Disheroon
Disheroon Corporation
7452 Precinct Line Road
Dallas, TX 76388-0055

PROJECT 11-3 WRITE A MEMORANDUM

Explain how to process both incoming and outgoing mail (Objective 2)

You have received the following correspondence in today's mail. Ms. Portosky is out of town; she has asked that you handle all mail. Explain how this mail should be processed. Using the memorandum form on DCD11-03, write a memorandum to your instructor telling her or him how you would process this mail.

1. An interoffice memorandum from Wayne Wixom to Jana Portosky.

2. An e-mail marked urgent from Wayne Wixom to Jana Portosky.

3. An e-mail from Wayne Wixom requesting a meeting with Ms. Portosky on Tuesday of next week. You know that she will be out of town for two days of this week (Monday and Tuesday); she will be back on Wednesday.

4. A letter from a contact in Australia saying that he is coming to the United States in May of this year and would like to meet with Ms. Portosky.

5. A letter to Ms. Portosky from Australia that came as EMS mail.

PROJECT 11-4 WRITE A REPORT

Describe copier types and features (Objective 3)

In groups of three or four, visit one office supply company that carries copiers. Check out the features on one high-volume and one low-volume copier. Write a short report to your instructor giving the features of the copier and the name of the office supply you visited.

PROJECT 11-5 WRITE A REPORT

Explain the benefits of recycling to organizations and our environment (Objective 4)

Research the benefits of recycling for organizations and the environment; use the Web for your research. Write a short report on your findings; cite the references that you used.

Submit the report to your instructor.

PROJECT 11-6 ADD TO YOUR PROFESSIONAL GROWTH PLAN

Explain the importance of ethics and etiquette when making copies (Objective 5)

Add to your Professional Growth Plan that you began in Chapter 1 by writing a paragraph on how you will observe appropriate ethics and etiquette when making copies.

Save your plan on your Professional Growth Plan disk as PGP11-6.

COMMUNICATION POWER

Use DCD11-b to assist you in improving your grammar skills.

ASSESSMENT OF CHAPTER OBJECTIVES

Now that you have completed the chapter and the projects, take a few minutes to review the chapter learning objectives. For your convenience, the objectives are repeated here. Did you accomplish these objectives? If you were unable to accomplish the objectives, give your reasons for not doing so; be specific and concise. Your instructor may prefer that your answers be submitted to her or him. If so, DCD11-c contains the Assessment of Chapter Objectives. Complete the Assessment of Chapter Objectives; submit your results to your instructor.

1. Identify USPS mail services and mail classifications; identify private mail services. Yes ☐   No ☐

_____

_____

_____

2. Explain how to process both incoming and outgoing mail.   Yes ☐   No ☐

_____

_____

_____

3. Describe copier types and features.   Yes ☐   No ☐
_____

_____

_____

4. Explain the benefits of recycling to organizations and our environment.   Yes ☐   No ☐
_____

_____

_____

5. Explain the importance of ethics and etiquette when making copies.   Yes ☐   No ☐
_____

_____

_____

CHAPTER 12

TRAVEL ARRANGEMENTS

Learning Objectives

1. Explain the global nature of corporate America.
2. Make domestic travel arrangements.
3. Make international travel arrangements.
4. Explain organizational travel procedures and the administrative professional's responsibilities before and after a trip.
5. Exhibit respect for other cultures.
6. Maintain a high achievement attitude.

Image 100

> CORPORATE AMERICA— A GLOBAL ENTERPRISE

United States companies/corporations and organizations often have locations in a number of different cities within the United States. Additionally, the global nature of our world results in companies having locations multinationally. An excellent example of a global corporation is General Motors, with 317,000 employees around the world. General Motors has manufacturing operations in 32 countries, with its global partners including Fiat Auto SpA of Italy and Fuji Heavy Industries Ltd. and Suzuki Motor Corporation of Japan, to name a few. GM also has technology collaborations with companies in South Korea, Germany, China, and numerous others.[1] This example is merely one of many companies and organizations in the United States that not only have international but also multinational businesses. The United States, along with other countries, considers land, labor, and technical expertise not only in the United States but also in other parts of the world when deciding where to produce a product.

Even though the majority of businesses in the United States are not international or multinational, numerous businesses have subsidiaries in other cities or states, which require their executives to travel frequently within the United States. Also, executives are often members of professional organizations that conduct statewide or nationwide conventions at least once each year. As an administrative professional, you may be a member of an organization such as the International Association for Administrative Professionals (IAAP). IAAP holds a national meeting yearly within the United States; and because the organization is also international, you may have the opportunity to travel abroad.

---

[1]"Company: General Motors Corp. (NYSE: GM)," <http://www.gm.com/company/corp_info/profiles/> (accessed June 17, 2005).

Many United States corporations are international.

Because of this national, international, and multinational presence of U.S. companies and organizations, executives often make trips for business purposes. As an administrative professional, you will probably be responsible for handling travel arrangements for your employer—arrangements within the United States or outside the United States. You also may have the opportunity to work in an international location for your company.

If you are to handle travel arrangements effectively, you must become familiar with the types of services available. This chapter will help you understand your options when making travel arrangements and also understand your responsibilities while your employer is out of the office.

> DOMESTIC TRAVEL

Because time is an extremely important commodity for business executives, almost all their travel is done by air. Executives generally do not have the time required to travel by car or rail. Thus, the emphasis in this chapter is on air travel, although car and rail travel are mentioned briefly.

> Air Travel

During a flight, busy executives are able to use their time productively by reading their mail, newspapers, and professional periodicals. They also may use cell phones and computers before takeoff and after landing, but, as of this writing, not during the flight. A flight attendant announces when technological equipment may and may not be used. Federal Communications Commission (**FCC**) and Federal Aviation Administration (**FAA**) rules and regulations specify that no technology that emits a signal is acceptable during a flight.

Flight Classifications

There are three classes of flight—first class, business class, and economy/coach class. Some airlines offer all three classes. Airlines, such as Southwest Airlines, JetBlue Airways, and American Eagle (all three are considered **regional jets**—flying to specific parts of the country) offer only one class of flight. Additionally, Southwest does not have reserved seating; it is on a first come, first serve basis. However, such is not true for the majority of airlines; generally seat numbers are assigned when you purchase your ticket.

At the opposite end of the spectrum from the regional jet is the luxury jet, which transports small groups of people (approximately 4 to 20) in country club style to almost all parts of the world. These luxury jets are very expensive and provide many amenities, including several attendants to handle the needs of the traveler, spacious seating, and lavish food and beverages. Obviously, only a small portion of the population is able to use luxury jet transportation.

First-Class Accommodations. **First-class accommodations** are the most expensive of the three classes and the most luxurious. The seats are wider and farther apart, and services are greater. Alcoholic beverages are offered without additional cost and are generally served in glass containers. Since 9/11, however, airlines have experienced considerable financial difficulties and services have been cut, even in first class. Meals are not always available in first-class; however, they are available on longer flights. Cloth napkins, tablecloths, silverware, and china dinnerware are used. Headsets for listening to music are provided at no additional cost. The seats are generally wider and more legroom is provided. There are also more flight attendants per customer than in coach/economy or business, which means greater attention is given to each flyer. First-class customers are allowed to board and exit first. Attendants take passengers' coats and hang them up; they also store passengers' parcels in overhead bins.

Business-Class Accommodations. **Business-class accommodations** are a level between first class and economy/coach class. Business class is not available on all aircraft or on all flights. Business-class passengers typically board the plane before economy class passengers and enjoy larger seats. These seats may be fully reclinable to the sleeping positions; however,

there may be a surcharge for such a seat. Seats may have footrests. Personal video, laptop power port, and satellite phones may be available. Coffee and juices are served. Meals are available on international flights. Business-class fares are more often available on cross-country and international flights.

Economy/Coach-Class Accommodations. **Economy/coach-class accommodations** (economy is the term that is used more often at the present time; coach is still used by some airlines) are in the main cabin area and are typically the lowest-priced seats on the airplane. Seats are closer together than in first class and generally than in business class. Fewer flight attendants are available to serve the needs of the customers.

After 9/11, the airlines experienced a loss of dollars because of the fear of flying by individuals, and because of businesses cutting back on their national and international flights. Numerous cost-cutting measures were taken by airlines. Generally, the only food served on flights within the United States is snack food, such as a package of crackers or nuts. Soft drinks, juice, coffee, tea, and water are also provided. Some airlines have begun serving sandwiches or salads and some breakfast foods at a cost to the passenger, with costs being approximately $3 to $5, depending on the food.

Security Precautions

Since 9/11 America's airports have operated under unprecedented levels of security. Being knowledgeable about security measures can help you know how long you need to be at the airport before your plane leaves, understand what not to pack, and help you feel more confident and secure as you travel. Listed here are several security precautions that are in place at airports across the United States.

1. Air marshals are on a number of flights.

2. Only ticketed passengers are allowed beyond the screening checkpoint.

3. All laptops and video cameras must be removed from their cases. They are subjected to both x-ray and physical inspection.

4. Passengers are required to have a government-issued ID when checking in for a flight.

5. Passengers are required to remove their shoes before going through the electronic screening device.

6. Shoes are subjected to x-ray inspection, as are briefcases, billfolds, purses, metal belts, luggage, and other items that passengers are taking on the flight.

7. If you bring a prohibited item such as weapons, explosives, and/or incendiaries, you may be criminally or civilly prosecuted and/or at least asked to rid yourself of the item. A screening agent or a Law Enforcement Officer will make this determination depending on what the items are and the circumstances. Bringing a prohibited item to a security checkpoint, even accidentally, is illegal.[2]

Security precautions have been increased since 9/11.

© Photodisc

In an effort to continually make our airports safer, agencies such as the Transportation Security Administration conduct tests. For example, security testing has been conducted at selected airports across the nation. Because of the concern for safer air travel, passengers at some airports have undergone screening by an explosives detection document scanner.[3] It is anticipated that this type of security testing will continue indefinitely.

With the increased number of security measures being implemented at airports, it is important to arrive approximately an hour before your flight leaves—longer if it is an international flight. It is also important for you as an individual to take certain precautions. For example, you should:

▶ Watch your bags and personal belongings at all times.

---

[2]"Travelers & Consumers Prohibited Items," <http://www.tsa.gov/public/display?theme+177> (accessed June 15, 2005).

[3]Industry Partners Security Technology Deployment, "TSA and Technology: Working Better Together for You," <http://www.tsa.gov/public/display?theme=70> (accessed June 17, 2005).

- Not accept packages from strangers.
- Report unattended bags or packages to airport security.
- Check to be certain that you have all your belongings before leaving the security area—wallet, keys, jewelry, cell phone, computer, and so on.

Company-Owned Planes

Large corporations may have their own plane or fleet of planes if the amount of travel within the company makes it advantageous to do so. Pilots employed by the organization fly the planes, which are housed adjacent to local airports.

Airline Clubs

For the frequent business traveler, membership in an airline club may be a worthwhile investment. Major airlines provide these clubs in large airports, and membership is available through the individual airline. Membership fees vary. A variety of services are available in the clubs, including the following:

- Computer equipment, fax, and copy machines
- Conference rooms and lounge space
- Reading material
- Complementary soft drinks, juice, and coffee
- Alcoholic beverages
- Pastries and snacks
- Assistance with airline reservations

Parking Services

Large airports generally provide free shuttle service from airport parking locations; however, you are charged for parking your car. The fee is based on the location of your car, with parking lots closer to the airport being more expensive, and the time your car is in the lot.

Because parking at an airport for an extended period can become expensive, private shuttle services in large cities occupy a profitable business niche. Shuttle buses take you to and from the airport. These buses run frequently, with generally no more than a ten-minute wait between runs.

Ticketing

The **e-ticket** is the common form of ticketing, usually online. The most common method of delivering e-tickets to customers is by e-mail or fax. E-tickets may be presented at airport ticket counters to obtain the boarding passes. Also, most large airports now have self-service kiosks set up in proximity to the airline ticket counters. You insert your flight information from your e-ticket and receive a boarding pass from the machine. This option eliminates standing in lines at the airline ticket counter.

Changes or Cancellations

Occasionally it is necessary to change or cancel flight reservations. Generally, you are charged a penalty for changing to another flight. The policy for changes or cancellations is usually made clear online. Some airlines will let you bank the ticket for future flights, with a small penalty charged. When a change is made because of airplane mechanical difficulty, or some other issue that causes the airline to change or cancel the flight, you are not charged. Since you are usually inconvenienced by such a change, the airlines attempt to make the situation as painless as possible. If the change results in your having to stay overnight, the airlines will usually pay for your hotel and give you vouchers for food.

▷ Ground Transportation

Once executives arrive at their destination, they may need some type of ground transportation to their hotel. That transportation may be a taxi or shuttle bus. When making arrangements, you should check taxi costs and the availability of shuttle services. Some hotels provide free shuttle service to and from the airport. Shuttle services are also available from private vendors, which may be less expensive than taxi service.

If executives must attend meetings at several locations during their stay, renting a car may be the most economical and convenient method of ground transportation. Car rental agencies are available at most airports. Cars may also be rented through airlines or travel agents or on the Internet. When renting a car, specify the make and model preferred, along with the date and time the car will be picked up and also the date and time the car will be returned. Most car rental agencies have age restrictions. Check with the specific rental agency to determine the age requirements. Some may require the renter to be at least 21; others may require the renter to be at least 25 years old, for example.

Domestic Car Travel

If an executive is traveling only a few hundred miles, she or he may prefer to travel by car. Most top-level executives use cars furnished by the company; gasoline expenses are paid by the company. Other executives are reimbursed on a per-mile basis for any

Take a few minutes now to check your understanding of what you have learned to this point concerning air travel within the United States. Answer the following questions:

1. List and describe the classes of air travel in the United States.
_____
_____

2. List and describe several security measures that are in effect at airports since 9/11.
_____
_____

job-related travel. Your responsibilities for a trip by car may include determining the best route to follow, making hotel reservations, and identifying restaurants along the way. The American Automobile Association (**AAA**) provides map services, along with hotel and restaurant information. However, it is necessary to be a member of AAA to get these services. Mapquest.com gives directions between two driving points. You may also make car rental and hotel reservations on the Mapquest.com site.

> Domestic Rail Travel

Although rail travel is a rarity for an executive to use, there may be times when rail travel is necessary. Amtrak is available on the Web at www.amtrak.com. Rail travel is available to many parts of the United States. First-class and sleeping accommodations are available, as well as coach accommodations for more economical travel.

> INTERNATIONAL TRAVEL

Many organizations now have international interests, with senior executives making trips to the organization's sites abroad. As an administrative professional, you need to know how to make arrangements for an international trip. You also need to become knowledgeable concerning the cultural differences of the countries your employer is visiting.

> Cultural Differences

A basic understanding of the culture of the people in the country where your employer is traveling will help you make appropriate travel arrangements.

Additionally, such knowledge can be advantageous as you work in a global world and encounter people from extremely different and diverse backgrounds. Information about countries can be obtained from a variety of sources, some of which are listed here.

1. Consulates of the country to be visited. Consulate websites are available. Information concerning the Consul General of the country, basic information about the country, and how to contact the Consul General is given on these sites.

2. Travel books. These books are available in libraries and bookstores, and generally contain information about local customs and business practices.

3. Seminars and short courses. Local colleges and universities often provide short courses or one-day seminars on the culture of various countries, along with tips on doing business with particular countries.

4. The Internet. Numerous articles are available on cultural differences internationally.

Several general rules for international travel are given in Figure 12-1.

The administration of JWay Nu-Systems Tech is proceeding with its plans to expand to Australia next year and to Taiwan within the next two years. Here is some general information concerning the culture of both countries.

Australia
English is the official language of Australia; grammar and spelling are a mix of British and American patterns. Christianity is the dominant religion, with the

GENERAL RULES FOR INTERNATIONAL TRAVEL

1. Learn the appropriate greeting for the country you will be visiting.

2. Learn how to say *please* and *thank you* in the language of the country.

3. Have business cards printed with your name and your company name in both English and the language of the country you are visiting.

4. Do not criticize the people or customs of the country you are visiting. Show appreciation for the music, art, and culture of the country.

5. Remember that business generally is more formal in other countries than it is in the United States.

6. Dress appropriately; this generally means business suits for men and conservative dresses or suits for women. Although dress in the United States has become more casual than in the past, you cannot assume that is true for international organizations. Casual business dress generally does not imply a professional image. It may be seen as sloppy dress.

7. Eat the food that is offered you; do not ask what you are being served; show appreciation to your host.

8. Be courteous and respectful at all times.

▶ Manual labor enjoys relatively high prestige.
▶ High standards of cleanliness exist.
▶ Direct communication is preferred and expected.[5]

Spotlight on CULTURAL DIFFERENCES

Cultural differences are to be accepted and understood—not evaluated.

Taiwan

Taiwan's population is primarily Taiwanese and mainland Chinese. The culture is generally closed to outside information but willing to consider data that are important to Taiwan's interests. Confucianism has a great influence on the society; there is a rigid ethical and moral system that governs relationships. Decisions are made by consensus, with the oldest members having the most control. It is an individual's duty not to bring shame on a family or organization of which the person is a member. Businesses are competitive, with heavy emphasis on entry level skills and the importance of each individual getting along in a group. Although Taiwan is still a male-dominated society, there is a strong women's movement.[6]

By American standards, the Taiwanese can take a long time to reach a business decision. A handshake is customary; a slight bow shows respect, but it should never be overdone. It is acceptable to arrive shortly before or after the scheduled time for an appointment. Meals are elaborate, with toasts common. A small gift is appropriate when visiting a family in their home. Both hands should be used when handing a gift or other object to another person; thank-you notes are a must. Discussions of mainland China and local politics should be avoided.[7]

▷ Appointments

If you are involved in setting up appointments or meetings for the executive, remember time zone

population equally divided between Anglicans and Roman Catholics. However, Muslims, Buddhists, and Jews are also present. Australia has one of the world's highest rates of urbanization, with approximately 85 percent of the people living in the cities. Judeo-Christian ethics pervade all behavior; however, material progress is more important than humanistic progress.[4]

Australians and Americans enjoy a number of cultural similarities. Several of them are given here.

▶ Australians like to be given a firm handshake and be called by their names.
▶ Punctuality is extremely important.
▶ Executives at all levels will generally hear what employees have to say.

[4]Terri Morrison, et al., *How to Do Business in Sixty Countries: Kiss, Bow, or Shake Hands* (Massachusetts: Adams Media Corporation, 1994), pp. 8–10.
[5]Roger E. Axtell, editor, *Do's and Taboos Around the World* (New York: John Wiley & Sons, Inc., 1993), pp. 84–85.
[6]Morrison, et al., pp. 374–375.
[7]Ibid., pp. 96–97.

Self

1. Explain several cultural similarities between Australia and the United States.

_____
_____
_____

2. Explain several cultural differences between Taiwan and the United States.

_____
_____
_____

differences. **Jet lag** (the feeling of exhaustion following a flight through several time zones) can limit an executive's effectiveness. Since it takes the body approximately a day to adapt to the new environment for each time zone crossed, give the executive an extra day to recover from the trip before scheduling meetings.

If executives do not have the luxury of a full day before appointments, they can take advantage of certain techniques to help with jet lag. For example, if they are traveling west, they can postpone the time they usually go to bed by two or three hours for two days before the flight. If they are traveling east, they can retire a couple of hours earlier than usual. At the same time, they can also start shifting mealtimes to those of the destination city. Their body clock will not be fully adapted to the new time when they land, but they will have made a start in the right direction.

You should not schedule appointments the day before the executive leaves on a trip or the day the executive returns from a trip. The day before a trip is usually a busy one in preparation for the trip. When the executive returns from a trip she or he must again contend with time zone changes.

▷ Business Gifts

In some countries, business gifts are expected; in others business gifts are not particularly welcomed. If a business gift is given, it should be a small one, a nice pen or some memento representative of the United States. However, executives must be aware of customs and taboos when giving gifts to avoid offending someone without knowing it. Figure 12-2 lists some gift giving information in Australia and Taiwan.

▷ Business Practices

Business practices can differ greatly from country to country. Before taking a business trip abroad, the business practices of that country need to be carefully studied. Several of the business practices of Australia and Taiwan are given in Figure 12-3.

▷ Flight Classifications

International flight classifications are the same as domestic air travel. Classes of flight are first class

Figure 12-2	**BUSINESS GIFT GIVING IN AUSTRALIA AND TAIWAN**

Australia

Australians do not generally give gifts in a business context. However, if you are invited to a home for dinner, you may give a small gift of flowers, wine, or chocolates. Folk crafts from home are also welcomed.[8]

Taiwan

Gift giving is practiced in business settings. Acceptable gifts include items with small company logos on them. Be certain the products were not manufactured in Taiwan. Other popular gifts to business people include imported liquor, gold pens, and magazine subscriptions.[9]

---

[8]Morrison, et al., pp. 10–11.
[9]Ibid., p. 380.

Figure 12-3 BUSINESS PRACTICES IN AUSTRALIA AND TAIWAN

Australia

- Before beginning a business meeting, spend some time in small talk.
- Australians generally do not like high-pressure sales. One is expected to present the case in a straightforward manner, both the good and the bad.
- Business presentations should not be filled with hype.
- Be as brief as possible when presenting the business plan.
- Decision-making occurs in consultation with top management. It generally takes more time to make a decision in Australia than it does in the United States.[10]

Taiwan

- The basis of a business relationship in Taiwan is respect and trust.

- Business tends to take place at a slower pace than in North America or Europe. North Americans must be patient.
- The negotiating team should include persons with seniority and a thorough knowledge of the company. Taiwanese believe that when a senior executive is sent, the corporation must be serious about doing business with them.
- It is still rare to have women participate in business in Taiwan. Foreign women will have the additional challenge of overcoming this initial hesitancy. When women are to be included in teams, be certain to discuss this intent with the Chinese contact before the meeting is to take place. Allow the contact some time to adjust to the idea.
- Chinese women will rarely shake hands. Western men should not try to shake hands with Chinese women. Western women will have to initiate a handshake with Chinese men.
- When negotiating, it is important to be sincere and honest. Humility is a virtue.[11]

and economy/coach, with business class available on many international flights. Weight and size restrictions for luggage may vary slightly from one airline to another. When traveling abroad, executives must arrive at the airport earlier than normal; most airlines suggest arriving two hours before the flight.

≥ Passports

A **passport** is an official government document that certifies the identity and citizenship of an individual and grants the person permission to travel abroad. A passport is required in most countries outside the United States. Check with a local travel agent to determine if the country being visited requires a passport. For example, Canada and Mexico do not require passports. However, even if a country does not require a passport, having one is a good idea because it shows proof of citizenship.

Passport application forms can be obtained from the Web at http://travel.state.gov/passport. Only the U.S. Department of State has the authority to grant, issue, or verify United States passports. To obtain a passport for the first time, you must go in person to

a passport acceptance facility (federal, state and probate courts, post offices, some public libraries, and a number of county and municipal offices) located throughout the United States. You must take with you two photographs of yourself, proof of U.S. citizenship, and photo identification, such as a driver's license. You can renew a passport by mail, with the following stipulations:

- If the passport has not been altered or damaged
- If you received the passport within the past 15 years
- If you were over age 16 when it was issued
- If you still have the same name
- If you can legally document your name change

A passport is valid for ten years from the date of issue. As soon as the passport is received, it should be signed, rendering it valid. Also, the information in the front pages should be filled out, which includes the address of the bearer and names to be contacted in case of an emergency. Travelers should always carry passports with them while abroad; they should never be left in hotel rooms.

---

[10]Morrison, et al., p. 11.
[11]Ibid., pp. 376–377.

▷ Visas

A **visa** is a document granted by a government abroad that permits a traveler to enter and travel within a particular country. A visa usually appears as a stamped notation on a passport indicating that the bearer may enter the country for a certain time.

▷ Currency

Before leaving the United States, the executive can exchange money from certain banks and currency exchange offices for the currency of the country being visited. The rate of exchange for various countries is published in the newspaper. If the executive prefers, he or she can exchange a small amount of money in the United States and exchange more money upon arrival at the country of destination. Any currency left over at the end of a trip can be exchanged for U.S. currency. It is always a good idea to be aware of the exchange rates before traveling to another country and to pay attention to the exchange rates once in the country. Exchange rates are not always the same; for example, the exchange rate at a bank may be more favorable than the exchange rate at an airport.

Since January 2002, the **Euro** has been physically in circulation; these banknotes have replaced the old European currencies, such as the French Franc and the German Mark. The Euro is the currency of twelve European member states at the time of the writing of this textbook, with these being

The Euro (common currency of 12 European countries) has been in circulation since January 2002.

© Digital Vision

Belgium, Germany, Greece, Spain, France, Ireland, Italy, Luxembourg, the Netherlands, Austria, Portugal, and Finland.[12] However, the status of the Euro in the future is presently in question, with some countries considering withdrawing because of the inadequacy of a single currency in the face of the economic slowdown, the loss of competitiveness, and the job crisis in certain European markets.[13]

▷ Health Precautions

Before leaving for a country abroad, the executive should check with a physician concerning any medications needed. The environmental factors may be different from those in the United States; and there is a possibility of developing an illness as a result of the food, water, or climate of the country. For example, a physician can prescribe medications for stomach-related illnesses or colds. Vaccinations may be required in certain countries.

If you are staying with a host family in a country where there are health precautions that must be taken or you personally have some health issues that do not allow you to eat certain foods, you should politely explain these issues to your host. For example, if you have an allergy to fruits such as mangos, tell your host of this allergy as soon as you arrive. If it is not safe to drink water from the faucet, bottled water is usually available. If your host does not provide bottled water, you can buy it at a local store. Most restaurants and markets serve and sell purified water, which is the same as what people in the United States are accustomed to drinking. Tap water in another country is not necessarily contaminated; however, it may contain different flora and fauna than in the United States, thus causing possible digestive problems. To be safe, it is important to use purified water at all times, even when brushing your teeth, washing your hands, or rinsing raw foods. For the same reasons, you may want to avoid using ice that is served in drinks.

▷ Hotel Reservations

Hotel reservations can be made through travel agents or airlines at no additional cost. Hotel reservations may also be made online. Most hotels have rooms that are equipped with computers, copiers, faxes, and so forth. However, cellular phones, PDAs, and/or

[12]"The Euro—Europe's single currency," <http://www.eubusiness.com/topics/Euro> (accessed June 18, 2005).

[13]"Euro facing meltdown as Italy considers backing out," <http://thescotsman.scotsman.com/index.cfm?id=611492005> (accessed June 17, 2005).

laptop computers are standard equipment for many traveling executives. Meeting rooms are also available in most hotels. If you are making hotel reservations directly for your employer, let the hotel reservations clerk know what equipment and/or meeting rooms are needed. If the executive is going to be arriving late, it is important to give that information to the hotel clerk. Rooms can be released at a certain hour if reservations have not been confirmed for late arrival.

▷ International Car Rental

Cars are readily available to rent. Travel agencies can arrange for car rentals before executives arrive in a country. An executive can also rent a car after arrival. In most countries, a U.S. driver's license is sufficient. You may obtain an International Driver's License from AAA. Travelers must have appropriate insurance. Travelers should also familiarize themselves with the driving regulations if they are going outside the United States. Driving conditions are sometimes quite different from those in the United States. For example, in England, Scotland, and Wales you must drive on the left-hand side of the road and pass on the right-hand side. Steering wheels are also mounted on the right-hand side of the car.

▷ International Rail Transportation

Many countries have excellent rail service, particularly in Europe. A traveler can go from one city in Europe to another in a relatively short period of time with a limited amount of inconvenience. Trains are generally clean, and the accommodations are comfortable. Underground rail is also available in a number of countries in Europe.

> ORGANIZATIONAL TRAVEL PROCEDURES

How travel arrangements are made depends on the business/organization where you work. Some companies use one travel agency to schedule all travel. This agency becomes knowledgeable about the needs of the organization and is able to provide what the executives need with limited assistance. Other organizations, particularly small ones, ask that individuals make their own travel arrangements.

Regardless of how travel arrangements are made, as an administrative professional you will have a role. Before an executive takes her or his first trip, talk with the person about travel preferences. If you are to

be an effective agent for your employer, you must have the information you need. Figure 12-4 gives pertinent information that is necessary for you to know if you are going to be effective. It is a good idea to set up a folder when the executive first tells you about an upcoming trip. You should place all notes and information relating to the trip in the folder. It is then available for instant referral when needed.

Figure 12-4 INFORMATION NEEDED FROM THE EXECUTIVE ON TRIP PREFERENCES

- ▶ Dates and times of travel

- ▶ Cities to be visited

- ▶ Hotel preferences—price range, number of nights, single or double room, size of bed (full, queen, king), smoking or nonsmoking room

- ▶ Car rental preferences—type of car, size, make and model, number of days of usage, pick-up and drop-off locations

- ▶ Reimbursement—reimbursement policies of the company (per diem for meals and other travel expenses)

- ▶ Arrangements for transportation to airport or train station

- ▶ Appointments to be made and where and when

- ▶ Materials—business cards, cell phone, PDA, computer

- ▶ Person in charge while the executive is away

- ▶ Correspondence and calls—how they will be handled in the executive's absence

- ▶ Executive's credit card number or company account number for charging tickets, hotel, and car rental

If an executive is traveling by air, you need to know:

1. The name of the preferred airline (if the executive has a preference) as well as his or her **frequent flyer** number (an incentive program that provides a variety of awards after the accumulation of a certain number of mileage points; awards may include upgrades from coach to first-class and free airline tickets).

2. Whether the flight is to be direct (if possible) or whether the executive is willing to change planes, which can often mean less expensive flights.

3. The class of flight—first-class, business, or economy/coach.

4. Seating preference—aisle or window.

5. Meal preference if international flight. As you have already learned, food is not served free of charge on many flights at the present time, except perhaps in first class. Some airlines are providing food, with a charge. Most airlines do provide cold or hot drinks and snacks free of charge.

If you are making arrangements for more than one top-level executive to travel to the same location at the same time, company policy may dictate that the executives fly on separate airlines. In case of a serious accident when both executives are on the same plane, both might be lost to the company.

▷ Arrangements by Travel Agencies

Travel agencies can make all travel arrangements for the executive. Travel agencies are particularly helpful when the executive is traveling internationally. They can schedule the flight, obtain tickets, make hotel reservations, and arrange car rental. They will also deliver the complete package to your organization. Part of their service includes providing an **itinerary** that gives flight numbers, arrival and departure times, hotel reservations, and car rental.

▷ Arrangements by the Administrative Professional

If you are making the travel arrangements, the Web becomes your friend. All major airlines have their own websites. In addition to flight reservations, you can make hotel and car reservations on these sites. There are also several websites, such as www.travelocity.com, www.orbitz.com, and www.priceline.com, that are independent from the airlines. These websites can give you prices for several airlines, along with hotel and car rental information; they also give you all price information. The Web becomes a one-stop entity for flights, hotels, and car rentals.

In addition to the duties already mentioned in assisting the executive with travel arrangements, such as determining passport/visa requirements, checking on currency needs, determining health issues in the country to be visited, making hotel reservations,

arranging car rental, and arranging rail transportation, you may be responsible for the following:

- ▶ Preparing a complete itinerary
- ▶ Obtaining travel funds
- ▶ Preparing and organizing materials for the trip
- ▶ Checking the executive's calendar
- ▶ Confirming appointments
- ▶ Assembling trip items
- ▶ Understanding how matters are to be handled in the executive's absence

Prepare an Itinerary

The itinerary is a must for you and your employer. If you are working with a travel agency, the agency will prepare an itinerary that includes flight numbers, departure and arrival times, car rentals, and hotels. However, an agency does not have the information on appointments and other special information. The executive needs to have an itinerary that reflects all activities on the trip.

You will want to prepare multiple copies of the itinerary:

1. One for the executive

2. One for the executive's family

3. One for the administrator who will be in charge while the executive is away

4. One for the files

Figure 12-5 shows a partial itinerary prepared by the administrative professional.

Obtain Travel Funds

Organizations differ in how they handle funds for trips. Most of the time airline tickets are charged directly to the organization. Hotel, meals, and car rental may be charged on a credit card provided by the organization. Another practice is for the individual to get a cash advance to cover all expenses of the trip. To do so, the individual fills out a travel form before leaving, indicating how much money she or he will need for lodging, meals, and so on. The company advances the money to the employee before the person leaves on the trip. Another practice is for the executive to pay the expenses; she or he is then reimbursed by the company upon returning from the trip. Company policies generally require employees to turn in a receipt for an expense above a certain amount.

Figure 12-5 **SAMPLE ITINERARY (PARTIAL)**

ITINERARY (Partial)
JANA PORTOSKY
November 6-12, 20XX
Sidney, Australia

MONDAY, NOVEMBER 6
DALLAS, TEXAS, TO SIDNEY, AUSTRALIA

8:25 p.m., November 6	Leave DFW International Airport on American Flight 57 (e-ticket in briefcase)
8:15 a.m., November 7	Arrive Sidney Airport, Sidney, Australia Hotel Reservations at Gold Mansion 300 Mark Street Confirmation 848992

If an executive is traveling abroad, he or she may take traveler's checks. Traveler's checks may be purchased from most local banks and travel agencies. However, because credit cards are readily acceptable in international locations, it may be easier for the executive to use a credit card. If using traveler's checks, know that they come with two receipts, which serve as records of the checks' serial numbers. One copy of the receipt should be kept in the files at the office, and the other copy should be given to the executive. If checks are lost, the individual is reimbursed by producing the receipt. Therefore, the receipts should not be kept with the checks.

Prepare and Organize Materials

Any number of items may be needed for a trip. If it is an international trip, items such as passports, medications, business cards, and small gifts are standard. Whether the trip is domestic or international, several items usually must be prepared, such as proposals, reports for meetings, and presentation materials. Here is a list of items that may be included in the executive's briefcase.

- E-ticket
- Itinerary
- Calendar
- Credit cards, traveler's checks
- Hotel confirmation
- Special materials, reports, or appointment schedule
- Presentation notes

- Cell phone, personal digital assistant, or laptop
- Reading materials
- Business cards
- Passport

Check the Calendar

Check your employer's electronic and desk calendars, along with your calendar, to see if any appointments have been scheduled for the period in which the executive will be gone. If so, find out if these appointments are to be canceled or if someone else in the company will handle them. Then, notify the people involved. Also check other files, such as tickler files or pending files, to see if there are matters that should be handled before the executive leaves.

Confirm Trip Appointments

E-mail or call people the executive plans to see during the trip to confirm appointments. It is wise to do so before preparing the itinerary. Obtain or verify addresses and directions from the hotel to the location of all meetings. Make a note of these addresses and directions on the itinerary.

Assemble Trip Items

The administrative professional is responsible for assembling all items the executive needs for a trip. Here is a representative list of items:

- Plane tickets
- Itinerary
- Travel money and credit cards
- Cell phone
- Business cards
- Hotel confirmation
- Information on organizations to be visited
- Copies of correspondence, presentations, reports, and so on
- Reading materials about the country and culture if visiting an international organization

Know How Matters Are to Be Handled

Find out who will be in charge during your employer's absence. Check to see if your employer is expecting any important papers that should be forwarded. Be certain you understand how to handle all incoming mail. For example, your employer may want you to refer all mail that must be answered immediately to another executive within the workplace. Or, your employer may ask that you answer the routine mail and refer the non-routine mail to a designated executive.

▷ Role of Administrative Professional During and After the Executive's Absence

You may be tempted to tell yourself that you have worked hard in getting the executive ready for the trip so you deserve a little time off. However, such is not the case. The pace may be more relaxed while the executive is away. Conversely, it may even be more hectic since you have added responsibilities of seeing that all important items are handled.

Handle Messages, Appointments, and Correspondence

Executives may e-mail or call the office on a daily basis while they are away on trips. If the executive prefers to call, determine the approximate time of day the call will be so you can have all messages and items reviewed and be ready to discuss them. Always keep urgent messages and correspondence in an established place on your desk so you can refer to them quickly.

While the executive is away, you may need to set up appointments for people who want to see her or him after the trip. Remember that the executive will probably already have a full day of work to handle on the first day back. Thus, it is not a good idea to schedule appointments for that day. Also, remember that if the trip has been an international one, the executive probably will have some jet lag. If an appointment is absolutely necessary on her or his first day back, schedule it in the afternoon rather than the morning. Not scheduling early morning appointments is also a good idea in case of delayed return flights.

It is important that correspondence be handled. You may be responsible for seeing that all mail is given to the person in charge; you also may be required to assist the person in answering the mail. Additionally, you may have the responsibility for answering routine correspondence. If so, keep a copy of the correspondence and response for your employer to review after he or she returns. You may find it helpful to keep a log of all items that need to be discussed with your employer.

Make Decisions

You have the responsibility of making wise decisions within the scope of your responsibility during the executive's absence. You should know what matters to refer to someone else in the company and what matters to refer directly to the executive through an e-mail, a fax, or a telephone call. Certainly you do not want to place an excessive number of calls to the executive while she or he is away, but there may be matters that the executive must be informed of immediately.

Post-trip Briefing

When the executive returns, you must brief her or him on what occurred in the office during the trip, providing all necessary information. You should also inform the executive of the appointments you set up and the telephone calls, e-mail, and other correspondence you received.

Additionally, the executive may need to write several follow-up letters as a result of the trip. Thank-you letters are often sent. Information on products or services may need to be sent to customers or prospective customers. You also may be given several receipts (meals, car rental or taxi, hotel, restaurant, and incidental expenses) that need to be included on the expense report.

The administrative professional is responsible for briefing the executive when she or he returns from a trip.

© Photodisc

Maintain Your High Achievement Focus

High achievers maintain a **positive attitude** (ability to maintain a pleasant outlook even when negative situations occur). They believe they can perform their job well, make a difference on the job, and solve problems; they are consistently striving and active. Conversely, people with a low achievement focus tend to be more of a follower and less concerned with high achievement.[14] When your employer is gone, you need to retain that high achievement focus and a positive attitude. The pace may be a little slower or it may even be more hectic, but the need to produce high quality work remains the same.

---

[14]Mark Mallinger and Ileana Rizescu, Winter 2001, "Personality Traits and Workplace Culture," <http://gbr.pepperdine.edu/011/culture.html> (accessed June 22, 2005).

SUMMARY

Reinforce your learning in this chapter by studying this summary.

▸ Many United States' companies/corporations and organizations often have locations in a number of different cities in the United States. Additionally, the global nature of our world results in companies having locations multinationally.

▸ Executives, because of the national, international and multinational presence of their organizations, make trips abroad for business purposes.

▸ Flight classifications include first class, business class, and economy/coach class.

▸ Since 9/11, America's airports have operated under unprecedented levels of security.

▸ Executives travel by commercial air and company-owned planes.

▸ When traveling internationally, executives need to be knowledgeable of the culture of the country where they are traveling.

▸ Currency in other countries is different from that in the United States.

▸ When traveling abroad, executives need to take appropriate health precautions.

▸ The administrative professional's responsibilities before the executive travels include the following: preparing an itinerary, obtaining travel funds, preparing and organizing materials for the trip, checking the calendar, confirming trip appointments, assembling trip items, and knowing how matters are to be handled during the executive's absence.

▸ After the executive leaves the administrative professional is responsible for handling messages, appointments, and correspondence; and making decisions.

▸ When the executive returns, the administrative professional is responsible for doing a post-trip briefing and helping the executive with any matters that must be completed because of the trip.

▸ It is important for an administrative professional to consistently maintain a high achievement orientation and a positive attitude.

GLOSSARY

AAA—American Automobile Association.

Business-class accommodations—Level between first class and economy/coach class. It is not available on all aircraft or on all flights. Business-class passengers generally have larger seats that may recline and have footrests. Personal video, laptop power ports, and satellite phones may be available. Meals are available on international flights.

Economy/coach-class accommodations—The least expensive of the three classes of flight, usually with fewer flight attendants and the seats are less comfortable.

E-ticket—Ticket provided online by most airlines.

Euro—Banknotes that have replaced the old European currencies in 12 countries (at the time of the writing of this textbook). The status of the Euro in the future is presently in question, with some countries considering withdrawing.

FAA—Federal Aviation Administration.

FCC—Federal Communications Commission.

First-class accommodations—Most expensive of the three classes of flight and the most luxurious.

Frequent flyer—Incentive program with a variety of awards after the accumulation of mileage points.

Itinerary—Gives necessary information for a trip; e.g., flight numbers, arrival and departure times, hotel reservations, car rental, and appointments.

Jet lag—The feeling of exhaustion following a flight through several time zones.

Passport—Official government document certifying the identity and citizenship of an individual and granting the person permission to travel abroad.

Positive attitude—Ability to maintain a pleasant outlook even when negative situations occur.

Regional jets—Planes that fly to specific parts of the country.

Visa—Document granted by a government abroad that permits a traveler to enter and travel within a particular country.

CHECKPOINT

Check your understanding of these terms by completing DCD12-a on the Data CD.

DISCUSSION ITEMS

These discussion items provide an opportunity to test your understanding of the chapter through written responses and/or discussion with your classmates and your instructor.

1. Explain the global nature of corporate America.

2. List and explain the three main classes of domestic flights.

3. Discuss five security precautions present at airports since 9/11.

4. Identify four responsibilities of the administrative professional when planning an international trip.

CRITICAL THINKING CASE

Juan Gonzales, an assistant that you employed about three months ago, is Puerto Rican. He was born in Mexico and came to Texas when he was a teenager. He has an associate degree from a community college in Texas. He is fluent in both English and Spanish. Juan is extremely outgoing and will grab you in bear hugs when things are going well. Lin Basan is from Taiwan and has been in the United States only one year. She learned English in Taiwan, but she does not always understand expressions. She is quiet and reserved. Lin works for Wayne Wixon's assistant.

When Ms. Portosky decided to go to Taiwan, she asked to speak to Lin concerning the culture. Lin accepted the invitation graciously. She said that in her culture older people are greatly respected. She also stated that she was surprised when she discovered the way young people talk to their elders in the United States; she considers it disrespectful. She mentioned to Ms. Portosky that the Taiwanese do not engage in public displays of affection.

Juan heard about her talk; he decided that he must have offended Lin on numerous occasions without realizing that he was doing so. He asked you if he should apologize to Lin or at least try to talk with her about her culture. What advice would you give Juan?

A

The correct answers are as follows:

1. First-class accommodations are the most expensive of the three classes and the most luxurious. The seats are wider and farther apart, and services are greater. Business-class accommodations are a level between first class and economy/coach class. Business class is not available on all aircraft or on all flights. Business class passengers generally have larger seats that may recline and have footrests. Personal video, laptop power ports, and satellite phones may be available. Meals are available on international flights. Economy/coach-class accommodations are in the main cabin area and are typically the lowest-priced seats on the airplane, with less comfortable seats and fewer flight attendants.

2. Security precautions include:
   a. Air marshals on a number of flights.
   b. Only ticketed passengers allowed beyond the screening checkpoint.
   c. Removal of all laptops and video cameras from their cases. They are subjected to both x-ray and physical inspection.
   d. Passengers required to have government-issued ID when checking-in.
   e. Shoes are subjected to x-ray inspection, as are briefcases, billfolds, purses, metal belts, luggage, and other items that passengers are taking on the flight.
   f. If you bring a prohibited item such as weapons, explosives, and/or incendiaries, you may be criminally or civilly prosecuted.

B

The correct answers are as follows:

1. Cultural similarities between Australia and the United States are: English speaking; direct in communication; executives (no matter what level) will generally hear what employees have to say; manual labor enjoys relatively high prestige; high standards of cleanliness; punctuality is important.

2. Cultural differences between Taiwan and the United States are: Culture generally closed to outside information; Confucianism has a great influence; rigid ethical and moral system that governs relations; decisions made by consensus; duty not to bring shame on family or organization.

WORKPLACE PROJECTS

PROJECT 12-1 PREPARE AN ITINERARY

Explain the global nature of corporate America (Objective 1)

Make international travel arrangements (Objective 3)

Explain organizational travel procedures and the administrative professional's responsibilities before and after a trip (Objective 4)

Exhibit respect for other cultures (Objective 5)

Maintain a high achievement attitude (Objective 6)

Your employer, Jana Portosky, is going to Taipei, Taiwan, on November 10 and returning on November 15. Determine flight times, hotel arrangements, and costs by checking a website. The President of Taiwan Technology will pick her up at the airport. Her schedule will be as follows:

November 12, 9 a.m. appointment with Kuo Lu
November 13, 10 a.m. appointment with Sheng Mo
November 13, 2 p.m. appointment with Ming Su
November 14, 2 p.m. appointment with Chan Yi

Prepare an itinerary, listing the appointments. Note the number of hours of travel time on the itinerary; also note the differences in time between Dallas and Taiwan. Ms. Portosky asks that you schedule two appointments for her when she returns; she told you to get the appointments as soon as possible. One appointment is with George Hooks of Reynolds Technology; the second one is with Robert Williamson of Papp Electronics. Assume that you have scheduled the appointments and write her an e-mail with the dates and times.

Prepare a note to yourself of what you should do when Ms. Portosky is out of the office and when she returns. Explain how you will effectively use your time. Turn in the information to your instructor, along with the itinerary.

Ms. Portosky asks that you check business culture in Taiwan; using the Web, check at least three sources.

Pay particular attention to the status of females in the Taiwan culture. Write a memorandum to Ms. Portosky, listing your findings. Cite your resources. Turn in your findings to your instructor, using report format and a cover page. DCD12-01 contains a memorandum form.

 PROJECT 12-2 DETERMINE DOMESTIC FLIGHT TIMES

Make domestic travel arrangements (Objective 2)

Ms. Portosky plans to go to New York on business on December 1 through December 3. She wants to go at approximately 10 a.m. on December 1 and return after 5 p.m. on December 3. Using the Web, check out the times available and the costs. She does not want you to do an itinerary at this point; she merely wants an e-mail with the times and cost. (The e-mail should be sent to your instructor; if the instructor prefers, use a memorandum form—DCD12-02.)

PROJECT 12-3 ADD TO YOUR PROFESSIONAL GROWTH PLAN, RESPECT FOR OTHER CULTURES

Exhibit respect for other cultures (Objective 5)

Maintain a high achievement attitude (Objective 6)

Add to your Professional Growth Plan by describing how you will continue to demonstrate respect for other cultures and maintain a high achievement attitude. Save your plan as PGP12-3.

 COMMUNICATION POWER

Use DCD12-b to assist you in improving your grammar skills.

ASSESSMENT OF CHAPTER OBJECTIVES

Now that you have completed the chapter and the projects, take a few minutes to review the chapter learning objectives. For your convenience, the objectives are repeated here. Did you accomplish these objectives? If you were unable to accomplish the objectives, give your reasons for not doing so; be specific and concise. Your instructor may prefer that your answers be submitted to him or her. If so, DCD12-c contains the Assessment of Chapter Objectives. Complete the Assessment of Chapter Objectives; submit the results to your instructor.

1. Explain the global nature of corporate America. Yes ☐ No ☐

_____

_____

_____

2. Make domestic travel arrangements. Yes ☐ No ☐

_____

_____

_____

3. Make international travel arrangements. Yes ☐ No ☐

_____

_____

_____

4. Explain organizational travel procedures and the administrative professional's responsibilities before and after a trip. Yes ☐ No ☐

_____

_____

_____

5. Exhibit respect for other cultures.   Yes ☐   No ☐
   _____
   _____
   _____

6. Maintain a high achievement attitude.   Yes ☐   No ☐
   _____
   _____
   _____

CHAPTER 13

MEETINGS AND CONFERENCES

Learning Objectives

1. Explain the frequency and cost of meetings.
2. Describe the various types of meetings.
3. Explain the characteristics of effective meetings.
4. Determine meeting formats.
5. Describe the responsibilities of the executive in meetings.
6. Describe the responsibilities of the administrative professional in assisting with meetings and conferences.
7. Develop conflict resolution skills.

Image 100

> MEETINGS—A WAY OF LIFE IN THE WORKPLACE

Meetings are a way of life in the workplace. In a business environment that is downsized, multinational, and driven by technology (with e-mail, telephone, and faxes providing for quick communication both nationally and globally), one might expect fewer meetings. However, in reality, the opposite is true. As more work is handled by teams, the number of meetings is increasing rather than decreasing.

According to one study, the average CEO in the United States spends 17 hours a week in meetings, with senior executives spending 23 hours a week and middle managers spending 11 hours per week in meetings.[1] Another study details the cost of meetings to United States corporations as more than $37 billion annually. This study also gives the following information regarding meetings:

- ▶ Business managers spend nearly 80 percent of their time in meetings.
- ▶ U.S. corporations hold 15 million meetings per day.
- ▶ The average business trip consumes $1,400 in hard costs and more than $3,000 in total costs, including personnel time.
- ▶ Business professionals rate at least 40 percent of meetings as unproductive.
- ▶ Meetings are responsible for more than $30 billion in productivity losses each year.[2]

As you can readily see, meetings are costly to organizations. With teams increasingly becoming a standard method of operation, it is

---

[1]Jon Jenkins and Gerrit Visser, "Meetings Bloody Meetings," <http://www.imaginal.nl/mgtonlinemeetings1.htm> (accessed July 1, 2005).
[2]"Smarter Decisions.Faster," <http://www.groupsystems.com/site/statis/pdfs/gs-sales-sheet.pdf-Microsoft> (accessed July 1, 2005).

imperative that meetings be effective. This chapter will help you develop the knowledge and skills you need to assist your supervisor in holding meetings that are productive for all participants. Additionally, as a team member and even a team leader on occasion, the chapter will also help you develop the skills not only to run an effective meeting but also to be a productive team member.

> TYPES OF MEETINGS

Typical meetings within an organization include Board of Director Meetings, staff meetings, committee or task force meetings, project team meetings, customer or client meetings, and international meetings.

▷ Board of Director Meetings

Most large corporations and organizations operate with a board of directors. There are usually **bylaws**, written policies and procedures that clearly define how board meetings are to be conducted. Boards may meet once a month or less. The chairperson of the board conducts the meeting, and strict procedures are usually followed. An agenda is distributed before the meeting, indicating the items to be discussed. If the organization is a public entity in which the open meetings rule applies, notice of the meeting is posted according to legal procedures. Participants generally follow parliamentary procedures as set forth in *Robert's Rules of Order*.

▷ Staff Meetings

Staff meetings are common within organizations. Staff meetings are scheduled on a regular basis, with an executive meeting with members of his or her staff. For example, an executive may meet with his or her six direct reports as a group every week. The purpose of staff meetings may be to review directions, plans, or assignments, or to handle routine problems.

▷ Committee/Task Force Meetings

In most organizations, committees or task forces are created. A **task force** is formed to deal with a specific issue or problem. Once the problem has been handled or solved, the task force is disbanded. In other words, the task force has a specific beginning and ending. It is organized for a purpose; once the purpose is accomplished, it no longer exists. A **committee** is generally established for an ongoing purpose. For example, your workplace may have a safety committee that meets regularly (perhaps every month) to identify and address safety concerns. Since safety is an ongoing concern, the committee usually functions from year to year.

▷ Project Team Meetings

Project teams are frequently used in organizations to accomplish a specific task. For example, a project team may be organized to determine the type of software that will be used in an organization or to implement quality control policies within a company. Once the project has been completed, the team is disbanded or takes on another project.

▷ Customer/Client Meetings

Some employers hold meetings with customers or clients. These meetings are generally small, including only one or two people. For example, a lawyer may meet with a client to discuss the evidence in a case. An engineer may meet with a customer to discuss the design of a product.

International meetings are common in our global economy.

© Digital Vision

▷ International Meetings

With many organizations being international in scope, meetings with staff in locations outside the United States are common for upper-level administrators.

Also, as organizations within the United States continue to broaden their international scope, meetings to pursue international opportunities are held with business leaders in numerous other countries. In international meetings, it is imperative that you understand the culture of the countries involved and honor that culture. Figure 13-1 lists several important areas to consider when conducting international meetings.

> EFFECTIVE MEETINGS

Well-run and well-thought-out meetings are an important forum for keeping open channels of communication and providing a vehicle for sharing ideas and information. However, in spite of the usefulness of meetings, there are situations when a meeting is not the best choice. Before a meeting is called, the administrator or staff person should ask the following questions of herself or himself.

- Is a meeting the most effective vehicle for communicating the necessary information?
- Have alternatives to a meeting been considered? Would an e-mail or a phone call be just as effective or maybe more effective?
- Does the meeting leader have the necessary facilitation skills? Is the facilitator capable of handling a challenging group?
- Are the right people going to be in attendance?
- Is there a clear agenda?
- Are there supporting materials; i.e., facts and figures needed?

Figure 13-2 gives several suggestions for conducting effective meetings. A meeting effectiveness evaluation is given in Figure 13-3.

---

[3]Michael Ochs and Rini van Solinger, "Making Meetings Work," <http://www.stsc.hill.af.mil/crosstalk/2004/02/04020chs.html> (accessed July 1, 2005).

Figure 13-3 MEETING EFFECTIVENESS EVALUATION

Directions: Rate the statement on a scale of 1 to 6, with 6 being most effective and 1 being least effective.

1. Participation	All members are encouraged to participate.	6 5 4 3 2 1
2. Communication	Thoughts freely expressed.	6 5 4 3 2 1
3. Conflict	If it occurs, it is dealt with properly.	6 5 4 3 2 1
4. Roles and Assignments	Assignments are clear and involve all members.	6 5 4 3 2 1
5. Creativity	Breakthrough or creative ideas are encouraged.	6 5 4 3 2 1
6. Project/Problem Solving Tools	Tools are used to assist team in project management, in solving problems, and in coming up with new ideas.	6 5 4 3 2 1
7. Meeting Process	The meeting process is effectively managed to produce team results.	6 5 4 3 2 1
8. Facilitator	The facilitator was effective in providing guidance and support to the team.	6 5 4 3 2 1

COMMENTS

Please comment on how improvement might be made.[4]

_____

_____

> MEETING FORMAT

The meeting format is most often **face to face.** Organizations will continue to have numerous face-to-face meetings because of the increase in teamwork within organizations and the need for these teams to share information in a face-to-face format. Audio conferencing (although an older technology) remains a viable type of meeting format. However, in our technological world, videoconferencing and webconferencing are growing significantly. The growth rate has been 15 to 20 percent each year, with companies combining on-the-road activities with teleconferencing and webconferencing to maximize collaborations and increase business for organizations while decreasing costs.[5] Each of these meeting formats is explained in more detail in the next sections.

▷ Face-to-Face Meetings

Even though we live in a technological world, the traditional face-to-face meeting is still common. These meetings are ones where people gather for face-to-face discussion of issues or problems at one location. Advantages of face-to-face meetings include the following:

- ▶ A creative, interactive group discussion is more likely to take place because of the ability of individuals to be in close proximity to each other; the participants can touch, see, and hear all group members.
- ▶ Body language of participants can be closely observed.
- ▶ People generally feel more relaxed in this type of session because its format is more familiar.
- ▶ The atmosphere generally allows people to deal more effectively with difficult items.
- ▶ Widespread participation among group members is more likely.

Figure 13-4 gives several disadvantages of face-to-face meetings.

[4]"Meeting Effectiveness Evaluation," <http://hra.co.sacramento.ca.us/quality/Quality/meeting.htm> (accessed July 1, 2005).
[5]Mary K. Pratt, "Teleconferencing Seen Moving From Novelty to Necessity," <www.netspoke.com/articles/bbj111904a.html> (accessed July 1, 2005).

Audioconferencing

An **audioconference** is a type of conference in which an unlimited number of participants use a voice input unit to participate in a meeting. An audio conference differs from a telephone conversation in that it involves more than two people in at least two locations. The unit may be as simple as a speakerphone or as elaborate as a meeting room with microphones, speakers, and bridging technology. Bridging services, supplied by telephone and communication service companies, allow multiple locations to dial in to a single phone number that is bridged into one auditory space.

Videoconferencing

A **videoconference** is a system of transmitting information through a video camera, a microphone, and speakers mounted on the individuals' computers. As participants speak to one another, their voices are carried over the network and delivered to the other participants' speakers. The images that appear in front of the video camera appear in a window on the other participants' monitors. Multipoint videoconferencing allows three or more participants to sit in a virtual conference room and communicate as if they were sitting right next to each other.[6]

In our technological and global world, videoconferencing is an accepted format for business meetings.

© Digital Vision

Webconferencing

Three types of webconferencing are introduced here—the webmeeting, the webcast, and the webinar.

Webmeeting

A **webmeeting** is just that—a meeting that takes place over the Web. Through a webmeeting, you can hold real-time conversations and share documents. These meetings can be fully interactive, allowing participants to converse in real time and information to be exchanged between individuals.

Webcast

The **webcast** is a type of broadcast that is similar in nature to a television broadcast, except it takes place over the Web. However, the broadcasting nature of this type of conferencing means that there is little opportunity for the presenter and delegates to interact; it is primarily a presenting tool, which can be broadcast simultaneously to hundreds of recipients.

Webinar

The **webinar** allows you to conduct a seminar over the Web. It enables the presenter to conduct question and answer-type sessions with delegates, but it

---

[6]"Videoconferencing," <http://isp.webopedia.com/TERM/V/videoconferencing.html> (accessed July 1, 2005).

does not provide the same degree of interaction as a webmeeting.

◫ Advantages and Disadvantages of Audio, Video, and Webconferencing

Audio, video, and webconferencing have both advantages and disadvantages just as face-to-face meetings have.

Advantages include:

▶ Savings in travel time and costs, including meals and hotel rooms.
▶ Bringing people together who have expertise in a number of different areas with a minimum of effort.

Disadvantages include:

▶ Less chance for effective brainstorming on issues.
▶ Less spontaneity among individuals because of a structured environment.
▶ No chance for the interaction before or after the meeting that is often so effective in face-to-face meetings.

Spotlight *on*

MEETINGS

Schedule meetings only when necessary. A meeting with no purpose results in a waste of employees' time, frustration for meeting participants, and unnecessary costs for the organization.

> INTERNATIONAL MEETINGS

Throughout this text, you have been introduced to the importance of understanding differences in cultures. You certainly may be involved in setting up and/or participating in electronic meetings with individuals from other countries. Remember that cultural differences do exist; these differences must be understood and respected. Otherwise, you may be dealing with an international incident rather than getting a resolution on an important contract or

issue. It is important for you and your employer to do your homework before the meeting. Find out as much as you can about the culture or cultures that will be represented. Then, be sensitive to the needs of the individuals in the meeting. International meetings are always more formal in nature. You must understand hierarchical considerations and use proper greetings and amenities. Figure 13-5 gives several suggestions for what to do and not to do in international meetings.

> MEETING RESPONSIBILITIES

As you help plan and organize a meeting, remember that several individuals play an important part in assuring that the meeting is effective. These individuals include the executive who calls the meeting; the person who makes arrangements for the meeting; the leader who facilitates the meeting; the participants; and the administrative professional who assists in planning and preparing materials. Each individual or group has specific roles and responsibilities that help ensure an effective meeting environment.

Figure 13-5 APPROPRIATE AND INAPPROPRIATE BEHAVIORS IN INTERNATIONAL MEETINGS

1. Greet each person properly in all meetings.

2. Do not use first names of participants. Even though using first names is common in U.S. meetings, rarely is it an appropriate practice in other countries.

3. Recognize the leader of the other group(s). For example, if the presidents of companies are involved, they should be recognized first and speak first.

4. Disagree agreeably; some cultures consider it offensive to be contradictory.

5. Avoid gesturing with your hands. Many people take offense at such gestures.

6. Watch your body language; remember that body language has different meanings in different cultures.

7. Respect the hierarchical nature of the international participants.

≥ Executive's Responsibilities

The **executive** (an individual who has managerial authority in an organization) has a variety of responsibilities when planning meetings. She or he must determine the purpose of the meeting, set the objectives, determine who should attend and the number of participants, plan the agenda, and establish the time and place. The executive may work closely with the administrative professional in accomplishing these tasks.

Determine the Purpose of the Meeting

Every meeting must have a purpose; without it, there is no need for a meeting. Generally, the executive calls the meeting, so it is his or her role to determine the purpose. When meeting notices are sent out, the purpose should be clearly stated. All participants must understand why the meeting is occurring. Although the administrative professional is not responsible for determining the purpose, she or he must understand the purpose so that appropriate arrangements can be made. Without this understanding, errors can occur.

Spotlight *on*

MEETINGS

If there is no carefully thought-out purpose for a meeting, a meeting should not be called.

Set the Objectives

Every meeting should have specific written objectives. Objectives should clearly define the purpose and delineate what is to be accomplished. For example, if the general purpose is to establish a strategic plan for the next year, the objectives might be:

▶ Evaluate the accomplishment of objectives for the current year.
▶ Establish objectives and timelines for the next year based on the three-year strategic plan.
▶ Determine the resources needed to meet these objectives.
▶ Determine responsibility for carrying out all objectives.

Meeting objectives must be shared with the **participants** (individuals who take part in a meeting) before the meeting. The attendees may be a group of executives, a group of non-managerial employees, or a mixed group of both managerial and non-managerial employees. Sharing the objectives with the participants will not only provide them with an understanding of the purpose of the meeting, but also allow them to be prepared for the meeting. If they have questions about the purpose, they will have the opportunity to clarify meaning before the meeting begins.

Determine Who Should Attend

Individuals who are invited to the meeting are those who:

1. Have knowledge that can contribute to meeting the objectives.

2. Will be responsible for implementing the decisions.

3. Represent a group who will be affected by the decisions.

In the previous situation with the purpose to establish a strategic plan for the next year, all managers in the department must be invited to the meeting.

Now, assume that another meeting is being called, with the objective of brainstorming international expansion into three or four new countries in addition to Australia and Taiwan. The people who should attend are the officers of the company; this decision is a top level one that will, after consideration by the officers, be presented to the Board of Directors for approval.

In determining who should attend a meeting, consideration should always be given to the purpose of the meeting and to whom is most affected by the issue or problem that is to be discussed. Also, consideration needs to be given to the background of each individual being asked to attend. For example, a **heterogeneous group** (a group with dissimilar backgrounds and experiences) can often solve problems more satisfactorily than a **homogeneous group** (a group with similar backgrounds and experiences). Since a heterogeneous group will usually bring varying views to the problem, creative thinking is more likely to occur than in a homogeneous group.

Determine the Number of Participants

In the two examples given previously, the participants have been determined by their expertise in the matter being discussed. Now, assume a very different type of meeting. This meeting is one in which the group is to determine new product lines for JWay Nu-Systems Tech to pursue. You want an extremely creative group to brainstorm. One way to accomplish your goal is to reach across departments and classifications. In other words, include individuals from a cross-section of JWay, with different backgrounds, education, and experiences. Generally, a heterogeneous group will bring varying views to the issue/problem.

The ideal number of participants is based on the purpose of the meeting, with the number of people invited who can best achieve the purpose. The best size for a problem-solving and decision-making group is from 7 to 15 people. This size group allows for creative **synergy** (the ideas and products of a group of people developed through interaction with each other). There are enough people to generate divergent points of view and to challenge each other's thinking.

Small groups of seven people or less may be necessary at times. For example, if the purpose of the meeting is to discuss a personal matter, the human resources director and the supervisor may be the only ones in attendance. If the purpose of the meeting is to discuss a faulty product design, the product engineer, the manager of the department, and the technician may be the only persons in attendance. Advantages to having only a few people in a meeting are:

▸ Participants may be assembled more quickly since there are fewer.
▸ The meeting can be informal and thus provide for more spontaneity and creativity.
▸ Group dynamics are easier to manage.

The disadvantages of a small group include the following:

▸ Points of view are limited because of the size of the group.
▸ There may not be enough ideas to create the best solution to the problem.
▸ Participants may not be willing to challenge each other's point of view if they are a close-knit group.

Plan the Agenda

The executive's role is to plan the **agenda**. The agenda, which should be distributed before the meeting, provides participants with the purpose and objectives of the meeting. The agenda should include the following specific information:

▸ Name of the group, department, or committee
▸ Date of the meeting
▸ Start and end times
▸ Location of the meeting

Additionally, the agenda should include:

1. The agenda item, in order of presentation.
2. The individual responsible for presenting the agenda item.
3. The action expected on the agenda item; i.e., approval, information only.
4. Background materials (if needed).

A well-planned agenda saves time and increases productivity in a meeting. By providing participants with the proper information before a meeting, the leader can use time in the meeting effectively and decisions can be made in a timely manner. Figure 13-6 gives additional suggestions for creating an effective agenda.

Establish the Time and Place

The executive is responsible for establishing the approximate time of the meeting and the general location for the meeting. For example, the executive may tell the administrative professional that the meeting will take place on Thursday morning, but not give a specific time. The executive also tells the administrative professional that the meeting will be held in-house. The administrative professional then has the responsibility of checking with other participants (or their administrative professionals) to determine the most appropriate time. The administrative professional may have access to an online calendar of meetings scheduled in the organization; such a calendar saves time and effort if it is kept up-to-date. Additionally, the administrative professional checks to determine an appropriate conference room available at the particular time needed. If the meeting is a routine meeting that occurs each month, a time and place is usually established when the first meeting is held. Such an approach eliminates work for the administrative professional and also keeps the administrators from having schedule conflicts.

Figure 13-6 **CREATING AN EFFECTIVE AGENDA**

- ▶ Send an e-mail or memo stating there will be a meeting, including the goal of the meeting and the administrative details, such as when and where the meeting will be held.

- ▶ Ask participants requesting an agenda item to contact you no less than two days before the meeting with their request and the amount of time they will need to present it.

- ▶ Summarize the agenda items in an appropriate format, with the headings: **Agenda Item, Presenter,** and **Time.** Make certain all agenda items are directly related to the goals of the meeting.

- ▶ If someone sends an agenda item that does not relate to the meeting, suggest that the person send an e-mail instead or recommend that the agenda item be discussed in another meeting.

- ▶ Be realistic concerning the time needed for the agenda item. Do not cram more items into the agenda than the time allows.

- ▶ Send the agenda to all meeting participants at least two days in advance.

- ▶ Follow the agenda during the meeting.

Source: "How to Create an Agenda, Step by Step," <http://www.effectivemeetings.com/meetingplanning/agenda/agenda.asp> (accessed July 1, 2004).

▷ Leader's Responsibilities

The **leader** (individual who is in charge of the meeting) is generally your supervisor. Since teams are used extensively in organizations today, you (as an administrative professional may be the **team leader** (individual who heads a team that is charged with getting some type of task accomplished) in a meeting. Additionally, you may also be a **co-leader** (one member of a team of two members who are in charge) with another administrative professional in the organization. Team leaders have the following responsibilities when leading a meeting.

Clarify the Purpose and Objectives of the Meeting

Have you ever been in a meeting where there was no apparent purpose? Most of us have been to a number of such meetings, and we know that people's time

and energy are wasted. We usually walk away from such meetings saying, "I wonder why I bothered to attend?" It is extremely important to establish the purpose and the objectives of the meeting. Without attention to these important details, people invited to the meeting do not know what to expect and cannot be properly prepared. The meeting purpose should be sent out in writing to the participants, along with the objectives of the meeting—what must be accomplished. The leader is also responsible for establishing the timeframe of the meeting—how long it will take to meet the objectives of the meeting and whether the meeting is in the morning or the afternoon. A detailed agenda should be prepared and sent, along with the announcement of the meeting. The agenda should include the items, the names of the people who are responsible for presenting information on each of the items, and the projected timeframe for each item.

Adhere to the Agenda

When the meeting begins, the leader should reiterate the purpose of the meeting. The leader should also let the participants know what outcomes are expected. For example, if the purpose of a meeting is to establish a direction for the unit for the next year, the expected outcomes of the meeting may be to determine at least four unit objectives. If participants stray from the agenda, the leader is responsible for sensitively, but firmly, bringing them back to the topic at hand. The leader might say, for example, "Thank you for your comments concerning this issue. We can put it on the agenda for our next meeting. Now, let's continue discussing the unit's objectives for this next year."

Manage Time

Meetings should begin on time, even if several people are late in arriving. Waiting for others is not fair to the individuals who have made an effort to be on time. Timeframes (both beginning and ending) are established when the meeting notice is sent out.

In addition to beginning on time, the leader is responsible for ending on time. Have you ever been in a meeting that was to last for one hour and you were still sitting there two hours later? Most of us have, and most of us would say that allowing a meeting to run over significantly from the time scheduled is poor management on the part of the leader, in addition to insensitivity to the needs of the participants. With our fast-paced business world, calendars are generally tightly scheduled. To allow one meeting to go longer than scheduled generally means that participants are late for another commitment. In fact, if a meeting goes longer than scheduled, it is perfectly acceptable to excuse yourself by making the following statement to the leader, "I am so sorry, Jim or Jean (the leader of the group), as you will recall, I mentioned to you when I agreed to be at this meeting that I had another meeting today. Unfortunately, that meeting is starting in ten minutes, and I must leave. I promise to read the minutes very carefully so that I may be informed as to what I have missed." Such a statement shows the group that you care and that you did inform the leader that you had another meeting when you accepted the invitation. It demonstrates your desire to fulfill all of your commitments. It also lets the other participants know that you are not being rude or inconsiderate—you are merely fulfilling another obligation.

Encourage Participation

Before participants are invited to a meeting, the leader should give considerable thought to who should be at the meeting. The people in attendance should be the best people in the organization to solve the problems, discuss the issues, or determine the directions. The leader is responsible for seeing that all individuals participate and that no one dominates the discussion to the exclusion of the remainder of the group. The leader should help individuals feel secure enough to say what they think. If, as the meeting gets under way, several people have not spoken, the leader may make statements similar to these:

▶ "Maria, what direction do you think we should take?"
▶ "Lin, we haven't heard from you on this issue. What are your thoughts?"

Let each participant know that you and the group value her or his opinion. Encourage everyone to contribute. Respect participants and the comments they make. You might make statements such as these:

▶ "Thank you for that contribution."
▶ "That's an excellent idea."
▶ "Your idea definitely has possibilities. Can you explain it more?"

The leader is also responsible for seeing that one or two people do not dominate the conversation,

even if their contributions are beneficial. The leader might use the following types of statements.

1. "Diana, that is an excellent idea. Eduardo, how could it be implemented in your area?"

2. "Thanks, Roger; Michael, what direction do you think we should take?"

The leader needs to (1) keep the participants focused on the agenda, (2) encourage participation from everyone in the meeting, (3) limit the domination of any one person, (4) positively reinforce all individuals for their contributions, and (5) keep the discussion moving to accomplish the outcomes desired.

A leader keeps the meeting participants focused on the agenda.

Reach Decisions

The leader is responsible for helping the participants reach a decision about an issue, problem, or direction. The leader must carefully assess all alternatives that have been discussed. Next, the leader needs to push for a decision on the issue. For example, the leader might say, "We seem to have identified each issue and the possible solutions. Does anyone else have anything to add? Are we overlooking anything? Are there problems we haven't seen?"

If the group seems to be comfortable with the alternatives that have been discussed, the leader can move to resolution by saying, "Now of the two solutions that have been proposed, let's determine which solution will work better for our group. Let's take a quick vote to help clarify which alternative the group thinks is better." In this situation, the leader has been supportive of the group members by listening carefully to alternatives that were presented and then has helped the group make a decision by calling for a vote on the alternative considered the better of the two presented.

Evaluate the Meeting

Generally, with informal meetings within an organization, no formal evaluation is necessary. However, an informal evaluation by the leader (and possibly the participants) should be done. Participants are usually forthright; they may tell the leader that the meeting was not as successful as they had hoped. When participants make this type of statement, the leader should seek clarification on exactly what was meant. The leader may want to ask two or three individual participants how the meeting went. The leader will also want to ask the questions given in Figure 13-7 of himself or herself.

▷ Participants' Responsibilities

Just as a leader has responsibilities, so do the participants. Their role is much broader than attending the meeting. Their responsibilities begin before the meeting and continue after the meeting.

Before the Meeting

Participants are responsible for reading the meeting notice, responding to it promptly, and reading any materials sent out before the meeting. Participants are also responsible for understanding the purpose of the meeting and reviewing the materials. Each participant must take seriously her or his responsibility to contribute to the success of the meeting, which means that the participant must be prepared. No one appreciates the person who comes to a meeting late and opens up the pack of materials for the first time—clearly not having prepared for the meeting.

During the Meeting

The participants are responsible for being on time to the meeting and for contributing thoughtful,

---

Figure 13-7 **EVALUATION QUESTIONS FOR THE LEADER TO ASK AFTER A MEETING**

1. Were the participants participatory?

2. Was the nonverbal behavior positive?

3. Were the participants creative problem solvers?

4. Did the participants exhibit a high energy level?

5. Was the purpose of the meeting satisfied?

6. Were appropriate decisions made?

7. Can I improve in how I handled the issues, the people, or the meeting?

---

well-considered, or well-researched comments. Other responsibilities include these: listening nonjudgmentally to others, respecting the leader's role, and being courteous to each individual.

Although making these types of contributions sounds simple, it is not always so. Your mind tends to wander, focusing on other work-related tasks or on personal issues. However, your contributions can be the very ones that get the meeting back on track if individuals stray or help the leader keep the meeting focused. Your obligation is always to contribute in a positive manner to the success of the meeting.

After the Meeting

A participant's responsibilities do not necessarily end when the meeting is over. The participant may have

---

CHECK A

Self

Check your understanding of the leader's role in a meeting by listing six responsibilities below.

1. _____

2. _____

3. _____

4. _____

5. _____

6. _____

been asked to research a topic or work with a group of individuals to bring back a recommendation on a particular item for the next meeting. Although these types of after-meeting assignments are time consuming, the assumption is that the contribution made from the assignments will positively affect the organization.

▷ Administrative Professional's Responsibilities

In planning meetings (whether they are face-to-face or some type of electronic meeting), the administrative professional has a number of responsibilities. You must work with the supervisor to determine the purpose of the meeting and the duties you are expected to perform. When you first join an organization or begin to work with a different supervisor, you should take time before each meeting to understand his or her needs and preferences. As you learn the supervisor's preferences, you will need to spend less time in discussing the details of the meeting. However, you should continue to discuss the purpose of the meeting. Otherwise, you may make decisions about details that cause problems.

Confirm the Date and Time

At times, the executive will request to hold a meeting on a specific date and at a specific time. At other times, one or both of these decisions will be left up to the administrative professional. You will probably want to avoid scheduling meetings on Monday mornings and Friday afternoons. Employees often use Monday mornings to get an overview of the week and handle any pressing items that may have occurred over the weekend. Friday afternoons are often used to complete projects.

When determining the time of a meeting, avoid selecting a time immediately after lunch or near the end of the day. Meetings generally should last no longer than two hours. People get restless when they must sit longer than two hours. However, if a long meeting cannot be avoided, schedule short five- or ten-minute breaks for participants.

Select and Prepare the Meeting Room

Room arrangements should be made immediately after you know the date and time. Organizations generally do not have a large number of conference rooms, and these rooms are usually booked quickly for meetings. If various size conference rooms are available; you will want to book one, if possible, that meets your seating needs. For example, if you have 10 people coming to the meeting and you schedule a conference room that seats 30, participants may feel lost in the room. Conversely, if you choose a room that is too small, participants will feel crowded.

Check the temperature controls before the meeting. Remember that bodies give off heat, so the room will be warmer with people in it. A standard rule is to aim for approximately 68°F. A hot, stuffy room or a room that is icy cold is a big distraction for people who are trying to make important decisions. Be certain you understand how to change the thermostat if the room becomes too hot or cold. Although maintenance personnel are generally available, it may take them a while to get to the room, and usually the task is a simple one.

Determine the Seating Arrangement

The seating arrangement of the room depends on the objectives of the meeting. The five basic seating arrangements are rectangular, circular, oval, semicircular, and U-shaped. Figure 13-8 shows these arrangements.

The **rectangular arrangement** allows the leader to maintain control because she or he sits at the head of the table. This arrangement is also effective when participants will be talking in groups of two or three. Individuals seated next to or opposite each other have a chance to discuss issues as they arise. However, if discussion is important, the table should not be too long. A long table may make communication difficult because people cannot see the nonverbal behavior of other participants. A long table may also prevent the leader from taking part in discussions if she or he is seated away from other participants. The rectangular arrangement is most effective in formal meetings.

The **circular** and **oval arrangements** work best when the purpose of the meeting is to generate ideas and discussion in a relatively informal meeting. These arrangements encourage togetherness, shared communication, and participation. Participants can make direct eye contact with everyone else in the group. Communication channels are considered equal among all participants because no one person is in a dominant position.

The **semicircular** and **U-shaped arrangements** work well for small groups of six to eight people. The leader retains moderate control because she or he is in a dominant position. The two arrangements are also good for showing visuals because the visual can be positioned at the front of the configuration.

Figure 13-8 **FIVE BASIC SEATING ARRANGEMENTS**

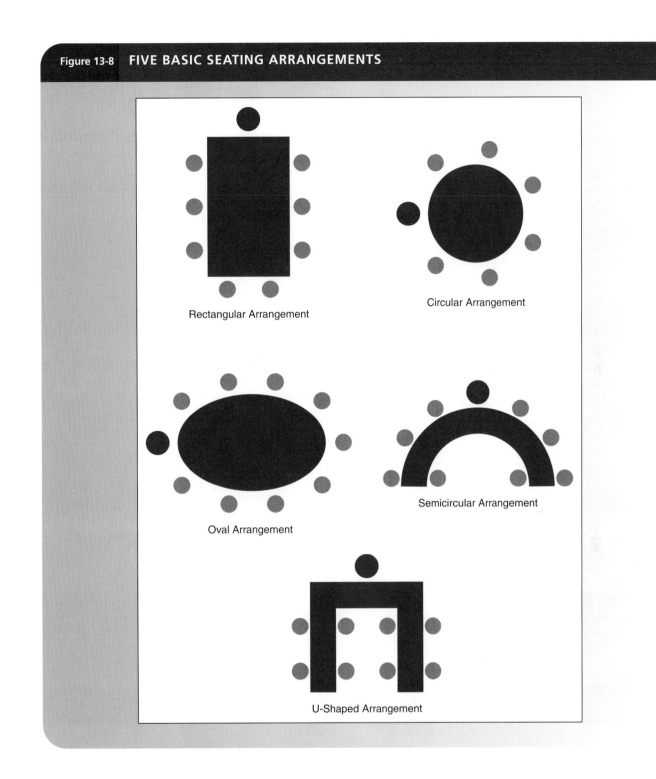

Rectangular Arrangement

Circular Arrangement

Oval Arrangement

Semicircular Arrangement

U-Shaped Arrangement

Make certain you have enough chairs for the number of participants who are scheduled to attend. You do not want to have extra chairs; they just get in the way, and it appears as though some people failed to attend. You also do not want to have too few chairs; it appears as though you did not plan properly.

Prepare the Meeting Agenda

All meeting participants should know the purpose and plan of action before coming to a meeting. An agenda is an outline of what will occur at the meeting. Participants should receive the agenda at least two days and preferably a week before the meeting. The agenda should include the following information:

- Name of the meeting or the group
- Date of the meeting
- Start and end times
- Location
- Order of agenda items
- Person responsible for presenting each agenda item
- Action expected on each agenda item
- Background materials (if needed)

In addition, you might also allocate a particular time for the presentation of each agenda item. Although this process is not essential, it does remind people of the importance of time and adherence to a schedule. If timeframes are not listed, the facilitator of the meeting may need to move the meeting along. The order of the agenda items can vary. Some people feel that the most difficult items should be presented first so participants can deal with them while they are fresh. Others think the difficult items should be presented last. Check with your supervisor to find out which order she or he prefers. A partial agenda is shown in Figure 13-9.

Notice that the word ACTION is listed after certain agenda items. This word indicates that a decision should be made. This approach helps participants know that they should come to the meeting prepared to make a decision.

Prepare the Meeting Notice
If the meeting is scheduled within the organization, notify participants by e-mail, with the meeting agenda sent as an attachment. If you have access to employees' online calendars, you can check the schedules of meeting participants to determine whether they are free at the time of the meeting. The meeting notification should include the following information:

- Names of participants
- Purpose and objectives of the meeting
- Meeting agenda
- Location, date, and time
- Background information
- Assigned materials for preparation

You may be responsible for following up on meeting notices. Although you have asked people to let you know if they cannot attend, not everyone will respond. E-mail the people who have not responded to determine if they will be present. You also need to let your supervisor know who will be attending the meeting and who will not be. If a number of people are unable to attend, your supervisor may choose to change the meeting time and/or date.

Prepare Materials for the Leader
Materials for the leader include:

- The meeting notice with a list of the people who will attend.
- Materials needed for the meeting.

If the leader is a participant in an off-site meeting, you may need to include directions to the

---

Figure 13-9

MEETING AGENDA
Planning Meeting
Conference Room A
March 22, 2006
10 a.m.–12 noon

1. Review of departmental objectives (30 minutes)	All Managers
2. Proposed budget for next year (30 minutes)	Lin Baysin
3. Goals for next six months (1 hour) ACTION	All Managers
4. Objective planning timelines (30 minutes) ACTION	Lin Baysin

meeting. Using a website such as www.mapquest.com, you can get maps and driving directions.

Prepare Materials for Participants

Background materials (if needed) should be sent to participants with the meeting notice and agenda. If handouts are to be distributed during the meeting, prepare them well in advance of the meeting. If handouts are made up of several pages, place them in individual folders. Sometimes participants may need to take notes. You might put a pad of paper in the folder, along with a pen.

Order Equipment

Determine what equipment, if any, is needed for the meeting. For example, if PowerPoint slides are going to be shown, you will need to have a computer available along with a screen. Follow through to make sure the equipment is available. It is a good idea to make a list of the necessary equipment and to note on the list the arrangements that have been made. List the person responsible for obtaining each item. If it is your responsibility, note that. Before the meeting begins, take your list to the room and check it against the equipment there.

Order Food and Beverages

For a morning meeting, coffee, tea, and juice may be provided for the participants. Water should also be available. For an afternoon meeting, you may want to provide soft drinks and coffee. Providing beverages is not mandatory, however. Check with your supervisor to see what she or he prefers.

For a luncheon meeting, you may have the responsibility of selecting the menu, calling the caterer, and arranging for the meal to be served. Avoid a heavy lunch if you are expecting people to work afterward. A salad or light entrée is more appropriate for a working lunch. For a dinner meeting, you may have the responsibility of working with an outside caterer. Sometimes there are health issues to consider. If you know the participants, provide food that meets their needs. If you do not know the participants, ask the caterer to recommend several meals to you and select from one of these meals. Be certain to ask your supervisor what the budget allocation is for the meal.

For a dinner meeting at a hotel, you can expect assistance from the hotel staff. You will usually be responsible for selecting the menu. If the event is formal, you might wish to have table decorations and place cards. You should know the group when

selecting the seating arrangement; your supervisor can advise you.

Handle Duties During the Meeting

The administrative professional's responsibilities during the meeting are varied. You may be expected to greet the participants and to introduce individuals if they do not know each other. Your courteousness, warmth, and friendliness can go a long way toward making people feel comfortable and getting the meeting off to a good start.

Your main responsibility during the meeting will probably be to take the **minutes** (a record of a meeting). Sit near the leader so you can clearly hear what she or he says. You may wish to use a laptop computer to take notes.

Minutes should contain a record of the important matters that were presented in the meeting. You do not need to record the minutes verbatim (with the exception of motions), but you do need to record all pertinent information. Items that should be included in the minutes are given in Figure 13-10.

Figure 13-10	**ITEMS TO BE INCLUDED IN MINUTES**

- ▶ Date, time, and place of the meeting
- ▶ Name of the group
- ▶ Name of the presiding officer
- ▶ Members present and absent
- ▶ Approval or correction of the minutes from the previous meeting
- ▶ Reports of committees, officers, or individuals
- ▶ Motions made, including the name of the person who made the motion, the name of the person who seconded it, and an indication of whether it passed or failed
- ▶ Items on which action needs to be taken and the person responsible for taking the action
- ▶ A concise summary of the important points of discussion
- ▶ The date and time of the next meeting (if one is scheduled)
- ▶ The name and title of the person who will be signing the minutes, along with a signature line

Follow Up After the Meeting

Your duties after the meeting include seeing that the meeting room is left in order, preparing the minutes, and handling other details.

Routine Tasks. These routine tasks are essential after a meeting.

1. Return all equipment. See that additional tables and chairs are removed from the room. Clean up any food or beverage leftovers, or notify the cleaning staff if the room needs a general cleaning.

2. Write items that require future attention by you or your employer on your calendar.

3. Send out any necessary follow-up memos.

4. Evaluate the meeting. Review what happened; consider how you might improve the arrangements for the next meeting. Make notes for review before the next meeting. If you used a caterer, make notes about the quality of the food, the helpfulness of the staff, and other items that you need to remember.

5. Keep files on meetings long enough to refer to them when planning the next similar meeting. Your notes will help ensure future success. You might also keep names and telephone numbers of contact people.

Preparation of Minutes. If minutes are necessary, they should be prepared and distributed within 24 to 48 hours of a meeting. Prompt preparation and distribution of minutes reminds participants of what they must do before the next meeting. Nonparticipants may also get copies of minutes from a meeting. For example, minutes from a company board meeting may be made available to all executives within a company.

Sample minutes from a meeting are shown in Figure 13-11. Although there is no set format for writing minutes, general guidelines are given here.

▶ Minutes are single-spaced. Margins should be at least 1 inch. If the minutes are to be placed in a bound book, the left margin should be 1½ inches.
▶ The heading should be keyed in all capital letters and centered.
▶ Subject captions should be used as paragraph headings; subject captions usually correspond to the agenda topics.
▶ Minutes may or may not be signed. Minutes of board meetings and professional organizations are generally signed. If minutes are to be signed, a signature line should be provided.
▶ Minutes must be stored for future reference. In addition to computer storage, you will

---

Self CHECK B

Take a few minutes to check your understanding of the administrative professional's role in planning meetings by listing and explaining six responsibilities in the space provided below.

1. _____
_____

2. _____
_____

3. _____
_____

4. _____
_____

5. _____
_____

6. _____
_____

Figure 13-11

MINUTES, BOARD OF DIRECTORS MEETING

MANAGEMENT ASSOCIATION

Dallas Chapter

December 14, 2005

TIME AND PLACE OF MEETING

The regular monthly meeting of the Board of Directors of the Management Association was held on December 14 at the Regent Hotel at 6:30 p.m. The meeting was called to order by the President, Marjorie Martin. All 12 board members were present.

READING OF THE MINUTES

The minutes of the November meeting were approved without reading because each member received a copy prior to the meeting.

TREASURER'S REPORT

Edwardo Rejuan reported that he received acceptance from Harold McLean to speak at the March meeting; his picture and vita have been sent to the Publicity Committee.

NEW BUSINESS

Membership Committee: The application of Theresa Pulliams for membership was unanimously approved.

Service Committee: It was suggested that the merit award qualifications be included in the Chapter Bulletin for the first week of February.

Program Committee: William Farr, Chairperson of the Speakers Bureau, reported that he and the committee are planning to increase the number of programs at the winter seminar. He also reported that the committee agreed on "Ethics in International Business" as the theme for the seminar.

ADJOURNMENT

The meeting was adjourned at 8:30 p.m.

Respectfully submitted,

(leave space and sign)

Patricia McIntosh
Secretary, Dallas Chapter

probably want to store the minutes in hard copy form in a notebook. In addition, the agenda and all pertinent materials presented in the meeting should be stored with the minutes.

Organization—The Key

Regardless of what your responsibilities are, the key is organization. Know what you have to do, and stay organized in doing it. As you plan a meeting, continue through the process of the meeting, and oversee the follow-up activities. Ask yourself these questions.

1. How can I best organize my time and efforts?

2. When should each task be completed?

3. Who is responsible for each activity?

4. What should I discuss with my supervisor?

5. What can I do on my own?

> CONFERENCES

A conference is much larger in scope and has more participants than a meeting. Executives may belong to a professional organization in a particular field of expertise, such as accounting, engineering, or human resources. Many of these organizations hold at least one major conference each year. Most companies encourage their executives to participate in conferences as a means of broadening their knowledge.

As an administrative professional, you may be a member of one of these organizations: International Association of Administrative Professionals (IAAP), the National Association of Legal Professionals (NALS), the American Association for Medical Transcription (AAMT), ARMA International, the Association for Information Management, or the National Association of Educational Office Professionals (NAEOP). As a member, you may attend and/or help to plan some of their conferences.

▷ Before the Conference

Preparing for a regional or national conference takes months of work. Good planning ensures a smooth, successful conference. Poor planning results in a disorganized, ineffective conference. One of the major responsibilities of planning is to determine the location and meeting facilities for the conference. You may wish to contact the chamber of commerce in the city being considered to ask for information about the city and appropriate conference facilities. You may also request conference planning guides from the hotels and conference centers that you are considering. These guides usually give floor plans of the facilities, dining and catering services, price list of rooms, and layout of meeting rooms.

Your task will not be to invite someone to speak unless you are working on a conference where you are a member and assisting with the planning. However, you may contact presenters to make travel and lodging arrangements. If you are responsible for making hotel arrangements for a presenter, you should determine the types of accommodations that the presenter would like to have, within the cost limitations of the budget because presenters' expenses are usually covered, at least in part, by the host organization. For example, does the presenter prefer a queen- or king-size bed? If the conference is not at a hotel, you might give the presenter a choice of two or three hotels (within your price range) in the area. If you are making flight reservations, you need to know anticipated arrival and departure times and rental car needs.

Pre-registration is held before the conference; you may be involved in setting up the pre-registration in addition to actually registering individuals. Most registration is now done online. Thus, your role may be to design the online registration process and put the appropriate information online. Also, you may be involved in preparing packets of information for the registrants. Often, program information, a list of participants, and a small gift or two are included in the registration packet.

▷ During the Conference

Your responsibilities during the conference may include running errands, delivering messages to participants, and solving problems that may occur. Other responsibilities may include checking room arrangements, equipment needs, meal arrangements, and a multitude of other last-minute details that always occur. Since you are a representative of the company for which you work or the organization of which you are a member, it is imperative that you present a positive image at all times. You also need to keep a smile on your face and handle even the most difficult situations, which may even involve resolving conflicts with the hotel, the caterers, or the participants. The last section of this chapter on conflict resolution will help you be successful at these difficult tasks.

▷ After the Conference

After the conference, your basic duties involve cleaning up and following up. These responsibilities include seeing that all equipment is returned, presenters are assisted with transportation to the airport, letters of appreciation are sent to presenters and others as appropriate, expense reports are filled out, and bills are paid. You may also be responsible for seeing that the proceedings of the conference are published and mailed to participants. Many times, presentations are

The administrative professional needs to be patient even when difficult situations occur at a conference.

© Photodisc

recorded on CDs, with the participants given an option of buying the CDs. You also may be responsible for mailing the CDs to the appropriate individuals.

Conference Evaluation

A post-conference evaluation session should be held with all individuals who worked on the conference. At this meeting, you will need to review what was successful and what was not. A formal evaluation of the conference may have been filled out by participants. If so, evaluations need to be tallied and presented in the post-conference evaluation session. Notes of all issues and/or problems need to be taken and passed on to the organization president so that people involved in the next conference will have the benefit of your experiences. No one ever wants to make the same mistake twice. A record of the problems or issues recorded and passed on to the president will help the next group avoid some mistakes.

> CONFLICT RESOLUTION

Conflict resolution is so needed in our world that seminars and entire books are written on the subject. Numerous companies have personnel in the human

resources offices or in other parts of the organization that specialize in resolving workplace conflicts.

As a successful administrative professional, you will find that you must possess and use conflict resolution skills frequently. You must use these skills with executives and other administrative assistants, in internal meetings with people working in the same organization, on the telephone, or the Web as you communicate with customers or prospective customers. You will also use these skills in your written correspondence with both internal and external audiences. Too many people try to avoid conflict (a noble effort but impossible to totally avoid in the workplace) rather than dealing with it in a positive manner.

If you are to be successful in conflict resolution, you need to develop an attitude of openness and **empathy** (identification with and understanding of another's situation, feelings, and motives) with others. Additionally, you must treat all people equally, never showing favoritism even if the person is your friend. You must continually practice effective conflict resolution skills. Read carefully the next section and commit to becoming an administrative professional who resolves rather than encourages conflict.

Openness

Be open to what others think and feel. State your feelings and thoughts openly without being negative. In other words, use "I" statements about how you feel and what you think should happen. For example, if a conflict erupts about the type of meeting that should be held, you might say, "I suggest we try an online conference rather than a face-to-face meeting. It will save both money and time." You should not say, "You're not thinking! A face-to-face meeting would not be productive in this situation. Twenty people would have to travel from all over the United States, costing both time and money."

Do you see the difference between these two statements? In the first one, you have used an "I" statement and you have stated your reason for suggesting an online conference in a very straightforward but non-threatening manner. In the second statement, you begin by accusing the others involved of not thinking. Such a statement immediately puts the individuals on the defensive.

Empathy

Listen with empathy to what others are saying. Express your concern and support for the other person's opinions. Check your empathy by stating, in your own words, what you understand the other person is saying. You might even say, "This is what I heard you say," and repeat what you believe the person said. Then, you might ask, "Did I hear you correctly?" Do not be closed to the opinions of others. Be willing to change your position if others present appropriate reasons for doing so.

▷ Equality

Give other people time to express their feelings. Evaluate all ideas equally. Do not base your opinion of an idea on whether the person is a friend of yours or whether you like or dislike the individual. Adhere to the communicator's pledge, which is:

> Whether or not I agree or disagree with what you say, I will respect your right to say it and I will try to understand it from your point of view. This, in turn, helps me to communicate my point of view to you more effectively.[7]

▷ Practice Your Skills

This section has given you several suggestions for successfully solving conflicts that may occur in your organization. However, reading by itself will not make a difference; you must *practice* your skills daily if you are to become a truly effective administrative professional—one who not only cares about others but also constantly seeks ways to make the workplace environment more productive. Commit to practicing these ideas daily in your work and school environment. Start by taking one of the suggestions and practicing that suggestion for one week until it becomes part of your method of operation. Then, move to the next suggestion and practice it for one week, along with continuing to practice the first suggestion. Move through the list in this manner until the suggestions have become a part of how you daily respond to your workplace and school environment. Several conflict resolution suggestions are given in Figure 13-12.

| Figure 13-12 | CONFLICT RESOLUTION SUGGESTIONS |

1. Identify what is causing the conflict. Is it power, resources, recognition, or acceptance? Many times our needs for these items are at the heart of the conflict.

2. Determine what each person needs or wants. Ask questions to determine what the other person wants. Be willing to listen to the other person. Everyone feels a deep need to be understood. By satisfying that need in the other person, you may be able to lessen the conflict. If you do not understand what the other person is saying, paraphrase what you think you hear and ask for clarification. Be open to what the other person tells you.

3. Identify points of agreement. Work from these points first. Then identify the points of disagreement.

4. Create a safe environment. Establish a neutral location and a tone that is accepting of the other person's view and feelings. Behind anger may be fear. Let the other person tell you how he or she is feeling. Watch how you position yourself physically in the room. Remember, you have a more difficult time competing with someone who is sitting next to you than with someone who is across the table or room. A circular seating arrangement may be appropriate if you have several individuals involved in a conflict.

5. Do not react. Many times individuals act too quickly when a conflict occurs. Step back, collect your thoughts, and try to see the situation as objectively as possible.

6. Do not seek to win during a confrontation. Negotiate the issues, and translate the negotiation into a lasting agreement.

7. Actively listen. Watch the individual's eyes; notice his or her body language.

8. Separate people from the issue. When the people and the problem are tangled together, the problem becomes difficult to solve. Talk in specifics rather than general terms.

---

[7]Kris Cole, *The Complete Idiot's Guide to Clear Communication* (Australia: Pearson Education, 2000), p. 89.

SUMMARY

Reinforce your learning in this chapter by studying this summary.

- Meetings are a way of life in the workplace, with the number of meetings increasing in organizations rather than decreasing.

- The types of meetings include Board of Directors' meetings, staff meetings, committee/task force meetings, project team meetings, customer/client meetings, and international meetings.

- Effective meetings are well run and well thought out.

- The meeting format is most often face-to-face. However, in our technological world, audio conferences, videoconferences, and webconferences are relatively common.

- With our global business world, international meetings are relatively common. These meetings may be face-to-face meetings or through one of the technological venues.

- The executive's role and responsibilities in meetings include determining the purpose of the meeting, setting the objectives, determining who should attend, determining the number of participants, planning the agenda, and establishing the time and place.

- The leader's role includes being clear as to the purpose and objectives, adhering to the agenda, managing time, encouraging participation, reaching decisions, and evaluating the meeting.

- The participants' responsibilities include being prepared by reviewing the materials provided before the meeting, actively listening and making contributions during the meeting, and doing the necessary work after the meeting such as researching a particular topic and preparing recommendations for the next meeting.

- The administrative professional's responsibilities include confirming the date and time, selecting and preparing the meeting room, determining the seating arrangement, preparing the meeting agenda, preparing the meeting notice, preparing materials for the leader, preparing materials for participants, ordering equipment, ordering food and beverages, handling duties during the meeting, and following up after the meeting (including returning equipment, reviewing what went right and what went wrong in the meeting, and preparing minutes).

- As an administrative professional, you may be responsible for helping organize a conference for your business organization and/or for your professional organization.

- To resolve conflicts that can occur in meetings, an administrative professional needs to develop conflict resolution skills. These skills include being open to what others think and feel, listening to others with empathy, and giving other people the chance to be heard and understood.

GLOSSARY

Agenda—An outline of what will occur at a meeting.

Audioconference—Type of conference in which an unlimited number of participants use a voice input unit to participate in a meeting.

Bylaws—Written policies and procedures that clearly define how board meetings are to be conducted.

Circular and oval arrangements—Work best when the purpose of the meeting is to generate ideas and discussion in a relatively informal meeting.

Co-leader—One member of a team of two members who are in charge.

Committee—Established for an ongoing purpose; e.g., a workplace may have a safety committee that meets regularly to identify and address safety concerns.

Empathy—Identification with and understanding of another's situation, feelings, and motives.

Executive—An individual who has managerial authority in an organization.

Face-to-face meetings—Interacting with people who are in the room with you.

Heterogeneous group—A group with dissimilar backgrounds and experiences.

Homogeneous group—A group with similar backgrounds and experiences.

Leader—Individual who is in charge of the meeting.

Minutes—A record of a meeting.

Participants—Individuals who take part in a meeting.

Project teams—Teams frequently used to accomplish a specific task.

Rectangular arrangement—Allows the leader to maintain control because she or he sits at the head of the table.

Semicircular and U-shaped arrangements—Work well for small groups of six to eight people.

Synergy—The ideas and products of a group of people developed through interaction with each other.

Task force—A committee formed to deal with a specific issue or problem. Once the problem has been handled or solved, the task force is disbanded.

Team leader—Individual who heads a team that is charged with getting some type of task accomplished.

Videoconference—System of transmitting information through a video camera, a microphone, and speakers mounted on the individuals' computers.

Webmeeting—A meeting that takes place over the Web.

Webcast—A type of broadcast that is similar in nature to a television broadcast, except it takes place over the Web.

Webinar—Allows for conducting a seminar over the Web. It enables the presenter to conduct question and answer-type sessions, but does not provide the same degree of interaction as a webmeeting.

CHECKPOINT

Check your understanding of these terms by completing DCD13-a on the Data CD.

DISCUSSION ITEMS

These discussion items provide an opportunity to test your understanding of the chapter through written responses and/or discussion with your classmates and your instructor.

1. List and explain the types of meetings.

2. List and explain three types of meeting formats.

3. Define the role and responsibilities of the executive in meetings.

4. Define the leader's responsibilities in meetings.

5. Define the administrative professional's responsibilities in meetings.

6. List and explain how conflict might be resolved.

CRITICAL THINKING CASE

You are the leader of a team of administrative professionals at JWay Nu-Systems Tech. Your team is charged with reviewing ten applications that have been submitted for a position as an entry-level administrative professional to work for a newly appointed vice-president in the office to be established in Australia by the end of this year. The vice-president wants the administrative professional to be knowledgeable about the home office before assuming the job in Australia. Advertisements were placed in both the

Sydney papers and the Dallas papers. There are two applicants from Australia and eight from Dallas. Your team is to interview the Australian applicants via a videoconference setup. The applicants from Dallas will be interviewed in person. As the leader of the group, you are charged with developing a process for interviewing and the questions that you will use. You will need to research questions that are legal and questions that are illegal. Once a candidate is selected, your team is also to suggest a training process for the new person to learn about JWay. Work with two of your classmates on this project; submit your interviewing and training processes to your instructor, using a report format. Also submit a list of the sources you used.

RESPONSES TO SELF-CHECK

A
The correct responses are:

1. Clear as to the purpose and objectives of the meeting.

2. Set the timeframe of the meeting to accomplish objectives.

3. Adhere to the agenda.

4. Manage time.

5. Encourage participation.

6. Reach decisions.

7. Evaluate the meeting.

B
The correct responses are: (Any six of the following may be given.)

1. Confirm the date and time. Mondays and Friday afternoons generally should be avoided.
2. Select and prepare the meeting room. Room arrangements should be made immediately after the date and time are known. Select a room that is of the appropriate size—not too small or too large. Check the temperature controls; be certain that the lighting is adequate and appropriate equipment is available.
3. Determine the seating arrangement. The five basic seating arrangements are rectangular, circular, oval, semicircular, and U-shaped.
4. Prepare the meeting agenda. The agenda should be sent out at least two days before the meeting and preferably a week before. The agenda should include the following information: name of the meeting or group, date, start and end times, location, order of agenda items, person responsible for presenting each agenda item, actions expected on each item, and background materials.
5. Prepare the meeting notices. The meeting notification should include the purpose and objectives of the meeting; meeting agenda; location, date, and time; background information; and assigned materials for preparation.
6. Prepare materials for the leader. The materials should include the meeting notice with a list of the people who will attend and materials needed for the meeting.
7. Prepare materials for participants. Background materials (if needed) should be sent to participants. Handout materials (if appropriate), pads of paper, and folders with pens are often necessary.
8. Order equipment. Make a list of the equipment needed and who is responsible for obtaining each item.
9. Order food and beverages. For a morning meeting, coffee, tea, and juice can be provided. For an afternoon meeting, soft drinks and coffee are generally appropriate. For a luncheon meeting, you will probably have the responsibility of selecting the menu and making arrangements with the caterer. For a dinner meeting at a hotel, you can expect assistance from the hotel staff.
10. Handle duties during the meeting. Your main responsibilities during the meeting include taking minutes.
11. Follow-up after the meeting. Handle routine tasks such as returning equipment, sending out follow-up memos, and evaluating the meeting.
12. Prepare minutes. If minutes are necessary, they should be prepared and distributed within 24 to 48 hours of a meeting.

PROJECT 13-1: PREPARE A REPORT

Explain the frequency and cost of meetings (Objective 1)

Describe the various types of meetings (Objective 2)

Using the Web, research the various types of meetings that businesses conduct, along with the frequency and estimated cost of meetings. Prepare a short report for your instructor (two to three pages), using footnotes for your sources. In addition, check with an administrator in your college concerning the types of meetings conducted in the college (online, face-to-face, etc.) and the estimated cost of these meetings. Include this information in the report that you submit to your instructor.

PROJECT 13-2 PREPARE A REPORT

Explain the characteristics of effective meetings (Objective 3)

Describe the responsibilities of the executive in meetings (Objective 5)

Describe the responsibilities of the administrative professional in assisting with meetings and conferences (Objective 6)

Develop conflict resolution skills (Objective 7)

Rebecca Edwards was promoted to office manager for JWay Nu-Systems Tech four months ago. One of her duties is to meet with all administrative professionals once each month. The first month, she was so inundated with work that she did not have a meeting of the administrative professionals. She has called a meeting the last three months. She has not sent out an agenda for the meetings; her feeling was that the group needed to decide what they wanted to discuss. The first meeting was set for 10 a.m.; half the group was not there at 10, so Rebecca suggested to the group that they wait for the others before beginning the meeting. At 10:30, all members finally appeared. Rebecca opened the meeting by saying that she did not have an agenda; she asked that the group talk about their needs and issues. People said very little, although a few "gripes" were stated. Rebecca (at approximately 11 a.m.) dismissed the group.

At the next meeting, Rebecca again did not send out an agenda; she felt the group needed more time to get to know each other before they began to participate in a significant manner. Although the time for the second meeting remained at 10 a.m., again the group members did not appear on time. The meeting actually

started at 10:35 a.m. More members entered into the session by talking about their complaints and naming "names" of individuals that they felt were incompetent. Two of the administrative professionals talked extensively about their perceived inefficiency of JWay management. Again, Rebecca listened. By the third meeting, Rebecca decided that the group was a "bunch of complainers" and she suggested to the group that they meet only twice each year. The group responded that they really saw no reason to be meeting at all. Rebecca did not accept their suggestions, stating that it was important to meet at least twice each year.

If you were the leader of the group, what would you do differently? As you answer, explain the characteristics of an effective meeting, describe an appropriate meeting format for the meeting with the administrative professionals; describe the role and responsibilities of the participants (in this case the administrative professionals at JWay). Explain how Rebecca can get the meetings with the administrative professionals "on track." Describe Rebecca's role in these meetings. Submit your answers to these questions to your instructor in report format.

PROJECT 13-3 PREPARE A REPORT

Describe the responsibilities of the executive in meetings (Objective 5)

Describe the responsibilities of the administrative professional in assisting with meetings and conferences (Objective 6)

Attend a meeting of a professional organization—either a club you are a member of at your college or a professional organization. Take notes at the meeting, and key your notes in the form of a report. Describe the role and responsibilities of the leader/executive, the role and responsibility of the assistant (person taking notes), and the role and responsibilities of the participants. Evaluate the success of the meeting and the effectiveness of the leader and the participants. Were visuals used, such as PowerPoint slides? If so, were they effective? Report your findings to the class and submit your report to your instructor.

PROJECT 13-4 ADD TO YOUR PROFESSIONAL GROWTH PLAN

Develop conflict resolution skills (Objective 7)

Add to your Professional Growth Plan by determining how you will develop conflict resolution skills. Save your plan as PGP13-4.

COMMUNICATION POWER

Use DCD13-b to assist you in improving your grammar skills.

ASSESSMENT OF CHAPTER OBJECTIVES

Now that you have completed the chapter and the projects, take a few minutes to review the chapter learning objectives. For your convenience, the objectives are repeated here. Did you accomplish these objectives? If you were unable to accomplish the objectives, give your reasons for not doing so; be specific and concise. Your instructor may prefer that your answers be submitted to her or him. If so, DCD13-c contains the Assessment of Chapter Objectives. Complete the Assessment of Chapter Objectives; submit your results to your instructor.

1. Explain the frequency and cost of meetings.　　　　　　　Yes ☐　　No ☐

　　_____

　　_____

　　_____

2. Describe the various types of meetings.　　　　　　　　Yes ☐　　No ☐

　　_____

　　_____

　　_____

3. Explain the characteristics of effective meetings.　　　　Yes ☐　　No ☐

　　_____

　　_____

　　_____

4. Determine meeting formats.　　　　　　　　　　　　　Yes ☐　　No ☐

　　_____

　　_____

　　_____

5. Describe the responsibilities of the executive in meetings.　Yes ☐　　No ☐

　　_____

　　_____

　　_____

6. Describe the responsibilities of the administrative professional in assisting with meetings and conferences.　　　　　　　　　　　　　　　　　Yes ☐　　No ☐

　　_____

　　_____

　　_____

7. Develop conflict resolution skills.　　　　　　　　　　Yes ☐　　No ☐

　　_____

　　_____

　　_____

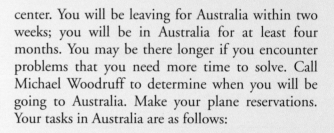

PART V: MAIL, TRAVEL, MEETINGS, AND CONFERENCES

Integrated Project

Note: You are to work in a team of three on this project.

You have been asked to take a position as office manager for JWay Nu-Systems Tech. You have worked for JWay for one year and enjoy your job tremendously. You believe you do a good job, and the president, Jana Portosky, has told you a number of times that you have supervisory skills. She is encouraging you to take the position; she has assured you that it will be challenging and that you will also have additional growth opportunities from this position.

Because you are not certain that you want to be in a supervisory position, you have asked Ms. Portosky if you might work on two or three projects that involve managing people and tasks. You feel that such an experience would give you a greater understanding of what a full-time job in this area would entail and whether or not your skill sets are the right ones for such a position. Ms. Portosky readily agrees that your idea is a good one; she asks that you check with human resources to determine what projects they might have available for you to do. You agree to tell Ms. Portosky in four months whether or not you are interested in a full-time supervisory position.

After talking with human resources, you accept your first supervisory task. Here is what you are asked to do.

Your Assignment

As you know, JWay will open a center in Australia at the end of this fiscal year. You will report to the manager for this center, Michael Woodruff. He is already in Australia and has located a building that JWay has purchased; this building will house the call center. You will be leaving for Australia within two weeks; you will be in Australia for at least four months. You may be there longer if you encounter problems that you need more time to solve. Call Michael Woodruff to determine when you will be going to Australia. Make your plane reservations. Your tasks in Australia are as follows:

Task I   Develop your job description after your discussion with Michael Woodruff.

Task II   You will need to employ three call center assistants; one of the assistants must speak Chinese. (Note: In the Integrated Project for Part IV, you were asked to develop a job description and a training program for call center assistants. The job description and training program were accepted by management. Review your suggestions before you begin this assignment. Assume that your recommendation in Part IV was that one call center assistant should speak Chinese.) You will interview and hire three call center assistants for the office in Australia.

Task III   Train the assistants using the plan you developed in Integrated Project IV; if you discover necessary modifications to the plan, make the modifications.

Task IV   As you work in this new supervisory capacity, start a daily log of what went right and what did not, what you are learning about management, and where your skills need to be improved.

Jana Portosky has asked to receive copies of all correspondence that you have with Mr. Woodruff.

As a group, submit your report to your instructor.

José Rego
President
truVOICE Consulting, Inc.
Miami, Florida

SPOTLIGHT *on Success*

establish myself in the training and development field. With the coaching of a mentor, I began to take small steps in creating a portfolio that would reflect the qualifications that would help me achieve my objective.

TO WHAT DO I ATTRIBUTE MY SUCCESS?

Right out of high school with the ability to type 92 wpm, my first job was as an assistant to my father's secretary. Many of the principles my father has taught me are the solid rocks upon which I have built my career. And to say that "I have built my career" is something that brings up an incredible sense of pride in me. What success I enjoy today I attribute to a combination of influential factors that continue to play an important role in my day-to-day life, and the important realization that in order to maintain a steady flow of in-bound success and accomplishments, I *must* constantly be giving back.

WHAT IS MY BACKGROUND?

In the nearly 20 years that I worked as an administrative professional in corporate America, I had the opportunity to work with some pretty spectacular corporations. And even though it took that long to recognize what my true career calling was, I could not bear considering the possibility that all that time had been wasted, as my new profession had little relation (if any) to the administrative career in which I had invested so much time and effort. By the time the year 2000 rolled around, I made it my number one objective to make a change in my career and

TO WHAT PROFESSIONAL ORGANIZATIONS DO I BELONG?

I remember how joining the International Association of Administrative Professionals® (IAAP) benefited me professionally. Membership in professional associations that focus on the field we are a part of has proven to provide added knowledge and skill that allow you to succeed in that field. I took all the necessary steps to become a member of the American Society for Training & Development (ASTD), the leading organization for training professionals, and focused on learning as much as possible about the training industry. At the recommendation of my sponsor, I attended a National Speakers Association (NSA) convention in Philadelphia.

WHAT DOES HAVING A SPONSOR/ MENTOR MEAN?

Having a *sponsor/mentor* is not a luxury, but an important element of success. My mentor never advised me on what to do, but rather what *not* to do—especially in those instances when I was about to take on more than I could handle or projects in areas in which I did not have enough expertise. My mentor is a trainer and speaker who tailors her efforts and programs strictly to the administrative profession. She invested time and energy in our friendship and guided me though the process of realizing my life calling. While she helped me to see what my career path opportunities were, she also helped me understand that the knowledge and skills I had gained as an

Chapter 14:	*Job Search*
Chapter 15:	*Teleworker/Virtual Assistant*
Chapter 16:	*Leadership Skills*

administrative professional were not to be taken for granted. Today I constantly look for the opportunity to sponsor or mentor people at different stages of their career, in the hope that they can find the same satisfaction in their work that I have found.

As a result of my hard work, focus, and clearly defined objectives, I was offered a fantastic opportunity as an instructor with the world's largest train-the-trainer company—Langevin Learning Services—which I have the pleasure and honor to represent today. I most certainly still work very hard, and there are still days filled with last-minute decisions and challenges . . . but I face them with a smile on my face and joy in my heart because I am following my heart's desire and my true calling. As an instructor with Langevin, I spend about 70 percent of my time traveling to conduct workshops all around the world. I have had the opportunity to visit Canada, Australia, Mexico, Indonesia, and other destinations. I have enjoyed getting to know many wonderful cities. When I am not traveling, I work from home, preparing lesson plans, customizing workshop agendas for private clients, and helping other instructors prepare their workshops. The background and experience I acquired during my many years in the administrative profession were key elements in helping me establish my home office and performing my administrative responsibilities. Without that experience I would not be able to stay organized and handle the stack of paperwork on my desk.

WHAT IS THE MOST FUN PART OF MY JOB?

I have the most fun when I encounter a challenge in the training class or at speaking engagements, which motivate me to work even harder. I know I will receive the same positive energy back in return for my effort. I have learned that life is like a boomerang and what I send will return to me ten-fold. When we do something we love, it ceases to be "work" and becomes an adventure and a discovery expedition toward who and what we are to become. Knowing this helps me deal with a stressful travel schedule and the increasing demands of the industry I love so much.

WHAT IS THE MOST CHALLENGING PART OF MY JOB?

It is indeed a true challenge to maintain my full-time job with Langevin (as it remains my primary source of income) while I grow my own business . . . but I simply cannot resist the desire to share with others the magnificent lessons and experiences that life has bestowed upon me. Emptying my bucket into others' with all the incredible tools, knowledge, and skills I have learned only serves as a conduit for refilling my bucket again and again. I believe that every person has a *gift* or *talent* that sets him or her apart from everyone else. I also believe that the only way to keep and grow that gift is to share it with others. A gift is not a "gift" until it is given . . . if all we do is keep it to ourselves, then it remains simply a possession.

WHAT ADVICE WOULD I GIVE SOMEONE JUST BEGINNING THIS PROFESSION?

When people ask me what my advice would be for the future I tell them, "Use the future to energize you, but don't dwell in it. Use the present to increase your skills and abilities. If you are unhappy or feel unfulfilled with your current professional situation, find something you absolutely LOVE to do—something that complements your values and gives you the opportunity to be the best YOU you can be."

JOSÉ REGO—CASE STUDY

I recently conducted a three-day workshop. As I started to get acquainted with the participants, it became clear that this was a group of extroverts and highly participative people. They enjoyed discussions and voicing their opinions.

One of the participants had a substantial amount of experience, resulting in his undermining the perspectives and opinions of the other participants at his table. All of his comments were about "when I did this," or "this is what I did."

The other participants at his table believed that he was being too controlling, unwilling to consider anybody else's perspectives. The group dynamics at his table became so difficult for other people to handle that I had to change seating arrangements three times on the first day of the workshop. I even approached him individually. I explained how valuable his years of experience were to the process and asked him to allow others to participate as well. He agreed but the situation did not change much. Basically, he was determined to voice his "expertise" at all times (including breaks).

On the second day of the workshop, he was at a new table—again. This time one of the younger and less experienced participants, who was determined to get the most out of the workshop experience, was sitting at his table. While the group was debriefing an exercise, our "expert" had a comment or rebuttal about anything anyone said. When it came time for his table to participate in the debriefing, the young woman sitting in the group attempted time and time again to voice her perspective, each time being interrupted by our "expert." After noticing her frustration over and over, I made a point to address her attempts to voice her opinion. I looked straight at her and asked, "What was the perspective you wanted to offer?" She promptly replied, "Well, I was going to say something, but I have been interrupted so many times, I forgot." And with that said, I called a ten-minute break.

What happened? What turned the expert around? See page 433 for the case solution.

CHAPTER 14

JOB SEARCH

Learning Objectives

1. Review your skills, abilities, and interests.
2. Identify sources of job information.
3. Become familiar with various organizations.
4. Prepare a letter of application and a résumé.
5. Develop job interview skills.
6. Commit to living your values in the workplace.

© Getty Images/Photodisc

> REVIEW YOUR SKILLS AND INTERESTS

Throughout this course, you improved your skills and positioned yourself to become an administrative professional. Stop now and reflect for a few minutes on your skills. And, as you reflect on both your hard skills (computer competency, writing skills, presentation skills, and others) and your soft skills (interpersonal, teamwork, and verbal communication, for example), you need to analyze what all of this means for your career path. Where do you think your hard skills and soft skills will best fit? What type of organization interests you? Long term, where do you want your career path to go? The days when an organization took care of its employees' career development are over. Your grandparents and possibly your parents may have worked for one organization all of their lives. However, it is highly unlikely you will do so. You will be responsible for your own growth and career path; sometimes changing jobs is a part of that growth. You need to develop proficiency in not only looking for a job, but also in finding one that will make the most of your strengths and the directions you wish your career to go. Stop for a few moments to review your strengths and your weaknesses and consider where you want to be in five or ten years.

Once you have seriously taken the reflective step of thinking about what your skills are and where you want to go, you are ready to begin thinking about the steps you must take to identify a job that fits your skills and what you want to achieve. Complete Self Checks A and B on page 344 now.

> DETERMINE SOURCES OF JOB INFORMATION

One of the first things to do as you look for a job is to get all the information you can about available job opportunities. Information is available through the sources listed here.

- ▶ The Web
- ▶ Networking
- ▶ College placement offices
- ▶ Newspaper advertisements
- ▶ United States Federal Government, United States Postal Service, and state governments
- ▶ Employment agencies
- ▶ Walk-ins

▷ The Web

The Web has a variety of resources for job seekers, including tips for résumé and cover letter preparation and interviewing. Additionally, many organizations now allow you to post your résumé directly on their website. You will learn more about writing and posting résumés on the Web under the section titled "Electronic Résumé."

Here are several websites that provide job search information and allow you to post your résumé.

- ▶ www.careerbuilder.com
- ▶ www.careerjournal.com
- ▶ www.JOBcentral.com
- ▶ www.flipdog.com
- ▶ www.hotjobs.yahoo.com
- ▶ www.monster.com
- ▶ www.eurojobs.com

These websites allow you to browse by company, industry, location (country, state, city), and by pay. Additionally, on these sites you may post your résumé, network, and get advice on successful job application techniques. Figure 14-1 shows sample information that you may find in an administrative professional job opening.

CHECK A

As you reflect on your skills (both hard and soft), ask yourself these questions.

1. What are my strengths?

_____
_____
_____

2. What are my weaknesses?

_____
_____
_____

CHECK B

Where do I want to take my career?

1. What type(s) of organization will fit my skills best?

_____
_____

2. What do I want to achieve in the future? Where do I want my career to go?

_____
_____
_____

Figure 14-1 ADMINISTRATIVE PROFESSIONAL JOB OPENING

Credentials
Two to five years of relevant work experience

Duties and Responsibilities
Accounts receivable/accounts payable
Management of internal database reporting
Management of human resource activities, policy, and guidelines
Data entry/invoicing/database management
Correspondence with management, sales team, and advisors

Requirements
Full-time position
Salary based on experience
Medical benefits and retirement plan

▷ Networking

You have probably heard any number of times about the importance of networking when searching for a job. How is networking defined? Here is one definition.

Definition

Networking may be defined as any face-to-face contact with a person who hires or supervises a person with your skills—even if they are not presently able to extend a job offer.[1] Most of us already have an extensive social network including our relatives, friends, and others. Your task as you begin to think about looking for a job includes developing a job-working network. How do you do that? Here are some suggested steps.

Steps

Step 1: Let people know that you are searching for a job. Contact individuals you know who work for firms where you would like to work. Ask for leads and referrals.

Step 2: Contact professional organizations. For example, you may contact the local chapter of IAAP. Contact administrative professionals who are already employed. Contact managers that you know; ask for referrals for any job openings that exist. Try to obtain at least three or four names from each person with whom you speak.

Step 3: Ask administrative professionals who are employed in the field how they obtained their positions and what they like or dislike about their jobs.

Step 4: Keep a record of every person with whom you talk—his or her e-mail or telephone number and any comments.

Figure 14-2 gives additional networking tips.

▷ College Placement Offices

Many colleges and universities have placement offices. The counselors in these offices aid students

Figure 14-2 NETWORKING TIPS

- ▶ Make yourself visible.

- ▶ Attend and volunteer to work at professional conferences.

- ▶ Have a positive attitude and talk positively about your skills.

- ▶ Develop a portfolio.

- ▶ Be honest about yourself.

- ▶ Be persistent and patient.

- ▶ Be articulate.

- ▶ Capitalize on your strengths.

- ▶ Decide to be a winner.[2]

---

[1]"Career Center, Networking," <http://career.boisestate.edu/networking.html> (accessed July 9, 2005).
[2]Ibid., (accessed July 9, 2005).

Networking can help you find a job that fits your abilities and interests.

© Photodisc/Keith Brofsky

in career planning. Job fairs are a relatively common type of service offered to students. Business people invited to these fairs include representatives from major companies in the area who are seeking employees.

Additional services offered by placement offices include:

▶ Materials on specific careers.
▶ Writing assistance for application letters and résumés.
▶ Interviewing assistance.
▶ Testing.

You will want to visit the placement office in your college (assuming one is available) for assistance that the personnel in this office can provide.

▷ Newspaper Advertisements

Although job advertisements are carried in most newspapers all week, the Sunday newspaper is generally

the paper that carries the most possibilities. Look in the Jobs Section and under Administrative Professionals and/or Secretaries for the jobs.

▷ United States Federal and State Government

Federal government jobs are available through their website—http://www.usajobs.opm.gov. This website allows you to choose the location you desire (U.S. Government jobs throughout the world are listed), the job category, and the salary range or pay grade range desired.

You may also want to review the positions available on the United States Postal Service website and state government positions available through individual state government websites.

▷ Employment Agencies

There are two types of employment agencies—private and state-operated. Tax dollars support **state-operated employment agencies.** You can take advantage of the free services provided by these agencies. **Private employment agencies** charge a fee for their services. When private employment agencies advertise jobs in newspapers, they may include the word **fee-paid,** meaning the employer pays the fee. However, you may be responsible for paying the fee. If you go to a private employment agency, ask who is paying the fee and the amount. If you are, ask the amount. You may be required to sign a contract with a private agency. The contract should include the fee, if required. Read the contract carefully before signing it. However, you may not be asked to pay a fee; the employer often pays the fee. Private employment agencies are responsible for approximately 3 percent to 5 percent of all hires nationally.[3]

Some agencies also provide temporary work possibilities. If you are uncertain about the type or size of organization where you want to work, you might want to work in several organizations as a temporary employee for a period of time. Without any long-term commitment, you can gain an understanding of where you want to work as a full-time employee.

▷ Walk-Ins

If you are interested in obtaining a position with a certain organization or in a particular type of business, going directly to the business or organization may yield successful results. Individuals who are

---

[3]ACAP: Employment Assistance, <http://www.acap.army.mil/transitioner/presep/chapter3/3m.cfm> (accessed July 9, 2005).

most successful using this approach are those who have a gift for selling themselves. Before you engage in this approach, find out as much as you can about the organizations you plan to visit. Knowledge of the organization where you are applying is always helpful, no matter what job approach you select. Never restrict your job search to walk-ins only. It can be a time-consuming process, often with little success. Additionally, you must be able to handle rejection. However, you cannot take rejection personally; you may receive more "we have no openings" than "we are hiring for several positions." If you do use the walk-in approach as one of your approaches, be certain to dress professionally and take several copies of your résumé. Prepare to make a professional impression.

> BECOME FAMILIAR WITH VARIOUS ORGANIZATIONS

Once you have identified organizations of interest to you, spend time learning about the organization—its mission and vision, its financial history, its products or services, its reputation, the length of time it has been in business and how it treats employees. How do you do this? There are several possibilities. However, with so many organizations having websites today, the best place to start is probably the company's website. Read everything on the site, paying particular attention to its mission and vision statement and the directions of the organization. Other suggestions for finding information about the organization include:

▸ Reading periodicals that profile organizations within the United States. *Fortune* provides a list of the 200 *Best Companies to Work for in America, 100 Fastest Growing Companies, America's Best Companies for Minorities,* and *America's Most Admired Corporations. Working Mothers Magazine* lists the *100 Best Companies for Working Mothers. Latina Style* lists the *50 Best Companies for Latinos to Work for in the USA.* Forbes lists *The 200 Best Small Companies.*
▸ Ask friends, relatives, and acquaintances what they know about the organization.
▸ Obtain an annual report of the company; usually you can get one by asking the company to send it to you.
▸ Consult your local chamber of commerce.
▸ Ask your college placement office for information.

Spotlight on

JOB PREPARATION

Give thought to the type of organization in which you would like to work. Then spend time researching organizations by checking out websites and asking friends about organizations.

When evaluating an organization, you will probably want to find answers to the following questions:

1. What is the organization's service or product?
2. Is the organization multinational? Does the organization have branches in other states?
3. What has been the profit picture of the organization for the last several years?
4. Is the organization financially secure?
5. Is the organization growing?
6. What is the reputation of its chief executive officer?
7. Does the organization have a good reputation in the community?
8. Is there a good relationship between the employer and employees?
9. Is the organization an equal opportunity employer?
10. Are there opportunities for advancement?

> PREPARE YOUR LETTER OF APPLICATION

The letter of application is generally the first contact you have with a potential employer and the key, along with your résumé, to obtaining an interview. It is a sales letter, with the purpose being to sell your abilities. The person reading your letter gets a favorable or unfavorable impression of you from the content of your letter, your writing skills, and the format of the letter. Certainly, this letter must be free of keying or spelling errors. If you make mistakes in the letter, you have little chance of getting an interview. Think of this letter as your chance to say to a prospective employer, "I am the person who can do the job; my work is always well written and free of errors." Conversely, a poorly written letter, with keying and English errors, suggests that you are disorganized, sloppy, unfocused, and ill suited for employment.

The basic goals of a letter of application are as follows:

- State your interest in the position.
- Provide general information about your skills (specific information appears in your résumé), and sell your skills (let the reader know you have something to offer the organization).
- Transmit your résumé.
- Request an interview, providing your contact information.

▷ Use Proper Format

If you need a review of letter and punctuation styles, refer to page 414 of the *Reference Guide.* Standard block style is the most commonly used style; however, modified block style is also appropriate. Mixed punctuation, with a colon after the salutation and a comma after the complimentary close, is the most often used punctuation style. Figure 14-3 gives several tips for writing application letters. You may be posting your letter and résumé online. This possibility will be discussed in a later section of this chapter.

Figure 14-4 provides an example of a letter of application for your review. Notice that the three basic goals of a letter of application are followed carefully in the three paragraphs of the letter. Notice that the top of the letter includes your address, telephone number, and e-mail. Your résumé will also include this information; however, if your letter and résumé get separated, this approach allows the organization to contact you.

▷ Address the Letter Appropriately

Be certain that you address the letter appropriately. Reread the address several times and proof the address that you have keyed against the position advertisement. Clearly, you do not want to key the wrong title, misspell the recipient's name, or even send it to the wrong person. Never use *To Whom It May Concern* as a salutation. If a name is not given in the job vacancy notice, use the organization and address given, with *Ladies and Gentlemen* as a salutation.

▷ Refrain from Using *I* Frequently

The use of the word *I* excessively may cause the reader to think you are self-absorbed, pushy, or boastful. You do not want to portray these characteristics in your letter. Notice that in Figure 14-4, *I* is used only three times.

Figure 14-3   TIPS FOR WRITING APPLICATION LETTERS

1. Research the organization before writing your letter. One good source of information for most organizations is their website.

2. Key the letter in proper form using an acceptable letter style.

3. Print your letter on high-quality bond paper. Office supply stores sell paper recommended for use in writing letters of application and résumés.

4. Use correct spelling, punctuation, capitalization, and grammar. Use the spell and grammar check on your computer.

5. Keep the letter short; put details in the résumé.

6. Address the letter to a specific person. Do not address an application letter "To Whom It May Concern." If you do not have a name, call the company or check with the placement office, agency, or person who told you about the job.

7. Send an original letter for each application. Do not send photocopies. Do not assume one letter is appropriate for all organizations. Personalize each letter by reading and writing to the job notice published by the organization.

8. Do not copy a letter of application from a book. Make the letter representative of your personality.

9. Use three paragraphs—an opening paragraph in which you provide a brief statement of your interest, a middle paragraph in which you describe your abilities, and a closing paragraph in which you request an interview, providing your contact information.

10. If you do not own a printer that produces quality work, have your cover letter and résumé professionally printed.

Figure 14-4 **LETTER OF APPLICATION**

2445 Edgecliff Road
Dallas, TX 75034-1859
vre5@web.com
972-555-6655

May 21, 2006

Ms. Jean LeJuan
Human Resources Department
JWay Nu-Systems Tech
1510 Eastern Drive
Dallas, TX 75275-0356

Dear Ms. LeJuan:

Your announcement for an administrative assistant posted on the Employment Opportunities page of your website is most appealing to me. After reading the qualifications you are seeking, I believe my skills and experience make me a strong candidate.

My qualifications include the following:
▸ An associate degree in administrative systems from Mountain Peak College
▸ One year of work experience in the field
▸ Excellent human relations and communications skills
▸ Knowledge of computer software, including Microsoft Word, Excel, and PowerPoint

My résumé, which gives further details about my experiences and skills, is enclosed. May I have the opportunity to discuss my qualifications with you? I will call you next week to arrange a meeting at your convenience.

Sincerely,

Vivian R. Edwards

Vivian R. Edwards

Enclosure: Résumé

> PREPARE YOUR RÉSUMÉ

The **résumé,** a concise statement of your background, education, skills, and experience, is an important part of your job application packet. Just as the letter of application is a sales letter, so is the résumé. It represents a very important product—you. Today, résumés are often posted on the Web. "Electronic Résumé," a section later in this chapter, deals with several of the nuances of posting online. Although much of the information included on a traditional résumé is the same as should be included on an online résumé, there are some differences. This section covers submitting the résumé by mail or in person. A number of résumé writing tips are given in Figure 14-5. Figure 14-6 lists a number of action verbs that might be used.

There are three general types of résumés—chronological, functional, and targeted/combination style. In determining the type of résumé to prepare, you must consider your purpose and your background.

> Chronological Résumé

The **chronological résumé** is the most common and most preferred format for a résumé. In a chronological résumé, your work experience is presented in reverse chronological order (your most recent jobs presented first). This style works well for showing progress and growth if the jobs listed reflect increasing responsibility. Figure 14-7 illustrates the format of a typical résumé in chronological order. Just as there is an appropriate use of the chronological résumé, so is there an inappropriate use. Figure 14-8 gives several appropriate and inappropriate uses of a chronological résumé.

> Functional Résumé

The **functional résumé** allows you to concentrate on those skills and abilities that are more applicable to the job you are seeking. In this type of résumé, the same information is included as in a chronological résumé; however, the organization is different. Your education, experiences, and activities are clustered into categories that support your career goals. The functional résumé works well for individuals who have good educational backgrounds and skills but little or no work experience. It also works well if there are periods when an individual did not work; for example, if a woman took a break from her career to have a

---

Figure 14-5 TIPS FOR PREPARING RÉSUMÉS

Target your résumé to each job. Highlight those areas of your background or work experience that fit the position you want.

▸ If you are a recent graduate and have held only part-time jobs, list them.

▸ If you have not had any paid work experience, list volunteer jobs or leadership positions you have held. Do not insert a category and write "none" under it. If you have nothing to list under the work experience category, omit it from your résumé.

▸ Be accurate and honest.

▸ Keep the résumé concise—one or two pages preferably.

▸ Do not use personal pronouns (I, me, you). They are unnecessary and detract from the impact of the résumé.

▸ Describe your qualifications and skills in specific terms; avoid vague language.

▸ Check your spelling and grammar usage. Many employers discard a résumé if just one spelling, typographical, or grammatical error appears. Do not rely totally on the grammar and spell check feature on your computer. This program does not find all errors, and some errors noted are not errors. You must pay careful attention to the grammar and format. Read and reread the résumé several times, and ask someone else who is a good proofreader and grammarian to read it also.

▸ Avoid using abbreviations, with the exception of your degree.

▸ Take advantage of professional help in writing your résumé. Check Web sources, talk with your college placement representatives, and visit a bookstore or library for materials on résumé preparation.

▸ Print your résumé on quality paper.

▸ Emphasize action verbs; Figure 14-6 lists a number of action verbs.

▸ Never use an email address such as fungirl@msn.com or partyhappy@msn.com, or some equally unprofessional address. Do use a professional, neutral email address, such as rlsmith@yahoo.com.

Figure 14-6 ACTION VERBS

Listed here (by categories) are a few action verbs that might be used.

Creative Skills	Communication	Technical skills
Acted	Arranged	Adapted
Composed	Authored	Applied
Created	Composed	Assembled
Designed	Defined	Calculated
Illustrated	Described	Designed
Initiated	Edited	Developed
Modified	Influenced	Installed
Planned	Involved	Maintained[4]

child. The functional résumé de-emphasizes the gaps and emphasizes skill sets. Figure 14-9 shows a functional résumé. Figure 14-10 lists several appropriate and inappropriate uses of the functional résumé.

⊳ Targeted/Combination Résumé

The **targeted/combination résumé** allows you to target a specific position through the use of an objective. The subsequent information provided allows you to support that objective.

The targeted/combination résumé is appropriate to use in the following situations:

▸ You know exactly which position or type of job you are pursuing.
▸ You are considering several different fields of work and are willing to compose separate résumés for each different job you may pursue.
▸ You know the type of work you want to pursue and your work history may be sketchy.
▸ You want to present related skills and experience gained through volunteer work, school projects, or internships.

A targeted/combination résumé is not appropriate in these situations:

▸ You prefer to use only one résumé for a variety of jobs.
▸ You are not clear about your job direction.

Figure 14-11 gives an example of a targeted/combination résumé.

⊳ Résumé Parts

The résumé has seven basic parts:

1. Heading
2. Career objective
3. Education
4. Relevant skills/professional skills
5. Work experience/employment history
6. Accomplishments
7. Professional affiliations (if there are numerous affiliations that relate to the job) and military service

These headings may have different names. In preparing your résumé headings, pay attention to the words that most clearly state your credentials. Also, these headings may appear in different order on the résumé. Figures 14-7, 14-9, and 14-11 give examples of different types of résumés. Notice on these résumés that the sections are not labeled exactly the same. However, the types of information included are quite similar and correspond to the seven basic parts listed here.

Although there is some disagreement among writers in the field, many experts advocate not putting references on your résumé. The résumé is a place to highlight work experiences and skills. However, you should have a list of references prepared. The reference list should be taken with you to all job interviews; you may need to list them on an application, or the interviewer may ask you for them.

---

[4]"Action Verbs Checklist," <http://www.careers.pitt.edu/cybercounselor/jobtoolboxresumes.htm> (accessed August 2, 2005).

Figure 14-7 CHRONOLOGICAL RÉSUMÉ

VIVIAN R. EDWARDS
2445 Edgecliff Road
Dallas, TX 75034-1859
972-555-6655
e-mail: vre5@web.com

CAREER OBJECTIVE
A position as an administrative assistant with the opportunity to use technology and human relations skills

EDUCATION
Mountain Peak College, Dallas, Texas, August 2004 to May 2006
Associate Degree in Administrative Systems
Courses studied: Business communications, organizational behavior, management, English, psychology, administrative procedures, and computer software

COMPUTER SKILLS
Keyboarding at 100 wpm; proficient in Word, Excel, Access, PowerPoint, Internet research, and Web page design

EMPLOYMENT HISTORY
Intern, Admissions Department, Mountain Peak College, September 2004 to May 2006

- Prepared spreadsheets using Excel
- Keyed correspondence using Microsoft Word
- Prepared first draft of admission letters for students
- Filed correspondence on hard drive and disks
- Handled student inquiries
- Answered the telephone
- Assisted in designing class schedules

Records Management Assistant, LakeSide Manufacturing, September 2000 to August 2004

- Maintained computer records for entire company
- Assisted new clerical employees in setting up appropriate records storage methods

Receptionist, Martin Technology, Inc., January 1997 to August 2000

- Greeted visitors
- Answered the telephone
- Keyed correspondence

ACTIVITIES/HONORS

- Speech Club
- Service Learning—tutored two 10th-grade girls
- Delivered food for the Meals on Wheels program
- Most Outstanding Student, Business Department

Figure 14-8	APPROPRIATE AND INAPPROPRIATE USES OF THE CHRONOLOGICAL RÉSUMÉ

Appropriate Use

1. You have a good record of job stability (minimum of two years for each position held).

2. You want to emphasize your strong abilities and stability.

3. You are interested in several different types of positions.

4. You have held a few jobs over a long time.

5. The name of your employers will add credibility to your credentials.

Inappropriate Use

1. Your work history demonstrates a lack of job stability.

2. You are seeking your first job.

3. You are re-entering the workforce after a long time.[5]

Get in touch with your references before a job search. Let them know you are looking for a job, and ask whether you can use them as a reference. Confirm the addresses and phone numbers of your references, as well as their current employment and job title/duties. A thoroughly completed reference section on an application can be a determining factor in the hiring of one applicant over another.

Electronic Résumé

The term **electronic résumé** can have a number of different meanings including the following:

- A résumé that is pasted into the body of an e-mail message
- A file sent as an e-mail attachment

- A résumé posted on a job hunting database or website such as Monster.com.
- A Web page created by a jobseeker

A study conducted in 2004 showed these statistics concerning Internet hiring.

1. Employee referrals and the Internet accounted for 61.3 percent of all external hires in 2004, up from 53.6 percent in 2002.

2. Employee hires from online employment destinations accounted for 39.7 percent of all hires. According to employers, 53.3 percent of new hires came via the Internet to their corporate website.[6]

Additionally, according to research conducted by another source, 92.4 percent of all people looking for a job are likely to visit a corporate website.[7]

Spotlight on ONLINE RÉSUMÉ

Target your online résumé for the particular job for which you are applying. Read the job announcement carefully and respond specifically to what it asks. Do not send in a general résumé.

If you do not wish to spend hours filling out Web forms, you can let a service such as Resume Rabbit work for you. Here are several advantages of posting on the website.

1. Fill out one form and get immediate postings on over 70 major career websites, such as Monster.com, HotJobs, and Headhunter.net.

2. Password access to check the status of your site postings.

3. An easy résumé builder if you do not have a résumé handy.[8]

---

[5]Phyllis Pinter, "A Winning Resume in a Changed Employment Market!" <http://64.233.161.104/search?q=cache:wcySZzPcvwcJ:www.askhrs.com/Winning-Resum.> (accessed July 31, 2005).

[6]"Employers rely on Internet & referrals to hire." *The Career News.* March 21, 2005. <http://www.thecareernews.com/newsletter.php?ID=449> (accessed July 31, 2005).

[7]Katherine Hansen, "Internet Job-Hunting Turns a Corner: A Quintessential Careers Annual Report, 2005," <http://www.quintcareers.com/Internet_job-hunt_report.html> (accessed July 31, 2005).

[8]ResumeRabbit.com, "Be seen by 1.5 million employers & recruiters instantly!" <http://www.iversonsoftware.com/careers/employment/cj/resumerabbit.html> (accessed July 31, 2005).

Figure 14-9   **FUNCTIONAL RÉSUMÉ**

EDWARDO M. ROMANO

2380 Highland Drive
Fort Worth, TX 73456-2389
817-555-0698
e-mail: er85@web.com

CAREER OBJECTIVE
A position as an administrative assistant with the opportunity to use my technology, written communication, and human relations skills.

EDUCATION
Grand Haven College, August 2004 to May 2006
Associate Degree in Administrative Systems

SKILLS

Leadership

▶ President of Phi Theta Kappa
▶ Vice President of the Student Union
▶ Vice Chairperson of Service Learning Association

Service to Others

▶ Coordinated activities for children in the YMCA program
▶ Participated in Adopt-A-Highway Program

Technology

▶ Computer—Word, Excel, Access, PowerPoint, Internet research, Web page design
▶ Keyboarding—90 wpm with high level of accuracy
▶ Filing system—established an electronic records management system while working for one semester in the President's office

Communication

▶ Excellent writing skills
▶ Experience composing letters and reports

Human Relations

▶ Served on numerous teams, including YMCA teams and academic teams

WORK HISTORY
▶ Student Assistant in Business Department, September 2004 to May 2006
▶ Served in United States Army, June 2002 to July 2004
▶ Clerk at Rogers Hardware, January 1999 to May 2002

HONORS
▶ Phi Theta Kappa
▶ Dean's List
▶ Most Outstanding Student, Business Department
▶ Medal of Honor, United States Army

Figure 14-10

APPROPRIATE AND INAPPROPRIATE USE OF THE FUNCTIONAL RÉSUMÉ

Appropriate

1. You are a recent high school or college graduate with minimum work experience.

2. You are re-entering the workforce after a prolonged absence and are open to a variety of positions.

3. You do not have much actual paid experience, but want to emphasize skills gained through volunteer work, school projects, or internships.

4. You may not want to show experience from all previous jobs.

Inappropriate

1. You have a strong work history.

2. You can easily target the job of your choice.

3. You are using only one résumé for a variety of jobs.

4. You are not clear about your job direction.[9]

When you submit your résumé online, your résumé will have a greater chance of being read if you adhere to the following suggestions.

1. Make your résumé scannable. Scannable résumés are résumés that are designed to withstand the automated screening process that human resource departments use to make their jobs easier. Without résumé scanning, employers had to read through hundreds or thousands of résumés to find qualified candidates.

2. Use the right key words. Today, an employer can use a computer to weed out applicants whose résumés do not meet the criteria of the employer. Your résumé must have the *right key words.* For example, if you are applying for an administrative assistant, use the term several times in your résumé. Additionally, use action words such as *wrote, organized, managed, collaborated,* and *designed.*

3. Pay attention to the words in the job advertisement or job description and use these words as in your application.

4. Put your name, address, phone number, and email on their own separate line. If you have a résumé of longer than one page, put your name [and page number] at the top of the additional page.

5. Use one of the following font faces: Helvectica, Arial, Times New Roman, Palantino, or Courier.

6. Keep your font size between 10 and 14 points.

7. Do not use italics, underlines, lines, shadows, or excessive formatting.

8. Avoid multiple column formats.

9. Do not exceed 65 characters per line.

10. Put a space between slashes: Finance / Accounting.[10]

If you are applying to an individual organization online, read carefully the information provided by the organization online. For example, here is information from one organization's website concerning the online employment application process.

Preparing to Fill Out the Online Employment Application

Before continuing this job application, you need to be prepared to complete the following information: Name, address, phone number, driver's license information, criminal background record (if any), military service information, education, other languages spoken, work history, job-related qualifications, and skills.

We suggest you gather this information before continuing with the application because the application will time-out after 20 minutes of idle time, possibly causing you to lose the information you have already submitted.[11]

> COMPLETE THE EMPLOYMENT APPLICATION

You may fill out an **employment application** form provided by the prospective organization before or after the interview. In some organizations, all

---

[9]Phyllis Pinter, "A Winning Resume in a Changed Employment Market!" <http://64.233.161.104/search?q=cache:wcySZzPcvwcJ:www.askhrs.com/Winning-Resum.> (accessed July 31, 2005).

[10]"Online Job Applications," <http://www.vuw.ac.nz/st_services/careers/publications/career_editorials/online_job?application.html> (accessed July 31, 2005).

[11]Official Web Site for the City of Fort Worth, Texas, <http://www.fortworthgov.org/hrapp1/frontdoor.asp> (accessed July 31, 2005).

Figure 14-11   TARGETED/COMBINATION RÉSUMÉ

Gloria Mercado
3809 North Road
Colleyville, TX 76034-3400
817-555-0234
e-mail: gm6@web.com

CAREER OBJECTIVE: Administrative Assistant, Human Resources Management

EDUCATION
Oxford County Community College, August 2004 to May 2006
Associate Degree in Administrative Systems

PROFESSIONAL SKILLS
Excellent writing skills, strong teamwork skills, adept at promoting and maintaining harmonious environments, assisted with creating training programs for staff. Leadership skills, excellent keyboarding skills (100 wpm); proficient in Word, Excel, PowerPoint, Access, and Web page design.

EMPLOYMENT HISTORY

- Three years of experience as administrative assistant in Human Resources Department, People Pharmaceuticals.
- Assisted in developing and conducting training programs for human resources personnel.
- Coordinated and edited a human resources monthly newsletter.
- Assisted with writing human resources policies.
- Researched human resources policies and procedures through the Web.
- Supervised three administrative assistants in a human resources department.

ACHIEVEMENTS

- Implemented a Quality Team program for clerical and administrative assistant staff. Surveys revealed that 76 percent of employees experienced increased job satisfaction and improved work-life quality.
- Recognized as an outstanding human resources employee by People Pharmaceuticals.

Read the entire job application carefully before starting to complete it.

© Photodisc

applicants fill out the form. Other firms ask only those people who are seriously being considered for a position to fill out the application. Follow these suggestions when completing an employment application.

1. Read the entire application before starting to complete it.

2. Print unless your handwriting is extremely neat.

3. Answer every question completely. If a question does not apply to you (such as military experience), put NA, meaning "not applicable." Leaving a space blank can give the impression that you overlooked the question.

4. Check your spelling. Carry a pocket dictionary so you can look up words you do not know how to spell.

5. Have all information with you that you need to fill out the form—dates you attended college, dates of employment, complete addresses of employers, and references. Carry your social security card with you.

6. Be honest. State accurately the experience and skills you have. Do not falsify any information. To do so could be grounds for firing. However, do try to state what may be negative information in a positive manner. For example, most applications include a question asking why you left your last job. If you were fired from the job, you must indicate so. However, you can make the statement positively by stating that your skills did not match those needed by the organization.

> DEVELOP JOB INTERVIEW SKILLS

The interview will not be an ordeal if you adequately prepare for it. Knowing what to do and what to say help eliminate a great deal of nervousness. In the interview, the employer will judge your appearance, personality, human relation skills, self-confidence, and other traits. The interviewer will question you about your experience and abilities, as identified in your letter of application and résumé. The interview is an opportunity for the prospective employer to get to know you and for you to get to know the interviewer and to learn more about the organization.

▷ Portfolio Information

You may wish to prepare a portfolio of your work to take with you to the interview. A **portfolio** is a compilation of samples of your work. The work should be arranged attractively in a binder. Some possible items for inclusion are:

▶ Letters you have written that demonstrate your writing style.
▶ Research reports you have produced to demonstrate your ability to conduct research and present the research in an attractive format.
▶ Spreadsheets, graphics, and PowerPoint slides you have created to demonstrate your knowledge of software.

Be certain that the work you choose is of the highest quality. Have someone who is knowledgeable in your field review your work carefully. Take seriously the individual's critique and make the necessary changes.

You may prefer to prepare an **ePortfolio** (one sent on the Web to prospective employers) as part of your total application package, which includes your résumé and possibly your letter of application.

▷ Pre-interview Nervousness

It is natural to feel nervous before an interview. Most people have such feelings. In fact, nervousness can cause productive behavior; you probably will prepare better because you are concerned that you will not do well. However, you want to control your nervousness. Here are several suggestions that will help.

1. Research the organization.

2. Practice interviewing by having a friend ask you questions. Figure 14-12 gives several questions that might be asked of the recent college graduate.

3. Research carefully the typical salaries for administration professionals. You can get some information from the Web on national salaries. For example, IAAP usually has information on their website, www.iaap-hq.org, for salaries of various job titles for administrative professionals.

4. Use stress reduction techniques, such as exercising, getting the proper amount of sleep, and engaging in positive self-talk.

5. Plan something to do the night before the interview so you do not spend your time worrying about the interview. Go to a movie or dinner with a friend.

6. Do not place all of your hopes on one interview. As you conduct your job search, select several organizations of interest to you. The more interview experiences you have, the more you will learn. View each interview as a learning experience. After the interview, write down what went right and what went wrong. Concentrate on the positives; try not to make the same mistakes a second time.

▷ Know Your Credit Rating

Some organizations run credit checks on you. Employers may assume that debt and other red flags such as a bad reference check impact job performance and are clues to poor character or inadequate management skills. If you do not know your credit rating, it is a good idea to find out before going on a job interview. Equifax, Experian, and TransUnion are the three major credit bureaus that keep track of your credit history. Credit scores range from 300 to 850, with the median score being 720. The easiest route to get credit reports from all three bureaus and your score is to go to www.myfico.com and order the package; there is a small charge.

If you have a negative credit rating, defuse it in the interview. For example, if you are asked about your credit rating, you might say, "It is not perfect, but here is the reason." Then, give a rationale, which may be educational expenses you incurred or hospital costs. If not and you have merely been a poor money

---

Figure 14-12 · **QUESTIONS ASKED OF THE RECENT COLLEGE GRADUATE**

1. How do you describe yourself?

2. What do you see yourself doing in the next five years?

3. What do you really want to do in life?

4. What are your long-term objectives and how do you plan to achieve them?

5. Why did you choose your college?

6. What are the most important rewards you expect to gain from your career?

7. What do you expect to be earning after you graduate?

8. What do you consider to be your greatest strengths and your weaknesses?

9. What motivates you to go the extra mile on a project?

10. Why should I hire you?

11. How do you define success?

12. What qualities do you have that will make you successful?

13. How will you make contributions to our company?

14. What is your GPA? Are you happy with it? Explain.

15. Do you feel you work well under pressure?[12]

---

manager, admit that you have recognized your errors and are now a prudent money manager.[13]

▷ Location of Interview

Be certain you know the exact time and location of the interview. Do not rely on your memory. Write down the time, address, telephone number, and person's name you are to see; take it with you. When traveling to the interview location, allow time for unexpected delays. You do not want to be late for an interview. Excuses for being late will not change the poor impression you have made by your lateness.

---

[12]"Creative Job Interview Tips," <http://view/atdmt.com/VON/iview/brstmvon0410000049von/direct/01746?click+http://www.> (accessed August 2, 2005).

[13]"Know Your Credit Before Job Interviews," *Grand Rapids Press,* July 10, 2005.

⊳ Number of Interviews

You may have more than one interview for a particular position. For example, a human resources professional may interview you first. Next, you may interview with your prospective supervisor. Finally, you may have a group interview with your prospective team members.

⊳ Team Interview

A team interview may be with two or three or even five or six people. Although this type of interview sounds intimidating, it need not be. Tips for a successful team interview are:

▸ When introductions are made, pay careful attention to the individuals' names.
▸ Focus on each individual as the person asks questions.
▸ Listen carefully to the questions asked and answer them succinctly.
▸ When you ask a question, ask it of the group. If one group member asks you a question you did not understand, address that person and ask for clarification of the question.
▸ Make eye contact with all individuals when answering a question.
▸ If you find yourself getting nervous, glance occasionally at individuals who have given you positive feedback—ones who have a friendly face, open body language, and positive reactions to your responses. Say to yourself, *This person likes me; I am doing well.*
▸ Thank the group when the interview is completed. Use their names if possible; it shows you were paying attention.

Team interviews may be with two or three people or even five or six.

© Digital Vision

⊳ Virtual Interview

Occasionally organizations will conduct a **virtual interview** (an employee is interviewed via technology by an interviewer at a distant location). Assume you are applying for a job in Washington, D.C.; however, rather than traveling to the job site, you are being interviewed in Dallas, Texas, where you live. The organization makes arrangements for you to go to a facility that has teleconferencing capabilities.

If you are going to take part in a virtual interview, you need to be well-prepared. When a camera is involved, most people get nervous. However, your goal is to relax and treat the situation as if the person interviewing you were in the same room. Figure 14-13 gives several suggestions for a successful virtual interview.

Figure 14-13 | **SUGGESTIONS FOR A SUCCESSFUL VIRTUAL INTERVIEW**

1. Dress in colors that look good on you and on camera. Black or gray generally does not come across well on camera. Do not wear jewelry that jingles. The noise on camera is even more noticeable than in person.

2. Greet the interviewer warmly and with a smile (remember you are on camera). Repeat the interviewer's name. You might say, "I am happy to meet you, Ms. VanderVeen."

3. Sit in the chair provided; sit back in the chair, not on the edge of your seat. Sitting on the edge of the chair can connote nervousness.

4. Try to forget the camera is there; do not concentrate on it. Concentrate on the interviewer and the questions you are asked.

5. Pay attention to body language and small nuances of the interviewer. Do not spend an inordinate amount of time answering any one question. Be warm and informative but also concise.

6. Enunciate carefully. Poor enunciation is more pronounced on camera than in person.

7. Once the interview is over, thank the person and leave the room.

8. Read the hints for traditional interviews given in the next section. Many of these also apply to the virtual interview.

▷ Helpful Interview Hints

Observe these suggestions to help you make a good impression during the interview.

Before the Interview

1. Get a good night's rest so that you will be alert.

2. Have your hair professionally styled and cut (if needed).

3. Determine what you should take with you. You should have several copies of your résumé in a folder. Also, put a list of your references, with their full name, address, e-mail address, and telephone number in the folder.

4. Prepare your briefcase. Women should try to do without a purse; it is merely an extra item to juggle. Put your résumé, references, billfold, cell phone, makeup, and so forth in the briefcase. Put a pad, ink pen, and pencil in your briefcase in the event you need to take notes or fill out an application. A small pocket dictionary can also be helpful. Do not fill your briefcase to overflowing. Arrange your briefcase in an orderly manner so you do not have to shuffle papers during the interview.

5. Plan your driving time so that you will not be late. You will probably want to make a trial run to the interview site a few days before the interview. Make this run at the same time that you will have the interview so that you understand how much time to allow for traffic. Determine a close parking lot where you might park your car. If you have parking meters in your area, be certain to have the appropriate change for the meter. You do not want to be frantically looking for a place to get change when you need to be focusing on being on time for the job interview.

Dress and Grooming

1. Dress conservatively, even if you are applying for a position in an organization that is in a creative line of work, such as art and design. For both men and women a suit is appropriate; women may also wear a conservative dress. Wear a color that looks good on you. Keep your jewelry to a minimum. Do not wear dangling earrings or bracelets that jingle.

2. For women, do not wear excessive makeup or perfume.

3. For men, do not wear excessive cologne or after-shave.

4. If you wear an overcoat, hang it in the reception area. Do not take it into the office in which you are being interviewed. You do not want to be burdened with numerous belongings.

5. Be sure to keep cell phones turned off or left on mute.

Greetings

1. Greet the receptionist with a friendly smile, stating your name and the purpose of your visit.

2. If you have to wait for the interviewer, pick up a magazine if one is on a table next to where you are sitting. It will give you something to do and help control any nervousness. If the receptionist offers you a magazine, thank the person.

3. Once you are in the interviewer's office, shake his or her hand with a firm (but not tight) grip. Wait to sit down until invited to do so. Maintain appropriate eye contact with the interviewer.

During the Interview

1. Show genuine interest in what the interviewer says; be alert to all questions.

2. Do not talk too much. Answer questions both thoroughly and concisely.

3. Be enthusiastic; demonstrate pride in your skills and abilities.

4. Be positive. Do not criticize former employers, instructors, schools, or colleagues.

5. Do not tell jokes.

6. Do not argue.

7. Do not brag; you may be seen as overselling yourself!

8. Try to understand your prospective employer's needs and describe how you can fill them.

9. Be prepared to tell the interviewer about yourself—a commonly asked question at the start of the interview. Keep the conversation on a professional level.

10. Express yourself clearly.

11. Do not smoke even if you are invited to do so; most companies have no-smoking policies.

12. Do not chew gum.

13. Answer questions carefully and truthfully. Several commonly asked interview questions are given in Figure 14-14. A number of interview mistakes are given in Figure 14-15.

At the Close of the Interview

▸ Attempt to determine what the next step will be. Will there be another interview? When can you expect to hear the results of the interview?

▸ Reiterate your interest in the job (that is, if you are still interested).

▸ Smile pleasantly and thank the interviewer.

▸ Smile and thank the receptionist as you leave.

Interview Follow-Up

After the interview, promptly write a follow-up letter. A sample letter is shown in Figure 14-16. The letter should include the following: (1) a thank-you for the opportunity to interview, (2) a recap of your skills and abilities, (3) a statement of your continued interest in the job (if this is true), and (4) a reminder of the next steps you agreed on in the interview, such as when the decision is going to be made.

If no action is taken concerning your application within a reasonable time (one to two weeks), a second follow-up letter or a call may be advisable. The second letter should merely remind the employer of your continued interest in the job. Depending on the situation, you may want to make a third contact with the organization. Being persistent shows your interest in the job, and the organization views it as a plus. However, you do not want to annoy the employer. Use good judgment in determining how many follow-ups are appropriate in each job situation.

Figure 14-14   COMMONLY ASKED INTERVIEW QUESTIONS

Questions in Regard to Job and Organization Interest

▸ What do you know about our organization?

▸ Why are you interested in our organization?

▸ Why do you want this position?

▸ What do you consider the ideal job for you?

Questions Regarding Education

▸ Why did you choose your major area of study?

▸ What was your academic average in school?

▸ What honors did you earn?

▸ In what extracurricular activities were you involved?

▸ Which courses did you like best? Least? Why?

▸ How have the classes you completed as part of your major helped you prepare for your career?

Questions Regarding Your Ability to Fit into the Organization

▸ If you disagree with something your supervisor asked you to do, what would you do?

▸ What type of work atmosphere do you prefer?

▸ Is a sense of humor important at work? Why or why not?

▸ Tell me about a conflict you have had with someone in the work environment. How did you handle the conflict?

▸ How do you handle pressure?

▸ How would your previous employers and coworkers describe you?

Questions Regarding Experience

▸ Have you ever been fired or asked to resign from a position?

▸ Why did you leave your previous job?

▸ Have you had any problems with previous supervisors?

▸ What are your greatest strengths?

▸ What do you not do well?

▸ Why should I hire you?

▸ What salary do you expect?

Note on Salary: You should have an idea of an appropriate salary range before the interview. You can check the job advertisements of your local newspaper for area salaries and the Web for national salaries. Your school placement office is another good source for local salary information.

Figure 14-15 FREQUENT INTERVIEWING MISTAKES

1. Being late.

2. Not making eye contact.

3. Criticizing past employers.

4. Asking questions about salary and benefits immediately.

5. Not answering questions concisely.

6. Being too self-assured (having a cocky attitude).

7. Failing to demonstrate interest in the position by asking few questions.

8. Providing a résumé with grammar and typographical errors.

9. Failing to bring a list of references.

10. Not articulating interest in the position.

After the interview, you may decide you are not interested in the position. In that case, you should promptly send a courteous letter expressing your appreciation for the interview and explaining that you do not wish to remain a candidate for the position. Although you are not interested in the present position, you may be interested in a position with the company in the future. You do not want to close all doors.

Interview Evaluation

If you are interested in a job but do not get it, you may receive a generic reason from the organization. Most organizations do not give you exact reasons because of legal problems that may occur. You may also do very well in the interview and still not get the job. There simply may have been someone more qualified or with more experience than you have.

In any case, play back the experience in your mind. Note the questions you had trouble answering, the questionable reactions from the interviewer, and any errors that you believe you made. Think about how you can correct errors before the next interview. Review your thoughts with a trusted adviser. Ask the person how you might improve. A job rejection is no reason to become depressed. Do not lose confidence in your skills and abilities. Learn from each interview situation. Maintain a positive attitude.

Job Offer Evaluation

In addition to evaluating yourself in the interviewing process, you need to ask yourself if the organization lived up to your expectations. When evaluating whether you want to work for the organization, ask these questions:

▶ Do my skills and the position match?
▶ Is the work environment one in which I will be happy and will prosper?
▶ Will I have a chance to work with people I can respect and admire?
▶ Will the work be interesting?
▶ Will I be able to learn from the job duties and the people?
▶ Are the benefits and compensation packages acceptable?

Keep in mind that your goal is to find the right position for you. You will spend the major part of each week on a job, and you need to feel happy and productive in your job.

> ADVANCE ON THE JOB

Once you have successfully completed the interviewing process and have accepted a job offer, your task is to combine your skills and knowledge in performing the job well. Listen to what coworkers and supervisors tell you. Observe and learn what is expected and accepted in the workplace. Make certain you have a clear understanding of your job duties and how you will be evaluated. Most companies provide job descriptions that detail the responsibilities of particular jobs. If you are not given one, ask for it. If a job description does not exist, ask your supervisor to go over your duties with you.

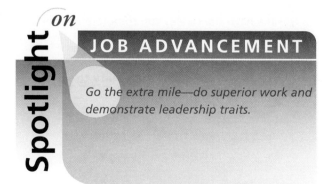

Spotlight *on* **JOB ADVANCEMENT**

Go the extra mile—do superior work and demonstrate leadership traits.

Figure 14-16   **SAMPLE INTERVIEW FOLLOW-UP LETTER**

2445 Edgecliff Road
Dallas, TX 75034-1859
May 24, 200X

Ms. Jean LeJuan
Human Resources Department
JWay Nu-Systems Tech
1510 Eastern Drive
Dallas, TX 75275-0356

Dear Ms. LeJuan:

Thank you for giving me the opportunity to interview for the administrative assistant position that is open in the human resources department. I appreciate the time you spent with me, and I enjoyed learning more about JWay Nu-Systems Tech.

Because of my education and experience, I am confident I can be an asset to the company. My skills in technology, communications, and human relations will help me perform at a high level. The interview today reinforced my interest in joining your team. I was extremely impressed with what I heard from you about JWay Nu-Systems Tech's philosophy of management and the international directions being taken by the company. I welcome the chance to be a part of the organization.

You may reach me by calling 972-555-6655 or by email at vre5@web.com. Thank you for your graciousness. I look forward to hearing from you within the next two weeks.

Sincerely,

Vivian R. Edwards

Vivian R. Edwards

⊳ Perform Successfully

Listen to what your supervisor and coworkers tell you. Pay attention to what is happening in the organization and learn daily from the people with whom you work and your supervisors within the organization.

Listen, Observe, and Learn

Observe workplace expectations and acceptable behaviors. Ask about the directions of your department. If a strategic plan for the organization exists, read it. Establish a plan of action for what you intend to accomplish for the next three to six months. Review your plan with your supervisor. Modify the plan when needed.

Live Your Values

Throughout this course, the importance of values has been emphasized—values for the organization and values for the individual worker. After several months on the job, you need to ask yourself several value questions.

- Are the organization's values clear?
- Do my values mesh with those of the organization?
- Is this an organization where I can continue to live my values, learn, and grow in my job?

Assume Responsibility

It is your responsibility to know what your job is and to do your job with commitment and professionalism. A professional does not wait for her or his employer to describe every aspect of the job. As a professional, you are responsible for not just doing what is expected of you but exceeding expectations. Be certain that you consistently produce quality work in a timely manner. If you are not able to complete a task in the assigned timeframe, do not blame someone else. Accept the fact that you did not complete the task on time and look for ways that you can be more efficient. Ask yourself a series of questions:

- Did I understand the scope of the task?
- Did I seek information that I needed to complete the task?
- Did I work efficiently?
- Did I use my time wisely?
- If I encountered unexpected problems that I could not solve, did I ask for help?
- Did I let my employer know that I would not be able to complete the task on time?

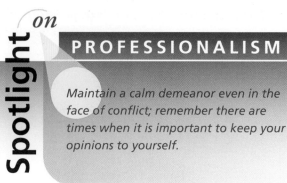

Spotlight *on* **PROFESSIONALISM**

Maintain a calm demeanor even in the face of conflict; remember there are times when it is important to keep your opinions to yourself.

- Did I volunteer to work after hours to get the job done?

Grow from the Performance Appraisal

How often performance appraisals are done varies from company to company and even from position to position. However, if you are a new employee, a performance appraisal is usually done at your six-month anniversary. Some organizations provide employees with evaluation procedures during a new employee orientation process. If you do not receive information concerning evaluation procedures, ask your supervisor. If a form is used, ask for a copy.

Listen and learn during the performance appraisal process.

© Photodisc/Ryan McVay

A fairly common procedure during the performance evaluation is to ask you to evaluate yourself, paying attention to the job description that you were provided when you first took the job and any planning documents of the company that detail goals that need to be accomplished. For example, if your unit has a planning document, you and your supervisor may have used it as a basis to determine your job responsibilities and establish your goals. Then, during the evaluation period, use the planning document to determine if you have accomplished your goals. Read the evaluation tips given in Figure 14-17 to help you understand how to conduct yourself during an evaluation and ways that you can grow and learn from the experience.

| Figure 14-17 | **EVALUATION TIPS** |

1. Listen to what the evaluator is saying.

2. Discuss the issues openly and honestly.

3. Maintain a calm and professional demeanor.

4. Provide the evaluator with important in formation relating to your performance—information the evaluator may not have.

5. Maintain eye contact with the evaluator.

6. Accept negative comments as a criticism of your performance, not of you as an individual.

7. Resolve to correct your mistakes. Tell the evaluator you will do so.

8. Discuss with your evaluator how you can improve your performance.

9. If the evaluator is not clear about the direction you should take in the future, ask for clarification. Writing objectives that fit the unit's strategic plan can help you know what you should accomplish.

10. Accept praise with a smile and a thank you.

> LEAVE A JOB

You may decide to leave a job voluntarily, or you may be given no choice. Whatever your reasons for leaving (whether you are unhappy with a position and decide to leave on your own, you are looking for greater opportunities than you are being provided, or you are forced to leave), you must be professional in handling the exit.

▷ The Exit Interview

Most companies conduct an **exit interview** with the employee. An impartial party (such as a staff member in the human resources department) generally conducts the interview. Your immediate supervisor is not involved.

This exit interview is not a time to get even, to make derogatory remarks about your supervisor, or to unduly criticize the company. Keep in mind the old adage about not burning your bridges. If you are leaving on your own, you may wish to return some day. Regardless of your reason for leaving, you will probably need a reference from the company. Be honest and professional in the exit interview. For example, if you are leaving for a job that has greater opportunities for growth, say, "I've decided to accept a position with greater responsibilities." You do not need to give detailed reasons for your move.

▷ A Layoff or Termination

In your career, you may have to face the situation of being laid off or fired. Assume first you are being laid off. The situation may be a downsizing of the company where other jobs are being eliminated in addition to your own. Keep in mind that you did not cause the situation. Even though the situation is difficult, the skills, abilities, and experience you gained from your job will help you find another one. Remain positive and begin to think about what you want to do next.

Now assume you have been fired. Your feelings of fear, rejection, and insecurity are normal. However, it is not a time to blame yourself or feel sorry for yourself. It is time to take a hard look at what skills you have. Listen to what your employer tells you about your performance. What can you learn for the future? What steps do you need to take to ensure that you do not find yourself in the same situation again? In what areas do you need to improve? Talk with family, friends, and your closest advisers. Realize that the job may not have been the best one for you. Commit to finding a job that will better match your skills and abilities.

SUMMARY

Reinforce your learning in this chapter by studying this summary.

▸ Sources of job information include the Web, networks, college placement offices, newspapers, the government, employment agencies, and walk-ins.

▸ When you have identified an organization for which you would like to work, spend time learning about the organization.

▸ The letter of application is a sales letter; since it is generally the first contact you have with a potential employer, it is an extremely important document.

▸ The résumé represents your skills and abilities; it lets the employer know your educational background and your work history. The three general types of résumé are the chronological, functional, and targeted/combination style résumé.

▸ The interview is an opportunity for the prospective employer to get to know you and for you to get to know the interviewer and learn about the organization.

▸ Preparing a portfolio of your work can help a prospective employer know something about your abilities.

▸ Pre-interview nervousness is common. You need to take steps, such as exercising and getting the proper amount of sleep before the interview, to offset the nervousness.

▸ Team interviews are conducted in some organizations.

▸ Virtual interviews, with a candidate being interviewed via technology, are sometimes used in our technological world.

▸ Pay attention to grooming and dress for the interview. Spend time collecting your thoughts on what you want to say during the interview. Be prepared!

▸ During the interview, be professional and be prepared to talk about your background and your reasons for wanting to work for the organization.

▸ Follow-up after the interview with a thank-you letter.

▸ Advancing on the job includes listening, observing, and learning; living your values, assuming responsibility, and growing from the performance appraisal.

▸ If you leave a job for whatever reason (promotion to another position, leaving the organization, or termination), behave professionally. Consider carefully how you will handle the situation.

GLOSSARY

Chronological résumé—Work experience is presented in reverse chronological order, with the most recent work presented first.

Electronic résumé—Résumé presented on the Web, in the body of an e-mail message or as an attachment.

Employment application—An application that is provided the job applicant by the organization where he or she is applying.

ePortfolio—One sent on the Web to prospective employers.

Exit interview—An interview conducted by the employer as an employee leaves a job.

Fee-paid—The employer pays the fee rather than the job applicant.

Functional résumé—The functional résumé allows an applicant to concentrate on skills and abilities that are applicable to the job sought by presenting the applicant's education, experiences, and activities in categories that support career goals.

Networking—Any face-to-face contact with a person who hires or supervises a person with the appropriate skills—even if they are not presently able to extend a job offer.

Portfolio—A compilation of samples of your work.

Private employment agencies—Agencies that charge a fee for their services.

Résumé—Concise statement of your background, education, skills, and experiences.

State-operated employment agencies—Employment agencies supported by tax dollars from the state.

Targeted/combination résumé—This résumé allows a job applicant to target a specific position through the use of an objective. The subsequent information provided allows the applicant to support the objective.

Virtual interview—Being interviewed via technology by an interviewer or interviewers at a distant location.

CHECKPOINT

Check your understanding of these terms by completing DCD14-a on the Data CD.

DISCUSSION ITEMS

These discussion items provide an opportunity to test your understanding of the chapter through written responses and/or discussion with your classmates and your instructor.

1. Define your major skills.
2. Identify five sources of job information.
3. Identify where you would like to work and why.
4. Explain what should be included in a résumé.
5. List ten helpful hints for making a good impression during the interview.
6. Explain the importance of living your values on a job.

CRITICAL THINKING CASE

Robin McKnight was graduated with a two-year degree a year ago. Robin was an A student; however, she was very shy and introverted. She was considered a loner by most of her classmates. She stayed away from all extracurricular activities. Because she was not certain where she wanted to work, she decided to try a number of different types of jobs through a temporary agency. During this past year, she worked for four companies. Her supervisors always praised her work; she was offered full-time employment at two of the organizations. Robin has gained confidence in her social skills. In fact, she was given a party by her colleagues and supervisor when she left three of the organizations. She has decided that she wants to work as an administrative assistant in a health-related facility—either a hospital or a research facility. She has applied for two jobs recently, both in her preferred field; however, she was not offered either job. Robin had these experiences during the interviews.

1. When asked about her present job, Robin stated that she did not work at the present time. She did not explain her work experiences during the past year.

2. When asked about her college experiences, Robin said that she made good grades but did not do anything outside of her classes.

CRITICAL THINKING CASE *(continued)*

3. When asked about her strengths, Robin said that she was a capable employee, but she had much to learn.

4. When she was asked by the interviewers if she had any questions, she replied, "No."

5. Robin was very nervous during each interview.

Robin knows she is capable; she has proven that in her performance at four different companies during the last year. However, she is still not very confident. What advice would you give Robin?

RESPONSES TO SELF-CHECK

A and B

Each response will be different. Ask yourself these questions about your self-check responses:

What steps are you taking to correct your hard and soft skill weaknesses?

Do you now know what direction you want to take your career?

If you cannot answer these questions with thoughtful answers at this point, you need to give serious thought to your workplace future. You might want to talk with professionals in the field and read job vacancy notices on the Web and in the newspaper.

WORKPLACE PROJECTS

PROJECT 14-1 WRITE A PAPER

Review your skills, abilities, and interests (Objective 1)

As you have learned in this chapter, before applying for a job you must spend time identifying your skills, abilities, and interests. Find a quiet place where you can spend quality time with yourself thinking through what you have to offer an organization in the workplace. Using three sheets of paper, put the word *skills* at the top of one sheet, *abilities* at the top of the next sheet, and *interests* at the top of the remaining sheet. Thoughtfully, put in your answers. Put the piece of paper away for a day or two. Then, go back and review it. Change, delete, or add as necessary. Turn in your analysis of your skills, abilities, and interests only if your instructor asks that you do so. The purpose of this assignment is for you to spend time thinking through your job capabilities and interests.

PROJECT 14-2 WRITE A REPORT

Identify sources of job information (Objective 2)

Become familiar with various organizations (Objective 3)

Using the Web and newspapers, identify six positions that fit your areas of expertise. From these job vacancy notices, research (via the Web) information concerning three of the organizations. Determine which two organizations you would like to work for and why. Prepare a report giving this information; include appropriate headings in your paper. Submit your report to your instructor.

PROJECT 14-3 WRITE A LETTER OF APPLICATION AND A RÉSUMÉ

Prepare a letter of application and a résumé (Objective 4)

Using one of the administrative assistant jobs you found in Project 14-2, apply for the position. Prepare a résumé and a letter of application. Use whatever résumé format best fits your background and experience. Save your résumé on a disk; print a copy. Prepare the same résumé as an electronic résumé making the necessary changes to fit the online format. Print a copy of your electronic résumé. Submit both résumés and your letter of application to your instructor.

PROJECT 14-4 ROLE PLAY AN INTERVIEW

Develop job interview skills (Objective 5)

Work in teams of four on this project. Review the pages in your text on interviewing before beginning this project. Using the position you applied for in Project 14-3, assume you are going on an interview. Role-play that interview with your classmates with one of you being the employer, one being the interviewee, and the other two observing. When you have finished, the two observers are to critique your performance. Go through the steps again until each member of the team has played every role.

PROJECT 14-5 ADD TO YOUR PROFESSIONAL GROWTH PLAN

Commit to living your values in the workplace (Objective 6)

Add to your Professional Growth Plan by determining how you will live your values in the workplace. Save the file as PGP14-5.

COMMUNICATION POWER
Use DCD14-b to assist you in improving your grammar skills.

ASSESSMENT OF CHAPTER OBJECTIVES

Now that you have completed the chapter and the projects, take a few minutes to review the chapter learning objectives. For your convenience, the objectives are repeated here. Did you accomplish these objectives? If you were unable to accomplish the objectives, give your reasons for not doing so; be specific and concise. Your instructor may prefer that your answers be submitted to her or him. If so, DCD14-c contains the Assessment of Chapter Objectives. Complete the Assessment of Chapter Objectives; submit your results to your instructor.

1. Review your skills, abilities, and interests.   Yes ☐   No ☐

_____

_____

_____

_____

2. Identify sources of job information.   Yes ☐   No ☐

_____

_____

_____

_____

3. Become familiar with various organizations.   Yes ☐   No ☐

_____

_____

_____

_____

4. Prepare a letter of application and a résumé.   Yes ☐   No ☐

_____

_____

_____

_____

5. Develop job interview skills.   Yes ☐   No ☐

_____

_____

_____

_____

6. Commit to living your values in the workplace.   Yes ☐   No ☐

_____

_____

_____

_____

CHAPTER 15

TELEWORKER/VIRTUAL ASSISTANT

Learning Objectives

1. Define teleworking, teleworkers, and virtual assistants.
2. Identify the job growth of teleworkers.
3. Identify the advantages and disadvantages of telework.
4. Describe the individual qualities and skills necessary for success.
5. Describe office space essentials.
6. Practice self-management behaviors.

© Getty Images/Photodisc

> TELEWORKING, TELEWORKER, AND VIRTUAL ASSISTANT DEFINED

Teleworking is the general term used to describe working full- or part-time in the home or in some mobile-type work environment. Several major types of telework are significant. These types include:

▶ Teleworking that is based partly in the home and partly on the employer's premises;
▶ Teleworking that is based entirely in the home but that is carried out exclusively for a single employer;
▶ Teleworking that is based entirely in the home but that is carried out by freelance workers for a number of different employers or clients[1]; and
▶ Teleworking that allows an employee to work at a remote site for part or all of the working hours.[2]

If you work in any of the four situations mentioned here, you would be called a **teleworker,** a person who works partly or totally at an off-site location (other than the standard workplace), one who is employed by a single employer, or one who is employed by a number of different employers or clients.

Still another type of teleworker is the **virtual assistant,** a teleworker who *is an independent entrepreneur offering business support services in a virtual environment.* The term "virtual assistant" came into being in 1995 because of a number of factors, including the growth of the Internet, changing

---

[1]"Networks and New Ways of Working: Human Aspects," <http://www.accart.nom.fr/Conferences/NewWays.html> (accessed August 6, 2005).

[2]Lisa Kleiman, "Telecommuting Primer," <http://www.stc-src.org/newsletter/0505/feature1.htm> (accessed August 6, 2005).

demographics, corporate downsizing, evolution of telecommuting relationships, and the expansion of the field of virtual services. Recent research indicates that the majority of virtual assistants are based in the United States, although Australia and the United Kingdom are now experiencing growth in this area. Projections are that virtual assistants will grow rapidly in the future in English-speaking countries in particular as Internet use spreads.[3]

The virtual assistant falls under the broad category of teleworker, with two special distinctions. First, the virtual assistant by definition is *always an independent entrepreneur*, whereas, the general teleworker can be employed by an organization or as an independent contractor. Second, virtual assistants *offer business support services and are the equivalent of office administrative assistants working for their clients offsite and performing a variety of administrative tasks.*[4] Throughout the remainder of this chapter, teleworker will be used as the generic term that includes virtual assistants. Virtual assistant will be used when referring exclusively to the independent entrepreneur who offers business support services.

As a future administrative assistant, you have more choices today in how you work than ever before. You may choose to work in a traditional office situation in a building with others. You may choose to work as a teleworker for an organization and work part-time in an office building and part-time at home. Or, you may choose to work for an organization and work full-time at home. Still another choice is to become a virtual assistant, an independent entrepreneur offering business support services in a virtual environment.

> JOB GROWTH

As more and more individuals become "wired," the trend for working anytime and anyplace will continue. Surveys indicate that the number of individuals involved in the various types of telework has grown over the past few years, with statistics showing the following:

- In 2004, there were 44.4 million teleworkers in the United States, with 20.3 of these teleworkers self-employed.[5]
- The Federal government had 102,921 teleworkers in 2003, which represents a 93 percent increase since April 2001.[6]
- Telework is growing not only in the United States but also in many countries throughout the world, including Denmark, Finland, France, Germany, Ireland, Italy, Netherlands, Spain, Sweden, and Great Britain, to name a few.[7]
- Projections are that by 2006 half of U.S. workers (67 million) will work remotely at least some of the time.[8]
- It is estimated that 5,000 individuals internationally are using the term "virtual assistant" to describe the type of work they do.[9]
- A recent study by the International Telework Association & Council indicated that 16.6 million teleworkers in the United States alone are self-employed. Other estimates are that 33 million Americans are now working for themselves. These statistics suggest that the virtual career trend is probably much larger than has been officially estimated.[10]

Another interesting statistic is the growth of virtual businesses, with a sharp increase in companies choosing to operate the majority of their businesses online. Examples of business that are maintaining a solely online presence (although by no means an exhaustive list) include law firms, market researchers, auditors, florists, journalists, and real estate firms.[11]

> ADVANTAGES/ DISADVANTAGES OF TELEWORK

Telework, as in most all types of work, has both advantages and disadvantages for the individual workers, the organization, and society. Several of these advantages/disadvantages are listed here.

[3]"The VA Profession," <http://www.ivaa.org/virtual-assistance-profession.htm> (accessed August 6, 2005).

[4]"Virtual Assistant—FAQs," <http://www.virtuallyyourz.com/virtualassistantdef.php> (accessed August 6, 2005).

[5]"Telework Facts," <http://www.telcoa.org/id33_m.htm> (accessed August 6, 2005).

[6]Telecommuting Surveys, "Telework growth in Federal agencies," <http://www.langhoff.com/surveys.html> (accessed August 6, 2005).

[7]"Share of Teleworkers Will Rise to 11 Percent of the Labour Force by 2005," <http://www.ecatt.com/statistics/madrid-pmle.html> (accessed August 6, 2005).

[8]Telecommuting Surveys, "Mobile Workforce Growing," <http://www.langhoff.com/surveys.html> (accessed August 6, 2005).

[9]"The Virtual Work Experts," <http://www.msvas.com/FAQ.htm> (accessed August 6, 2005).

[10]"Virtual Heroes: The Growth of the Virtual Assistant," <http://ezinearticles.com/?Virtual-Heroes:-The-Growth-of-the-Virtual-Assistant&id+5400> (accessed August 7, 2005).

[11]Ibid.

▷ Advantages to the Individual Worker

1. Enhances employee productivity and work quality

2. Improves morale and job satisfaction

3. Provides a greater degree of responsibility

4. Provides greater lifestyle flexibility in meeting family and job demands

5. Reduces transportation costs[12]

6. Provides greater autonomy

7. Increases flexibility for two-career couples to work for different employers many miles apart (even cities or states apart)

8. Less distraction from coworkers

9. Savings in time and commuting costs[13]

10. Provides financial savings from at-home versus restaurant lunches and wardrobe costs

11. Eliminates commuting aggravations, such as rush-hour traffic and parking

12. Provides opportunity to move from one part of the country to another and still work for the same organization

▷ Disadvantages to the Individual Worker

1. Isolation from the office team; can be a lonely environment

2. Lack of organizational identity—few or no ties with an organization

3. No support group—teleworker is responsible for all aspects of her or his job

4. Little or no support for telecommunication problems

5. Lack of access to equipment

6. Loss of fringe benefits, such as paid vacations and insurance coverage if you are a self-employed teleworker

Teleworking reduces commuting time and stress.
© Photodisc

7. Conflict between work and home responsibilities

8. Interruptions and distractions if in a home environment

9. Family stress and turf problems; possible spousal resentment of the stay-at-home partner

10. Telecommuter track: Fear of being left out of the loop and ignored for future promotions[14]

▷ Advantages to the Organization

1. Enhanced employee productivity and work quality. According to one study done in 2003, AT&T realizes approximately $150,000,000 in annual savings by teleworking; $100,000,000 through direct employee productivity, $35,000,000 through reduced real estate costs, and $15,000,000 through enhanced employee retention[15]

2. Reduced absenteeism[16]

3. Increased retention and loyalty of employees

4. Improved employee morale and job satisfaction

5. Increased workforce diversity by widening the labor pool

6. Reduced overhead costs

7. Reduced employee sick leave and absenteeism

8. Expansion of the labor pool with the ability to attract a wider range of workers[17]

---

[12]"Virtual Heroes," Kleiman, (accessed August 7, 2005).

[13]"What is telework or telecommuting?" <http://www.ccohs.ca/oshanswers/hsprograms/telework.html> (accessed August 15, 2005).

[14]Ibid., Kleiman, (accessed August 7, 2005).

[15]"Telework Facts," <http://www.telcoa.org/id33_m.htm> (accessed August 7, 2005).

[16]Ibid.

[17]Ibid., Kleiman, (accessed August 7, 2005).

9. Increased productivity

10. Increased number of potential candidates for a job[18]

▷ Disadvantages to the Organization

1. Difficulty in effectively managing teleworkers

2. Possibility of increased training costs

3. Difficulty in evaluating employees effectively

4. Difficulty in providing opportunities for teleworkers to remain a part of the total workforce team

These disadvantages are ones that are particularly true for organizations in the infancy of their efforts in telework. If an organization is going to commit to long-term telework, planning must be done to avoid these disadvantages. The supervisors of teleworkers must manage these workers differently from traditional workers. The next paragraph offers some suggestions concerning management techniques. Additional suggestions are given in Figure 15-1.

When providing telework opportunities, the organization must think differently about the management role. How can managers not only measure the productivity of the worker, but also help the worker to feel a part of the total organization while working in isolated locations? Consideration must be given to employing the right people in telework situations

and then giving them the proper support. There are no easy answers, but many organizations are making the arrangement work effectively.

Some organizations use video conferencing, telephone conferencing, and computer conferencing to link individuals from their remote locations to individuals in the traditional office setting. Also, a number of organizations include teleworkers in biweekly or monthly staff meetings on site at the organization. **Virtual teams** are also used (dispersed workers who come together through telecommunications technology to accomplish a task). Before the teleworker begins any task, both the manager and the teleworker must be clear about project expectations and timelines. Because teleworkers receive less informal feedback than do other employees, they must receive adequate information during formal evaluation sessions.

The concerns and techniques given here address only a few of the myriad management issues. An organization that supports teleworkers must continually study and improve its support structures to assure the productivity of its teleworkers.

▷ Societal Advantages

Telework encourages entrepreneurial activity. Individuals can set up and maintain home offices at relatively low costs. Current technology and the Internet provide new business opportunities that were not available in the past. To understand the relevance of this statement, you merely need to scan the Web to discover the number of entrepreneurs who have businesses on the Web. Additionally, more opportunities are available for caregivers because telework allows them to maintain a successful business operation while juggling family and home responsibilities.

Telework also provides for increased community stability and less pollution of our environment

Figure 15-1 SUCCESSFUL TELEWORKER MANAGEMENT TRAITS

1. Have an open and positive attitude toward telework.

2. Establish clear and measurable performance objectives.

3. Communicate well with potential teleworkers and the team.

4. Provide a system for timely and constructive feedback.

5. Use employee input in generating solutions.

6. Trust the employee to perform duties when away from the supervisor's direct contact.

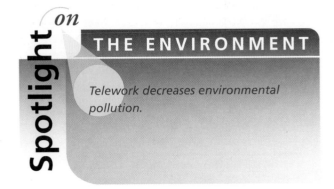

Spotlight *on* THE ENVIRONMENT

Telework decreases environmental pollution.

---

[18]"What is telework or telecommuting?" <http://www.ccohs.ca/oshanswers/hsprograms/telework.html> (accessed August 15, 2005).

according to a study conducted by AT&T in 2000. In fact, AT&T research showed that AT&T teleworkers avoided 110 million miles of driving, saving 5.1 million gallons of gasoline. Less driving by teleworkers resulted in reduced emission of air pollutants, including 1.7 million tons of carbon monoxide, 220,000 tons of hydrocarbons, 110,000 tons of nitrogen oxides, and 50,000 tons of carbon dioxide.[19]

> TRAITS/SKILLS

As you have already learned, the benefits of telework are many. However, before choosing telework as a way to work, you need to consider the traits and skills necessary to be a happy, productive teleworker. Several of these traits/skills are being productive and disciplined, setting objectives and being a self-starter, being organized, and having excellent oral and written skills. In addition the teleworker must be proficient in various types of workplace technology.

▷ Is Productive/Disciplined

Working as a teleworker requires that you be productive and disciplined. Your workplace will usually be your home, where you may have a number of distractions, including your friends and pets. Often, you have to help both your friends and family understand that even though you work at home, you have deadlines to meet just as anyone else does in a work situation. You are not always free to chit-chat with friends or to engage in activities with your children or your spouse. Setting objectives and being a self-starter are two ways to ensure that you are productive and disciplined.

Sets Objectives

One way of ensuring that you are productive and disciplined is to set objectives for yourself. Just as you have timelines to meet in the traditional workplace, you also have timelines in the home or off-site office. Before you quit work each afternoon or evening, write down on your computer the objectives you need to accomplish for the next day, including how long you believe it will take you to complete the task. Obviously, some projects will take more or less time than you envision; however, establishing estimated times keeps you focused on the task.

Is a Self-Starter

A self-starter knows what needs to be done and is eager to get it done. A self-starter is the opposite of a procrastinator. A procrastinator always has an excuse as to why a project cannot be started or cannot be completed. A self-starter generally has a number of items on her or his to-do list and not only gets them accomplished, but feels a sense of satisfaction at marking the items off the list. The self-starter is eager to begin the next to-do list, enjoying a sense of pride and accomplishment from being able to do a number of tasks well.

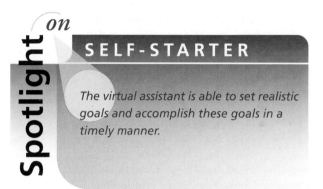

Spotlight *on*

SELF-STARTER

The virtual assistant is able to set realistic goals and accomplish these goals in a timely manner.

▷ Is Organized

Organization is important on any job, but it is particularly important in a telework environment. The teleworker must be able to plan and organize time well and to implement time management techniques such as setting priorities, organizing the workstation, and handling paperwork as few times as possible.

When working at home, you need to establish a routine just as you would in a traditional workplace. Make a to-do list each afternoon and check it each morning. Check your e-mail and voice mail on an established scheduled. For example, you may check your e-mail at 9 a.m., 11 a.m., and 3 p.m. Shut your office door at night. The teleworker can overdo the work hours just as the traditional employee can. Determine the number of hours you will spend working and then stick to that number. Remember that the most productive worker is a balanced worker, one who knows how to effectively handle work, family, and play.

▷ Has Excellent Oral and Written Communication Skills

Throughout this text, you have been reminded of the importance of being a good communicator and continuing to grow in your communication skills. As a

---

[19]"Telework Reaches All Time High at AT&T," <http://www.att.com/telework/artlib/alltime-high.html> (accessed March 6, 2001).

teleworker, your communication skills are crucial. For example, you may never see a customer face-to-face; however, you will probably communicate frequently through e-mail or the telephone. You may also be writing a number of reports for your various customers. Thus, both your oral and written skills are crucial.

▷ Maintains Technology Skills

Technology skills are essential for all administrative assistants. However, as an administrative assistant in the traditional office, you usually have assistance available to you if there is a malfunction of your computer, copier, or fax. Unfortunately, as a teleworker/virtual assistant, you do not generally have someone who can assist you with technology problems. You must become a good troubleshooter—one who is able to determine what the problem might be, even if you are not able to fix it. Often, in our technology driven world today, you can find assistance through the telephone or the Web to solve many of your technological problems. However, in finding this assistance, you must be able to adequately define and/or describe the problem. In identification of

your technological problem, you must not only be a good troubleshooter, but also a good problem solver, and a good communicator.

As telecommunication equipment continues to become more sophisticated, you must continue to upgrade your knowledge and skill. You can do so by reading computer periodicals, by checking upgrades on equipment through the Web, and by talking with other teleworkers about what they are using.

Figure 15-2 lists the traits of the teleworker personality as identified by International Telework Association & Council (ITAC).

Figure 15-2	**TELEWORKER PERSONALITY TRAITS**

- ▶ Self-motivated, responsible, and conscientious
- ▶ Self-disciplined and able to work independently with a limited need for assistance but able to ask for it if necessary
- ▶ Proven performer with strong past job reviews and success in current position
- ▶ Trusted by supervisor/manager
- ▶ Highly organized and proficient at time management
- ▶ Good oral and written communication skills
- ▶ Strong decision-making and problem-solving skills
- ▶ Appropriate home life
- ▶ Committed to teleworking[20]

Self CHECK

Answer these questions with a *yes* or *no*.	Yes	No
1. I set objectives for myself.	☐	☐
2. I am a self-starter.	☐	☐
3. I am organized.	☐	☐
4. I have excellent oral and written communication skills.	☐	☐
5. I have excellent technology skills.	☐	☐

---

[20]"ITAC What We Do," <http://www.workingfromanywhere.org/about/index.htm> (accessed August 8, 2005).

> TELEWORK CHALLENGES

Certainly, as you have already learned, there are many advantages to being a teleworker; however, as in any job, there are challenges also. Four of these challenges are presented in this section.

> Isolation

To a great degree, the environment of a teleworker is one of isolation. If you have been accustomed to working in a traditional environment, you will understand the differences immediately. You are not able to get a cup of coffee with a coworker and exchange small talk. You do not have access to someone with whom you can discuss a work problem. You miss little things, such as walking into work with someone from the parking lot. The degree to which isolation bothers you depends to a certain extent on your personality traits. Are you an introvert or an extrovert by nature? Certainly an extrovert can be a successful teleworker, but the person must give consideration to how she or he can satisfy a need to interact with others. For example, an extroverted teleworker may decide to join a health club and sign up for an exercise class. Here are several additional suggestions for feeling less isolated.

1. Make arrangements to have lunch occasionally with someone in a similar business.

2. Go to a deli or coffeehouse where you can chat with people.

3. Exchange pleasantries with the merchants with whom you deal; for example, your mailing service, your office supply store, and your grocery store.

4. If you are a teleworker employed by an organization, take advantage of company-sponsored professional development activities and company social events.

5. Turn on the television to a news program during your lunch to get in touch with what is happening in the outside world.

6. Schedule jogs or walks with a neighbor who also exercises.

7. Go to an occasional movie in the afternoon.

> Noise

Noise around the home can be a challenge because of a number of factors generally outside the control

Join a health club; take an exercise class.

© Photodisc

of the teleworker. Here are a few of the noise detractors: noisy neighbors, garbage trucks, car and ambulance alarms, barking dogs outside the home, pets within the home making noise, and neighbors doing yard work or having pool parties.

Because noise can be a distraction, you should attempt to lower the noise level around the house. Here are several suggestions for doing so:

▶ Install acoustic foam on your walls.
▶ Put in double-pane glass windows.
▶ Add wall-to-wall carpeting.
▶ Add noise-reducing ceiling tiles.

> Family Issues

Dealing with conflicting job and home demands can be difficult for the teleworker. If you are interested in becoming a teleworker and you are married, have a family, or live with other family members, you need to discuss your interest with your family. Your family may have misconceptions about what working from home means. To some people, it means not being involved in real work. If your family has this perception of telework, they may expect you to have the time to take on additional responsibilities around the house. It is a good idea to have serious talks with your family about what teleworking actually is. You might explain that you are serious about your work and that you cannot be a full-time parent or housekeeper and maintain a full-time work schedule as a teleworker.

Each member of the family needs to understand his or her role in the new arrangement. You will probably need to talk with your family about each person's responsibilities in this new work arrangement. For example, here are questions that need answers.

- Who does the cooking?
- Who does the cleaning?
- Who buys the groceries?
- What are the spouse's responsibilities?
- What are the children's responsibilities?

All family members need to understand their household responsibilities.

© Photodisc/Ryan McVay

Other suggestions for keeping family issues to a minimum include taking steps to make your environment as non-chaotic as possible. These suggestions can keep your homework surroundings less stressful so that you can enjoy your work and your family.

- Find a housecleaning service or an individual who can come in when needed. Hire someone full-time to do the housecleaning if your workload becomes overwhelming.
- Decide if you need someone to help with the children either full-time or after school. If you do, call a child-care referral service and/or ask friends for recommendations. You need to be assured that you have a competent, caring individual looking after your children.
- Keep the lines of communication open with your family. When you believe someone is not

doing his or her fair share, communicate your feelings.
- Do not expect perfection from your family as they perform their tasks. Be grateful they are chipping in to do their share of the work.
- Try to keep your home a low-maintenance one. Do not buy furniture or carpet that requires constant cleaning, such as glass tables or white carpet.

With both family and friends, continue to communicate what your needs and expectations are. Be certain they know your working hours, just as if you were going to the traditional office each day. To help your family understand when you cannot be disturbed, you may do one of the following:

1. Close your office door.

2. Put a "Do Not Disturb" sign on the door.

3. Put a sign on a bulletin board in a place the family uses frequently to indicate your working hours for the day or week.

Refer to your home office as your workplace. Do not let family and friends think you can take on extra community projects because you are a teleworker. Give a business reason for your refusal. For example, you may say, "I am sorry but I have an important project to finish. I simply do not have the time."

▷ Work/Life Balance

Just as you cannot let family and friends interrupt your work to the point that you get nothing done, you also cannot ignore family and friends to the point that all you do is work. There must be a balance between family and work. What is that balance? You must answer that question for yourself. What is important is that you understand what a healthy balance is for you and maintain that balance. People obviously vary in how much work they can handle and what the balance needs to be in order to be a success not only in your chosen career but also with your family.

You may have heard the old saying, "All work and no play makes Jack (or Jill) a dull person." The statement has great validity. If you allow work to become all-consuming, you can develop stress levels that make you physically and emotionally sick. If you never spend time with your family and friends, read a book, listen to a news program, or learn something new outside of your job, you may find that you have fewer good ideas and less creativity in your work projects. Several questions concerning work/life balance are given in Figure 15-3. If you answer *yes* to four or more of these questions, your life may be out of balance.

Figure 15-3 **WORK/LIFE BALANCE QUESTIONNAIRE**

1. Have you stopped seeing friends because it seems like a waste of your time?

2. Are family members complaining that they see too little of you?

3. Have you missed important family occasions because of work?

4. Do you see fewer movies/concerts/plays and sporting events because of work?

5. Do you find yourself feeling bored or empty when you are not working?

6. Are you unsure of what to do with yourself when you are not busy?

7. Does relaxing make you feel guilty or nervous?

8. Do you have trouble making conversation that isn't about your job?

9. Do you work to the point where you are simply too tired to do anything else?

10. Do you evaluate your day strictly by the amount of work you accomplish?[21]

> HOME WORKSPACE

Before considering what type and size of workspace you need, ask yourself these questions: What type of work will I be doing? Will I be working on highly technical material that requires a distraction-free environment? How much space do I need to accomplish the work? What furniture and equipment do I need? Will I be meeting clients or customers in my workspace? What environmental factors are important to me; for example, do I need to be close to a window so I can see the outdoors? Can I share my space with my spouse? If you have a spouse who is a teleworker, is it possible to have a two-person office? Once you answer these questions, you are ready to consider size and location.

▷ Workspace Location and Size

If you need a distraction-free workspace, locate your office away from the family living area of your home. A spare bedroom or a basement room may be the answer. If clients, customers, and/or coworkers will be meeting with you occasionally, the space should be close to an outside entrance. If you have extremely noisy neighbors on one side of your home, locate your workspace on the opposite side of the house or as far away from the noise as possible.

How large does your space need to be? If you are a telecommuter who is working at home only one or two days per week, you can be less concerned about workspace. Your space may be a small area you set up with a minimal amount of equipment in a corner of a room. If you are working at home full-time, consider what type and size of desk you need and the space required for a copier, a computer, a printer, file cabinets, bookshelves, and any other necessary equipment.

The location you choose must have adequate lighting for your equipment. You do not want to locate your computer so close to a window that the outside light causes a glare on your computer screen. Your location also needs to have sufficient electrical outlets and telephone jacks to accommodate your equipment. The electrical outlets must be in proximity to your equipment. Stringing extension cords across a room can be dangerous.

You want to be able to control the heating and cooling in the room. Working in an environment that is too hot or too cold contributes to lessened productivity.

The color of your office can make a big difference in your productivity. We know from color research that colors affect our well-being. Research reveals all human beings make a subconscious judgment about a person, environment, or item within 90 seconds of initial viewing and that between 62 percent and 90 percent of that assessment is based on color alone.[22] Color carries important associations in the human brain. Figure 15-4 shows some of the effects of color on individuals.

---

[21]Alice Bredin, *The Home Office Solution* (New York: John Wiley & Sons, 1998), p. 126.

[22]"Alive and in Color: Your Workplace," <http://www.steelcase.com/na/knowledgedesign.aspx?f510258&c510960> (accessed August 15, 2005).

Figure 15-4 · EFFECTS OF COLOR IN THE WORKPLACE

- Red incites excitement, passion, and activity but also anger, dominance, and rebellion; it may not be the best color for team work-spaces.

- Orange is a welcoming color and carries connotations of informality and even playfulness.

- Pink has a soothing effect and could work well in high-stress environments such as call centers.

- Yellow carries associations of happiness and energy, but researchers have found it is processed in the same part of the brain that controls temper and anxiety. Its effects are complex.

- Blue can actually help lower your blood pressure and pulse rate. It is considered a relaxing color. It is not best for high-tempo offices, but better for learning environments or relaxation areas.

- Green is considered a restful and rejuvenating color for almost anywhere.[23]

▷ Furniture and Equipment

When determining the type of furniture and equipment you need, pay attention to ergonomic factors. **Ergonomics** is defined as the applied science of equipment design intended to maximize productivity by reducing operator fatigue and discomfort.[24] Several ergonomic guidelines that should be followed when you are working at a computer are listed here.

1. The height of your chair should be adjusted so that your knees are slightly lower than your hips.

2. Your feet should rest firmly on the ground or on a foot rest, if needed.

3. The monitor should be about the same height as your eyes and about 18 to 24 inches from your face.

4. The angle of your elbows should be at 90 degrees as you work at the keyboard, with your arms held close to your sides.

5. Keep your wrists flat when you are keying.

6. Keep the mouse and keyboard as close together as possible to eliminate unnecessary reaching.

7. Support your lower back. If your chair does not have good support, use a pillow.

8. Take a break for a few minutes every hour.[25]

Spotlight on ERGONOMICS

Be certain that you have a desk chair that is the proper height for you and that supports your lower back.

Your equipment should include the basics—a computer, printer, fax, and copier. To help you determine what equipment will best meet your needs, do the following:

- Conduct Web research; many equipment and software manufacturers advertise their products through the Internet.
- Shop your local computer stores.
- Talk with people who use technology. Discuss the best buys with other teleworkers, computer technicians, or friends who are computer literate.

▷ Workplace Safety

Be conscious of the need for security. Because you are often working home alone using computer technology and other expensive hardware, you want to do what you can to maintain a theft-proof environment. Here are several suggestions for keeping your workplace safe.

1. Install simple locks on windows so they cannot be forced open from the outside.

2. Install a security system that contacts the police if there is a break-in.

3. Install a deadbolt on the office door.

---

[23]"Alive and in Color: Your Workplace," <http://www.steelcase.com/na/knowledgedesign.aspx?f+10258&c=10960> (accessed August 8, 2005).

[24]*The American Heritage College Dictionary*, Fourth Edition (New York: Houghton Mifflin Company), p. 474.

[25]"Practical Ergonomics," <http://www.homeandoffice.hp.com/hho/cache/766-0-0-225-121.html> (accessed August 17, 2005).

4. Draw the shades when you are working at night.

5. When traveling for a few days, leave a few lights on and put other lights on automatic timers.

6. Be certain your office furniture and equipment are insured for the proper amount.

> HEALTH, LIFE INSURANCE, AND RETIREMENT BENEFITS

If you are a self-employed teleworker, you need to purchase health and life insurance and set up a program for retirement. Talk with several health and life insurance companies, and research the benefits available. You must also consider how you will provide for yourself during your retirement years. Options include **IRAs** (individual retirement accounts), investments in **mutual funds** (funds that include a combination of stocks and bonds purchased through a mutual fund company), or individual **stocks** (documents representing ownership in a company) and **bonds** (documents representing debts owed by organizations). Also, insurance companies offer **annuities** (contractual relationships with an insurance company[26]), which will provide a stream of income upon your retirement.

You should carefully research the options available to you. You may find it helpful to consult with a financial planner or an investment counselor. Some cities have special organizations dedicated to securing benefits for small businesses. You may want to investigate whether such a service is available in your area.

> SURVIVAL STRATEGIES

As a teleworker, the following skills are essential: creativity, self-management, productivity, strategic thinking, and continued learning.

Certainly, these skills are many of the same ones the traditional workplace demands. However, in the traditional workplace, you have the luxury of receiving input from your coworkers about your strengths and weaknesses and taking advantage of organization-sponsored staff development events. As a teleworker, these opportunities are not as easily available to you. Thus, it behooves you to take care of yourself. You cannot keep up a pace of constant, effective work production if you do not also give yourself the

opportunity for renewal. You do not want to become **insular** (narrow or provincial in outlook). How do you provide that opportunity of renewal? Here are some suggestions.

▷ Take a Walk in the Woods

Give yourself breaks—breaks of 30 minutes and breaks of an hour or two. These breaks do not reduce your productivity; they improve it by giving you a chance to renew and think more creatively. Take a walk in the woods for an hour; notice the beauty of nature. Go to a park; observe the children playing and the dogs enjoying their walks. Let your mind be free of the stresses of work for a period of time.

© Photodisc/Doug Menuez

Enjoy nature; revel in its beauty.

Reward yourself with longer breaks from your routine where you have the chance to enjoy a beautiful setting and also work. That setting may be a month in a cottage on the shores of Lake Michigan or two weeks on Kona Beach in Hawaii. Remember,

---

[26]Gordon K. Williamson, *Getting Started in Annuities,* (New York: John Wiley & Sons, Inc., 1999), p. 3.

the teleworker can work from almost any setting as long as he or she has access to telecommunications. You may be surprised at how much work you actually accomplish and how creative and refreshed you feel for allowing yourself the opportunity for renewal. Growth comes when we let ourselves thoroughly experience the world.

> Schedule Relaxation

If you are not very good at taking that walk in the woods—you never quite find the time or you just forget about it—schedule the walk on your calendar, along with other relaxation activities. Schedule ten minutes to read or watch television every evening, or schedule an hour at a local club every week to play tennis with a friend. Schedule a vacation without your laptop; spend two weeks relaxing, without even thinking about your work. Although scheduled relaxation appears to be an **oxymoron** (a combination of contradictory terms), many of us have become so conditioned to accomplishing what is on our calendars that the only way we take advantage of a relaxing activity is to schedule it.

> Exercise

Numerous studies have shown the importance of regular exercise for our bodies and minds. Yet most Americans ignore the studies and fail to exercise on a regular basis. Here is why exercise is so important. The task of the cardiopulmonary system is to pump oxygen into your blood and then to pump the blood to all parts of your body. When you are sitting and breathing quietly with your heart at rest, less oxygen and blood are flowing to your brain than when you exercise. Your brain activity naturally slows because blood and oxygen are in lower supply.

The exercise should be aerobic. **Aerobic exercise** means the body uses oxygen to produce the energy needed for the activity. For an activity to be aerobic, it must meet three criteria. It must be brisk, sustained, and involve a repeated use of large muscles. Walking, jogging, swimming, stationary cycling, and jumping rope are examples of aerobic exercise.

Both starting and maintaining an effective exercise program are hard tasks but well worth the effort—the payoff is not only a healthier body but also a more creative, productive brain. Here are some tips to help you sustain an exercise program.

- Write on a calendar the days you plan to exercise each week.
- Mark off the days you exercise as the week goes by.
- At the end of the week, count the number of times you exercised. Did you meet your goal?
- Make arrangements for family or friends to exercise with you.
- Find an indoor location where you can exercise in extreme weather conditions.

> Eat Properly

Eating properly may be more of a challenge for the teleworker than the traditional office worker. Why? It is easy to take a break in the kitchen and reach for whatever snack is available. It is also easy to get involved in a project and reach for a snack to break the tension. Most of us use food in a variety of ways—to feel better, to be sociable, and to reduce boredom. Although food cannot solve our emotional and mental issues, we attempt to fool ourselves that it can. Certainly a major part of the way we treat food has to do with what we learned about food growing up. Did our parents allow us candy if we cleaned our room? Were we rewarded with a special meal celebration if we brought home good grades? To get our eating under control, we may have to undo the patterns we learned as children.

One of the tricks to get your eating under control is to refrain from buying candy, cookies, and other snacks at the grocery store. If the food is not in the house, you cannot eat it. As you or another family member prepares the weekly grocery list, make certain it is replete with fruits and vegetables. Learn to cut out a major part of the fat that is in your diet, and reduce sugar and caffeine consumption. Excessive intake of fat, sugar, salt, and caffeine contributes to poor health. With caffeine, moderation is the key. Most experts agree that 300 mg of caffeine is a moderate intake. Because research is ongoing concerning the effects of caffeine, it is wise to talk with your doctor for guidance about your consumption. Some people are more sensitive to caffeine's effects than others and may feel effects at smaller doses.[27]

> Get Adequate Sleep

The proper amount of sleep is essential to mental and physical health. Studies make it clear that **sleep deprivation** (overall lack of the necessary amount of

---

[27]McKinley Health Center, University of Illinois at Urbana-Champaign, "Caffeine," <http://www.mckinley.uiuc.edu/health-info/drug-alc/caffeine.html> (accessed August 15, 2005).

sleep[28]) is detrimental to your health. Although the amount of sleep needed varies among individuals, medical studies indicate that seven to eight hours a night appears to be the best amount of sleep for adults.[29]

A number of us have problems getting the proper amount of sleep because of our busy schedules and stressful lives. The teleworker may go back to the "office" at the end of the day for three or four additional hours of work.

Teleworkers may also go to bed thinking about their projects for the day or their projects planned for the next day and find that sleep does not come for an hour or so after going to bed. Practicing the following techniques may help you fall asleep.

- Set aside the hour before bed for quiet activities such as reading.
- Take a hot bath.
- Turn off the TV in the bedroom and/or turn down the TV in an adjoining room.
- Practice deep-breathing exercises.
- Create a relaxing scene in your head—waves rolling up on a beach or a mountain stream.
- Be certain your mattress and pillow are right for you—the proper firmness or softness.
- Pay attention to the amount of coffee, tea, cola, or hot chocolate you are consuming; these drinks can lead to sleep deprivation.

▷ Reward Yourself

In the traditional work setting, rewards can come from your supervisor or from your coworkers in the form of a smile and a thank you or a pat on the back, with the statement "Good job," or from a promotion and/or increase in salary.

When you are a teleworker, you must remember to give yourself rewards. That may not be easy for you to do. However, success in life demands that you not only recognize your strengths but also reward yourself for them. You need to feel good about your work and your accomplishments. How do you reward yourself? Try these techniques.

1. Make a to-do list of what you plan to accomplish each day. Mark off your accomplishments at the end of the day.

2. Share your accomplishments with others. Tell your spouse, your children, and your close friends about what you have achieved. Remember, however, that confidential information you may have access to should not be shared.

3. Reward yourself. Give yourself a night out at the theatre or buy something for yourself you have been wanting. Take the time to read a novel, go to a concert, or enjoy a meal at a restaurant with family or friends.

> CAREER GROWTH OF THE TELEWORKER/ VIRTUAL ASSISTANT

As a teleworker, you are often responsible for your own career growth. You may not have the luxury of staff development activities often provided by organizations. If you are a virtual assistant, a self-employed teleworker, you certainly have no help from an organization in providing career growth. It is up to you to determine what you need. How do you find assistance? Part of the answer is to become a member of professional associations. Additionally, for the virtual assistant, a certification program is available.

▷ Professional Associations

One professional association, available for the independent entrepreneur offering business support services, is the International Virtual Assistant Association (IVAA). This association is only a few years old, with its beginnings in 1995, when Internet sites began to appear advertising Web-based staffing solutions. Figure 15-5 contains the organization's mission statement. IVAA also has a code of ethics, with a portion of the code of ethics presented in Figure 15-6.

Another professional association available for all teleworkers, managers, and telework leaders is the International Telework Association & Council (ITAC). This association was founded in 1993 as a not-for-profit organization dedicated to advancing the growth and success of work independent of location. The five basic membership categories are as follows:

1. Sole proprietor/education/non-profit (available to self-employed individuals, educational institutions

[28]Dictionary, LaborLawTalk.com, <http://encyclopedia.laborlawtalk.com/Sleep_deprivation> (accessed September 10, 2005).

[29]University of Wisconsin, School of Medicine, Department of Medicine, "Sleep Medicine," <http://www.medicine.wisc.edu/mainweb/DOMPagesText.php?section=sleepmed&page=sleepdynamicactivity. > (accessed September 10, 2005).

Figure 15-5 — MISSION STATEMENT OF IVAA

The mission of IVAA is to

- Provide access for Professional Virtual Assistants worldwide to the leading virtual assistant organization.

- Educate the general public and the business community on the role and function of Virtual Assistants.

- Promote and require high professional standards through member commitment to the code of ethics.

- Provide members with cutting-edge professional certification programs and reward the completion of this rigorous program with the esteemed IVAA CVA designation as tribute to demonstrated professionalism, skill levels and ethical business practices.

- Assist members to operate their VA practices more efficiently and profitably by providing education and benefits that promote the entrepreneurial work ethic, strengthen their wealth capacity, and enhance general economic development.

- Build strategic alliances, coalitions and affiliations to foster networking opportunities while promoting innovative and effective changes in the business culture to reflect the Virtual Assistant profession.

- Serve as a resource for businesses seeking Professional VAs by maintaining a free, easily accessible on-line database to simplify the task of locating the best-qualified VA for their needs.[30]

Figure 15-6 — CODE OF ETHICS

- Members shall always exercise integrity, honesty and diligence in carrying out their professional duties and responsibilities.

- Members shall safeguard the interest of their colleagues and clients, and shall not knowingly be a part of any illegal or unethical activity.

- Members shall enter into no agreement nor undertake any activity which may be in conflict or give the appearance of conflict with the legitimate interest of their client, or that would prejudice their capacity to perform their professional duties.

- Members shall protect any confidential information obtained in the performance of their duties, and shall not use such information for personal gain nor in a manner that would be detrimental to their client or any other party.[31]

---

such as colleges and universities, and non-profit organizations)

2. User (available for any company or organization that has a primary interest to promote telework within the organization)

3. Agency (for government offices at the federal, state, and local level that promote telework)

4. Vendor (for companies that offer telework solutions including consultants, technology companies, telecommunication companies, and telework centers)

5. Telework Top Tier (designed for telework leaders)[32]

Telework associations also exist worldwide. Listed here are associations in six countries:

Spain: Associacion Espanola de Teletrabajo
France: Association Francaise du Teletravail et des Teleactivites
Canada: Canadian Telework Association
Portugal: Portuguese Association for Telework Development
United Kingdom: TCA (Telecenter, Telework, Telecottage Association-UK)
Germany: Verband Telearbeit Deutschland e.V.[33]

▷ Certification

Virtual Assistant Certification is the joint effort of three leaders in the virtual assistance industry—The International Association of Virtual Office Assistants (IAVOA), AVirtual Solution (AVS), and Virtual Assistance U (VAU). Leaders in these organizations were determined that a certification system should be designed to weed out individuals with

---

[30]IVAA, "Mission Statement," <http://www.ivaa.org/iva-mission-statement.htm> (accessed August 16, 2005).

[31]IVAA, "IVAA Code of Ethics," <http://ivaa.org/ivaa-code-of-ethics.htm> (accessed August 16, 2005).

[32]"Advancing Work from Anywhere, ITAC What We Do," <http://www.workingfromanywhere.org/about/index.htm> (accessed August 16, 2005).

[33]Telework Connection, "Telework Associations," <http://www.telework-connection.com/associations.htm> (accessed August 16, 2005).

marginal skills and experience from those with higher skill levels and more experience.

There are two levels of certification—the PVA (Professional Virtual Assistant) and the MVA (Master Virtual Assistant). The PVA is the first level of certification. PVAs have good skills and experience in the field. The MVA is the pinnacle of the certification program. These individuals have expanded their education with additional courses pertaining to their practice and have more depth of experience in a variety of tasks and projects than the PVA.[34]

⊳ Virtual Assistant Programs

A few colleges have programs for the training of virtual assistants. Courses required include general business courses such as accounting, desktop publishing, small business management, and marketing. Special courses in virtual assistant topics are also part of the curriculum. These programs may be offered in the traditional mode (attending classes in person at a college) or online. The projection is that these programs will become increasingly viable in the future.

---

[34]"What is Certification?" <http://www.vacertification.com/introduction.htm> (accessed August 26, 2005).

SUMMARY

Reinforce your learning in this chapter by studying this summary.

▶ As a future administrative assistant, you have more choices today in how you work than ever before. You may choose to work in a traditional office situation or as a teleworker working part time or full time from your home.

▶ Surveys show that the number of individuals involved in telework has grown. Projections are that by 2006 half of U.S. workers (67 million people) will work remotely at least some of the time.

▶ Virtual businesses are growing, with a sharp increase in companies choosing to operate the majority of their businesses online.

▶ Telework has various advantages for the individual worker, with some of those advantages being enhanced employee productivity, work quality, improved morale and job satisfaction, a greater degree of responsibility, greater flexibility, reduction in transportation costs, greater autonomy, fewer distractions from coworkers, savings in time and commuting costs, financial savings such as lunch costs, and the opportunity to move to other places and still work for the same company.

▶ Disadvantages to the individual worker include isolation from the office team, lack of organizational support, lack of access to equipment, possible loss of fringe benefits, conflict between work and home responsibilities, interruptions and disruptions if in a home environment, family stress and turf problems, and the fear of being left out of the loop for information and promotions, to name a few.

▶ Several advantages of telework for the organization include enhanced employee productivity and work quality, reduced absenteeism, increased retention and loyalty of employees, improved employee morale and job satisfaction, increased workforce diversity, and reduced overhead costs, reduced employee sick leave, expansion of the labor pool, and increased potential for candidates for a job.

▶ Disadvantages to the organization include difficulty in managing teleworkers, possible increased training costs, difficulty in effectively evaluating teleworkers, and difficulty in providing opportunities for teleworkers to be a part of the total team.

▶ Societal advantages include new business opportunities, additional opportunities for women, increased community stability, and less pollution of the environment.

▶ Teleworkers need to be clear concerning their goals. One way to establish this clarity is to write a personal mission statement.

▶ A successful teleworker must be productive and disciplined, which demands setting objectives and being a self-starter.

▶ Additionally, a teleworker must be creative, organized, and have excellent oral and written communication skills, as well as excellent technology skills.

▶ Telework challenges include isolation, noise, family issues, and work/life balance.

▶ When determining home workspace, consider the following: location and size, furniture and equipment, and safety factors.

▶ If you are a self-employed teleworker, it is essential that you determine the health, life insurance, and retirement benefits that you will need. Once you determine your needs, you must establish a plan that meets your needs.

▶ Survival strategies for the teleworker include a walk in the woods, scheduled relaxation, exercise, eating properly, the appropriate amount of sleep, and rewarding yourself.

▶ Career growth can include joining professional telework/virtual associations, achieving virtual assistant certification, and ongoing education through virtual assistant programs and/or other college programs.

GLOSSARY

Aerobic exercise—Exercise that causes the body to use oxygen to produce the energy needed for the activity.

Annuities—Contractual relationships with an insurance company that provide a stream of income upon retirement.

Bonds—Documents representing debts owed by organizations.

Ergonomics—The applied science of equipment design intended to maximize productivity by reducing operator fatigue and discomfort.

Insular—Narrow or provincial in outlook.

IRAs—Individual retirement accounts.

Mutual funds—Funds that include a combination of stocks and bonds purchased through a mutual fund company.

Oxymoron—A combination of contradictory terms.

Sleep deprivation—Overall lack of the necessary amount of sleep.

Stocks—documents representing ownership in a company.

Teleworker—Person who works partly or totally at an off-site location, is employed by a single employer, or who is employed by a number of different employers or clients.

Teleworking—General term used to describe working full- or part-time in the home or in some mobile type work environment.

Virtual assistant—An independent entrepreneur offering business support services in a virtual environment.

Virtual teams—Dispersed workers who come together through telecommunications technology to accomplish a task.

CHECKPOINT

Check your understanding of these terms by completing DCD15-a on the Data CD.

DISCUSSION ITEMS

These discussion items provide an opportunity to test your understanding of the chapter through written responses and/or discussion with your classmates and your instructor.

1. Research the role of teleworkers/virtual assistants in the workworld.

2. Discuss the job growth of teleworkers.

3. List five advantages and five disadvantages of telework for the individual. List five advantages of telework for the organization.

4. Explain five qualities and skills necessary for success as a teleworker.

5. When planning home office space, what should be considered?

6. List and explain five survival strategies for the teleworker.

CRITICAL THINKING CASE

Aldarado Jiminez has been working as an administrative professional for three years. She is married and has two children. She has recently decided to set up a home office and work as a virtual assistant. Aldarado has talked with three businesses that are interested in using her skills immediately. She is excited about being able to stay home with her children; they are two and five years old. However, she does have some concerns. She knows it will be difficult to take care of her children while she works; however, she believes she can manage it as she begins her job. She thinks she can handle the initial work that she has been promised in approximately 20 hours per week. However, she wants to grow her business to approximately 40 or 50 hours per week. Her husband is extremely pleased that she will be staying home; he has told her he is looking forward to a hot dinner on the table by 6 p.m. every evening.

CRITICAL THINKING CASE *(continued)*

Aldarado has not given much consideration to how she will set up her office. She has a computer at home, but no copier or fax machine. She has a small home with two bedrooms. She has thought of setting up her office in the bedroom that she and her husband share, since it is a fairly large room. Another option is to set up her office in a small space off the kitchen or to set it up in a corner of the living room.

As Aldarado starts her new virtual assistant position, what suggestions would you make to her concerning her workload, office arrangement, caring for her children, and cooking and cleaning for family?

RESPONSES TO SELF-CHECK

The self-check is designed to help you consider traits and skills that you might want to improve. Individuals' answers will differ.

WORKPLACE PROJECTS

PROJECT 15-1 PREPARE A REPORT

Define teleworking, teleworkers, and virtual assistants (Objective 1)

Identify the job growth of teleworkers (Objective 2)

Research the role of teleworkers/virtual assistants in the work world. Use the latest information you can find, preferably within the past three years. Additionally, determine the job growth of teleworkers in the past three-to-five years. Prepare a report using the information you have discovered. As a conclusion to your report, project (from the data you have found) the number of teleworkers/virtual assistants ten years from now. Document all sources of information. Present your report to your instructor.

PROJECT 15-2 PREPARE A GROUP REPORT

Identify the advantages and disadvantages of telework (Objective 3)

Describe the individual qualities and skills necessary for success (Objective 4)

Describe office space essentials (Objective 5)

As a group of three or four, search the Web for information on the advantages and disadvantages of telework and the qualities and skills necessary for success as a teleworker. If you know someone who is a teleworker, you might also interview this person; however, the interview is not a requirement because you may not have access to a person who is a teleworker. If you are able to talk with a teleworker, ask these questions:

▶ Why did you decide to become a teleworker?

▶ What adjustments did you have to make from the typical office situation?

▶ Are you self-employed and offering business support services (a virtual assistant) or do you work for an organization?

▶ Has working at home (or in an offsite workspace) been a problem for you? If so, what were the problems and how did you handle them?

▶ Has your family had issues/concerns about your working at home?

▶ How did you set up your offsite office? Did you have problems finding office space in your home? What would you suggest the beginning teleworker consider as he or she is setting up an office in the home?

Using the presentation skills that you are developing, present the information to the class. Use PowerPoint if the equipment is available to you. Offer your classmates a chance to interact with your group by inviting them to comment and/or ask questions at the end of the presentation. Prepare and distribute to your classmates a group evaluation sheet. Prepare a written report for presentation to your instructor.

PROJECT 15-3 ADD TO YOUR PROFESSIONAL GROWTH PLAN

Practice self-management behaviors (Objective 6)

Add to your Professional Growth Plan that you began in Chapter 1 by assuming you are a virtual assistant and describing how you will practice self-management behaviors; file your plan as PGP15-3. Then practice these behaviors for one week. Congratulate yourself if you were successful. You may be asked to report on your success.

COMMUNICATION POWER

Use DCD15-b to assist you in improving your grammar skills.

ASSESSMENT OF CHAPTER OBJECTIVES

Now that you have completed the chapter and the projects, take a few minutes to review the chapter learning objectives. For your convenience, the objectives are repeated here. Did you accomplish these objectives? If you were unable to accomplish the objectives, give your reasons for not doing so; be specific and concise. Your instructor may prefer that your answers be submitted to her or him. If so, DCD15-c contains the Assessment of Chapter Objectives. Complete the assessment of Chapter Objectives. Submit your results to your instructor.

1. Define teleworking, teleworkers, and virtual assistants. Yes ☐ No ☐

_____

_____

_____

_____

2. Identify the job growth of teleworkers. Yes ☐ No ☐

_____

_____

_____

_____

3. Identify the advantages and disadvantages of telework. Yes ☐ No ☐

_____

_____

_____

_____

4. Describe the individual qualities and skills necessary for success. Yes ☐ No ☐

_____

_____

_____

_____

5. Describe office space essentials. Yes ☐ No ☐

_____

_____

_____

_____

6. Practice self-management behaviors. Yes ☐ No ☐

_____

_____

_____

_____

CHAPTER 16

LEADERSHIP SKILLS

Learning Objectives

1. Define leadership and describe effective leadership characteristics.
2. Define management and describe essential management responsibilities.
3. Determine your leadership values.

© Getty Images/Photodisc

> LEADING AND MANAGING

As you assume positions of greater responsibility in the workplace, you may have one or more people reporting to you. Being an effective manager, one who is able to inspire people to produce at their maximum, means that you understand and apply basic leadership and management theory. Even if you do not become a manager or supervisor, you may have the opportunity to assume leadership roles in other areas. You have learned, throughout this text, that teams are used extensively in organizations today. You will probably have an opportunity to lead teams. Additionally, you may serve as an officer in a professional organization, and/or assume leadership positions in civic and church organizations. By studying this chapter, you will develop an understanding of effective leadership characteristics.

> EFFECTIVE LEADERSHIP DEFINED AND PRACTICED

In defining leadership, the research and writings of four well-known, often quoted, and prolific writers in the field of leadership—Robert Greenleaf, Peter Senge, Peter Drucker, and Stephen Covey—are highlighted in this chapter. Because of the page constraints of this chapter, only a very limited portion of their writing is included. However, you can learn much about leadership by exploring their works and practicing their concepts.

▷ Robert Greenleaf on Leadership

Greenleaf coined the term **servant leadership** in an essay titled *The Servant as Leader.* One of Greenleaf's major premises is that the true leader is a servant-leader, one who is servant first. He writes, "It begins with the natural feeling that one wants to serve, to serve first. Then conscious choice brings one to aspire to lead. The best test is do those served grow as persons; do they, while being served, become healthier, wiser, freer, more autonomous, more likely themselves to become servants? And, what is the effect on the least privileged in society; will they benefit, or at least, not be further deprived?"[1]

The servant leader understands and lives the concept that true leadership involves serving others. True leaders are both leaders and followers; they understand how to move back and forth between leading and following. These leaders help others to grow and take on leadership responsibilities.

True leaders understand the importance of serving others.

© Digital Vision

⊳ Peter Senge on Leadership

Another individual who is a prolific writer in the field of leadership is Peter Senge. In his writing, he encourages leaders to build learning organizations— organizations in which a shared vision of the future allows the organization to move forward in the accomplishment of significant goals and objectives. He suggests that visions that are shared take time to emerge. According to Senge, ". . . visions that are genuinely shared require ongoing conversation where individuals not only feel free to express their dreams, but learn how to listen to each others' dreams. Out of this listening, new insights into what is possible gradually emerge."[2]

⊳ Peter Drucker on Leadership

Peter Drucker in his writing tells this story of a true leader.

A favorite story . . . is that of the three stonecutters who were asked what they were doing. The first replied, *I am making a living.* The second kept hammering while he said, *I am doing the best job of stonecutting in the entire country.* The third one looked up with a visionary gleam in his eyes and said, *I am building a cathedral.*[3]

The third person is the true leader—a person with a vision and the ability to make that vision happen.

⊳ Stephen Covey on Leadership

Covey views leadership from the perspective of principle-centered individuals. He identifies the following as characteristics of principle-centered leaders. They are:

▶ Continual learners.
▶ Service-oriented.
▶ Synergistic, with synergy defined as, " . . . the state in which the whole is more than the sum of the parts."[4]

The leaders:

▶ Believe in other people.
▶ Have a vision.
▶ Lead balanced lives.
▶ See life as adventure.
▶ Have positive energy.[5]

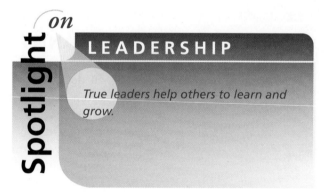

Spotlight *on* LEADERSHIP

True leaders help others to learn and grow.

[1] R. K. Greenleaf, *Servant Leadership* (New York: Paulist Press, 1977), p. 23.

[2] Peter M. Senge, *The Fifth Discipline: The Art and Practice of the Learning Organization* (New York: Currency Doubleday, 1990), pp. 217–218.

[3] Peter F. Drucker, *The Essential Drucker* (New York: Harper Business, 2001), p. 113.

[4] Stephen R. Covey, *Principle-Centered Leadership* (New York: Fireside, 1991), p. 37.

[5] Ibid., pp. 33–39.

Although these writers in the field of leadership have looked at leadership in different ways, there are similarities in their characterization of true leaders, with these similarities being commitment to others through:

- Service.
- Visionary leadership.
- Continual learning.
- Synergy.

> LEADERSHIP TODAY

Throughout this course, you have been reminded that change is constant today. You have also learned that we must consider ourselves part of a global community. Even if we wanted to think of the United States in isolation, we cannot do so. Technology allows us to communicate daily on a worldwide basis, pulling together people of diverse backgrounds and cultures. Many organizations are multinational in scope, demanding that we learn how to communicate effectively with people throughout the world.

In the previous section, you were introduced to four writers in the field of leadership and their perspectives of the characteristics of a true leader. In the next section, you will be introduced to several more characteristics of an effective leader. As you enter the workforce for the first time or as a returning worker, you need to pay careful attention to developing the skills that will assist your growth in your job and in obtaining positions of greater authority and influence.

> LEADERSHIP TRAITS

What are the traits of an effective leader in this global world of constant change? Here are a few important ones.

▷ Lives by a Set of Values

When we look back over history, we discover that values have been important topics of discussion among many leaders and philosophers. The writings and teachings of both Socrates (469–399 B.C.E.)[6] and Plato (428–348 B.C.E.)[7] asserted that virtue and

ethical behavior were associated with wisdom. After the rise of Christianity, Catholic theologians, such as St. Augustine (354–430)[8] and St. Thomas Aquinas (1225–1274),[9] dominated ethical thinking. Correct behavior in both personal and business dealings was necessary to achieve salvation and life after death.

Today, ethical behavior in business remains the accepted practice. The tough part becomes how that ethical behavior is lived in the business organization. What practices are ethical? What practices are not ethical? Even though it can be difficult to determine what is and is not ethical in specific instances, few of us would disagree that our leaders must stand firmly on moral principles. Leaders must work within the organization to identify and define those principles and ensure that they are carried out in the daily activities of the organization. When difficult decisions must be made, leaders must stand on their values; they must walk the talk. Effective leaders understand this principle. They know that establishing and living a set of values must begin with the top leaders and permeate through every level of the organization.

▷ Builds a Shared Vision

The ethical organization has visionary leaders, ones who are able to build a shared vision in the organization. Building this vision means employees at all levels of the organization must be involved. It means that leaders help employees consider these questions:

1. What values does the organization have? What values should it have?

2. What contributions should the organization make to the community?

3. What reputation does the organization have? What reputation should it have?

4. Who are the clients and customers of the organization?

5. How do people work together within the organization?

6. Do the values of the individuals within the organization match the values of the organization?

7. What contributions do individuals within the organization make to the community?

---

[6]"Socrates (469–399 B.C.E.)," <http://www.philosophypages.com/ph/socr.htm> (accessed August 21, 2005).

[7]"Plato (427-347 B.C.E.)," <http://www.philosophypages.com/ph/plat.htm> (accessed August 21, 2005).

[8]"Augustine, Saint (354–430)," <http://www.ccel.org/a/augustine/> (accessed August 21, 2005).

[9]"Saint Thomas Aquinas," <http://plato.stanford.edu/entries/aquinas/> (accessed August 21, 2005).

Effective leaders help employees understand the organization's vision and how their individual goals and objectives support that vision. These leaders publish the organization's vision statement so employees are aware of it. Additionally, a number of organizations today publish their vision/value statement on the Web to inform the public of what is important to their particular organization.

▷ Commits to Service

Effective leaders consider service to others primary. In other words, effective leaders are not concerned first with building a career for themselves, but in understanding how they can serve the organization and its employees as well as the external community. For example, a leader's values may include a commitment to helping people grow, a commitment to diversity, and a commitment to helping the world become a better place. Figure 16-1 presents Starbucks' Mission Statement, with its community comment highlighted.

▷ Empowers Others

Power is the capacity to influence others. Power can flow in any direction in an organization and can apply to both individuals and groups.[10] **Empowerment** can be defined as "putting power where it is needed."[11]

Figure 16-1	STARBUCKS MISSION STATEMENT

Establish Starbucks as the premier purveyor of the finest coffee in the world while maintaining our uncompromising principles while we grow.

The following six guiding principles will help us measure the appropriateness of our decisions:

Provide a great work environment and treat each other with respect and dignity.

Embrace diversity as an essential component in the way we do business.

Apply the highest standards of excellence to the purchasing, roasting and fresh delivery of our coffee.

Develop enthusiastically satisfied customers all of the time.

Contribute positively to our communities and our environment.

Recognize that profitability is essential to our future success.[12]

Leaders empower people when they take these actions:

1. Provide employees with access to information that will help them increase their productivity and effectiveness.

2. Allow employees to take on more responsibility.

3. Allow employees a voice in decision making.

Empowered employees feel a sense of ownership and control over their jobs. They understand they are responsible for getting their jobs done. Empowered employees usually are happier individuals; they trust the organization, feel a part of it, and enjoy the rewards the job provides.

The leader who empowers people has a core belief in people, believing that people are basically good, honest, and well intentioned. The leader believes that people will do the right thing when they have the resources available to accomplish a task. She or he understands that leadership is operating from a central core of values, even in the most difficult situations.

▷ Rewards Risk Taking

Organizations of today, with change as a constant, face risks daily. They do not accept conformity to the norm nor security in the past. Successful organizations must be willing to seek new answers to problems, try new approaches, and be flexible. Successful leaders also encourage risk taking in others. These leaders know that risk taking does not always result in success. However, they are willing to take calculated risks, knowing that the status quo can result in failure.

Some of the keys to successful risk taking are:

1. Trusting in your own abilities,

2. Being open-minded,

3. Overcoming fear of mistakes, and

4. Developing support teams.

▷ Moves Through Chaos

Because chaos is an inevitable part of leadership today, effective leaders learn from it—from the good and bad experiences that happen. Leaders practice

---

[10]"Definition of Power," <http://www.csupomona.edu/~msharifzadeh/mhr318/power.htm> (accessed September 25, 2005), p. 1.

[11]Ibid., p. 5.

[12]"Starbucks Mission Statement," <http://www.starbucks.com/aboutus/environment.asp> (accessed August 21, 2005).

the art of meeting individuals where they are and moving them forward to bring about the desired outcomes. They understand that each situation is different and may be difficult. However, they do not ignore the situation; they move it from the unacceptable to the acceptable.

▷ Knows How to Follow

The effective leader knows the importance of stepping back and being a follower when the situation demands it. This person understands that leaders are sometimes followers and followers are sometimes leaders. A **bilateralness** (affecting or undertaken by two sides equally)[13] exists, with the leader not only understanding the importance of following but also having the trust in others to know that they, given the proper opportunities and training, can be leaders also.

Women and men who lead at the highest level have many extraordinary traits; they continue to develop additional skills throughout their lives. Figure 16-2 lists several additional traits of successful leaders.

> LEADERSHIP AND MANAGEMENT CONTRASTED

Leadership and management are related but different in concept and definition. Numerous writers have dealt with the differences; Figure 16-3 gives closely related but different definitions of leading and managing. The effective leader operates around a clearly defined set of values, with those values centering on what is right for an organization and its employees. Effective leadership relies on the leader

Spotlight *on* **LEADERSHIP**

Effective leaders learn from both good and bad experiences.

Figure 16-2	**KEY TRAITS OF SUCCESSFUL LEADERS**

1. Emotional stability. Good leaders must be able to tolerate frustration and stress. They must be well-adjusted and have the psychological maturity to deal with anything they are required to face.

2. Dominance. Leaders are often competitive and decisive and usually enjoy overcoming obstacles. They are assertive in their thinking style as well as their attitude in dealing with others.

3. Enthusiasm. Leaders are usually seen as active, expressive, and energetic. They are often very optimistic and open to change. Overall, they are generally quick and alert; they tend to be uninhibited.

4. Conscientiousness. Leaders are often dominated by a sense of duty and tend to be very exacting in character. They usually have a very high standard of excellence and an inward desire to do one's best. They also have a need for order and tend to be very self-disciplined.

5. Social boldness. Leaders tend to be spontaneous risk-takers. They are usually socially bold and generally thick skinned. Overall, they are responsive to others and tend to be high in emotional stamina.

6. Tough-mindedness. Good leaders are practical, logical, and to the point. They tend to be low in sentimental attachments and comfortable with criticism. They are usually insensitive to hardship and, overall, are very poised.

7. Self-assurance. Self-confidence and resiliency are common traits among leaders. They tend to be free of guilt and have little or no need for approval. They are generally secure and are usually unaffected by prior mistakes or failures.

8. Compulsiveness. Leaders were found to be controlled and very precise in their social interactions. Overall, they were very protective of their integrity and reputation and consequently tended to be socially aware and careful, abundant in foresight, and careful when making decisions or determining specific actions.[14]

---

[13] *The American Heritage Dictionary*, Third Edition (Boston: Houghton Mifflin Company, 1993), p. 136.

[14] SBA Women's Business Center, "Key Traits of Successful Leaders," <http://www.onlinewbc.gov/docs/manage/traits.html> (accessed August 21, 2005).

Self CHECK A

List the characteristics of an effective leader that you believe you already possess.

____

____

List the characteristics you would like to work on during the remainder of this course.

____

____

Figure 16-3 LEADERSHIP AND MANAGEMENT DIFFERENTIATED

Management is efficiency in climbing the ladder of success; leadership determines whether the ladder is against the right wall.[15]

Management maintains a focus on:

1. Planning and organizing.
2. Controlling and problem solving.
3. Focusing on outcomes.

Leadership maintains a focus on:

1. Creating a vision and developing strategies.
2. Engaging, motivating, and inspiring people.
3. Building trust and having courage.
4. Creating action.[16]

bringing the appropriate set of values to the work environment.

There is no real way to assess the values of the leader in isolation. The values become apparent only as the leader guides an organization to accomplish its goals, which benefit not only the organization but also the external community and the individuals within the organization. The importance of leadership cannot be diminished. Management can be considered a subset of leadership. The functions of management include planning, organizing, leading, and controlling. These activities are relatively concrete and can be quantified, measured, and assessed. If an organization is to be successful, these functions must be understood and carried out effectively. Although the characteristics of effective leaders and the responsibilities of effective managers are presented separately in this textbook, understand that the most effective managers are also effective leaders. Conversely, effective leaders are also effective managers.

> MANAGEMENT RESPONSIBILITIES

If you are to be successful in a supervisory role, you need to understand how to effectively perform the basic management functions, including planning, organizing, managing information, recruiting and employing, training, controlling, motivating, delegating, and evaluating. These responsibilities are presented here.

Planning

Planning is a crucial function of management. Without proper planning, an organization and its employees do not know where they are going. A major part of the planning process is setting goals and objectives. Although most organizations have goals and objectives, they may be very loosely defined or not defined at all. Defining them in writing and establishing measurable results is a process that was recommended by Peter Drucker over 50 years ago. In a seminal work entitled *The Practice of Management,*

[15]Leadership Quotes: Voices of Wisdom and Experience, Stephen R. Covey, *The Seven Habits of Highly Effective People,* "Leadership vs. Management," <http://ebiz.netopia.com/learntolead/voicesofexperiencequotes/> (accessed August 21, 2005).

[16]Leadership Quotes: Voices of Wisdom and Experience, Leadership vs. Management, Trish Jacobson, "What It Takes To Be an Effective Leader," *Canadian Manager,* Winter 2002 "Leadership vs. Management," <http://ebiz.netopia.com/learntolead/voicesofexperiencequotes/> (accessed August 21, 2005).

Drucker set forth the process that came to be known as Management by Objectives (**MBO**).[17]

Strategic thinking (addressing the values, philosophical convictions that guide the organization, and the vision of what the organization should be in the future)[18] leads to **strategic planning** or **long-range planning** (a comprehensive management tool designed to help organizations assess the current environment, anticipate changes in the environment, increase effectiveness, develop the organization's mission, and reach a consensus on strategies and objectives for achieving the mission). Organizational plans are generally written for two time frames—a one-year period (**tactical planning**) and a three- to five-year period (strategic planning or long-range planning).[19] In the past, organizations sometimes wrote plans for a ten-year period. However, our world is changing so rapidly today that it is difficult to write ten-year plans.

The overall goals of an organization may be set by boards of directors and top-level administrators (presidents and executive vice presidents). Once these goals have been determined, they are distributed to the managers in the organization. The managers, along with their workgroups, then set objectives for their work units. Managers are held responsible by upper administration for achieving the objectives established.

Assume you are a supervisor of two administrative support staff. What is your involvement in the planning process? First, you review the strategic plan with the personnel who report to you and go over the long-range objectives. You then talk with them about the directions the unit needs to take to support the strategic plan. Next, as a unit you set objectives that support the overall objectives of the organization. The unit, with your leadership, then develops a tactical plan that specifies how the objectives will be accomplished—what actions will occur, who is accountable, when the tasks will be completed, what financial resources are necessary, and how the tasks will be evaluated.

Once the plan is developed, you hold the employees who report to you responsible for completion of the tasks. You help your staff get past any roadblocks that occur. You support them in the accomplishment of their tasks that support the overall goals of the organization.

▷ Organizing

Once the planning occurs, the work is organized. Organization involves bringing together people and systems to accomplish the organizational goals in an effective manner.

Teams

As you have learned throughout this book, teams are used extensively in organizations today. Once a team receives an assignment, the team members determine the responsibilities of each team member and accomplish the tasks in a timely manner. If a team member does not perform her or his portion of the task, it is the responsibility of the team leader to discuss the issue with the individual.

Teams can be more effective when these conditions are present:

▸ The task is clear.
▸ The team works together well.
▸ Information is shared.
▸ Each individual has the knowledge and skill needed to perform his or her portion of the task.
▸ Resources are available to accomplish the task.
▸ Teams are given appropriate authority to accomplish the work.

Teams are hindered or ineffective in the following conditions:

▸ The task is not clear.
▸ Resources (both people and monetary) are not provided to accomplish the task.
▸ Managers **micromanage** (do not give people the information and authority to do the tasks assigned; over monitor and assess every step). The result of micromanagement is often an ineffective team—one that is unable to get the task done because of the ineffectiveness of the manager.
▸ Team members are not willing to take risks.

Systems

A **system** is a dynamic and complex whole that interacts as a structured functional unit with information flowing between the different elements that compose the systems.[20] Systems thinking is almost

[17]Peter Drucker, *The Practice of Management* (New York: Harper and Row, 1954), p. 122.
[18]George W. Morrisey, *Morrisey on Planning: A Guide to Strategic Thinking: Building Your Planning Foundation* (San Francisco: Jossey-Bass, 1996), p. 4.
[19]Ibid., pp. 100–106.
[20]Wikipedia, "Systems Thinking," <http://en.wikipedia.org/wiki/Systems_thinking> (accessed September 25, 2005).

synonymous with organizational learning. The leader of the unit helps unit members understand the organization as a system in which everyone's work affects the activities of everyone else. If the systems within an organization are not well defined and easily accessible by people within the organization, the effectiveness of the organization is reduced significantly.

For example, assume that your organization is becoming a multinational organization, expanding to New Zealand within the next three years. Your manager has asked your workgroup to determine whether or not a call center will be set up in New Zealand; and if so, the number of employees who will be needed in the operation. After considerable research and discussion of the directions the organization is taking (through reviewing the organizational plan), your group recommends that a call center be set up and staffed initially with five employees. You also project that within two years, assuming the organization is effective, additional personnel will be needed—four is the projected number. When your recommendations go to your supervisor, he reviews them with human resources and discovers that no budget exists for expansion of call centers.

What happened? Your workgroup did not take into consideration all the systems within the organization that were needed in helping you to define the parameters of your task. Perhaps systems were not well defined and possibly not easily accessible to all employees within the organization. You were given a task; you accepted that task, thinking that you had the latitude to get the task done. You were not told that there were financial constraints, and you did not check with human resources. There was lack of definition in the task; thus, your effectiveness was reduced. However, one positive aspect of this situation emerges—learning from failure contributes greatly to a learning organization.

▷ Managing Information

A major task of management is managing information. Think for a minute about the amount of information generated by organizations. This information includes product information, research information, personnel information, financial information, and so forth. If information is to be of value to organizations, their boards, their clients and customers, and their employees, it must be accurate, complete, relevant, and timely. Systems must be developed that allow this information to be stored properly, used effectively, and distributed to the necessary **stakeholders** both inside and outside the organization. Examples of stakeholders include project teams, human resources, purchasing agents, top management, government agencies, subcontractors, customers, and stockholders—if the organization is a publicly-held one. This list of stakeholders is not meant to be all inclusive; certainly, there can be numerous other stakeholders depending on the organization and the information generated.

▷ Recruiting and Employing

Organizations usually establish procedures through their human resources departments that outline how they will recruit employees. Managers and supervisors within departments then have the responsibility for recruiting and employing. If supervisors are to do so effectively, they must be aware of recruitment sources and laws that impact recruiting and interviewing. For example, when placing advertisements, companies must not discriminate against any group of people. Discrimination statutes prohibit advertisements that show preferences in terms of race, religion, gender, age, or physical disabilities. An employer cannot advertise for a particular age group. Expressions such as *young person* or *retired person* are illegal in advertisements. If you are recruiting employees, check with the appropriate individuals within your company (usually human resources) to make certain you are observing the organization's rules and legal guidelines.

Spotlight *on*

RECRUITING

When recruiting individuals for a job, employers must become familiar with and follow laws that prevent discrimination in hiring.

Organizations use three major screening and selection tools when employing people; these are:

▸ Résumés.
▸ Interviews.
▸ Testing.

The manager or a team of people may review the applications. If you are part of that team, you should be clear about the skills, education, and experience you are seeking in job applicants. All of this information should have been determined before the job description was written and the job vacancy notice posted. With the criteria in mind, screen the applications and select the most qualified individuals to interview, noting specifically the information in the résumé.

You may choose to conduct one-on-one interviews, team interviews, or a combination of the two. Before the interviewing process begins, compile a list of questions to ask of each candidate. Such a list keeps you and the team on target as you begin the interviewing process and helps you treat all interviewees with fairness and consistency. Additionally, the list helps remind you that certain questions are not legal. The following questions are unlawful to ask during the interview:

Are you married? Single? Divorced? Separated?

What is the date of your birth?

Is your spouse a U.S. citizen?

Where were you born?

To what clubs do you belong?

What are the ages of your children?

What church do you attend?

Have you ever belonged to a union?

You must keep up with the latest laws concerning discrimination and interviewing procedures. Otherwise, you may inadvertently place your organization in jeopardy of a discrimination suit.

Set aside enough time for a thorough interview. You will probably need to spend an hour or more with each applicant. Do not consider this time wasted. Hiring the right person for a job is one of the most important things you will do as a manager.

The third screening tool is the test. Here, too, legal considerations are important. The test must measure the person's qualifications for the job. If you are employing an administrative professional, for example, and a requirement of the job is that the person is able to key at a certain rate with an established degree of accuracy, you can give the person a keyboarding test. You can also give applicants grammar and spelling tests because they must produce documents free of grammar and spelling errors. You cannot ask the applicant to take a math proficiency test unless the use of math is necessary in performing the job. If you decide to test, you must give the same test to all candidates. You cannot select

You can ask an administrative professional to take a keyboarding test.

© Photodisc/Ryan McVay

certain applicants to test and certain others that you do not test.

▷ Training

Once a person is employed, the next step is to assist that person in gaining the necessary knowledge of the organization and the job that she or he is to perform. To be successful, the person must learn about proper company procedures. As a manager, you have an obligation in this area. New employees need to know the history of the organization, the policy and procedures of the organization (usually there is a policy and procedures manual), and evaluation procedures, such as when evaluations occur and what criteria and evaluation forms are used. Other entry-level training includes assistance in the day-to-day procedures of the administrative professional's job, such as using records management systems and technology.

Some organizations assign new employees **mentors** (counselors or teachers).[21] The mentor meets with the new employee regularly, introduces the new employee to other people within the organization,

---

[21] *The American Heritage Dictionary,* Third Edition (Boston: Houghton Mifflin Company, 1993), p. 851.

answers questions, and helps the employee learn both the job and the organizational procedures. In addition to entry-level training, ongoing training is necessary because of the rapid changes in technology.

▷ Controlling

Organizations exercise a variety of controls in measuring the performance of the organization and individuals within the organization. One of these measures is **benchmarking** (comparing one's performance with the best performance in the industry or with the best anywhere in the business).[22] Organizations may benchmark anything; for example, the time needed to produce products, and the quality of the products.

Still another very different type of control can be exercising control over dysfunctional politics within the workgroup. When attempting to control politics, leaders must be aware of the causes and techniques used within the workgroup. For example, during a downsizing, the chief executive officer can be alert to backstabbing that might take place and/or attempts to please him or her. Open communication in such instances can reduce the amount of dysfunctional politics. When communication is open between management and employees, it makes it much more difficult for gossip to be used as a political weapon.[23]

▷ Motivating

Motivation may be **extrinsic** (originating from the outside)[24] or **intrinsic** (relating to the essential nature of a thing).[25] An example of an extrinsic factor is a salary increase; an example of an intrinsic factor is something that is done because it is right and fits the individual's values. Figure 16-4 lists both intrinsic and extrinsic motivational factors.

▷ Delegating

Delegation refers to assigning tasks to others and empowering them by providing the necessary information to get the job done. Delegation can be difficult for a manager, particularly one who has a need to control all aspects of a job. Yet no manager can possibly do it all; managers must delegate. Once a task is delegated, employees should be trusted to perform.

Figure 16-4 · MOTIVATIONAL TECHNIQUES

1. **Set objectives.** Help employees you supervise establish challenging, measurable objectives. Then, help them commit themselves to achieving the objectives. This approach requires follow through and planning on the part of the supervisor. You must not only know the objectives, but also follow up to see that the employee has achieved the objectives.

2. **Give recognition.** As a supervisor, you need to become sensitive to the accomplishments of others. You can give recognition in a number of ways: verbal praise for a job well done, a thank-you letter written to an employee, and recognition in the organization's newsletter.

3. **Develop a team.** Individuals need to be an accepted member of a group. As a supervisor, you can capitalize on this need by building a team of people who work together well. Productivity can be increased when each person in the group contributes to the overall effectiveness of the team.

4. **Pay for the job.** As a supervisor, know what your employees do and then pay them fairly for their work. Reward employees who consistently give you outstanding performance with good salary increases.

5. **Delegate work.** Employees enjoy doing meaningful and challenging work. Provide them this opportunity by delegating important projects.

▷ Evaluating

The evaluation step is an important one. Without it, plans may not be carried out, with no one asking why. Organizations suffer, and even go out of business, because of an inability to adhere to plans and deliver a product or service that customers need. Still another important area of evaluation is that of employees. Evaluation of personnel is never easy. As a manager, you should have a carefully defined evaluation system, one that all employees understand and all administrators uphold. Individuals are evaluated in most organizations at specified periods of time. Teams may also be evaluated by the manager and/or by other team members. In addition, the entire workgroup may be a part of the evaluation process.

---

[22]Peter F. Drucker, *The Essential Drucker* (New York: Harper Business, 2001), p. 104.

[23]Andrew J. DuBrin, *Leadership: Research Findings, Practice, and Skills* (New York: Houghton Mifflin Company, 2004), pp. 220–221.

[24]*The American Heritage Dictionary*, Third Edition (Boston: Houghton Mifflin Company, 1993), p. 486.

[25]Ibid., p. 712.

Spotlight *on* MANAGEMENT

Management empowers others by providing them with the necessary information to get the job done.

Team members may evaluate each other after working on a project.

Suggestions for administering effective evaluation systems are given in Figure 16-5.

Individuals

Individual evaluations are essential even if team evaluations occur. Most companies use forms and processes developed by the human resources department. This department may use a team within the company to develop the evaluation system. Once the evaluation process is developed, it should be consistently followed throughout the organization. Usually, the process involves an employee completing a self-evaluation and the supervisor preparing an evaluation. At the evaluation conference, both evaluations are discussed and a final evaluation document is prepared. If the employee provides information that the supervisor does not have, the supervisor should note that information on the form.

Teams

Some companies use team evaluations in which employees who work together as a team are asked to evaluate each other. These team evaluations may be given by the supervisors of the people involved in the team or by the individual team members only. If the team members discuss the evaluation, the team leader needs to take a strong position in the process to ensure that the team evaluation session does not become one of fault-finding or blaming others. Guidelines should be given to the team before the evaluation occurs. The team leader should stress that the evaluation is to determine whether the team completed its tasks successfully and what contributions were made by individual members to the task.

Workgroups

Workgroup evaluations may also be a part of the evaluation process. Workgroups should set measurable objectives that are related to the overall goals established by the organization. The manager and the workgroup might also evaluate what needs to be improved during the next six months or year by using a total quality approach. Here are some questions they might ask.

1. What needs to be improved?

2. What actions should the workgroup take to improve the areas identified?

Self CHECK B

List the management characteristics that you need to acquire.

_____

_____

_____

Figure 16-5 **EMPLOYEE EVALUATION TECHNIQUES**

▶ When a new employee is hired, explain the organization's evaluation system within the first week of employment. If the formal evaluation process is in writing (and it is a good idea to have it in writing), give the employee a written copy and go over how often evaluation will occur. Ask the employee if he or she has any questions; take the time to answer the questions.

▶ Never rely on only formal evaluation. On a daily or weekly basis, give an employee feedback. For example, if there is an error in a piece of correspondence, show the error to the employee. Make certain the employee understands how to correct the error. Give positive feedback concerning projects that are done well; do not confine yourself to only negative feedback.

▶ Involve all employees in strategic planning for the unit. Ask that each employee determine what activities he or she will perform in support of the plan.

▶ Allow adequate time for formal evaluation. You need to spend an hour or two with each employee. Hold the evaluation conference in an appropriate place. If you are using your office, ask that you not be interrupted and close the door to ensure privacy.

▶ In the formal evaluation session, establish ground rules at the beginning of the session. For example, you might say, "I will discuss your performance on each objective of your plan and then give you an opportunity to tell me what your assessment is."

▶ During the formal evaluation session, praise the employee for work well done. Too many managers consider an evaluation period as a time for criticism only. It is not. In what areas is the employee performing in an exemplary manner? In an average manner? Below expectations?

▶ During the session, stay focused on the topics at hand. It is a time to discuss both contributions and the need for improvement. If you are asking for improvement from the employee, give examples of what you expect. Make certain that you are clear about your expectations.

▶ Give the employee an opportunity to talk. An evaluation session should be a time when both the manager and the employee have an opportunity to discuss performance. Encourage the employee to tell you how you may help the employee grow in the job. If the employee makes negative comments, try to understand and accept the employee's feelings.

▶ An evaluation session is not a time to talk about personal areas for either the evaluator or the person being evaluated. Do not become involved in an employee's personal life. Do not confide in the employee concerning your own personal issues.

▶ If the employee has numerous areas of improvement that must be made, ask her or him to develop a plan in writing. Review the plan with the employee and modify as appropriate. The plan should clearly address what the employee must do to improve. If the employee shows improvement, praise the person. If the employee does not show improvement, schedule a session to discuss why improvement is not occurring. If the employee has major problems, the next step may be firing the individual. No caring supervisor does this lightly. The employee must be given appropriate information and help to improve. However, if the employee (after a period determined by you and understood by the employee) does not improve, termination may be the only possible step. It should always be the last resort and made only after giving the employee time and help.

▶ Take notes during the performance evaluation and urge the employee to do the same. Offer the employee an opportunity to add comments to the final written evaluation, which becomes a part of his or her file.

3. Who does what and when is it done? Once these questions have been answered, a plan is developed. The plan should include specific tasks to be achieved, including who is responsible for each task identified and when the task will be completed.

4. Is the plan working? Once the action plan is implemented, it is monitored to determine if the desired results are being achieved.

5. What has been learned? Areas where difficulties occurred should be reviewed so performance can improve.

> THE RIGHT TO LEAD

Leadership in an organization is an earned right—a person is not born with leadership characteristics.

One must work at developing them. You have also learned that a leader lives by a set of values. If a leader is to be effective, the organizational values and the leader's values must be aligned. Value-driven leaders understand that success does not come from merely talking about values; success comes from consistently putting values into action. When organizational tasks are aligned around values and when goals are lived by individuals within the organization, ordinary people can and do accomplish extraordinary results.

Needless to say, not all individuals have the characteristics mentioned in this chapter and not all individuals are interested in developing these traits. The process of learning how to lead is a continual

Spotlight *on* **LEADERSHIP**

Leadership is not a birthright; it is developed through hard work, living by a set of values, and aligning the values and goals of the organization.

one. Individuals who consistently demonstrate a commitment to the skills defined in this chapter earn the right to lead.

SUMMARY

Reinforce your learning in this chapter by studying this summary.

▸ Robert Greenleaf coined the term servant leadership, with the premise that the true leader is a servant first.

▸ Peter Senge encourages leaders to build learning organizations—organizations in which a shared vision of the future allows the organization to move forward in the accomplishment of significant goals and objectives.

▸ Peter Drucker defines the true leader as a person with a vision and the ability to make that vision happen.

▸ Stephen Covey views leadership from the perspective of principle-centered individuals. He

believes these principle-centered leaders are continual learners, service-oriented, and synergistic.

▸ Leadership traits include living by a set of values, building a shared vision, committing to service, empowering others, rewarding risk taking, moving through chaos, and knowing how to follow.

▸ Management is a subset of leadership. The functions of management include planning, organizing, leading, and controlling.

▸ Leadership is an earned right—a person is not born with leadership characteristics. One must develop them through hard work and living by a set of values.

GLOSSARY

Benchmarking—Comparing one's performance with the best performance in the industry or with the best anywhere in the business.

Bilateralness—Affecting or undertaken by two sides equally.

Delegation—Refers to assigning tasks to others and empowering them by providing the necessary information to get the job done.

Empowerment—Putting power where it is needed.

Extrinsic—Originating from the outside.

Intrinsic—Relating to the essential nature of a thing.

MBO—Management by Objectives.

Mentors—Counselors or teachers.

Micromanage—Not giving people information and the authority to do the tasks assigned; over monitor and assess every step.

Power—The capacity to influence others.

Servant leadership—One who is servant first, then leader.

Stakeholders—Those to whom information is often distributed: project teams, human resources, purchasing agents, top management, government agencies, subcontractors, customers, and stockholders.

Strategic planning or **long-range planning**—A comprehensive management tool designed to help organizations assess the current environment, anticipate changes in the environment, increase effectiveness, develop the organization's mission, and reach a consensus on strategies and objectives for achieving the mission.

Strategic thinking—Addressing the values and philosophical convictions that guide the organization, and the vision of what the organization should be in the future.

System—A dynamic and complex whole that interacts as a structured functional unit.

Tactical planning—Planning that is done for one year.

CHECKPOINT

Check your understanding of these terms by completing DCD16-a on the Data CD.

DISCUSSION ITEMS

These discussion items provide an opportunity to test your understanding of the chapter through written responses and/or discussion with your classmates and your instructor.

1. Research leadership and discuss three writers in the field of leadership.

2. Describe effective leadership characteristics.

3. Define management.

4. Describe essential management responsibilities.

CRITICAL THINKING CASE

Two months ago, JWay Nu-Systems Tech offered you a position as a manager in the recently opened Australia office of JWay. After four months of doing an internship in Australia, studying leadership, and talking with leaders you respect in JWay, you decided to accept the position.

You are responsible for supervising three call center employees—two are Australian and one is Chinese. These employees went through a month-long training program before working with customers. You feel that your training program was a good one. However, one of the Australians is not effective with customers. You have already had two serious complaints from customers. You have talked with your supervisor about your concerns; he has told you to give the employee more time to learn the job. You have talked with the employee about the complaints, offering her a few suggestions for how she might do the job better. You have assured her that you know she can learn the job and you are counting on her to be successful. This week you have had three complaints about her inability to deal with customers. These customers have told you that she is rude, non-responsive, and sometimes "yells" at them. You have decided that you must be more direct with her; the situation must change. What should you do? Remember that your employer has asked you to give her more time.

A

Your responses should indicate the effective leadership qualities you possess presently and indicate leadership growth areas.

B

Your responses should indicate your management skills and designate growth areas for you to pursue.

WORKPLACE PROJECTS

PROJECT 16-1 CONDUCT RESEARCH AND PREPARE A REPORT

Define leadership and describe effective leadership characteristics (Objective 1)

Define management and describe essential management responsibilities (Objective 2)

Work as a team with three of your classmates on this assignment. Research effective leadership and management, using four references. Two of your references may be Greenleaf, Senge, Drucker, or Covey. All of these people have written extensively, and you will have no problem finding material outside the textbook. Determine at least four characteristics of effective leaders and managers (other than the ones presented in your textbook). Summarize your findings in a report to your instructor. Submit your report to your instructor.

PROJECT 16-2 ADD TO YOUR PROFESSIONAL GROWTH PLAN

Determine your leadership values (Objective 3)

Add to your Professional Growth Plan by determining the leadership values that are important for your development. Save your plan as PGP16-2.

Review your Professional Growth Plan. Have you met all your objectives? If not, which ones do you need to meet or refine? Think about your future and decide what steps you need to follow to prepare yourself even better for your career. List those steps. If your instructor asks, present your plan in an interview situation with him or her.

COMMUNICATION POWER

Use DCD16-b to assist you in improving your grammar skills.

ASSESSMENT OF CHAPTER OBJECTIVES

Now that you have completed the chapter and the projects, take a few minutes to review the chapter learning objectives. For your convenience, the objectives are repeated here. Did you accomplish these objectives? If you were unable to accomplish the objectives, give your reasons for not doing so; be specific and concise. Your instructor may prefer that your answers be submitted to her or him. If so, DCD16-c contains the Assessment of Chapter Objectives. Complete the Assessment of Chapter Objectives; submit your results to your instructor.

1. Define leadership and describe effective leadership characteristics.　　Yes ☐　　No ☐

_____

_____

_____

_____

_____

2. Define management and describe essential management responsibilities.　　Yes ☐　　No ☐

_____

_____

_____

_____

_____

3. Determine your leadership values.　　Yes ☐　　No ☐

_____

_____

_____

_____

_____

PART VI: YOUR CAREER

Integrated Project

Note: You are to work individually on this project.

In the Integrated Project for Part V, you began work in Australia. Your supervisor has been extremely pleased with your work and has urged you to continue in an administrative position; he has assured you that you have a future in the company in this area. You have enjoyed your work and feel that it is challenging and exciting. You have discovered that your training skills are good and that employees respond positively to you. You feel that you can help people learn and grow, while serving the needs of JWay and its customers. The Taiwan office is opening within the next few months. Your supervisor wants you to consider helping JWay open this office and train the new customer service representatives. He has told you that you can expect to spend two years in Taiwan; after that time, he feels you will have other opportunities available to you within JWay.

Your Assignment

You have enjoyed your supervisory role, and you feel that you have learned much. However, you still need to learn more about training, motivating, and evaluating others. You have told your supervisor that you will take the opening in Taiwan. You know that, in addition to expanding your supervisory skills, you need to learn more about the history of Taiwan and its culture. As you research its history and culture, consider how you will use this information in becoming a more effective supervisor.

Task I
- Research the areas mentioned and write a memorandum to your instructor advising her or him how you will improve your training, motivating, and evaluating skills and how you will use your research on Taiwan as you employ and work with the Taiwanese.

Task II
- Write a job description for a customer service representative; include languages that need to be spoken.

Task III
- Submit a proposal for training activities for the customer service representatives, identifying essential training areas and personnel needed to deliver the training; e.g., you may choose to use an outside firm.

CONTENTS

REFERENCE GUIDE

The Reference Guide provides grammar and punctuation rules and basic formats for letters and reports that you use daily in written and verbal communication. To help you review the basics, read through the Reference Guide at the beginning of the course. You can also refer to it as questions arise when you are preparing materials for this course. Additionally, as you complete the Communication Power on the Data CD for each chapter, use the materials to review specific rules. The parts of the Reference Guide are as follows:

▶ Abbreviations
▶ Bias-Free Language
▶ Capitalization
▶ Collective Nouns
▶ Letters and Envelopes
▶ Number Usage
▶ Often Misused Words and Phrases
▶ Parallel Construction
▶ Passive Voice
▶ Plurals and Possessives
▶ Pronouns
▶ Punctuation
▶ Report Format
▶ Spelling Rules
▶ Subject and Verb Agreement
▶ Word Division
▶ Proofreaders' Marks

> ABBREVIATIONS

1. Use standard abbreviations for titles immediately before and after proper names.

   ### Before the Name

   Periods are used in abbreviations before the name.

   > Dr. Cindy Bos
   > Mr. Michael Khirallah
   > Rev. Thomas McIntrye

   ### After the Name

   Academic, military, and civil honors follow a name and are preceded with a comma. Academic degrees are abbreviated in uppercase with periods, or the periods may be eliminated. The titles *Reverend* and *Honorable* are spelled out if preceded by *the*.

   > The Honorable Marjorie Popham
   > Patricia LaFaver, Ph.D.
   > Nathan Portello, MS
   > Bryant McAnnelley, J.D.
   > Helene Chen, PhD
   > Bryon Edwards, MD

   Civil titles are abbreviated in uppercase with no periods.

   > J. Hansel LeFevre, CLU

   Personal titles such as *Rev., Hon., Prof., Gen., Col., Capt.,* and *Lieut.* may be abbreviated when they precede a surname and a given name. When only the surname is used, these titles should be spelled out.

   > Prof. Mark Huddleston
   > Professor Huddleston

2. Many companies and professional organizations are known by abbreviated names. These abbreviated names are keyed in capital letters with no periods and no spaces between the letters.

   > IBM   International Business Machines
   > YMCA Young Men's Christian Association

3. Certain expressions are abbreviated.

   > e.g. exempli gratia (for example)
   > etc. et cetera (and so forth)
   > i.e. id est (that is)

4. Names of countries should be abbreviated only in tabulations or enumerations and should be written in capital letters; periods may or may not be used in these abbreviations.

   > U.S.A. or USA
   > U.S. or US

   Note: *United States* may be spelled out as a noun and abbreviated as an adjective.

   > The United States 2000 Census gave us updated statistics concerning our population.
   > The median age of the U.S. population is 35.6 years.

5. Abbreviations for government agencies are usually written in capital letters with no periods and no spaces between the letters.

   > FTC   Federal Trade Commission
   > CIA   Central Intelligence Agency

6. Abbreviations containing a period falling at the end of a sentence use only one period. In sentences ending with a question mark or an exclamation mark, place the punctuation mark directly after the period.

> The play began at 8:15 p.m.
> Does the class start at 9:30 a.m.?

7. The following categories of words should not be abbreviated unless these words appear in tabulations or enumerations.

- ▶ Names of territories and possessions of the United States, countries, states, and cities
- ▶ Names of months
- ▶ Days of the week
- ▶ Given names, such as *Wm.* for *William*
- ▶ Words such as *Avenue, Boulevard, Court, Street, Drive, Road, Building*
- ▶ Parts of company names (such as *Bros., Co., Corp.*) unless the words are abbreviated in the official company name
- ▶ Compass directions when they are part of an address; use *North, South, East, West. NW, NE, SE,* and *SW* may be abbreviated after a street name, however.
- ▶ The word *number* unless it is followed by a numeral.

> BIAS-FREE LANGUAGE

In the last few years, we have become aware of the effects language can have when used to describe characteristics such as gender, race, and physical characteristics. As we speak and write, we must carefully consider the words we use. This section offers suggestions for avoiding communication biases in three areas—gender, race, and physical characteristics.

▷ Gender Bias

Inclusive usage in language (incorporating both sexes) is extremely important in writing. Exclusive language (words that by their form or meaning discriminate on the basis of gender) should be avoided. Examples of exclusive language include words such as *craftsman, weatherman, fireman, policeman,* and so on. Other examples of exclusive language include such statements as these.

> *The teacher asked everyone to state his name.*
> *The executive answered his phone.*

In writing and speaking, gender bias statements should be eliminated. For example, *weatherman* becomes *weatherperson, policeman* becomes *police officer.*

> *The teacher asked everyone to give his or her name.*
> *The executive answered the phone.*

Strategies for avoiding pronoun gender problems include the following:

- ▶ Use the plural of the noun and pronoun.
- ▶ Delete the pronoun altogether.
- ▶ Replace the masculine pronoun with an article *(the).*
- ▶ Use *he* or *she* (but only sparingly).

▷ Ethnic and Racial Bias

Acceptable terms for various races and ethnicities change over time. It is the writer's and speaker's responsibility to be aware of the most acceptable terms. Presently these terms are the ones to use.

- ▶ *African American* (Some African Americans prefer *black.*) The phrase people of color has been used recently.
- ▶ *Native Americans* or *American Indians*
- ▶ *Hispanic* (Some individuals prefer *Latinos/Latinas,* with the masculine form ending in *o* and the feminine form ending in *a.*)
- ▶ *Asian* may be used as a general term when referring to people from the Far Eastern region of the world. Citizens of China are *Chinese,* never Orientals.

▷ Biases Based on Physical Characteristics

The most recent terms for individuals with disabilities is *physically challenged.* Some groups (but certainly not all) prefer to use *visually impaired* for the blind and *hearing impaired* for the deaf. Since terms do change, you must be aware of current usage.

> CAPITALIZATION

1. The first word of every sentence should be capitalized.

2. The first word of a complete direct quotation should be capitalized. The first word of an indirect quotation

is not capitalized. (The word *that* frequently introduces indirect quotations.)

> Mary reported that "the group is angry over the intolerance of several group members."

If words like *yes* and *no* are not direct quotations, they are not placed in quotes.

> He answered no to every question he was asked.

3. The first word of a salutation and all nouns used in the salutation should be capitalized.

4. The first word in a complimentary close should be capitalized.

5. The first word after a colon is capitalized when the colon introduces a complete passage or sentence having independent meaning.

> Jacques made this statement: "The survey shows that consumers are satisfied with the product."

If the material following a colon is dependent on the preceding clause, the first word after the colon is not capitalized.

> I present the following three reasons for changing: the volume of business does not justify the expense; we are short of people; the product is decreasing in popularity.

6. The names of associations, buildings, churches, hotels, streets, organizations, and clubs are capitalized.

> The Business Club, Merchandise Mart, Central Christian Church, Peabody Hotel, Seventh Avenue, Administrative Management Society, Chicago Chamber of Commerce

7. All proper names should be capitalized.

> Great Britain, John G. Hammitt, Mexico

8. Capitalize names derived from proper names.

> American, Chinese

Do not however, capitalize words derived from proper nouns that have developed a special meaning.

> pasteurized milk, china dishes, moroccan leather

9. Capitalize special names for regions and localities.

> North Central States, the Far East, the East Side, the Hoosier State

Do not, however, capitalize adjectives derived from such names or localities used as directional parts of states and countries: far eastern lands, the southern United States, southern Illinois

10. Capitalize names of government boards, agencies, bureaus, departments, and commissions.

> Civil Service Commission, Social Security Board, Bureau of Navigation

11. Capitalize names of the deity, the Bible, holy days, and religious denominations.

> God, Easter, Yom Kippur, Genesis, Church of Christ

12. Capitalize the names of holidays.

> Memorial Day, Labor Day

13. Capitalize words used before numbers and numerals, with the exception of common words, such as *page, line,* and *verse*.

> We are on Flight 1683.
> He found the material on page 15.

14. Any title that signifies rank, honor, and respect and that immediately precedes an individual's name should be capitalized. Do not capitalize a title that follows a name.

> She asked President Harry G. Sanders to preside.
> Dr. Carter is president of the company.

15. Capitalize titles of high-ranking government officers when the title is used in place of the proper name in referring to a specific person.

> Our Senator invited us to visit him in Washington.
> The President will return to Washington soon.

16. Capitalize military and naval titles signifying rank.

> Captain Meyers, Lieutenant White, Lieutenant Commander Murphy

17. Capitalize the first words of list items when they are set apart from the text; do not capitalize the first words of list items in running text.

The appendix includes the following parts:

► Abbreviations
► Capitalization

Before preparing a presentation, the presenter should consider these areas: the intended audience, the age of the audience, the number of people who are anticipated, and the interests of the audience.

18. Personifications of abstractions are usually capitalized.

> In the autumn, Nature treats us to beautiful colors of gold, orange, and auburn.

19. Names of buildings, monuments, and public places are usually capitalized.

    Buckingham Palace
    the Statue of Liberty
    the Great Wall of China

20. Titles of laws, bills, and historical documents are capitalized when the full title is used.

    the Gettysburg Address
    the Constitution
    the Declaration of Independence
    the Civil Rights Act

21. Proper nouns referring to a supreme being and other deities are capitalized.

    the Messiah
    Buddha
    Jehovah
    the Prophet Mohammed
    Jesus

22. Proper names of clubs, societies, associations, and institutions are capitalized.

    Girl Scouts of America
    Better Business Bureau

23. Names of teams, leagues, divisions, and conferences are capitalized.

    the Dallas Cowboys   the Davis Cup
    the Olympic Games   the World Series

> COLLECTIVE NOUNS

A collective noun is a word that is singular in form but represents a group of persons or things. For example, the following words are collective nouns: *committee, company, department, public, class,* and *board.* These rules determine the form of the verb to be used with a collective noun.

When the members of a group are thought of as one unit, the verb should be singular.

The *committee has* voted unanimously to begin the study.

When members of a group are thought of as separate units, the verb should be plural.

The *staff are* not in agreement on the decision that should be made.

If the sentence seems unclear or awkward, you may address the problem by inserting the word

members after the collective noun and using a plural verb.

The *staff members are* not in agreement on the decision that should be made.

> LETTERS AND ENVELOPES

This section provides a review of letter and punctuation styles, placement of letter parts, envelope addresses, and letter insertion.

▷ Letter and Punctuation Styles

Letters may be keyed in block or modified block style. Figure 1 shows block style with blocked paragraphs. (When using block letter style, the paragraphs must be flush left.) Notice in the block letter style that every line begins at the left margin. Figure 2 shows modified block style with indented paragraphs. (When using modified block style, the paragraphs may be blocked or indented.) Notice in the modified block style that the date line and the closing lines begin near the horizontal center of the page.

With open punctuation, no punctuation appears after the salutation or complimentary close. With mixed punctuation, a colon appears after the salutation and a comma appears after the complimentary close. Notice the open punctuation style in Figure 1 on page 415 and the mixed punctuation style in Figure 2 on page 416.

▷ Placement of Letter Parts

▶ Date line—Key a double space below the last line of the letterhead or 2" from the top of the page without a letterhead.
▶ Inside address—Key four lines (a quadruple space) below the date.
▶ Attention line—Key as the first line of the address.
▶ Salutation—Key a double space below the letter address.
▶ Subject or reference line—Key the subject line in ALL CAPS a double space below the salutation.
▶ Body—Key a double space below the salutation or a double space below the subject line.
▶ Second-page heading—Key 1" from the top. Key the addressee's name, the page number, and the date in a three-line block at the left margin. Or use a one-line arrangement, and key the addressee's name at the left margin, center the page number, and position the date flush at the right margin.

Figure 1   **BLOCK LETTER STYLE, OPEN PUNCTUATION**

MCGREGORY INTERIOR DESIGN
1818 Neiwander Street
New Albany, OH 43254
614-555-1832

April 18, 20XX

Attention Mr. Harold Chad
Tricounty Building Corporation
2395 36th Street
Ada, MI 49301

Ladies and Gentlemen

Thank you for your order for three executive chairs and three desks. The order will be shipped to you on March 5. I understand you are interested in working with one of our designers on furniture for a new building that you anticipate completing in October. As manager of the department, I will be calling your office in the next week to schedule an appointment with you.

We are pleased you are using our furniture, and I look forward to working with you on furniture designs for the new building.

Sincerely

Allen McGregory

Allen McGregory
Manager, Interior Design

lc

Figure 2   **MODIFIED BLOCK LETTER STYLE, MIXED PUNCTUATION**

THE NATIONAL MANAGEMENT ASSOCIATION
3406 North Drive
Kalamazoo, MI 49031
269-555-1306

April 25, 20XX

Mrs. Helena Andrews
Fetzer Foundation
2356 Old Kent Road
Kalamazoo, MI 49003

Dear Mrs. Andrews:

The National Management Association is sponsoring a community seminar on management techniques for not-for-profit organizations. Would you be interested in speaking at this seminar? I know your expertise would add greatly to the quality of the seminar.

I will be calling you within the next week to talk about this possibility.

Sincerely,

Eduardo Heminez

Eduardo Heminez
Vice President, Community Relations

lc

- Complimentary close—Key a double space below the last line of the body.
- Name and title of writer—Key a quadruple space below the complimentary close.
- Reference initials—Key a double space below the name and title.
- Enclosure—Key a double space below the reference initials.
- Postscript—Key a double space below the reference initials or the last keyed line.
- Copy notation—Kay a double space below the reference initials or the last keyed line. If a copy notation and a postscript are both used, the postscript is a double space below the copy notation.

▷ Envelope Addressing

Software packages have envelope addressing tools that allow for correct placement of both the letter address and return address on an envelope. However, you should be aware of the correct placement in case you need to key an envelope address manually.

OCRs (optical character readers) used by the U.S. Postal Service are programmed to scan a specific area, so the address must be placed appropriately. With a No. 10 envelope (the standard size used in offices), the address is placed 2″ from the top of the envelope and 4″ from the left edge. The address is keyed in all capital letters with no punctuation. Two-letter state abbreviations should be used, along with the nine-digit ZIP Code.

Notations to the post office, such as REGISTERED, should be keyed in all capital letters below the stamp, approximately ½″ above the delivery address.

Notations such as HOLD FOR ARRIVAL, CONFIDENTIAL, and PLEASE FORWARD should be keyed in all capital letters a double space below the return address.

▷ Letter Insertion

Standard Size Envelopes (No. 10–9½″ × 4⅛″)

Fold in the following manner:

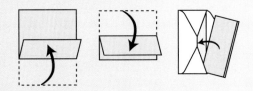

Small Envelope (No. 6¾—6½ × 3⅝″)

Fold in the following manner:

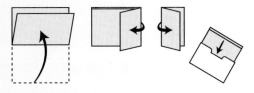

> NUMBER USAGE

1. Spell out numbers 1 through 10; use figures for numbers above 10.

   We ordered nine coats and four dresses.
   About 60 letters were keyed.

2. If a sentence contains related numbers above and below nine, either spell out all numbers or key all numbers in figures. If most of the numbers are below nine, use words. If most are above nine, use in figures.

   Please order 12 memo pads, 2 reams of paper and 11 boxes of envelopes.

3. Numbers in the millions or higher may be expressed in the following manner in order to aid comprehension.

   3 billion (rather than 3,000,000,000)

4. Numbers are spelled out at the beginning of a sentence.

   Five hundred books were ordered.

5. If the numbers are large, rearrange the wording of the sentence so the number is not the first word of the sentence.

   We had a good year in 2003.
   Not: Two thousand and three was a good year.

6. Indefinite numbers and amounts are spelled out.

   A few hundred voters turned out for the local election.

7. All ordinals (first, second, third, and so on) that can be expressed in one or two words are spelled out.

   The store's twenty-fifth anniversary was held this week.

8. When adjacent numbers are written in words or figures, use a comma to separate them.

   On car 33, 450 cartons are being shipped.

REFERENCE GUIDE

9. House or building numbers are written in figures. However, when the number one appears by itself, it is spelled out. Numbers one through ten in street names are spelled out. Numbers 11 and above are written in figures. When figures are used for both the house number and the street name, use a hyphen preceded and followed by a space.

> 101 Building
> One Main Place
> 21301 Fifth Avenue
> 122 - 33d Street

10. Ages are usually spelled out except when the age is stated exactly in years, months, and days. When ages are presented in tabular form, they are written in figures.

> She is eighteen years old.
> He is 2 years, 10 months, and 18 days old.

> | *Name* | *Age* |
> |---|---|
> | Jones, Edward | 19 |
> | King, Ruth | 21 |

11. Use figures to express dates written in normal month-day-year order. Do not use *th, nd,* or *rd* following the date.

> May 3, 2005
> *Not:* May 8th, 2005

12. Fractions that can be expressed in two words are spelled out unless they are part of mixed numbers. Use a hyphen to separate the numerator and denominator of fractions written in words when the fraction is used as an adjective.

> three-fourths   5¾

13. Amounts of money are usually expressed in figures. Indefinite money amounts are written in words.

> $1,000
> $3.27
> several hundred dollars

14. In legal documents, numbers may be written in both words and figures.

> One Hundred Thirty-four Dollars ($134)

15. Express percentages in figures, spell out the word *percent.*

> 10 percent

16. To form the plural of figures, add *s.*

> The 2000s will be challenging.

17. In times of day, use figures with *a.m.* and *p.m.;* spell out numbers with the word *o'clock.* In formal usage, spell out all times.

> 9 a.m.
> 10 p.m.
> eight o'clock in the evening

> OFTEN MISUSED WORDS AND PHRASES

1. *A* or *an* before the letter *h*

   The letter H when following the article "a" or "an" has either a hard sound or a silent sound. When H has a hard sound, the article "a" is correct. When H has a silent sound, the article "an" is correct. Notice the differences in a hard sound and a silent sound shown in the table below.

Hard Sound	*Silent Sound*
A horse	An honor
A harmonica	An honest person
A historical event	An heirloom

2. Awhile, a while

   A while is a noun meaning a short time; *awhile* is an adverb meaning a short time.

   > We plan to go home in a while.
   > She wrote the poem awhile ago.

3. About, at

   Use either *about* or *at,* not both.

   > He will leave about noon.
   > He will leave at noon.

4. Accept, except

   To *accept* an assignment is to agree to undertake it.

   To *except* someone from an activity is to excuse that person from the activity.

5. Accessible, assessable

   If something is *accessible,* it can be reached or attained.

   An object whose value can be estimated is *assessable.*

6. Advice, advise

   Advice is a noun meaning a recommendation; *advise* is a verb meaning to counsel.

She did not follow my advice.
The counselor will advise you.

7. All, all of

Use *all; of* is redundant. If a pronoun follows *all,* re-word the sentence.

Check all the items.
They are all going.

8. All right, alright

All right is the only correct usage; *alright* is not appropriate for business usage.

9. Among, between

Among is used when referring to three or more persons or things; *between* is used when referring to two persons or things.

The inheritance was divided among the four relatives.
The choice is between you and me.

10. Appraise, apprise

Appraise means to set a value on; *apprise* means to inform.

The house was appraised at $300,000.
I was apprised of the situation by Jack.

11. Bad, badly

Bad is an adjective; *badly* is an adverb.

He feels bad about losing.
The football team played badly tonight.

12. Biannual, biennial

Biannual means occurring twice a year; *biennial* means occurring once every two years.

The Conseco Board meets biannually.
Tactical planning occurs biennially.

13. Bimonthly, semimonthly

Bimonthly means every two months; *semimonthly* means twice a month.

Our IAAP chapter meets bimonthly.
We put plant food on our flowers semimonthly.

14. Can, may

Can means to be able to; *may* means to have permission.

The diskette can be copied.
You may leave when you finish your work.

15. Capital, capitol

Capital is used unless you are referring to a building that houses a government.

Austin is the capital of Texas.
We toured the United States Capitol in Washington.

16. Cite, sight, site

Cite means to quote; *sight* means vision; *site* means location.

She cited the correct reference.
That is a pleasant sight.
They sighted a whale.
The site for the new building will be determined soon.

17. Complement, compliment

Complement means to complete, fill, or make perfect; *compliment* means to praise.

His thorough report complemented the presentation.
I complimented Jane on her new dress.

18. Council, counsel

Council is a noun meaning a governing body.

Counsel can be a noun or a verb. As a noun, *counsel* means a person with whom one consults about a matter. As a verb, *counsel* means to advise.
The council meets today.
Dr. Baker's counsel helped Chris overcome her fears.
Counsel was consulted on the case.
He is there to counsel you.

19. Desert, dessert

Desert, as a noun, means a barren or arid region with low rainfall; *desert,* as a verb, means to abandon. *Dessert* is a confection often served at the end of a meal.

We traveled through the desert of Arizona.
He deserted his family.
We had ice cream for dessert.

20. Farther, further

Farther refers to distance; *further* refers to a greater degree or extent.

The store is a mile farther down the road.
We will discuss the matter further on Saturday.

21. Good, well

    Good is an adjective. *Well* is typically used as an adverb but may be used as an adjective when referring to the state of a person's health.

    > I feel well. (adjective)
    > I will perform the task as well as I can. (adverb)
    > She feels good about her job.

22. Got, gotten

    Got is preferred to *gotten* as the past participle of get. It is informal when used for *must* or *ought*.

    > I've got to get up at 6 a.m.
    > Improved: I must get up at 6 a.m.

23. In, into

    In means located inside an area or limits; *into* means in the direction of the interior or toward something.

    > She is sitting in the room.
    > She went into the room.

24. Its, it's

    Its is the possessive form of *it; it's* is the contraction of *it is.*

    > The family had its reunion yesterday.
    > It's probably going to rain.

25. Percent, per cent; percentage

    Percent is always spelled as one word; *per cent* is incorrect.

    Percentage is also one word and is the preferred word when a number is not used.

    > He received 56 percent of the vote.
    > The percentage of votes he received is not known.

26. Principal, principle

    Principal as an adjective means *main;* as a noun, *principal* means the main person or a capital sum.

    Principle is a noun meaning a rule, guide, truth; it never refers to a person directly.

    > The principal character in the play was John.
    > The principals in the case are present.
    > She held steadfast to her principles.

27. Respectfully, respectively

    Respectfully means in a courteous manner; *respectively* refers to being considered singly in a particular order.

    > She respectfully asked for her grade report.
    > The first, second, and third awards will go to Richard, Sarah, and Christine, respectively.

28. Stationary, stationery

    Stationary means stable or fixed; *stationery* is writing paper.

    > The ladder seems stationary.
    > Order three boxes of stationery.

29. That, which

    Both *which* and *that* are relative pronouns used to refer to places, animals, objects, ideas, and qualities. To improve clarity, many writers make this distinction: The word *which* is used to introduce nonessential information, and a comma is placed before the word. The word *that* is used to introduce a clause containing essential information, and no comma is used.

    > The presentation, which would have worked well for managers, had little appeal to the teachers. In ten minutes, Harry solved the problem that I had been working on for hours.

30. Who, whom

    Who is used as the subject of a verb; *whom* is used as an object of a verb or as a preposition.

    > Ken is the one who will be at the meeting.
    > Ken is the one whom I will hire.
    > It does not matter who did what to whom.

> PARALLEL CONSTRUCTION

Parts of a sentence that are parallel in meaning should be parallel in structure. Writers should balance a word with a word, a phrase with a phrase, a clause with a clause, and a sentence with a sentence. Notice the examples given below.

Incorrect:	The parents tried pleading, threats, and shouting.
Correct:	The parents tried pleading, threatening, and shouting.
Incorrect:	In undeveloped countries, don't drink the water; in developed countries, the air is dangerous to your health.
Correct:	In underdeveloped countries, don't drink the water; in developed countries, don't breathe the air.

> PASSIVE VOICE

Voice is the form of a verb indicating whether the subject is engaging in the action or receiving the action. A verb is in the **active voice** when the subject performs the action.

> Max **caught** the basketball.
> The voters **chose** the delegates.

A verb is in the passive voice when the subject receives the action.

> The basketball **was caught** by Max.
> The delegates **were chosen** by the voters.

Notice that the passive voice places the emphasis on the result of the action or the receiver of the action. The active voice is generally more appropriate to use than the passive voice.

> PLURALS AND POSSESSIVES

1. When a compound word contains a noun and is hyphenated or made up of two or more words, the principal word takes an *s* to form the plural. If there is no principal word, add an *s* to the end of the compound word.

   > commanders-in-chief
   > runners-up
   > write-ins

2. The plural of letters is formed by adding *s* or *'s*. The apostrophe is unnecessary except where confusion might result.

   > CPAs
   > dotting the *i*'s

3. Singular nouns form the possessive by adding *'s*. If a singular noun has two or more syllables and if the last syllable is not accented and is preceded by a sibilant sound *(s, x, z)*, add only the apostrophe for ease of pronunciation.

   > the person's computer   The boss's office
   > the department's rules   for goodness' sake

4. Plural nouns form the possessive by adding an apostrophe if the plural ends in *s* or by adding *'s* when the plural does not end in *s*.

   > ladies' wear
   > the children's bicycles

5. When a verb form ending in *ing* is used as a noun (gerund), a noun or pronoun before it takes the possessive form.

   > Mr. Ware's talking was not anticipated.

6. To form the possessive of a compound word, add the possessive ending to the last syllable.

   > Her mother-in-law's gift arrived.
   > The commander-in-chief's address was well received.

7. Joint possession is indicated by adding the possessive end to the last noun.

   > We are near Jan and Mike's store.
   > Drs. Edison and Martin's article was published this week.

8. In idiomatic construction, possessive form is often used.

   > a day's work   two weeks' vacation

9. The possessive form is used in cases where the noun modified is not expressed.

   > Take it to the plumber's. (shop)

10. The possessive form of personal pronouns is written without an apostrophe.

    > This book is hers.
    > She will deliver yours tomorrow.

> PRONOUNS

1. A pronoun agrees with its antecedent (the word for which the pronoun stands) in number, gender, and person.

   > *Roger* wants to know if *his* book is at your house.

2. A plural pronoun is used when the antecedent consists of two nouns joined by *and*.

   > *Marty* and *Tomie* are bringing *their* stereo.

3. A singular pronoun is used when the antecedent consists of two singular nouns joined by *or* or *nor*. A plural pronoun is used when the antecedent consists of two plural nouns joined by *or* or *nor*.

   > Neither *Elizabeth* nor *Johann* wants to do *her* part.
   > Either the *men* or the *women* will do *their* share.

4. Do not confuse certain possessive pronouns with contractions that sound alike.

Possessive	*Contraction*
its	it's (it is)
their	they're (they are)
theirs	there's (there is)
your	you're (you are)
whose	who's (who is)

As a test for the use of a possessive pronoun or a contraction, try to substitute *it is, they are, it has, there has, there is,* or *you are.* Use the corresponding possessive form if the substitution does not make sense.

> *Your* wording is correct.
> *You're* wording that sentence incorrectly.
> *Whose* book is it?
> *Who's* the owner of the laptop?

5. Use *who* and *that* when referring to persons. *Who* refers to an individual person or group; *that* refers to a class or type.

> He is the boy *who* does well in history.
> She is the type of *person that* we like to employ.

6. Use *which* and *that* when referring to places, objects, and animals.

> The card *that* I sent you was mailed last week.
> The fox, *which* is very sly, caught the skunk.

7. A pronoun in the objective case functions as a direct object, an indirect object, or an object of a preposition. Objective pronouns include *me, you, him, her, it, us, them, whom,* and *whomever.*

> The movie was an emotional experience for *her* and *me.* (The pronouns *her* and *me* are in the objective case since they function as the object of a preposition.)

8. A linking verb connects a subject to a word that renames it. Linking verbs indicate a state of being *(am, is, are, was, were),* related to the senses, or indicate a condition. A pronoun following a linking verb renames the subject, so it must be in the subjective case. Subjective pronouns include *I, you, she, be, it, we, they, who,* and *whoever.*

> It is I who will attend the play.

9. The pronouns *who* and *whoever* are in the subjective case and are used as the subject of a sentence or clause.

> *Whoever* is in charge will be required to stay late.

10. At the beginning of questions, use *who* if the question is about the subject and *whom* if the question is about the object.

> *Who* is going to the party?
> *Whom* can we expect to give the welcoming address?

11. Reflexive pronouns reflect back to the antecedent. Reflexive pronouns include *myself, herself, himself, themselves,* and other *self* or *selves* words.

> I intend to do the painting *myself.*

> PUNCTUATION

Correct punctuation is based on accepted rules and principles rather than on the whims of the writer. Punctuation is also important if the reader is to correctly interpret the writer's thoughts. The summary of rules provided here will be helpful in using correct punctuation.

▷ The Period

The period indicates a full stop and is used in the following ways:

1. At the end of a complete declarative or imperative sentence.

2. After abbreviations and after initials that represent a word.

> acct.   etc.   Ph.D.
> U.S.   p.m.   c.o.d.
> Jr.   i.e.   pp.

However, some abbreviations made up of several initial letters do not require periods.

> FDIC (Federal Deposit Insurance Corporation)
> FEPC (Fair Employment Practices Committee)
> AAA (American Automobile Association)
> YWCA (Young Women's Christian Association)

3. Between dollars and cents. A period and cipher are not required when an amount in even dollars is expressed in figures.

> $42.65 $1.47 $25

4. To indicate a decimal.

> 3.5 bushels   12.65 percent   6.25 feet

▷ The Comma

Use the comma:

1. To separate coordinate clauses that are connected by conjunctions (such as *and, but, or, for, neither, nor*) unless the clauses are short and closely connected.

> We have a supply on hand, but I think we should order an additional quantity.
> She had to work late, for the auditors were examining the books.

2. To set off a subordinate clause that precedes the main clause.

> Assuming no changes will be needed, I suggest you proceed with your instructions.

3. After an introductory phrase containing a verb form. If an introductory phrase does not contain a verb, it usually is not followed by a comma.

   > To finish his work, he remained at the office after hours.
   > After planning the program, she proceeded to put it into effect.
   > After much deliberation, the plan was revoked.
   > Because of the vacation period we have been extremely busy.

4. To set off a nonrestrictive clause.

   > Our group, which had never lost a debate, won the grand prize.

5. To set off a nonrestrictive phrase.

   > The beacon, rising proudly toward the sky, guided the pilots safely home.

6. To separate from the rest of the sentence a word or group of words that breaks the continuity of a sentence.

   > The administrative professional, even though his work was completed, was always willing to help others.

7. To separate parenthetical expressions from the rest of the sentence.

   > We have, as you know, two people who can handle the reorganization.

8. To set off names used in direct address or to set off explanatory phrases or clauses.

   > I think you, Mr. Bennett, will agree with the statement.
   > Ms. Linda Tom, our vice president, will be in your city soon.

9. To separate from the rest of the sentence expressions that, without punctuation, might be interpreted incorrectly.

   > *Misleading:*   Ever since we have filed our reports monthly.
   > *Better:*   Ever since, we have filed our reports monthly.

10. To separate words or groups of words when they are used in a series of three or more.

    > Most executives agree that dependability, trustworthiness, ambition, and judgment are required of workers.

11. To set off introductory words.

    > For example, the musical was not as lyrical as the last one I saw.

Thus, both the man and the boy felt a degree of discrimination.

12. To separate coordinate adjectives. Coordinate adjectives are two or more adjectives that equally modify a noun.

    > The large, insensitive audience laughed loudly at the mistake.

13. To set off short quotations from the rest of the sentence.

    > He said, "I shall be there."
    > "The committees have agreed," he said, "to work together on the project."

14. To separate the name of a city from the name of a state.

    > Our southern branch is located in Atlanta, Georgia.

15. To separate abbreviations of titles from the name. Personal titles Jr. and Sr. may appear without the comma if the person prefers it.

    > William R. Warner, Jr.
    > Ramona Sanchez, Ph.D.

16. To set off conjunctive adverbs such as *however* and *therefore*.

    > I, however, do not agree with the statement.
    > According to the rule, therefore, we must not penalize the student for this infraction.

17. To separate the date from the year. Within a sentence, use a comma on both sides of the year in a full date.

    > The anniversary party was planned for June 18, 2005.
    > He plans to attend the management seminar scheduled for April 15, 2007, at the Hill Hotel.

18. Do not use a comma in numbers in an address even when there are four or more digits.

    > The house number was 3100 Edmonds Drive.

19. Do not use a comma in a date that contains the month with only a day or the month with only a year.

    > The accident occurred on June 10.
    > The major event for June 2003 was the ethics seminar.

▷ Comma Splices

A comma splice is a sentence that contains two or more independent clauses joined by only a comma.

Comma splice: Take your raincoat with you, rain is predicted today.

The two cures for a comma splice are to:

1. Make two complete sentences with a period. *Take your raincoat with you. Rain is predicted today.*

2. Separate the clauses with a semicolon. *Take your raincoat with you; rain is predicted today.*

▷ The Semicolon

The semicolon should be used in the following instances:

1. Between independent clauses when either of the clauses contains a comma.

   He was outstanding in his knowledge of technology, including telecommunications and computers; but he was lacking in many desirable personal qualities.

2. Between compound sentences when the conjunction is omitted.

   All individuals in the group enjoyed the meal; many of the group did not enjoy the movie.

3. To precede expressions (such as *namely, for example* or *e.g., that is* or *i.e.*) used to introduce a clause.

   We selected the machine for two reasons; namely, it is reasonably priced and it has the necessary features.
   There are several reasons for changing the routine of handling mail; i.e., to reduce postage, to conserve time, and to place responsibility.

4. In a series of well-defined units when special emphasis is desired.

Emphatic:	Prudent administrative professionals consider the future; they use their talents to successfully attain their desired goals.
Less emphatic:	Prudent administrative professionals consider the future and use their talents to successfully attain their desired goals.

▷ The Colon

The colon is recommended in the following instances:

1. After the salutation in a business letter except when open punctuation is used.

   Ladies and Gentlemen:
   Dear Ms. Carroll:

2. Following introductory expressions (such as *the following, thus, as follows,* and other expressions) that precede enumerations.

   Please send the following by parcel post: books, magazines, newspapers.
   Officers were selected as follows: president, Helen Edwards; vice president, Mark Turnball; treasurer, Ralph Moline.

3. To separate hours and minutes when indicating time.

   2:10 p.m.   4:45 p.m.   12:15 a.m.

4. To introduce a quotation of more than one sentence.

   This quote from Theodore Roosevelt is a favorite of mine: "No man needs sympathy because he has to work. Far and away the best prize that life offers is the chance to work hard."

5. To introduce a list after phrases such as *the following*.

   His holiday gifts included the following: a cruise, a computer, a new suit, and ten books.

▷ The Question Mark

The question mark should be used in the following instances:

1. After a direct question.

   When do you expect to arrive in Philadelphia?

   An exception to the foregoing rule is a sentence phrased in the form of a question when it is actually a courteous request.

   Will you please send us an up-to-date statement of our account.

2. After each question in a series of questions within a sentence.

   What is your opinion of the Orlando division? the Phoenix division? the Boston division?

▷ Exclamation Point

The exclamation point is used to express command, strong feeling, emotion, or exclamation.

   Don't waste supplies!
   It can't be done!
   Stop!

▷ The Dash

The dash is used in the following instances:

1. To indicate an omission of letters or figures.

   Dear Mr. —   The dollar amounts are —

2. To indicate a definite stop or as emphasis.

> This book is not a revision of an old book—it is a totally new book.

3. To separate parenthetical expressions when unusual emphasis is desired.

> These sales arguments—and every one of them is important—should result in getting the order.

4. Around appositives if the use of commas might cause confusion.

> Concern over terrorism—biological warfare, attacks on cities, and attacks on government buildings and personnel—is demanding much media attention.

▷ The Apostrophe

The apostrophe should be used in the following instances:

1. To indicate possession.

> the boy's coat
> the ladies' dresses
> the girl's book

To the possessive singular, add 's to the noun.

> man's work
> bird's wing
> hostess's plans

An exception to this rule is made when the word following the possessive begins with an s sound.

> for goodness' sake   for conscience' sake

To form the possessive of a plural noun ending in an s or z sound, add only the apostrophe (') to the plural noun.

> workers' rights   hostesses' duties

If the plural noun does not end in an s or z sound, add 's to the plural noun.

> women's clothes   alumni's donations

Proper names that end in an s sound form the possessive singular by adding 's.

> Williams's house   Fox's automobile

Proper names ending in s form the possessive plural by adding the apostrophe only.

> The Walters' property faces the Jones' swimming pool.

To indicate the omission of a letter or letters in a contraction.

> it's (it is)
> you're (you are)
> we'll (we will, we shall)

2. To indicate the plurals of uncapitalized letters and uncapitalized abbreviations.

> Don't forget to dot your i's and cross your t's.
> The girls wore their holiday pj's.

▷ Quotation Marks

The following rules should be applied to the use of quotation marks:

1. When a quotation mark is used with a comma or a period, the comma or period is inside the quotation mark.

> She said, "I plan to complete my program in college before seeking a position."

2. When a quotation mark is used with a semicolon or a colon, the semicolon or colon is placed outside the quotation mark.

> The treasurer said, "I plan to go by train"; others in the group stated they would go by plane.

3. When more than one paragraph of quoted material is used, quotation marks should appear at the beginning of each paragraph and at the end of the last paragraph.

4. Quotation marks are used in the following instances:

Before and after direct quotations.

> The author states, "Too frequent use of certain words weakens the appeal."

To indicate the title of a published article.

> Have you read the article "Anger in the Workplace"?

To indicate a quotation within a quotation, use single quotation marks.

> The instructor said, "Read the chapter 'The Art of Listening' to prepare for tomorrow's discussion."

▷ Omission Marks or Ellipses

Ellipses marks (. . .) are frequently used to denote the omission of letters or words in quoted material. If the material omitted ends in a period, four

REFERENCE GUIDE

omission marks are used (. . . .). If the material omitted does not end in a period, three omission marks are used (. . .).

He quoted the proverb, "A soft answer turneth away wrath, but . . . ."

She quoted Plato, "Nothing is more unworthy of a wise man . . . than to have allowed more time for trifling and useless things than they deserved."

▷ Parentheses

Although parentheses are frequently used as a catchall in writing, they are correctly used in the following instances:

1. When amounts expressed in words are followed by figures.

   He agreed to pay twenty-five dollars ($25) as soon as possible.

2. Around words that are used as parenthetical expressions.

   Our personnel costs (including benefits) are much too high.

3. To indicate technical references.

   Sodium chloride (NaCl) is the chemical name for common table salt.

4. When enumerations are included in narrative form.

   The reasons for his resignation were three: (1) advanced age, (2) failing health, and (3) a desire to travel.

> REPORT FORMAT

▷ Title Page

Include the title of the report, the name and title of the person writing the report, and the date of the report. Center all items on the page. Key the title of the report in all caps 2" from the top of the page. Space down 5 inches, and key the name and title of the person writing the report. Key the date approximately 9" from the top of the page.

▷ Table of Contents

Center *Table of Contents* approximately 2 inches from the top of the page. Key main headings and subheadings in order, using leaders (periods every other space) to the page number. Use a combination of double and single spacing. Key the page number in lowercase Roman numerals centered either one inch or 0.5 inch from the bottom of the page.

▷ Body of the Report

Center the title of the report 2 inches from the top of the page. Set the left margin for 1½ inches if left-bound, 1 inch if unbound; use 1 inch top and bottom margins. Number the first page of the body 1 inch from the bottom at the center, or do not number at all. Number all other pages of the report using Arabic numerals keyed 1 inch from the top of the page at the right margin or centered 1 inch from the bottom. The report may be double or single spaced.

▷ Footnotes/Endnotes

Follow an acceptable style for formatting endnotes/footnotes.

Endnote (Chicago Style)

The endnote style requires a superscript number when the reference is noted in the text. However, no information about the work is given until the end of the paper in a section referred to as "Works Cited."

Footnote (Chicago Style)

At the point where the reference is mentioned, a superscript number is placed in the text and a footnote is placed on the same page as the superscript number.

Your body sends messages to your mind to meet its needs. One of the most important signals the body sends is that of hunger.[1]

APA and MLA Documentation Style

Both the APA (American Psychological Association) and the MLA (Modern Language Association) format style use internal citations. These citations are placed in the report itself within parentheses. The details of

[1]Deepak Chopra, *Grow Younger, Live Longer* (New York: Harmony Books, 2001), 77.

the source are then given in a section titled "Works Cited" (in MLA) or "References" (in APA).

In the report itself, the documentation is given in the following ways:

APA Style: According to Chopra (2001), the essence of flexibility is the willingness to let go.

MLA Style: Deepak Chopra suggests that the essence of flexibility is the willingness to let go (15).

Note: When the authority is first introduced, the first name and the surname are used. In subsequent citations by the same authority, only the surname is used.

▷ References/Works Cited Section

1. At the end of the report (APA documentation style), a section entitled "References" gives information on all sources quoted. The format of the section is as follows:

   Chopra, D. (2001). *Grow younger, live longer.* New York: Harmony Books.

2. At the end of the report (MLA documentation style), a section entitled "Works Cited" gives information on all sources quoted. The format of the section is as follows:

   Chopra, Deepak. Grow Younger, Live Longer. New York: Harmony Books, 2001.

3. At the end of the report (Chicago style) with footnotes or endnotes, a section entitled "Bibliography" gives information on all sources quoted. The format of the section is as follows:

   Chopra, Deepak, *Grow Younger, Live Longer.* New York: Harmony Books, 2001.

▷ Tables, Charts, and Graphs

Number the tables, charts, and graphs consecutively throughout a report. Identify all tables, charts, and graphs with the word *Figure* followed by the number. Give each graphic a title.

> SPELLING RULES

1. Put *i* before *e* except after *c* or when sounded like *a* as in *neighbor* or *weigh*. Exceptions: *either, neither, seize, weird, leisure, financier, conscience.*

2. When a one-syllable word ends in a single consonant and when that final consonant is preceded by a single vowel, double the final consonant before a suffix that begins with a vowel or the suffix *y*.

run	running
drop	dropped
bag	baggage
skin	skinny

3. When a word of more than one syllable ends in a single consonant, when that final consonant is preceded by a single vowel, and when the word is accented on the last syllable, double the final consonant before a suffix that begins with a vowel.

begin	beginning
concur	concurrent

   When the accent does not fall on the last syllable, do not double the final consonant before a suffix that begins with a vowel.

travel	traveler
differ	differing

4. When the final consonant in a word of one or more syllables is preceded by another consonant or by two vowels, do not double the final consonant before any suffix.

look	looked
deceit	deceitful
act	acting
warm	warmly

5. When a word ends in a silent *e*, generally drop the *e* before a suffix that begins with a vowel.

guide	guidance
use	usable

6. When a word ends in a silent *e* , generally retain the *e* before a suffix that begins with a consonant unless another vowel precedes the final *e*.

hate	hateful
due	duly
excite	excitement
argue	argument

7. When a word ends in *ie*, drop the *e* and change the *i* to *y* before adding *ing*.

lie	lying
die	dying

8. When a word ends in *ce* or *ge*, generally retain the final *e* before the suffixes *able* and *ous* but drop the final *e* before the suffixes *ible* and *ing*.

    manage   manageable
    force   forcible

9. When a word ends in *c*, insert a *k* before adding a suffix beginning with *e*, *i*, or *y*.

    picnic   picnicking

10. When a word ends in *y* preceded by a consonant, generally change the *y* to *i* before a suffix except one beginning with *i*.

    modify   modifying   modifier
    lonely   lonelier

11. When a word ends in *o* preceded by a vowel, form the plural by adding *s*. When a word ends in *o* preceded by a consonant, generally form the plural by adding *es*.

    folio   folios
    potato   potatoes

12. When a word ends in *y* preceded by a vowel, form the plural by adding *s*. When a word ends in *y* preceded by a consonant, change the *y* to *i* and add *es* to form the plural.

    attorney   attorneys
    lady   ladies

> SUBJECT AND VERB AGREEMENT

This section presents a review of basic rules concerning subject-verb agreement.

1. When the subject consists of two singular nouns and/or pronouns connected by *or, either . . . or, neither . . . nor,* or *not only . . . but also,* a singular verb is required.

    Jane or *Bob has* the letter.
    Either *Ruth* or *Marge plans* to attend.
    Not only a *book* but also *paper is* needed.

2. When the subject consists of two plural nouns and/or pronouns connected by *or, either . . . or, neither . . . nor,* or *not only . . . but also,* a plural verb is required.

    Neither the *managers* nor the *administrative assistants have* access to that information.

3. When the subject is made up of both singular and plural nouns and/or pronouns connected by *or, either . . . or, neither . . . nor,* or *not only . . . but also,* the verb agrees with the noun or pronoun closest to the verb.

    Either *Ms. Rogers* or the *assistants have* access to that information.
    Neither the *men* nor *Jo is* working.

4. Disregard intervening phrases and clauses when establishing agreement between subject and verb.

    One of the men *wants* to go to the convention.
    The *request* for new computers *is* on Mr. Woo's desk.

5. The words *each, every, either, neither, one, another,* and *much* are singular. When they are used as subjects or as adjectives modifying subjects, a singular verb is required.

    Each person *is* deserving of the award.
    Neither boy *rides* the bicycle well.

6. The following pronouns are always singular and require a singular verb:

    anybody   everybody   nobody   somebody
    anyone   everyone   no one   someone
    anything   everything nothing   something

    Everyone plans to attend the meeting.
    Anyone is welcome at the concert.

7. *Both, few, many, others,* and *several* are always plural. When they are used as subjects or adjectives modifying subjects, a plural verb is required.

    Several members *were* asked to make presentations.
    Both women *are* going to apply.

8. *All, none, any, some, more,* and *most* may be singular or plural, depending on the noun to which they refer.

    Some of the supplies *are* missing.
    Some of the paper *is* needed.

9. *The number* has a singular meaning and requires a singular verb; *a number* has a plural meaning and requires a plural verb.

    A number of people *are* planning to attend.
    The number of requests *is* surprising.

10. Geographic locations are considered singular and used with a singular verb when referring to one

location. When reference is made to separate islands, the plural form is used with a plural verb.

> The Hawaiian Islands has been my vacation spot for years.
> The Caribbean Islands have distinct cultures.

> WORD DIVISION

1. Divide words between syllables.

   moun-tain
   base-ment

2. Do not divide words of five or fewer letters (preferably six or fewer).

   apple
   among
   finger

3. Do not divide one-syllable words.

   helped
   eighth

4. If a single-letter syllable falls within a word, divide the word after the single-letter syllable.

   regu-late
   sepa-rate

5. If two single-letter syllables occur together within a word, divide between the single-letter syllables.

   continu-ation
   radi-ator

6. Divide between double consonants that appear within a word. Also, when the final consonant of a base word is doubled to add a suffix, divide between the double consonants.

   neces-sary
   commit-ted

7. When a base word ends in a double consonant, divide between the base word and the suffix.

   tell-ing
   careless-ness

8. Divide hyphenated compound words at existing hyphens only.

   two-thirds
   self-control

9. Avoid dividing a date, a personal name, or an address. If it is absolutely necessary, maximize readability by doing the following:

   Divide a date between the day and the year.
   Divide a personal name between the first name and surname.
   Divide an address between the city and state.

10. Do not divide figures, abbreviations, and symbols.

    $20,000
    YMCA
    #109

11. Do not divide contractions.

    he'll
    wouldn't

12. Divide no more than three or four words on a page.

13. Avoid dividing words at the end of the first and last lines of a paragraph.

14. Do not divide the last word on a page.

15. Do not divide a word when a one-letter syllable is the first syllable. Do not divide a word when the last syllable contains two letters.

    around (not a-round)
    lately (not late-ly)

REFERENCE GUIDE

> PROOFREADERS' MARKS

Symbol	Meaning	Marked Copy	Corrected Copy
∧	Insert	two people _or three_	two or three people
℘	Delete	the man ~~and the woman~~	the man
⊏	Move left	human relations	human relations
#	Add space	follow these	follow these
/	Lowercase letter	in the Fall of 2002	in the fall of 2002
⌒	Close up space	sum mer	summer
∿	Transpose	when is it	when it is
⊐	Move right	skills for living	skills for living
∨	Insert apostrophe	Macs book	Mac's book
∨∨	Insert quotation marks	She said, No.	She said, "No."
⊔	Move down	falle n	fallen
⊓	Move up	straigh t	straight
¶	Paragraph	¶ The first and third page	The first and third page
No ¶	No new paragraph	No ¶ The first and third page	The first and third page
◯ sp	Spell out	Dr. sp	Doctor
stet or	Let it stand; ignore correction	most efficient worker	most efficient worker
___	Underline or italics	Business World	_Business World_ _Business World_
⊙	Insert period	the last word ⊙	the last word.

CASE SOLUTIONS

> PART 1
ALVERTA HARTY—CASE SOLUTION

The first thing I did was write down all the problems that were causing my stress and frustration. This helped me to focus on the problems without my emotions making them worse. Then I discussed my problems with my original director. He understood and when I told him I needed to speak with the president, he agreed. My discussion with the president went very well, because most of the senior staff had complained about some of the same problems I had in addition to problems on the management level. He asked me to hold on for a little while because management was working on a solution, but it would take some time. He also said that my credibility was still intact, and everyone knew that I was not causing the problems.

I did not want to leave the company, but I knew I could not continue the way things were going. However, by talking with my managers and the president, they let me know that they were aware of the problems and were working on a solution. That director was asked to leave a few months later, and a new director was brought in. I'm still Executive Assistant/Department Coordinator for both departments, but it's a much better working environment.

> PART 2
NILDA CAMPBELL—CASE SOLUTION

Because the new PA is going to work with me and I am the most senior PA, I took the initiative and offered assistance. I asked her what information was given to her so I could use that as a basis for any additional information I could provide her. I found out that there was practically no information of substance that was passed on to her.

I provided her with information such as the organizational chart, goals for the year, various lists of committees, working groups, government agencies we deal with, government officials (Cabinet and Members of Parliament), information on where to find things, staff agreements and other information which I find helpful to make her work easier. I gave her a road map of New Zealand for the December holiday season.

When the manager came back from the holiday, she talked to me and asked how the new PA was progressing. I told the manager honestly and in fairness to both parties the problems encountered and the reasons why it happened that way. I told the manager what I did. The manager took note of the materials and information I provided, which eventually will be added on to the information provided for new hires.

The new PA was very appreciative of the assistance I provided her and so was the manager.

> PART 3
JANET RADOSEVICH—CASE SOLUTION

After 18 months, it became evident to management that my replacement would not be able to meet their expectations and needs in this high-level administrative position. The individual was given another position within the company and I retained my previous position, plus the additional responsibilities I had taken on. It was communicated to me that it was clear my skills were required for the efficient support of the department. For this reason, my pending layoff status was cancelled. It was noted that my dedication and contributions to the department were appreciated.

This was a difficult time for me, but I believe I grew from the experience. I became a stronger person by believing in myself and doing the best job I could in this situation. During this time I received great moral support from my husband, family, and friends. I became aware of how important networking is, and decided to join a professional organization. I believe that through my involvement with IAAP I have grown both personally and professionally over the past 12 years.

> PART 4
LAVETTA HUNLEY—CASE SOLUTION

Having previously completed a course on team leader/facilitator training, I applied several of the techniques I learned in that course. To increase my training knowledge, I completed various other training courses, including a train-the-trainer and workshop design courses. I applied several combined techniques from those courses as well as my knowledge in Microsoft. I developed individual, 4-hour training classes for each of the 36 manuals (12 in each of the three skill levels) and facilitated the monthly classes. I used all of my skills to complete the training program.

The planning meeting for the Water Department to implement the OPTIONS Training Plan was held in May 2004; classes started in June. It was well received. As a result, approximately 40 members of the administrative staff enrolled in the courses. This is the first ever training program specifically designed for administrative staff to be implemented in the city organization. Success of the program could be the foundation for the implementation of an administrative training program for all of the city's administrative staff. If not citywide, we definitely look forward to continuing the training within the Water Department.

> PART 5
NANCY UPCHURCH—CASE SOLUTION

I presented a proposal to the company showing all the different types of computers and software used nationwide and how much time was expended learning each one when they were transferred from jobsite to jobsite. My proposal was to standardize computers and software, alleviating the frustrations of transitioning from one type of computer and software and bringing continuity to the company. At this time, my company was a nationwide company with $200 million in annual revenue, and I was the "new kid on the block," so selling my proposal and my knowledge was a daunting task.

My proposal was taken into consideration, but the final decision to "standardize" did not take effect until five years later. Having the knowledge and skills gained through my "life-long" learning gives me pride in knowing that I was part of bringing our nationwide, now $2-billion-a-year company into the "technology" era.

Now, more than ever, businesses are relying on administrative professionals to bring direction and efficiency to the workplace. The days are gone when typing speed and shorthand skills were the sole marks of a good admin.

Today, administrative professionals must demonstrate a much broader range of skills: in language, making decisions, in working with other associates, and, of course, understanding and using this technology. If there is any value we cling to most dearly, it is in our belief that we, as professionals, can do much to ensure the excellence of the workforce. I strive to be that administrative professional.

> PART 6
JOSÉ REGO—CASE SOLUTION

Although our "expert" continued to grace the rest of the workshop with his insights, he kept his comments brief and relevant, seeming to keep in his mind everyone else's need to participate and contribute to the learning.

Our "expert" realized beyond a shadow of any doubt that the comment made by the young woman was directed at him. I often find that after a trainer has done everything possible to control group dynamics, the participants may choose to handle situations on their own by taking the initiative to address issues directly. I believe this is a result of the trainer carefully but skillfully reminding people that a workshop is only as effective as they want it to be and that participants must take ownership of their personal experiences if they are to gain the most from the workshop.

One of the lessons I learned in my years of administrative work is that sometimes the best thing to do is nothing at all—except to provide opportunities where others can become empowered and handle the situation themselves.

INDEX

INDEX

INDEX

INDEX

INDEX

INDEX